Media Ethics

Should journalists be impartial and objective? How should the public's right to know be balanced against an individual's right to privacy? How should the media be regulated? Is there a justification for spin-doctors and cheque-book journalism?

The role and responsibilities of the media are constant subjects of public debate. *Media Ethics* brings together philosophers, academics and media professionals to discuss the pressing ethical and moral questions faced by journalists and the media and to examine the basic notions such as truth, virtue, privacy, rights, offence, harm and freedom, underlying them.

The contributors explore issues of impartiality and objectivity, the ethics of political journalism, the regulation of privacy and media intrusion, and the justification of censorship. They discuss the relationship between journalism and public relations, war reporting and military propaganda in the Gulf War, media portrayals of sex and violence, photojournalism and the tabloid press. *Media Ethics* includes a chapter by Martin Bell on responsible journalism and war reporting in Bosnia.

Contributors: David Archard, Martin Bell, Andrew Belsey, Noël Carroll, Ian Cram, Anthony Ellis, Gordon Graham, Bob Franklin, Richard Keeble, Matthew Kieran, Brian McNair, Mary Midgley, Rod Pilling, Nigel Warburton.

Editor: Matthew Kieran is Lecturer in Philosophy at the University of Leeds. He is the author of *Media Ethics: A Philosophical Approach* and co-author of *Regulating for Changing Values*, a report for the Broadcasting Standards Commission. He has published articles in media ethics, aesthetics, ethics and social philosophy.

Media Ethics

Edited by Matthew Kieran

 Routledge
Taylor & Francis Group

LONDON AND NEW YORK

First published 1998
by Routledge
2 Park Square, Milton Park, Abingdon, Oxon, OX14 4RN

Simultaneously published in the USA and Canada
by Routledge
270 Madison Ave, New York NY 10016

Reprinted 2000, 2002, 2003

Transferred to Digital Printing 2005

Routledge is an imprint of the Taylor & Francis Group

Selection and editorial matter © 1998 Matthew Kieran
Individual chapters © 1998 the contributors

Typeset in Sabon by
J&L Composition Ltd, Filey, North Yorkshire

British Library Cataloguing in Publication Data
A catalogue record for this book is available from the British Library.

Library of Congress Cataloging in Publication Data
Media ethics/edited by Matthew Kieran.
　　p.　　cm.
　　Includes bibliographical references and index.
　　1. Mass media–Moral and ethical aspects.　I. Kieran, Matthew, 1968–
P94.M358　1998
　　175–dc21　　97–39544

ISBN 0–415–16837–6 (hbk)
ISBN 0–415–16838–4 (pbk)

Contents

vi   *Contents*

Notes on contributors

David Archard is Reader in Philosophy at the University of St Andrews. He has published *Marxism and Existentialism* (Blackstaff, 1980; Gregg Revivals, 1992), *Consciousness and the Unconscious* (Hutchinson, 1984), and *Children: Rights and Childhood* (Routledge, 1993), as well as a number of articles and book chapters. He has completed a book on sexual consent and is currently researching the concept of community in relation to the family and the nation.

Martin Bell was on the staff of BBC TV news from 1965 to 1997 and during this period covered assignments in over eighty countries, including eleven wars, from Vietnam to Bosnia. He was voted Royal Television Society reporter of the year in both 1977 and 1993, the latter for his work in Bosnia. He became MP for the constituency of Tatton in 1997.

Andrew Belsey is Lecturer in Philosophy at the University of Wales, Cardiff, and a member of Cardiff's Centre for Applied Ethics. He is editor (with Ruth Chadwick) of *Ethical Issues in Journalism and the Media* (Routledge, 1992) and (with Robin Attfield) of *Philosophy and the Natural Environment* (Cambridge University Press, 1994). He is currently engaged on a study of British philosophy of science in the nineteenth century.

Noël Carroll is Monroe Beardsley Professor of the Philosophy of Art at the University of Wisconsin at Madison. He has written widely in aesthetics and film theory; his most recent book is *A Philosophy of Mass Art*, published by Oxford University Press.

Ian Cram is Lecturer in the Faculty of Law at the University of Leeds. His research interests include civil liberties and administrative law. He is currently writing a book on the law and practice of reporting restrictions in criminal trials.

Anthony Ellis is Professor of Philosophy at Virginia Commonwealth University and was formerly Senior Lecturer and Head of the Moral

Philosophy Department at the University of St Andrews. He is the author of many articles in ethics, political and social philosophy and also edits *Philosophical Books*.

Bob Franklin is Reader in Media and Communications at the University of Sheffield. He is the author of many publications, including *Televising Democracies* (Routledge, 1992), *Newszak and News Media* (Arnold, 1997) and *Making the Local News* (with David Murphy, Routledge, 1998).

Gordon Graham is Regius Professor of Moral Philosophy at the University of Aberdeen. He has held visiting positions both in the United States and Europe and his publications include *Contemporary Social Philosophy* (Blackwell Publishers, 1988), *The Idea of Christian Charity* (University of Notre Dame, 1990), *Ethics and International Relations* (Blackwell Publishers, 1996), *The Shape of the Past: a Philosophical Approach to History* (Oxford University Press, 1997) and *Philosophy of the Arts* (Routledge, 1997). He is a regular contributer to *The Scotsman* newspaper, and to BBC Radio Scotland.

Richard Keeble is Director of the undergraduate programme at the Department of Journalism, City University, London. He worked on local papers in Nottingham and Cambridge and edited *The Teacher* from 1980 to 1984. He is the author of *The Newspapers Handbook* (Routledge, 1994) and his study of the press coverage of the 1991 Gulf conflict is to be published by Libbey.

Matthew Kieran is Lecturer in Philosophy at the University of Leeds. He is the author of *Media Ethics: A Philosophical Approach* (Praeger, 1997) and co-author (with David Morrison and Michael Svennevig) of *Regulating for Changing Values: A Report for the Broadcasting Standards Commission* (BSC, 1997). He has also published articles in media ethics, aesthetics, ethics and social philosophy.

Brian McNair is Senior Lecturer in Film and Media Studies at the University of Stirling. He is the author of many books, including *Glasnost, Perestroika and the Soviet Media* (Routledge, 1991), *An Introduction to Political Communication* (Routledge, 1995) and *News and Journalism in the UK* (Routledge, 2nd edn, 1996).

Mary Midgley is a moral philosopher with many publications to her name, including, more recently, *Utopias, Dolphins and Computers* (Routledge, 1996), *The Ethical Primate* (Routledge, 1994) and *Science as Salvation* (Routledge, 1992). Her writings often appear both in the academic arena and national newspapers. She was formerly Senior Lecturer in Philosophy at the University of Newcastle.

Rod Pilling is Head of the School of Media and Communications at the University of Central England and a former journalist.

Nigel Warburton is Lecturer in Philosophy at the Open University, Milton Keynes. He has published articles on the philosophy and history of photography in the *British Journal of Aesthetics*, *Ratio* and *History of Photography* and has edited a book on the photographer Bill Brandt (Clio Press, 1994). His forthcoming book, *The Philosophy of Photography*, is to be published by Routledge. He is also the author of *Philosophy: The Basics, Thinking from A to Z* and *Philosophy: The Classics*, all published by Routledge.

Introduction

The media clearly have a strong and complex influence upon how we understand and shape our world. From news reporting and investigative journalism to the broadcasting of soaps, dramas and films, they provide us with information, entertainment and seek to enhance our understanding of the world. Hence, in often indirect ways, the media engage with and affect our beliefs, values and fundamental commitments. Naturally, then, given the media's increasing presence and influence within our world, there arise a host of ethical and social questions that need to be addressed.

Indeed, there has been increasing public debate about such matters, usually motivated by outrage against some perceived wrong committed by a section of the media. Accusations of bias, press cynicism, media manipulation, condemnations of journalistic intrusions into privacy, worries about the damaging or distortive effect of the televisual medium and hotly contested pronouncements about the appropriate forms of media regulation or censorship have all hit the headlines with ever greater frequency. The aim of this collection is to focus upon some of the key questions about the media's ethical responsibilities and rights. For only by critical reflection upon what, rationally, we may legitimately demand of the media, in terms of their duties and responsibilities, can we hope to arrive at any substantial basis for claiming that a particular press intrusion or media programme is immoral.

As most of the readers of this collection will notice, the majority of the essays in this collection are philosophical. This is for a good and important reason. Although sociology, psychology and legal studies are informative, for example, about what people's actual preferences are, how those preferences come about and how legal restrictions actually apply, they are, essentially, non-normative. They do not and cannot tell us what, for example, people's preferences ought to be and why, rationally speaking, this is so. It may be that many people assume political spin-doctoring, cheque-book journalism or the broadcasting of pornography on satellite channels are immoral and thus should be prohibited. But even if there were a social consensus about such matters, it does not follow that these things are indeed wrong. For, as we are all aware, people's preferences and moral judgements can be mistaken. Hence, in order to understand what the ethical issues involved are, what responsibilities, rights or duties exist and how they might conflict, we need to pursue a philosophical analysis of things like the nature of objectivity, privacy, the influence of sexual and violent programming and censorship. As it happens, as a recent report for the Broadcasting Standards Commission has shown,[1] there isn't even a consensus on such matters, except perhaps regarding the public's views on rights to privacy, so there are pressing conceptual and pragmatic reasons for trying to resolve such issues rationally. This is not to deny that other disciplines have something to contribute to such matters. They do. But, as can be seen from the nature of the collection, their primary role is to explain what is actually happening and why. Such considerations are important since they need to be taken into account when reasoning philosophically about such matters. After all, if privacy or state censorship laws are clumsy instruments, then this must be taken into account when considering, philosophically, whether they are justified or not.

The first article, by Andrew Belsey, focuses on whether it even makes sense to think we can make ethical demands of journalism. For journalism, by necessity, seems to involve muck-raking, deceit and intrusions into privacy, amongst other things, in order to achieve the function of getting the all-important story. Perhaps we have good reason to exempt journalists from the ethical responsibilities, such as the duty to tell the truth, which obtain in ordinary life. But despite such considerations, and the recognition that journalism is a major industry, Belsey argues that journalism's responsibilities, as well as special rights, arise from appropriately conceiving of journalism as occupying a distinctive facilitating role in the democratic process. Hence journalists must serve the public interest in a virtuous manner. Unethical journalistic activity, such as habitual muck-raking or deceit, will undermine the public's trust in the media and without that relationship of trust journalism's democratic function cannot be fulfilled.

This theme clearly relates to the next two articles, by Martin Bell and myself, which focus on the assumption that journalists should aim to be impartial and objective. Bell argues that far from being distanced, neutral observers, journalists are implicated within the events they are reporting and should not avoid making and reporting evaluative judgements about them. But, though understood by some as an argument against objectivity, it is no such thing. For, as I argue, objectivity is a matter of arriving at the appropriate report, interpretation *and* evaluation of a state of affairs. Impartiality, unlike neutrality, does not preclude evaluative judgements. For good journalism should not just describe how and why an event happened but seek to show its true nature; and often what is most important is to highlight, in the case of a war massacre for example, the truly evil and horrific nature of what has been perpetrated. It is through the symbiotic process of reflective equilibrium, rationally considering one's

judgements in regard to the basic principles of interpretation and evaluation, that objectivity can be achieved. To deny this would be to reduce,
falsely, all journalism to the status of propaganda – which is a perversion
of journalism proper. For journalists do indeed have a duty to strive for
impartiality and thus objectivity.

Such considerations tie in with Mary Midgley's article because the
culture of journalism seems to presume, falsely Midgley argues, that
impartiality requires journalists to focus upon the failings and possibility
of hidden motives in public characters. Midgely traces how such cynicism
has evolved from Strachey's revolution in biography. Yet, as Midgley points
out, hypocrisy is not always vicious. A failure to live up to publicly
espoused ideals may only reflect human fallibility rather than vicious
hypocrisy. Indeed, even where the hypocrisy is vicious, it may be of greater
social value to concentrate on a public character's good aspects rather than
his failings in order to avoid, falsely, damaging a valuable cause.

Such issues, of course, are particularly pertinent when considering the
interrelationships between journalism and politics. A consideration which
may cut against Midgley's argument, in the sphere of party politics, is the
emerging network of systems contemporary political parties use to get the
most favourable 'spin' on a story for their respective party. Although many
complain about the media's confrontational style of political journalism,
and the presumption of cynicism, McNair argues that if we understand the
game properly, it is clear that journalists need to maintain this approach to
combat the politicians' attempts to control the news agenda in a way
which serves their interests, as distinct from the public's.

In the light of these arguments concerning matters of impartiality,
objectivity and the public interest, Richard Keeble's article serves as a
warning that such values may be very difficult to realise. In focusing
upon the media coverage of the Gulf War, as personalised in the figure
of Saddam Hussein, Keeble argues that the media played a distorting role
in constructing our understanding of the war. Hence, at the very least, we
always ought to ask whose interests are served by reporting an event in this
way. A failure to do so can only reinforce the false assumption that we are
always told the truth – something which, if Keeble's analysis is plausible,
turns out to be a very dangerous assumption indeed.

Moving on to the issue of privacy, David Archard outlines concerns
about the nature of privacy and the public interest justification for infring-
ing it. Indeed, where the right to privacy is trumped by considerations of
public welfare, it is far from clear that a right has been infringed at all.
However, most of us assume that where there is no direct public interest,
construed in terms of harm, there can be no justification for media intrusion. Yet, interestingly, Archard sketches an argument which cuts against
this presumption. Gossip, for example, can and does play a significant role
in the moral life of a community, by reinforcing the normative dispositional force of certain moral prescriptions and prohibitions. Thus, for

example, perhaps the perverted sex life of a private individual ought to be exposed, not merely for his or her own good but to stand as an example of what flourishing human sexuality should not aim towards. Moreover, exposing the private lives of the rich and powerful can reinforce a sense of egalitarianism which tends, rather healthily, to dissolve their mystique, which can so easily be abused.

Nonetheless, despite Archard's powerful argument, some people may remain worried about the moral nature of gossip as such and, more importantly with regard to the media, the effects such intrusion may have upon the private lives of celebreties and royals alike. The deaths of Diana, Princess of Wales, Dodi al-Fayed and their driver in August 1997 tragically highlighted the way such figures are often hounded by the news media to the extent that they can have little privacy or peace regarding even the most intimate aspects of their lives. It may be thought that such media intrusion is far from justifiable. But to challenge Archard's argument it must be shown that there is a clear division between the public interest and what the public is interested in. If, however, there is a link between the two, as Archard suggests, then the media attention devoted to the lives of the royals and celebrities is morally justifiable (even though we may rightfully deplore the form such intrusion may take in a particular case).

Ian Cram's article outlines how the piecemeal nature of the legal protection of privacy interests was found wanting by the Calcutt Committee report and the nature of its recommendations. Cram argues that, given a lack of political will to institute a direct right of privacy, enforceable by the courts, it is worth paying greater attention to the non-legal forms of privacy protection provided by regulators and current codes of media practice. Importantly, Cram goes on to consider how the European Convention on Human Rights and Fundamental Freedoms could, if incorporated into domestic law, provide the most substantial means by which to protect privacy.

Bob Franklin and Rod Pilling's article examines whether there has been a discernible move towards more tabloid orientated journalism and how this has affected both contemporary news values and the role of proprietors and regulatory authorities in attempting to curb such market-driven excesses. They go on to examine the likely effectiveness of increasing legal restrictions and the costs and benefits of self-regulation. Especially when gossip comes to be seen to constitute news as such, the problem arises as to the forms of redress ordinary people, unable to avail themselves of the legal and regulatory avenues open to those better off, have open to them when their privacy and lives have been abused by the press.

Nigel Warburton switches focus to ethical problems arising from the nature of the photographic medium. Many people are worried about the ethical problems which new media technology seems to raise. For example, the possibility of creating flawless images may undermine the trust we place in photojournalism as bearing faithful witness to an event as it happened. But Warburton argues that such worries are based on a mis-understanding of the nature of the photographic medium and a naïve presumption that, prior to the electronic age, photographs could not be manipulated and thus were, in a straightforward sense, transparent windows on to the world. What it does show, however, is that news photographers must retain a commitment to retaining the causal link from the resulting image back to the originating event. For the point of photojournalism is to retain a link to the actual world so that we can understand what was true of an actual event.

Noël Carroll's concern, by contrast, is a cluster of misgivings people have voiced about the nature of the televisual medium. These worries basically amount to three claims. Firstly, that television's realistic nature carries with it, falsely, a certain rhetorical force. Namely, that it cultivates in viewers, falsely, the assumption that how things are depicted is, in fact, the way things must be. Secondly, that television indulges a fantastical, morally dubious form of escapism. Thirdly, that as a medium television precludes the use of our imagination. But, Carroll argues, these worries turn out to be unfounded. Essentially, they fail to take account of the complex ways in which we understand and respond to television, or rely on an overly simplistic view of the nature of our emotions. Thus, Carroll concludes, the television medium or image is not inherently immoral though we may nonetheless have worries about the content of certain programmes.

Gordon Graham's target is the form of argument that suggests that representations of sex and violence, both in reporting and fiction, cause harm. The premise that watching such programmes will cultivate a tendency to be violent is, Graham argues, highly debatable for all but a very few. Moreover, even were harm to result from such programmes, this would not legitimate censorship. After all, we know that allowing cars on the road will directly lead to the deaths of a number of individuals each year. But the freedoms at stake are more important than the resultant harm. The interesting point about reports or films which make gratuitous use of violent or sexual imagery, Graham argues, is their failure to engage our interest in order to deepen our understanding. Thus we should, perhaps, ask why it is that our artistic and journalistic communities are failing us.

The last article in the collection, by Anthony Ellis, follows on to address arguments over censorship and the media. Obviously freedom of speech is valuable and ought to be protected, to some extent, against government interference given the primary importance of individual freedom. Ultimately, he argues, the harm involved in such restrictions is so great that even proven harm resulting from free speech should not be prohibited unless it is of a very high degree. But Ellis also goes on to consider whether not just harm but offence can constitute grounds for prohibition. Yet the notion of offence is intrinsically tied to morality. Given this link, at least within a liberal framework, offence cannot constitute sufficient grounds for censorship because the liberal state has no business in legislating for morality. Indeed, deeply held beliefs and moral convictions often need to be attacked. Legislation to protect the feelings of those who cherish certain beliefs is, at best, mistaken, and at worst, deeply pernicious. A culture that legislates against offence is one that not only fails to protect our basic freedoms as individual persons but one likely to stagnate and infantilise its citizens.

The articles in this collection show that there are some deep ethical and social issues in journalism and the media which require careful thinking through, with regard both to their philosophical complexity and to their pragmatic aspects. Of course, the arguments here do not constitute the last word. But they do at least help to elucidate some of the central ethical issues in the media and provide arguments which must be taken into account in justifying our judgements. Thus, at the very least, they help us to understand more deeply what responses are rationally open to us and what the ethical responsibilities of the media are. It is to be hoped that the collection may play a small part in focusing the debate and emphasising the need for rational justification in such matters, as opposed to the rhetoric, prejudices and emotional responses that so often seem to hold sway.

I would like to thank all the contributors for accepting the invitation to contribute to this collection and for responding courteously to editorial requests. I would also like to thank all the speakers and participants at the media ethics conference held at the University of Leeds, in September 1996, from which this collection sprang and gratefully acknowledge sponsorship for the conference from the Society for Applied Philosophy and Yorkshire and Humberside Arts.

Matthew Kieran
Leeds, May 1997

Note

1 See Matthew Kieran, David Morrison and Michael Svennevig, *Regulating for Changing Values* (London: Broadcasting Standards Commission, 1997).

1 Journalism and ethics
Can they co-exist?

Andrew Belsey

Introduction

Both the image and the essence of journalism are hard to pin down because each appears to contain contradictory strands. By 'image' I mean the way in which journalism is generally regarded by the public. By 'essence' I mean the reality that lies behind (or apart from) the image. It is well known that journalism has a poor image with the public. They do not regard it highly. They are suspicious of journalists and the way they practise their trade. Journalists are regarded in much the same way as politicians, as disreputable, untrustworthy and dishonest, pushing a personal or sectional interest rather than the facts of the case. If people are told that the essence of journalism is truth-telling, they will react with some scepticism or derision. If they are told that the practice of journalism is founded on ethical principles they will either laugh or, if they are prepared to take the matter seriously, point out that the typical tabloid story is trivial, scurrilous or invented.

But all this is contradicted by another image of journalism, illustrated by the most extraordinary event of the British General Election of May 1997. This was the election of Martin Bell as Member of Parliament for the Tatton constituency. Until about a month before the election, Mr Bell was a television journalist – a respected journalist, let it be said – working for the BBC, reporting from the war-torn zones of the world with an immediacy and an integrity that made a considerable impact. To cut a long story short, Mr Bell stood as an anti-corruption (or as the media put it, 'anti-sleaze') candidate against Neil Hamilton, the previous MP for the constituency, who was alleged to have been involved in financial dealings ethically incompatible with the status of a Member of Parliament. When Mr Hamilton refused to stand down and was renominated by his party, the candidates of the other major parties withdrew to give Mr Bell a clear run, and he was elected as an Independent with some ease.

This was an unusual situation. It is unusual for non-party candidates to be elected to the House of Commons. It is even more unusual for major parties to stand aside to assist a non-party candidate. But what was most unusual was that this non-party candidate, standing on a platform of public and political honesty, was a journalist, a member of a profession usually mistrusted as much as politicians themselves. But here was the public, or at least that part of it represented by the electors of Tatton, putting their trust in Mr Bell as the right person to stand up against political corruption, or any suspicion of it.

Part of the reason for this is the character of Martin Bell himself, as he is well known to the television audience who have been able to assess him as a person of integrity. But there is more to it than this. It is not that there is a general mistrust of journalists, but with Martin Bell as the sole exception. There is a different and competing image of journalism, which can indeed be focused on reporters like Martin Bell. Journalists who, for example, stand in bullet-strewn areas at considerable risk to themselves, telling the viewers via the camera what exactly is going on, are regarded as brave and honourable, and almost certainly doing their honest best to present an objective and truthful account of what is happening and why.

There is, perhaps, a difference between television and newspaper journalism here. Many people rely on television as the main source of information for news, current affairs, world events, consumer matters and the like. Being able to see the journalist or presenter and whatever else is on the screen means that the audience can to some extent trust its eyes rather than rely solely on the word. Of course, in one sense this means that there is even greater scope for manipulative propaganda if the control of television broadcasting is in the wrong hands, so the audience will also take the source into account. In the United Kingdom the BBC is more trusted than channels with purely commercial (profit-seeking) interests, which is one reason why the maintenance of public service broadcasting is socially and politically important. Still, although of course anyone would be foolish to place absolute trust in anything that appears on television, there is a contrast with the newspaper world, where there is the suspicion among readers, justifiably based on actual cases that have been exposed, that journalists sit in their offices and invent stories. Newspapers are also known to be politically biased and to treat their readers unscrupulously, so why should they be trusted? But it is not just intentional bias that is regarded as a danger. Although both television images and written stories are taken in through the eyes, there is an enormous difference in their reception, for words are known to be deceptive, always at a remove from a reality that can be depicted directly.

It would, however, be a mistake to rely on there being an intrinsic difference between television and newspaper journalism. Although stories have been invented by some newspapers, it is usually other papers that have exposed these deceptions of the public. And the alleged corruption against which Martin Bell offered himself as a symbol was brought to light by a lengthy and sustained campaign by newspaper journalists, and one that was legally dangerous, given the severity of British libel law. And as for the deceptiveness of the written word, this is not the place to go into this ancient and extraordinarily deep philosophical issue, so let me just say that it is a problem that we mostly manage to overcome at a pragmatic level in our daily lives. Whenever we are offered information, whether by newspapers, television, the Internet or any other source, we have no option but to use our everyday intelligence to assess it for reliability. This applies as much to a depiction as to a word or written text.

There is then no general assurance of the soundness of journalism. Just as nowadays the practice of television journalism is satirised on television, so there is a long tradition of satire against the foolishness of the newspaper industry before the television age (Evelyn Waugh's *Scoop*, for instance). But there have always been journalists who have stood out from the crowd because their virtue (if not always their judgement) seems unimpeachable. There are examples this century from George Orwell and James Cameron down to the investigative journalists of recent years, who have recognised that the proper practice of journalism must sometimes be subversive and anti-establishment, and expose what those in power would rather keep concealed from the public to whom they should be accountable.

The point, however, is not that there are exceptional individuals like Orwell, Cameron and Bell who escape the public suspicion and distrust of journalists. It is rather, as I have already hinted, that there is a different and competing image of journalism, one that contradicts the low esteem in which journalism is held. No doubt there is a good deal of Hollywood in this image, but it is more than a myth. This alternative image presents the journalist as the fearless investigative reporter standing up against the mob or the dishonest city boss, determined to expose the corruption because 'the public has a right to know'. More generally this is an image which sees journalism as serving a useful, even indispensable function in society, providing the information, the analysis, the discussion and the comment without which a modern complex society could not operate. This takes us straight to the underlying political justification for the existence of journalism and for such notions as 'the freedom of the press', that the free circulation of news and opinion is a requirement of a democratic society.[1]

Journalism as an industry

Corresponding roughly to the double image of journalism is a two-sided reality but one in which the two sides contradict rather than complement each other. On the one hand journalism is an industry, a major player in the profit-seeking market economy, and journalists are merely workers in that industry, driven by the need to make a living. On the other hand journalism is a profession, a vocation founded on ethical principles which direct and regulate the conduct of the practitioner. Since trying to live in both these realities is difficult, if not contradictory, deeper explanation and analysis is called for.

There is no doubt that journalism is a major industry. Indeed, journalism is too narrow a term: this is the age of the media. The media are multifarious, transnational and interlinked: newspapers, magazines, television, radio, film, video, cable, communication satellites, the Internet are increasingly coming under the control of a handful of corporations which are based nowhere and everywhere and which seek greater market share, greater profits and greater global influence. In spite of the variety the media is, in defiance of grammar, a singular phenomenon, and one which has universal effect. Once upon a time social theorists were concerned with material production and with the means of production, the farms, forests, factories, fleets and mines which constituted the economy. Today we are sometimes urged to forget these old-fashioned concerns and to realise that this is the age not of production but of information, and that it is the means of information that now dominate economic and social life and provide an insight into its heart and mind.

In such an industry media workers are like any other workers. They are concerned with getting a job, job security, working conditions, future prospects, and, quite rightly, personal satisfaction. They are under the usual pressures of work in the 1990s: line management, downsizing, deskilling ('shorthand not required') and reskilling ('Windows 95^{TM} and PageMaker^{TM} required'). It is market share and the 'bottom line' that rule, and sales figures, circulation figures, audience figures and keeping the advertisers happy dominate the thoughts and actions of the executives who manage the various branches of the corporation. This ethos soon permeates the whole structure of the media industry, including, it must be stressed, that part of it still theoretically devoted to the public service. In a competitive market audience figures and the urge towards growth are as inescapable in 'non-commercial' organisations as in the explicitly profit-seeking ones.[2]

Let me admit that this is not the whole story, for, whatever other age we live in, it is also nominally the ethical age, not just in medical ethics and other traditional areas of moral concern but in environmental ethics, professional ethics, business ethics. Corporations – not necessarily from the best of motives but because they recognise and fear the power of the concerned consumer – include ethical objectives in their statements of principle, and emphasise their commitment to environmental responsibility, the rights of indigenous people, meeting the needs of the customer, personal (or personnel) development, parental leave, crèches, and all the other symbols of the modern caring corporation. But while admitting all this it is not too much of an exaggeration to say that overall it has little effect against the overwhelming demands of competition and the requirement for growth as the only means to survival in a heartless world. The market is either amoral or immoral (or perhaps both at different times), and this affects the media industry as much as any other.[3]

What then of ethics in the media? Inasmuch as workers of all sorts are required to 'perform', financial objectives predominate and there seems to be little scope for ethics, irrespective of the worker's own personal motives and desires. Perhaps it could even be argued that in journalism the situation is worse, because the doctor who exploits a vulnerable patient for sexual favours can be struck off and lose the privilege of practising, and an accountant who steals from clients can be sent to prison, but a journalist who misbehaves may get a scoop and a promotion. The theoretical and practical difficulty, however, lies in deciding what constitutes journalistic misbehaviour.

There are two contradictory pressures on journalists. On the one hand they are subject to the attention of the lobbyists and the publicity-seekers, who not only want their story told but want their own slant on it. This is an ethically-fraught area (especially if the lobbyist happens to be also the owner of the newspaper or television channel). But it is the other hand which is even more ethically interesting and puzzling here, because a lot of journalism consists of discovering and printing information about something or some situation that those involved in would rather keep secret. (Sometimes, of course, the two hands come together: journalists are deliberately given a misleading story to print but recognise it for what it is and have to investigate for themselves what the real story is.)

To make the situation even more complicated, this second aspect of journalism can itself be divided into at least two parts. First, much of the practice of discovering and printing information that some people would wish to keep secret is absolutely and legitimately central to journalism. Investigative journalism, finding out what is really going on in society, keeping people well informed about political, economic and other matters, providing information, analysis and comment, is precisely what a responsible press is supposed to do in a democracy in order to serve the public interest. But where are the boundaries of the public interest? That is the question. They do not coincide, as has often been pointed out, with what the public is interested in.

The second part of discovering and printing what some people would prefer to keep secret often involves information that the public is interested in, but should not be, from an ethical point of view. This is what is not legitimately part of journalism. This can involve any combination of ethically dubious content, presentation and investigation. The content may be what is properly secret, or at least private (the two are not the same).[4] Thus personal privacy should be respected, and although it is difficult to draw the line, there are some things clearly on the wrong side of it, like invasions of private grief and suffering. But well beyond this private people are entitled to a private life; the difficulty is always in deciding who are these 'private people'.[5] Then there is the question of presentation. Dubious material is usually presented in dubious ways, involving trivialisation, sensationalism, obscenity, vulgarity, racism, sexism and homophobia. But even legitimate material can be presented in ways that are ethically offensive, a point often overlooked in discussions of media ethics.

Methods of investigation have traditionally received more ethical attention. There are technological aids, like long-range cameras, telephone taps and electronic eavesdropping devices of all sorts, used to spy on people and pry into their affairs. Of course, modern technology cannot be blamed for unethical journalism, since deception, lying and trespass have always been open to journalists. We know, of course, that journalists often behave in such unethical ways, and if it is unethical, then they should not do it. It is as simple as that.

If only it were as simple as that! The point is that words like 'deception', 'lying' and even 'spy' and 'pry' have the ethical evaluation, the condemnation, built into them. But should activities like this, only without the condemnation, be contemplated by journalists? Let us revisit the distinction between the content, the material of journalism, and the method of investigation. Could the end justify the means? In the investigation of crime or corruption, or just incompetence, perhaps the journalist has to resort to some deception.[6] These are areas where the people involved would rather keep things secret but where the public really does have a right to know. There is a long and honourable tradition (perhaps dying now) of investigative journalism, in which the journalist cannot come straight out with the questions. Much investigative journalism (like much police work) is not glamorous but consists of the minute analysis and comparison of thousands of documents. But then some first-hand investigation might be called for, in which a bit of deception, a touch of electronic eavesdropping, is the only available means – but with words like 'deception' and 'eavesdropping' shorn of their condemnatory ethical undertones.

But can we play about with the meanings of words like this? In this context the question is part of a much larger and central ethical issue about the relation of ends and means, and the related problem of dirty hands. Can we do good by doing bad? If we are doing good, then perhaps we are not doing bad. The issue usually comes up in discussions of issues much more difficult than journalism, like war and violence. Is bombing a city justifiable if civilians will be killed? Is it morally right to assassinate the evil dictator?[7] (It is worth remembering, however, that for journalists not lucky enough to work in liberal democracies, this last question might be practically pressing rather than merely theoretical, especially when the dictator is not only willing and able to assassinate them, but preparing to.) But even in liberal democracies journalists can find themselves investigating evil and ruthless people, when prudence if not morality calls for deception. But how can the gangster, the drug pusher, the corrupt politician, the fraudulent businessman be exposed, except by methods which in other contexts would be questionable? Perhaps in these journalistic contexts such methods are morally required.

So far in this section I have been concerned with 'industrial' journalism, in which journalism is just a job and the journalist is subject to all the usual pressures to 'perform' for the sake of the corporation. I have already strayed into ethical matters but will postpone further discussion of them until the next section, when I shall deal with them more directly. Before that, what can we conclude about industrial journalism? Corporate pressures, the search for sales, the search for audience, promote the production of material that the public is interested in, rather than that which is in the public interest. So as not to appear too unconspiratorial, I should say that 'what the public is interested in' is not fixed, a given, eternal, immutable fact of nature. The appetite is rather, and largely, constructed by the very media that feed it, in a glorious circle of supply creating demand and demand creating supply.

One symptom of the resulting trivialisation of social life and the representation of it in the media is the failure to distinguish between secrecy and privacy, and a resulting failure to understand the ethical significance of the distinction. Neither term is well defined, and I do not intend to stipulate once-and-for-all definitions of them, but instead to try to bring out the differences significant in the context of journalism. Although private individuals can have secrets, I take secrecy in the political sense to be the concealing of information by those public individuals and organisations with power, when it ought to be available to ordinary people as part of the democratic process, for reasons of accountability. Privacy, on the other hand, although the term is often misused in connection with what organisations try to keep hidden,[8] is something that only individual persons can have, and only in so far as they are engaged in private and not public activities.

These definitions solve few problems; there is an element of circularity, and they do not provide criteria for distinguishing what may be kept hidden legitimately, whether it be a matter of secrecy or privacy. Just as there are no doubt legitimate areas of privacy for individuals so no doubt there are legitimate areas of secrecy for organisations, but they are much smaller than is often taken for granted. (Consider the long struggle in the United Kingdom against official secrecy and for freedom of information.) But industrial journalism, in league with supposed public demand, too often confuses the two areas, and connives with the powerful to keep secret what ought to be exposed, while invading the privacy of those who neither wish for nor deserve such treatment. This is an over-generalisation, of course. Lots of individuals love the attention of the media and are quite willing to be on the receiving end of the publicity. And at the other end of the scale there is still serious journalism dedicated to serving the public interest and to keeping the public informed as part of the democratic process. But the reality of industrial journalism is to be found largely inhabiting an ethics-free zone.

Ethical journalism

So journalism is just a job in a market economy in which the usual pressures of work discourage practice based on ethical principles. But there is another reality in which journalism is a profession based on ethical principles, indeed constituted by ethical practice. However exaggerated the claims about this reality have sometimes been, it is not just a myth, a self-serving piece of propaganda put about by those with lots to hide and lots to gain. Nor is it just an ideal, never to be attained. It is a reality illustrated (rather than proved) by the experience of Martin Bell in Tatton, a journalist getting the support and confidence of the public in direct competition with a politician. Ethical journalism even has a sort of physical embodiment in the *Code of Practice* issued by the Press Complaints Commission (as well as in similar codes all over the world), even though such codes fail to be sufficient from an ethical point of view.[9]

But before fully considering the claims of journalism to have an ethical existence, we should look at the question of professionalism.[10] Ethics and professionalism are often seen as co-requisites. What then is a profession? Traditionally a profession involved the giving of a service by a certified expert to an individual client, for a fee and on the basis of mutual trust and respect. In areas like law and medicine the client has to trust the expertise and the good faith of the practitioner, who in turn respects the needs and vulnerability of the client. The professions are policed in the sense that a practitioner who transgresses against the ethically based standards of practice is punished in some way, with expulsion from the profession as the ultimate sanction.

On this account journalism doesn't sound like a profession, but then neither do many other occupational areas that today claim professional status. (Almost every occupational area claims professional status.) Even the traditional professions often fail to match their traditional image, as social, economic and technological changes alter the relationship between the service-seeker and the service-provider. Perhaps then the emphasis should be on the ideas of ethical practice and adherence to an ethical code. Indeed, it is the proliferation of such codes among occupational groups that is used to justify the claim to professional status. Presumably, the spread of such codes, inasmuch as they have a genuine and serious effect, should be welcomed, as it means that the idea of ethical practice permeates further into society. But if all occupational groups are code-based professions, professional status no longer points to any significant ethical distinction between one occupation and another.

A further (yet related) account of professionalism is in terms of each profession's essence, which links the practice of the profession to the attainment of some intrinsically worthwhile end. Thus it is claimed that the essence of medicine is the promotion of health, of accountancy the insistence on financial probity, of law the pursuit of justice, of social work the enhancement of client autonomy, of the Church the cure of souls, etc. On this approach the essence of journalism is telling the truth, or, to put it in different terms, journalism is constituted by truth-telling. Essentialism of any sort is not these days universally popular as a method of explanation and illumination, and these examples show some of the reasons why. For a start, we might expect all the transactions of everyday life to be based on telling the truth, so there is nothing distinctive about journalism on these grounds. Furthermore, while we might be able to deal with the truth and nothing but the truth, the whole truth is altogether more difficult. All information is selected from an infinite whole, and all information has to be presented in one way or another. And then much journalism is concerned with opinion, argument, debate and discussion, where notions of objectivity and fairness are central, rather than truth. Furthermore, essentialism of this sort is not very helpful because it is over-general and thus somewhat vague. It provides no way forward when the rights and interests of different people conflict. There is a very great deal in the practice of medicine, for example, which is not illuminated by generalities about the promotion of health. This so-called essence does not help much on questions about abortion and euthanasia. Similarly, the notion of truth-telling in journalism does not answer the problem, already discussed, of using dubious methods to obtain the truth. This does not, of course, suggest that telling the truth is not important in journalism.

We have not, so far, tracked down what is meant by speaking of journalism as a profession, except in so far as ethical practice is necessary, but not sufficient, for a profession. But this should be of little concern, as it is the ethical practice and not the designation 'profession' that is important. So long as any occupation, or indeed any activity, is based on sound ethical principles, why should we worry whether it is a profession or not? As I have already suggested, professional status tends to be a self-awarded honorific these days, a fact that is of more sociological than ethical significance. What clearly is of ethical significance is the ethics of the activity, whether it be journalism or anything else.

What then of the reality of ethical journalism? Analogies with traditional professions obstruct rather than assist understanding. A journalist is not (except perhaps in a very few, exceptional cases) an individual service-provider with an individual client. Nevertheless, journalism can best be thought of as providing a service. Journalists provide a vital service to society as a whole, but it is a political service. Journalism is part of the political process. Now of course there are dangers in such a statement. Journalists are not legislators and neither are they governors. It is bad for society and for journalism if journalists are tempted to be either. They should be considered, rather, as facilitators, to use the jargon of the modern age to make a very traditional point.

They facilitate the democratic process. It is not true that we have just moved into the information age, because even the drafters of the American Bill of Rights recognised that information oils the wheels of democracy when they laid down that 'Congress shall make no law . . . abridging the freedom of speech, or of the press' (First Amendment to the Constitution of the United States of America (1791)). Autocratic governments control information, and regard secrecy as a important weapon – and not only autocratic governments. But if a government is to be accountable to the people it must know what is going on; if the people are to cast their votes wisely and rationally they too must know what is going on. Information is necessary (though not of course sufficient) for a successful democracy, inasmuch as it requires the free circulation of news, opinion, debate and discussion. Hence the incorporation of freedom of expression and freedom of information in international charters like the Universal Declaration of Human Rights. A democratic necessity is transformed into a human right.

As commentators on the American Constitution have pointed out, the traffic is not one way, and the privileges guaranteed to journalists by the First Amendment should be reciprocated by the responsibilities of journalists.[11] The privileges are granted to enable journalists to facilitate the democratic process without hindrance, and so they license conduct which is directed towards actually facilitating it, and not just any old conduct. It is in this political area that the reality of ethical journalism is located, since journalism as part of the democratic process can only be ethically informed journalism. The point is obvious, in that the ends of democracy cannot be served by media that are full of untruths, lies, invasions of privacy, scurrility, obscenity, triviality, distortion, bias and all the other sins that industrial journalism actually exhibits. All the virtues associated with ethical journalism – accuracy, honesty, truth, objectivity, fairness, balance, respect for the autonomy of ordinary people – are part of, and required by, journalism as located within the democratic process.

If the media are to be part of the democratic process because of their role in the origination and circulation of information and opinion, then the quality of that information and opinion is going to be a vital issue. Quality here is meant in a typically ethical sense, so that the ethics and the politics of the media are not really different or separable issues. Ethical journalism serves the public interest. One good reason for putting the point in terms of virtues is that although virtues might become ingrained dispositions they are not arbitrary or irrational but based on sound ethical principles. Virtues are not algorithms, but the very nature of their principle-based flexibility enables them to deal more successfully with novel situations than can a set of rules embodied in a code of practice. And a democratic society, especially one in a technological age, will constantly produce situations and opportunities which are ethically novel.

This then is the reality of ethical journalism, journalism based on the idea of virtuous conduct, facilitating the democratic process and serving the public interest. Cynics will say that this is myth-making and that there is no reality behind it. The less cynical might say that it is an ideal of what ought to be, and a long way in advance of what actually is, although we might aspire to make some further progress towards the ideal. The cynic, I wish to argue, goes too far, although given the nature and power of industrial journalism one can understand why there is an apparent justification for such cynicism. The lesser cynic is correct in approach, although, as I have argued, ethical journalism is not just an ideal but a reality, just as much a reality as industrial journalism.

Journalism is a two-sided reality, in which the two sides contradict rather than complement each other. Is this a helpful way of putting the point? I hope so. Industrial journalism exists, and so does ethical journalism. They both co-exist and contend, battling for supremacy in a recreation of an ancient and eternal struggle. Each is armed with different weapons. Industrial journalism can call on the amoral power of the transnational corporation, but ethical journalism is undefeated, being able to rely on the undiminished strength and perennial appeal of virtue.

Co-existence?

But enough of these Manichean metaphors! What is the ordinary journalist to do in his or her everyday working life? No doubt journalists, especially when young and entering the profession, wish to be good journalists, to do a good job, and to obtain at least some degree of personal satisfaction. But they will have mixed motives and expectations, some material, some ethical. It is unlikely that many journalists are motivated directly by a desire to serve the public interest, yet they are likely to have some such notion occupying an underground area of their thoughts.

The pressures of work keep it underground, mostly. Journalists do behave unethically. Yes, they have invented stories, invaded privacy, harassed the unfortunate, used sexist images and generally behaved badly. The image of journalism held by the public, according to which journalists are a shifty, untrustworthy bunch of unprincipled self-servers, has plenty of justification. And yet not all journalists suffer from this image, as is shown by the example of Martin Bell, not only in his habitual role of respected journalist but also in his unexpected role of victorious politician. There is a delicious irony in the fact that it was a journalist who stood for and was elected to Parliament on an ethical ticket.

The pressures of work that prevent ethics from having a firm place in journalism are not all that different from the pressures on anyone else.

There is a job to be got, promotion to be obtained, so the story has to be written and the methods necessary to obtain the story used. The story must sell, the managers must be satisfied, the growth targets met. The market must be chased, so there is a constant temptation (more than a temptation) to print trivial stories, salaciously presented and obtained by suspect methods. Personal beliefs and desires do not come into it. Journalists are often thought to be hypocrites when those who are committed Labour voters work for or even edit newspapers that are little more than Conservative Party propaganda sheets. This has happened, and probably the other way round as well. How can they do it, people wonder, failing to recognise that the necessity of making a living makes a mockery of most people's highest ethical aspirations. Compromise is part of living in the world as it now is.

Does this mean that there is no place for moral integrity in journalism? No, I am far from arguing that, having claimed that ethical journalism is as much a reality as industrial journalism. But of course ethical journalism is under pressure, as is ethics in almost any walk of life, because we live in a world dominated by economic considerations and an economy driven by market forces. Moral motivations and moral intentions are good, but they can be powerless in practice, or misled. They are powerless when the pressures of the system are too great for them to prevail against. They are misled when, for example, journalists find themselves justifying their unethical conduct in terms of their own unblemished intentions to do good, though employing dubious means. This is the doctrine of the double effect, and it is as fallacious in journalism as it is everywhere else.[12]

But fortunately it is not necessary to draw a totally pessimistic conclusion. In spite of all the pressures ethics is entrenched in journalism, and so it will never disappear completely. There is a tradition of truth-seeking, objective reporting and fair and reasonable presentation which is sufficient to challenge if not to defeat industrial journalism. There is also a tradition, though not one that is as strong as it should be, of reasoned discussion of such matters. It is an interesting coincidence that the same Martin Bell, shortly before his sudden transformation into a successful politician, was attracting media attention not because of his own work in the media but because of his theoretical discussion of some of the principles on which it was based. The point he was making was that there is not the conflict that many people assume must exist between objectivity in reporting and commitment to values, because journalists should not try to take a neutral stand between right and wrong. The war reporter in the world of today cannot avoid witnessing an appalling collection of atrocities, massacres, torture and other crimes, and must not pretend that these are neutral events of no moral significance. Such pretence involves a failure to be objective.

This is surely correct, and it illustrates some of the problems of ethical journalism. It is relatively easy for journalists based in liberal democratic countries to be objective about unsavoury military dictators in other parts of the world, but objectivity does not come so easily when the unsavoury character is your own boss. The case of Robert Maxwell demonstrates both the farcical and the tragic side of this. The sight of the sycophants of the living Maxwell intoning moral condemnations over his corpse was amusing for the uninvolved spectators but not for those whose pensions disappeared with Maxwell over the side of the boat.

But there is, I fear, no resolution of the contradiction, no solution to the paradox of industrial journalism co-existing with ethical journalism. Yes, good intentions are fine, but they can only operate within the existing system. But systems are rarely monolithic and thus they fail to be monopolistic. There is scope for good intentions, after all. But good intentions are not sufficient, as they need to be matched by corresponding good actions. This is why I put the emphasis on virtue in journalism, as virtue is a disposition to act in ethically correct ways, even in novel situations. And whatever the difficulties caused by co-existing with industrial journalism, there is still scope for the tradition of ethical journalism to live and develop.

Notes

1 See Judith Lichtenberg (ed.), *Democracy and the Mass Media* (Cambridge: Cambridge University Press, 1990).
2 For a wide-ranging discussion of the issues raised in this paragraph, see James Curran and Jean Seaton, *Power without Responsibility: The Press and Broadcasting in Britain*, 4th edn (London: Routledge, 1991).
3 The current state of business ethics is surveyed in Peter W. F. Davies (ed.), *Current Issues in Business Ethics* (London: Routledge, 1997).
4 See Sisela Bok, *Secrets: On the Ethics of Concealment and Revelation* (Oxford: Oxford University Press, 1982); and F. D. Schoeman (ed.), *Philosophical Dimensions of Privacy* (Cambridge: Cambridge University Press, 1984).
5 This is discussed further in my article 'Privacy, publicity and politics', in Andrew Belsey and Ruth Chadwick (eds), *Ethical Issues in Journalism and the Media* (London: Routledge, 1992), pp. 77–92.
6 See Bok, *Secrets*, pp. 249–64; and Jennifer Jackson, 'Honesty in investigative journalism', in Belsey and Chadwick, *Ethical Issues in Journalism*, pp. 93–111; and on the wider issues, Sisela Bok, *Lying: Moral Choice in Public and Private Life* (Brighton: Harvester, 1978).
7 Jonathan Glover provides an illuminating introduction to such moral issues in *Causing Death and Saving Lives* (Harmondsworth: Penguin Books, 1977). See also Richard Norman, *Ethics, Killing and War* (Cambridge: Cambridge University Press, 1995).
8 See Bok, *Secrets*, esp. p. 13.
9 Press Complaints Commission, *Code of Practice* (London, Press Complaints Commission, September 1994). There is an analysis of the PCC Code in Andrew Belsey and Ruth Chadwick, 'Ethics as a vehicle for media quality', *European Journal of Communication* 10 (1995), pp. 461–73. See also Nigel G. E. Harris, 'Codes of conduct for journalists', in Belsey and Chadwick, *Ethical Issues in Journalism*, pp. 62–76.

10 See Ruth Chadwick (ed.), *Ethics and the Professions* (Aldershot: Avebury, 1994).
11 This issue is discussed in Stephen Klaidman and Tom L. Beauchamp, *The Virtuous Journalist* (New York: Oxford University Press, 1987), esp. pp. 5–14. My thinking on ethics and journalism owes a great deal to the clarifications and insights of Klaidman and Beauchamp's book.
12 See Glover, *Causing Death and Saving Lives*, esp. pp. 86–91.

2 The journalism of attachment

Martin Bell

I write as a war reporter of some antiquity – that is, more than thirty years in the business, from the killing fields of Vietnam to the *barrios* of Nicaragua to the savage hills and valleys of central Bosnia. It was not a calling that I ever chose; rather, I would say that it chose me. One day a long time ago in a BBC newsroom, I happened to be the reporter nearest the door when a foreign war broke out. Having survived one war zone I would then be asked to take my chances in another – and then still more, until today I have discovered that a journalist can be typecast just as much as an actor. I am well on the wrong side of 55 and had wished to end my career with a stint as peace correspondent, if such a job were to exist; but sadly I have concluded that it does not. I even tried to resign, but was vigorously dissuaded.

Have the wars themselves changed? Hardly at all. The modern high-tech high-intensity conflict exemplified by the Gulf War was probably the exception. The Bosnian War was more typical; in it civilians were targeted on a massive scale and the weapons used were essentially those of the First World War battlefields: rifles, machine guns, mines, trench mortars and artillery. They were just as lethal: an old trench mortar can ruin your day just as effectively as a bright shining new cruise missile. Sometimes as I stood amid the mud and barbed wire of these wasted emplacements it seemed to me that we had learned nothing and forgotten everything, and that we were revisiting history all the way back to 1914, pausing only to fail to absorb the lessons of 1938. The only new ingredient was television.

But our way of reporting the wars has changed fundamentally, and not only because of television and its satellite dishes, those concave discs which we pitch almost on the front lines themselves and which uplink all our tragedies and bind us to them. Our attitudes and ways of working have also changed. When I started out as a war reporter in the mid-1960s I worked in the shadow of my distinguished predecessors and of a long and honourable BBC tradition of distance and detachment. I thought of it then as objective and necessary. I would now call it *bystanders' journalism*. It concerned itself more with the circumstances of wars – military formations, tactics, strategies and weapons systems – than with the people who provoke them, the people who fight them and the people who suffer from them (by no means always the same categories of people).

I am no longer sure about the notion of objectivity, which seems to me now to be something of an illusion and a shibboleth. When I have reported from the war zones, or anywhere else, I have done so with all the fairness and impartiality I could muster, and a scrupulous attention to the facts, but using my eyes and ears and mind and accumulated experience, which are surely the very essence of the subjective.

This is not an argument for campaigning or crusading journalism. That has its place, from William Cobbett in the last century to G. K. Chesterton, George Orwell, John Pilger and many others in this, but its place is in political and polemical literature and not in the daily chronicling of the news. I am old-fashioned enough to insist on the distinction between them. Besides, it is my experience that the campaigners and crusaders tend to find what they are looking for, ignoring inconvenient evidence to the contrary and the unstructured complexity of what is actually out there. Rather, I have found it useful to do the opposite and seek out the unfavoured spokesmen of unpopular causes, whether the Afrikaners in South Africa, the loyalist paramilitaries in Northern Ireland, or the Serbs in Bosnia; they will often hold the key to a conflict and its possible resolution.

In place of the dispassionate practices of the past I now believe in what I call the *journalism of attachment*. By this I mean a journalism that cares as well as knows; that is aware of its responsibilities; that will not stand neutrally between good and evil, right and wrong, the victim and the oppressor. This is not to back one side or faction or people against another. It is to make the point that we in the press, and especially in television, which is its most powerful division, do not stand apart from the world. We are a part of it. We exercise a certain influence, and we have to know that. The influence may be for better or for worse, and we have to know that too.

In my one and only book, which was mainly about the Bosnian War and which touched on this issue, I cited a story from Sarajevo which I hope is apocryphal but I believe is not.[1] It was about a journalist who wished to write a profile of a front-line sniper. It did not matter on which side the sniper operated, because both sides had them and each feared the other's as much as it valued its own. The reporter made his arrangements with the man's commander and visited the front line. The sniper was peering out from between two bricks in his forward defences. The reporter asked, 'What do you see?' The sniper replied, 'I see two people walking in the street: which of them do you want me to shoot?' It was at this point that the reporter realised, too late, that he had embarked on a project which was inherently lethal and which he should not even have considered. So he urged the sniper to shoot neither of them, made his excuses and turned to leave. As he did so, he heard two shots of rapid fire from the position just behind him. He turned and looked, questioning. 'That was a pity,' said the sniper, 'you could have saved one of their lives.'

I use this example because, even at the level of theory or hypothesis, it disposes of the myth of the journalist as neutral observer and witness, the candle-holder who looks on. There are other instances which occur almost daily in the known, real world of war reporting. Which of us has not, during a tour of the trench lines in quieter times (which is when such facilities are usually offered), been asked by a soldier whether we would like him to blaze away, with rifle or machine-gun, for the camera's sole benefit? On one occasion an entire battery of 105 millimetre field guns would have been fired for my benefit, had I wished. To have accepted the offer would greatly have increased the marketability of what I had to offer my news editor later in the day. But the answer to all such invitations had to be a firm and principled 'No'.

Is that always the case? I somehow doubt it. I am fortunate in having worked for a news organisation, the BBC, in which – despite all its trials and travails – a culture of truthfulness still prevails, and which is not driven by the commercial imperative of maximising profits. (The interesting comparison here, not on the point of truthfulness but of profit-chasing, is with another great but troubled institution, Reuters.) The differences which have arisen between the BBC and myself, one of its foot soldiers in the trenches of news – differences on a range of issues from 'objective' reporting to rolling news to the censorship of real-world violence – are essentially a falling out between friends on matters of perspective rather than principle.

These are exactly the same differences that occur, on a field of battle, between an army's front-line soldiers and its staff officers. We see things that they do not see. We know things that they do not know. We have been where they have not. Yet they command and deploy us. This discrepancy of view is even greater in television, because of the technical advances in recent years that have so much extended its reach, if not its grasp. Our staff officers – the programme editors and network executives – are on the receiving end of such a flood of information both verbal and visual that they *think* they see and they *think* they know and they *think* that they have been there. The news itself takes on an aspect of virtual reality; it may be that the problem lies partly in the proliferation of computer screens, and in journalists whose eyes are directed downward at the screens in front of them, rather than outward at the wider world beyond. So the screens become screens also in the traditional sense, of blocking the view and filtering out the light.

The differences between us were brought home to me most forcefully in November 1996, when I attempted to explain my 'journalism of attachment' to an audience of television news people in Berlin. I was invited, not by the BBC but by my friends in German television, to take part in a session on the ethics of television journalism; I contributed a few brief, and moderate, remarks about the limits of objectivity. I was not in fact proposing anything new and revolutionary, although there were some present who saw it as that, but merely articulating a change in the practice of news reporting. I pointed out that the BBC's guidelines require its reporters to be objective and dispassionate. I am no longer sure what 'objective' means: I see nothing object-like in the relationship between the reporter and the event, but rather a human and dynamic interaction between them. As for 'dispassionate', it is not only impossible but inappropriate to be thus neutralised – I would even say *neutered* – at the scene of an atrocity or massacre, or most man-made calamities. I was not dispassionate at Ahmici in Bosnia in 1993, just as Jeremy Bowen was not at the bombed bunker in Baghdad in 1991, and for that matter even the great Richard Dimbleby himself was not at the liberation of Belsen in 1945 (and he was operating in a much more restrictive broadcasting climate).

There is a time to be passionate and a time to be dispassionate – a time and a season for all things; and I would not report the slaying of innocent people in the same tone and manner that I would use for a state visit or a flower show or an exchange of parliamentary insults.

It is a matter of common sense. It is also a matter of tone and tact rather than language, for television resists the flourishes of rhetoric and fine writing. It is a cool medium which answers best to understatement and requires the sparest of commentaries, especially alongside powerful and emotive pictures. Adjectives themselves are hardly necessary, since our images are our adjectives. Lately I have come to be merciless even with the verbs. The hardest technical discipline of all is the writing of silence.

I was in the process of explaining some of this to my colleagues in Berlin, when I was set upon from the floor by a middle-ranking BBC executive who clearly saw me as a heretic and backslider from long-established truths. He compared me to a priest who had grown weary of the long years of celibacy and had resolved to explore the carnal pleasures hitherto denied. (The term that he used was less felicitous, but executives do not necessarily rise through the ranks by having a way with words.) He then countered my argument for a principled journalism with the old and Shakespeare-derived notion of the function of news being to hold a mirror up to nature, or in this case to events in the world about us.

But the analogy is, of course, a false one. It is false for this reason, that the mirror does not affect what it reflects, the television image does. This is a clear and consequential distinction. One of its consequences is that journalism – not only in the war zones and amid human suffering, but perhaps especially there – is not a neutral and mechanical undertaking but in some sense a moral enterprise. It must be informed by an idea of right and wrong. It operates frequently on morally dangerous ground. It makes a difference. It has to be aware, as in the story of the reporter and the sniper, of what that difference might be.

I happen to believe – and I admit this to be a comforting, even convenient belief – that especially in the case of television the difference is mostly benign. I know there are critics who hold otherwise, and that in situations of incipient riot and civil commotion the very presence of television can be inflammatory. This certainly has been so on some occasions, though people tend to hold to their own realities. I remember a long time ago during a serious loyalist riot in East Belfast being approached by an old lady who bore down on me, with voice and umbrella raised, through a hail of missiles. She accused me of filming something that wasn't happening. She had her reality, I had mine: we were apparently not even witnesses of the same event.

But for most of the early 1990s I spent my working life in an environment rather less agreeable than civil commotion: the projectiles were harder edged and moving faster. I make no exaggerated claims here; but that time served in the war zones has left me with the settled conviction that the effect of television, even as its impact and influence have grown, has been to make things a little *less worse* than they would have been without it.

To take the simple example of prisoner exchanges: there was no deal between the three peoples and armies of Bosnia more likely to be undone, no business or transaction between them more fallible, than the handing over and retrieving of prisoners. It brought out their deepest dislike and distrust of each other, as well as a distinctively Balkan sense of the value of human life. So it was that at quite an early point in the war they came to insist on the presence of a foreign television crew at the handover point, as a means of holding each other to honour agreements already reached. Sometimes it worked and sometimes it didn't. But the television camera made failure less inevitable.

On a broader canvas, I would argue from experience that the presence of television in the satellite age makes war crimes harder to commit, and certainly harder to get away with than in the darker ages preceding it. This may seem a difficult case to make from a war which was waged with peculiar brutality and included the massacres at Srebrenica, Ahmici and Uzdol (only one of these, incidentally, involving the Serbs); but it was one of the many lessons of the Bosnian War that, in this decade of the dish, a military victory can swiftly turn into a political defeat. So it was with the Serbs. Their siege of Sarajevo held, and their enemies' attempts to break it were beaten back repeatedly and at terrible cost. But the killing and maiming of civilians, under the eye of the camera, left the Serbs friendless and isolated. The major bombardments of Sarajevo over a three and a half year period were viewed all over the world on the day that they happened. The counter-attacks, by Bosnian government forces, were either not viewed, or seen as acts of defence by a people cruelly besieged. The Serbs' case was lost in the court of world opinion before ever a war crimes tribunal was even mooted.

Of course in all such cases a tide of lies will wash over the airwaves; the perpetrators of war crimes will attempt to cover their tracks; and as television grows more consequential it will find itself increasingly blocked, cajoled and manipulated. But sooner or later the truth will come out, or a sufficient outline of it, as most notoriously it did many months after the massacre at Srebrenica. The war crimes will do most damage, over the long term, to those who commit them.

The same applies to the indiscriminate targeting of civilians; a point may actually have been reached where television is changing the conduct of wars and the ways in which they are waged. The British Army's staff college regularly introduces into its war games (the theoretical scenarios of future conflict) an element of media intrusion, in which an alliance's cohesion or an army's willingness to fight may be weakened by a public relations disaster: the bombing of an orphanage, perhaps, instead of an arms dump. 'Collateral damage' – as dreadful a euphemism as 'ethnic cleansing' – can now be decisive in a military campaign. This may be a heretical notion to introduce, but I have come to wonder whether, had satellite television existed in 1945, the carpet-bombing of Dresden and Hamburg by the British and Americans would have been politically possible; or would the tens of thousands of civilian casualties have turned allied opinion against the prosecution of the war by such ruthless means? Further back still, could the sacrificial strategies of the Battle of the Somme in 1916 even have been contemplated? They would be unthinkable today.

In our own time, much ink has been spilled on the relationship between television and diplomacy – the so-called 'CNN effect', which for reasons of regimental pride I should prefer to call the 'BBC effect'. That there is such a connection is now accepted by all but a few unreconstructed British diplomats of the old school. I remember an American colleague telling the story of President Bush's Chief of Staff, usually a man of meticulous punctuality, arriving late for his appointment with him; he explained that CNN had just screened some dramatic footage from Kurdistan, and the administration was therefore revising its policy towards the Kurds.

The British establishment tends to resent such pressures as an impudent challenge to its wisdom by an upstart medium. When Douglas Hurd was Foreign Secretary, he pointed out that murder, warfare and the forced migration of peoples were nothing new; they had always been with us. What was new was that, mainly through television, they were much more widely known than they had been before; and so politicians were challenged to take action on issues that were not of their choosing, and on priorities set by the box in the corner of the living room. Mr Hurd was rather scathing about the 'Something Must Be Done Club'.

He was speaking with the Bosnian example specifically in mind. I am, I suppose, a founder member of his 'Something Must Be Done Club'. I find the company I keep there more honourable, and easier to live with, than those who associate with the opposing faction, the 'Nothing Can Be Done Club'. Besides, I never openly advocated intervention in Bosnia (except once, and inferentially, with a parallel exposition of the risks). I did not need to. The images did it for me. But if, as a result of the television reporting from Bosnia, governments were moved to take action which they would not otherwise have taken, and people were helped who would not otherwise have been helped, I see nothing there for which we need apologise. For all the failures and retreats of the UN's involvement there, it probably saved a hundred thousand lives. Is anyone maintaining that those lives were not worth saving?

To me this is another case of television doing more good than harm. But since I am concerning myself here with the moral ground on which it operates, I will add a note of warning about a tendency which, if it persists, could do more harm than good. I am not referring here to the ratings-driven downmarket drift of the news agenda, especially on the commercial and satellite channels, although that is troubling enough. I mean the representation of real-world violence.

It is a long-running argument. What we should show and what we should not show are issues that cause more difficulty to a television reporter in a war zone than any others, except getting access in the first place. I have even wondered, occasionally, whether it isn't easier to deal with the warlords than the editors. At least I am face to face with the warlords and understand them; we are sharing the same slivovitz. The editors are a thousand miles away; they are cautiously determined not to cause offence; we are negotiating about raw footage that I have seen and they have not, and working to guidelines that are vague and variable.

I find myself at one end of this argument, and usually standing alone. I do not believe that we should show everything that we see. Some images of violence – as for instance most of the pictures of both the market-place massacres in Sarajevo – are almost literally unviewable and cannot be inflicted on the public. But people have to be left with *some* sense of what happened, if only through the inclusion of pictures sufficiently powerful at least to hint at the horror of those excluded. To do otherwise is to present war as a relatively cost-free enterprise and an acceptable way of settling differences, a one-sided game that soldiers play in which they are seen shooting but never suffering. The camera shows the outgoing ordnance, but seldom the incoming.

This actually connects with the sort of world in which the old-style 'dispassionate' war reporter could ply his craft quite comfortably. No need to be unflinching, because nothing is left in the coverage that he has to flinch from. No need to be compassionate, because nothing is left in that he has to care about. What remains? Neither evil nor suffering nor bloodshed nor grief, nor anything from the darker shores of the human condition – but just a passing show, an acceptable spectacle.

The argument is more one of degree than of principle. But I believe that we have retreated too far, certainly in British television – practices vary from country to country and network to network – and that a measure of course-correction is now in order. We should flinch less. We should sometimes be willing to shock and to disturb. We should show the world more nearly as we find it, without the anaesthetic of a good-taste censorship. And if we do not, then perhaps we should ask ourselves whether we are merely being considerate, or *indifferent*. And in a world where genocide has returned in recent years to haunt three continents we should remind ourselves that this crime against humanity requires accomplices: not only the hatred that makes it happen, but *the indifference that lets it happen*.

I have a friend, a Bosnian soldier who spent more time in Bosnia than any other, who chides me for having let the Bosnian War get at me too much. 'There you go again,' he says when he sees me at work, 'bleeding all over your typewriter.' (Yes, I still use a typewriter: it keeps me honest.) Maybe he is right. It is certainly easier to take the reporter out of the war zone than the war zone out of the reporter. But the soldiers themselves have also been deeply affected by what they have seen there, and are not less effective as soldiers because of it. We, and they, are battle-softened veterans of a foreign war.

These are issues which seem to me to deserve more attention than they commonly receive. Should we really be expected, in the most powerful news medium ever devised, to be indifferent to its consequences? Is objectivity even possible? Should it be one of our imperatives not to upset people? What do we believe in? What in the end is our vaunted technology *for*? And what is the justification for a disengaged journalism which would requires its practitioners, as special people with special privileges, to close their hearts to pity?

This is a phrase with a certain historical resonance. There was in this century a military commander who urged his generals to do just that – to close their hearts to pity. He enjoyed a measure of success for a while. His name was Adolf Hitler.

Note

1 Martin Bell, *In Harm's Way: Reflections of a War Zone Thug* (London: Hamish Hamilton, 1995).

3 Objectivity, impartiality and good journalism

Matthew Kieran

Introduction

It is a commonplace assumption of journalism that the media have a fundamental duty to be impartial in order to achieve the goal of an objective report or analysis of current events. Of course, certain kinds of feature journalism or polemical programming do not have such a duty but I am unconcerned with those here. Rather, my focus is upon news reports, investigative journalism or current affairs programmes. This supposed duty, to impartiality and objectivity, arises from conceiving of the media as an unofficial fourth estate.[1] One of the functions the media must fulfil is to report and evaluate, appropriately, events that affect our lives as members of society. Hence, for example, the media must inform us about significant political matters, criminal proceedings, social affairs, corruption and vicious hypocrisy. Thus, in covering such matters appropriately, it seems to follow that the media must be impartial in their approach in order to arrive at and report upon what is, in fact, the case. This explains precisely why, above all else, journalists prize their reputation for impartiality. To accuse a journalist of being biased is to impugn his journalistic integrity in the deepest possible sense. For it is to claim that a journalist is, intentionally or otherwise, not adhering to the truth-respecting methods required for him to achieve the proper goal of journalism: arriving at the truth of the matter. Hence when Nick Robinson, a BBC political correspondent, heard rumours that media managers in the Labour Party were whispering that he had his own political motives and agenda his response was the following: 'I've had ten years as a journalist in the BBC and nobody's ever accused me of bias and if they do I'll pursue it.'[2]

However, it has become increasingly fashionable, within cultural, media and even journalistic studies, to dismiss claims concerning objectivity. Infamously, at the time of the Gulf War, Baudrillard claimed that the war was only a media event.[3] In a similar vein Glasser claims that journalists striving for objectivity rely, falsely, upon a 'naively empirical view of the world, a belief in the separation of facts and values, a belief in the existence of *a* reality – the reality of empirical facts.'[4] Of course, construed in one sense, such claims are clearly false. There are facts of the matter which can be faithfully reported. The Gulf War did happen and any report which claimed it didn't is obviously false. However, we can construe the claim in a more interesting fashion. The basic thought is that news events inevitably give rise to a number of different legitimate reports which are not reducible to one underlying complete and consistent report. This is because news reports rest upon commitments to fundamental moral, social and political principles. Yet these principles are not themselves open to dispute but are presumed to be inaccessible to critical questioning.[5] One could hold to this claim on the grounds that fundamental beliefs are ideological and thus determined by the socio-economic structure or discourse we are implicated within. I believe this presumption to be typically false but will not examine it here.[6] A more interesting argument which might underwrite such a position can be derived from the work of Richard Rorty. The basic thought is that since our most fundamental beliefs and values are contingent, they are not amenable to rational justification:

> As long as we think that there is some relation called 'fitting the world' . . . which can be possessed or lacked by vocabularies-as-wholes, we shall continue the traditional philosophical search for a criterion to tell us which vocabularies have this desirable feature. But if we could ever become reconciled to the idea that most of reality is indifferent to our descriptions of it . . . then we should at last have assimilated what was true in the Romantic idea that truth is made rather than found, and that truth is a property of linguistic entities, of sentences.[7]

The subjectivity of interpretation

News is essentially value-laden. Given that journalists bring to bear their fundamental value assumptions in making a report, any event is open to innumerable redescriptions in different terms. Thus it is pointless to seek rational justification in order to privilege one news report over any other. For, the claim is, description is interpretation-laden and interpretation itself is evaluatively driven. Any given event is open to many possible interpretations which are appropriate given different kinds of evaluative concerns and commitments. So journalists who claim to search for 'the right' description, interpretation and evaluation of states of affairs are, on such a view, misguided and misleading. Much of the force of the critique of objectivity derives, in relation to media analysis, from the way it apparently captures the nature of journalism's pre-reflective practice. For over different newspapers, broadcast bulletins, individual journalists and the time-span of a story we seem to end up with divergent reports of the same event. The nature of an event, it is claimed, partly depends upon those who interpret it.

Consider, further, the following example. When the ceasefire in Northern Ireland was announced on 30 August 1994, there was obviously a huge demand for stories about the ceasefire that would symbolise the incipient hopes for the peace process. On the day itself Crispin Rodwell, a photographer acting for Reuters, was asked to get an image to go with the hopeful news. He spent some time traversing Belfast and came upon a freshly painted slogan, 'Time for Peace, Time to Go.' So he started photographing the slogan whilst people walked by. Whilst he was doing so a young boy started playing brick-a-bat against the wall, which he managed to capture on film (see Figure). He then sent a batch of the photographs through to Reuters, including one of the boy in front of the slogan. Now, importantly, Rodwell cropped the photograph so that the second half of the slogan, 'Time to Go', did not appear. Reuters's executive editor rang Rodwell to check that the photograph had not been artificially set up in some way, for example by paying for the slogan to be painted. Once satisfied that this was not the case, Reuters syndicated the photograph around the world and it was the predominant image used on the front pages of most British newspapers to go with the story about the ceasefire.

Now, of course, however one interprets the image and its use, certain low-level descriptions of what the photograph is of are true. The slogan had been painted on the wall and the boy had played brick-a-bat against it.

Figure

But, we might think, such low-level descriptions can be interpreted and evaluated in rather different ways. Thus journalists generally are not so much after *the* rational assessment and report of a story but, rather, different ways of interpreting and evaluating the same event in ways in which the relevant audience will find appropriate.

The point is that, as Rodwell and the Reuters executive editor presumably knew, 'Time for Peace, Time to Go' is an oft-used Irish Republican slogan. It is, in such a context, tantamount to writing 'Brits Out'. The slogan effectively asserts British troops should withdraw from Northern Ireland if there is to be peace. But through the cropping of the image and its subsequent use, next to headlines announcing the ceasefire, the same slogan came to symbolise the hopes, both in the province and Britain, that the ceasefire would lead to permanent peace. The very same slogan, depending on the use to which it is put, seems to give rise to different interpretations and evaluations. On this view, it is not the case that one interpretation is 'the' right one. For both interpretations can appeal to objective features of the image and basic beliefs or evaluative commitments. Rather its meaning seems to depend upon its use and the context it is placed within. The meaning of the image, and of events generally, so it is claimed, depend upon how they are framed by the interpretative and evaluative commitments of those who are reporting upon it.

It is important to recognise the exact claim being made here. One should not confuse it with a far weaker epistemic claim: namely that though there is a truth of the matter, over how an event should be interpreted and evaluated, we might not know what that truth is. For example, in the Bosnian War many claims and counter-claims were made about massacres by both sides. But the media were often not able to find out whether they really had happened or not. But, reasonably enough, you might think, we presume there is a truth of the matter; there either was or was not a massacre at Srebrenica. Similarly, we might be unable to determine whether increasing violence on television bears a causal relationship to increasing violence in society. This may be because there are so many other factors, variables and multiple causes that research will never be able to prove the matter one way or the other. Yet we might presume that there is a truth of the matter, it's just that we cannot determine what it is.

But the critique of objectivity involves a much stronger claim. Obviously events are significantly independent of us, so certain low-level descriptions are true of them. But, the claim is, how we should interpret the image or event, and construe its significance, depends upon the categories, interpretative framework and evaluative commitments we bring to bear upon it. Thus the meaning of Rodwell's photograph depends upon the conceptual context and framework it is placed within. Of course, we can still evaluate the different possible interpretations and evaluations in terms of their consistency, coherence and adequacy to the low-level descriptions. But where interpretations differ, because of different basic beliefs and evaluative commitments, there is no resolvable dispute.

The subjectivity of evaluation

Such disputes are irresolvable because there is no morally neutral stance from which the distinct sets of basic commitments can be impartially weighed up and evaluated. Hence when there are contradictions in news media coverage that run down to the foundational level they are irresolvable. So (according to Rorty), once we recognise 'that anything can be made to look good or bad by being redescribed' we should renunciate 'the attempt to formulate criteria of choice between final vocabularies' and must perforce become committed ironists.[8] We should, on this view, recognise that 'the truth of the matter' is relativised to the basic commitments involved.

On such a view we should not be surprised that news media reports often diverge over both how certain facts and which facts are salient. Consider, although it is not clear cut, the US media coverage of the O. J. Simpson trial. Apart from the shift of focus in media attention due to the ebb and flow of the legal process, there were striking differences in the coverage of the trial, depending on who reported it. The mainstream media concentrated on the circumstances of Simpson's initial arrest, whether he had received favourable treatment because of his star status and what the circumstantial evidence was. Conversely, the black media focused upon possible racial angles to the case and whether Simpson had been set up because of his colour and star status. By contrast, the women's press made much of the allegations of wife beating and abuse by Simpson of Nicole Brown. It would seem, then, that the same event affords a plurality of different possible legitimate news reports which cannot be meaningfully contrasted with one another in terms of some higher-order interpretative principle. For the radical divergence in news reports merely reflects something fundamental about the basic interests and values concerned.

If the critique of objectivity is sound then it obviously has fundamental consequences for the nature and practices of news reporting. Journalism proper aims at the appropriate description and interpretation of current events. Hence a journalist's news report should aim to persuade the audience that his or her description and interpretation is the rational and appropriate one. But given that what constitutes appropriateness is, on this view, relativised to fundamental beliefs and evaluative commitments, we cannot distinguish between reasons as causes of belief change and other non-rational causes. Although we can distinguish between rational and non-rational forms of persuasion relative to our foundational commitments, ultimately which beliefs and values we assent to is a contingent matter. Hence a Rortian journalist would be someone who fulfils three conditions: (1) she has radical and continuing doubts about the final vocabulary she currently uses, because she has been impressed by other vocabularies, vocabularies taken as final by people or books she has encountered; (2) she realizes that argument phrased in her present vocabulary can neither underwrite nor dissolve these doubts; (3) in so far as she philosophizes about her situation, she does not think that her vocabulary is closer to reality than others.[9]

Rortian journalists who recognise the contingent nature of their fundamental values and vocabularies are committed to the claim that ultimately the distinction between good and bad news coverage, like the commitments it depends on, is contingent, wholly arbitrary and thus an illusion. Hence they cannot be committed to conveying 'the' truth about world affairs but only deeply sceptical about the validity of any news report, including their own. To condemn a particular news report as shoddy, irrelevant or inappropriate would only serve to point out that we do not share the news values being addressed rather than to claim there is a fundamental mismatch between the report and the actual nature of the event being covered. For all reports, on this picture, are necessarily contingent and biased. Thus if objectivity is, as a matter of principle, impossible then the news media can't in any meaningful sense have a duty to be objective.

Objective constraints upon interpretation

However, though the critique of objectivity may seem plausible there is good reason to think it flawed. Let us return to Rodwell's photograph of the slogan 'Time for Peace, Time to Go'. Pre-reflectively we might well ask why we should presume that just because the media have used it in a certain way that it is appropriate to do so. After all, if the slogan was intended to have a certain meaning, and was publicly understood to have that meaning in the relevant context, then surely to present it as if it had a different meaning is surely to misrepresent it. I remember reading, when I was younger, *Bright Lights Big City*, a novel by Jay McInerney about New York yuppies, literary sets and their cosmopolitan nightlife. Throughout the novel the central character made various detours to the restroom in several clubs. I thought it highly civilised that clubs in New York had rooms where people could go and rest, away from all the noise of the music, chat and take their drugs. But it was only years later when I actually went to the United States and found myself wandering around the airport looking for the toilet that I finally realised that 'restroom' actually meant 'toilet'. The point here is that though the words in the novel could give rise to the interpretation I had given them, this is only because I did not have the relevant background knowledge. Had I possessed the relevant background knowledge I would not have misconstrued the semantic meaning of the word. Similarly, readers who interpreted the slogan in Rodwell's photograph as concerning the ceasefire lacked the relevant background information about what the slogan was intended to and taken to mean. The slogan's meaning is not altered, but rather misrepresented, by the new context and use to which it is put. Meaning is not straightforwardly reducible to use. For we can misuse and misinterpret the meaning of something, whether because we lack an understanding of the appropriate context or because we misunderstand the publicly governed rules which determine how a concept or term ought to be applied.

Of course, there is something to the thought that what the image is expressive of is determined by its context and use. Even though the slogan itself clearly means 'Brits out', nonetheless the image of the boy playing brick-a-bat against the phrase 'Time for Peace' does seem to express the hopes many had for the peace process at that time. But it is crucial to note the difference between something's meaning and what it can be used to be expressive of. Clearly such use in and of itself does not change the meaning of the slogan. But the image of the slogan was adapted to reflect the hopes of the newspapers' readers. Before an after-dinner speech in January 1994, John Major had his head in his hands in order to think out his speech in verse. The correct interpretation of what John Major was doing concerns what his intentions in acting thus were. But the photographs of him in this pose were used by the media to express the general perception that both he and his government were in trouble. Representations of events can be used to express general perceptions, hopes and fears. But, used as such, the image should not necessarily be understood as an interpretation and evaluation of the nature of the event it is of. To construe the use of Rodwell's photograph as conveying the meaning of the slogan is to misunderstand what it's being used for. The slogan's meaning, and the appropriate interpretation of it, is an objective matter in the sense that one can be mistaken or misrepresent it. Indeed, one might think that had such images as 'Time for Peace, Time to Go' not been used so prolifically in the way they were at the time of the ceasefire, and had people understood that the photograph was merely expressive rather than relaying what was actually meant, then the British public would not have been so naïve about the prospects for the ceasefire.

The Rorty critique of objectivity falsely reduces all journalism to the status of propaganda. But propaganda is a perversion of journalism proper. Propaganda, as can be seen from the history of journalism in the old USSR, covers events in terms of assumed basic commitments and values which are not considered open to critical revision.[10] Hence even when a propaganda report is true it does not constitute good journalism because truth is conceived of merely as a contingent means for the promotion of the presumed basic commitments. A propagandist need not be a liar but cannot be, as journalists should be, committed to truth-respecting methods. The idea that what is true is somehow constituted out of the news report itself naturally and viciously lends itself to thinking of all news as exercises in rhetoric: it is only a question of whose rhetoric is, ultimately, more powerful. Whichever type of news coverage wins out will, according to Rorty, effectively remake reality in its own image: a chilling thought reminiscent of George Orwell's *Nineteen Eighty-four*.

But the thought is only chilling precisely because what people may be told and come to believe can, *pace* Rorty, come apart from what is actually the case. The fact that, in *Nineteen Eighty-four*, the chocolate ration is reported to have gone up does not make it so. Commonsensically we do draw a distinction between good and bad news reports on a rational basis in a non-arbitrary manner. For our understanding of the news media as committed to reporting the truth entails a distinction between non-rational means of persuasion and rational ones. The fact that there may be fundamental differences between news reports driven by distinct beliefs and values does not entail that the resultant reports are equally sound. Of course, different news reports might focus upon different aspects of a story because they are addressed to different concerns and audiences. But even news reports that speak to different concerns ought to cover the central aspects of an event which make it a news story. Hence we can and do sometimes criticise news reports for failing to focus upon the central facts and issues of a story whilst distracting readers with peripheral features. That there may be distinct emphases in news reports and analyses of events shows at most that news stories may legitimately speak to the distinct social concerns of different groups. The Rorty critique of objectivity is inherently flawed because it fails to allow for the possibility of misinterpreting an event (and thus precludes the possibility of much substantial media criticism).

Objective contraints upon evaluation

Conflicts in news reporting usually occur because there are differences in judgement as to what really constitutes a news story, how a story should best be covered and what the public ought to have their attention drawn to. The end of journalism itself, relaying the news about events that affect and concern the public, is hardly disputed and it is unsurprising that differences in coverage reflect differences in social values and commitments. But none of the news media involved, including the most radical ones, will dispute that what they are after is the appropriate description and analysis of the news story. Only by recognising the goal internal to journalism can we make sense of the claim that certain reports might be mistaken or inadequate in focus or tone.

What must be emphasised is that there are facts and features of an event which are independent of the reporting of them and the foundational commitments involved. Hence any report must attempt to take account of the facts about the events they are seeking to cover. News reports are diagnostic, in that they seek to identify the essence of the story and possible underlying causes, and prescriptive, in that they suggest what the significance of the event is and even sometimes how such an event might be prevented again. Of course, some events may only be construed as news given a certain agenda or be news by virtue of the news media's role. But it doesn't follow from this that news coverage is wholly determined by foundational values in a way that is immune to critical analysis. The standards by which we assess the value of a news report concerns adequacy to the facts and the cognitive virtues of rational coherence, plausibility and explanatory value.

Returning to coverage of the Simpson trial, the different reports should be conceived either as emphasising distinct aspects of the case or, if each asserts that its report is the appropriate and complete description, in direct conflict. Thus black media reports, whilst dwelling on the strain of racial issues running through the case, need not deny or occlude the central question of Simpson's guilt or innocence. However, where reports do conflict each is committed to the claim that the others are inadequate to the facts, misconceived or biased. Such conflicts are, in principle, testable by adducing the known facts and evidence for the report, the reliability of sources, the consistency, coherence and plausibility of the reasoning involved. Hence the responsibility of journalists to make clear their attribution of sources, provide evidence for their report, make clear the reasoning involved, relevant background beliefs and the possible motives of key players. Then the public has a clear basis for judging for themselves whether the report appears to be objective, i.e. it relies upon an impartial evaluation of the facts and bears the mark of an appropriate description of the events concerned.

The core features of a news story which should structure the journalist's report are fixed (let us number these features F1 . . . F12). A news report, and the claims made within it, are assessable as true or false by drawing on the chronology of events, the motives and nature of the characters involved, source attribution, the historical background and the norms and wider beliefs implicit in the report. Hence we can and do make sense of the claim that reports can be mistaken. Thus the radical diversity of news reports concerning the same event is merely apparent. Indeed, it is striking that news reports of most events, as distinct from feature articles, hardly diverge at all except in atypical cases such as the Simpson trial. Monism in news reporting is the rule rather than the exception. A thorough news report, unhindered by exigencies of time, production constraints and different audience interests, would explain the diversity of the news coverage in terms of a fundamental comprehensive report.

Of course, this still allows for different possible reports as legitimate. For we might be interested in distinct aspects of the same story, say the racial issues in the Simpson case (F1 . . . F4), which constitute only a cluster of the story's features. But although the emphasis and tone of different legitimate reports may be distinct, as in the news coverage of the Simpson case, nonetheless they may all be correct in some respect. They may be true regarding what is covered but fail to refer to other relevant aspects of a story, say questions of Simpson's actual guilt or innocence, the wife beating angle or his true character (F5 . . . F12), hence they are incomplete. Such incomplete reports can be combined, as a matter of principle, into one single complete report. Thus, in principle at least, we could capture the single correct interpretative framework which fits a news story in a way which would include the specification of the distinct aspects open to the journalist to focus on in making his report. The plurality of different correct reports of a story are the upshot of incomplete reports which can be subsumed under a minimal, empirically grounded, coherent and comprehensive report. Thus the different legitimate reports are, essentially, not different interpretations at all but incomplete sketches of the correct report.

It is important to emphasise that I am not claiming that a clear apprehension of the facts of the matter are necessarily sufficient to yield the correct interpretation and evaluation of the relevant states of affairs. Given that our understanding is necessarily mediated by our interpretative and evaluative frameworks the facts of the matter underdetermine the correct report. However, we clearly can and should critically examine the relevant facts, our considered judgements concerning them and our general principles of interpretation and evaluation. For our construal of the facts, judgements and even general principles of interpretation and evaluation may be inconsistent or incoherent. In applying our principles of interpretation and evaluation we can symbiotically examine our judgements and assessments in the light of each other. The process of reflective equilibrium enables us to strive for a position where our considered judgements and assessment cohere with our considered principles of interpretation and evaluation.[11] Where this is so the report will be able to explain what the relevant facts are and their relationship to one another in a consistent, coherent and explanatory manner. Indeed, such a process should be able to help the reporter explain why alternative possible assessments may be in error. Now it may be true that even having gone through such a process convergence on the same report has not been achieved. But this is merely to recognise that objectivity does not necessarily guarantee convergence. It may be that given all the relevant facts and critical reflection the event may legitimately admit of more than one possible evaluation which, on their own terms, are equally consistent, coherent and explanatory. Hence reasonable disagreement can still arise. Nonetheless, a strong degree of objectivity still pertains to both reports and, moreover, the possibility of one correct report remains. It is just that the correct and complete report would specify both those alternative assessments which are reasonable and rationally grounded.

This is not to say that journalists must always capture the complete story in their report or even always aim to do so. For the nature of journalism, in getting information about events out quickly, is necessarily a time- and production-bound business. We cannot expect anything other than rough sketches of history. But it is crucial that we do not confuse the pragmatic constraints on arriving at an understanding of the truth of an event with the false claim Rorty would have us believe, that there is in essence no truth to be had. This claim leads dangerously close to conflating fact and fiction: something which would only serve the interests of governments, public figures, business men and those in positions of power and influence with something to hide.

True, as Rorty points out, we cannot reason from nowhere. But the fact that we must reason from somewhere does not entail that foundational beliefs and journalistic reports are unamenable to rational assessment. At any given time certain beliefs and presumptions must be taken as given, otherwise journalistic practice could not get going and news reports would be interminably long and tedious. But these presumptions and beliefs are open to examination in the light of other beliefs and values we hold, hence reason can lead to a change both in fundamental commitments and the way a news story is being covered. Hence the news media in the USA during the Vietnam War came to reassess and modify their evaluative commitments, leading to a shift in coverage from the uncritical acceptance of US policy to often downright hostile news reporting.[12] Closer to home the shift in the way the bovine spongiform encephalitis scandal has been covered in the mid-1990s provides an interesting example of how, in the light of increasing evidence and critical reflection, journalists shifted from dismissing warnings about human contamination as the allegations of cranks to talking of a credible potential disaster. Seeking consistency, coherence, simplicity and informative explanations in news reports may have to start from somewhere, but it does not follow that the implicit beliefs and values are immune to critical revision.

Objectivity, impartiality and good journalism

This is not to claim that the questions at issue are simple or easily resolvable. For example, only late in the Simpson case did it become obvious to many that the racial strand to the story was very important indeed. Yet it is a feature of news events that they are highly complex. But this is due to the messy nature of human reality and not to some putative incompatibility between the basic values and commitments implicit in different news agendas. In other words we may not be able to know in some cases which of the conflicting reports is the most accurate and we may remain ignorant about relevant facts. But this is an epistemological matter, a question of whether we can find out what is the case, and does not touch the point that there is a truth of the matter which journalists properly aim at.

Of course, there may be fundamental disagreements in how to cover a story. For example should, in covering the Gulf War, reporters have worked with the military pool groups or, like Robert Fisk, worked independently? Journalists have different techniques, strategies and methods of uncovering stories and, if nothing else, they are driven by commitments to both the means and ends of their journalism. Similarly, at the broader institutional level, the in-depth coverage of politics by the worthy broadsheets and the tabloid concentration upon the rich and famous reflect different emphases. Yet although journalists must bring to bear their own understanding, assumptions and values in reporting an event, it does not follow that there are radically different correct interpretations of the world. Take the *Sunday Times* report about Michael Foot's alleged spying activities.[13] What the *Sunday Times* 'discovered' was that Michael Foot had met a KGB agent and spied for the USSR. Obviously the natural interests, agenda and prejudices of the *Sunday Times* were driving the reporters' perception of the facts they had available. But we do not think that the actions of Michael Foot in this regard are open to a plurality of interpretations. Rather, we recognise that the facts of the case – how he was approached, how he acted, what his motives were – determine which of the ways in which his actions should be construed. In journalism, as distinct from fiction, there is a truth of the matter and this is what objectivity in journalism aims at. Thus how a journalist reports a news story may come apart from what the story actually is. Hence it is not just illegitimate but immoral to reconstrue news events merely because a journalist's prejudices, interests or news agenda suggests things should be otherwise. So, in the Michael Foot case, we should condemn the *Sunday Times* not just for being mistaken but for, at best, only carelessly respecting the journalistic practices that aim at objectivity, and for allowing their own assumptions and thirst for a good story to override the proper journalistic goal of aiming at the truth. It is precisely because we can and should understand journalism as aiming toward an objective report upon states of affairs, and thus what we have good reason to believe, that we can criticise the news media where this goal is clearly not aimed at or where a report fails to realise this goal through carelessness or lack of critical assessment.

Of course, in recognising distinct aspects of journalism's internal goal we should not lose sight of the idea that there are different means of informing the public about their concerns and interests. This is why, in some ways, the craft of journalism is akin to an art rather than a science. Nonetheless, like science, journalism as a practice aims at truth and it is relative to this fundamental aim that we classify news reports as good or bad. Good journalism aims at discovering and promoting the audience's understanding of an event via truth-promoting methods. This is, indeed, why impartiality is important. For a journalist must aim to be impartial in his considered judgements as to the appropriate assessment of particular events, agents' intentions, why they came about and their actual or potential significance. A failure of impartiality in journalism is a failure to respect one of the methods required in order to fulfil the goal of journalism: getting at the truth of the matter.

Conversely, bad journalism is truth-indifferent and fails to respect truth-promoting practices. Whether the *Sunday Times*'s Michael Foot story was bad journalism depends not just upon its falsity but whether claims concerning their poor research and methodology are sound. If speculation was treated as fact, if their research and methodology were poor, then truth-promoting methods were abandoned and the truth was not sought. Honesty, discipline and impartiality are required to be a good journalist. The danger of taking Rorty's critique of objectivity to heart is not just an abstract one, but very real. Where reporting turns away from the goal of truth and journalists treat events as open to many interpretations, according to their prejudices, assumptions, news agenda or the commercial drive toward entertainment, the justification and self-confessed rationale of journalism threatens to disappear. The intelligibility and rationality of the practices and activities of news journalists themselves depend upon recognising journalism's internal goal, informing the public about significant events in the world, and this goal requires journalists to strive to be impartial and thus objective.

Notes

1 See, for example, Matthew Kieran, *Media Ethics: A Philosophical Approach* (Westport, CT: Praeger, 1997), ch. 2, and John Locke's *A Letter Concerning Toleration* (New York: Prometheus, 1990) where he stresses that citizens need to know how they are being governed in order to judge the actions of those who exercise power on their behalf.
2 Quote taken from a 1996 BBC *Panorama* programme on political spin-doctors and the media.
3 Jean Baudrillard, 'The Reality Gulf', *Guardian*, 11 January 1991.
4 Theodore L. Glasser, 'Objectivity and news bias', in Elliot D. Cohen (ed.) *Philosophical Issues in Journalism* (New York: Oxford University Press, 1992), p. 183.
5 See, for example, Richard Rorty, *Contingency, Irony and Solidarity* (Cambridge: Cambridge University Press, 1989), Paul Ricoeur, *Hermeneutics and the Human Sciences*, trans. J. B. Thompson (Cambridge: Cambridge University Press, 1981), Gaye Tuchman, *Making News: A Study in the Construction of Reality* (New York: Free Press, 1978), Andrew Edgar, 'Objectivity, bias and truth', in A. Belsey and R. Chadwick (eds) *Ethical Issues in Journalism and the Media* (London: Routledge, 1992), pp. 112–29, and John Fiske, *Media Matters* (Minneapolis, MN: University of Minnesota Press, 1994), pp. 125–90.
6 For arguments against the ideological construal of this claim see Matthew Kieran, 'News reporting and the ideological presumption', *Journal of Communication*, 47/2 (1997), pp. 79–96.
7 Rorty, *Contingency, Irony and Solidarity*, pp. 6–7.
8 ibid., p. 73.
9 ibid.

10 See Brian McNair, *Glasnost, Perestroika and the Soviet Media* (London: Routledge, 1991).
11 John Rawls, *A Theory of Justice* (Oxford: Oxford University Press, 1972), pp. 48–51.
12 See Stanley Karnow, *Vietnam: A History* (New York: Viking Press, 1983).
13 'KGB: Michael Foot was our agent', *Sunday Times*, 19 February 1995, for which Foot was eventually awarded substantial damages and received a printed apology from the paper.

4 The problem of humbug

Mary Midgley

The pleasures of denunciation

Cynicism has its own morality. Cynics are moralists as much as the rest of us, indeed they can often be heard being quite self-righteous. What cynics feel righteous about is the need to expose hypocrisy: to point out yawning gaps between our ideals and our practice. It is no trouble finding those gaps; they open up almost everywhere. Since most reformers are human beings, they can usually be convicted of inconsistency. Sooner or later, they can be caught tolerating things which should not really be tolerated, things which may be every bit as bad as the evils they are attacking.

Thus, in the early nineteenth century, people in Britain who campaigned to abolish black slavery in the USA were attacked as hypocrites for picking on this particular evil while ignoring others which might be worse. Defenders of slavery, such as Carlyle, asked why the abolitionists didn't occupy themselves with the evils of industrial slavery nearer home. In the same way, more recently, during the era of apartheid, spokesmen for the South African government used to point out that people in countries that criticised them were themselves allowing inhumane practices in their own territories. They asked why the critics did not attend to their own business and clean up their own backyards.

This kind of counter-attack has a real point. But some tricky principles are involved. The obvious conclusion is that outsiders who attack a bad practice are hypocrites unless they are above reproach themselves. This seems rather too simple. The objection to casting first stones is strong and genuine, but it is not quite right for this kind of case.

Jesus, when he made his point about stone-casting, was talking about the status that is needed if one is to *punish* people for past offences.[1] People prepared to do this need to be irreproachable and indeed properly authorised. But if we demanded the same kind of status before allowing people to make protests about ongoing evils such as slavery and apartheid we would make such protests impossible. In practice, hardly anybody has hands clean enough for completely satisfactory stone-casting.

The question is, how central do we want to make this issue of hypocrisy in our moral spectrum? It does not usually follow the simple pattern displayed by classic literary hypocrites like Tartuffe[2] and Mr Pecksniff.[3] These straightforward plotting villains exist but they are relatively rare. The pervasive problem of everyday hypocrisy is not exemplified in such extreme characters but, rather, arises from the appalling mixedness of our ordinary human nature.

One can see how tempting it is for journalists, and the media generally, to assume that hypocrisy really is a simple and straightforward matter which should always be exposed. The stereotypical picture of a hypocrite is one who professes to do something for an honourable, publicly declared motive while really doing it from a disreputable hidden one. So any possible extra motive can be pounced on for exposure. Thus, as Raymond Snoddy points out, the suspicion of such a motive led the *Mail on Sunday* to feel justified in publishing a quite irrelevant story about Peter Bottomley's sexual inclinations after he had tried to help a social worker.[4]

Much of the news agenda, from political interviewing to investigative journalism, concentrates on suspicions of this kind. It is supposed to be motivated by a stern drive to expose hypocrisy. By a curious coincidence, however, it seldom explores the whole range of possible outside motives, which might really be quite interesting. Instead, it focuses pretty steadily on a few exciting private motives, chiefly sex. In the last few years, for instance, much of this kind of attention has been directed against Prince Charles's marriage. His critics have contrasted the shortcomings of his private life with the (often impressive) views that he expresses on public matters. Wasn't this barrage of accusation itself somewhat hypocritical?

The obvious way to test this would be to ask the journalists involved – and still more the proprietors of their papers – whether they would be willing to have the details of their own private life exposed to the public over many years with the same thoroughness and the same venom. And would they (incidentally) expect a marriage to survive well in such circumstances? The usual reply to this query is that people in powerful positions must expect to endure more public scrutiny than the rest of us. But newspaper proprietors certainly wield more real power today than the heir to a constitutional monarchy. And clearly, the kind of scrutiny that is appropriate for power should concern, not private life, but matters directly relevant to public affairs on which that power is deployed.

The mixedness of motives

The interesting thing about this whole argument is that the defenders of intrusive journalism evidently see the exposure of this supposed kind of hypocrisy as a general justification for all their activities. They take it that all our actions, from the best to the worst, have multiple sources. We never act from one motive alone. That is why such charges can never be disproved. If we did insist on having rulers who were moved only by patriotic motives, we would need to wait a long time to find them. And if we ever did find them, they might well be so unlike the people whom they govern that they would find their job unintelligible.

As things are, then, we know that practically nobody manages to summon up the perseverance needed for success in any profession – let alone one as bruising as politics – without the help of outside motives which don't appear on its work-specification. The commonest and most obvious of these motives are ambition, pugnacity and sociability of particular kinds, such as a fancy for drinking in particular bars. But there are always a heap of others as well. Non-political motives are bound to direct people's interests, playing some part in the choice of particular policies to support. There is absolutely nothing wrong with this so long as their owner keeps checking these motives steadily to see that they correspond with duty to the public. All this, naturally, applies in journalism too.

It surely is true, then, that in politics practically no individual, however idealistic, is faultless and certainly no country is so. All nations and all groups either tolerate some injustice and oppression within them or at least draw advantages from the practices abroad, advantages such as cheap food and cheap labour – 'guest-workers' and so on. Even when reformers do confine themselves to their own backyards, trying to improve things within their own nation, they still meet the same sort of difficulty. If they want to get anything done they have to find someone to work with. They can hardly ever choose their allies. They also have to concentrate their fire, selecting certain causes and turning their backs on others. They cannot deal with all ongoing needs at once. So they must turn a blind eye to some of the evils around them and accept some colleagues of whom they bitterly disapprove. Biographies of even the most thorny and scrupulous reformers, such as Mill and Gandhi, illustrate this painful necessity.

Strachey's crusade

Does this mean that, since we are all miserable sinners, none of us is ever in a position to express outrage and shout that things ought to be made better? This is surely not a sensible proposition. But there is a genuine conflict here. We need both to be honest about admitting how bad things actually are and also to give due credit to the efforts that are being made to make them better. This often means praising imperfect people and denouncing people who are by no means wholly odious. Indeed it can sometimes mean denouncing and praising the very same people.

This conflict is a real problem for journalists, and there are lots of forces at present pushing them towards simplifying things by sneering at everybody. This is not just because scandals sell better than eulogies. On top of that, we all have a tendency to feel that portraits *ought* really to be as dark as possible, with plenty of warts. There is a sense that there's something wrong and embarrassing about a wart-free nose, about praising anything or anyone at all strongly. This fashion set in when Lytton Strachey reversed the conventions of biography, ruling that discreditable facts about public figures should normally take precedence over creditable ones. Putting it crudely, Strachey's idea – much influenced by his reading of Freud – was that disreputable qualities always underlie good ones and represent a deeper truth. In general, therefore, the more enlightened and intelligent one is, the worse one's opinion will be of one's fellow human beings – however admirable their actual conduct may be.

In theory, Strachey's innovation was meant chiefly as a counter-balance to its opposite. It was meant to complete the picture, balancing whole shelves-full of biographies that had been straightforward eulogies by putting in the shadow-side. But, like many projects that aim at balance, it didn't work out that way. Post-Stracheyan biographies and biographical articles in magazines have tended *not* to form a balanced picture. Instead they substitute one kind of simplification for another. They concentrate attention on people's faults and weaknesses to the point where their exhausted readers sometimes begin to wonder why these particular people's lives were ever worth writing about.

More generally, our whole journalistic culture has been skewed this way, focusing on people's failures and weaknesses of character without the concomitant drive to understand why they have these faults, what the context is, and how they link up with their strengths and virtues. Sometimes a whole profession is guyed in this way. For instance, the genuinely absurd remarks that stupid judges sometimes make get generalised into a dismissive stereotype for the whole profession.

The immediate reaction to these particular remarks is appropriate enough. But the phenomenon is limited. We must have judges, and if we write them off wholesale because of such scandals we deprive them of the respect which is necessary to make their difficult work possible at all. Clearly, the kind of pedantry and narrowness which causes these scandals are the sorts of faults which, in human beings, do tend to go with the sort of quiet care, persistence and learning which judges need. And, so far at least, all our judges are human beings. Of course this kind of expectedness does not excuse the faults. But it means that they don't call for the astonished denunciations of the whole profession.

Pioneers, projects and personalities

This over-personal, melodramatic writing may well be useful in making us more aware of bad motives, which is a genuinely important topic. But the price of this insight has surely been a difficulty in being realistic about good ones. It imposes a narrowness, a distorted emphasis which blocks a wider understanding of how human projects work. Of course everybody is grossly imperfect, but some of these imperfect people – both past and present – manage to think up projects that are hugely valuable to the rest of us. In the case of biography, if we want to know about these people at all, we do so primarily because we want to know how they managed to do these surprising things, what was the thinking behind the feats that roused our curiosity in the first place. Initially, we need to see them simply as part of that project, in a role to which their faults and weaknesses are irrelevant for much of the time.

In relation to today's press and media, this need is especially strong when the project is still continuing. People who want to understand a new and honourable movement need to see it personified, crystallised in the figures of those who lead it. This is not a demand for a lie but for relevant selection. The natural human tendency to look for examples to follow is not hypocritical. It is just a simplification, a concentration on crucial achievements which leaves other, less relevant details in the background.

Concentration of that kind certainly can easily result in the build-up of mythical, heroic figures such as those whom Strachey debunked, figures such as Florence Nightingale and Gladstone, or more recently Gandhi, Einstein, Albert Schweitzer, Freud himself. Strachey hoped that, by smashing these icons, he could dispel the myth that surrounded them, revealing the naked truth behind it. But naked truths are harder to find than that. This approach surely displayed an extraordinary short-sightedness about both the power and the usefulness of myths. What it actually managed to do was simply generate a new myth centring on a new set of stereotyped figures, an imaginary bunch of naïve Victorian hypocrites.

By stressing the faults of the reformers Strachey made it look as if these people had been quite exceptionally crude and obtuse, bizarrely short of self-knowledge. He made it seem that they had belonged to an inferior tribe morally, an extinct species of alien pre-Freudian moralists who were really of no interest to enlightened thinkers in the Modern Scientific Age, because modern thinkers no longer go in for self-deception. Thus Strachey's story gave great force to the wider myth that the twentieth century itself was an entirely fresh start, the cannibalistic myth of 'modernity' which so grossly distorted thought early in that century, the myth which is now finally being castigated under the name of modernism.

This simplified, monolithic, debunking approach is a part of that self-consciously 'modern' tradition, a part which still persists to a surprising extent today. Many people still have a quite disproportionate terror that they will be guilty of hypocrisy if they are caught out approving of anything or anybody. They feel that their prime business ought always to be to look for the faults in any public person or enterprise and, when they have found them, to denounce the whole as a sham.

A striking example of this was the bizarre front-page story that the *Sunday Times* ran in 1995 accusing Michael Foot of having worked for the KGB.[5] Not surprisingly, this had to be hastily and completely retracted when he at once made it clear that he had only met a KGB operative in Moscow, something that had happened to virtually every prominent politician who visited the city at that time. More generally, however, almost all political interviewers fall into a ludicrous habit of interviewing people as if they were detectives grilling suspects at the scene of a crime, instead of trying to find out what these people actually mean and think. Readers and listeners have to endure constant repetitions of familiar charges and equally familiar rebuttals while the interviewer desperately tries to winkle out some secret crime.

The place of idealisation

This attitude surely operates with a quite unreal notion of the moral scene. It assumes that public figures must be black if they are not pure white, whereas we know very well that most people and most movements are parti-coloured, brownish or piebald. If we treat people who are leading a movement with respect, that does not have to mean that we are taken in and believe them to be perfect. We know that the picture which shows these people as idealised figures is selective. It is a symbolic simplification. But we still stick with it when we can because it saves us from wasting time on personal criticisms which are simply not relevant to the main project.

At the end of the last century, Parnell lost his career, and Ireland lost a precious chance of relief from its oppressions, because of an adultery that had absolutely nothing to do with the political issues that he stood for. Would we be able to avoid this mistake today? Suppose that, when the negotiations for the new South Africa hung in the balance, Mandela or de Klerk had been subjected to this sort of allegation, could it have been put aside and ignored? Surely it should have been, yet it is not clear that it could. Today's journalistic conventions make such ignoring very hard. Yet these conventions do change. Lloyd George's sex life enjoyed remarkable immunity. At the other end of the scale, Greek and Roman statesmen used to accuse each other of every possible sexual abomination so loudly and habitually that the public presumably took no notice of such charges at all. Our present difficulty is that we combine an unbridled interest in these personal matters with a determined pretence that public figures live lives far purer than the rest of us are ever expected to.

Where do we want to place ourselves on this wide spectrum? Morally speaking, people are always mixed. But – to mention a truism – since the officially acknowledged good side of them which involves their declared ideals, aims and projects is often of special importance for the rest of us, there is always a reason for taking those good intentions seriously for a start, a reason to give them credit for genuineness initially, before starting to suspect their faults. This is even more obviously true of societies and nations than it is of individuals, because societies are even more obviously bound to be morally mixed and full of conflicts.

When a whole society is accused of hypocrisy – like nineteenth-century Britain in the case of slavery or prostitution – the main point usually is that some of its members are still committing the crime while others are denouncing it. In that case there is not much point in personifying the whole nation as one enormous hypocrite, an outsize Tartuffe or Pecksniff. Personification encourages fantasies of a personal vendetta that can only be satisfied by total destruction. It generates indulgence in self-righteousness of a kind which blinds one to the relevant details.

It is also possible, of course, that the rest of the citizens are in a confused, self-deceiving state which they need to clear up. It can then be quite useful for outsiders to point out this unevenness and to demand more consistency. They can indeed sometimes do this by accusing them of hypocrisy, or of some more general form of humbug. In the case of slavery it was certainly also reasonable to tell people who were campaigning against it abroad to do something about the form of it that they were countenancing at home.

How far is consistency possible?

The kind of consistency which involves a realistic sense of priorities in matters like these is indeed important. Sometimes, relatively trivial moral issues do seem to absorb a quite disproportionate amount of public attention. For instance, it is surely reasonable to ask the people who now campaign against abortion as the most serious moral problem of the age whether they really consider it a worse evil than the deliberate manufacture and sale of land-mines, which not only kill far more innocent people at a more crucial stage of their lives but also mutilate many and make great areas of land useless to survivors. If, then, one is 'pro-life', should one not treat it as the worse evil of the two? Similarly, the kind of intense indignation that is felt against the use of drugs is usually not extended to the over-prescribing of tranquillisers and anti-depressants, nor to alcohol and tobacco.

In such cases, the temptation is always to confine one's indignation to exciting things done by groups other than one's own, without asking how these activities rank in the whole range of evils which one might be able to object to. And because, in a fast-changing age, the shape of this larger range is inclined to shift, sticking to these established targets does make moralising much easier. Undoubtedly we ought to resist this seductive kind of inconsistency. We should struggle to get our priorities clear. Yet it is surely not to be expected that we could ever reach complete consistency here.

What would it be like to have a policy which followed completely consistent and defensible priorities? Could we find one which never left us open to the charge of fiddling while Rome burns or of Pharisaically picking on our neighbours while ignoring our own crimes? In order to do this we would need a carefully researched chart of all the currently pressing evils with their relative urgency and closeness to our own responsibilities duly assessed and placed in order. Presumably we would then work steadily outwards from the nearest and most urgent ones towards those further off, making sure at each stage that our own hands were clean on each point before we dared to criticise our neighbours.

No doubt there would be a lot to be said for this kind of self-discipline and it would certainly provide a living for plenty of hungry researchers. But it would surely mean that it was a long time before we got round to shouting about Tibet or Nigeria. By contrast, what we actually do is to respond simultaneously and somewhat unpredictably to certain ongoing scandals which happen to strike us as being horrible beyond what we are prepared to tolerate. This kind of selective response is now expressed in the idea of *human rights* – the idea that, never mind the enormous differences between the various earthly cultures, there are some things which should not be done anywhere to anybody.[6]

Though some academics worry about the use of the civic, legalistic word 'rights' here, I think that, at the everyday level, most people today accept it, not only in the Enlightenment-driven West but all over the world. Oppressed peoples appeal to it, not, I think, merely using it as a foreign language but as a kind of genuinely universal moral concept. This is surely good. But the need to select such cases lays on journalists a great responsibility, which many of them feel profoundly, for telling us about these things so that we may have the chance of exploding constructively.

What, me?

When we do explode, the governments accused always feel injured and say that we don't understand their circumstances. And, as many cases that have come before the European Court have shown, British governments are no exception. Nobody likes being accused by outsiders, and if the outsiders were perfect they wouldn't actually like it any better than they do today when (as they often complain) their accusers are not perfect at all. At present, of course, Europhobia intensifies this habitual prickliness in Britain to an absurd degree, as is evident over the BSE (bovine spongiform encephalitis) scandal of 1996. (It is indeed increasingly clear that BSE might as well have meant Blame Someone Else.) Yet this kind of accusation is absolutely necessary. Between nations as between individuals, there do have to be charges brought and the local conscience cannot possibly be trusted to bring them. In the case of nations it is specially vital that outsiders – however imperfect – should sometimes take up this role because culpable governments can so easily suppress their internal critics.

Clean hands among these accusers do indeed make the charge far more telling, and dirty ones beyond a certain point can destroy its political force. But, strictly speaking, counter-accusations about the state of accusers' hands are never a defence against the original charge. The validity of an accusation does not depend on the accusers' merits, and is certainly not destroyed by suspicion about their motives. The only proper reply to accusations is to answer them directly. This is what makes the constant nagging exchange of counter-accusations between political parties so inexcusably irrelevant and exasperating. There is, moreover, no reason why the press and other news media should let themselves become involved in these games. They are there to examine the actual issues, the policies and the nature of their impact on ordinary members of the public. If they discuss any new proposal without reference to this kind of impact, treating it simply as a ploy used by one party to attack the other, they are neglecting this primary duty completely.

Priority trouble

What, however, about the matter of fiddling while Rome burns? We cannot, of course, dismiss complaints about relatively minor abuses as humbug on the ground that these things are trivial compared with worse ones. The fact that an abortion is not a land-mine does not show that it does not matter at all. The difficulty is to get one's priorities right in each kind of case. It is interesting that the charge of triviality is often made against those who campaign on behalf of animals. How (their critics ask) can you devote time and money to this matter while so many human beings are suffering?

Thus people often cite the mid-nineteenth-century case where an American mother was prosecuted for grave cruelty to her child, but the prosecution had to be brought under a recently passed law forbidding cruelty to animals, since the child was being treated in a way that this act made illegal for an animal. What a scandal (people say) that animals were protected before children! In fact the situation here was rather different. The position was that children had indeed had plenty of legal protection before that time, but there was a loophole in it. The existing law had not licensed the prosecution of *parents* for cruelty, since it mistakenly regarded them wholly as their children's protectors. After this case, that loophole was of course closed. Animals, however, had had no protection at all before the law in question had been passed and continued to have very little after it.

This is one of many cases in which people tend to exaggerate what is actually done for animals because they have not quite decided whether they are prepared to attend to them at all. There are, for instance, quite often complaints about the collection of money by animal charities. At present these charities take around 2 per cent of the total subscribed to charitable causes in Britain. Is that total too high? If so, what ought it to be? Point seven? One point three? Can anybody give a reasoned answer? Here again, objectors seem to operate with the idea of an ideal chart which would list the causes we could subscribe to in strict order of priority.

Sometimes, when I contemplate the bewildering flood of appeals that I receive from various causes, I wish there was indeed such a list. Would I do better if I picked out one – Oxfam, Amnesty or Greenpeace – and threw all the rest away? Doing this does save time and stamps, but it doesn't solve the problem. Unfortunately, the idea of a single order of urgency is not workable. There are a thousand *kinds* of things that need doing. And if we all picked out one of them as the most urgent this week and worked to support it, we might make it less urgent. Should we all then turn over to something different?

Here again, what we actually do is somewhat idiosyncratic and arbitrary, but not unworkable. We tend to specialise. Some of us devote ourselves thoroughly to particular causes, usually not because we have checked that nothing else is more urgent, but simply on the positive grounds that we can see the importance of this one. And as supporters we similarly attach ourselves more or less lastingly to particular projects.

That kind of attachment has the crucial advantage of giving these organisations the kind of continuity without which they cannot work at all. A more spasmodic, chronically critical approach would make effective campaigning impossible. Without covenants and bankers' orders, charities would have to spend their entire time trying to raise funds for the next day's work. This network of habits does have the disadvantage of making it hard for new causes to get started and for existing ones to change direction, which is a serious nuisance in a fast-changing world. It can also sometimes lock people into obsessions with things that are genuinely trivial. But the idea of replacing it by a scientifically-calculated table of priorities is a non-starter.

Consistency and shame

The point here is that we should be wary of assuming that the press and news media ought to conform to a single scale of news values, as if one could lexically order stories according to their significance. Some philosophers, such as Rawls and the Utilitarians, have tried to formalise significance by this kind of calculus, but after a very rough beginning their formulae always run into the sand. There really are many kinds of things that we are and ought to be interested in and know about. Perhaps one of the troubles with the news media is its excessive concentration on narrowly political matters. As most of us recognise, many issues and events are of central importance to people in ways that are not directly related to politics at all.

Altogether then, it does not make much sense to dismiss pronouncements as humbug either on the grounds that they are not consistent with that ideal priority system or that they are being made by people whose own lives don't fully live up to them. There is surely something particularly odd about the suggestion that mere inconsistency between the accusers' theory and practice could invalidate accusations. If consistency here were all that mattered, they could easily produce it by simply dropping their attempt at reform. It is not difficult to be a consistent scoundrel or a whole-hearted lump of apathy.

People who are attacking hypocrisy sometimes do talk as though this kind of consistency were indeed all that they were after, as though they would be satisfied if (for instance) the slave-owners or other oppressors simply dropped their pretensions to be morally respectable. This would, as moralists sometimes say, make them 'at least honest'. But this kind of honesty scarcely seems to be worth much. The attackers' real target in these cases is of course not that kind of honesty but its opposite. They want to close the yawning gap between theory and practice upwards, not downwards. Their cry is not really 'Why don't you profess what you are doing?' but 'Why don't you do what you profess?'

The interesting thing here is what gives protest its foothold in this inconsistency between theory and practice, that is, humbug, which is therefore, in a strange way, a necessary stage in the process of reform. This is what people mean by saying that hypocrisy is the tribute which vice pays to virtue.[7] If we try to imagine what a society would be like that was totally unpretentious morally – a society which really had no ideals that were any higher than its actual practice – we shall probably find it hard to make any sense of the possibility. Even the Mafia, for instance, has quite demanding standards. Similarly immoralism, as Nietzsche conceived it, is a most exacting way of life.[8] Because human impulses continually conflict, any sort of workable existence has to involve priorities among its standards and aims which lie far beyond its present practice.

Ideals and practice are, in fact, always some way apart, even among people whose ideals are quite unpretentious. They are linked by a longish piece of elastic on which we can pull in either direction, upwards or downwards. The tension is usually quite strong because there is a genuine wish not to be totally inconsistent. People who pull downwards, trying to lower the ideals, are not necessarily cynics. They may still be idealists themselves. (Nietzsche did a good deal of it.) As we have just seen, these down-pullers may be aiming at honesty, though they don't always make it clear why honesty should be thought so important when other, larger ideals are dropped. Or these people may think that some of the current ideals really are misconceived. But very often the pull is intended to work upwards by shaming the majority into greater efforts towards aims that it already acknowledges, and into acknowledging further ones which it hasn't yet admitted.

This process of progressive shaming can be clearly seen at present over our concern for and reporting of environmental issues. Since the 1960s or 1970s we have reached an extreme stage of rampant hypocrisy about this, a stage where even the crustiest of unrepentant sinners has to give the matter lip-service, and where the gap between this talk and practice sometimes seems to be immeasurable. All the same, there is some strength in the elastic. Some things do get done; how effectively, we shall see in the next few decades. Meanwhile the smell of humbug sometimes does become almost intolerable. But if we had skipped this hypocritical stage, it's not clear how we would ever have got started at all.

Conclusion

I have been trying to understand a bit more fully the respectable motives that can bring people near to cynicism. Because cynicism itself is paralysing, I think it may be important to sort out the sensible parts of these motives from the unworkable bits. I have suggested that Strachey's revolution in biography has taught us a habit of rather mindless denigration, which current conventions in our news media tend to pander to and encourage. This habit did have a point, but it has become so habitual as to be fairly meaningless. I want to counter the still-persisting sense that there is something hypocritical in straightforward praise – the embarrassment about articulating ideals – the fear of seeming naïve if one says the morally obvious.

I am sometimes struck by the situation in which someone British is too embarrassed to make what is plainly the right and appropriate moral comment on a particular situation while someone American does it directly and without self-consciousness. Journalism is always open to these temptations, because anyone who has to write something in a hurry, from a school-child to an overworked leader-writer, always finds it easier to grouse than to grasp the real problem. But the moral fashion that made this approach seem positively laudable is surely about due for retirement.

Notes

1 John 8: 7.
2 In Molière's play of that name.
3 In Charles Dickens's *Martin Chuzzlewit*.
4 Raymond Snoddy, *The Good, the Bad and the Unacceptable* (London: Faber, 1992), pp. 1–8.
5 *Sunday Times*, 19 February 1995.
6 On this crucial and difficult subject see Timothy Dunne and Nicholas Wheeler (eds), *Human Rights, Human Wrongs* (Cambridge: Cambridge University Press, 1997) and Ken Booth, 'Human wrongs and international relations', *International Affairs* 71/1 (1995), pp. 103–26.
7 Duc de La Rochefoucauld, *Maxims and Moral Reflections* (Letchworth: Arden Press, 1910), p. 233.
8 See, for instance, Nietzsche's *Beyond Good and Evil*, p. 226: 'We immoralists! . . . we are spun into a strict network and hairshirt of duties; we cannot get out. In this we are men of duty, even we.' Compare p. 228, 'Isn't moralizing . . . immoral?' and his *Ecce Homo*, ch. 6, on the fierce difficulties that face Zarathustra.

5 Journalism, politics and public relations

An ethical appraisal

Brian McNair

Introduction

At the end of the twentieth century the citizens of western democracies have access to more information about politics than at any previous time in human history. Journalistic media proliferate, and politics is high on their agenda. Politicians are acutely aware of this, and work hard to influence public opinion through those media. A supporting network of professional communicators strives to ensure that political messages are accurately and widely disseminated, in the face of a journalistic profession which becomes more aware of, and resistant to, such efforts by the year.

Through print, television and radio, with mass access to digital broadcasting and the Internet now imminent, we – the electorate, to whom all this communicative activity is ultimately directed – have access to a continuous flow of political information in all its forms – news, current affairs, debate shows, phone-ins, commentaries, satirical comedy – from early in the morning until late at night.

Are we then, as a consequence, more knowledgeable about politics, and thus more powerful as citizens (assuming that Francis Bacon was right and knowledge is still power) than ever before? Or are we merely passive witnesses of a media spectacle beyond our control, in which the quantity of information communicated is high, but its quality as a resource in opinion-forming and political decision-making is low?

In posing the question in these terms we enter a debate which is not new, but which has acquired new urgency as the sheer quantity of political communication in circulation increases, and the debate about its effects on the democratic process intensifies. In both Britain and the United States in recent years the role of political communication in electoral victory and defeat has been crucial. Quantifying that role is difficult, but it is beyond dispute that effective political communication played a large part in saving Bill Clinton's second term, and that it greatly helped the British Labour Party to its first government in eighteen years.

If few would challenge the underlying truth of these observations, many are concerned about their implications for the conduct of democratic politics. Three general concerns are voiced:

- first, that the style and content of political journalism is not, as it should be, supplying the citizenry with useful information, but on the contrary is actually obstructing the communication of political messages;
- second, that political actors no longer formulate their policies on grounds of principle and rational argument, but do so in consideration of the perceived need to 'play well' in the media, and to please 'public opinion', itself often argued to be largely a media creation;
- and third, that the communicative work of both journalists and politicians has become distorted by the influence of what Edward Bernays in 1923 called 'press counsellors', and who are better known today as 'spin-doctors', 'communications advisers', 'media consultants' or 'PR gurus'.

Taken together, it is argued, these developments have undermined the integrity of the public sphere, and rendered the late twentieth century's apparent participation of the masses in the democratic process illusory. Worse, they have encouraged mass apathy and growing non-participation in politics, as exemplified by the American case[1]. Such criticisms identify three groups of actors whose communicative ethics we should be concerned with:

- the politicians, in and out of government, for whom information flows are important power resources;
- the journalists who monitor, report, scrutinise and analyse the politicians' actions and rhetoric;
- and the group occupying a place in the communicative process somewhere between the first two: the aforementioned public relations advisers and spin-doctors.

Political communication is, to a large extent, both the process and the result of interaction and negotiation between these groups, each of which has its own ethical codes, defined in relation to the normative principles of liberal democracy. Politicians in a democracy are supposed to communicate (professionally, at least) for the purpose of ensuring good government, presenting citizens with political choices, laying claim to political power, and informing citizens honestly and openly about the administration of government.

The public relations practitioner (whether in the guise of lobbyist, spin-doctor, or Whitehall press officer) aspires to facilitate the effective communication of a message from a political actor to a wider public, in most cases through the media, since these are the channels through which the vast majority of people receive their political information. He or she also communicates in the other direction, lobbying politicians on behalf of organisational clients such as companies, trade unions and single-issue pressure groups. Because the public relations industry (including its political wing) is young (very much a twentieth-century phenomenon) it has developed ethical codes and practices which are designed to enhance its status and prestige as a *profession*, and thus to legitimise its existence as a necessary and worthwhile element of the contemporary media environment. The deliberate telling of lies on behalf of a client, for example, is not regarded as ethical.

Journalists, finally, are considered a key source of the information on which the integrity of the public sphere depends. But they are also expected to monitor the political environment on the citizens' behalf, and keep a watchful eye out for the abuse of power. This has been their 'fourth estate' role since the time of Edmund Burke.

These roles and functions are, of course, ideals. They describe things as they should be, and not necessarily as they are. But they are ideals taken seriously by all three professional groups, and reflected in standards of communicative behaviour which we as citizens are entitled to see applied, even if imperfectly. When they are not, then the democratic condition of an authentic public sphere, supported by rational information flows, through channels open and accessible to all, is called into question. This essay assesses the form and content of contemporary political communication from the perspective of the politician, the public relations professional, and the journalist respectively, in the context of the ethical standards which they have set themselves, and of the ongoing debate about these issues which so occupies academic and professional observers at the present time.[2]

Communicating politics

We begin with the politicians, since it is they who stand at the apex of the communicative pyramid, and compete most aggressively for the prizes awarded in the game of democratic politics. They do so, at this point in capitalism's evolution, in a uniquely public way, subject to the approval of a genuinely mass electorate. It is, after all, only eighty or so years since women were excluded from this electorate, and not too long before that, that men without the approved wealth and education qualifications were also deprived of the vote. Now, regardless of class, sex, ethnic or religious background, all are equal in the privacy of the polling booth. Politicians must compete for our support, using the channels of mass communication at the centre of our cultural lives to project their ideas, values and policies. To the extent that politicians require public support political communication is largely about publicity. Where feudal lords (and their contemporary counterparts in China, Iraq and elsewhere) imposed their will on powerless subjects, politicians who claim to be democratic leaders must win popular consent, and be seen to have won it. They must have *legitimacy*, or they cannot govern.

There are two stages to winning legitimacy. One is to be seen and heard in the public sphere, by securing a requisite *quantity* of media coverage. As one observer notes, 'the struggle for visibility is at the centre of all politics'.[3] Civil servants and party functionaries prefer anonymity and secrecy, but the ambitious politician must be seen and heard, if the highest reaches of office are to be his or hers.

As many politicians know to their cost, however, not all publicity is good publicity. A second stage in winning democratic legitimacy in today's political environment is to secure *qualitatively* favourable coverage, which accentuates the positive and downplays negative features of a politician's or a party's public identity. This fact has led politicians to develop increasingly sophisticated means of managing the media so as to secure such coverage. In the process, argue the critics, the communication activity of politicians has become artificial, manipulative, even deceitful. The rational content of political discourse has been subordinated to the needs of public opinion management.

Jurgen Habermas's framing of the argument continues to be influential. For Habermas, 'publicity' as we understand the term today is the harmful by-product of democratic politicians' perceived need for favourable media visibility. Because *favourable* publicity is desired, the presentation of information tends to be selective and dishonest. As he puts it, 'publicity work is aimed at strengthening the prestige of one's own position without making the matter on which a compromise is to be achieved itself a topic of public discussion' (1988, p. 200). Publicity seeks to divert the attentions of the public from critical debate about the real business of politics (the issues), and towards passive consumption of symbols (personality and style). If publicity is, in normative terms, the process of informing the public on important matters, in current conditions of mass mediatised politics it has lost its educative and critical functions. Through publicity 'arguments are transmuted into symbols to which one does not respond by arguing but only by identifying with them' (p. 206). Political decisions are made 'for manipulative purposes and are introduced with consummate propagandistic skill as publicity vehicles into a public sphere manufactured for show' (p. 221).

Habermas wrote these words in the 1960s, but recent events lend support to his central argument. Bill Clinton's political resurrrection and eventual victory in the presidential election of November 1996 was the result not least of his highly public, highly visible abandoning of some hitherto cherished policies, and the adoption of others previously associated with the US right. As Clinton's communications adviser Dick Morris (1996) boasts in his account of the Clinton first term, this 'positioning' of the president in a place somewhere between traditional notions of left and right was done deliberately to attract voters, a strategy which – despite Whitewater, Hillarygate, 'Slick Willie' and all the other personal scandals which afflicted his first-term administration –

was successful, if measured by the proportion of votes cast. Clinton's ideological principles and instincts were sacrificed to the greater goal of retaining political power, much to the anger of ordinary Democratic party members who, despite their pleasure at the prospect of a second Clinton term, accused him of betrayal of the causes on which he had first been elected in 1992.

In Britain, similar accusations have been made of the Labour Party since the election of Tony Blair as leader in 1994. Here, too, it is alleged that political principles have been sacrificed in the pursuit of power; that policy has been formulated and communicated with an eye on public opinion rather than what is right for the country; that 'New Labour' is all style and no substance, masking what amounts to a historic betrayal of British socialism and of the British working classes. The fact that New Labour won a General Election in 1997 does not invalidate the criticisms of those who hold such views, nor mollify their feelings of betrayal since, they would argue, a left-of-centre party in power without a principled approach to government is hardly a better prospect than another Conservative term of office.

Elsewhere I have argued that criticisms of this type are naïve, betraying a romanticised, patronising view of both the social democratic left (which has by definition never been 'socialist' in any theoretically rigorous sense) and the working classes, who have consistently rejected 'authentic' socialist policies and who, on the contrary, have sustained right-wing governments in Britain for most of the century (McNair 1995, 1996). Intepretations of policy aside, however, can the politicians who have led these 'betrayals' be fairly accused of unethical behaviour in their ever more managed and calculated approach to the communication of their messages?

An answer to this question can only be given on the basis of specific circumstances. If politicians, in the content of their communication, knowingly deceive the electorate, then we are certainly entitled to criticise their ethical standards. When politicians, in government or opposition, lie about their motives, ambitions and decisions; when they suppress information which the public has a right to receive; when they 'leak' aggressively and unfairly against opponents and colleagues, they are behaving unethically, and there have been instances of all three in recent British history, on all parts of the party political spectrum. If, on the other hand, they are simply using the available repertoire of communicative techniques and instruments to project ideas which may deviate from traditional norms, but which are a sincere response to changed political and socio-economic circumstances, then the charge of ethical violation seems excessive. No individual politician, or party, can be blamed for the fact that considerations of image and style are today as important to political success as the detail of policy, and none can be blamed for participating enthusiastically in 'the game' as it is now played. On the contrary, failure to do so, in the manner of the Labour Party before the arrival of Peter Mandelson as communications director in the mid-1980s, might be viewed as a greater evil, since it deprives the electorate of meaningful choice and makes minority government more sustainable. Commentator Anna Coote, para-phrasing the French sociologist Pierre Bourdieu, points out that

> as traditional differences between left and right break down, so the notion of faith [in politicians] becomes increasingly important: what matters to voters is not what politicians promise, or even what they stand for, but whether they can be trusted. That, in turn, depends on the personality of the politician and the character of the relationship with the voter. These are expressed largely by means of image and style.[4]

Greater emphasis on 'image and style' is, in short, the price of mass democracy in a late capitalist, post-Cold-War environment, whether one likes it or not.

Managing political communication: the ethics of political public relations

Whether politicians are ethical or not, the design and execution of their media performances are increasingly delegated to professional advisers and consultants: specialists in political public relations, marketing, lob-bying and advertising who are employed, usually behind the scenes, to advise on and manage the communication process. The names of the best-known members of this profession – George Stephanopoulos, James Carville, Dick Wirthlin and Dick Morris in the United States; Brendan Bruce, Tim Bell, Peter Mandelson, Alistair Campbell in Britain – have become, for their critics, emblems of the ethical decline in political life, and generated a major sub-genre of political journalism devoted to the discussion of their alleged crimes. These include manip-ulation and intimidation of the media to advance the politicians' pub-licity goals, pressurising politicians to denude themselves of principle and integrity in deference to presentational gloss and, in the worst cases, of usurping the place of the politician and becoming major political players in themselves. The worst offenders in this regard are said to be the 'spin-doctors', a new breed of communicator who does not facilitate the flow of political information (a long-standing and respected function ideally carried out in a disinterested manner by civil service functionaries and other 'apolitical' staff) so much as 'doctor' it for media, and then public consumption. Journalist Simon Heffer contrasts the more traditional function of press officer with that of the spin-doctor in the following terms:

> The press officer, even if he was a party rather than a government employee, would mainly concern himself with the provision of facts and background information . . . The spin doctor is concerned mainly

with spin. His role goes beyond the facts; it is to outline to journalists exactly what he feels the thrust of their story should be; it is to persuade them to accentuate the positive and ignore or at least play down the negative.[5]

The term was imported from the United States in the 1980s, and has since come to be used as a form of mild abuse, surrounding those to whom it is applied with a slightly sinister air of magic and mystery. Spin-doctors seek to manipulate press coverage by controlling access to senior politicians and, in particular, denying it to journalists who do not seem amenable to the 'persuasion' mentioned by Heffer. Their main weapon is aggressive lobbying, accompanied by punitive action against dissenting journalists. They are often accused of being arrogant and overbearing. Columnist Iain MacWhirter complains that the 'media minders cruise the lobbies these days like celebrities. No longer are they the servants of the press, whose function it is to get the party message across as clearly and as widely as possible. They now regard themselves as players in their own right'.[6] Labour's Peter Mandelson and Alistair Campbell have been the most frequently attacked in these terms, most famously in relation to the fax sent to the BBC newsroom when the verdict of the O. J. Simpson trial was announced. They were concerned about the possibility of having a Tony Blair speech driven down the BBC's running order by the news from Los Angeles, and the fax was a blatant attempt to influence editorial policy.

The attempt failed, in so far as the fax became a news story in itself, making more transparent and newsworthy the process of political news management. In October 1996 the *Panorama* current affairs magazine marked the Labour conference by devoting an entire edition to the work of spin-doctors, much to the anger of Campbell and Mandelson. The fax incident, and others like it, thus led to a new policy of increased vigilance on the part of BBC producers, reducing the ability of political news managers of all parties to influence journalistic agendas.

In his defence, Alistair Campbell has repeatedly maintained that the notoriety of the Simpson fax shows how rare is conflict of this kind between journalists and party news managers and that, in any event, the activity of 'spinning' is not a qualitatively new or unethical feature of democratic politics. 'Spinning' may have grown in importance and visibility alongside the growth of the political media, but it dates back at least as far as the reign of Charles II, who employed Samuel Pepys to act as his 'press handler'. Responding to the *Panorama* programme in which he featured prominently as one of Clare Short's 'people who live in the dark' Campbell pointed out that:

We live in the media age. There are more newspapers, magazines, television and radio stations than ever before. They all have space to fill, and they look to politics to fill a good deal of it. The political party that does not understand the needs of the media is doomed. Much of the work involves ensuring all outlets are spoken to, a consistent line is taken, and our central points communicated. None of that stifles debate.[7]

This seems reasonable, provided that it is communication rather than intimidation to which journalists are exposed. If Campbell, Mandelson and their colleagues can be blamed for a bullying and over-zealous approach to ensuring 'consistency' of policy presentation – and even they admit that they *have* been guilty of this on occasion[8] – then they should also be given the credit for instilling professionalism and coherence in their employer's communication management, with all that has subsequently flowed from this in terms of electoral success. Whether the price of this success has been too high will perhaps be clearer at the end of Labour's first term.

Lobbying

One branch of the political public relations industry whose ethical standards have been most directly and deservedly challenged in recent years are the lobbyists. Such organisations as Westminster Strategy, the Communication Group, Government Policy Consultants, and the now infamous Ian Greer Associates, exist to advance the interests of extra-parliamentary clients in the House of Commons. They 'lobby' for some acts of legislation and against others, by using a variety of formal and informal communicative tactics. In the case of Ian Greer Associates and certain Conservative MPs, as was revealed by the press in 1995 and 1996, this involved passing brown envelopes full of money in exchange for said MPs asking official questions of ministers. The 'cash for questions' scandal, and other examples of 'sleaze' documented in the early 1990s were clear violations of the ethical standards of the professions involved.

On the other hand, most political lobbying companies do not seek to bribe politicians, and most politicians would not accept bribes if they were offered. That some do, have then been exposed by the press, and have seen their careers damaged by the resulting waves of criticism, might be interpreted to mean that the British political system is not yet in the same league of corruptibility and criminality as those of many other comparable countries. Nevertheless, this dimension of the political communication process requires continued monitoring, not just by the various parliamentary committees and watchdogs which have been set up in the wake of the 'sleaze' scandals of the 1990s, but by the political media. In this respect the *Guardian* and the *Sunday Times*, which led the investigative reportage of the Hamilton affair, have played an exemplary role, and one which should be viewed as a model for the role of the 'fourth estate'.

The ethics of political journalism

Unfortunately, the praise which legitimately accrues to some newspapers for their exposure of unethical practices in the political arena is more than matched by persistent criticism of the media's role in degrading and trivialising the democratic process. Some of these criticisms raise the issue of ethical standards, since they concern features of political journalism that are deliberate and intentional. Others highlight trends which are the product of factors beyond individual journalistic control but which, intentionally or not, are alleged to damage the quality of public political discourse.

The press and political bias

In relation to the press, two ethical criticisms are made most frequently. The first concerns the long-standing issue of bias, and the tendency of so many newspapers to act as propagandists for right-of-centre political masters. This bias results, it is argued, not only in editorial support for the ideas and values of the right, and against those of the left, but dishonest and inaccurate reportage. Well-known examples include the 1980s coverage of the activities of the 'loony left' in London, the *Daily Mirror*'s false accusations of Arthur Scargill's 'links' with Libya in its coverage of the 1984–5 miners' strike, and a succession of British General Elections in which the Labour Party was unable to secure a fair hearing from the vast majority of the press. Although empirical evidence for a pro-Tory effect of this coverage is difficult to assemble, many commentators have argued that the seventeen-year hold of the Conservative Party on government was not unrelated to the degree of unquestioning support which it enjoyed from all but a few broadsheet and tabloid newspapers over this period.[9]

Former Conservative minister Lord Wakeham is among those in his party who frankly concede that the role of the press was crucial in securing electoral victory in 1992. In his view, 'the sharpness of the pro-Conservative newspapers' comments and the depth and breadth of their reporting undoubtedly helped to ensure some of the movement towards us in the last weeks of the campaign' (1995, p. 5). The 'sharpness' and 'depth' referred to by Wakeham included such stories as the *Daily Mail*'s 'tax bombshell' coverage, and the *Sun*'s day-of-poll headline, 'If Kinnock wins today, will the last person to leave Britain turn out the lights'.

Anti-Labour press bias was not new in 1992, but it reached unprecedented heights and may, in the view of many observers, have made a crucial difference to the result. For leading Tory fundraiser Lord McAlpine, writing in the *Sunday Telegraph* a few days after John Major was returned to office, the press were 'the heroes of [the 1992] campaign'.

> Never has the attack on the Labour Party been so comprehensive. They exposed, ridiculed and humiliated that party, doing each day in their

pages the job that the politicians failed to do from their bright new platforms. This is how the election was won.[10]

The press in a democracy has, of course, the right to say what it likes within the law, but the self-proclaimed ethical standards of the journalistic profession may be thought to preclude efforts to 'fix' elections by the deliberate distortion and misreporting of political information. There is, as Noam Chomsky and others have persuasively argued, little difference between the Soviet-era propaganda sheets and those newspapers of the 'free press' which volunteer themselves as cheerleaders of one political party over another, irrespective of 'the truth'. The fact that the period between 1992 and 1997 saw a decline of pro-Conservative press bias, attributable in large part to sustained and skilful courting of the Murdoch titles by the Labour Party, does not alter the underlying argument: that journalists in a democracy – even those working on tabloids – have a responsibility to pluralism and diversity of political debate, and to refrain from peddling myths and lies about groups who may be viewed in certain quarters as 'subversive'. The fortunes of the Labour Party in government will be significantly shaped by how seriously the British press take this responsibility in the coming years.

The tabloidisation of political journalism

If the period between 1992 and 1997 was one in which the press became less like the collective house organ of the Conservative Party, it was also one of unprecedented reportage of political scandal, much of it affecting the Conservative Party itself. It may be that the two phenomena are related, and that Messrs Murdoch, Black, Montgomery *et al.* found it increasingly difficult to give unbending support to a party so apparently prone to moral lapses. In vigorously reporting the numerous cases of alleged ethical misconduct amongst politicians which have been revealed in recent years, however, the press has been accused of undermining faith in the political system itself, and of itself behaving unethically.

I referred above to the 'cash for questions' scandal, and the widely welcomed reportage of those newspapers which exposed it. Less welcome, for many observers, have been the many exposures of alleged sexual and 'lifestyle' misconduct amongst MPs. These have included serial philandering (Steven Norris), bizarre sex practices (the tragic death of Stephen Milligan), closet homosexuality (Jerry Hayes), alcoholism and drunk driving (Nicholas Scott). Almost all of these accusations involved the Conservative Party, and many required ministerial resignations, contributing much to the decline of the government's poll ratings after 1992. In reporting these stories, newspapers have been accused of masking the pursuit of commercial advantage (in an extremely competitive press market) behind pious concern for the nation's morals. Politicians, it is argued, have a right to privacy in so far as their private activities do not interfere with their public duties. What, for example, has Jerry Hayes's sexual preference got to do with his parliamentary life, given that he has been a liberal on gay rights in any case?

The royal family, too, has seen its private problems and difficulties relentlessly exposed in the press, leading to a climate in which its future as the pillar of the British constitution is under serious threat.

The ethical defence of such expository journalism is usually presented as follows. Regardless of the motivations behind it (and there can be little doubt that commercial rather than public interest considerations have been prominent in the thinking of tabloid editors) the press has a right, indeed a responsibility, to expose hypocrisy in public life. When politicians who on conference platforms preach about the social evils presented by single motherhood, or who choose to campaign around 'back to basics' moral values, turn out to be unfaithful to their wives, or neglecting their illegitimate children, the voters have a right to know. The conduct of private life in such cases has a clear relevance to public policy, and contradictions between the two are the proper subject of political journalism.

Revelatory coverage of the royals also has a public interest defence. Andrew Neil justified the *Sunday Times* serialisation of Andrew Morton's biography of the late Princess of Wales by arguing, firstly, that it was the product of Diana's own desire to have her side of the story reported, and furthermore, that the public has a right to know of matters which have serious constitutional significance, even if these are painfully private. He favourably contrasted the media visibility of the Charles–Diana marital split with the secrecy and widespread public ignorance which surrounded the abdication of Edward VIII in 1936.

The above justifications for a political journalism which is, whatever else it may be, undeniably titillatory, voyeuristic, and commercially successful, are indeed consistent with the ethical standards of a profession which since its emergence from the ruins of feudalism in early modern Europe has aspired to watch over the powerful. If the public's estimation of the political class suffers as a result, we might argue, then whose fault is it but their own?

Some media sociologists complain that the resulting coverage is 'part of a tendency to distract the public from matters of principle by offering voyeuristic pseudo-insights into individual matters' (Gripsund, 1992, p. 94). Others positively welcome the (unintentionally) subversive effect of such material appearing on our breakfast tables each morning, creating as it does an 'informed popular scepticism' (Fiske, 1992, p. 61) towards the powerful.

Readers of this book will have their own views on the impact of 'sleaze' journalism on our political culture. There are, clearly, some cases where the revelatory reportage of élite misbehaviour is consistent with the ethical codes of liberal journalism, and others where it is not. Distinguishing between the two is the task, firstly, of the journalists themselves, if they do not wish their already low reputation as a professional group to sink even further; of those who buy the newspapers concerned, and who give such coverage commercial value; and of the industry regulators, the Press Complaints Commission, whose judgements on these matters have not always been consistent or effective, prompting demands for legal measures to prohibit the worst excesses. Most journalists, including those who would not touch a toe-sucking royal story if it were handed to them on a plate, agree that it would be a pity if these demands led to legislation, since the law would be used most aggressively by the powerful to censor the legitimate, wholly ethical exposure of élite corruption and abuse.

Broadcasting

Broadcast political journalism has, until relatively recently, avoided the ethical challenges confronted by the print media. In Britain and many other countries, broadcast journalism has been strictly regulated to ensure that it is not biased towards one political party or another, and serves the public as a whole with political information and analysis of the quality demanded by modern democratic procedures. As a consequence, even in countries with almost entirely commercial systems, such as the United States, broadcast news has an image of neutrality and non-partisanship – a reputation for standing above and back from the party political fray – which gives it a distinctive role in the public sphere. Increasingly in the 1990s, however, broadcast journalists have been accused of abusing this role, and of damaging the political communication environment in the process.

Referring back to an earlier stage of the discussion, the growth of broadcast media, and television in particular, has been held responsible by many for the ascendancy of political style as an element in voter decision-making. Broadcast journalism, because of its space limitations and the brevity it imposes on political discourse, has produced what the senior BBC correspondent Nicholas Jones describes as 'a media environment habituated to the relentless pursuit of the soundbite' (1995, p. 51). The American James Fallows, editor of *The Nation*, accuses his colleagues in broadcast news of 'a relentless emphasis on the cynical game of politics' (1996, p. 31) which 'threatens public life itself'. Although individual broadcasters can hardly be blamed for an environment which they confront as a pre-given of their work, broadcasters as a group are the third essential strand of the politician–spin-doctor–journalist web, and as such implicated in the transformation of political communication into the deployment and manipulation of neat catchphrases (soundbites) and pleasing images (photo-opportunities).

Many variants of these criticisms exist in the literature, but they can perhaps be summarised in the claim that, for reasons of commerce, technology and professional vanity, the style of political journalism has gradually come to take precedence over substance. As the quantity of broadcast political communication available to viewers and listeners has grown exponentially, its quality has declined.

The ethics of broadcast style

Walter Cronkite, for example, has attacked what he sees as 'the trend towards trivialising "infotainment"'.[11] The increasingly revelatory and voyeuristic content of press journalism about politics was discussed earlier. Now, the argument goes, as broadcasting systems become more commercialised and competitive, similar features are becoming apparent in television and radio journalism.

Cronkite's reference was to America, but it applies also to Britain where, with cable, satellite and digital technologies quickly coming on stream, broadcasting is undergoing rapid change. Will this be accompanied by a 'tabloidisation' of broadcast journalism? If so, for Jon Snow of Channel 4 News, 'the whole fabric of democracy is threatened. In a world in which debate is replaced by exchanged seven second soundbites, the content of politics falls victim to the more easily communicated evidence of human frailty'.[12]

Criticism is focused not only on the familiar evil of 'tabloidisation'. Broadcast political journalism also stands accused of developing a repertoire of stylistic traits which, though intended to connote authority, balance, neutrality, and so on, actually inhibit the communication of substantive information. The media analyst Bryan Appleyard observes of television news that 'the cult of seriousness has become a style in itself . . . there has been an extraordinary blooming of technical and representational style, driven by a highly competitive market that demands the maximum impression of significance and sensation'.[13]

Nowhere is this more apparent than in the 'cult' of the 'star' presenter, exemplified in Britain most notably by Jeremy Paxman and John Humphrys and, on occasion, Sue MacGregor, James Naughtie and others who have acquired reputations for increasingly aggressive adversarial interviewing styles. At regular intervals in recent years these individuals have been accused of being excessively confrontational in their dealings with politicians, and of turning political interviews into sterile exchanges of accusation and counter-accusation which may entertain, but do not inform. The interview, it has been argued by politicians and broadcasters alike, becomes a test of a politician's ability to engage in verbal jousting rather than the articulation of policy.

The subject of political journalism becomes the *game* of politics, rather than the issues; the *process*, rather than the policies. As James Fallows observes, the 'context that gives meaning to information' (1996, p. 130) is sacrificed to make way for ratings-friendly drama.

For the 'stars' themselves, on the other hand, hostile interviewing is wholly consistent with their ethical responsibilities to the audience. John Humphrys, in rejecting politicians' criticisms of his style, has argued that broadcasters like himself play a key role in exposing the gap between what politicians say and what they do. In an increasingly managed communication environment, the in-depth political interview allows an element of unpredictability and challenge to be reintroduced, to the benefit of the citizen. The results may often lack rationality and coherence, but 'interviewing politicians is an important bridge between the electorate and their political leaders. We have to distil the national argument, to represent the voters' concerns'.[14] Michael Cockerell agrees that while Humphrys (and the other 'star' interviewers) 'may sometimes deploy a terrier-like persistence in his interviews that can sometimes be counter-productive . . . his aim is to strip away the public relations gloss and use his own sharp teeth to counter pre-rehearsed soundbites'.[15]

The ethics of political interviewing is a subject which, perhaps understandably, has mainly preoccupied the politicians who are most regularly subjected to the techniques developed by Humphrys and his colleagues. For that reason alone, we should be cautious before endorsing calls for a journalistic retreat from the confrontational style. Occasional examples of presenter-vanity and 'hyperadversarialism' (as James Fallows calls it) are a small price to pay for a journalism which is not intimidated by the powerful.

Conclusion

Each of the three groups whose communicative behaviour we have examined in this essay is participating in a competition – a game, to use the metaphor frequently applied in this context. The politicians and the journalists compete to set the news agenda, and to have their perspectives on events reported. The spin-doctors act as coaches and managers on behalf of the politicians, and as technical assistants in realising the desired communicative effects. We, the voters, are positioned as spectators, with occasional walk-on parts. At the end of each electoral cycle we are asked to choose whom we think has performed best during the preceding period, and who is likely to perform best in the forthcoming one.

The politicians ask us to make that decision on the basis of the policy options which they lay out before us. Their spin-doctors and communication advisers operate on the assumption that we will also be influenced by the presentation, as well as the policy content of the message, a consideration which places great emphasis on the political performers' style and image. The journalists, meanwhile, probe this confection of policy-substance and image-surface, exposing and widening the gap between rhetoric and reality, laying bare the contradictions, drawing our attention to the existence of the game and the artifice employed by its participants.

None of this is incompatible with the respective ethical standards of each group. Politicians advocate, media consultants advise, journalists scrutinise. They are all, in that sense, merely doing their jobs. The difference between now and earlier times – and what has made this such a burning issue – is principally that the game is, from the viewpoint of the players, more competitive and managed. For us as spectators it is more omnipresent, even intrusive, than ever before. At times we come to feel that we have overdosed on politics. We grow weary with the politicians' posturings, the journalists' probings, and the spin-doctors' efforts to pull the wool over our collective eyes. Yet the luxury of excess is not one which we should take for granted. Less than one hundred years ago, as was noted above, women did not have the vote in Britain. Free from the gaze of electronic media, politicians and other élite groups could pursue their business relatively free from journalistic intrusion. As recently as the 1950s the journalistic norm in dealing with politicians was (as seen from this distance in hilarious black and white newsreel footage) embarrassing, laughable deference. As for the world beyond the countries of advanced capitalism, many populations still live under criminally corrupt or authoritarian regimes, where a Jeremy Paxman, a James Naughtie, and even a Kelvin Mackenzie would not last ten minutes.

Of course there are excesses, and none of what has been said thus far is intended to lessen the significance of ethical lapses when they occur. Politicians lie. Journalists pursue confrontation for confrontation's sake, and expose the private failings of public figures for no more noble cause than the commercial advantage of their proprietor. Spin-doctors overdo it with threatening faxes and bullying phone calls.

The encouraging thing in all this, however, is how often we come to know about these abuses of the political communication machinery, how often they are exposed and themselves become part of the evidence and information on which we make our political judgements. This essay on the ethics of political communication could not have been written without reference to the vast quantity of media debate about – the ethics of political communication. We exist – largely thanks to the media – in a state of informed 'knowingness' which does much to protect us from the politicians' tendency, assisted by their professional media advisers, to dissemble, deceive and manipulate. And, of course, we have our own reservoirs of experience against which to compare everything that the political communicators say and do. The media supply a large part of the information on which we base our political behaviour, but by no means all.

We cannot reverse the communicative trends discussed in this essay, nor, I would argue, should we wish to. We inhabit the most media-literate, information-rich society in human history, where it is ever more difficult for élites to keep secrets, and to suppress debate, should ethical failings predispose them to do so. We *are* probably overloaded with political information, much of it trashy and superficial, but better that than the inhibited, boot-licking media of a few short decades ago.

As we enter the era of digital television and the Internet, we face another expansion of the political media, as hundreds of new channels come on air or on-line with space to fill. In meeting that challenge we as citizens should be vigilant, and ensure that our journalists are vigilant on our behalf, maintaining their own ethical standards, those of the politicians on whom they report, and the spin-doctors who seek to influence their coverage. We should encourage media education in schools and universities, so that the citizens of the twenty-first century learn the skills of critical reading and viewing as part of their preparation for civic responsibility. We should demand freedom of information and governmental openness. We should support appropriate restrictions on media ownership, so that the means of political communication are not open to monopolisation by wealthy individuals, and the potential for one-sided press bias is minimised. We should defend public service broadcasting, while accepting that it must adapt to meet the demands of new technologies and new viewing and listening patterns. And if all of that is not enough, we will simply have to exercise our right not to play the game: to switch off, withdraw our support, and call it to a halt.

Notes

1 The French philosopher Jean Baudrillard says, for example, that 'for some time now, the electoral game has been akin to TV game shows in the consciousness of the people. The people enjoy, day to day, like a home movie, the fluctuations of their own opinions in the daily opinion polls. Nothing in all this engages any responsibility. At no time are the masses politically engaged in a conscious manner', in *In the Shadow of the Silent Majorities . . . or the End of the Social* (New York: Semiotext, 1983), p. 38.

2 Although the opinions expressed are entirely my own, the argument draws on work funded by the Economic and Social Research Council on political communication and democracy currently being undertaken by the author in collaboration with colleagues at the Stirling Media Research Institute of Stirling University, Scotland.

3 M. Woollacott, 'When invisibility means death', *Guardian*, 27 April 1996.

4 A. Coote, 'Labour puts its neck on the line', *Sunday Times*, 29 September 1996.

5 S. Heffer, 'Spinning for a living . . . who cares?', *British Journalism Review* 6/4 (1995).

6 I. MacWhirter, 'Not what the spin doctor ordered', *The Scotsman*, 9 August 1996.

7 A. Campbell, 'Auntie's spinners', *Sunday Times*, 22 September 1996.

8 In an interview given to the *Guardian* in February 1997 Campbell conceded that his and his colleagues' response to Clare Short's 1995 statements on tax had been inappropriate and unfair (J. Mulholland, 'Labour's Mr Media', *Guardian*, 17 February 1997).

9 See Martin Linton's *Guardian* lecture, 'The battle for Jennifer's ear', given at Nuffield College, Oxford, on 30 October 1994. In it he asserts that 'Labour has never won an election when it was more than 18 per cent behind the Tories in

press share' (reported in M. Linton, 'Sun-powered politics', *Guardian*, 30 October 1995).

10 Quoted in D. McKie, 'Fact is free but comment is sacred', in I. Crewe and B. Gosschalk (eds) *Political Communications: The General Election Campaign of 1992* (Cambridge: Cambridge University Press, 1995), p. 128.

11 W. Cronkite, 'More bad news', *Guardian*, 27 January 1997.

12 J. Snow, 'More bad news', *Guardian*, 27 January 1997.

13 B. Appleyard, 'Please adjust your mind set', *The Independent*, 9 February 1994.

14 J. Humphrys, 'In the firing line', *Guardian*, 24 May 1995.

15 M. Cockerell, 'Whose fingers on the mike?', *Guardian*, 27 March 1995.

6 The myth of Saddam Hussein

New militarism and the propaganda function of the human interest story

Richard Keeble

The making of the Gulf War myth

It could be argued there was no Gulf War of 1991. In the way in which the term is generally used and understood, what took place in the Persian Gulf in January to February 1991 was not a 'war' at all. It was nothing less than a series of massacres. This is not a mere semantic quibble. The distinction (and the accompanying notion of the 'war' myth) has profound theoretical and analytical implications for any study of the press coverage. There was no credible enemy. The Iraqi army was constantly represented in the British and American press in the run-up to the conflict as 1 million strong, the fourth largest in the world, 'battle-hardened'[1] after the eight-year war with Iran, led by monster madman Saddam Hussein. When, in January and February 1991, Iraqi soldiers were deserting in droves and succumbing to one slaughter after another, Fleet Street still predicted the largest ground battle since the Second World War. Stories of enormous Iraqi defensive structures with massive berms and a highly sophisticated system of underground trenches filled the media. In the end there was nothing more than a walk-over, a rout, a barbaric slaughter buried beneath the fiction of heroic warfare.

The nature and significance of the war sprang out of the realms of myth, rhetoric and media spectacle. Focusing on the conflict as a construction in this way can draw attention to the broad political and economic factors, the nature of the militarism of the states involved and the propaganda role of the mainstream media within those states. More particularly, it can highlight the propaganda function of the sensationalist, human interest story.[2]

Major, high-profile wars are no longer fought as merely military events. People are slaughtered, children and soldiers are traumatised, buildings, hospitals, radio stations, tanks are destroyed. But major wars are now fought as media spectacles for largely non-strategic purposes. The Gulf War had little to do with getting Iraqi soldiers out of Kuwait. It had little to do with protecting Saudi Arabia from an Iraqi invasion. It had little to do with protecting the oil supplies. The conflict had little to do with getting rid of Saddam Hussein. He was supported by the international élites of the East and West in the decade leading up to August 1990, he was supported by the CIA even after August 1990[3] and no doubt a powerful faction in the allied élite still supports his regime.[4]

Kicking the Vietnam syndrome, constructing the Saddam myth

A major war needed to be constructed – to be seen to be fought and won – in large part so that the US élites could eradicate the trauma of the Vietnam defeat from their collective memory.[5] A hastily constructed, mythical Saddam Hussein suddenly appeared as the perfect enemy against whom the perfect war could be waged. Since the collapse of the Soviet Union the massively resourced military industrial complex was facing a potential crisis and desperate to find a new enemy. Britain's Falklands adventure in 1982 over an insignificant group of islands populated largely by penguins set the precedent for the transformation of militarism into spectator sport.[6]

Then, following the Falklands precedent, Grenada (1983), Libya (1986) and Panama (1989) were dabbled in as enemies by the United States. But none could compare to Saddam Hussein. Moreover, the myth of the war was to prove all the more potent since it also served the interests of the Iraqi élite by resolving some of the contradictions of their old-style militarism. Since the ceasefire in the Iran–Iraq war of 1988, thousands of men were returning to cities from the front, ending up dissatisfied and jobless.[7] Many of them were engaged in revolts against the regime, especially Kurds and Shi'as.[8] A 'war' could eliminate large groups of them. As Faleh Abd al-Jabbar comments, 'The rout relieved Saddam of the most troublesome part of his army and preserved the most loyal divisions.'[9]

The media spectacle of the mythical war

The Gulf simulated war ended up like a motion picture spectacular[10] with the coalition forces acting each day as if according to a pre-arranged script. As Fuad Nahdi, one of the three *Los Angeles Times* reporters in Riyadh, commented, 'The first press conference of the day would be at 7.30 a.m. From then on you knew exactly what the line for the day was going to be. The script had been written beforehand and I felt like the reviewer of a good play or film.'[11]

So the censorship regime (the pooling arrangements, the denial of access to the front to journalists, the intimidation of reporters by the military) served essentially symbolic purposes. It was an expression of the arbitrary, monopoly power of the military over the conduct of war. Similarly the almost total monopoly of the pools by American and British media representatives symbolised these countries' dominance over the global communications networks.[12] The military, according to the dominant myth, went into the Vietnam War with their hands tied behind their back (by traitor-ous media and peace-freaks). Vietnam was a war that 'got out of control'. Desert Storm was the US military's attempt to wage the perfect war: to control and give it a contrived, happy ending. Censorship was used not so much to preserve military security as to promote a positive image of the massacres.

New militarism and the propaganda function of the press

The Gulf War can usefully be seen as a manifestation of a distinctly new kind of militarism. As James Combs argues over the Falklands adventure and the US invasion of Grenada:

> It is a new kind of war, war as performance. It is a war in which the attention of its *auteurs* is not only on the conduct of the war but also the communication of the war. With their political and military power to command, coerce and co-opt the mass media, the national security élite can make the military event go according to the script, omit bad scenes and discouraging words and bring about a military performance that is both spectacular and satisfying.[13]

Military strategy becomes essentially a media event, an entertainment, a spectacle. Warfare, moreover, is transmuted into a symbolic assertion of United States and to a lesser degree British global media (and military) power. Media manipulation becomes a central military strategy. This 'mediacentrism' is a pivotal element of new militarist societies.[14]

Instead of mass active participation in militarist wars (such as 1914–18; 1939–45 and Vietnam), people are mobilised through their consumption of censored media (the censorship largely imposed by journalists themselves) whose job is to manufacture the spectacle of 'warfare'. People respond to the propaganda offensive with a mixture of enthusiasm, contempt, apathy and scepticism. Yet, most crucially, media consumption and public opinion polling provide the illusion of participation just as satellite technology provides the illusion of 'real live' coverage of the war.

MacKenzie has described the 'spectacular theatre' of nineteenth-century British militarism, when press representations of heroic imperialist adven-tures in distant colonies had a considerable entertainment element.[15] Featherstone, too, has identified the way in which the Victorian 'small' wars of imperial expansion in Africa and India were glorified for a doting public by war correspondents such as William Russell, G. A. Henty, Archibald Forbes and H. M. Stanley.[16]

But Victorian newspapers and magazines did not have the social pene-tration of the mass media of today. And Victorian militarism was rein-forced through a wide range of institutions and social activities: the Salvation Army, Church Army, and uniformed youth organisations, rifle clubs, ceremonial and drill units in factories. MacKenzie comments, 'In all these ways, a very large proportion of the population came to have some connection with military and paramilitary organisations.'[17] By the 1970s this institutional and social militarism had given way to a new media-centric, consumerist, entertainment militarism in which the mass media, ideologically aligned to a strong and increasingly secretive state, had assumed a dominant ideological and propaganda role. Indeed, the manu-factured new militarist wars of the 1980s deliberately served to reinforce the power of the political and economic élites within the national security state and the marginalisation of the mass of the public.

Unlike militarist wars which lasted years, new militarist wars are over quickly. As Benjamin Bradlee, former executive editor of the *Washington Post* commented bluntly of the events of January–February 1991, 'The trouble with this war was it was so fucking fast.'[18] But the 42-day Gulf conflict was a long war in new militarist terms. The military become, then, the primary definers of the fast-moving event while journalists, kept far from any action, are in no position to challenge their inventions.

Moreover, the strategic imperatives of new militarism mean that wars become inherently difficult to report. They are fought by planes (to which journalists have no access), at high altitude and often at night. New weapons incinerate their victims, making calculations of casualties even more difficult. The emphasis on computer games in military planning means the distinction between 'real' and Nintendo-style wars becomes blurred.

The media myth of defence

The dominant view reproduced in the mainstream media represents the state as having fought defensively only in exceptional cases since 1945. The Gulf War, accordingly, was represented as a legitimate, defensive response to an unprovoked attack by Saddam Hussein on innocent, vulnerable, tiny Kuwait (and, by implication, on vulnerable western civilisation). Such an interpretation significantly obscures the offensive (and often covert) ele-ments of the UK and US state systems and military strategies.

In fact, since 1945 the UK and the USA have deployed troops somewhere in the globe at least once every year, usually away from the media's glare. Rose argues that since 1945 British troops have been involved in more wars in more places across the globe than those of any other country.[19] And Steve Peak identified the Falklands War as the 88th deployment of British troops since 1945.[20] In the case of the USA, Cecil Currey finds that since 1950 America has used either force or its threat about 500 times.[21] Former CIA agent John Stockwell suggests that the agency has been involved in 3,000 major operations and 10,000 minor operations which have led to the death of 6 million people worldwide.[22] Pentagon adviser John M. Collins, in his seminal analysis of strategy in these largely secret wars, known as low intensity conflicts (LICs), isolates just 60 examples this century.[23]

The dominant media view fails to acknowledge the inherent aggression of the state, representing the short, sharp attacks (or defensive actions as argued by the administration of the day) of the USA on Grenada, Libya and Panama in the 1980s as the typical form of warfare. In fact, the reverse is nearer the truth. Some 57 per cent of Collins's sample lasted under five years but 33 per cent exceeded 10 years. For instance, he points out that the LIC against Libya has been going on since 1970. The eleven-minute attack on Libyan targets in April 1986 (a manufactured crisis staged as a media event and co-ordinated to coincide with the beginning of the 7 p.m. news in the USA, according to Kellner[24]) was just a tiny feature of this multi-pronged conflict.

Most warfare of new militarist societies clearly avoids the use of massive armies of the size the coalition forces assembled in Saudi Arabia, during the lead-up to the 1991 conflict. Instead permanent warfare (driven by the demands of the military industrial complex to which the media are closely aligned) is conducted through special force intervention, the support of proxy forces and leaders, through diplomatic, trade and other economic sanctions, through secret service destabilisation and assassination.[25]

The making of the Saddam myth

Central to the construction of the Gulf War myth, then, was the sensationalist demonisation of Saddam Hussein. Yet the press construction of the myth of Saddam Hussein first began in the months leading up to August 1990 and only then completely dominated the coverage throughout all the British media. Before the Kuwait invasion, the principal bogeyman in the Middle East for the mainstream press was Iran. Searle demonstrates how the *Sun*'s racist venom was directed at this country throughout the 1980s. On 18 October 1987, after the USA destroyed two Iranian ex-oil rigs in the Gulf, it commented, 'The Americans have enough firepower in the Gulf to render the country a wasteland. Maybe that would not be a bad thing for the rest of humanity.'[26]

During the Iran–Iraq war (1980–8) Iraq was, in general, referred to simply as Iraq or Baghdad. As significant sections of the West tilted towards Iraq so Saddam Hussein was covered by the media in favourable terms. Robert Freedman highlights stories in the western press which spoke approvingly of Saddam's moves to privatise the economy in the mid-1980s and he was even compared to Thatcher in this context.[27]

The myth of Halabja

Even the press coverage of the chemical bombing of Kurds in Halabja on 16 March 1988 was notable for its comparative restraint.[28] Yet more than 5,000 civilians were killed and another 7,000 maimed for life. Timmerman suggests the gas was a hydrogen cyanide compound the Iraqis had developed with the help of a German company.[29] Made in the Samarra gas works, it was similar to the poison gas the Nazis had used to exterminate the Jews more than 40 years earlier. Survivors interviewed by Human Rights Watch, Middle East confirmed that the bombs were dropped from Iraqi and not Iranian planes, since they flew low enough for their markings to be legible.[30] Human Rights Watch also lists 60 Kurdish villages attacked with mustard gas, nerve gas and a combination of the two over the previous two years.[31]

Little blame was levelled personally at Saddam Hussein in the press for the Halabja atrocity. No Hitler or Nazi jibes emerged. The *Guardian* of 17 March 1988 was typical: 'It is hard to conceive of any explanation for the chemical bombardment of Halabja other than one which Iranians and Kurds offer – revenge.' The madness of Saddam Hussein, his lust for power was nowhere identified as the cause of the outrage. While a 24 March editorial defined the atrocity as 'Iraq's latest and greatest war crime' it mirrored the government's position on the war, taking no side and calling for a ceasefire.

At the same time the press gave considerable prominence to US government claims that Iranians were also responsible for the chemical attacks. *The Times* carried prominently the report headlined 'US evidence suggests Iran also use chemicals', while the *Guardian* quoted a Reuters report of US State Department spokesman Charles Redman claiming, 'There are indications that Iran may have also used chemical artillery shells in the fighting.'

Six weeks after the attack, a UN report, made by a Spanish military doctor, Col. Manuel Dominguez Carmona, concluded it was impossible to say whether Iraq or Iran or both were to blame.[32] In February 1990, a US Army War College report concluded that Iraq was not responsible for the Halabja massacre and that 'it was the Iranian bombardment that had actually killed the Kurds'.[33] Was this mere US government-inspired misinformation because Iraq was then a close ally? Certainly the media at the time of Halabja raised serious questions about the supposed guilt of Iraq. These doubts were completely absent in the coverage of the 1990 crisis and later massacres. The Halabja bombing, rather, featured prominently in all the demonisation propaganda directed at the Iraqi leader.

Bazoft ambivalences

The ambivalence of the élite's approach to Saddam Hussein at this time was most apparent in the coverage of the hanging of the *Observer* journalist Farzad Bazoft on 15 March 1990. An explosion had destroyed the al-Hillah plant north of Baghdad on 17 August 1989 and Bazoft had travelled there with an English nurse, Daphne Parish, taking photographs and even soil samples.[34] After being arrested by Iraqi security police he had 'confessed' to being an Israeli spy. Immediately after the hanging British

intelligence leaked information that Bazoft had stolen £500 from a building society ten years earlier. According to John Pilger, MI5 was acting on
behalf of the Thatcher government 'desperate for any excuse not to suspend its lucrative business and arms deals with Saddam Hussein'.[35]

The *Sun*'s 'exclusive' headline went: 'Hanged man was a robber'; the
Mail's: 'Bazoft a perfect spy for Israel'; *Today*'s: 'Bazoft was an Israeli
agent'. A *Sunday Telegraph* editorial condemned Bazoft as a spy, likening
investigative journalism to an offence against the state. The investigative
journalist Simon Henderson also argued that Bazoft was a spy. He concluded, 'At no time did the British admit that Bazoft had been spying, nor
did Iraq flesh out its allegations. The reason was clear: if Britain admitted
to the spying the two countries would have had to break off diplomatic
relations.' Neither country wanted this. 'So the Bazoft incident was left to
die down.'[36]

The propaganda function of the human interest story

After the Iraqi invasion of Kuwait of August 1990, the personality of a
mythical Saddam Hussein became the prime focus of sensationalist press
coverage. Hussein, in effect, became Iraq. In this way, the human interest
bias, which is deeply embedded in journalists' culture, served a crucial
propaganda function, simplifying an enormously complex history, seriously distorting the representation of the conflict and drawing attention
away from other important social, political, geostrategic, religious and
economic factors.

As Curran, Douglas and Whannel argue, human interest is not simply a
neutral window on the world but embodies a particular way of seeing.[37]
Accordingly, the possibility of basic structural inequalities is rejected while
non-historical forces of 'luck, fate and chance' are represented as dominant
within a given, naturalised world. Paul Kennedy sees the human interest
bias as an indication of the potency of the conservative historical ideology
which prioritises human interest factors above deeper underlying, contex-
tualising factors.[38]

This view is reinforced by Sparks who says, 'The popular conception of
the personal becomes the explanatory framework within which the social
order is presented as transparent.' The media fail to convey the 'social
totality' comprising 'complex mediations of institutional structures, economic relations and so on'.[39]

Ultimately, the hyper-personalising of the crisis served the crucial propaganda function of directing all blame on to the one man: Saddam. Thus,
when during the 1991 conflict the allies bombed the Almeriyya shelter in
Baghdad or the retreating conscripts on the road to Basra, causing hundreds of deaths, there was one simple, predictable response: it was all
Saddam's fault. The allies in the massacre-speak were always 'kicking

Saddam's arse', his conscripts were always reduced to non-people, animals; Iraqi civilian deaths were either 'inevitable' or 'mistakes'.

Hitler Hussein

Another central feature of the demonisation strategy and the construction of the mythical Saddam was the representation of him as the new Hitler. The *Telegraph*, of 3 August, was typical. It wrote, 'President Hussein's decision to invade Kuwait is proof of his Hitlerian determination to get his own way.' Robert Harvey, in a leader page feature, contributed, 'For once the overworked comparison with Hitler is apposite.' The *Mail* editorial of the same day commented, 'Like a rerun of Hitler's invasion of Czechoslovakia in the 1930s, the Iraqi dictatorship has flouted international opinion and grabbed a small but wealthy neighbour. Nothing justifies this outrage.' In the *Sun* of 4 August, Dr John Laffing, described as an expert on Arab affairs, wrote that 'power-crazed tyrant Saddam Hussein was exposed yesterday as a Führer freak who models himself on Adolf Hitler' and had set up a shrine to Hitler.

On 5 August, the *Sunday Times* said of the Iraqi invasion, 'It was a strategy on Hitlerian lines: the annexation by *blitzkrieg* of a weak neighbour.' The *Observer* editorial of the same day commented, under the heading 'Why this Hitler of the Gulf has to go', 'It is going to be desperately difficult to get out of this one without the exchange of rocket fire. If the comparison with Hitler holds good, it may prove impossible.' And the editorial continued, 'Comparing people to Hitler can be counter-productive as Sir Anthony Eden (over Nasser) and Nicholas Ridley (over Chancellor Kohl) both found to their cost. But in Saddam Hussein the world is facing another Hitler . . . He has the same kind of expansionist ambitions and brutal lack of humanity. Like the German Führer he has an underlying vision of an all-powerful Iraq funded by oil and backed by force.'

The Independent of 3 August editorialised, 'The appetites of dictators grow with what they feed upon as Europe learnt to its cost when dealing with Hitler.' And its profile of 11 August began, 'In the overworn comparison with Hitler and Stalin there is a kernel of truth. For he shares the secret of great dictators – he understands the psychotic relationship between fear and love.' The *Mirror* intoned, 'Saddam Hussein is the Adolf Hitler of the Arab world. If he isn't stopped now the West will pay a heavy price.'

A similar focus occurred in American press coverage. The Gannett Foundation study found 1,035 mentions of Saddam Hussein as Hitler from 1 August to 28 February 1991 in the print media.[40] On both sides of the Atlantic the analogy was reinforced in cartoon representations. Macarthur comments, 'Hardly any reporters were heard challenging the President in his Hitler comparisons at press conferences.'[41]

Yet the Hitler angle did not appear to politicians and the press 'naturally'; it served a number of important ideological, propaganda purposes. With the collapse of the Soviet Union, the spectre of the 'communist threat' could no longer be raised as a justification for US military action. As a propaganda tool the Hitler threat was remarkably efficient: it was simple and seemingly unproblematic. In popular rhetoric, Hitler has been transformed into an enormous symbol of evil and danger. Focusing on the enemy as a Hitler could only serve to direct massive emotional negativity to that single person, and at the same time elevate the moral purity of the forces lined up against him. As *The Independent* leader of 3 August commented with commendable clarity, 'Since the changes in Russia some people have been lamenting the lack of a convincing enemy. Here he is.' Saddam Hussein was and remains a brutal dictator. The paper's profile of 11 August remarked, 'President Saddam has achieved the apotheosis of the totalitarian ideal.' Yet for ten years the superpowers were happy to cultivate Iraq as a 'friend'. During those years there were many opportunities for the press to put the Hitler label on Saddam. The Ba'ath party, indeed, had Fascist origins, being formed in Damascus in 1941 out of an aid committee set up by Alflaq and Bitar to assist Rashid Ali's Nazi-backed revolt in Iraq.[42] One of the first mentions of Saddam Hussein as Hitler appeared on 16 September 1988. Hazhir Temourian wrote, 'Saddam Hussein, the little psychopath who clearly believes he will get away with emulating his hero, Hitler, must be punished with the powers of the civilised world.' But this was in the leftist *New Statesman and Society* (pp. 20–2).

All the post-August 1990 Hitler hype sought to say implicitly, 'There have been many horrible dictators since 1945 but Saddam Hussein is the worst of all.' By no sensible historical criteria could the validity of that assertion be assessed; it was merely serving rhetorical, ideological and ultimately political/military purposes.

The endlessly repeated Hitler analogy represented a highly selective, ideologically motivated use of history by the USA and its prominent allies. For its essential purpose was to draw on pre-Cold War rhetoric to silence many histories, in particular the imperial roles of the USA and UK in the Middle East and more globally. As Bennett comments, 'The vivid, personalised framing of Saddam Hussein as Hitler made a clean historic break with past administration policies toward Iraq and established a new historical and emotional reference from which opinion formation could begin anew.'[43]

The Hitler analogy also served a critical role in the complex, multifaceted propaganda project to highlight the military option above the diplomatic one; after all Hitler was removed only by force.[44] As Christopher Layne says, 'The 1930s analogy rests on the assumption that 'aggression' must be resisted, not appeased whenever it occurs because it will snowball unless firmly stopped.' It was a sort of variation of the Cold War/

old order domino theory which drove the USA into the débâcle of Vietnam.[45] Those who questioned the Bush agenda were thus labelled 'appeasers' (returning again to pre-1939 rhetoric) and saddled with all the negative connotations of that word. It served to highlight Saddam Hussein and the country he was supposed to run as a powerful, global threat which needed to be tamed or destroyed if President Bush's 'new world order' was to be established.

After the Kurdish massacres, with Saddam still in power (and with the USA maintaining its pre-invasion policy of ambivalence towards the Iraqi regime) the Hitler analogies suddenly disappeared from the media. The analogy was exposed as an ideological device to legitimise the US and allied stance.

Madman Saddam

Along with 'Saddam' as Hitler, the other dominant aspect of the coverage of Iraq after the Kuwait invasion was to represent Saddam as mad and evil. On 7 August, John Kay wrote in the *Sun*, 'Britain's élite SAS regiment could assassinate crazed Iraqi President – and defuse the growing Gulf crisis in one blow.' The *Guardian* editorial commented, 'In the two years since the Gulf War ended it has been at times hard to decide which of the two damaged regimes that staggered out of that bloody conflict was the more deranged or the more dangerous.' The *Mail* of 3 August, in a centre-spread headlined 'A new Hitler plots his empire', described Saddam Hussein as a megalomaniac. The *Express* headlined, 'Mad despot who wants to rule the Arab world'. The story beneath gave prominence to a piece of Mossad misinformation which was to feature regularly in the press in the lead-up to the massacres. It reported, 'This week an Israeli graphologist who examined his handwriting at the request of the secret service Mossad – without knowing the identity of the author – ruled that he is in urgent need of psychiatric treatment.'

Linked to this representation was the emphasis on Saddam (and by association those who supported him) as being barbarous and brutal. In effect, the press was portraying him as a monster, non-human, uncivilised and thus worthy of any treatment dealt him.

The *Mirror* profiled him on 3 August: 'Already he is a mass murderer, a man guilty of genocide, a monster who has used gas and chemical weapons on civilians and enemy troops and whose war with Iran cost half a million lives.' On 7 August, the *Sun* evoked the animal metaphor in this disreputable way: 'A stone lifted at the Iraqi embassy in London yesterday and a reptile crawled out.' It was referring to ambassador Shafiq Al-Salih who supposedly shrugged when asked the fate of British hostages in Iraq. The paper continued, 'We hope an American B-52 wipes the crooked smile from his lips.' In much of the coverage Saddam is presented as the embodiment of evil. The *Mail* of 3 August: 'Hussein is known to approve 30 types of torture. They include mutilation, gouging out of eyes, cutting off the nose, sex organs and limbs, hammering nails into the body, burning with hot irons and roasting victims over flames.'

What is striking about this dominant genre of Saddam profiling is the way in which he is represented as existing in a natural state of bloodthirsty anarchy where none of the normal human factors operate. The history of British and American imperialism, political, religious, environmental dynamics play no part in this biography. It is completely untouched by history. There is little concept of Saddam Hussein as a diplomat. Thus the dominant representation remains extraordinarily two-dimensional and consistent throughout the crisis and massacres.

As Prince argues on these anti-historical projections and images, 'Iraq was thereby exiled from the modern world and the 20th century, banished to a nameless, pre-civilised period, effectively distanced in spatial, temporal and moral terms from the West.'[46]

Saddam trapped within the frame of popular culture

The crisis, with all its immense complexities, was from the outset represented within the dominant frames of popular culture which represent reality as a simple fight between good and evil. As Gilbert Adair said, 'Saddam Hussein himself has become a concentration of pure malevolence, of a type instantly, irresistibly, reminiscent of the villains in James Bond movies.'[47] And Roy Greenslade, editor of the *Mirror* during the massacres of the Kurds, later commented, 'We covered the war in a fairly mainstream, tabloid way. Here was a recognisable enemy. Saddam was an evil man. That was the great assumption.'[48]

John Schostak develops this theme. He writes,

By evoking the experiences now overlaid with the mythology of the Second World War, Hussein's actions and the West's counter actions could be explained simply and simplistically to the public. The complex history of involvement by the West in Middle Eastern affairs, which had allowed tyrants to arise and be supported was largely glossed over. The invasions and subversions carried out by Western powers all over the world could be ignored in this simplistic drama echoing the fight of good over evil.[49]

According to William F. Fore, the mass media are the devices used by the controllers of our culture to keep it simple.[50] In this they reproduce the rhetoric of the political élite. For instance, President Bush told Congress, 'I have resolved all moral questions in my mind: this is a black versus white, good versus evil.' This moralistic, anti-historical rhetoric, reproduced in the press, helped portray the Kuwait invasion as an inexplicable and irrational undertaking.

Press construction of the Kurdish myth

Press representations of Saddam Hussein since the war have shown significant fluctuations. The 1991 Kurdish revolt served to portray a nation, previously marginalised in the media, as suddenly heroic in their liberation struggle, while the suppression of this revolt and that of the Shi'as in the south reinforced the image of Saddam as ruthlessly oppressive.

Yet the romantic presentation of the Kurdish plight (which fitted so neatly into dominant simplistic goodie versus baddie representational frames) shrouded the CIA's covert involvement in the Kurd's history, past and present, which was always marginalised in the media.[51] As Heikal commented on the Kurds and Shi'as, 'If the two uprisings had been truly motivated by the desire for radical changes in the structure of Iraq, they might have succeeded; as it was, many of those involved were merely trying to exploit a chaotic situation for reasons of greed and revenge.'[52]

Moreover, while the press represented Prime Minister John Major as being forced by the pressure of public opinion and media coverage to dream up the enclave idea to protect the Kurds from the marauding Saddam, other political factors had far more impact.[53] In particular, the Turkish leadership feared that the mass of Kurds fleeing over their borders would add support to the growing revolt of Turkish Kurds, spearheaded by the Marxist-oriented Partia Karkaris Kurdistan (PKK), so coverage of this group was either non-existent or marginalised in the media.

Given their support during the war, the Turkish leaders probably felt that they had reason to expect some favours from the USA. In fact, the Turkish President Turgut Ozal first suggested the Kurdish haven on 7 April.[54] Major's proposal came only the following day. In the south, Saudi concern over Iranian, Shi'ite advances into Iraq probably doomed the Shi'ite revolt to defeat.

How Saddam is transformed into a naughty schoolboy

For long stretches since March 1991 Saddam has disappeared from sight in the press. One section of the western élite is clearly happy that he remains in power (countering Iranian expansion and serving as an easy 'enemy' to bomb at appropriate times). Another section wants him out and uses exclusion zones, covert action and the occasional symbolic bombing raid to put pressure on his regime. But Saddam is no longer represented as a global threat worth the trouble of fighting heroic wars to dislodge.

Significantly, during the January and June 1993 risk-free air attacks on Iraq by the USA, all blame was again levelled at Saddam.[55] But from being 'worse than Hitler' he was transformed into a naughty little schoolboy worth a 'spanking'.[56]

Conclusion

The 1991 Gulf conflict was America's manufactured 'big' war in which it supposedly finally kicked the Vietnam syndrome. Saddam was always the monstrous global threat the allies were fighting. Around his personality a crucial narrative was manufactured to help legitimise the allied stance. In this way the human interest bias of the press, rooted in journalists' everyday routines but located in this study in its historical and political context, came to serve a crucial propaganda role.

As Reese and Buckalew conclude, 'The most pervasive, powerful and difficult to counter illusion [of real warfare] emerged from the routine, structural workings of the media system.' And they add, 'The interlocking and reinforcing triangle of government, news media and corporate needs works together to further a culture supportive of military adventures such as those in the Gulf.'[57]

Significantly, US military interventions since 1991 have not been hyped as acts of heroic warfare in the press. New militarist warfare, as identified here, is a very specific, mediacentric, spectacular phenomenon. When the conditions are not right for major, overt conflict, then this style of warfare is pursued in secret (as in Bosnia), or given low-key coverage and called 'peacekeeping' (as in Somalia and Haiti) or 'punishing Saddam' (as during the US bombing of Iraq in September 1996).

Indeed, as western élite rhetoric about Saddam Hussein fluctuates, so the consensual voice of the press follows meekly in its wake.

Notes

1 Iraqi troops were known to have performed badly in the 1980–8 war with Iran when thousands had deserted. See A. Abbas, *The Iraqi Armed Forces, Past and Present in Saddam's Iraq: Revolution or Reaction?* (London, CADRI/Zed Books, 1986), p. 220 and Norman Friedman, *Desert Victory: The War for Kuwait* (Annapolis, MD: Naval Institute Press, 1991).
2 See, for example, Noam Chomsky and Edward Hermann, *Manufacturing Consent* (London, Vintage, 1994).
3 Alan Friedman, *Spider's Web: Bush, Saddam, Thatcher and the Decade of Deceit* (London, Faber, 1993), p. 172.
4 Helga Graham, 'How America saved Saddam', *New Statesman and Society* (20 September 1996), pp. 24–6 and Richard Keeble, 'How the West pulls punches against its favourite demon', Gemini News Service (London, 14 January 1997).
5 There were many other factors driving the USA (and its allies) towards the construction of a mythical war. For example: it could serve to bring some sense of unity to deeply fractured societies and legitimise the media, military and industrial élites in the eyes of the public; it was needed by the USA to assert militarily its primacy in the 'new world order' against the growing economic strength of Germany and Japan; it could destroy the social and economic infrastructure of Iraq which, while posing no threat to the West, was seen as a threat by the Israeli élite; it could serve as an obscenely macabre testing ground for new weapons with humans and a society's infrastructure as targets;

it could help President Bush banish his 'wimp' image for good and help his re-election prospects.

6 See Robin Luckham, 'Of arms and culture', *Current Research on Peace and Violence* (Tampere, Finland) iv/1 (1983), p. 18 and Michael Mann, *States, Wars and Capitalism* (Oxford: Blackwell Publishers, 1988).

7 Efraim Karsh and Inari Rautsi, 'Why Saddam Hussein invaded Kuwait', *Survival* (January/February 1991), pp. 18–30.

8 John Pilger, 'Who killed the Kurds?', *New Statesman and Society* (12 April 1991), pp. 6–7.

9 Faleh Abd al-Jabbar, 'Why the uprisings failed', *Merip* (Washington DC; May/June 1992), pp. 2–14.

10 George Gerbner, 'Persian Gulf War: the movie' in Hamid Mowlana, George Gerbner and Herbert Schiller (eds), *Triumph of the Image: The Media's War in the Persian Gulf – a global perspective* (Boulder, CO: Westview Press, 1992), pp. 243–65.

11 Interviewed London, June 1992.

12 For example, only three places in the pools went to reporters from countries other than the USA or UK.

13 James Combs, 'From the Great War to the Gulf War: popular entertainment and the legitimation of warfare', in Robert Denton (ed.) *The Media and the Persian Gulf War* (Westport, CT: Praeger, 1993), pp. 257–84. See particularly p. 227.

14 This definition of mediacentrism differs from that promoted by Philip Schlesinger and Howard Tumber, *Reporting Crime: The Media Politics of Criminal Justice* (Oxford: Clarendon Press, 1994). They apply it to studies of the media which focus on media content and journalists' relationships with sources. For this approach they substitute a 'source-media analysis' model.

15 John MacKenzie, *Propaganda and Empire: The Manipulation of British Public Opinion 1880–1960* (Manchester: Manchester University Press, 1984).

16 Donald Featherstone, *Victorian Colonial Warfare: Africa* (London: Blandford, 1993) and *Victorian Colonial Warfare: India* (London: Blandford, 1993). See also Raymond Sibbald, *The Boer War: The War Correspondents* (Stroud, Glos.: Alan Sutton, 1993).

17 MacKenzie, *Propaganda and Empire*, pp. 5–6.

18 John R. Macarthur, *Second Front: Censorship and Propaganda in the Gulf War*, 2nd edn (Berkeley and Los Angeles, CA: University of California Press, 1993), p. 147.

19 Stephen Rose, 'Spend, spend, spend – on military only', *New Statesman* (3 January 1986).

20 Steve Peak, 'Britain's military adventures', *The Pacifist* 20/10 (1982).

21 Cecil Currey, 'Vietnam: lessons learned', in Phil Helling and Jon Roper (eds) *America, France and Vietnam: Cultural History and Ideas of Conflict* (Aldershot: Avebury, 1991), pp. 71–90.

22 John Stockwell, *The Praetorian Guard: The US Role in the New World Order* (Boston: South End Press, 1991), pp. 70–3.

23 John M. Collins, *America's Small Wars* (Washington and London: Brassey, 1991).

24 Douglas Kellner, *Television and the Crisis of Democracy* (Boulder, CO, San Francisco, Oxford: Westview Press, 1990), p. 138.

25 See also Asaf Hussain, *Political Terrorism and the State in the Middle East* (London and New York: Mansell Publishing, 1988), p. 45.

26 Chris Searle, *Your Daily Dose: Racism and the Sun* (London: Campaign for Press and Broadcasting Freedom, 1989), p. 36.

27 Robert Freedman, *Middle East from the Iran–Contra Affair to the Intifada* (Syracuse, NY: Syracuse University Press, 1991).

28 Steven Rose and Abraham Baravi, 'The meaning of Halabja: chemical warfare in Kurdistan', *Race and Class* 30/1 (1988), pp. 74–7.

29 Kenneth R. Timmerman, *The Death Lobby: How the West Armed Iraq* (London, Fourth Estate, 1991), p. 293.

30 Human Rights Watch, Middle East, *Iraq's Crime of Genocide: The Anfal Campaign against the Kurds* (New Haven, CT and London: Yale University Press, 1995), p. 70.

31 Ibid., pp. 262–5.

32 John Bulloch and Harvey Morris, *No Friends but the Mountains: The Tragic History of the Kurds* (London: Viking, 1992), p. 144.

33 Stephen Pelletierre, Douglas Johnson and Leif Rosenberger, *Iraqi Power and US Security in the Middle East* (Washington, DC: US Army War College, Strategic Studies Institute, US Government Printing Office, 1990). See also Martin Yant, *Desert Mirage: The True Story of the Gulf War* (Buffalo, NY: Prometheus, 1991), p. 109.

34 Daphne Parrish gives her version of events in *Prisoner in Baghdad* (London: Chapmans Publishers, 1992).

35 John Pilger, 'Shedding crocodile tears', *New Statesman and Society,* 20 March 1992, p. 10.

36 Simon Henderson, *Instant Empire: Saddam Hussein's Ambition for Iraq* (San Francisco: Mercury, 1991), pp. 214–16.

37 James Curran, Angus Douglas and Gary Whannel, 'The political economy of the human interest story', in Anthony Smith (ed.) *Newspapers and Democracy: International Essays on a Changing Medium* (Cambridge, MA: MIT Press, 1980) pp. 288–316.

38 Paul Kennedy, 'A. J. P. Taylor and profound causes in history', in Chris Wrigley (ed.) *Warfare, Diplomacy and Politics: Essays in Honour of A. J. P. Taylor* (London: Hamish Hamilton, 1986), pp. 14–29.

39 Colin Sparks, 'Popular journalism: theories and practice', in Peter Dahlgren and Colin Sparks (eds) *Journalism and Popular Culture* (London, Newbury Park, CA, New Delhi: Sage, 1992), pp. 24–44.

40 Gannett Foundation, *The Media at War: The Press and the Persian Gulf Conflict* (New York: Columbia University, The Freedom Forum, 1991), p. 42.

41 Macarthur, *Second Front*, p. 72.

42 John Bulloch and Harvey Morris, *Saddam's War* (London: Faber, 1991), pp. 53–4.

43 Lance Bennett, 'The news about foreign policy', in W. Lance Bennett and David L. Paletz (eds) *Taken by Storm: The Media, Public Opinion and US Foreign Policy in the Gulf War* (Chicago: University of Chicago Press, 1994), pp. 12–40. See particularly p. 32.

44 Glasgow University Media Group, 'The British media and the Gulf War', research working paper (Glasgow, 1991), p. 3.

45 Christopher Layne, 'Why the Gulf War was not in the national interest', *Atlantic Monthly* (July 1991), pp. 615–81.

46 Stephen Prince, 'Celluloid heroes and smart bombs: Hollywood at war in the Middle East', in Robert Denton (ed.) *The Media and the Persian Gulf War*, pp. 235–56. See particularly p. 244.

47 Gilbert Adair, 'Saddam meets Dr Strangelove', *Guardian* (29 January 1991).

48 Roy Greenslade interviewed in London, May 1994.

49 John Schostak, *Dirty Marks: The Education of Self, Media and Popular Culture* (London: Pluto, 1993), p. 85.

50 William Fore, 'The shadow war in the Gulf', *Media Development* (October 1991), pp. 51–3. See particularly p. 52.
51 See Phil Agee, *Covert Action: What Next?* (London, Agee Hosenball Defence Committee, 1976); Bulloch and Morris, *Saddam's War*, p. 31, and William Blum, *The CIA: A Forgotten History – US Intervention since World War Two* (London: Zed Books, 1986), p. 278.
52 Mohamed Heikal, *Illusions of Triumph: An Arab View of the Gulf War* (London: HarperCollins, 1992), p. 320.
53 For example, Martin Shaw, *Civil Society and Media in Global Crises: Representing Distant Violence* (London: Pinter, 1996), pp. 79–96, argues that the British media, in particular television, played the dominant role in persuading John Major to promote the Kurdish 'safe havens' proposal.
54 Eddie Abrahams (ed.) *The New Warlords: From the Gulf War to the Recolonisation of the Middle East* (London: Larkin Publications, 1994), p. 40 and David McDowall, *The Modern History of the Kurds* (London and New York: I. B. Tauris, 1996), p. 375.
55 Douglas Kellner, 'Gulf War II, the media offensive', *Lies of our Times*, May 1993, pp. 17–19 and Douglas Kellner, 'The US media and the 1993 war against Iraq', in Yahya R. Kamalipour (ed.) *The US media and the Middle East* (Westport, CT: Praeger, 1997), pp. 105–18.
56 Norman Fairclough, *Media Discourse* (London and New York: Edward Arnold, 1995), p. 95 and Richard Keeble, 'From butcher to bad boy' (London: Gemini News Service, 19 January 1994).
57 Stephen D. Reese and Bob Buckalew 'The militarisation of local television: the routine framing of the Persian Gulf War', *Critical Studies in Mass Communication* (Annendale, VA, 1995), vol. 12/1, pp. 40–59. See particularly p. 41.

7 Privacy, the public interest and a prurient public

David Archard

Going public: what is an invasion of privacy?

A mass circulation newspaper publishes the photograph it has obtained of a prominent public person engaged in what is evidently an intimate sexual encounter with another identifiable individual. The photograph, which is explicit but not offensively pornographic, is accompanied by a news report which spells out the significance of the image. Let us suppose that the newspaper can offer some plausible reason for publishing this story; what kinds of reason they might offer will be considered in due course. The paper does not publish it simply because it is a titillating image. Indeed let us allow that *only* the publication of the image would serve as sufficient support for the report it accompanies.[1] In short, publication of the photograph is not gratuitous. What is wrong with publishing the image and report?

First it might be wrong if the manner in which the photograph had been obtained was clearly impermissible. This would be the case if, for instance, the photographer had trespassed on private property to take the picture or a photograph lawfully taken (say by friends of the couple) had been stolen by the newspaper.[2] There might be a worry about permissibility if the photograph had been obtained clandestinely, that is, without its subjects knowing that it was being taken. 'Clandestine' also means 'underhand' and 'surreptitious', suggesting that the secrecy involved was somehow wrong or unfair. The wrongness, we will assume, is not of a kind already discussed. It could be that the subjects of the photograph not only did not know they were being photographed but might reasonably expect not to have been photographed. No one bathing on a deserted private beach of an uninhabited island miles from any other territory can expect that photographers lie undetected off shore with long-lens cameras. But a person's reasonable expectation not to be photographed is not necessarily a rightful expectation that she should not be. The press cannot, for obvious reasons, always advertise to those it is investigating when, where and whether they are conducting the investigation.

Publication of the photograph might be thought wrong if taking it formed part of a pattern of clear, persistent and intrusive harassment of its subject. A photographer who follows his quarry day and night wherever she goes, never letting her out of his sight, and photographing her every move, behaves unreasonably. It is proper that such behaviour should be the subject of a legal injunction to desist. The taking of the published photograph is not of itself wrong. After all, it might have been the one and only shot taken at a single opportune moment. It is the pattern of harassment which led to the taking of the photograph which is unacceptable.

The taking and publishing of the photograph would arguably be wrong if it breached confidentiality. If someone enters into a confidential relationship with another person, who reveals to others information which is obtained only through that relationship, then that person is in breach of an obligation of confidentiality. That obligation can arise through either an express or tacit contract. Princess Diana sued for breach of confidence when in 1993 a tabloid newspaper published photographs of her working out in a gymnasium which had been obtained without her knowledge or consent and with the connivance of the owner of the gym. This law was not used, but might have been, in the similar case of the publication by the *Sunday Sport* in 1990 of photographs of the actor Gorden Kaye while he lay injured and barely conscious in a hospital bed. Some have argued that the law of confidentiality might be used in Britain to cover invasions of privacy.[3] However, it is not plausible to think that every photograph whose publication gives rise to worries about invasion of privacy need have been obtained in a manner which breached confidence.

Finally, the photograph's publication might give cause for moral concern if the choice of image or the language accompanying it were clearly intended to humiliate, ridicule, belittle, or unfairly stigmatise the subject, or if the story's publication formed part of a pattern of reporting with such an intention. Here it is reasonable to think that a story goes beyond the reporting of a newsworthy event and fair comment upon it. There is a point at which *Schadenfreude* at another's failings, which may be regretted if not condemned, passes into unacceptably vindictive persecution. Many had the feeling that this occurred with the tabloids' reporting of Sarah Ferguson's long fall from grace in 1996.

Let us assume that the photograph of our example does not fall foul of any of these kinds of worry. If there is still felt to be something wrong with publishing it then that worry will most likely be expressed along the lines of its being no business of the press what this person freely does in private with another consenting individual. It is this worry which is captured by the notion of a wrongful invasion of privacy. What follows is an attempt to make sense of that worry when it is set against arguments which purport to justify such an invasion.

Privacy has to do with keeping personal information non-public or undisclosed. Personal information is that set of facts about oneself that a person does not wish to see disclosed or made public. The facts need not take the form of written statements. Personal information is contained within or can be inferred from a photograph or sound recording. Obviously what one person strives to keep private another may be happy to see as common knowledge. Some of us are shy about revealing our age, others unembarrassed. Most of us would probably think of our sexual and financial affairs as properly private.

This understanding of privacy is not the only one possible.[4] Privacy has been defined in terms of being let alone, control of access to one's body and personal space, autonomy in personal matters, and solitude. No one of these definitions enjoys universal acceptance and each is subject to familiar criticisms and counter-examples. The most obvious, and frequently defended, alternative to the definition offered here is that which speaks of privacy in terms of a person's control over access to herself and to her personal information.[5] A newspaperman who obtained personal information about me, perhaps in an entirely licit fashion, but who did not make it public would on this definition, but not on mine, be breaching my privacy.

There are at least three reasons for preferring my definition in the present context.[6] The first is that it is reasonable to prefer a 'non-reductionist' definition of privacy, that is, one which cannot be fully rendered in terms of other concepts.[7] If privacy is to be accounted a distinct interest (and its invasion a distinct wrong) then it should not be defined in terms of more fundamental interests. Defining privacy in terms of control over access to oneself is defining it in terms of the more fundamental interest of autonomy. If I am wronged in losing control of access to my personal information this is so inasmuch as my desire to keep control of this information is overridden.

The second reason is simply that an unexploited loss of control over one's personal information just does not seem to amount to an obvious violation of my privacy. If I no longer have exclusive access to my personal information but that information is undisclosed, not made public, then it does not appear as if my privacy has been invaded. Of course it is true that safeguarding control of personal information increases, and loss of that control diminishes, the extent to which one's privacy is protected. But it would be a mistake to confuse what may serve an interest with the interest itself.

Third, in the present context of discussing the putative wrongness of the press publishing certain stories or photographs it is my definition that best captures what it is that is invaded when it is said that a person's privacy has been invaded by publication.[8]

A disclosure of personal information may follow upon an invasion of privacy according to the non-standard definitions. If, for instance, my telephone is bugged or my private behaviour filmed by a secret camera, then I am likely to have suffered trespass and a loss of control over access to my personal space. Yet it would be the publication of the taped phone calls or film that would constitute the invasion of my privacy.

What I take to be a paradigmatic invasion of privacy in my sense is the publication of the details of someone's personal circumstances: that someone is gay, is HIV positive, is having an extramarital affair, engages in a certain kind of sexual activity, has an illegitimate child, and so on. These constitute just the sorts of revelations that constitute the stories beloved of the tabloid press and that give rise to moral concern about the privacy of individuals. I do not propose to tackle the question of what legal or official regulative procedures might be appropriate, whether for instance there should be a law of privacy. Nor shall I even presume that there is a right to privacy. I shall, for the moment, assume only that each individual has a strong interest in her privacy and that any breach of a person's privacy must be shown to be justified by the display of good reasons for the breach. Such good reasons must meet the proviso that making public something that is private should not merely serve a valued end but be the only thing that does and can serve that end. Revealing a Cabinet Minister's sexual peccadilloes can effectively display his hypocrisy and unsuitability for high office. But if drawing attention to his public acts does as good a job of discrediting him then the disclosure of his private affairs is gratuitous.

No one is naïve enough to deny that journalists may rationalise their behaviour. The disclosure of a politician's sexual affairs may indeed serve a useful purpose, such as revealing him to be a liar or untrustworthy, but such a disclosure also pleases a paying public who are titillated by learning the details of another's sexual behaviour. Claiming that a noble end warrants a disclosure which is intended to satisfy the ignoble tastes of the readership is hypocritical but hardly surprising or rare. Such rationalisation reflects poorly on the character of editors and reporters but it does not, of itself, show the publication of a story to be illicit.

I shall also assume that we can distinguish between what may be wrong with breaching privacy and what may wrong in the manner in which that breach is achieved. To publish what should be private is one kind of possible wrong; to find out what is private by illicit means is another kind of wrong. Thus, the wrong of bugging a telephone to tape the conversations between David Mellor and his mistress or of stealing a letter from Paddy Ashdown's solicitor detailing his extramarital affair can be separated from the putative wrong simply of revealing the details of the affair in either instance.[9]

Finally, I take for granted a background presumption in favour of the freedom of the press to report what it deems appropriate. The relevant freedom is one to publish what the press deems to be sufficiently attested facts. The freedom to publish opinions is one that is famously defended by J. S. Mill in chapter 2 of his *On Liberty*. That defence invokes considerations of the truth and the role that an unconstrained plurality of expressed views may play in securing the truth. One could of course argue similarly that the truth of any matter can only be reached if all relevant information bearing on its determination is made public.

Whereas the Millian argument might seem to presume that the truth is valuable for its own sake, it could be urged that making all known pertinent facts available to the public serves a valued political purpose. This is that the citizens of a democracy are the better able to make sound judgements – both of what is for their own good and what is for the common good – the more informed they are about all relevant facts. The ability to make sound judgements on these matters is what ensures that democratic procedures yield desirable political outcomes.

Whatever the arguments for such a presumption in favour of a freedom of the press, the point is that such a general presumption exists. It works in favour of the press's activity, even before a newspaper has need to invoke a ground for the publication of a story charged with an invasion of privacy. Thus a newspaper might claim that spiking such a story not only violated the freedom of the press but ignored the particular ends served by this one story.

If there is a countervailing presumption in favour of respecting a person's privacy it will be, I assume, a fairly strong one. But it need not be, I also take for granted, an overwhelmingly strong one. Those who defend a right to privacy do not defend it as an absolute right. What sorts of reasons are offered in justification of breaching an individual's privacy? I shall consider three: (1) when somebody is or becomes a public person she, by that very fact, loses her privacy; (2) where a proven public interest can be shown to be served by the disclosure of the private; (3) where the public is interested in knowing what is private. The first two are familiar and often cited as good reasons. The last is cited only to be contrasted with the second and dismissed as an evidently bad reason. I want to offer critical comments about the first two and then suggest some grounds for thinking the third reason has been too quickly rejected.

The public figure as not entitled to privacy

Consider this extract from the famous, influential article on the right to privacy by Samuel Warren and Louis Brandeis: 'to publish of a modest and retiring individual that he suffers from an impediment of his speech or that he cannot spell correctly is an unwarranted, if not unexampled, infringement upon his privacy, while to state and comment on the same characteristic found in a would-be congressman would not be regarded as beyond the pale of propriety.'[10] Assuming that both individuals have an interest in keeping these disabilities private there are two ways of understanding the claim that the aspirant politician has less reason to complain if his defect is publicised. The first lies in arguing that a speech impediment or inability to spell bears on his suitability to serve in a public office. He would be the worse congressman for having these failings and an electorate is entitled to know any material facts that would influence their preferences for one candidate for office over another. The second way of understanding the claim of Warren and Brandeis is to think that someone who enters public life thereby rightly suffers a loss of privacy. To become a public person is to undergo a change in one's status, associated with which is a lesser degree of privacy. On the first understanding of the claim it is said that whatever bears on your public role ceases to be properly private; on the second understanding it is said that a public person is less private simply in virtue of his or her public status.

Let me now consider this second understanding. Many who achieve fame speak – some in protest, others in grudging acceptance – of the loss of privacy that comes with the territory of fame. Clearly it is harder to keep your life private if you are a public person. Others, and not just the press, have an interest in knowing more about you and your life, an interest which is not displayed towards the ordinary citizen. However, the question is whether what a public person can keep private should be so kept.

One set of considerations that appears to speak in favour of the non-privacy of public persons has to do with fairness. The idea is that it is somehow only fit and proper that public persons should not have privacy. There is a general version of this thought and one specifically having to do with the role of publicity. Let me consider the particular version first. In a 1977 case where the Court of Appeal dismissed an injunction against a former press agent revealing secrets about his charges, a ground for the decision was 'that those who seek and welcome publicity, so long as it shows them in a good light, cannot complain about invasions of privacy which show them in an unfavourable light'.[11] If the bad publicity followed accidentally from the effort to secure good publicity – one sought to look one way and ended up appearing another – the claim would hardly be contentious. Equally there might be merit in it if the good publicity was secured fraudulently, by means, for instance, of a significant lie about the person or the false disparagement of another.

But a wrong has been done by the invasion of privacy. It is not enough simply to say that doing such a wrong is warranted by its resulting in an evil (the bad publicity) cancelling out the good (the favourable publicity) which has been sought and secured. Consider the argument: someone who chooses to wear clothes that show her in a good light cannot complain if she is made to wear clothes that show her in an unfavourable light. Or, those who choose to play a sport which shows their talents in a good light cannot complain if they are forced to play a sport which shows their talents in an unfavourable light. They are not compelling arguments. Neither is that which says good publicity somehow deserves bad.

The general argument is that a loss of privacy is the fair price a famous person pays for her fame. The rewards of fame are large – wealth, social status, public recognition, power and influence, and so on – so why, it might be suggested, should there not have to be a cost exacted in return, that cost being a lesser degree of privacy than the ordinary person? This is unconvincing. A plausible principle of fairness might reasonably allow that a person's public status is simply earned outright and does not morally require a compensating cost. A public status, unlike a job, university place or election victory, need not be thought of as something which can be unfairly acquired at a cost to specific others who lose out. That the general public choose to make the untalented famous is the good luck of the latter; such celebrity is not somehow undeserved. A principle of rectification is inappropriate in this context. Consider how the lucky lottery winner might respond to the suggestion that her good fortune in gaining so much demanded a compensating repayment of a significant part of her winnings.

Imagine that the relevant principles of fairness are grounded in some shared understanding as to what fame should entail, an understanding which could be reached without knowledge by the parties to it of who in fact will be or become famous.[12] Where would be the agreement that public status comes at the price of a loss of privacy? Such a 'contract' would be refused by all who aspire to that status and it would be grossly burdensome to those who have no choice in the matter, those who are born to fame or have it thrust upon them. Imagine that you become a public person despite yourself: you are a relative of the Prime Minister, witness a major crime, survive a disaster. You endure unchosen costs due both to what it is that made you famous and that very public status. You are now told that society understands this status further to require that you lose your privacy. Who, it will be asked, shares in *that* understanding?

A loss of privacy as serving the public interest

The idea that, in fairness or by agreement, public status comes with a loss of privacy is unpersuasive. Far more persuasive is the thought that a person's privacy may be breached if the information disclosed serves a proven public interest. A code of press practice may specify the various conditions that could count as involving a genuine public interest in publication, such as detecting or exposing crime, protecting public health, preventing the public from being misled. Showing public officials to be corrupt, grossly inefficient, criminally negligent, or dishonest is certainly in the public interest, provided that these failings bear directly on their performance of their public duties. Thus, for example, revealing that a minister is a highly paid non-executive director of a company which regularly seeks contracts with the government is a matter for public concern. However, the majority of cases where privacy is breached touch on matters of sexual morality and it is that much harder to see how the public interest is served by their disclosure.[13] Let me rehearse a number of distinct arguments in respect of the publication of the details of a minister's sexual misconduct – all of which, in one form or another, should be fairly familiar.

Before doing so it is important to be clear what role is played by any sexual impropriety as such. In some cases what may be decisive in discrediting a politician is that his sexual misbehaviour is illegal, such as sex with persons below the age of consent. Or such misbehaviour may compound other and perhaps more serious failings. David Mellor was probably forced to resign in 1992 less on account of his extramarital affair with Antonia de Sancha than because of the subsequent revelation that he had enjoyed a holiday at the expense of Mona Bauwens, whose father was a funder of the Palestine Liberation Organisation. What reasons might then be given for thinking that the disclosure of a person's sexual misconduct serves the public interest?

There is, first, the view that any kind of private immorality disqualifies a person from public office. An adulterer is not fit to be a Minister of the Crown for no other reason than that adultery is wrong and fitness for public office requires a morally untarnished character. The view has a charming Victorian resonance to it and is as utterly removed from reality as that period is from our own. We should set the standards of public office high but not so high as to require of our officers that they be angels.

Second, we might argue that the adulterer is a hypocrite. He may be. Posing in public as a family man and defending the values of the family as an electoral gambit, whilst entertaining a mistress in private, is hypocritical. But how important is it to learn that our minister is a hypocrite? There may be little or no reason to believe he is a hypocrite in all matters, especially those that are central to the discharge of his duties. Further, the significance of his hypocrisy in this particular matter is diminished by the thought, surely shared by most of us, that few live up to their proclaimed ideals in this area of their life.

There is a dangerous kind of hypocrisy. Imagine that Smith is in a position to influence policy in some area where the private consensual behaviour of citizens is at issue. Imagine further that the way in which he publicly chooses to influence policy is directly at odds with his own private preferences and behaviour. Then it can be argued that his public actions penalise those with whom he in fact shares a common interest. Those who share that interest may, with justice, view his hypocrisy as harmful and deserving of exposure. The most obvious instance of this kind of reasoning is to be find in the statements of Outrage, whose members seek to bring out from the closet those politicians and clergy whose public words and deeds gainsay (and betray) their private homosexual identity.[14]

A third claim is that a man who lies to his wife will also deceive his country; a man who breaks his marriage vows will break the oath of office. David Mellor's father-in-law publicly attacked him in the media with the claim, 'If he'll cheat on our girl he'll cheat on the country.'[15] If he is a liar and a cheat in all matters let this be shown. Nothing in the pattern of human dissembling reveals the adulterer, simply in virtue of his adultery, to be any less trustworthy or reliable in general. Most people can recognise the difference – in moral significance and motivation – between a personal betrayal and public treachery. Of course someone may be exposed as untrustworthy for the manner in which he has conducted an affair, or has sought to conceal it. Cecil Parkinson, in October 1983 for instance, was probably fatally damaged by the fact of his broken promise to divorce his wife and marry his mistress, Sarah Keays. He might have survived the disclosure of his adultery, but his failure to honour the pledge did supply grounds for resignation.[16] Even so, a man may be dishonourable in business, friendship, and many other matters beside love alone.

The fourth thought is that an adulterous minister is distracted by his adultery from his duties or is less capable, in consequence of his affair, of performing them. That may be so. But so he may be also in virtue of being a conscientious family man,[17] or because of playing golf, reading books or a hundred and one other private pursuits. Claiming this kind of reason[18] as a ground for publicising private immorality has the desperate air of self-serving rationalisation.

Gossip and the interest of the public

There may be personal information which, if disclosed, serves the public interest but most of the reasons given for thinking that the private sexual behaviour of public figures is that kind of information seem tendentious. This brings us to the third reason that might be given for breaching an individual's privacy. This is simply that the public is interested in knowing – not that there is a public interest in knowing, but just that most people would like to know and would derive some pleasure from knowing.

Normally a clear distinction is made between a story being in the public interest and a story being one that interests the public, and the latter is quickly dismissed as a good reason for publication. In my view this distinction and dismissal is too hasty. I do not intend to suggest that there is no distinction and that the public's interest in knowing something does constitute a public interest in knowing that thing. It is rather that society's interest in knowing about the private lives of its public figures may have value and thus, in a way hitherto ignored, help to define the moral space in which the press operates. It is not that a presumption in favour of individual privacy can only be defeated by showing in some specific case that invasion of this person's privacy serves a particular public interest. It is that a general norm of privacy is shaped and constrained, in the first instance and at a prior level, by an opposing general norm of social interest in knowledge. The best way to appreciate this is by thinking of journalism as print gossip.

The differences between leaning across the garden fence to whisper the details of a neighbour's improprieties and publishing them on the front page of a popular newspaper are several. One, apparently trivial but important to the American courts, is that print gossip is written whereas neighbourhood gossip is oral.[19] Another is the scale of subsequent knowledge. Neighbourhood gossip, like a secret, is normally characterised as being told to only one person, but one person at a time and in the confident expectation that the information disclosed will be passed on seriatim. The front-page story spreads its information instantaneously and over a much larger population. It follows that the subject of print gossip is incapable of avoiding the knowledge that his private business is public knowledge. In the case of neighbourhood gossip everyone may also know but he need not know that they do. Yet another difference is that neighbours are understandably far less cautious about the laws of slander and defamation. Newspaper gossip is, normally, better researched, more likely to be true, even if no less malicious in intent. Finally, there is the difference that the newspapers do our gossiping for us. In the neighbourhood we are the agents of its transmission. This difference is moderated by the thought that newspapers sell on the basis of those stories it judges its public want to hear. As readers we may not actually start the gossip but we play our role in ensuring that it is started.

These differences are not so great as to obscure the fact that the journalistic exposure of private lives is a kind of gossip – and is thought distasteful for that reason. Yet closer scrutiny of gossip sheds a different light on its morality. Consider, first, two kinds of reason one might find gossip distasteful: the motives of those who gossip and its effects on those who are the victims. Gossip proper is 'idle', it is aimless and effortless, done with no purpose other than its own enjoyment.[20] Of course, it can be gloating, full of *Schadenfreude*, or vicious; it can serve manipulative purposes such as the blackmailing or stigmatisation of its victim. But so can any kind of talk which concerns other people, and it is these contingent features of the gossip that make gossip objectionable not the mere fact that it is gossip. Gossip may harm those whose private deeds it exposes to public scrutiny. But note that gossip, like any talk about others, can be condemned for falsely defaming those it speaks of. To say that we have an interest in keeping our private lives private and are harmed when this is not so is just to say we have an interest in privacy. It does not follow – and indeed it is just this which is in question – that society does not also have a distinct interest in knowing what individuals would like to keep private. Finally it should be obvious that some general practice may have bad effects for some within it and be motivated (always, sometimes) by viciousness but nevertheless be a good thing on the whole.[21]

Gossip should not then be condemned out of hand for the wrong reasons. It would also be a mistake to ignore the possibly valuable social purposes served by gossip. Let me sketch three such purposes – bearing obvious relationships to one another – which have been noted in anthropological studies of gossip.[22] The first is that gossip plays a role in defining a community and maintaining its unity. Whom one gossips about and with whom is one of the ways in which the insiders of a group differentiate themselves from outsiders. Learning the rules of gossip, acquiring the substance of previous gossip, are how someone may be inducted into a group.[23]

The second and probably most important purpose gossip can serve has to do with the shared values of the community in which it is conducted. There are a number of ways in which this is so. Gossip bears on conduct which is evaluable by these values and it bears on such conduct *because* it is evaluable.[24] Gossip is a way of testing out or rehearsing these values by exposing conduct that they would seem to proscribe.[25] In gossip these values, and thereby also the identity and unity of the group which professes them, may be reaffirmed.[26] Finally, gossip exposes the wrongdoer to public shame or ridicule and consequently functions as a deterrent to such wrongdoing.[27]

The third purpose gossip serves is an egalitarian one. Gossip demystifies the pretensions of public status; it can expose the ordinariness of the famous by showing them to be no more and no less capable of avoiding the failings we know ourselves to display all too often. There is a mystique that surrounds the rich and famous whereby the mundane – both in shortcoming and in achievement – seems beyond them. Gossip is a testing of that mystique. A frequently made observation is that the antics of the 'younger royals' faithfully recorded by the popular press finally stripped the British royal family of any remaining aura it might once have possessed. As sympathetic royalists have commented, that aura, if it is needed, can only now be sustained by the construction of an artificial wall around the activities of royalty.

It is also true that the intimate and personal aspects of people's lives are more revealing of their true character than their public behaviour.[28] Exposing such aspects – which gossip may alone be capable of doing – thus sheds light on the real nature of those whose fame and public status might represent them in other and misleading ways. It is not simply that the famous are just like us and that it is important to know this; it is that fame of itself would suggest otherwise, a suggestion which gossip can very effectively rebut.

In suggesting that gossip serves these social purposes I do not ignore the immediate response that these purposes in turn need to be shown and not just assumed to be valuable. Deference to the rich and famous may be thought an estimable feature of society; an egalitarian demystification of their true nature may be deemed socially destructive. One could object that the very moralism of gossip is what makes it unappealing and agree with Oscar Wilde that whereas 'gossip is charming . . . scandal is gossip made tedious by morality'.[29] One might argue that it is dangerous to assume that a community does share a single set of values; that anything which may be represented as enforcing or asserting such a set of values is to be, for that reason, deprecated as dangerously conservative. Such comments can and should be made.

However the following also needs to be said. First, that gossip might serve any valuable social purpose is too often ignored. The preceding was intended to show that, at the very least, it might. Second, the messenger should not be shot for communicating an unwelcome message. The problems which attach to the possession by a community of values – shared, disputed or absent – should not be attributed to the medium, gossip, in which these values can be publicly communicated. Indeed it is to the credit of gossip that it brings into the light of publicity the lights by which a society claims to live. An important consequence of doing this is that we can learn the true value of our values. Rightly or wrongly, for instance, we expect our public figures to exemplify in their own behaviour the standards of conduct which we think our community tries to live by. Realising that they can no more live by these ideals than we can may lead us to suspect that we have got these values wrong. We may, of course, think that standards in public life are declining (and be right to think so). However we may also think that the standards have been set so high that a falling short of them – even by public exemplars of virtue – is inevitable. Such thinking, fuelled by gossip, will play its part in an invaluable debate about what the values of our community ought to be.

However, it does seem unfortunately true that a particular obsession with the *sexual* behaviour of public figures reveals a characteristically British puritanical prurience, an unresolved unhealthy combination of fascination with and revulsion at sexual activity. Too much of the reporting of private sexual behaviour seems to indulge the vicarious tastes of a public who want to have their moralistic cake and to eat it as well. As many commentators have noted, the British obsession with the sexual behaviour of their public figures contrasts unfavourably with the comparative indifference of the Europeans.

Conclusion

So far nothing has shown that there is a specifiable set of circumstances in which it would be justified for the press to invade a person's privacy or what such circumstances might ever be. Nothing has been said about the value to us, and its foundations, of our privacy. The concern has been to review the sorts of reasons one might give for believing that privacy could justifiably be invaded. The conclusions have been as follows. There is no warrant for thinking that a person loses his privacy in virtue of becoming a public person. The public interest may be served by disclosing the private behaviour of a public person. But where the disclosure is of the sexual affairs of a public person the arguments to show that disclosure is useful are often unconvincing.

Most interestingly, the public's interest in knowing what public figures do in private – an interest which print gossip serves – should not be dismissed as morally valueless. Such an interest is not a legitimate public interest as that term is properly understood. Rather, gossip provides a forum wherein we affirm our identity as a community, assure ourselves that everyone can behave badly and explore the force of our moral conventions which determine what is and is not bad behaviour. That is not enough to show that the public's interest does warrant invasions of privacy. It shows only that there is a further dimension – one which has been unjustly neglected – to the moral space in which such invasions are evaluated.

The surprising thought, then, is that a public's interest in the private conduct of its public figures is a reason of sorts for disclosure. It is not that interest as such which justifies the disclosure. Rather it is that such an interest serves a socially regulative purpose – reminding us that we are all very much alike in our private affairs and informing collective reflection upon the standards we claim to share and live by. And this in turn prompts a final thought. The more confident a community is in the standards it expects its members – whether public persons or ordinary citizens – to live by and the more assured it is that everybody, famous or no, is as fallible as anybody else in trying to live by these standards, then the less likely it is that the community's media will feel pressed to meet a public need to learn what our public figures do in private. That, one suspects, may be a lesson to be learnt from comparing the British press with others.[30]

Notes

1   The photograph is not, in the words of guidance by Lord Wakeham to the press on privacy and the public interest, 'merely illustrative'. See Roy Greenslade, 'Privacy on parade', *Guardian*, 25 November 1996, G2 p. 17.
2   Raymond Snoddy, *The Good, the Bad and the Unacceptable* (London: Faber, 1992), p. 35, provides the example of 'snatchmen' who 'accompany reporters on interviews with relatives in tragedy stories and snatch – steal – pictures of the dead from the mantelpieces'. I am grateful to Matthew Kieran for pointing out this reference to me.
3   M. P. Thompson, 'Confidence in the press', *The Conveyancer and Property Lawyer* 57 (1993), pp. 347–58.
4   For a useful collection of pieces on the subject see Ferdinand David Schoeman (ed.), *Philosophical Dimensions of Privacy: An Anthology* (Cambridge: Cambridge University Press, 1984).
5   Sissela Bok, *Secrets: On the Ethics of Concealment and Revelation* (Oxford: Oxford University Press, 1982), pp. 5–6, defines privacy as the condition of being protected from unwanted access by others; I. Altman, 'Privacy: a conceptual analysis', *Environment and Behavior* 8 (1976), pp. 7–8, defines it as selective control over access to oneself or to one's group; and E. Van den Haag, 'On privacy', in J. R. Pennock and J. W. Chapman (eds) *Privacy: Nomos XIII* (New York: Atherton Press, 1979), p. 149, defines it as the exclusive access of a person to a realm of his own.
6   Perhaps not decisive reasons but a full defence of any preferred definition would require a separate chapter.
7   J. J. Thomson, 'The right to privacy', *Philosophy and Public Affairs* 4 (1975), pp. 295–314, is a justly celebrated exposition of a reductionist account of the

interest of privacy as an amalgam of the interests of property, the person and confidentiality.

8 For a defence of this definition in the context of journalism see W. A. Parent, 'Privacy, morality, and the law', in Elliot D. Cohen (ed.) *Philosophical Issues in Journalism* (Oxford: Oxford University Press, 1992), pp. 92–109.

9 The bugging was morally dubious, but it was legal becuase done with the consent of the landlord of the flat the couple were using; the theft of the letter was a crime and punished as such.

10 Samuel Warren and Louis Brandeis, 'The right to privacy', *Harvard Law Review* 4 (1890), p. 205.

11 Thompson, 'Confidence in the press', p. 350. The case was *Woodward* v. *Hutchins.*

12 This is a rough-and-ready version of John Rawls's derivation of principles of justice from behind a 'veil of ignorance'; see his *A Theory of Justice* (Oxford: Oxford University Press, 1972), Part I.

13 As Matthew Parris's entertaining book *Great Parliamentary Scandals, Four Centuries of Calumny, Smear and Innuendo* shows, politicians in Britain have regularly been brought low by sexual scandals, even if their financial improprieties have also regularly, if less often, done the same (assistant eds David Prosser and Andrew Pierce; London: Robson Books, 1996).

14 Consider, by contrast, the statement by Peter Tatchell of Outrage about the press exposure in January 1997 of the Conservative MP Jerry Hayes as a homosexual: 'Jerry voted to equalise the gay age of consent and scrap the ban on homosexuals in the armed forces. His private behaviour is consistent with his public pronouncements', *Guardian*, 9 January 1997, p. 2.

15 Quoted in Parris, *Great Parliamentary Scandals*, p. 304.

16 For the circumstances of his resignation see, for instance, Hugo Young, *One of Us: A Biography of Margaret Thatcher* (London: Macmillan, 1991), pp. 343–5.

17 'Spending more time with my family' has become the favoured recent public reason for resigning from high office, with the implication, whether intended or not, that a full domestic life is incompatible with the performance of one's official duties.

18 As was done in the case of David Mellor's affair with the actress, Antonia de Sancha.

19 For discussion of this and other differences see Robert Post, 'The legal regulation of gossip: backyard chatter and the mass media', in *Good Gossip*, ed. by Robert F. Goodman and Aaron Ben-Ze'ev (Lawrence, KS: University of Kansas Press, 1994), pp. 65–71.

20 See Gabriele Taylor, 'Gossip as moral talk', in *Good Gossip*, pp. 34–46.

21 Ronald de Sousa makes the explicit comparison with capitalism according to a familiar line of reasoning, 'In praise of gossip', in *Good Gossip*, p. 27.

22 I am grateful to Joanna Overing for making me aware of such material.

23 Max Gluckman, 'Gossip and scandal', *Current Anthropology* 4/3 (June 1963), pp. 307–16, esp. p. 313.

24 'gossip dwells on those features of behaviour which call cultural rules into play – those items of information that enable people to make evaluations', John Beard Haviland, *Gossip, Reputation and Knowledge in Zinacanton* (Chicago: Chicago University Press, 1977), p. 5.

25 'Zinacentecos, through gossip, continually test ordinary rules and evaluative words against actual behaviour', ibid., p. 55.

26 'gossip and scandal have important positive virtues. Clearly they maintain the unity, morals and values of social groups', Gluckman, 'Gossip and scandal', p. 308.

27 'By generating shame in those who violate social standards, [gossip] helps to enforce agreed-upon values', P. M. Spacks, *Gossip* (New York: Knopf, 1985), p. 141, quoted in Ronald de Sousa, 'In praise of gossip', p. 32.
28 Aaron Ben-Ze'ev, 'The vindication of gossip', in *Good Gossip*, p. 15.
29 Cecil Graham gives voice to this claim in Act III of Wilde's *Lady Windermere's Fan* (first performed 1892 and published 1893).
30 I am grateful for the comments and questions of participants at the Leeds University Media Ethics Conference, September 1996, where a first version of this chapter was delivered. I am also grateful to Matthew Kieran for his helpful editorial suggestions.

8 Beyond Calcutt
The legal and extra-legal protection of privacy interests in England and Wales

Ian Cram

Introduction

In April 1989, against a background of increasing parliamentary and public concern about unwarranted intrusions by the press (particularly some tabloid newspapers) into the private lives of individuals,[1] the Conservative government announced the setting up of an 'Inquiry into Privacy and Related Matters', to be chaired by David Calcutt QC. This inquiry was to be confined to an examination of intrusions by the print media and the adequacy of remedies for press intrusion. During its deliberations, the inquiry was presented with a clear example of the sort of conduct which had given rise to concern: it occurred when a journalist and a photographer from the *Sunday Sport* managed to obtain access to the hospital room in which Gorden Kaye – a well-known actor – was recuperating after receiving injuries to his brain as a result of a car crash. Mr Kaye apparently agreed to talk to the men and be photographed. Medical evidence subsequently showed that Mr Kaye could not have given fully informed consent to the interview and photographs. In the subsequent legal action to restrain the publication of statements made by the plaintiff or pictures of him, Lord Justice Bingham said that the newspaper's conduct towards Mr Kaye was

> a monstrous invasion of his privacy. . . . If ever a person has the right to be let alone by strangers with no public interest to pursue, it must surely be when he lies in hospital in no more than partial command of his faculties. It is this invasion of privacy which underlies the Plaintiff's complaint. Yet it alone, however gross, does not entitle him to relief in English law.[2]

Although Mr Kaye succeeded in preventing publication on other grounds,[3] Lord Justice Bingham expressed the hope that the inquiry then in progress might prove fruitful in establishing a more satisfactory means of privacy protection. The Report of the Committee on Privacy and Related Matters (hereafter *Calcutt I*)[4] which followed in June 1990 made a series of recommendations which, despite being largely ignored by the

Major government, have nevertheless, in that government's own words, 'served to set the framework for the debate on press regulation and privacy ever since.'[5] In January 1993 a review of the effectiveness of the print media's voluntary self-regulation conducted by (the newly-ennobled) Sir David Calcutt QC was published. The report, entitled *Review of Press Self-Regulation*[6] (*Calcutt II*) examined whether a key recommendation of *Calcutt I* – the creation of the Press Complaints Commission – had been effective. Other contributions to the privacy debate appeared shortly thereafter. A consultation paper from the Lord Chancellor's Department and the Scottish Office entitled *Infringement of Privacy*[7] was issued in July 1993. Two years later, the government's own response, *Privacy and Media Intrusion*,[8] was published.

This article takes as its starting-point the piecemeal nature of legal protection of privacy interests which *Calcutt I* found wanting. It then considers the recommendations in *Calcutt I* to rectify matters and the Major government's response. It will be argued that, given the apparent lack of political will to create a direct, court-enforceable right of privacy, attention should, in the short term at least, focus upon the utility or otherwise of non-legal forms of protection of the sort encountered in media codes of practice. By way of conclusion, the level of protection offered by the European Convention on Human Rights and Fundamental Freedoms will be considered. The commitment of the subsequent Labour government to incorporate the Convention into domestic law means that this may well prove to be the most likely avenue by which the protection of privacy is to be attained. To begin with however, something needs to be said about why privacy is important.

The importance of privacy

It is clear that within much liberal thinking, considerable importance is attached to safeguarding the autonomy of individuals. The notion that individuals be given the conditions within which to pursue their own particular version of the good life – the idea of privacy or a protected sphere of private life within which the individual is free from interference from others and can determine who has access (and in which circumstances) to personal information – seems a useful means of promoting autonomy and thereby the conditions needed for human flourishing. The converse position, in which the individual has little or no control over the disclosure of personal information may diminish the prospects for entering into meaningful relationships with others and playing a fuller part in community life. Of course, it would be wrong to conceive of privacy as an absolute value. It may, for example, as Feldman reminds us, be necessary to interfere with a parent's privacy rights in order to protect the rights of children to be free from abuse.[9]

Legal protection for privacy interests

That English law provides no general protection against the disclosure of personal information in the form of a right of privacy is well known. Anyone who wishes to prevent such a disclosure must bring his or her claim within another recognised remedy heading, such as defamation, nuisance, confidence, etc. These indirect forms of privacy protection may be divided into two broad categories: criminal and civil remedies. The scope of the principal remedies within each category will now be sketched.

Criminal remedies

At first glance, the range of remedies provided by the criminal law do not appear very useful in a privacy context, since they are concerned primarily with the punishment by the state of certain forms of conduct rather than with preventing the disclosure of information. One recent text on the subject[10] manages to avoid reference to the criminal law altogether, and so arguably misses the important role played by the subject in regulating the conduct of the media in trying to obtain information for publication. A brief glance at the criminal law reveals that the following conduct is subject to penal sanction: the intentional interception of communications by post or the public telecommunications system;[11] the 'watching or besetting' of a place (or approach to such a place) where a person resides or happens to be;[12] the pursuit of a course of conduct[13] which amounts to the harassment of another and ought reasonably to be recognised as such.[14] Those involved in 'media scrums' might equally in theory be charged with a number of offences revolving around the unreasonable use of the highway, such as the statutory offence of wilful obstruction of the highway[15] and public nuisance at common law.[16]

Civil remedies

From the perspective of the victim of media intrusion, this class of remedies is initially more attractive for two reasons. First, breach of any entitlement in civil law normally entitles the injured party to seek compensation from the injuring party (defendant). Second, the courts may, in appropriate circumstances, issue an interlocutory injunction before the trial of the main action against the defendant to prevent the publication of material which will feature in the main action. In what follows a bare outline of each of the principal civil law remedies that might afford a measure of protection for individual privacy is presented.

(1) *Trespass*: If a defendant enters or remains on land contrary to the wishes of the plaintiff who has exclusive possession of the land, an action for trespass will lie. The remedy offers no assistance, however, to cases such as Gorden Kaye's, where the person whose privacy is being interfered

with does not enjoy exclusive possession of the land.[17] Nor does it avail when, in the era of the telephoto lens, photographs of individuals are taken from a vantage point outside the property which that individual possesses. One ameliorating feature of the trespass action is that, unlike private nuisance which is discussed below, the plaintiff need not show that he or she has suffered any damage as a result of the trespass.

(2) *Private nuisance*: Where the conduct of the defendant interferes with plaintiff's enjoyment of his or her own land and the plaintiff can show that harm or discomfort was caused thereby, the plaintiff may sue in private nuisance. For the remedy to lie, the defendant's conduct must be of a continuous nature. Thus the taking of a single picture would not amount to nuisance whereas the constant aerial surveillance and photographing of the plaintiff's every activity would probably be actionable.[18]

(3) *Defamation and malicious falsehood*: A defamatory statement has been described as one which lowers the esteem in which the plaintiff is held by right-thinking members of the public or leads such people to shun, avoid or exclude him or her.[19] The defendant will however be able to resist the action if the statement was true, or made as a fair comment on a matter of public interest. A further defence exists where the statement attracts absolute privilege (thus allowing a statement to be made even where it is motivated by malice) or qualified privilege (the privilege is lost upon proof of malicious intent). Examples of absolute privilege include speeches and statements made in the course of parliamentary and judicial proceedings. Qualified privilege attaches to journalists' reports of parliamentary proceedings.

Aside from the fact that legal aid is not available in defamation cases, the major defect with this remedy is that it offers no protection from the publication (actual or threatened) of *true information* about the plaintiff. Moreover, it is unlikely that an interlocutory injunction will be granted to restrain publication in advance of the full trial when the defendant indicates that a plea of justification, fair comment or privilege will be entered in response.[20] However, if the plaintiff succeeds at the full trial, damages from a jury will be recoverable.

By contrast, the related action for malicious falsehood has been shown of late to possess several advantages over defamation although it should be said that it remains at best a marginal weapon against privacy infringements. The elements of this civil wrong are that the defendant has published maliciously false words about the plaintiff which have caused the latter special damage. Legal aid may be available to a litigant to pursue such a claim.[21] An interlocutory injunction may also be granted to restrain publication in the future where the plaintiff can show that the words which the defendant wishes to publish are clearly false. The value of malicious falsehood for persons in the public eye was demonstrated in the case of *Kaye v. Robertson*[22] which was noted earlier. There, Gorden Kaye was able to obtain an interlocutory injunction preventing the publication of material in the proposed article, which suggested falsely that he had given proper consent to being interviewed and photographed. No jury could reasonably have thought that such consent had been forthcoming. The court went on to consider what Mr Kaye's position would have been if, in the absence of an injunction, the *Sunday Sport* had published the story, representing that the plaintiff's informed consent was forthcoming. Such conduct would have constituted a malicious falsehood for which Mr Kaye would have been able to recover damages. The right to damages arose because of the special damage the plaintiff would have suffered in a financial sense if publication in the *Sunday Sport* occurred. After all, Mr Kaye's story was one which other newspapers would be willing to pay large sums of money for if exclusive rights were granted.

Calcutt I, which considered this ruling, deemed the action to be of little value for ordinary individuals since few persons would be able to point to the sort of special damage that Gorden Kaye was able to establish. There is the further and serious drawback that, like defamation, the action requires there to be a false statement.

(4) *Confidence*: Increasingly, lawyers in practice are looking to actions for breach of confidence to provide protection for privacy interests. Outside of situations where confidentiality is protected in a contract (as in a commercial context), the plaintiff, to establish a breach of confidence, must show first that the information or material has the necessary quality of confidence about it.[23] Thus in the context of personal information, it is held that information concerning a person's sexual life may be protected by the law of confidence.[24] Second, the information must be confided in circumstances importing an obligation of confidence. This may occur where a pre-existing relationship exists such as that between employers and employees, doctors and patients, and banks and customers. Alternatively, the obligation of confidence may arise in a wider category of case where information is disclosed to another person on the understanding that it will be kept secret. Where information disclosed to the confidant is passed on a third party, the latter too may be restrained from publishing the confidential information.[25] Finally, there has to be an unauthorised use of the information which adversely affects the plaintiff. The ready availability of interlocutory injunctions preventing publication in confidence actions is also worth noting.[26]

Where the elements of the confidence obligation outlined above are present, it may be open to the defendant to avail him- or herself of the public interest defence or claim that the information is already in the public domain.[27] The public interest defence operates to override an obligation of confidence where there is just cause or excuse for disclosing the information, such as the disclosure to the police of information concerning alleged criminal wrongdoing.[28]

As a surrogate for a law of privacy however, the action for breach of confidence is not without its difficulties. These have been more fully addressed elsewhere.[29] Chief among the problems is the uncertainty over whether the absence of a relationship of confidence between the party who wishes to keep certain information private and the journalist who surreptitiously (by means of surveillance device or eavesdropping) or even accidentally acquires it, is fatal to an action.[30] If such a relationship is not required and a duty of confidence attaches purely by virtue of the *nature* of information, then a considerable obstacle will have been circumvented, although, in that event, separate questions over the scope of the defences of public interest would continue to occupy the courts.[31] That the judges seem content to develop the law in this direction is apparent from the recent ruling of the High Court in *Hellewell* v. *Chief Constable of Derbyshire*. In that case, Mr Justice Laws held that where someone with a telephoto lens takes from a distance and with no authority a picture of another engaged in a private act, disclosure of the photograph would be actionable as a breach of confidence, subject to the usual defences.[32]

(5) *Court reporting*: English law recognises the potential harm to children and young persons which can be caused by the publication of details of court proceedings in which the child or young person is involved as a witness, victim or defendant. Several statutes regulate media reports of court proceedings involving children by creating exceptions to the general rule from *Scott* v. *Scott*[33] that justice be done in public. In the case of youth court proceedings, there is a bar on the publication of material (including pictorial images) which may lead to the identification of a child concerned in those proceedings.[34] This prohibition may be lifted for the sole purpose of avoiding injustice to a child or young person. By contrast, where a youth appears as a defendant or witness before an adult court, the court has a discretion over whether to prevent the identification of the youth concerned.[35] In the case of adults, indirect protection of a privacy interest has occurred through both automatic statutory bars on the identification of persons who allege that they have been victims of sexual offences[36] and the issuing by the judges of anonymity orders. The latter have been employed to encourage witnesses to assist in criminal prosecutions and have included cases where it is necessary to protect the identity of a police informer,[37] and female witnesses in a pornography and procuring trial.[38] In both sets of cases, it is important to realise that the real motivation behind the grant of anonymity is not considerations relating to the convenience of witnesses etc. but rather the longer-term interests of the effective prosecution of offenders.

Calcutt I and *II*: proposals for reform

Calcutt I concluded that protection of privacy in domestic law would be improved by a combination of a new set of criminal law offences and more effective self-regulation by the press. The introduction of a new civil law remedy for the infringement of privacy was postponed so that an improved system of self-regulation might be given a final chance.[39] Three new criminal offences were proposed in *Calcutt I* to prevent physical intrusion by the press. These were (1) entering private property without permission with intent to obtain personal information with a view to its publication; (2) placing a surveillance device on private property without permission with intent to obtain personal information with a view to its publication; (3) taking a photograph, or recording the voice of, an individual who is on private property without consent with a view to its publication and with intent that the individual be identifiable. A defence to any of these offences would exist where the intrusive act was done for the purpose of preventing, detecting or exposing the commission of any crime; or other seriously anti-social conduct; or for the protection of public health or safety.[40]

As to an improved system of self-regulation a new body – the Press Complaints Commission (PCC) – was proposed to consider *inter alia* whether newspapers or periodicals had committed unwarranted infringements of privacy through published material or the obtaining of such material. This and other norms of ethical journalism were to be laid down in a code of practice. Breach of the code would lead to censure and require publication of the PCC's adverse findings. The new body was to be financed by the press industry. If the PCC was subsequently deemed to have failed to provide effective regulation, Parliament should create in its place a statutory press tribunal with a power in law to enforce its findings.

Calcutt II which followed in January 1993,[41] concluded that the PCC which the press industry had set up in response to *Calcutt I* was in crucial respects a weaker body than that proposed in *Calcutt I*.[42] For example, *Calcutt I* had wanted the new body to be composed of persons who were appointed by a body which was independent of the press. Instead, the PCC was appointed by a body which was part of the press industry. *Calcutt I* had also wanted the new body to initiate inquiries rather than wait for a complaint to be made. Moreover, the period since *Calcutt I* had witnessed further examples of press intrusions into the lives of individuals.[43] There was evidence that some complainants in this period were dissatisfied with the length of time taken for investigation. Others argued that because the press controlled the appointment of members to the PCC, it could not appear truly independent. Accordingly, *Calcutt II* proposed that a statutory complaints tribunal be created. It further recommended that the government consider the case for a new civil wrong (or tort) for the infringement of privacy. As any new tort would not be restricted to the press, the recommendation clearly went beyond Sir David's terms of reference. Shortly afterwards, however, both the Lord Chancellor's Department[44] and the National Heritage Select Committee[45] produced reports endorsing the creation of such a new tort. The ball was now firmly in the Major government's court.

The Major government's response

The government published its response, *Privacy and Media Intrusion*, in July 1995,[46] by which time the press industry had already taken a number of measures to fend off the chorus of voices calling for statutory intervention. In June 1993 it instituted a helpline for members of the public concerned about whether the code of practice was being breached in a press investigation relating to the public. In November 1993 the PCC announced that, in future, disciplinary action could be taken against journalists and editors who breached the revised code of practice. Under this code, intrusions into an individual's private life, including the use of long-lens photography to obtain pictures of persons on private property, were not 'generally acceptable'.[47] Where the PCC deemed there to have been a breach of the code, the publication in question was 'duty bound' to print the adjudication with due prominence. Clause 5 further stated that material obtained by 'clandestine listening devices' or intercepted telephone conversations should not be published unless justified by the public interest. Further provisions of the code prohibit harassment[48] and the obtaining of information or pictures through misrepresentation.[49] Special guidance is given to the relevant privacy considerations in published material involving children.[50]

After the promolgation of the code, efforts to improve the system of self-regulation continued. In January 1994 a Privacy Commissioner was created, with powers to investigate urgent complaints about breaches of privacy under the code. The Commissioner was also to have powers to initiate investigations on his own[51] and to report to the PCC (now constituted with a non-press majority) with his recommendations.

Reviewing the industry's efforts to improve self-regulation, *Privacy and Media Intrusion* concluded that there was now no compelling case for statutory regulation.[52] Whilst further improvements to the press industry's system could still be made, neither criminal nor civil legislation ought to be brought forward. In the case of criminal sanctions, the government said it had been unable to construct workable legislation.[53] As for the introduction of a new civil law remedy, the consultation exercise carried out by the Lord Chancellor's Office had yielded no consensus about the need for such a reform.[54]

Extra-legal protection: media codes of practice

To date, the Labour administration led by Tony Blair has given little indication that it wishes to enact further statutory protection for privacy along the lines advocated by *Calcutt II* and others. It is clear therefore that non-legal forms of privacy protection will remain vitally important in practice. In this section, the privacy protections contained in the codes of practice found in broadcasting are analysed more closely.

Earlier, aspects of the code of practice for journalists and newspaper editors were noted. In the case of broadcasters, the Broadcasting Act 1996 established the Broadcasting Standards Commission (hereafter BSC) which took over the regulatory functions hitherto undertaken by the Broadcasting Complaints Commission (the Commission) and the Broadcasting Standards Council (the Council). The BSC is required by the Broadcasting Act 1996, s.107(1) to draw up a code of practice which will give guidance on the

> principles to be observed and the practices to be followed, in connection with the avoidance of . . . (b) unwarranted infringement of privacy in, or in connection with the obtaining of material included in such programmes.

The Commission was criticised for its failure to adopt a principled approach to privacy issues in its adjudications. Gibbons, for example, has written,

> In a field where there is a rich literature about freedom of speech and the desirability of giving it special protection in constitutional and legal adjudication, the Commission has avoided drawing upon it to guide its thinking.[55]

The consequence of this failure, Gibbons argues, was that the Commission was not accepted by broadcasters, some of whom believed that it acted 'merely a censor'.[56] Robertson and Nicol have claimed that a survey of the Commission's Annual Reports reveals inconsistent and irreconcilable adjudications.[57]

Gibbons too has noted that the Commission has adopted more than one approach to the question of whether an unwarranted invasion of privacy has occurred in instances of 'doorstepping', where the journalist attempts to obtain a comment or statement by waiting outside the home or workplace of the person whose views are sought and then confronting the latter when he or she makes an appearance.[58] One line of rulings suggests that doorstepping is justified (and thus a warranted invasion of privacy) only in cases when all other measures to obtain an interview have been tried and failed. Another line of cases suggests that, even where no alternative means of obtaining an interview exists, a lengthy period of encampment combined with persistent attempts to get an interview might be sufficient to sustain a finding of an unwarranted infringement of privacy. A third line of cases allows factors such as the degree of disquiet about the intended interviewee's alleged activities to affect considerations of whether the privacy intrusion was warranted. It is to be hoped that this unhappy state of affairs can be avoided by the BSC which, under the 1996 Act, is under a statutory duty to expound and justify the values and norms which underpin its code and adjudications.

The new regulatory body may also wish to reflect upon the separate code developed by the Council which, although primarily concerned with standards of taste and decency, reminded broadcasters of the privacy interests of those whose lives are caught up (usually in an involuntary way) in events which become newsworthy. The code continued,

> In some cases lives afterwards have to be reconstructed or new lives built. Television and radio should do nothing through a disregard for privacy which makes that process even more difficult once the spotlight has moved away.

The Council also spoke of the need for a public interest justification where an intrusion into privacy occurred and further required that specific consent be sought for filming inside hospitals, factories, schools and other 'closed' institutions.

Like its predecessors, the BSC cannot force a broadcaster found to have breached the BSC code to apologise or provide compensation for any injury or distress caused as a result of the breach. Unlike the PCC it has no power to initiate investigations of its own.[59]

In the case of commercial television services (terrestrial, satellite and cable) licensed by the Independent Television Commission (ITC), section 2 of the latter's Code of Practice lays down guidance about the circumstances in which an individual's privacy interests ought to be respected.[60]

Privacy and the European Convention on Human Rights and Fundamental Freedoms

The manifesto commitment of the present Labour administration to incorporate the above Convention requires us to consider the type of protection it offers privacy interests. Article 8 of the European Convention states:

1 Everyone has the right to respect for his private and family life, his home and his correspondence.
2 There shall be no interference by a public authority with the exercise of this right except such as is in accordance with the law and is necessary in a democratic society in the interests of national security, public safety or the economic well-being of the country, for the prevention of disorder or crime, for the protection of health or morals, or for the protection of the rights and freedoms of others.'

It follows then that to establish a violation of an Article 8 privacy right, a complainant would have to show three things:

1 that the concept of a 'private life' included control over access to personal information;
2 that the *state* had failed to *respect* the complainant's right to private life by allowing a private individual or organisation to obtain and publish personal information; and

3 that the resultant interference with the complainant's private life was either
   (a) not in accordance with the law, or
   (b) not for a legitimate aim, or
   (c) not necessary in a democratic society.

As the European Court has not doubted that the concept of a private life does embrace the notion of control over access to personal information, the question arises whether a state has failed to respect the right to private life when it allows others to obtain and publish personal information. *In X & Y v. Netherlands*[61] the Court stated that Article 8 is not merely concerned with the negative obligations on states not to interfere with individuals' private lives, but can in a more positive sense require the state to take measures designed to prevent interference by other individuals. The choice of means employed to secure compliance with Article 8 is however a matter which falls within a state's margin of appreciation.[62]

In assessing whether the right to private life in a specific instance does require the state to take steps to protect it, the Court has regard to the nature of the complainant's interest and the burden which would fall upon the state if the right was to be recognised. Where the interest of the complainant is deemed to be slight and the burden of reform upon the state great, this would militate against the conclusion that the right to respect had been violated. For the government it may be argued that the interplay of nuisance law, breach of confidence law and other miscellaneous statutory and common law provisions provides a degree of legal protection which the Strasbourg Court should be slow to deem inadequate.

On the remaining requirements that the interference be in accordance with the law, has a legitimate aim and is necessary in a democratic society, it is far from clear that the United Kingdom would be able to satisfy the Court. For example, there would appear to be no specific legal mandate for the intrusive conduct of the media.[63]

Despite such positive omens for privacy advocates, it should be remembered that when asked on a previous occasion to rule on what was in essence a free speech versus privacy dispute, the Commission in *Winer v. United Kingdom*[64] ruled that the absence of a privacy right actionable in domestic law did not demonstrate a lack of respect for the applicant's private life and home. Winer had complained that a book which revealed information about his married life (some of it true, some false) had violated Article 8. Winer's claim was rejected. His right to privacy was not wholly unprotected as he was able to (and indeed did) have recourse to defamation law in respect of the false allegations contained within the book. What of course *Winer's* case does not tell us is what either the Commission or the Court would do when confronted with a case in which true information only was revealed and no domestic remedy existed to protect a complainant. One tendency of the Court in cases where Convention rights are in direct conflict is to concede a relatively wide margin of appreciation to a state, a stance which does little to advance the privacy interests of victims of media intrusions.

Conclusion

This article has considered the state of legal and extra-legal protection against media intrusion. Although the courts have tried to adapt existing legal remedies such as those provided by the law of confidence to the problem, successive governments have refused to countenance the introduction of a more general remedy for breach of privacy. For the time being, victims of intrusive media conduct will continue to be channelled along the improved, extra-legal remedy routes offered by the BSC, ITC and PCC. Whether these are sufficiently robust to handle further instances of intrusive misconduct remains to be seen. In the final analysis, it is likely that the jurisprudence of the European Court of Human Rights will determine where the balance between individual privacy and media freedom lies.

Notes

1 The measure of parliamentary concern may be indicated by the frequency of Private Members' Bills in the 1980s which unsuccessfully sought to enshrine in law varying degrees of privacy protection. At the time of the announcement of the government's inquiry in April 1989, the Right to Reply bill sponsored by Tony Worthington MP had secured support from all sides of the House of Commons and had reached its report stage. Public concern over press intrusion was amply demonstrated in submissions to the inquiry. A poll carried out for the *News of the World* by MORI in 1989 showed that 73 per cent of the public agreed that the press intruded too much into the lives of public figures.
2 *Kaye v. Robertson* (1990). Reported as Appendix I to the *Report of the Committee on Privacy and Related Matters*, Cmnd. 1102 (1990), London: HMSO. ('Cmnd.' reflects that this paper is laid by command of the Crown for consideration before Parliament.)
3 These are examined below.
4 *Report of the Committee on Privacy and Related Matters*, Cmnd. 1102 (1990), London: HMSO.
5 *Privacy and Media Intrusion: The Government's Response*, Cmnd. 2918 (1995), London: HMSO, para. 1.5.
6 Cmnd. 2135 (1993), London: HMSO.
7 (1993) HMSO.
8 Cmnd. 2918 (1995), London: HMSO.
9 D. Feldman, *Civil Liberties and Human Rights* (Oxford: Clarendon Press, 1993) p. 356.
10 R. Wacks, *Privacy and Press Freedom* (London: Blackstone Press, 1995).
11 Interception of Communications Act 1985, s.1. This act does not, however, apply to technical surveillance devices.
12 The prohibition was originally contained in a statute from the last century, the Conspiracy and Protection of Property Act 1875, s. 7. For the current form of this offence see the Trade Union and Labour Relations Act 1992, s. 241. *Calcutt I* thought it was unlikely that this provision would be used against the press,

although it should be noted that despite its title, it has been invoked outside of industrial disputes to gatherings outside abortion clinics.

13 That is at least on two occasions – Protection from Harassment Act 1997, s. 7(2).

14 Section 1. For the purposes of the Act, 'harassment' includes alarming or distressing the person and 'conduct' includes speech, s. 7(1) and (3).

15 Highways Act 1980, s. 137.

16 *Hubbard* v. *Pitt* [1976] QB142.

17 It would of course have been open to the hospital management to rely on this form of action.

18 *Bernstein* v. *Skyviews Ltd* [1978] 1 QB 479.

19 *Tolley* v. *Fry* [1930] 1 KB 460.

20 *Bonnard* v. *Perryman* [1891] 2 ch. 269; *Fraser* v. *Evans* [1969] 1 QB 349.

21 *Joyce* v. *Sengupta* [1993] 1 WLR 337.

22 *Report of the Committee on Privacy and Related Matters.*

23 *Coco* v. *AN Clark (Engineers) Ltd* [1969] RPC 41, 47.

24 *Stephens* v. *Avery* [1988] 2 WLR 1280.

25 *AG* v. *Guardian Newspapers Ltd* (No. 2) [1990] 1 AC 109.

26 *Calcutt I* observed, 'In England and Wales, an interlocutory injunction will more readily be granted in a breach of confidence case than for defamation. In particular, whereas a defendant in a libel action need say no more than he intends to plead justification and an interlocutory injunction will be refused ... by contrast in the case of breach of confidence he will need to make a strong case of public interest' (Cmnd. 1102 (1990), London: HMSO, at para. 8.10). The publication of photographs of the Princess of Wales (as she then was) exercising in the LA Fitness Centre, Isleworth Middlesex which appeared in the *Sunday Mirror* and *Daily Mirror* in November 1993 prompted lawyers acting for the Princess to obtain an interlocutory injunction, thus preventing further publication pending the outcome of her action for breach of confidence, contract and fiduciary duty. In the event the matter was settled out of court when the newspapers' owners paid the sum of £25,000 to a charity of Princess Diana's choice. One reason for the settlement may have been the fears of a consortium of newspaper owners that a victory for the Princess in the courts and the establishment of some form of privacy protection would seriously inhibit the newspapers' activities.

27 *AG* v. *Guardian Newspapers Ltd* (No. 2) [1990] 1 AC 109.

28 Although it should be noted that there is no need for any iniquitous conduct for the public interest defence to be available see *Lion Laboratories* v. *Evans* [1985] QB 526.

29 See Interception of Communications Act 1985 at pp. 55–6, 129–39.

30 For an assertion of the need for a prior relationship of confidence see the Law Commission, *Breach of Confidence*, Cmnd. 8388 (1981), London: HMSO. For the contrasting view that confidence can prevent disclosure upon the alternative principle of unconscionability see *Stephens* v. *Avery* [1988] 1 ch. 449, 456 *per* Browne-Wilkinson VC; and *AG* v. *Guardian Newspapers* (No. 2) [1990] 1 AC 109, 281 *per* Lord Goff. cf. *M & N* v. *Kelvin Mackenzie and News Group Newspapers Ltd.* (1988) (unreported). *Calcutt I* took the view that there had to be a prior relationship of confidence for the duty to attach (Cmnd. 1102 (1990) at para. 8.1).

31 *AG* v. *Jonathan Cape* [1976] 1 QB 752; *Woodward* v. *Hutchins* [1977] 1 WLR 760.

32 [1995] 1 WLR 804.

33 [1913] AC 417.

34 Children and Young Persons Act 1933, s. 49(1) as amended.

35 Children and Young Persons Act 1933, s. 39 as amended. There is an identifiable

trend in these cases towards allowing the identification of minors which has occurred mainly in cases involving extremely serious criminal conduct such as murder and rape. See for example, *R v. Lee (Anthony William) (A Minor)* [1993] 1 WLR 103.

36 Sexual Offences (Amendment) Act 1992. The bar is in force during the entirety of the alleged victim's lifetime regardless of whether the accused is subsequently convicted of the offence(s).

37 *R v. Reigate JJ ex parte Argus Newspapers* (1983) 147 JP 385.

38 *R v. Hove JJ ex parte Gibbons* (1981), *The Times* 19 June.

39 Hence the comment of the then Secretary of State for National Heritage (Rt. Hon. David Mellor QC MP) that the press was 'drinking at the last chance saloon'.

40 Where one or more of the new criminal offences had been committed, *Calcutt I* recommended that any person with 'sufficient interest' should be able to apply for an injunction to prevent the publication of information thereby obtained.

41 Cmnd. 2135 (1993), London: HMSO.

42 See further Cmnd. 2135 (1993), London: HMSO, at para. 3.94.

43 Ibid. at ch. 4.

44 Joint Report with the Scottish Office, *Infringement of Privacy* (1993), London HMSO.

45 *Fourth Report, Privacy and Media Intrusion* (1993), pp. 294–1.

46 Cmnd. 2918 (1995), London: HMSO.

47 Clause 4.

48 Clause 8.

49 Clause 7.

50 Clauses 12 and 13.

51 This had been recommended by *Calcutt I* in 1990 but had been rejected by the then chairman of the PCC, Lord McGregor of Durris.

52 Cmnd. 2918 (1995), London: HMSO, pp. 4–8. The PCC have since produced a Complainants' Charter, which commits the PCC to attaining specific standards of service in its dealings with the public.

53 Ibid. at para. 3.4.

54 Ibid. at paras 4.4–4.14.

55 E. Barendt, S. Bate, J. Dickens and J. Michael (eds), *The Yearbook of Media and Entertainment Law*, vol. 1 (Oxford: Oxford University Press, 1995), p. 134. One might add that a principled discussion of free speech must ask where the limits of this freedom lie.

56 Ibid.

57 Geoffrey Robertson and Andrew Nicol, *Media Law*, 3rd edn (Harmondsworth: Penguin Books, 1992) p. 554.

58 *Yearbook of Media and Entertainment Law*, p. 134.

59 In *R v. BCC ex parte Granada TV* (1994) *The Times*, 14 December, the Court of Appeal noted that the Commission had been given a wide latitude to determine what constituted 'privacy'. The courts would not, in other words, lightly interfere with the Commission's views on the matter.

60 The Broadcasting Act 1990, s. 7 states that the ITC must do 'all that it can to secure that the provisions of the code are observed in the provision of licensed services'.

61 (1986) 8 EHRR 235.

62 Within which the Court will not interfere.

63 See *Malone v. UK* (1985) 7 EHRR 14. A separate question – one not tackled here – is whether the interference is for a legitimate aim.

64 *No. 10871/84*, 48 DR 154 (1986).

9 Taming the tabloids
Market, moguls and media regulation

Bob Franklin and Rod Pilling

Self-congratulation and self-regulation

On 31 January 1996 Lord Wakeham, Chair of the Press Complaints Commission (PCC), hailed 1995 as 'a momentous year for the PCC' and for press self-regulation. 'We proved', said the carefully crafted press release, 'that the Commission is *independent* and that it can *bite* when necessary.' Few observers of the shaky progress of the Commission since its inception in January 1991 will have recognised Wakeham's description of the Commission as a forceful watchdog guarding against press misbehaviour; even fewer will have been moved to endorse Wakeham's self-congratulatory and bullish appraisal of the Commission's performance. Wakeham's confidence was undoubtedly boosted by a single high-profile case in 1995, which gave the PCC a considerable public fillip.

In April 1995 Britain's youngest tabloid editor Piers Morgan, then editor of the *News of the World*, ran a front-page story about the secret hospitalisation of Countess Spencer, under the splash headline 'Di's sister-in-law in booze and bulimia clinic'. This story must have promised, to Morgan, to be the latest in a line of royal and other scandals which had already won him and his paper three awards in his brief 16-months' tenure of the editorial chair. To Countess Spencer's husband, Earl Spencer, not surprisingly, it seemed very different. He complained to the PCC that it was an intrusion into his wife's privacy and a flagrant breach of the Commission's code of conduct. Given his celebrity and his fury, his complaint received media attention. Morgan tenaciously defended his decision to print, pointing out that the Spencers had sought favourable publicity in *Hello* magazine and that they must therefore be prepared for less favourable publicity. Morgan knew, of course, that the PCC's code of conduct provided a potential defence for such intrusions; he had used it in the past. It protected the publication of stories 'preventing the public from being misled by some statement or action of an individual or organisation'. His newspaper's defence had been forthright – a full-page article headed, 'Hypocrisy of the Earl Spencer . . . his privacy can be invaded for cash'. As the headline implies, his newspaper pointed out in no uncertain terms that the Spencers were very happy to receive – and even be paid for – certain types of publicity. It was therefore morally right for their public image to be investigated and exposed by the *News of the World*.

So far, this looked like a typical – if unusually heated – spat between a tabloid editor and a celebrity 'victim'. But then a significant exchange of letters elevated the débâcle to a new significance. Lord Wakeham took the unprecedented step of writing to the *News of the World*'s owner and publisher, Rupert Murdoch. The decision to involve the publisher was a new tactic in the PCC's limited armoury, although it had threatened such a strategy at the beginning of 1995. Murdoch, as so often, acted unpredictably. He astonished Morgan by giving him a ferocious dressing down and, on May 12, startled media commentators by making public his rebuke. He described Morgan as 'a young man' who had gone 'over the top'. Murdoch announced, 'I have reminded Mr Morgan forcefully of his responsibility to the code to which he as editor – and all our journalists – subscribe in their terms of employment.'[1] Morgan, evidently shocked by Murdoch's reprimand, publicly offered his 'sincere apologies' to Countess Spencer and accepted the PCC adjudication 'without reservation'. Lord Wakeham, well aware of his considerable public relations coup for the PCC and self-regulation, welcomed the intervention of the proprietor.

This incident, potentially a turning-point for the PCC, raises interesting questions about self-regulation. First, why is intrusion into privacy such an important issue and apparently so sensitive that it requires the intervention of a global media magnate? If the nature of PCC complaints can be considered as an indicator of public concerns, moreover, then newspaper accuracy – which accounted for 70 per cent of 1995's 2,508 complaints – is far more significant in public perceptions. Yet the PCC itself recognises the special importance of intrusion into privacy. It says in its 1995 annual report, 'Although only 12% of the complaints received by the Commission in 1995 related to intrusion into privacy, the task of ensuring that the provisions of the Code protecting the private lives of individuals are upheld is at the heart of the PCC's work';[2] this view is endorsed by the most powerful media figure in Britain, Rupert Murdoch. Why is this? One reason for this preoccupation is the PCC's sensitivity to the concerns of the Westminster establishment. There has been a succession of attempts to give some legal protection to privacy across the last decade, including unsuccessful bills introduced by back-bench MPs, the Calcutt inquiry of 1990, which recommended privacy legislation and the subsequent review of self-regulation in 1993 and, more recently, the revived proposal by the Lord Chancellor Lord Mackay for a civil tort of invasion of privacy.[3] The PCC is also responding to wider public concern about the role of the press. A MORI poll in 1992 echoed Westminster anxieties about press behaviour. Perhaps more significantly the PCC, and even Murdoch, recognises that issues of privacy are at the centre of widespread changes in journalism.

The old 'rumpy-pumpy': tabloid journalism and market pressures

It is widely argued that there has been a move toward a more tabloid agenda in journalism. A focus on celebrities – and especially titillating revelations about their private lives – has increasingly driven the news values of the popular tabloid newspapers.[4] The *Sun* and its sister paper the *News of the World* have been the undisputed market leaders in this development although they have spawned a range of imitators. A range of factors have triggered this development in news values. First, the key players in Fleet Street – especially Kelvin Mackenzie, the editor of the *Sun* during the 1980s – believed it was what readers wanted and that their sales success proved this. Mass circulation tabloids, which characteristically gain most of their revenue from their cover price, are very much driven by sales. Advertising success also rests principally on sales volume. The kiss-and-tell formula is popular and popularity is a prerequisite for the profitability of the tabloids. Second, the competition between tabloid newspapers is intense. The Bingo wars of the 1980s gave way to the price wars of the 1990s, especially marked by the *Sun*'s attack on the price front on 12 July 1993.

But the search for circulation-boosting stories has been constant. That search has often led journalists to explore people's private lives, those of celebrities if possible, but of pseudo-celebrities or others if not. The editors who were leading the field demonstrated this daily in their columns. A tabloid veteran told ex-*Daily Mirror* editor Roy Greenslade about the values that Piers Morgan was bringing from the *Sun* to *News of the World*: 'I must say, Piers loves the old rumpy-pumpy. We can't get enough to please him'.[5] This fierce competition between rival tabloids has developed in the context of the long-term decline in their sales in the post-war period combined with growing competition from radio and television as news sources. These latter media can deliver news more quickly than the tabloids but, because of the regulatory regime to which they are subject, are unable to compete on titillation. An important part of the tabloid response to these broadcast rivals has been the constant quest for 'rumpy-pumpy' or, expressed rather differently, a constant drive to intrude into other people's privacy. Broadly speaking, people's private lives, especially their sex lives, sell newspapers; such revelations always have. Some newspapers – notably the Sundays – have specialised in sex, crime and scandal since the middle of the nineteenth century.[6] A new feature of this long-standing obsession with the sexual habits of the famous and infamous is its rampant spread across most parts of the media.

This tabloid agenda has not been limited to Sunday or daily mass-circulation tabloid newspapers. Broadsheets have picked up many of the tabloid stories and run with them, as they have fought their own battles to retain and win a greater circulation in heated price wars. Lengthy features have been run in the 1990s on the late Princess of Wales's relationships with various men, while other stories have focused on film actor Hugh Grant's notorious liaison with Los Angeles prostitute Divine Brown; coverage of the latter story was greater in the *Guardian*, for example, than in any other paper.[7] The influence of the tabloids, moreover, does not seem to be limited to print media. Academics and regulators have criticised a shift in mainstream news programmes to a more tabloid agenda in which lighter stories about celebrities seem to be displacing coverage of serious foreign and other news stories.[8] Observers typically explain this preference for lighter stories by reference to the drive for ratings in a more competitive broadcasting environment and to lighter regulation. At the least-regulated end of broadcast news production – cable television – L!ve TV features the news bunny who signals approval or disapproval of news items by making thumbs up or thumbs down gestures; news bulletins are part of a schedule which includes topless (female) darts and 'lunchbox volleyball' which features young men in tight-fitting lycra shorts playing volleyball.

The gossip editor of the *National Enquirer*, Mike Walker, has noticed a different attitude towards gossip in the two years that his paper has been circulating in Britain and establishing an estimated 100,000 circulation. When invited on to television shows in 1996 he said he was no longer asked 'those questions about privacy, ethics and libel suits. Now they just introduce me as the *National Enquirer*'s "guru of gossip", and get right to the naughty bits: "Welcome back, Mike. So . . . who's doing Sharon Stone?"' If Walker is to be believed, the commodification of gossip is well advanced, and, unsurprisingly, he has a rationale for it: 'Gossip, after all, is just another word for news in a slinky red dress.'[9]

In defence of the indefensible

This move to a more tabloid agenda and the pressures it places on journalists to intrude into people's privacy explains the context in which issues of privacy became the most politically sensitive of public concerns about the press in the late 1980s and early 1990s.[10] The 'threat' of legislation to offer statutory protection of privacy undoubtedly underlies the importance and sensitivity which Wakeham and Murdoch attribute to the issue; both are eager to demonstrate that privacy is already adequately defended. In truth it is not. The limited protection of the press which prevails is contained in the PCC's *Code of Conduct*, a code agreed voluntarily by decision-makers in the newspaper industry, who also fund the PCC. The code specifically forbids intrusions 'into an individual's private life' except when it is in the 'public interest'. The 'public interest' can be established in three ways: by 'detecting a crime or a serious misdemeanour', by 'protecting public health and safety' or by 'preventing the public from being misled by some statement or action of an individual or organisation'.[11]

It was on the third of these criteria that Piers Morgan had largely based his defence for his intrusion into the life of the Spencers. He argued that they had voluntarily put their personal lives into the public arena and had made statements about it, so the *News of the World* report, which corrected their public image, was justified. The *News of the World* and other tabloids had cited the same defence in the discussion of a number of earlier stories that had involved intrusion. They were not alone in this. The notion that someone who seeks publicity is fair game for intrusive stories is bandied about on broadcast discussion programmes by journalists with enough regularity for an observer to conclude that it is an influential ethic in tabloid journalism. The *News of the World*, moreover, had received prizes rather than adverse adjudications for recent stories. Morgan and his colleagues had picked up awards from their fellow journalists for those efforts, which included several sexual scandals. To Morgan, Earl Spencer seemed to want to enjoy media attention on his own terms, only for positive self-promotion, and the code gave him the right to investigate and expose the 'hypocrisy' of that public image. To others, anxious about the right to privacy, this clause in the code seemed like a convenient loophole for almost every circulation-chasing story that invaded the private life of a celebrity or news-maker.

The PCC's rejection of Morgan's interpretation of the code clearly shocked him and some of his fellow journalists. This ruling seemed to throw some doubt over what had seemed clear-cut. Perhaps people who had enjoyed publicity, or had even been paid for it, were not necessarily fair game for intrusion. This conclusion is not inevitable; the PCC's ruling made clear it was distinguishing between Earl Spencer's rights to privacy and Countess Spencer's and that it was concerned by the intrusion into the latter's. However, 'ordinary' people may well conclude that the degree of protection from the code may depend on the complainant's connections and celebrity; not everyone has the high profile of Princess Diana's brother and sister-in-law. Geoffrey Robertson, the eminent media lawyer who chronicled the earlier failure of self-regulation in the Press Council, declared less than one month later that the PCC was a 'fraud and a con trick'.[12] But one point was inescapable: one of the most audacious of tabloid journalists – an opinion-leader – had been stopped in his tracks and the right to privacy had been publicly upheld.

Proprietorial pressures: the real regulatory power?

The way in which the right to privacy was defended, however, does raise a major issue concerning the role of the publisher in self-regulation. It was Murdoch's intervention which had proved crucial in securing Morgan's contrition and promised compliance with the PCC Code. This touches a nerve. Commentators on the generally unsuccessful Press Council have remarked that it only enjoyed a period of success when it had the support of two dominant publishers of that era, the so-called 'King–Thomson consensus'.[13] Conversely, accounts of the Press Council's least effective period, the mid- and late 1980s, show that more adjudications were registered against Rupert Murdoch's newspapers than against any other, without any apparent disapproval from the dominant Fleet Street proprietor. Indeed, at least one of these newspapers – the *Sun* under Kelvin Mackenzie's editorship – notoriously derided an adverse ruling of the Press Council and repeated the offending statements without any apparent reproof from Murdoch. It seems that self-regulation is not an independent system but depends on the support of those powerful individuals who are publishers and owners. This is a worrying form of accountability in a liberal democracy, one which is not expressed in constitutional form and is not a public process. It is also unreliable.

The support of a publisher is potentially fragile and fickle, as the highest profile PCC case of 1993, the so-called 'Di Spy' case, had shown. Mirror Group Newspapers (MGN) had withdrawn from the PCC after criticism from the then chairman, the late Lord McGregor, of the *Daily Mirror*'s decision to publish seven pages of photographs of the Princess of Wales wearing a leotard and cycling shorts and using an exercise machine. The photographs had been taken by a camera concealed in the gymnasium ceiling and had been sold to the *Daily Mirror* by the gymnasium owner. McGregor had decided to make an immediate personal statement in which he said that MGN was 'deliberately breaching the ethical boundaries which mark out an agreed competitive playing field for newspapers'.[14] The *Mirror*'s defence that the pictures illustrated a potential security risk for the Princess of Wales, that the gym was a public place and that the photographs had merely been purchased rather than taken by its own photographers, did little to placate McGregor or the *Mirror*'s competitor papers.[15] During the row, McGregor called for advertisers to boycott MGN newspapers, while the *Mirror* responded by describing McGregor as 'an arch buffoon'.

Within two days of initial publication, then *Mirror* editor David Banks announced that MGN were leaving the PCC. This would mean 25 per cent (by circulation) of Britain's national newspapers opting out of self-regulation, a loss to the PCC of MGN's contribution of over £100,000 and an end, effectively, to the credibility of self-regulation. The seriousness of the situation was marked by the importance of the peace negotiators. Interventions by Murdoch himself, and Sir David English, were crucial to the negotiation of a settlement between David Montgomery of MGN and Lord McGregor. Within 24 hours of leaving, the *Daily Mirror* returned to the PCC, which spent two hours discussing measures to enhance the credibility of self-regulation and prevent statutory regulation.[16] McGregor argued that the intervention of such senior figures was a demonstration of the strength of support for self-regulation but the incident also points to a worrying fragility. A system of regulation sustained and policed by the interventions of powerful individuals is potentially unsustainable, lacks any public accountability and seems to rest on arbitrary power rather than any legitimate authority. It also seemed, in this case, to be primarily determined by a desire to avoid the kind of regulation that was being threatened, a strategy to retain that power rather than submit it to authority.

Steering the blind goddess: directions for regulation reforms

If self-regulation is potentially unstable and if its success since the founding of the Press Council in 1953 has been at best patchy, what is the alternative? Is it further regulation? Journalists and editors have routinely mustered six arguments against statutory intervention. They believe: it is wrong in principle and constitutes censorship; it is impractical and unworkable; there are already too many statutory controls on press freedom; there is no evidence that it is necessary (for example, the PCC only found against newspapers 28 times in 1995); self-regulation is more flexible and allows a discourse, mediated by PCC, between readers and publishers; self-regulation offers the most effective sanction against potential offenders – namely peer review. British parliaments have also traditionally been wary of adding further legal restrictions on the press. Lord Wakeham, a veteran of Conservative regimes, said, on joining the PCC, 'As a Parliamentarian, I was *instinctively* in favour of self-regulation and opposed to statutory controls on the press.'[17]

Journalists are already subject to considerable regulation. William Waldegrave's 1992 White Paper *Open Government* listed 251 statutory instruments restricting disclosure of information which limit media competence to report government activity.[18] Newspapers are also subject to 46 legislative restrictions, including the various Official Secrets Acts 1911 to 1989 and the Prevention of Terrorism Act 1989.[19] This protection of information – and a readiness to impose injunctions preventing publication – is not balanced by statutory or constitutional rights to information. There is neither a general constitutional right of access to information in the public interest nor a Freedom of Information Act. The eminent media and civil rights lawyer, Geoffrey Robertson, has long believed that the general thrust of the law actually encourages kiss-and-tell intrusions into privacy and discourages public interest investigation: 'British law is the enemy of the British press. It circumscribes press virtues and comforts press vices. The blind Goddess of Justice raises her sword against the investigative journalist while her other hand fondles the Sunday muckraker.'[20]

Lawyers have notoriously been able to protect powerful people from disclosure by threatening litigation under various headings. Ironically, one of the most infamous of recent cases involves a media mogul. Robert Maxwell's small army of élite lawyers was successfully deployed to prevent publication by investigating journalists of allegations that he was abusing control of MGN pension funds. It was only after Maxwell's death that the long-suspected crimes came to light. Robertson would not have been surprised; he made this point about the 'blind goddess of British justice' more than ten years earlier: 'She suppresses the truth about crooked financiers, disreputable companies and hypocritical politicians on the pretexts of contempt of court, breach of confidence and infringement of copyright.'[21]

Robertson argued persuasively that the law made it easier to pursue kiss-and-tell stories than serious investigation. This adds a further powerful dynamic to that of the market in the shift toward a tabloid agenda, and a further pressure on privacy. The libel law has been a powerful and lucrative weapon for the wealthy; its high costs intimidate and counsel caution to even the bravest journalistic enquirer. Courts can punish inaccuracy with costly settlements, which most people cannot meet and yet the law of libel does not actually protect privacy. If a reporter can establish some aspect of a person's private life accurately, then it can be reported. There is, in effect, no legal protection for those aspects of the private lives of people that sell to newspapers. If a disgruntled lover, wife, husband or mistress wishes to retaliate by retailing accounts of a 'romance' to the tabloids, and they can provide adequate detail and substantiation, then there is little that the other parties can do to protect their own privacy. Conversely, an investigative journalist undertaking a serious enquiry into a matter of public concern has few rights of discovery of information and meets many obstacles to disclosure and publication.

Public and political concern with press behaviour in the late 1980s led to pressure for legislation to curb alleged intrusions. Regrettably, the effect of this legislation has been overwhelmingly to curb press behaviour and to give rights to people who were being written about, rather than to give journalists rights of enquiry and publication. Strong parliamentary support in 1989 for back-bench bills to give protection for privacy and a right of reply for victims of inaccuracy prompted the government to put the press on probation and to set up the Calcutt inquiry. The then Heritage Secretary, David Mellor, told the press that they were 'drinking at the last-chance saloon'. The Calcutt Report recommended closure of an ineffective Press Council, the introduction of a new self-regulatory body, which would itself be on probation for 18 months, and the introduction of civil laws to protect privacy.[22] The Press Council had few supporters and was closed at the end of 1990. The Press Complaints Commission replaced it but no privacy laws were introduced. The PCC was judged by Calcutt at the end of its probation to be 'ineffective' and he recommended a new statutory body with powers to fine and order corrections and apologies.[23] The government ignored his proposals. The PCC made changes, introducing some faster procedures, a new privacy ombudsman, more lay members and, after criticism of its chair, brought in Lord Wakeham, Mrs Thatcher's veteran political fixer, to revitalise the leadership of this regulatory body. But despite these piecemeal changes, many observers believed that the government should make a broader, more coherent, statement about reg- ulation. A White Paper promised since early 1993 was repeatedly delayed. In March 1994, the Association of British Editors (ABE), undoubtedly exasperated by the government's unwillingness to express an opinion, published 'an alternative white paper' entitled *Media Freedom and Reg- ulation.* It concluded that the British press was already unduly regulated and that it was unnecessary 'to create an entirely new wrong of infringe- ment of privacy'.[24] In reaching this conclusion, the ABE rejected Lord Mackay's green paper suggestion that a new civil tort of privacy should be established with maximum fines of £1,000 for infringement. In July 1995, the government finally published its views on privacy and press freedom; it concluded that statutory regulation of the press was not desirable.[25]

Media attention throughout this flurry of reforming activity centred on the Calcutt Report and the official responses it engendered. Wider parlia- mentary concern to reform press behaviour, however, was illustrated by the report from the National Heritage Committee which favoured a statutory press ombudsman as well as by the proposal from back-bencher Clive Soley. His Freedom and Responsibility of the Press bill was a rare attempt to give public interest reporting rights to press journalists as well as an attempt to impose a statutory regulator on the press along the lines of the Independent Broadcasting Authority. By 1996, however, there was no prospect of statutory regulation; Wakeham, the PCC and the newspaper industry had persuaded politicians and public alike that self-regulation offered a sufficient guarantee of privacy.

The clamour of editors against curbing 'press freedom' and against censorship enjoys a long and honourable tradition. Bentham expressed it vigorously: 'The Liberty of the press has its inconveniences, but the evil which may result from it is not to be compared to the evil of censorship.'[26] This tradition, moreover, takes strength from Macaulay's concept of the press as the fourth estate of a liberal democracy, with a role to report on the powerful and make public their actions. In the light of this perception, few would wish to subscribe to legislation which would curb exposure of the corruption of a government or a media mogul; indeed, many might wish to see legislation which strengthened the hand of the fourth estate in this sort of enquiry. Public and political concerns, however, do not cur- rently centre on the media as a fourth estate. There is a widely understood sense that we live in an age in which an individual's privacy has become a commodity which can be sold to a mass audience. A defence of tabloid journalism from the *News of the World* editor, Piers Morgan, illustrates the point: 'I'm not dictating to ordinary people, but say a married woman sleeps with the village policeman, her husband finds out, there's a fight and someone tells the *News of the World.* Then we'll run it. Is that wrong? Well, 4.9 million people thoroughly enjoyed the *News of the World* last week.'[27] In effect, says Morgan, the readers should have their titillation, unchecked apart from a voluntary code. The former *Daily Mirror* editor,

Roy Greenslade, writing about the very public media row over *Daily Mail* investigations into the private life of *The Independent* associate editor, Polly Toynbee, expressed concern about the consequences of this trade in private lives: 'intrusion into privacy is much less common than people believe. But when it happens it can have the most awful repercussions, ruining the victims' lives for ever.'[28] Greenslade points to a question central to the arguments about press regulation that have been occurring since the mid-1980s: 'Who is entitled to privacy?' The drive of market forces and the thrust of the law could well mean that very few – apart from media moguls – have this right. Journalism may be approaching a situation where news and gossip do become synonymous, and gossip editor Walker's view that 'Gossip, after all, is just another word for news in a slinky red dress' becomes widely accepted.[29]

Epilogue: the costs and rewards of self-regulation

What will be the cost to people's private lives of this trend towards tabloid reporting? And who will suffer? Clearly, celebrities will find themselves the subject of the greatest attention because their private lives are the most saleable. In 1996 television presenter Selina Scott complained to the PCC about a report headed 'My sex and smoked salmon with TV's Selina' which reported a relationship which allegedly happened 18 years earlier. But the most serious casualties of this journalistic trend will be ordinary people who, when their lives take some dramatic and often tragic turn, can find themselves at the centre of press interest. Lacking the financial and legal resources necessary to halt press intrusion, their everyday lives and experiences can be transformed into a commodity which can sell newspapers. Accounts of such ordinary 'tragedies' appear with increasing regularity in the tabloids; some 'survivors' argue that journalists' behaviour in reporting their story can be more distressing and damaging than the initial incident that triggered the media attention.[30] For ordinary people, self-regulation can prove a very costly business.

Those people who find themselves politically at odds with the too-evident partisan commitments of the tabloids will also find themselves the subject of investigation. In 1996 *The Independent*'s Polly Toynbee wrote in favour of divorce law reforms, which the *Daily Mail* was campaigning against. She discovered that the *Daily Mail* was researching her relationship with a married journalist who had separated from his wife. She presumed its response was not going to be a thematic rebuttal of her own arguments, but a portrayal of her as a marriage-wrecker and she responded by writing her own attack on the *Daily Mail*.[31] In late 1995 Labour's deputy leader, John Prescott, discovered that his past was being researched by the *Daily Mail*. He began to receive telephone calls from former shipmates from the 1950s and 1960s to warn him that they had been grilled by a *Daily Mail* journalist about the young John Prescott. The line of questioning showed little interest in his political qualities. It centred on whether he had girlfriends, went drinking, was a bully and so on.[32] Prescott, like Toynbee, decided to attack before this was published. He used a guest column in the *News of the World* to denounce the *Mail*'s 'blatant attempt to drag my name into the gutter with slurs, smears and innuendo'. The *Mail* explained that a human interest feature had been misunderstood. Both Toynbee and Prescott were able to use rival media to defend themselves. In Prescott's case this seemed to put an end to any feature; in Toynbee's it provoked the *Daily Mail* into a response, with a feature on the 'wronged wife'. It also provoked much media comment in other quarters. Barbara Amiel, a regular *Daily Telegraph* columnist and wife of its proprietor, Conrad Black, the Canadian newspaper magnate, showed little sisterly sympathy for Toynbee's plight. After attacking Toynbee's journalistic record and perspective, she prescribed the following remedy: 'As for gutter journalism, I have turned it to profit. My husband has been the target of many poorly researched and actionable stories . . . We have a deal. I get part of his settlement to spend on frocks. Since he has never lost an action, this has been helpful to my clothes budget. It's a minor point in the debate, but a major one for me.'[33] Media lawyer Geoffrey Robertson might express little surprise at this sentiment. He argued almost twenty years ago that libel was a particular source of protection, and further wealth, for the already wealthy and powerful, 'a tax-free bonus to assuage the *amour propre* of wealthy libelled litigants'.[34] Ms Amiel clearly feels adequately protected, as well as gracefully clothed, by the current situation, but what about those people who are not married to press magnates? What protection can they expect as gossip increasingly mimics 'news in a slinky red dress'?

Notes

1 Joanna Coles, 'Murdoch blasts his young editor who went over the top after press body attacks NoW's countess coverage', *Guardian*, 15 May 1995.
2 Press Complaints Commission, *Annual Report 1995* (London: Press Complaints Commission), 1995.
3 For a discussion of the various proposals for reform of press regulation see Bob Franklin, *Packaging Politics: Political Communications in Britain's Media Democracy* (London: Edward Arnold, 1994), pp. 45–9.
4 For a discussion of changing news values see Bob Franklin, *Newszak and News Media* (London: Arnold, 1997) and James Fallows, *Breaking The News* (New York: Pantheon, 1995).
5 Quoted in Roy Greenslade, 'The nuts and bolts of the Screws', *Guardian*, 17 April 1995.
6 See Matthew Engel's *Tickle the Public: One Hundred Years of the Popular Press* (London: Gollancz, 1996).
7 Steve Peak and Paul Fisher, *The Media Guide* (London: Fourth Estate, 1996).
8 Rod Pilling, 'Changing news values in ITN's bulletins for ITV', unpublished MA thesis, University of Keele, 1995.

9 Mike Walker, 'Panting for gossip? Just enquire within', *Guardian*, 27 May 1996.
10 Ray Snoddy, *The Good, the Bad and the Unacceptable* (London: Faber, 1992).
11 Press Complaints Commission, *Code of Conduct* (London: Press Complaints Commission, 1994).
12 Geoffrey Robertson quoted in Peak and Fisher, *Media Guide*, p. 24.
13 See Jeremy Tunstall, *The Media in Britain* (London: Constable, 1983).
14 Andrew Culf, 'Press counts the cost of outrage by Mirror', *Guardian*, 8 November 1993.
15 See David Banks, 'Put up or shut up', *UK Press Gazette*, 14 February 1993, p. 1 and Hugo Young, 'Privacy curbs would only be the half of it', *Guardian*, 11 November 1993.
16 Andrew Culf, 'Rivals press Mirror to rejoin Commission', *Guardian*, 10 November 1993.
17 Press Complaints Commission, *Annual Report 1995* (London: Press Complaints Commission, 1995).
18 Cited in Hugh Stephenson, *Media Freedom and Media Regulation* (London: Association of British Editors, 1994).
19 See Andrew Belsey and Ruth Chadwick, *Ethical Issues in Journalism and the Media* (London: Routledge, 1992).
20 Geoffrey Robertson 'Law for the press', in James Curran (ed.) *The British Press: A Manifesto* (London: Routledge, 1978).
21 Robertson, ibid.
22 David Calcutt, *Report of the Committee on Privacy and Other Matters*, Cmnd. 1102 (London: HMSO, 1990).
23 David Calcutt, *Review of Press Self-Regulation*, Cmnd. 2135 (London: HMSO, 1993).
24 Stephenson, *Media Freedom*, p. 12.
25 *Privacy and Media Intrusion: The Government's Response*, Cmnd. 2918 (London: HMSO, July 1995), p. 16.
26 Quoted in Alan Lee, *The Origins of the Popular Press in England 1855–1914* (London: Croom Helm, 1976), p. 23.
27 Piers Morgan, quoted in the *Guardian*, 17 October 1994.
28 Roy Greenslade, 'The Polly and Paul show', in the *Guardian*, 17 June 1996.
29 Walker, 'Panting for gossip?'.
30 For an account of how those involved in tragedies cope with the subsequent media reporting of that involvement see Anne Shearer, *Survivors and the Media* (London: Broadcasting Standards Council and John Libbey, 1992).
31 For details of this case see Greenslade, 'The Polly and Paul show'.
32 Seumas Milne, 'Wary of the Press Gang', *Guardian*, 22 January 1996.
33 Barbara Amiel, 'Publish and be damned by your cant Polly Toynbee', *Daily Telegraph*, 13 June 1996.
34 Geoffrey Robertson, 'Law for the press'.

10 Ethical photojournalism in the age of the electronic darkroom

Nigel Warburton

In the sceptical phase of his *Meditations*, René Descartes entertains the possibility that all his experiences might have been caused by the artifice of an evil demon: 'I will suppose that the heavens, the air, the earth, colours, shapes, sounds and all external things that we see are only illusions and deceptions which he uses to take me in.'[1] This evil demon manipulates Descartes's sensory inputs to give a convincing illusion of direct engagement with reality. Descartes gets the same sort of experiences he would have had had they been caused by engagement with reality; but it is all the work of the demon.

The evil demon finds its modern equivalent in the cynical photojournalist or picture editor who uses new electronic technology to manipulate what the viewer of a news photograph sees. Sophisticated computer technology which converts an image to pixels, each of which can be electronically controlled, allows almost anyone to manipulate photographs convincingly.[2] In a matter of minutes two photographs can be combined seamlessly to give the illusion that, for instance, John Major was rubbing shoulders with Tony Blair, when in fact they were standing on opposite sides of the room. Or, as actually occurred, two pyramids can be shunted electronically closer together in order to fit the portrait cover format of *National Geographic*[3]. Inconvenient details can be extracted without leaving any indication that they were ever there, and new details can be added from other photographs. In fashion photography it is now common practice for the photographs of models to be electronically altered: the pupils of their eyes are often enlarged, or their legs lengthened. We can't trust what we see in photographs any more.

Perhaps the only rational strategy in such circumstances is the Cartesian one of treating as false any belief acquired from looking at photographs, unless we can be absolutely certain that it is true. We have plenty of evidence that the demon-like picture editor is likely, on occasion, to deceive us. This casts doubt on the whole assumption of veracity which has traditionally been the starting-point of reputable photojournalism.

In newspaper and magazine journalism photography has traditionally played a major role, providing visual and memorable evidence for what the accompanying text described. War photography, for instance, illustrated more immediately than print ever could commonplace horrors and individual suffering. The Vietnam War lingers in many of our memories as a series of still photographs which provided evidence of particular events, but at the same time symbolised needless loss of life and cruelty. Malcolm Brown's image of a Buddhist monk's protest self-immolation, Eddie Adams's still of a police chief in Saigon executing a Vietcong officer with his pistol, and, of course, Huyn Cong Ut's unforgettable photograph of a naked girl, burnt by napalm, running towards the camera: these and other images had a profound effect on how that war was understood. But their effect depended upon their being reliable as documentary evidence for what they appeared to depict. Without the causal link back to a real event, these images would have been simply manufactured propaganda and would not have had the eyewitness status that they in fact did have. Readers of the magazines and newspapers in which they appeared quite reasonably took these to be photographs of real events, presenting in a legible way images of what actually happened. The convention of interpreting news photographs was based on trust: trust that the photographer wasn't duping picture editors about what his or her photographs really showed.

Now, in the age of the electronic darkroom, the informed viewer of a photograph should be sceptical about its origins, or perhaps even acknowledge that the old conventions of photography were based on an outdated cliché which we can no longer accept, that the camera never lies. In other words, from today photojournalism is dead. Theorists such as William J. Mitchell suggest that we have already moved into a post-photographic era.[4] It's just a matter of time before the newspaper-reading public catches on. Or so the story goes.

But this pessimistic view is mistaken. It is based on myths about the nature of photojournalism and the kinds of evidence it can provide, and about the kinds of evidence it has traditionally provided. The more optimistic line I want to take is that new technology should force photographers and picture editors to be far more aware of the moral implications of their practices.[5] Far from signalling the death of photojournalism, and particularly of ethical photojournalism, the electronic revolution could be the catalyst for its rejuvenation.

Is new photography different from old?

The claim that we are moving into a post-photographic era is based on the belief that electronic photography is fundamentally different from its optico-chemical forebears. With the new technology, so the argument goes, a new relationship between object, image and viewer is set up, and so the conventions surrounding photographic image production and reception must be transformed accordingly. The relevant features of new photography that distinguish it from old photography are:

(1) *Ease of manipulation*: Whilst the manipulation of photographs by means of cropping, dodging, burning in, composite printing and a whole range of darkroom procedures, has been possible for most of photography's history, the electronic darkroom facilitates such manipulation to an unprecedented degree. For instance, in order to produce a plausible photographic image of a footballer committing a handball offence in the penalty area, using as raw material a photograph of the same footballer with the ball at his feet, you would, if you used traditional optico-chemical methods, have to be a skilled photographic technician. Another way of producing a similar effect would be to use an airbrush; but, again, you would have to have quite a high level of skill to do this in a way that would be convincing. With computer-assisted manipulation of images, this sort of transformation of a photograph is relatively straightforward even for a novice. It could probably be done in a few minutes. One consequence of this is that virtually anyone with access to the appropriate machines can perform this sort of transformation.

(2) *Undetectability*: This has two aspects. First, the ways in which an image has been manipulated electronically can be undetectable. Seamless collage is a genuine possibility with the new media, whereas it was something less frequently achieved with the old. In the above example, no evidence of the original position of the ball would remain. Second, the electronic darkroom need not leave anything that you can go back to to check the accuracy of the print. Unlike the traditional forms of photography which, Polaroids and slides apart, left a negative as a touchstone against which subsequent manipulations of an image could be measured, video stills cameras need not leave any such objects. An edited picture file need not reveal that it has been edited, and the original can simply be deleted. Thus anyone attempting to demonstrate how an electronically produced photographic image has been manipulated has a difficult task.

(3) *Change from analogue to digital*: Traditional photographs are analogues of what they represent: every variation on the negative can in principle have a representational function. New photographs are digital, which means that they are genuinely reproducible, since the state of every pixel can be encoded. Perfect reproducibility is a new phenomenon for photography (even though at its inception old photography was hailed as intrinsically reproducible); however, it is not a relevant feature of photography for the present discussion.

(4) *Transmissibility*: New technology allows digitally produced images to be transmitted electronically without loss of quality. This has important implications for how photojournalists work, but is not relevant to the present discussion.

Of the four features of new photography outlined above, only the first and second, the ease and the undetectability of manipulation, are directly relevant to the issue of photographic truth. It should be noted that neither of these constitutes a difference in kind from traditional photography, only of degree. Everything that the new technology does in terms of manipulation has had its equivalent in pre-electronic photography. Skilful technicians have managed to produce equally undetectable images using traditional techniques. Besides which, most of the most successful deceptions using photography have been carried out outside the darkroom. Think of the case of the Cottingley Fairies which duped 'experts' for almost half a century,[6] or of Capa's 'Republican soldier at the very instant of his death', the authenticity of which has frequently been questioned, but never on the grounds of illicit photographic manipulation.[7] The new technology only speeds up what photojournalists could always do anyway: there is no relevant qualitative difference from this point of view between what the new electronic technologies can offer and what the optico-chemical ones always provided.

The ethics of news photography

So, the ethics of photojournalism in general is the real issue, not just of electronically based photojournalism. In order to address the central questions about the ethics of photojournalism, it is necessary to say something about photojournalistic conventions. Photography is clearly used in a wide variety of ways. Here I concentrate on news photography, and in particular on the use of photographs as evidence that an event took place. My concern is not with issues about the subject-matter of photographs, whether news photographers are insensitive, intrusive, irresponsible in their invasion of the private lives of public figures and so on. Rather I want to concentrate on the ethical questions about how they produce the images that they do, and whether or not they dupe viewers of those images about how they have been produced.

Imagine the following scenario. You pick up your morning tabloid on the way to work. On the front page is a photograph of a member of the royal family, a married princess no less, topless and in a compromising position with her bodyguard on a public beach. The picture is not in any way ambiguous. You can see who is involved and precisely what they are doing: no innocent explanation would be in the least bit plausible. The photograph is proof of what they did.

The photograph provides us with proof, or at least that is what we take for granted, because we have, consciously or unconsciously, acknowledged the conventions about how photographs are used accompanying news stories. We assume that the photograph really is a photograph of whoever the caption claims it is; we assume that what looks to be happening really was happening; we assume that the image before us is a photograph and not a skilfully executed painting, and so on. We might exercise a little healthy scepticism about how representative the depicted scene was of what was actually going on on the beach, but, as newspaper readers who have grown up with the conventions of photojournalism, we do not expect anything but a documentary photograph to accompany a news story. The photograph gives us convincing evidence of a special kind about what happened.

Now, consider how the image was made. The photographer climbed a tree with his camera and hung around for several hours until the couple emerged. He could scarcely believe what he was seeing through his tele-photo lens. He shot a roll of film, then sneaked off to have it developed, confident that he'd just made a year's salary in a few hours. To his dismay, a fault in the film meant that only half of the shots had come out; none of the more compromising ones were printable. But all was not lost; he scanned the photographs that had come out into his computer and within half an hour he had produced a composite picture showing more or less what he had seen through the telephoto lens. He felt justified in what he had done because he knew that the photograph was not misleading in any important way. He was committed to revealing the truth, and what better way to reveal the truth than with this striking image.

He sent the image electronically to the picture editor of his newspaper, who decided to make it the lead story. However, just to cover himself, the picture editor telephoned back to check that the photograph wasn't mis-leading. He asked the photographer whether it showed what really hap-pened; the photographer answered, honestly, that it did. So the photograph appeared on the front page of the newspaper the next day. None of the newspaper readers were aware of precisely how the photograph had been made, nor was the picture editor. They assumed that it was a straightfor-ward documentary photograph. Consequently they took it as incontrover-tible photographic evidence of the princess's misdemeanours.

Setting aside any issues of invasion of privacy, is there anything wrong with what the photographer did? The answer is surely yes. There are at least three reasons for this:

1 The image he sent down the wire to the newspaper wasn't *photographic evidence* for the action it seemed to show.
2 What the photographer did involved *deception* about how the image was made.
3 His deception took a step down a very *slippery slope* that could lead to the demise of news photography altogether.

We'll consider each of these reasons in turn.

Photographic evidence

Still photographs, because of reasonably direct and traceable causal links, can be good evidence for what they are indexically of (i.e. whatever was in front of the lens and left its trace on the light-sensitive film). Moving images tend to carry much more, and more accessible, information than still photographs; some aspects of most still photographs are ambiguous or indeterminate. But provided that you have external evidence about the conditions under which the photograph was taken, you may well be able to read off all kinds of information.

For instance, think of a photofinish in an Olympic 100 metres final; we can tell who crossed the line first, but only if we are confident that the camera angle is not misleading. We also have to know who was in which lane.[8] Aerial photographs can help us to construct maps if we know the height from which they were taken and possible distortions arising from weather conditions or other factors. X-rays and ultrasound images can give us a great deal of reliable information about the condition of bones, foetuses and internal organs, but they require specialist interpretation and are only usually produced in highly controlled conditions. And so on. The information in each case is there in virtue of such photographs being direct traces of their causes. We read information from these traces almost as if we were looking at the real things. Photographs picture their causes as well as being traces of them. But in some of the above cases appearances alone can be misleading, so we rely on other factual evidence from which we hypothesise the probable causes of the photographs' appearance.

However, most photojournalistic uses of photography differ significantly from the informational ones mentioned above. Typically the viewer does not have detailed information about the conditions under which photo-journalistic images were taken. Minimal information is usually carried in captions, accompanying text, or else is implied by the context of presentation. This point is well illustrated by a famous case in France. Robert Doisneau photographed a young woman in a café on the Rue de Seine drinking a glass of wine and sitting next to an older man. The photograph was used to illustrate the dangers of alcohol in a leaflet issued by the temperance league; it was then used to illustrate a story in the magazine *Le Point*, where it appeared with the caption 'Prostitution on the Champs-Elysées'.[9] In both uses, the photograph looked right: there were no incongruous details which undermined the interpretation suggested by the caption. However, in both cases the captions misled: neither of the people photographed was an alcoholic, and neither of them a prostitute. However, viewers of the photograph in these contexts would not have been able to read off these facts from the image itself.

Photojournalistic images have meaning in virtue of three interrelated aspects:

1 what they are of, in the sense of what caused them;
2 what they look to be of;
3 how they are used in a particular context.

The legibility of documentary photography depends on a relation of trust with the photographer or picture editor; in the case of news photography the viewer trusts that he or she is not being misled about the way the image was produced and what it appears to depict. The context of presentation communicates directly (through captions, accompanying stories, etc.) and indirectly (through implicit conventions) a way of interpreting the image. In most cases there is nothing within the photograph which will inform the viewer whether or not the photograph is of what the context of presentation suggests that it is. For example, as I suggested in relation to the Capa photograph of a Republican soldier, external evidence is needed to confirm our interpretation of it as of a Republican soldier at the very instant of his death and not, as has been claimed, of a Republican soldier stumbling in training. So we rely on the sincerity of the presenter and on any external evidence we might happen to have.

In the imaginary case of the photographs of the princess, the image that the photographer used wasn't direct evidence of the event. His wasn't an informational photograph about the event depicted (though if you knew enough about how he actually made the photograph you would no doubt be able to read off many factual details from the direct evidence which the image carries). Nor, however, was it a documentary photograph of the event, since the event did not play the appropriate and implied causal role in the image's construction. Its value as evidence for that event was on a par with an artist's sketch made partly from memory. It was a *pictorial* photograph of that event masquerading as a documentary one:[10] in fact it was a deliberately deceptive quasi-documentary photograph.

Deception

What is most disturbing in such cases is that the viewer is deceived – not deceived about what went on between the princess and the bodyguard, but deceived about how the photograph was made, and so about the kind of evidence being presented. The context of presentation on the news pages of a newspaper implicitly communicates to the viewer that the conventions of documentary news photography have been adhered to. But in fact they haven't. A set of conventions has grown up about photographic communication of news. Roughly, readers of daily newspapers expect that the photographs used alongside news stories are not just photographic illustrations, not simply pictorial interpretations of events, but are reasonably direct traces of what they depict. In other words, if a photograph of a princess and her bodyguard is presented as part of a news story, then the readers will quite naturally assume that they are being presented with a documentary photograph, one which was produced by taking a photograph of the couple in question while they were doing what they appear to be doing in the photograph. Clearly many photographs have the potential to be misleading about what was going on, so it is part of the picture editor's job to select images which are as unambiguous as possible, and at least not misleading on substantial issues. If you present a documentary photograph of a particular princess performing a particular act, then her performing that act must have played a direct causal role in the production of the photograph; if you got a look-alike to enact what had happened and photographed that, it could only serve as a photographic illustration of what happened.

Presenting photographic illustrations is acceptable, provided that you make clear from the context, or explicit in the caption that that is what you are doing. The effect of seeing a photograph apparently of a Second World War bomber crash-landed on the moon is, for most people, disbelief. The front page headline for the *Sunday Sport* on 24 April 1988 was 'World War 2 Bomber Found on Moon', but the headline was no more credible than the photograph accompanying it. This would have been so even if the photograph hadn't appeared on the front page of the *Sunday Sport*, but on the front page of, say, *The Independent*. The photograph reveals itself as pictorial because of the nature of the event it depicts as having actually occurred. It is largely irrelevant as to how the image was produced, whether by composite printing using conventional optico-chemical methods, or by electronic, digitally-based procedures. However, a front page photograph of the princess and the bodyguard would carry different expectations wherever it was published: the photograph depicts an event which could plausibly have taken place. This is the kind of news story deception that we should be concerned about: a form of lying by implication about the kind of visual evidence being presented.

The photojournalist in my example deliberately deceived the picture editor and thus the public about the nature of the photograph. What seems to be documentary evidence, is really just an illustration of the event it purports to reveal. It is a quasi-documentary photocollage. 'So what?', the photojournalist might say, 'I've laid bare a more important truth. What I've done is the equivalent to a white lie. A small lie to communicate a more important truth.'

His point is that the photograph may not be in a direct optico-chemical causal link back to the situation it depicts. Nevertheless it does actually convey what did in fact happen. The precise details of posture and nuance may be missing; but they would equally be missing from an eyewitness's testimony of the event, since the photographer did everything in his power to recreate the frame that he had expected to find on his reel of film when it was developed. The photograph communicated the important truth about the events, and that, surely, is what really matters in such cases.

Furthermore, parts of the photograph do have direct causal links to the situation depicted; no actors were involved, for instance, so there is fairly direct evidence about what the two were wearing, their hairstyles, and so on. In other words, parts of the photograph do carry the traditional sorts of photographic evidence. So there are some direct and some indirect causal links back to the depicted people and events, and the truth of what did happen is conveyed in a manner which remains, in all but minor incidental details, true to what took place.

Besides, it seems unreasonable to demand more than this, since in print journalism a certain amount of tidying up of quoted speech is tolerated and even encouraged. For instance, if a hesitant speaker included many 'ums' and 'ers' in his press briefing, no one would be likely to challenge a printed quotation that omitted these. What is important in print journalism is that the content of what was said is not distorted by the process of tidying it up. Newspaper readers don't usually want to read verbatim transcripts of speeches, but rather edited versions of them. Why then worry about whether a photograph presents direct evidence of what it depicts just so long as what it depicts did actually occur?

This sort of response rests on a misunderstanding of the conventions surrounding the use of news photographs and of the consequences of changing those conventions. These conventions include the toleration of minor deceptions in order to produce a legible image; it is usually acceptable to adjust contrasts, to 'burn in' important details and to crop out extraneous details. However, these conventions do not tolerate any manoeuvre which distorts the viewer's appreciation of the relationship between the photograph and its main subject. It is a matter of professional integrity for photojournalists to abide by these conventions. The role responsibilities of the photojournalist must surely include not deceiving the public about how your images were made. In my imaginary case of the princess, the bodyguard and the news photographer, it is not the fact that the photographer used electronic wizardry to produce the effect that makes it unacceptable; it is the fact that the photographer disguised the nature of the causal relationship between what happened and the photograph.

Quite apart from issues of personal and professional integrity, every case in which a deception like this is allowed into print (and subsequently exposed for what it is) serves to undermine the public's trust that the implicit conventions of photojournalism are generally being adhered to. This sort of point has frequently been made about lying in general. For example, it is the line taken by the philosopher G. J. Warnock:

> It is, one might say, not the implanting of false beliefs that is damaging, but rather the generation of the suspicion that they may be being implanted. For this undermines trust; and to the extent that trust is undermined, all co-operative undertakings in which what one person can do or has reason to do is dependent on what others have done, are doing, or are going to do, must tend to break down.[11]

In other words, what is wrong with lying is not that it tends to result in people acquiring false beliefs, but that it destroys the trust that is necessary for most co-operation and communication. Applying this sort of point to news photography we get the conclusion that what is wrong with what the photographer did in my example is that he contributed to the undermining of trust and thus of the possibility of photographic communication. If trust were substantially undermined in this area, there would no longer be any point in sending photographers out to take news photographs. Provide them instead with access to a picture library and a computer and they will be able to come up with plausible-looking illustrations of whatever story print journalists care to write up.

Slippery slope?

Toleration of minor deceptions for the sake of truth is the first step down a slippery slope towards general deception with total disregard for the truth. If you allow people to manipulate photographs without informing their viewers, then you will soon find yourself allowing photographers to invent reality. The force of this, like most slippery slope arguments, depends on whether or not you believe it is possible to arrest the descent and say 'Here and no further'. However, in most situations in which slippery slope arguments are used it is relatively easy to say how far down the slope we have already travelled. In the case of photographic deceptions, however, because they can be so difficult to detect, it is not easy to say on what kind of scale and to what degree such deceptions are currently being perpetrated. This in itself provides a reason for discouraging even minor sorties on to the slope.

Why have the conventions at all?

But why do we have a convention of presenting photographs which picture their causes in a legible way? Why not simply choose the best illustrations for news stories. In other words, what, if anything, is wrong with setting up a plausible tableau vivant and photographing it? What, if anything, is wrong with producing a composite picture by electronic means and publishing it on the front page of a newspaper? Both methods would serve to communicate a fact visually.

There are two principal reasons for preferring documentary photographs to pictorial ones in the context of news reporting. One is related to their status as evidence; the other to the psychology of looking at photographs.

Documentary photographs as evidence

Documentary photographs are themselves evidence, whereas pictorial ones are not themselves evidence; they are like implanted 'memories' which, even if their content happens to be true, are not genuine memories, no matter how realistic they seem to us. News photographs contain all sorts of information which wasn't consciously chosen by the photographer. However, one possible response to this point is that most of this information is inaccessible to the average viewer, requiring as it does a great deal of background information to interpret it. This suggests that there is more to documentary news photography than evidence alone. One additional aspect of news photography is the way that particular depicted events can take on a universal meaning, or at least the part can imply the whole in a kind of visual synecdoche. But this would still be possible if news photography were entirely pictorial. The further aspect of news photography that I believe is essential to understanding the impact of a documentary as opposed to a pictorial image is a feature of the psychology of looking at pictures that we know to be traces of what they depict.

The psychology of looking at relics

Because documentary photographs are traces as well as depictions, they have a reasonably direct causal contact with what they are of and this gives them the status of relics. This is equivalent to the effect of seeing the very shirt that Nelson wore at the battle of Trafalgar rather than a visually indistinguishable one. News photographs are relics of what has happened: events have left their trace on the world, albeit under the direction of a photojournalist. It is just a fact about human psychology that knowledge of such a direct link to events can have a profound effect on the viewer of news photographs. It's not just that the photographs seem to be declaring 'this happened', but rather that they give us the sense of being there when it did happen, and this not simply because of accuracy of detail.

Given the choice, most of us would prefer to have contact with the real world rather than a perceptually indistinguishable one produced by some evil scientist with a virtual reality machine. As Robert Nozick has put it:

> plugging into an experience machine limits us to a manmade reality, to a world no deeper or more important than that which people can construct. There is no *actual* contact with any deeper reality, though the experience of it can be simulated. Many persons desire to leave themselves open to such contact and to a plumbing of deeper significance.[12]

A benefit of contact with reality and not an imaginary version of what someone else takes reality to be is suggested by Harold Evans's remarks made in the context of discussing photographs after Auschwitz had been liberated:

> It is one of the central contributions of photojournalism that it goes beyond the limits of imagination. It makes the unbelievable believable.[13]

In exceptional cases news photography can make us realise the limits of our imagination. Some events are simply beyond our conception until we have seen photographs of them. This is not, of course, to say that the relation between a photograph and what it shows us is an unproblematic one: photographs aren't simply windows on to the past.[14] But they can carry a distinctive kind of evidence, and they can put us into a closer relationship with their subject-matter than any other kind of still picture; and this is why the conventions of documentary news photography are worth preserving even in the age of the electronic darkroom.[15]

Notes

1 René Descartes, *Discourse on Method and the Meditations*, trans. F. E. Sutcliffe (Harmondsworth: Penguin Books, 1968), p. 100.
2 For a useful bibliography on the subject of digital photography, see *History of Photography* 20 (1996), pp. 336–8.
3 For details of this case and others like it, see Fred Ritchin, *In Our Own Image* (New York: Aperture, 1990).
4 See, for instance, the subtitle of his book *The Reconfigured Eye* (Cambridge, MA: MIT Press, 1992): *Visual Truth in the Post-photographic Era*.
5 For a discussion of Susan Sontag's claim that photographs can't communicate moral knowledge, see Nigel Warburton, 'Photographic communication', *British Journal of Aesthetics* 28 (1988), pp. 173–81.
6 For a detailed and completely convincing account of how these photographs were produced and how so many people were taken in by them, see the series of articles by Geoffrey Crawley in the *British Journal of Photography*, from 24 December 1982 to 8 April 1983.
7 For a discussion of the philosophical implications of this photograph see Nigel Warburton, 'Varieties of photographic representation', *History of Photography* 15 (1991), pp. 203–10.
8 Joel Snyder and Neil Walsh Allen discuss the sort of evidence provided by the photofinish in their important article 'Photography, vision and representation', *Critical Inquiry* 2 (1975), pp. 143–69.
9 This case is described in Gisèle Freund, *Photography and Society* (London: Gordon Fraser, 1980), pp. 178–9.
10 For a discussion of the distinction between documentary and pictorial uses of photography see Warburton, 'Varieties of photographic representation'.
11 G. J. Warnock, quoted in Sissela Bok, *Lying: Moral Choice in Public and Private Life* (Brighton: Harvester, 1978), p. 287.
12 Robert Nozick, *Anarchy, State and Utopia* (Oxford: Blackwell Publishers, 1974), p. 43.
13 Harold Evans, *Eyewitness: 25 Years Through World Press Photos* (London: Quiller Press, 1981), p. 8.
14 For an attempt to show that we can quite literally see through photographs to what they are of, see Kendall Walton, 'Transparent pictures: on the nature of photographic realism', *Critical Inquiry* 11 (1984), pp. 246–77. For a critique of this view, see Nigel Warburton, 'Seeing through "Seeing through" photographs', *Ratio* NS 1/1 (1988), pp. 64–74.
15 I am very grateful for Matthew Kieran's comments on an earlier version of this essay.

11 Is the medium a (moral) message?

Noël Carroll

Introduction

The question to be addressed in this essay concerns the moral significance of the television medium. By 'medium' here I am not referring to television as a business that churns out countless stories. Rather, I am referring specifically to the historically standard image, especially in regard to fiction, and to the ways in which it is typically elaborated by structures like editing, camera movement, narrative forms, and the like. Moreover, I will be concerned with the moral status of the television image as such, irrespective of what it is an image of.

Though the distinction between form and content may be historically outmoded and ultimately unsatisfactory, perhaps I can at least provisionally demarcate my domain of interest by initially adopting the distinction and by saying that this is an essay about the putative moral significance of television from the viewpoint of some of its typical formal features – or, at least, from the viewpoint of a number of its formal features that are alleged to be typical.

Furthermore, throughout this essay, I shall be primarily interested with charges that, in some way or other, the relevant television forms are morally suspect – that they have moral implications or consequences that should be ethically worrisome. I dwell on the negative perspective of the medium, rather than on perspectives that see it as positive or beneficial, since negative prognostications represent the dominant tradition; most commentators prefer to scorn television rather than praise it.

I suppose that there can be little debate about whether television has some moral consequences, though there is certainly a legitimate disagreement about how extensive these are. On the positive side, there is evidence indicating that people can learn about alternative lifestyles from televison and that this can bring ethically significant changes in their everyday existence. People from Third World cultures can learn about ways of life in the First World and women can learn about male culture, and this exposure can encourage them to alter their lives. It is said that access through television to western ways of life contributed to the dissatisfaction and subsequent political resistance on the part of the citizens of the former Soviet empire. Likewise, a case can be made out that at least *sometimes* television befouls the moral atmosphere, perhaps by reinforcing oppressive social views. Obviously, certain programmes may traffic in outright propaganda and thereby stoke the flames of racism.

Such consequences as these, if and where they obtain, however, appear to be more a matter of the content of certain programming rather than the result of the historically typical forms of the medium. But the question before us is whether these historically typical forms of television – like the image – are morally significant. Specifically, are they inherently morally suspect?

Why would anyone think that they might be? Maybe one consideration has to do with the inordinate amount of time that the average viewer is said to spend watching the screen. These estimates seem to rise every year. One is often left with the impression that one's fellow citizens spend almost as much time watching television as they spend working and sleeping. Surely, the argument might go, it is reasonable to assume that if so much time is spent doing this, it must have some influence. Moreover, it also seems not implausible to assume – at least as a bit of armchair psychology – that part of that influence must be a result of the mode of presentation. For example, we often hear that the structure of programming has shrunk the audience's attention span, thus incurring a cognitive deficit. Analogously, one might conjecture that comparable moral deficits are also probable. Again, this hypothesis might be thought to be compelling just because television takes up such a large proportion of everyday life in the industrial world.

A second line of support for the view that the medium is morally significant might originate in the McLuhanite mantra that the medium is the message. That is, McLuhan urged a generation of researchers to look for the significance of television not at the level of its manifest content – its soaps and game shows – but at the level of its latent structure. McLuhan, himself, found a morally salutary message there: the prophecy of neo-tribalism and the global village. But since after half a century of television the world seems to many no better and perhaps worse, those who are convinced by McLuhan's mantra may begin to worry that the medium's message is far from wholesome. This is probably abetted by indulging the *post hoc, propter hoc* fallacy: since things have supposedly deteriorated morally to such a striking degree since the advent of television, it must be due, at least in part, to its emergence as a major medium of communication.

Of course, these suspicions are rather broad. The historically standard medium *might* have moral repercussions. Anything might. But before we become morally alarmed about these prospects, we want to be reassured that we are confronted by more than abstract possibilities; we want to have grounds for believing that some unsavoury moral possibilities are actually realised by existing television as we know it. This places a certain burden of proof on the critic. He or she must come up with some plausible compromising effect of the medium that is reasonably traceable to the traditional television formats (in the way that reduced attention spans at least *seem* to be a possible outcome of abbreviated televisual forms like advertisements, music videos and the rushed segmentation of game shows, headline news programmes, sit-coms and the like).

Another way to put this is that before we start being concerned that the medium carries untoward moral consequences, we will want to hear some concrete hypotheses about its likely immoral effects in conjunction with explanations of those features that are apt to bring these effects about. That is, we expect the critic to specify some mechanism that accords plausibly with an appropriate description of the medium and also seems of the kind likely to have unhappy consequences or implications for the moral life of viewers.

In this essay, I will consider three such hypotheses about such conjunctions of effects and mechanisms: what I call realism, escapism and hypnotism respectively. Though I believe that the tendency to resort to mechanisms like these is frequent in critical discourse about television, I also concede that my characterisations of them are ideal types. Television criticism is often quite fragmentary and elliptical, leaving many of its underlying premises unstated and unarticulated. What I will attempt to do is to give theoretical body to many of the intuitions that appear to be presupposed in some of the more frequently recurring diatribes against the medium. Thus, what follows is a rational reconstruction in theoretical form of what I take to be several of the leading anxieties about television's moral status.

However, since I intend to question each of these arguments against television, it might be objected that by 'rationally reconstructing' these viewpoints in order to confute them, what I am really doing is rigging the game from the start, assembling straw men for the purposes of igniting them. Against this, I would not only respond that these straw men are composed of real straws, gathered from the existing literature, but also that if there are better arguments than the ones constructed by either previous critics or me, then the burden of putting them forward now falls to the aspiring moralist.

The arguments about the degraded moral status of television that I am about to review – realism, escapism and hypnotism – are not peculiar to this medium. Some details derive from long-standing debates about popular art and media, especially visual media. Some elements in these arguments hark back to Plato and they have surfaced again and again in attacks on movies, comics, pulp literature, music and so on. In many cases, the recurring arguments against television seem to be a matter of far from new wine in very old bottles. This, of course, is to be expected, given the incremental evolution of culture, its tendency to accommodate the present by grafting it to elements of the past. But, if anything, this should lend more credence to my reconstructions of the arguments against television, since the gaps in those arguments can be so readily filled, in as much as they rely heavily on beliefs already abroad in the ongoing discussion of popular entertainment in culture.

Realism

The standard television image is pictorial – a close-up of Johnny Carson's face or a long shot of Deep Space-Nine. Pictures, moreover, are processed by the same visual capacities that we use in everyday life. Arguably we use pretty much the same perceptual processes to recognise typical pictures that we use to recognise their referents in, so to speak, 'nature'. Picture recognition may, in fact, be a hardwired perceptual capacity. This, in turn, may provide part of the explanation of how television can be so accessible to such wide numbers of people, since the basic images in its system of communication are things that nearly everyone has access to in virtue of their innate perceptual capacities.

Of course, even if we prefer to speak of codes or conventions of perception rather than of hardwired recognitional capacities, we may still agree that the so-called perceptual codes used with respect to pictures, on the one hand, and with respect to the world, on the other hand, are pretty closely related. It is in this regard that the television image (as standardly used) is realistic: the visual codes or recognitional capacities that we use to navigate its images are the same or pretty much the same as the ones that we use to navigate everyday life.

It didn't have to be this way. The early technologies that gave rise to television were developed in order to broadcast words and sentences – such as financial news – over great distances, such as oceans. Had its evolution continued under that programme, if it had become an art, then it would have been more in the tradition of the novel; it might have been a delivery system for novels rather than in the tradition of the theatre and film.

But that is not how things happened. And, as a result, the standard small-screen image is realistic in the sense that it is normally processed in much the same way that we view ordinary objects, as opposed, say, to the way that we read words. The medium trades in visual appearances and those visual appearances trigger perceptual processes akin to those triggered by their real-world referents.

The association of television as we know it with realism is also bolstered by its relation to camera technology. Television stands in the cultural lineage of photography and film; indeed much of its material is initially generated by means of cinematography. Moreover, such camera technologies are associated with recording – both historically, given some of the original purposes of photography, and formally, since whether made on film or video, television imagery is standardly a record of events in the world, even when the event is people acting out a drama or fiction. The relation of television to recording, then, supplies further grounds, though different grounds, for calling its image realistic, since it typically derives from reality, a reality that includes the acting out of scenes later to be taken as fictional.

According to Plato, picturing involves little more than holding up a mirror to nature. It deals in visual appearances (and, for Plato, for this very reason, picturing is epistemically defective when compared to the knowledge available from contemplating the Forms). Whether or not painters ever proceeded in such a mechanical manner, certain views of the television image are that it is little more than an affair of mirrors, mechanically or electronically recording, it might be said, the appearance of real things in such a way that our ordinary, low-level object-recognitional capacities are activated or triggered.

If we regard television realism in this way – as engaging ordinary, everyday perceptual capacities through processes that, in part, involve recording – the idea seems at least credible. However, critics believe that along with this variety of perceptual realism comes another effect, which we may call the naturalisation effect. Through realism of the previous sort – through verisimilitudinous appearances and recording – the image imbues whatever it presents with the aura of being natural, that is, of being a representation of the way things (really) are (and must be).

Realistic imagery in our previous sense, in other words, is said to carry a certain rhetorical force, namely it leaves the impression that what it depicts is the case. Perceptual realism tends to convince viewers, in some sense, of the veracity of what they are seeing. Thus, if television imagery presents racial stereotypes via perceptually realistic imagery, viewers, it is thought, will be disposed to accept those stereotypes as true representations, for example, of the behaviour of black people.

Images that proceed by means of perceptual realism, it is claimed, have a spillover effect that inclines viewers to greet them as, to speak loosely, representations of the way things are. Images of black men as confidence artists, lay-abouts and rascals, that is, are thought to confirm, by dint of their perceptual realism, that this is the way these kinds of people actually behave.

Furthermore, this spillover effect is supposed to be even stronger than I have thus far indicated. The thesis has a powerfully deterministic flavour, connoting not merely that what is depicted realistically is somehow the case, but also that it must be the case; that the relevant modality is not just actuality, but some kind of necessity. For example, repeated realistic representations of nuclear families in television sitcoms – from *The Dick Van Dyke Show* to *Roseanne* – not only are thought to imply that the nuclear family *is* the basic social unit, but that it *must* be – that this is a fact of human nature, that it is natural.

Hence the naturalisation effect ultimately is thought to engender in viewers convictions about the inevitability of existing social relations. This effect is particularly relevant for morality, since if it indeed obtains, then it would blinker the moral horizons of viewers. It would obstruct their recognition of alternatives to existing social arrangements. This causes especial alarm for moral reformers who, for example, oppose the notion that only heterosexual marriage is natural and so oppose any sort of representation that precludes the possibility of other sexual relationships. Thus, the putative naturalisation effect is of particular interest to reformers who worry that it is used in a way that inclines ordinary viewers toward complacency about existing immoral and unjust social relationships.

By means of perceptual realism, the television image is thought to lend credibility to various immoral and oppressive social relations. Ethnic, racial, sexist and heterosexist stereotypes are presented and naturalised as are all manner of other relations, such as: those between employer and employees; between the police, the criminal class, and law-abiding citizens; between doctors, nurses, and patients; lawyers, judges and clients; parents and children; and so on. Perceptual realism supposedly suggests to the audience that these relations are not only the way things are, but the way that things must be – that father indeed inevitably knows best (or, if not, mother does).

Moreover, if ought implies can, then the television world limits the viewer's conception of what is morally possible to whatever is endorsed by the putative rhetoric of perceptual realism. That is, if the spillover effects of perceptual realism suggest that things cannot be otherwise, then the image short-circuits moral reflection about the types of social and interpersonal relations it depicts.

Furthermore, if the hypothesis about the naturalisation effect is coupled with certain observations about recurring portrayals of social relations on television, then the medium as we know it presents a clear and present moral danger. For its 'world' is generally at great variance with the real world. There is far more violence there, more doctors, fewer poor people, a disproportionately large number of white males, and so on. Thus, the 'world' that television offers viewers in a perceptually realistic way is a distortion of society. Implicitly, it is a prescription masquerading – in the cloak of perceptual realism – as a description. Consequently, if some correlative, naturalising, spillover effect disposes audiences to view the 'television world' as the way that things must be, then the spectators' parameters for moral evaluation will be effectively undermined. Therefore, the television image as such comes to be regarded as morally problematic.

This hypothesis proposes both an effect – that the image inclines viewers to the conviction that things (especially social relations) cannot be otherwise, and a mechanism – naturalisation via perceptual realism. Both these postulations seem dubious. Let us look at the effect first.

Is it plausible to suppose that television disposes viewers to believe that things cannot be otherwise, specifically that they cannot be improved morally? This seems hardly likely as a generalisation about all television, since much of it is of a strongly reformist bent. Many movies made especially for it, for example, are 'problem films', presenting issues like racism, child abuse, wife-battering, AIDS and so on for the express purpose of convincing audiences that the relevant social ills can and should be remedied. I have little reason to disbelieve that these efforts are sometimes effective in moving some audiences morally. Therefore, it cannot be the case that by deploying perceptual realism, television cannot propose that things can be otherwise in morally significant ways.

Moreover, researchers in the area called cultural studies regard television as a site of resistance, by which they mean that viewers contest many of the implications of the programmes. For example, Native Americans may cheer when white settlers are massacred; they do not docilely accept the inevitability of white imperialism. Perhaps people in cultural studies exaggerate the amount of resistance that is abroad with respect to people's viewing. But they have established that there is some resistance and that is enough to call into question the hypothesis that the so-called naturalisation effect automatically reduces viewers to moral inertia.

Of course, one always wonders about the theoretical grounds for postulating the naturalisation effect. Supposedly perceptual realism gives rise to certain spillover effects: the impression that what is represented is how things are and, in consequence, how they must be. The first step in this deduction appears to ride on an equivocation.

Realism as a style, it might be said, implies a commitment to representing how things are; thus audiences take realistic representations that way. But *perceptual realism* is not realism in this sense. It is committed only to presenting things in such a way as to activate ordinary visual processes, specifically recognitional capacities. It carries no commitment to representing the world, especially the social world, accurately. This should be obvious, since it is, in principle, compatible with fiction. The audience realises that perceptual realism is not, in principle, committed to an accurate representation of the world. They know that Amos and Andy are not existing persons. So why suppose that viewers take perceptually realistic television images to show how things really are?

At this point, it might be said that it is not particulars that audiences take to be real, but rather certain social types and situation types. Audiences know that Andy and Amos do not exist, but perceptual realism convinces them that types, such as the ones portrayed by Amos and Andy, are accurate. But, even if we are not Platonists, the question remains as to why perceptual realism would have any special relation to shaping viewers' conceptions of types, since its domain is generally particulars: individual persons, actions, objects and events. What is the psychological mechanism that gets us from the appearance of particulars in whose existence we do not believe to types whose accuracy we accept?

If the connection between perceptual realism and the conviction that 'this is how things are' is doubtful, then the connection with the impression that 'this is how things must be' seems even more strained. Why should perceptual realism lend an aura of fatalistic determinism to what is represented? The application of our standing perceptual processes to events in the world does not come in concert with fatalism; when I see that my den is in a mess up, I do not surmise that it cannot be otherwise (or if I do, my wife doesn't). So why should the operation of our normal perceptual processes while watching television leave us convinced that things cannot be changed?

If the answer here is that it is not perceptual realism that secures this effect, but narrative structure, then we shall need to point out that television narratives often herald social change in morally beneficial directions. That is, many such narratives behave in a way opposite to that which proponents of the naturalisation effect predict.

Thus I conclude that anxieties about the moral status of the television image as such, which are based on the perceptual realism of the medium, are woefully ill-founded.

Escapism

One of the most frequent charges against television in the name of morality is that it is escapist. This charge is problematic at first blush because so many things can be meant by it, not all of which are bad. For example, if 'to escape' merely means to change one activity for another activity, which other activity may be rewarding (say, listening intently to classical music), then no necessary opprobrium should attach to the term. However, when television is called 'escapist' critics have something pejorative in mind.

One thing that might be labelled 'escapist' in the pejorative sense could be a tendency to do one thing when one should be doing something else. Shirking one's responsibilities and watching television instead would be escapist in this sense. This notion of escapism would appear to be in play when one is chided for spending too much time in front of the screen rather than improving oneself or undertaking political activity. But here the wrongness would appear to attach to one's avoidance behaviour and not to the medium itself, since it would be equally escapist in this sense to start working when one was supposed to be visiting a sick relative whom, perhaps, one dislikes. Thus when the label 'escapist' is used the critic must be referring to something else.

Perhaps it is this: escapism in this context has to do with the tendency to indulge in fantasy. Television, then, it is alleged, has something to do with inducing fantasy, where fantasy itself is regarded as morally disreputable. If this is what critics are arguing, then we need to know both what might be disreputable about fantasy and how it is that television, in particular, encourages it.

But what could be wrong with fantasising itself, especially where it is not the case that we are fantasising when we should be doing something else? One idea might be that fantasy involves decoupling our emotional responses from action. When we fantasise events – when we daydream – we undergo various emotional states, but these are divorced from action. We savour our indignation over various injustices around us, but we need not act; daydreaming disconnects affect from responsibility. This might be thought to be fraught with potential moral dangers, including: that by emoting indignation in our imagination, we deceive ourselves into thinking we have met the demands of morality; that we come to prefer emoting for the fantasised objects over real-world ones (for imagined poor people rather than real ones); that we come to prefer emoting over acting (putting watching television over community service).

But even if these specific problems are merely abuses that *might* arise from fantasy, it may still be argued that the bottom line is that it is of the nature of the structure of fantasy – its contents notwithstanding – to disconnect emotion and action. And this, it might be thought, is always a perversion of the normal function of our psychological system. Just as masturbation is alleged to pervert the sexual function, fantasy might be said to be a perversion of the emotion–action system. Detaching affect from action endangers the smooth functioning of the system; perhaps it makes us more likely not to respond to certain real-world events, just because we have accustomed ourselves to emoting without acting in our fantasy life. Thus, in so far as fantasy erodes or is likely to erode the linkage between emotion and action, and the linkage between emotion and action is essential for moral behaviour, fantasy as such – no matter what its contents are – is ethically suspect because it tampers with the conditions for moral activity. It leaves us satisfied with feeling the emotion without acting on it.

Moreover, it may be alleged that television is especially conducive to fantasy. That is, it encourages fantasy in a non-accidental way. Just as narcotics abet pure affective reveries divorced from action, so too does television. This is not simply a matter of people in certain circumstances turning to television when they should be otherwise engaged. The point about fantasy-encouragement is that it is supposed to be common to all television viewing, whatever the circumstances. It is about the medium as such and its inherent escapist proclivities. Moreover, this argument can be made without reference to any particular fantasy contents, such as the alluring (perhaps compensatory) imagery of wealth, sex and power. For the charge is that the medium itself encourages fantasy and fantasy as such is morally dubious.

But what is it about the medium that makes it complicit with fantasy? Here it may be argued that the its images are illusionistic. Their compelling perceptual realism cause us involuntarily to suspend our disbelief about the existence of a creature such as the 'primate worm' in the *X-Files* episode entitled 'The Host', and, as a result, we experience the thrill of fear without the impulse either to flee or to fight. Likewise we feel outrage at the treatment of children in a television movie such as *Miss Evers' Boys*, but we don't have to do anything about it. Moreover, this process is based on a deception: our acceptance of a false belief, i.e. that the illusion before us is a real, occurring event – thereby adding lying to the moral harm involved in this characterisation of escapism.

Illusion, then, is the mechanism that enables the television image to promote fantasy, where fantasy itself is an escapist tendency in the morally pejorative sense. Since Plato, there has been a disapproving correlation of the visual and the emotional, though in the present argument it is not the emotions themselves that are subject to moral criticism, but rather the condition of undergoing (and enjoying) emotions divorced from action and the responsibility to act. Television activates the emotions illusionistically, but in a way so as to function as a kind of electronic prosthetic fantasy – prosthetic in the sense that it does our imaging for us, but still a fantasy, since it requires no action on our part.

Television, then, is escapist because it encourages fantasy – an escape from the burden of action by its very nature – and it encourages fantasy through its deceptive or illusionistic imagery. But this argument seems flawed on two counts: both in its suspicion of fantasy and in its conception of the image as illusionistic.

The suspicion of fantasy seems to be based upon too narrow a conception of the psychology of the emotions. The emotions are typically connected to action and the linkage between the emotions and action is crucial to moral behaviour. However, this does not entail that entertaining emotions without acting is a perversion of human nature. The human capacity to undergo emotional states without the necessity to act is highly adaptive and, indeed, can make for more effective future action.

That children can be frightened by descriptions of counterfactual circumstances of danger prepares them for future predicaments. That we can envision future activities and undergo emotional responses with respect to our imaginings gives us information of what it would be like to do such and such, and, thereby, helps in making practical, and moral, decisions. Our capacity to emote without acting also enables us to simulate conspecifics and, in consequence, to modulate our responses to them, morally as well as prudentially. In all these cases, and many others, the capacity to decouple emotions and actions is an advantage to human psychology overall, not a perversion, and it is often relevant to, rather than disruptive of, moral behaviour.

Thus, where 'escapist' is opposed to 'adaptive', the bare faculty of fantasy is not necessarily escapist, nor is it necessarily alien to the moral life, since the capacity to imagine emotively without acting is at least relevant to deliberating morally about our own future actions; to learning to size up counterfactual situations, including morally significant ones, that may one day become factual; and for gathering information, including morally pertinent information, about others both in terms of what they are feeling and what they are likely to do. Thus there is nothing morally wrong with fantasy in principle, but only with specific fantasies.

Similarly, if there is any special connection between television and fantasy, there would be no problem then apart from the specific fantasies – abetted by specific programmes and their content – in question. And even if there is no special connection, but only a connection that television shares with other media, there is also no call to presuppose that everything it encourages us to imagine emotively is morally compromised. Indeed, if fantasy – imagining emotively – can be serviceable in moral living in general, then there are no grounds to think that television as prosthetic imagining can't be serviceable too. Perhaps responding emotionally to fictions depicting racism and sexism can prepare us to focus in emotionally appropriate ways on comparable real-world occurrences of racism and sexism.

Of course, there is also something wrong with the story rehearsed earlier about illusionism. Supposedly, the television image is an illusion which leads us to suspend our disbelief about whatever is represented. This makes it possible for us to respond emotionally, since it is supposed that an emotion requires belief, and the suspension of disbelief puts us in the requisite condition: it leaves us believing what we are seeing.

However, one wonders whether there aren't at least two steps too many in this scenario. For if emotions can be generated by imaginings – thoughts entertained in the mind but as unasserted with respect to truth – and if perceptual realism alone, without any supposition of illusion, can provide the grounds for imagining (for example, that Miss Evers' boys are being treated unjustly), then we can dispense with talk about both illusion and the suspension of disbelief at a stroke. And this would be all to the good anyway, since both ideas appear to suggest that viewers believe what they see before them, leaving it a mystery, then, why they don't match their emotions with actions.

Thus, the view that television is escapist because its illusionist image abets psychological perversity appears ill-advised, both because fantasy – emotive imagining decoupled from action – is not necessarily escapist in any morally pejorative sense and because the image in question is not illusionistic. The television image is typically perceptually realistic, but this does not involve one in taking on false beliefs, but only recognising what visual arrays represent. And though perceptual realism may support emotive imagining, the moral status of such imagining depends on its content, not upon the kind of mental state it is.

Here it might be argued that I have changed the terms of the argument by talking about imagining rather than fantasising. But if fantasising is just the name for naughty emotive imagining, then clearly once again it is the content of the state, not the category of the state that we are assessing.

It is true that television supports emotive imagining (though not by morally disreputable illusions), but since there is nothing wrong *per se* with emotive imagining, the medium as such is not escapist in any morally problematic way.

Hypnotism

If the problem cited in the escapism argument is that, in one sense, the medium encourages too much space for imaginative activity (abusively called fantasy), then the problem at issue in the hypnotism argument is that television allows virtually no room for the imagination at all. The hypnotism argument begins by taking note of the unexceptionable fact that the point of television is to draw our attention to it. Producers want us to watch it. In this they are no different from film makers.

However, in various respects, the movie maker has certain advantages over the television producer when it comes to compelling our attention. The film image is standardly much larger than the television one; the film screen is usually bigger than we are, whereas typically we tower over our television sets. Moreover, the resolution of the television image is typically not as bright or lustrous as the film image. Thus, along certain dimensions, the power of the former image can be said to be weak, particularly when compared to film. Whereas in a darkened screening room, our eyes are drawn to the large, illuminated film image – in truth we have little else to look at – in our living room, the duller, low resolution television screen competes for attention with other objects. It is easy for our attention to drift away from it. Thus, a primary task for the producer, given the tendency of our attention to drift, is to keep our eyes riveted on the screen.

A major resource for the television producer in this regard is the organisation of the image track. Our perceptual system is calibrated to be especially sensitive to change and movement. The obvious adaptive advantage of this is straightforward: movement in the environment in the early days of humankind was often the signal of the arrival of either predators or prey – of either danger or food. Thus our eyes are drawn to movement and change by reflex. The producer can make use of this in order to keep our attention on the screen by organising the image track structurally so that it bristles with movement and change.

Some of the relevant devices available for this purpose include: editing, camera movement, zooming, superimpositions, fades and so on. These sorts of visual devices, of course, are also available in film. However, their incidence in television – especially certain kinds (such as advertisements and music videos) – is often higher than it is in film. If we call the use of these devices 'structural articulations', then some commentators estimate that there are usually as many as eight to ten structural articulations per sixty-second interval in a commercial television programme and as many as ten to fifteen structural articulations per thirty-second interval in the average advertisement. Of course, the ration of structural articulations in commercial action programmes like *Miami Vice* can be even higher than the average for commercial programming, and cutting in music videos is frequently as high as nearly twenty shots per minute.

Needless to say, television not only deploys technical or structural changes of this sort. Fast movement inside the frame also commands our attention. This is why television loves basketball and football more than it loves baseball. Moreover, it is no accident that situation comedy is typically structured around rapid-fire repartee – trading insults in fast-paced *badinage* – because the cascade of punch lines, accompanied by rapid switching of shots from one person to another, holds our attention in the absence of compelling plot developments. Likewise, headline news programmes are always changing the story briskly, and cutting to the next visual, never giving our attention an instant to flag. Indeed, I have seen news reports where the visual cuts are repeated twice, presumably in order to maximise the number of cuts in the segment.

One pretty obvious function of the plethora of structural articulations on the visual track is to compel our interest in what is going on in the image by triggering our innate tendencies to fixate on movement and change. By means of structural articulations like cutting, the producer introduces movement and change into the visual array, often at a fairly pronounced pace. This is attention-grabbing; the structural articulations, so to speak, renew or rejuvenate our attention on almost a moment-to-moment basis, and they work against the tendency of our attention to drift away from the screen. The structural articulations, it might be said, trap our attention; they lure us into the imagery. They rivet our attention and stimulate our natural expectation that something significant is about to happen, since that is what our movement detectors are adapted to expect. Thus the structural articulations keep us watching and draw us ahead, deeper into the programme. Our attention, it is suggested, is locked involuntarily on the image track, as if we were in a hypnotic trance. Perhaps it might be added that this is part of the reason that people watch such an enormous amount of television.

But why, if structural features of the medium do function this way, is this morally problematic? Here it may be alleged that the way in which television holds our attention has us, in a manner of speaking, 'chasing after the image'. We have to keep up with the image track as one structural articulation comes fast on the heels of the previous one. We are so busy trying to deal with the onslaught of structural articulations that we have little time for thought – little time, for example, to exercise our powers of imagination. The exercise of our attention in tracking the rush of structural articulations squeezes out the opportunity for any other kind of cognitive activity.

That is, because producers exploit certain possibilities of their medium in such a way that the image captures attention to an extent that precludes or crowds out the operation of other relevant cognitive powers, television in its standard form, with its emphasis on a high incidence of structural articulations, is morally problematic. This judgement, of course, is connected to the specific cognitive powers that the critic alleges are thrust in abeyance by the intensive preoccupation of attention to the changing image track.

These cognitive powers are at least two in number: our critical powers and our imagining powers. The imagery purportedly goes by so fast that we are so busy keeping up with it attentively that we do not have time to assess it from the point of view of moral criticism. But an even more worrisome possibility is that the way in which attention is swamped with stimuli closes off the operation of our imaginative powers.

Here, the hypnotism argument shares a premise with the realism argument. The imagination is said to be an essential feature of moral thinking because it is the power to envision alternatives. Moral judgement presupposes the recognition that things could be otherwise. The rapid succession of structural articulations, like cutting, does not allow the spectator the time to imagine moral alternatives; one is so occupied in simply attending to the visual array that there is no space for the moral imagination to take root. Thus, by precluding the operation of the moral imagination with respect to fictional and documentary material that calls for moral judgement, the typical structuring of television imagery is morally suspect.

Both the realism argument and the hypnotism argument maintain that what is morally problematic about the television imagery is that it prevents the spectator from envisioning alternatives, from thinking that things could be otherwise than the way they are portrayed on the screen. However, the two arguments reach this conclusion by different routes. The realism argument alleges that this effect occurs through naturalisation – through imparting the impression that 'this is the way things are'. The hypnotism argument maintains that the imagination is stultified by overwhelming our attention with unrelenting sequences of structural articulations.

The hypnotism argument can also be connected to certain notions of escapism. If the concept of escapism that we have in mind is that behaviour is escapist when we are doing one thing when we should be doing another, then it may be alleged that television, organised breathlessly around the succession of structural articulations, contributes to escapism by, so to speak, holding our attention to the screen captive. It is not entirely our fault that we continue to watch when we should be doing other things – improving ourselves, engaging in political activities, and so on – because producers are, for their own purposes, manipulating features of our perceptual make-up in ways that reinforce inertia. In other words, it is not entirely a result of our own character failings that we are couch potatoes. We have been hypnotised by the way television is typically articulated, irrespective of the content of the imagery.

All those people who watch so much television are virtually trapped by televisual images. But not only are they held in thrall before the screen for hour after hour. While they sit there, their powers of imagination, notably their powers of moral imagination, are effectively anaesthetised. Their attention is so engaged negotiating the imagery that moral judgement goes on holiday. And this makes the typical television format morally problematic in its own right.

There is no question that the image track is structured so as to secure maximal attention from spectators. In this, the proponent of the hypnotism argument is on solid ground. However, the question is whether or not the hypnotism argument overestimates the effectiveness of the medium in this matter. In my view, the hypnotism argument vastly exaggerates the power of the image track to hold the audience spellbound. It may characteristically be designed as a solution to the problem of wavering attention, but it is hardly 100 per cent successful in this regard.

Much viewing occurs in a highly distracted way. As a successor to radio listening, television viewing is often pursued in concert with other activities, including household chores. As the family sits around the set, what is on the screen often takes a back seat to conversations. Some commentators characterise our typical way of looking at television as 'the glance' as opposed to 'the gaze'. The notion of the gaze refers to the intent looking that marks our attention to movie images in cinemas. The glance is a more casual mode of attention, such as that shown by students who look up from their homework and catch a glimpse of the programme before returning to their algebra. I would not wish to argue categorically that television viewing is always a matter of 'the glance' in contrast to movie viewing which is always a matter of the so-called gaze. Nevertheless, it does seem to me that the television image is not as hypnotic as critics argue. However much structural articulations incline us to continue watching, it is very easy to escape their grip, as should be clear from the fact that people often half-watch television while they are doing something else.

The fact that one can do this also raises doubt about the extent to which television really crowds out the possibility of other occurrent cognitive activities. Certainly it does not preclude imagining: one can easily indulge in a bit of daydreaming while following an episode of *Star Trek*. Indeed, it seems wildly wrong to suspect that television precludes imagining, since certain forms of imaginative activity are probably required or presupposed in order to understand what is going on in any given programme.

Television programmes are edited, often intensively edited, as we have already noted. But in order to assimilate the meaning of those edited arrays, the mind must be engaged in some form of constructive activity and this, presumably, involves the operation of the imagination. The structural articulations we have discussed cannot preclude the operation of the imagination entirely; we cannot merely be attending to the parade of structural articulations in a frenzy of cognitively impenetrable reflexes.

Otherwise the array would appear meaningless. But since these arrays characteristically appear meaningful, we must suppose that some form of constructive, imaginative mental activity is in play.

Moreover, not only is it the case that the operation of our constructive powers of imagination are engaged by watching television. Our powers of moral imagination must be in gear as well. Typical programmes – both fictions and news programmes – constantly call upon their audiences to make moral judgements. This presupposes the activity of the moral imagination. If we are to recognise that a certain character is evil, we must be able to recognise that his behaviour can be otherwise. How could typical TV programmes elicit the moral uptake they require in order to be intelligible if they, at the same time, shunt the moral imagination to the sidelines? Clearly, the moral imagination could not be so neutralised, if the programme is intended to communicate to viewers in a way that requires moral judgement. And just as clearly, the imagery does not neutralise our powers of moral imagination, since it does so frequently elicit the requisite moral judgements from viewers. In order to follow the programme, viewers must be making certain moral judgements. That they do follow such programmes indicates that their powers of moral imagination are suitably engaged. Following the image track in terms of attention, then, does not preclude following it with an alert moral imagination.

Nevertheless, here it might be argued that the moral imagination is shackled or constrained by television. We make moral judgements all right, but only the moral judgements that the producers want us to make about the content of their programmes. Yet this is palpably false. How could it be true at the same time that critics, including ordinary citizens, rage about violence and sex on television? Producers certainly are not happy about those moral responses, and did not intend them. Nor were the exercises of the moral imagination that were called on to make those responses in any way stultified by the organisation of the image track. In this regard, there is no reason to suspect that television as such, in its style of representation, necessarily poses a threat to the operation of the moral imagination. The hypnotism argument is no more compelling than either the realism or the escapism argument.

Nor does it seem very likely that the hypnotism argument explains why people watch so much television. The way the sequence of images is organised may draw attention to the screen, but its holding power is extremely limited; it takes a minuscule amount of effort to elude its grasp. That this is obvious perhaps explains why we often feel a guilty conscience for having overindulged our television habit.

If we watch too much television that is probably a function of the fact that in our culture we do not spend much time training people how to use the medium: how to integrate it in a fulfilling life-plan. This, of course, may itself reflect an unwillingness in certain societies to include as part of basic education thinking about how one might lead one's life and the habits one needs to develop to pursue such lives. The problem of excessive television viewing, then, is a moral problem, if it is a moral problem, because of a larger cultural failing. It is not an ailment to be attributed to the medium as such, nor to its characteristic stylistic elaboration of the image. Neither the medium nor the image is inherently immoral, though our systematic failure to educate people about how to use it may be socially irresponsible.

Bibliography

Carroll, Noël, 'Conspiracy theories of representation', *Philosophy of the Social Sciences* 17 (1987).

Carroll, Noël, *A Philosophy of Mass Art*, Oxford: Oxford University Press, 1998.

Dyson, Kenneth and Homolka, Walter (eds), *Culture First/Promoting Standards in the New Media Age*, London: Cassell, 1996.

Ellis, John, *Visible Fictions*, London: Routledge and Kegan Paul, 1982.

Fiske, John, *Television Culture*, London: Methuen, 1987.

McLuhan, Marshall, *Understanding Media*, London: Routledge and Kegan Paul, 1964.

Mander, Jerry, *Four Arguments for the Elimination of Television*, New York: Quill, 1978.

Meyerwitz, Joshua, *No Sense of Place*, Oxford: Oxford University Press, 1985.

Plato, *Republic*, Harmondsworth: Penguin, 1974.

Tester, Keith, *Media, Culture and Morality*, London: Routledge, 1994.

12 Sex and violence in fact and fiction

Gordon Graham

Controlling pornographic production

The claim that pornography, whether of a sexual or violent nature, leads to the real thing, forms the basis of the most common case made for its social regulation, a line of argument made famous by the representations of Catherine MacKinnon and Andrea Dworkin to the City of Minneaplois in 1983. This is an old and well-trodden line of thought, but it is one that has been put with increasing frequency of late, not merely because the volume of pornographic material is widely believed to have grown, but because there are new media deployed in its distribution: the VCR, satellite television and the Internet. These new media have extended the reach of pornography considerably, at the same time as weakening social systems for its control. Whereas formerly pornographic magazines, for example, could be seized and destroyed, it is not possible to make seizures on the Internet.

Forms of control adapted to the new media are actively being investigated, it is true. The government of Singapore, for example, has attempted to create restrictions on individual access to the Web, and there are systems of self-censorship under discussion by the chief suppliers of access in the USA and Europe. Experience suggests, however, that even the most determined states can exercise only limited control. Iran for instance has found it hard to block or restrict satellite television despite the perpetual vigilance of the religious authorities. Similarly, while children and young adults can be physically stopped from entering cinemas, it is much more difficult to prevent their watching television or videos in their own homes, bedrooms even, or discovering pornographic materials when surfing the Internet.

Combined with the scale and availability of the new media, there is, too, a widespread belief that because all these new media are largely visual, they are more dangerous, since the visual depiction of sex and violence is more powerful than the mere written word. With such a rising tide of pornography, is it surprising that sexual violence should also rise? Could there be any serious question but that we are confronting new dangers?

Spelt out in full, the argument against pornography runs like this:

1 The depiction of certain sorts of action causes occurrences of those actions.
2 These are actions of a socially harmful kind.
3 Society has the right to constrain the activities of individuals in order to prevent harm.
Thus:
4 Society has the right to constrain the activities of those who would produce and distribute pornography.
Consequently:
5 Society has a right to confine the activities of those who want to view it.

This argument has been given a new twist recently by its extension from fiction to fact. The multiple murders by Martin Bryant in Tasmania, Australia in 1996 followed so hard on the heels of the slaughter of children by Thomas Hamilton at Dunblane in Scotland a few months earlier, it was inevitable that someone should ask whether there might not be a connection between the two. At least one psychologist was reported as expressing the opinion that more discreet handling of Dunblane by television and newspapers would have reduced the chances of a repeat event in Tasmania. This, if true, seems to place a special burden of responsibility on reporters and editors. It implies, in effect, that their activities were a contributory cause to the deaths and injury of many people. This is a much more serious implication than those who draw it often seem to realise, one that needs to be weighed with the greatest of care.

The same charge is not less serious when it is made against pornographers. Though they are socially less respectable than (most) newspaper and television reporters, it is still a grave matter to accuse pornographers, previously thought of as seedy rather than vicious, of being responsible for the deaths of innocent people. In fact, the grounds upon which such an accusation might be made do not differ significantly between the factual and the fictional cases. The idea is just that the depiction of sex and violence in either fiction and fact can be a serious contributory factor in the production of social harms, and for this reason I shall use the label 'pornography' to cover both factual reporting and fictional imagery.

The argument as I have set it out rests upon a number of assumptions. In the first part of this essay I identify and examine some of these assumptions. I shall argue that once this is done, the argument is revealed as inherently weak. It follows that if reservations about the depiction of sex and violence are to be given a proper grounding, it is necessary to take another approach, one not based on the idea of causing harm, and in the second part of the essay I shall sketch what that approach might be.

Harm and pornography

The most obvious assumption at work in the argument is the truth of the first premiss: the depiction of certain sorts of action causes occurrences of those actions. How is this claim to be established or assessed? It is worth noting that abstract reason is no use to us here. People often say 'it stands to reason' that the more violence there is displayed on our screens, whether fictional or actual, the more there will be in our streets. When pressed for evidence, some have even argued that no evidence is needed. In this spirit Janet Daley writes,

> It is not necessary, nor is it possible, to establish a direct mechanistic link between the watching of a particular film and the carrying out of particular acts.
>
> There is nothing special, in this respect, about the relationship between video violence and actual violence. This is simply a universal truth about human psychology. No definitive causal link can ever be proved between any experience and any subsequent behaviour . . . [but] . . . If a link cannot ever be proved, then it does no damage to an argument not to have proved it. What is beyond dispute is that the saturation of popular culture with images of cruelty normalizes violence.
>
> This is not a statement that requires proof. It is self-evident.[1]

Philosophers generally hold that no factual proposition can be self-evident in the strict sense; such claims can only be made on the basis of empirical evidence. Daley, presumably, would deny this, but whatever the truth on the general point, her argument rests upon two important mistakes. First, even if it is true that we cannot establish a direct mechanistic link between the watching of a particular film and the carrying out of a particular act, it may yet be possible to make general statistical connections between images and actions of those types. Second, the fact that a statement by its nature is not *provable* does not release us from the obligation to believe it only if it has been shown to be *probable*. David Hume's dictum that we should proportion our belief to the evidence[2] applies just as well when there is an acknowledged absence of conclusive proof, and where all we have to go on is probability. Indeed, since most of our beliefs fall into this category, rationality requires us to make reasonable judgements of probability almost all the time.

A parallel which illustrates both these points will be found in the case of passive smoking. It is tempting to assume that if smoking damages health, 'it stands to reason' that other people's smoke will damage health as well. Many people do hold this to be self-evident, and faced with a demand for evidence, an adherent of this inference could rightly claim that given the multiplicity of factors, it is never possible to link some one bit of passive smoking with a particular death. Nevertheless, claims about passive smoking can be put to both clinical and statistical tests and so far the results seem to show that what is held to 'stand to reason' is not in fact very likely to be true.

Now it seems to be the case that convincing evidence of the harmful effects of pornography is also lacking.[3] No study has revealed any clear statistical connection, and even the seemingly plainest and most telling instances do not clinch the matter. This is partly because the theories of psychological motivation with which they must ultimately be supported allow interpretation in different directions. The most compelling examples usually cited are those of killings or rapes which appear to act out some video nasty. The difficulty is that even if we know of a connection in the mind of the person who acts out the fantasy, this in itself gives us no reason to regard it as that of cause and effect. It may as easily, and perhaps more plausibly be that the psychology of someone who is fascinated by such images is also the psychology of a killer or a rapist.

Something of the same is to be said about the extension of the argument from fiction to fact. From time to time it is alleged that the reporting of violence stimulates crimes by providing ideas and models for criminals, and provokes so-called 'copycat crimes'. For example, it is a familiar complaint that the BBC's *Crimewatch*, designed to alert us to and help catch thieves and criminals, actually suggests new ways of criminal behaviour to feckless viewers. On this theory, newspaper and television reports suggest ideas to would-be criminals, which they then set about realising in their own locality. It seems quite likely that this does indeed happen, but where crimes appear to be copycat, this shows only that their *form* has been determined by reports from elsewhere; it does not show that the impulse to crime itself has been prompted by the reporting. It seems not implausible that those waiting to commit crimes sometimes change their plans to imitate exploits of which they have read in the papers; it is much less plausible that until they picked up the newspaper no thought of crime had entered their heads. Once again, in order to establish a significant causal connection between the occurrence of crime and its depiction, whether in fact or fiction, we need hard empirical evidence, both about patterns of crime, and about the motivations of actual criminals. Claims of 'self-evidence' are not enough.

The example of Dunblane and Tasmania illustrates this. Martin Bryant, the Tasmanian murderer, may or may not have been mad, but at a minimum the evidence of his mentality shows it to be bizarre. In this it is like the mentality of most multiple murderers. Careful studies of the Boston Strangler, Jeffrey Dahmer, Dennis Nilson and so on, reveal that even where there is no clinically identifiable form of madness at work, the relation of belief, desire and action in such people is extremely hard to understand, if indeed it is intelligible at all.[4] A large part of the difficulty is the non-standard ways in which belief and action are related. The degree of importance that such people seem to attach to the wholly inconsequential, for instance, and strangeness of the desires and interests they have, puts their mental and emotional life at some considerable remove from the normal ways in which actions are motivated and controlled. Precisely because of this, however, it is naïve to imagine that we can estimate the contribution that watching television reports (or even pornographic videos) might make to the balance of forces within such a mind. The distinguished American psychiatrist Willard Gaylin has freely admitted that confronted with the strange mentality of the multiple murderer most experts 'are aware how trivial, ephemeral, descriptive and meaningless are psychiatric diagnoses' in these cases.[5] Accordingly, even if we knew that Bryant dwelt on the events of Dunblane with intensity, we could not attribute any clear causal weight to this. There is no more reason to think that this was the cause of his deranged state than that it was simply more evidence of it.

This line of argument may be applied more generally. It is a familiar thought that people whose newspapers and television screens are regularly filled with reports of violence will, so to speak, become inoculated against its horror, or worse, positively develop a taste for it. This is perhaps what Daley means when she says that images of cruelty normalise violence. That is certainly one possible outcome. It is equally possible, however, that the reporting of violence increases people's revulsion in the face of its consequences, and strengthens their repudiation of it. Neither one of these reactions is any more or less possible than the other, and that is as far as reasoning in the abstract can take us. To discover most people's actual, as opposed to possible, reaction we need solid, and extensive, social enquiry. This would provide some hard evidence, but it is evidence of a sort that we do not have as yet. Studies that have been attempted along these lines have resulted in very uncertain or conflicting conclusions.

There is reason to hold, I think, that violence begets violence. We ought not to confuse this with a quite different thesis, that the *depiction* of violence (factual or fictional) begets violence. This is a much more ambitious thesis, and one waiting to be established. Certainly pornography is to be found associated with violence, but the fact is that human history before radio, television and full colour magazines is littered with spectacular acts of cruelty, and most present-day violence can be causally connected with videos, television and so on in only the most tenuous way. Even today, in countries far too poor for any of these, truly staggering violence, rape and bloodshed can take place, as it did in Rwanda in 1995.

However, in order to expose the full weakness of the argument with which we began, let us suppose, contrary to these reflections, that there are some grounds for thinking that a proliferation of pornographic images leads to an increase in the real incidence of such actions. A second assumption at work in the argument we are considering is that these effects are necessarily harmful. This seems an odd assumption to question, but the fact is that the radically altered attitudes to sexual conduct which pornographic materials may induce are regarded by some as liberating rather than corrupting.[6] The once infamous Marlon Brando, Maria Schneider film *Last Tango in Paris* was hailed by the New Yorker's great film critic Pauline Kael as 'the most liberating movie ever'. It might be replied, of course, that while sexual pornography could be regarded as liberating, the same thing could hardly be said about the depiction of violence. The issue is not so clear, however. Long ago Aristotle argued that dramatic depiction can have a cathartic effect, dispelling emotions that would be harmful if given vent to in reality.[7] Now if it is true that the depiction of violence can have a cathartic as well as a provocative influence this means that as well as prompting violence, it forestalls it, by providing a fictional release for otherwise destructive emotions. In this sense, it too might be liberating, and if it is there will be a question whether the benefits do not outweigh the costs.

This line of thought can be expanded. Many people die as a result of motor vehicles on modern roads. The causal connection here is far better established than any connection between violence and pornography. But the public mind accepts these negative outcomes as a price worth paying for the benefits modern transportation brings. In principle the same point applies to VCRs, satellite television and the Internet. Of course, it is true that if one could have the benefits without the harms, this would be better still, but if we cannot, it may still be rational to accept the harms. It needs to be shown, therefore, that as things stand, the social and cultural condition to which we have been reduced is so bad as to warrant the elimination of much that is good.

The proponent of social controls will argue, of course, that this is not what is proposed. It is proposed only that society should, in the interests of self-protection, constrain the freedom of individuals with respect to the production and consumption of pornography. This reply reveals a further two assumptions. The first is that such controls can be effective. This I am inclined to doubt. The efforts of the western world to control illicit drugs is salutary in this respect. Many years of highly expensive law enforcement has resulted in a world in which trade in drugs is even more vigorous, as the enforcing agencies themselves declare. If there is a demand for pornography, which there obviously is, the black market will find ways of supplying it, and, if our experience with drugs is any guide, under legal proscription it will do so in even less well controlled ways, while at the same time generating the huge cost of an unsuccessful effort to contain it. This certainly was the experience under Prohibition in the United States. The attempt to make alcohol illegal simply pushed it underground.

The harm principle

But suppose effective control *is* possible, and that, further, we leave aside the question of who is to exercise it. A second assumption comes to the fore: that the prevention of harm is a sufficient justification for the exercise of social coercion. Here, we encounter the 'one simple principle' which John Stuart Mill elaborates in his classic essay *On Liberty*, a principle that has had considerable influence on public policy, notably in the reform of the law on homosexuality in England and Wales. Mill's principle still commands widespread assent, and yet philosophical discussion long ago revealed its weakness. The causing of harm to others is neither a necessary nor a sufficient condition of making something against the law. That is to say, to show that a class of action is harmful is not enough to satisfy the basic requirements of justified prohibition. Nor does harm in itself provide an adequate ground. Causing harm is not a necessary condition of unlawfulness because there can be violations of right that are not in any straightforward sense harmful – invasion of privacy is a good example – and it is not a sufficient condition because there are actions that seriously harm the interests of others which society must nevertheless permit; free competition in the market-place is one clear instance. I can invade your privacy without harming you, and I can seriously harm your means of livelihood simply by trading more efficiently and effectively.

The upshot of all this is that scarcely a proposition in the argument with which we began can be sustained. We cannot confidently assert that pornographic depiction is causally connected with the sort of action depicted; even if it were, we could not unequivocally declare those actions harmful; even if we could, the costs of attempting to control them might well outweigh the benefits; and in any case, the fact that something is harmful does not automatically justify its social proscription.

Once all these points are put together, the upshot is plain; the case against pornography on the grounds of the social harm it does is at best very weak. Possibly it is no case at all, and this is a rather striking conclusion since, as I remarked at the start, the appeal to the harm pornography does is the commonest case against it.

To draw or advance such a conclusion is often taken to mean that there is no reasoned case to be made against pornography, and that the root of objections to it must lie in personal revulsion. In turn this seems to imply that while people are entitled to express disgust, this is in all probability a matter of the residual feelings of older generations and should not be allowed to confine the activities of those who do not share these feelings. Such is the position, generally, of those who take a more relaxed attitude to pornography.

This retreat to subjectivism is not the only alternative, however. There are many social questions which bear thinking about in other terms. For example, we can reasonably object to the construction of drab and dreary towns and city centres, without supposing that there is only one question that matters to rational town planning: whether drabness leads to more domestic accidents or car crashes. Similarly, arguments about what sort of society it is rational to want to belong to need not confine themselves to physical or psychological harm. The argument about the harmfulness or harmlessness of pornography is essentially a legal-cum-political and social one. It takes the existence of graphic reporting and of a demand for pornography for granted, and then asks how far this is to be permitted and how far it is to be contained. One way of putting this is to say that it is concerned with the *external* control of pornographic material. A quite different approach lies in considering pornography from the point of view of the *internal* aims of the sort of human activity to which it belongs. This is the approach I now want to explore.

Pornography and creativity

The public view of pornography has moved a long way from the world in which the novel *Lady Chatterley's Lover* could be prosecuted as an obscene publication. In that trial, however, an issue was raised which continues to be relevant. Representations were made that *Lady Chatterley's Lover* could not be pornography because it was *art*, a line of thought frequently invoked in many other cases since then. What such a defence implies is that depictions are pornographic not so much because of their content or subject-matter, but because of the way this content is treated. In other words, pornographic productions fail to reach certain aesthetic standards. Early examples of pornographic literature bear out this contention. Almost without exception they have nothing of interest in the way of plot, character or dialogue, and for most readers their focus on the minutiae of sexual congress rapidly loses whatever appeal it might have had through the tedium of endless repetition. The same thing is true of the soft pornography novels which nowadays can be found on the paperback bookshelves of even mainstream booksellers. Though they may titillate, they are wholly without literary merit or distinction. So too with pornographic films in which repeated acts of sex without any narrative purpose quickly become boring. And the same can be said of stories and films that consist in repeated acts of violence.

By contrast, a book or a film which observes minimal literary standards, though it may contain sex and violence, will in fact *eschew* the purely pornographic. This is true of artistic creation that falls far short of anything aspiring to the grand title of 'Literature' or 'Art'. The reason is that literary creation of even a modest sort aims actively to stimulate new interest and value in its readers, and not merely to accept and exploit their pre-existent interests and values. Its hope is not simply to *serve* but to *create* its audience. In illustration of this point consider writing for entertainment. Among the great writers of this century who were without aesthetic pretension, P. G. Wodehouse and Eric Ambler must figure prominently. What these writers did, Wodehouse especially, was not to move from mere entertainment to high 'Art', but use their very considerable literary skills to generate a higher standard of entertainment. It is in this way that all truly creative writing, even writing whose sole purpose is entertainment, is educational (in a broad sense). It does not merely *pander* to taste but tries to *educate* it.

The language of pandering is unfashionable, and the idea of educating taste no less so. It is commonly assumed that about taste there can be no disputing, and by implication that all references to better or baser tastes is merely a cover for élitist prejudices. These assumptions are part of the subjectivism to which, as we have seen, the normal argument about pornography tends to lead. A convincing alternative, therefore, needs to challenge such assumptions, and in my view we have only to reflect briefly on one familiar area of human endeavour in order to make such a challenge convincing.

The pupil who first comes to the piano has practical abilities to learn. However boring they may be, scales and finger exercises, and those rather mechanical 'studies' which many first-rate composers have devised, are an essential part of mastering the techniques without which great works of music cannot be played. But this technical mastery is only a foundation. The main business of the music teacher lies elsewhere, partly in the development of musicality and partly in a knowledge of which pieces of music are most worth playing. It is essential to the relationship between pupil and teacher, that the teacher knows what the pupil does not. Accordingly, though (human beings being what they are) success will come more easily if pupils are quickly enabled to play the music they like, the purpose is to bring them to the point of playing music that is *worth* playing and being able to tell which music this is. It is at this point that they pass beyond the mere mastery of technique and are given a musical education. One way of putting this is to say that it is not merely the musical abilities but musical *taste* of pupils which must be educated.

Unfashionable though the idea of educated taste may be, its necessity in the real world of music, and the arts more generally, is undeniable. No good music teacher would take the preferences of the elementary pupil as sovereign; they await formation, and this is a major part of their musical education. Conversely, no sensible pupil would devote time and money to lessons if there were not valuable things to be learned. Consequently, the test of a good teacher, and of a good course of instruction, is not that pupils are pleased, or have their pre-existent preferences satisfied, but that they become good musicians. To be inducted into the world of music is certainly to be inducted into a world of pleasure and enjoyment (though in my view it is not only this). But it is also a matter of being taught which pieces of music are most worth enjoying, and which it is best to take pleasure in, a truth, I might add, which applies as readily to twentieth-century jazz as to eighteenth-century baroque. The crucial point to be observed is that the pupil–teacher relationship is one in which it is the informed taste of the teacher, not the natural taste of the pupil, which is sovereign.

It is not only, or even chiefly, those actually described as teachers who have this role and importance. Composers and other creative artists are also educators of taste in this sense, and can thus claim an authority that the mere player cannot. This is not a defence of artistic conservatism; the greatest artists are highly innovative. But it *is* a defence of discrimination, and hence an attack on the indefensible (and usually undefended) claim that the pre-formed or 'natural' taste of anyone and everyone is authoritative. There is plenty of prurience among potential audiences – of this there can be no doubt – but truly creative writing does not rest content with reflecting existing interests and desires, or worse, taking them as the principal basis of its appeal.

The same sort of point can be made about other media. Sex and violence will continue to make an appearance in films, theatre, and on television. This is not specially deplorable. There is sex and violence in Shakespeare, in the Norse Sagas, in *The Decameron*. What is to be feared is that the sex and violence come to dominate. They can do so, however, only to the extent that the internal aims of artistic endeavour itself are abandoned by those who work in these media. Such things as ratings wars, or box office competitions, can bring this about. It is easy for writers, directors and producers to succumb to popularity for its own sake, and economics often increases the pressure to do so. Nevertheless, in so far as the standards internal to good writing, television, theatre and so on are upheld, they bring a contrary pressure, one which militates *against* the depiction of largely gratuitous sex and violence. It is wrong to think of this pressure as a quite extraneous concern with something called 'morality', however. Rather, it is the special business of the creative artist to show us that there are matters *more* interesting, more entertaining, more arresting, than sex or violence, and that images of sex and violence are only fleetingly attractive unless they are set in one of these larger contexts.

If it is true that there is a rising demand for pornography, this is evidence that artists have to this extent failed the public. In this they have been assisted, I think, by declining standards of literacy, the need to fill countless hours of television time, and a widening gap between high art and folk art. Alarmists sometimes speak of a tide of pornography sweeping late twentieth-century culture. If so, it is not social policy which needs critical scrutiny so much as artistic endeavour. And there is some evidence that the failure of the artists is beginning to be more widely realised. The box office flop of the films *Jade*, *Showgirls* and *Striptease*, it has been argued, has had the effect of casting their hitherto celebrated scriptwriter Joe Esterhas in a rather less *marketable* light.

Media ethics

This same approach, in contrast to the harm argument, may also be applied to some effect in the case of reported as well as to imagined sex and violence. News reporting too has its own internal goods. To see what these are we need to ask what the point or aim of reporting is. A natural answer is 'to inform', but this as it stands is inadequate. 'The news' is not simply accurate information about what has happened recently. Otherwise the utterly trivial – the amount of petrol used by a bus between one stop and the next, say – would qualify as news; it happened, after all. A 'news story' is information in a context, and the context determines both the significance of the story and the relevance of the information it contains.

Now here, as in fiction, the writer seeks not merely to serve but to create a readership. It is editors and reporters who decide what is newsworthy. In doing so, like the artists they can adopt the role of panderer or of educator. In practice, of course, even the best journalism comprises some mix of the two. The question therefore is where the greater emphasis will fall. This is not a matter entirely for decision but something determined in large part by the history and traditions of the particular form of publication. A newspaper, journal or television programme must find and keep an audience. Consequently, what is known variously as the popular, tabloid or gutter press cannot be expected to give pride of place to investigative reporting. Nor can it reasonably be thought a failure because it does not. Nevertheless, there is still a crucial distinction to be drawn between populist newspapers and outright fiction and one which the editors and correspondents on such papers must continue to draw if they are to remain reporters in any sense at all.

Journalism, then, should be thought of as a spectrum and the question to ask is whether, at least at the higher end of the spectrum, the goods and norms internal to journalism place limits on how sex and violence are reported. At the other end of the spectrum is what is known as sensationalism. This is the publication of news items that shock, horrify and titillate. The standard of significance in such reporting is almost entirely extraneous: whatever will shock, horrify and titillate is newsworthy, and this can be true of isolated events that have no relevance to anything outside themselves. By contrast, the standard of newsworthiness in higher journalism is to a large extent internally generated. The purpose of serious news reports in the newspapers and on radio and television is not merely to recount what has happened, but to report events in a way that uncovers and explains their political, social and cultural significance. In turn, of course, this requires that some *conception* of significance be brought to the reporting, and hence to the reader.

Now the fact is that specific acts of sex and violence have relatively little significance of this sort. In fact, some of the most famous 'massacres' in history, which had enormous social and political repercussions, were modest affairs in terms of the number of deaths and injuries compared to spectacular murders such as those at Dunblane and Hobart. In the Boston Massacre, for example, which led to the American War of Independence and thus to the creation of the United States, only three people died. The same point may be made about the sex lives of political leaders. However lurid, they are generally not of any more consequence than other people's sex lives. More particularly, the express detail concerning both multiple murders and high society scandals has in general no social or cultural significance at all. Odd though it may sound, striking and shocking events can be of no moment. Thus to dwell on the details of reported sex and violence is a kind of prurience, and to devote a lot of space to it makes journalism passive rather than active in the public culture.

There is always, of course, the matter of readership to be considered. Journalism cannot succeed in a vacuum, or be forever talking down to those it hopes to make its audience. Even in what is generally called the 'quality' press, there is a need to appeal to existing interests and prejudices, and the task is to strike a balance between this necessity and the demands of good journalism itself. Nevertheless, there are, as it seems to me, some clear instances where this balance has not been correctly struck. For instance, it has always been common for court cases to be reported at length. In the past such reporting had a lot to do with matters of legal import, though some celebrated cases never had any significance other than their sensational character – nineteenth-century coverage of Dr Crippen is a good example. In recent years, however, the proportion of these has risen steadily, to the point where most cases reported in the quality press appear to be chosen for their lurid nature, not for their legal or social significance. When this is true journalism has failed by its own standards.

The truth of this claim is not specially important. I cite it chiefly as an example of the balance between the internal standards of and the external demands on news reporting, which is at the heart of anything properly called media ethics. If the public appears to have an insatiable appetite for true stories of sex and violence, this is something which journalists will accept and cater to only in so far as they have fallen into passivity and abandoned the creatively active role which is intrinsic to their profession. Just as there is something called artistic integrity, there is journalistic integrity, and it cannot be spelled out simply in terms of factual accuracy or the protection of sources. In short, if there is reason to be concerned about the level of depicted sex and violence in our culture, it is not protection from harm by government or law we should look for, but more active, less passive conceptions of journalism and the arts.

Notes

1 Janet Daley, *Daily Telegraph*, 26 June 1996.
2 David Hume, *Enquiries*, Section X, 'Of miracles', Part I.

3 A review of the evidence will be found in D. Howitt and G. Cumberbatch, *Pornography: Impacts and Influences* (London: HMSO, 1990).
4 See for instance Brian Masters, *Killing for Company: The Case of Dennis Nilson* (London: Jonathan Cape, 1985).
5 Quoted in Elliot Leyton, *Hunting Humans: The Rise of the Modern Multiple Murderer,* (Harmondsworth: Penguin Books, 1989).
6 A line of argument pursued by Nadine Strossen, *Defending Pornography: Free Speech, Sex and the Fight for Women's Rights* (London: Abacus, 1996).
7 Aristotle, *Poetics* 1449b28.

13 Censorship and the media

Anthony Ellis

Those who are in authority generally wish to regulate the views and sentiments that others express, for the power to do so makes their lives considerably easier; and this is nowhere more true than in the case of the government. It is a wish that has, in the western world, been increasingly frustrated in the last half century or so as the authority of government to regulate speech has been steadily diminished.

When we refer to freedom of speech we are, of course, not referring only to speech in the literal sense, nor just to speech and the press. There has been a growing awareness that most of the arguments in favour of freedom of speech will generalise to other forms of communication; in a recent US Supreme Court case, for instance, the Court held that nude, barroom dancing was entitled to some protection under the First Amendment – 'though barely', as Chief Justice Rehnquist put it. Article 10 of the European Convention on Human Rights speaks not of the freedom of speech but of the 'freedom of expression'.

Almost everyone agrees that speech must be protected, to at least some extent, from governmental regulation. But what are the arguments in favour of freedom of speech? And what are they supposed to show?

At this more specific level, there is, as one might expect, less agreement. As to what the arguments are supposed to show, we should note at least three differences of opinion. One concerns *scope*. There are those who think that the effective arguments show only that speech that has a political dimension should be protected; others think that they show that the protection must be more general. A second difference concerns the *weight* of the protection. The American tradition has, since the 1940s, tended to give greater protection to speech than have European jurisdictions. British common law seems now to have accepted as a principle that the value of freedom of speech should be given some weight, but the British Race Relations Act, for instance, would not pass constitutional muster in the United States. The third concerns the *nature* of the protection more generally. We could think of the protection as giving merely a negative right, the right, roughly, not to have one's speech interfered with in certain ways; or we could think of it as a positive right, a right imposing a duty on the government positively to promote freedom of speech. Taken in the latter way, as European traditions have tended to take it, the right might generate, for instance, a duty on the part of the press to make space available to some of those aggrieved by what they read therein; taken the former way, as the American tradition has tended to take it, it would not generate this right (and the US Supreme Court has refused to recognise a 'right to reply' against the press).[1] Let us briefly survey some of the more familiar arguments.

The argument that gives the least scope to the protection of speech holds that freedom of speech is necessary for the proper working of democracy.[2] This might be so for a number of reasons. One is that the government should be responsive to all preferences, and it can hardly be so if it denies some people the right to make their preferences known. Another is that, in a democracy, the government should be accountable to the people, and that it is more likely to be so, in fact and not just in theory, if it cannot stifle criticism. Another depends upon some version of the second justification, to which we shall turn in a moment: in general, it holds, we should expect political decisions to be more soundly based the more they depend upon true judgements rather than false ones, and freedom of speech is likely to conduce to the discovery of truth. There is surely something in all of these points, but few now would hold that protection for speech should be so narrowly circumscribed, offering, for instance, no protection for science and the arts except in so far as they may have political implications.

A second argument gives much greater scope. It is perhaps the most famous of the arguments and is often summed up in the slogan that the discovery of truth requires a free 'market-place of ideas'.[3] The argument has been stated in many ways, and often misunderstood; it is often ridiculed as depending on the obviously false claim that, if people are always allowed to speak their minds, then true ideas will necessarily triumph over false ones. But this misses the real point of the argument twice over. First, the argument does not depend upon the idea that the truth always drives out the false, nor indeed on the weaker claim that it generally does so. Nor does it depend upon the relativistic view that there is no such thing as truth other than what is socially accepted as 'true'. This is not to deny that some of the proponents of the argument have accepted these claims, but merely to point out that they are not essential to it. Indeed, in order to have considerable force the argument need not make a very general claim at all. The proponent of freedom of speech need not claim that speech is to be protected always and everywhere, and Mill, of course, did not claim that. All that needs to be claimed is that in our circumstances, in the modern, western democracies, allowing the government to hold a monopoly on speech is likely to hinder progress towards the truth. And that is surely true. Secondly, the argument should not in any case be stated in terms of truth, which would restrict its force unnecessarily, since we need not judge the worth of all communications – music and dance for instance – in terms of truth.

The previous two arguments have been, in the broadest sense, consequentialist: they hold that protecting speech will promote greater good. This does not mean, of course, that any particular item of speech is likely to do more good than harm, but only that allowing the government a general licence to regulate speech, or certain sorts of speech, is likely to do more harm than would the largely unfettered exercise of freedom of speech. Other justifications are quite different.[4] They depend upon the idea that in order for a government to respect the moral dignity of its citizens it must grant them fairly broad and deep free-speech rights – even if this involves considerable costs.

One argument of this type is found in Mill (though allegedly embedded in a utilitarian framework): it holds that the freedom to speak is intimately tied to the freedom of thought, and that a prohibition on what one can think is an attack on one's identity.[5]

Another non-consequentialist argument holds that to deny the freedom to speak is also to deny the freedom to *hear*, and that a democratic government must treat its citizens as responsible adults who must be trusted to hear dangerous opinions and who therefore have the right, within very large limits, to decide for themselves what they will hear.[6]

Another non-consequentialist argument would hold that we each have a moral responsibility – to others, or perhaps just to the truth – to express our views to others; in so far as the government denies us the freedom of speech it prevents us from carrying out that duty.[7]

It is perhaps a philosopher's tendency to seek the master-argument, the one argument that will do all that is necessary to justify a position. But this is unnecessary in the present case, for all of the arguments just canvassed can be thought to express a relevant truth. And the fact that some right to freedom of speech is so widely accepted may, perhaps, suggest that it has appeal from more than one point of view.

These arguments give freedom of speech different scope. The argument that rests its weight on the citizen's right to hear would clearly justify the US Supreme Court's view that nude barroom dancing is entitled to First Amendment protection, for it is as paternalistic of the government to try to protect willing consumers from this sort of expression as to protect them from political speeches.[8] It seems unlikely that the argument that emphasises the importance of speech for the democratic process would have that result. But clearly, taken together, the arguments give freedom of speech great scope.

What *weight* they give to freedom of speech is more complicated, and cannot be dealt with fully without taking account of more general issues in political and legal philosophy. No one thinks that any of them justifies absolute freedom. In the USA, for instance, any speech can be prohibited if the government has a 'compelling interest' in preventing the harm that it may cause. (Speech which, like barroom dancing, or burning one's draft card, has a substantial 'non-speech element' must pass a less stringent test: there must be a 'substantial' governmental interest.) But morality and history would suggest that, if the arguments are taken seriously, then they support considerable weight for the freedom of speech. History surely bears out the claim that government interference with the citizens' right to free expression generally produces baneful effects, and should labour under severe burdens. And in a political democracy we should surely place great weight on the claim that the government must respect the autonomy of its citizens, even at some cost to both.

The *nature* of the right to freedom of speech is also a complicated matter, not to be settled independently of general considerations about the nature of rights. I shall do little more than state a view: it is arbitrary to restrict rights to negative rights. Rights protect interests, and interests can be threatened by more than the interference of other agents. One's interest in expressing an opinion can be threatened by the lack of resources with which to do so just as much as by the positive interference of others; there seems little other than an overridable, broadly utilitarian, reason why the government should not be required to maintain, to some degree, a 'level playing field' in this area as in others. That requirement might well generate, for instance, a strong reason for allowing some right of reply against the press.

When may speech be restricted?

However weighty the right to freedom of speech may be, everyone agrees that it may legitimately be overridden. As we have seen, the USA requires that there be a 'compelling governmental interest' for ordinary speech, and a 'substantial' governmental interest for symbolic speech. The European Convention on Human Rights, Article 10 states,

> The exercise of [the freedom of expression], since it carries with it duties and responsibilities, may be subject to such formalities, conditions, restrictions or penalties as are prescribed by law and are necessary in a democratic society, in the interests of national security, territorial integrity or public safety, for the prevention of disorder or crime, for the protection of health or morals, for the protection of the reputation or rights of others, for preventing the disclosure of information received in confidence, or for maintaining the authority and impartiality of the judiciary.

Our question, then, is, 'When may the government legitimately override the right to freedom of speech?'

Harm

The most obvious justification for prohibiting speech arises when the speech causes significant harm. But what is to count as harm? And what is significant? If we take seriously the arguments of the first section, then one thing is relatively clear: we should expect the harm at issue to be restricted to speech that harms others; if there is speech that harms only the speaker, then it would be unacceptably paternalistic of the government to regulate it. Speech that harms others is, of course, a more complex matter.

Here is one slight complication. Speech may directly harm particular, specifiable people; that is the case with speech that libels individuals. It may, on the other hand, harm general social interests without harming any specifiable individuals; that will often be the case with speech that harms national security. Both are harms that the government has a legitimate interest in preventing, and so both can, in principle, generate legitimate restrictions on speech. The latter, for obvious reasons, are likely to be more problematic than the former, and we shall return to them in a moment.

The harm referred to plainly does not encompass all harms that speech may cause, but is limited to 'the substantive evils that [government] has a right to prevent'.[9] But this still leaves room for difference of opinion, since people differ about what harms it is permissible for the government to prevent. These differences, which touch on fundamental issues in political philosophy, obviously cannot be resolved here. We can, however, make some progress without resolving them, for there is considerable agreement about what concrete things count as harms even amongst people who differ about what abstract account of harm should be given. Thus few would disagree that, in principle, it is permissible for the government to restrict speech in order to protect any of the following: national security, territorial integrity, public safety, public order, public health, the reputation or rights of others, private information received in confidence, the impartiality of legal proceedings and the protection of the public from crime. (This is the list, minus one or two items to which we shall return, given in Article 10 of the European Convention on Human Rights.)

We should expect, then, broad agreement on the sorts of harms that the government may seek to prevent by restricting speech. That, of course, does not guarantee agreement about more particular issues, for the harm that is to be prevented must somehow be weighed against the harm involved in restricting speech, and people may disagree about the results of that weighing. Even here, however, we find considerable agreement. The UK has, for instance, libel laws which make it relatively easy for those who think that they have been libelled to win their cases. In the USA, by contrast, a 1964 ruling required that a public figure can win a libel case only if he can show that the libel was published with 'malice', i.e. knowing that it was false, or recklessly ignoring evidence that it was true.[10] The effect of this difference is clear. English libel law, though benefiting those who are libelled, has a discernibly chilling effect on what the media will print or broadcast about public figures, since a few unsuccessful libel suits could bankrupt even a large newspaper; it seems highly doubtful whether the resulting gains to public figures outweigh the loss to public life, and in fact few people do think this.[11]

It is also surely clear, and generally agreed, that the need to protect national security is frequently used to justify unacceptable restrictions on speech. In recent years, press coverage of war has provided ample illustration. It is widely thought that the United States lost the Vietnam War partly because television coverage critically sapped the support of the American public. Now, to the extent that the media coverage was fair and accurate, the enormous resentment that this belief fuelled was plainly out of place. Everyone would agree that press coverage may be restricted to protect military operations; protecting civilian morale is quite another matter, and a democratic people have a right to know what is happening in a war carried out in their name even if it does critically sap their support for it. That is surely clear. However, governments learned their lesson. When Britain entered the Falklands War in 1982 press coverage was severely restricted, and in ways which could not possibly have been justified by the need to protect particular military operations. The press was also used to disseminate militarily useful misinformation.[12] The American government followed the lead of Mrs Thatcher in the Gulf War in 1991.[13] In both of these cases citizens were prevented from learning information which, in a democratic society, they have a right to know.

Other cases are more difficult and there is therefore less agreement about them. There is, for instance, substantial difference between the USA and the UK in how the press is allowed to report legal proceedings. Crudely, the UK is more concerned with ensuring the integrity of legal proceedings whereas the USA is more concerned with protecting the freedom of speech. The EU countenances restriction of speech to safeguard 'the authority and impartiality of the judiciary';[14] we need not, perhaps, be overly concerned for the authority of the judiciary but the impartiality of legal proceedings is more troublesome. In the year-long 1996 murder trial of O. J. Simpson, a famous US footballer, the jury was effectively imprisoned for the duration of the trial to ensure that they could not hear the discussions which saturated the news and entertainment media. Sequestration of juries is one of the trade-offs for allowing more-or-less unfettered reporting of legal cases. Understandably, sequestration is not often practised in the USA, and it is tempting to believe that juries are often prejudiced by what they learn in the morning papers although they are typically instructed not to read them. On the other hand, there is little hard evidence to support this belief, and in the absence of good evidence it may well be that the value of free speech should prevail.

In cases such as these, hard or easy, a balancing of harms is called for. And in hard cases people will naturally differ about what the result of that balancing will be; and it may be that there will be many differences that are hard to resolve.

Some of these differences are empirical. That is so with, for instance, the continuing debate about sex and violence in the media, and particularly on television. One argument is that a continuous diet of entertainment in which violence and casual sex are a staple may contribute to the formation of attitudes in children which will later result in violent antisocial behaviour. The evidence, in fact, seems extremely thin, often relying upon fanciful definitions of violence, ways of measuring attitudes that leave much to be desired, and hasty inferences from short-term alterations in attitudes to long-term alterations. But there is nothing especially improbable about the hypothesis itself, and it should be taken seriously. And if credible evidence should be found to support it then everyone would agree that this would be relevant to the question of whether the government should impose some sort of restrictive legislation. How could it be denied? It would clearly be crazy to think that, *in and of itself*, our interest in publishing and receiving a particular sort of entertainment should trump our interest in bodily security. All that remains is the question of whether violent television entertainment actually does in fact make a significant contribution to the amount of real violence in society.

That question is largely empirical, but not wholly so. It asks whether violent, televised entertainment makes a *significant* contribution to the amount of real violence in society, and that is partly an evaluative question, requiring that we balance the value of freedom of speech against other values – bodily security, in the particular case. Here, people may differ. Those concerned with freedom of speech will, however, insist that speech must be accorded great value, much more than most of the things (alcohol, for instance) that may contribute to violence in society. Not to mince the matter, this means that we should require a higher rate of increase in crimes of violence or a higher probability of such an increase in order to justify regulating speech than to justify regulating alcohol. Speech, unlike alcohol, plays a crucial part in our political, social and personal lives, a role that requires that government leave it largely unrestricted, even at some cost to other values; or so the arguments for freedom of speech undertake to demonstrate.

Freedom of speech, then, has a cost. When the US Supreme Court decided that political life in a democracy demands sufficiently 'uninhibited, robust and wide-open' debate that public officials could not sue for libel unless they could show actual malice,[15] the justices presumably did not think that this would mean that, in each particular case, the harm to the democratic process would outweigh the harm to a libelled official, for this would clearly be false in any normal sense of harm. A cost has to be paid.[16] That emerges no less when we consider the different views about whether violent entertainment contributes to antisocial attitudes. There are those who argue that, if the evidence is unclear, caution should be our counsel and that some degree of censorship is legitimate. Those who value freedom of speech will take a different view: they will think that, if it is freedom of speech that is at issue, then this brings with it a more stringent demand that there be evidence for the harm to be prevented. They will also hold that not just any proven degree of harm legitimates regulating speech.

Blasphemy, profanity, vulgarity, indecency, obscenity

There are still many, in both the USA and the UK, who would like to restrict blasphemy (reviling God or religion), profanity ('swear words'), indecency and vulgarity in public life. Indeed, most of the complaints levelled against television programmes in the UK have concerned 'bad language'.

Here it is worth making a distinction. One may object to blasphemy, for instance, in different ways. One may think that cursing God (the traditional Jewish understanding) is simply wrong, independently of its effect on others, and that this is why it should be prohibited. By contrast, one might think that a major element in its wrongness is its tendency to offend and outrage others. A parallel distinction holds for profanity, vulgarity and indecency.

There is nowadays little support for restrictions on speech that does not adversely affect others; and in, for instance, English law, blasphemy has long been generally understood as involving the intent to outrage the feelings of others.[17] We may, then, think of blasphemy and so on merely as types of speech that give offence. Does such speech justify censorship?

Offence

Let us start with indecency and obscenity. Genuine obscenity is, and always has been, rare in the media, but indecency has not, for I take it that the public display of a woman's naked breasts for sexual titillation is indecent, as is the representation of intimate sexual behaviour common in films that are shown on television. Does the fact that people are offended by indecency give a legitimate reason for censoring it?

One response would be to say this: people certainly have a right to be protected from *bodily* assault; why should they not have a parallel right to be protected from assault on their *minds*?

This response, so far as it goes, is surely correct. I would certainly be doing you a wrong if, say, I caused you to fall into fits of pointless rage by putting drugs in your food, and this needs no argument. That the harm caused is to the mind rather than to the body is clearly irrelevant. But now we need some distinctions.

The first thing we need to do is to distinguish different ways in which things can be offensive.[18] A smell can be offensive and so too can the display of an attractive naked body. But these are not offensive in the same way. So-called 'offensive nuisances', such as smells and loud noises, are simply assaults – offences – on the senses; they are, in an important way, similar to the case mentioned above where someone's mental states are affected by drugs. To find the display of an attractive nude offensive is, however, quite different. This is no more than *to have a view* about the display; it is to think it morally inappropriate in some way, whether because it is boorish to cast off one's clothes with no thought of the embarrassment it might cause the guests at the vicar's tea party, or just because it is wrong in itself – shameful – to be naked in public. To censor such displays because they are found offensive is, then, simply to censor them because some people think them immoral. Is that a reasonable ground for censorship?

Here, we may perhaps need to remind ourselves of another distinction. There are different ways in which things can be immoral. Perhaps the most obvious is by causing harm. And when some people object to the presence of semi-naked pin-ups in newspapers they do so on the ground that it causes harm in some way, perhaps by fostering a climate in which sexual offences against women are more easily tolerated; again, people sometimes object to the display of sexual behaviour on television because it will encourage the young to experiment sexually to their, and others', detriment. We need not discuss the plausibility of such claims for they are all irrelevant at the moment; if such indecencies cause harm then *that* is the objection to them, and it was dealt with briefly in an earlier section. If the argument about offence is to bring in anything new it must be referring to a sort of immorality that has nothing to do with the allegedly harmful consequences of the displays in question. The thought that it is immoral to appear nude in public must be the thought that this is *intrinsically* immoral, simply morally inappropriate in itself, whether or not it leads to bad consequences.

Our question, then, is this: Is it reasonable to censor expression merely because some people think that it is intrinsically immoral?

I said above that there is little support for restrictions on speech that does not adversely affect others. If that is to mean anything then it must be implicit in it that speech does not 'adversely affect others' merely because they form a disapproving view of it. If it were not implicit, then we should have to accept the view for which, I said, there is little support: we must accept that speech can be censored simply on the ground that some people, perhaps a majority, disapprove of it, even though it has no (further) adverse effect on anyone. I think that most of those who campaign for more stringent standards of decency in our public life do indeed accept something like this, though often without fully realising it (for the dominance of consequentialist ways of thinking in public life have made it difficult for many to articulate their thoughts in a non-consequentialist way). But it is surely an unacceptable view.

First, we need to be clear that the argument cannot, without arbitrariness, be restricted to indecency; and this must carry with it an implication unwelcome even to those who profess to accept it. Their thought is that public nudity is just immoral, and ought not to be tolerated. That thought, however, can have no grip in our society until it has been through a democratic filter from which it will emerge as the thought that public nudity is *generally thought* to be immoral and so ought not to be tolerated; it must go through this filter, for it has to be decided whether public nudity is indeed immoral, and this must be decided in some democratic manner (by a democratically elected legislature, for instance). Now, of course, a corollary beckons: any expression, including for instance the expression of these intolerant views, could legitimately be censored if a majority disapproved of them. Such a view would effectively allow one to say only what the majority might decide that one may say. It therefore accords no value to freedom of speech whatever, for to think that freedom of speech is a value is at least to think that one's right to speak should not be dependent on majority approval. That is why the right to freedom of speech is, in the USA and the EU, enshrined in a constitution restricting the legislative powers of the government.

Even if the position under discussion could be restricted to indecency, it would still be unacceptable. Think again of some of the original arguments for valuing freedom of speech.

One of them – the idea of the 'market-place of ideas' – can be cast in terms of artistic freedom. It is unclear whether art progresses, but it certainly changes, constantly seeking the best that it can for its own time and place. This means that it must explore boundaries, and in the process it will often linger in dead ends which are variously silly and offensive; equally, it will often arrive at valuable destinations that required traversing ways which seemed, and perhaps were, silly and offensive. But the silly and the offensive are the price we pay for the sublime, for the best art does not emerge from the dictates of the majority (or from the dictates of a minority, for that matter). It is, of course, a value judgement to say that the price is worth paying. But if we deny that value judgement we should be clear about what it is that we are denying.

The argument about paternalism is also relevant here. I have often encountered things in the media of which I disapprove. But I would not, on the whole, wish for a society in which I was protected from them, even though my life might have been better in some ways if I had not encountered them. A society in which I was protected from them would inevitably be a society in which *others* decided what I should be protected from. That is not because I should need to encounter what I wish to be protected from before I could know that I wish to be protected from it, for often one wants to be protected from general types of things which can be specified adequately in advance. It is because I live in a society in which I do not myself make the relevant decisions about what I may and may not see; those decisions are made by a government more or less responsive to majority opinion,[19] and even if I had some desire to be protected from things that I myself disapprove of I should have no desire whatever to be protected from things that others disapprove of and think that I should disapprove of too. That some people, even a majority, disapprove of some expression is not, then, by itself a reasonable ground for censorship.

It may now be thought that I have misinterpreted the argument from offence. I have said that to be offended by something is to disapprove of it. But perhaps being offended is more than this, necessarily involving some unpleasant affect beyond that which is generally involved in having a disapproving view of something. The argument, it may be said, is not that the fact that people think something offensive is a ground for censorship, but the fact that they are actually *offended* by it, that they are caused feelings of indignation and outrage. Let us confine our attention, then, to things which cause offence in the sense that they cause *outrage*. Does this affect the argument in any way? Is it a reasonable ground to censor speech that it causes in some people outrage?

Here again a distinction needs to be observed. One reason for censoring speech that causes outrage is to protect the public order. This is, of course, a highly dangerous principle, and one that no government should normally countenance, for it creates the right to a 'heckler's veto': those who wish to silence speech may do so simply by threatening violence in response to it.[20] In any case, this reason is not relevant at the moment; its appeal is to *harm* that the speech may cause, and we have already dealt with that. The reason that would have to be at issue now would be that people simply have a right not to be caused outrage. But this principle is far from compelling. Our public life is disfigured by outrage on the part of too many who think they have a grievance or even just a worthy cause, and there seems little reason to honour it with legal protection. On the contrary, a healthy respect for the civic virtues requires, not only that one generally refrain from giving gratuitous offence, but that one should learn to control one's temper when it is given.

A further distinction may be worth commenting upon, though a fairly obvious one. Being offended is not the same thing as being embarrassed, though they are often confused in this context because one of the things that makes certain actions offensive is that they obviously cause embarrassment. Now, most people find it embarrassing to watch, say, representations of sexual behaviour on the television in the presence of their 11-year-old children. Such embarrassment is not at all unreasonable, and nor is the desire to be protected from it. But it does not generate any argument for censorship. The most that it justifies is a requirement of clear labelling. That can be accomplished in many ways. The BBC for many years operated with a '9 o'clock watershed'; nothing sexually explicit could be shown before 9 o'clock, when good children were supposed to be in bed. Many professed to find this inadequate on the ground that many children did not go to bed until much later. But, after all, viewers had been warned; they could send their children to bed if they did not want to be embarrassed (or, alternatively, go to bed themselves). But other methods would work better; some cable television stations in the USA, for instance, label the films that they show, indicating whether they contain nudity ('N'), brief nudity ('BN'), 'strong sexual content' ('SSC') and so on. Of course, one may switch ·

on the film after it has started and miss the label. But if one is subsequently embarrassed, that is one's own responsibility, just as it is if one drinks a bottle of paraquat not having had time to read the label.

We have been dealing so far with indecency, but we should now be able to see our way through the other issues that I mentioned. Let us turn to blasphemy.

Laws prohibiting blasphemy have never been ruled unconstitutional in the USA, but it would now be generally recognised that to prohibit blasphemy would violate two provisions of the First Amendment: the clause prohibiting the state from establishing a religion, and the clause prohibiting the state from abridging the freedom of speech. There has been no prosecution for blasphemy in the USA since 1971.

There is no such protection for blasphemy in the UK, and it remains a criminal offence in England and Wales.[21] However, the last prosecution for blasphemy in the UK was in 1976. Mary Whitehouse, a noted agitator for stringent standards of decency on radio and television, prosecuted a journal, *Gay News*, and its publisher for a poem celebrating a union of Christ and homosexuality. Though the conviction was upheld on appeal, many thought that the absurd affair was the dying cough of the law of blasphemy. It was resuscitated however, by two events in 1988. One was Martin Scorsese's film *The Last Temptation of Christ*, which suggested that Jesus had fathered children by Mary Magdalene. Reportedly described as 'the most blasphemous evil attack on the Church and the cause of Christ in the history of entertainment'[22] it caused immense outrage in many countries. (Even Franco Zeffirelli, whose *Jesus of Nazareth* had earlier been denounced as blasphemous, boycotted the film at the Venice Film Festival.) The other event was the publication of Salman Rushdie's *The Satanic Verses*, a long novel which many Muslims held to be blasphemous. It was widely banned and burned and eventually the Ayatollah Khomeini sentenced Rushdie (and the publishers) to death, promising an enormous sum of money to anyone who would murder them. Subsequent sales of the book have made Rushdie an enormously wealthy man, but he has ever since been forced to live in hiding, guarded by policemen.[23]

Both film and book undoubtedly caused much genuine offence, though, as is common with persecution for blasphemy, the hysteria over Rushdie's book was partly political, deliberately whipped up as part of an anti-western propaganda movement on the part of extremist Muslims. And the book, which in the normal course of events, would have been read by relatively few people, became an international best-seller. The most interesting aspect of all of this, however, was the impetus it gave to the movement to *extend* the blasphemy law in the United Kingdom, a movement supported by many politicians, church leaders and others. The idea, at its simplest, was to toughen up the blasphemy law and extend it to cover all religions and not just Christianity. The argument seemed to be twofold. First, in an increasingly multi-cultural society there is a public interest in preventing the sort of offence which might lead to civil discord; and second, people have a right to have their feelings protected from outrageous attacks on their religious beliefs or on the gods in whom they believe.

But we have already seen problems with these arguments. The first seems to legitimate the 'heckler's veto'. In the present context, however, it picks up other problems too. First, it has little to do with religion, and therefore gives little support to blasphemy laws specifically. Anyone minded to offend someone from a different culture will find little obstacle in a law prohibiting insulting references to his religion. Second, and a corollary, the argument would cast the net of prohibited speech very wide indeed, and such a law, if enforced, would almost certainly exact considerably greater costs to freedom of expression than any benefits to be reaped. Third, one might expect such a law to produce its own civil discord, as those who never liked a multicultural society in the first place vented their rage on those whose cultural differences were perceived as the root cause of this restrictive prohibition.

The second argument too we can now deal with fairly quickly. It should not be confused with the argument that says that it is intrinsically immoral to insult God or religion; that could be true, but we have already seen that the mere intrinsic immorality of speech will not generate a legitimate reason for censorship. Nor is that how it is nowadays usually intended. The idea is rather that what people have a right to be protected from is the hurt to their feelings caused by *outrageous insult*. But this cannot be right. First, if we were to acknowledge such a right, then it would be totally arbitrary to restrict it to the area of religion; we should thus not really be talking about blasphemy at all. Second, certain beliefs, some religious ones included, *call for* the sort of robust attack which their adherents will perceive as outrageous and insulting; it would be wholly inappropriate to censor such speech merely to protect the feelings of those adherents. Nor should we want to allow the government to decide which beliefs could be spoken of in that way and which could not.[24] Third, as I have already said, there seems in any case little reason to give protection against outrage caused by sentiments that one does not approve of.

Notes

1 *Miami Herald Co. v. Tornillo* 418 US 241 (1974).
2 See, for instance, Alexander Meiklejohn, *Free Speech and its Relation to Self-Government* (New York: Harper and Row, 1948). Meiklejohn gave absolute weight, however, to the narrowly defined speech that he thought was protected by the First Amendment.
3 See J. S. Mill, *On Liberty*, ch. 2 (*On Liberty and Other Writings*, ed. Stefan Collini, (Cambridge, Cambridge University Press, 1989); and Oliver Wendell Holmes's dissenting opinion in *Abrams v. US*, 250 US 616 (1919).
4 There is, of course, a technical method for expressing these other theories as consequentialist theories, but it does not hide the significant difference between them and the theories that it is more natural to refer to as consequentialist.

5 See Mill, *On Liberty*, p. 15; and Rodney Smolla, *Free Speech in an Open Society* (New York: Vintage Books, 1993), pp. 10f.
6 See Ronald Dworkin, *Freedom's Law: The Moral Reading of the American Constitution* (Cambridge, MA: Harvard University Press, 1996), p. 200.
7 Dworkin, *Freedom's Law*, pp. 200f.
8 However, obscene speech, as defined by *Miller* v. *California*, 413 US 15 (1973), has no constitutional protection in the USA.
9 *Schenck* v. *US*, 249 US 47 (1919).
10 *New York Times Co.* v. *Sullivan*, 376 US 254 (1964).
11 'The English law of civil defamation is widely regarded as unsatisfactory' (Eric Barendt, *Freedom of Speech* (Oxford: Clarendon Press, 1985), p. 178.
12 For a balanced account of press coverage in the Falklands War, see 'Information policy and the Falklands conflict' in Shimon Shetreet (ed.), *Free Speech and National Security* (Dordrecht: Nijhoff, 1991), pp. 143–54.
13 For a detailed account, see Smolla, *Free Speech in an Open Society*, ch. 10.
14 Article 10 of the European Convention on Human Rights. On this, issue see Barendt, *Freedom of Speech*, pp. 218–23.
15 *New York Times Co.* v. *Sullivan*, 376 US 254, 270 (1964). For an account of this case, see Anthony Lewis, *Make No Law: The Sullivan Case and the First Amendment* (New York: Vintage Books, 1991).
16 See Frederick Schauer, 'Uncoupling free speech', *Columbia Law Review*, 92 (1992), pp. 1321–57. Schauer points out that under current US First Amendment law, those who are injured by protected speech bear the full costs, costs which ought, in principle at least, to be borne by those who benefit from protecting speech, i.e. society at large.
17 However, the conviction in the *Gay News* case was upheld by the House of Lords in 1979, the majority of the justices holding that intent to offend was *not* a necessary part of the common-law crime of blasphemy. For an account of this case, see Leonard Levy, *Blasphemy: Verbal Offense against the Sacred from Moses to Salman Rushdie* (New York: Alfred A. Knopf, 1993), pp. 534–50.
18 I have discussed this in more detail in 'Offense and the liberal conception of the law', *Philosophy and Public Affairs* 13 (1984), pp. 1–23.
19 More or less because it takes only a small minority of people – such as the members of the National Viewers' and Listeners' Association – to have a significant effect on government bodies.
20 See Harry Kalven, Jr, *A Worthy Tradition: Freedom of Speech in America* (New York: Harper and Row, 1988), pp. 89ff.
21 Parliament repealed the 1698 Blasphemy Act in 1967, but it remains a common-law offence in England and Wales. There is no law of blasphemy in Scotland or Northern Ireland.
22 *The Economist*, 13 August 1988, p. 77.
23 Blasphemy has caused enormous offence in a different context; as I write, the city of Richmond, Virginia, is, probably unconstitutionally, desperately trying to cancel a contract for a concert with a Satanistic rock group known as Marilyn Manson; they had not realized, when the contract was made, the nature of the group's performance. The city councillors' outrage had been matched in many cities, and the University of South Carolina had shortly before, paid the group $40,000 not to perform a scheduled concert.
24 'If there is any fixed star in our constitutional constellation, it is that no official, high or petty, can prescribe what shall be orthodox in politics, nationalism, religion, or other matters of opinion', Justice Robert Jackson (*West Virginia State Board of Education* v. *Barnette* (319 US 624 (1943)).

Select bibliography

Altman, I., 'Privacy: a conceptual analysis', *Environment and Behavior* 8 (1976): 7–8.

Aristotle, *Nichomachean Ethics*, Harmondsworth: Penguin Books, 1953.

Aristotle, *Poetics*, Ann Arbor, MI: University of Michigan Press, 1970.

Attorney General's Commission on Pornography, *Final Report*, 2 vols, Washington DC: US Government Printing Office, 1986.

Barendt, Eric, *Freedom of Speech*, Oxford: Oxford University Press, 1985.

Barker, Martin and Petley, Julian (eds), *Ill Effects: The Media/Violence Debate*, London: Routledge, 1997.

Baudrillard, Jean, *In the Shadow of the Silent Majorities . . . or the End of the Social*, New York: Semiotext, 1983.

Baudrillard, Jean, *Selected Writings*, ed. Mark Poster, Cambridge: Polity, 1988.

Beauchamp, Tom L. and Pinkard, Terry P. (eds), *Ethics and Public Policy*, Englewood Cliffs, NJ: Prentice-Hall, 1983.

Bell, Martin, *In Harm's Way: Reflections of a War Zone Thug*, London: Hamish Hamilton, 1995.

Belsey, Andrew and Chadwick, Ruth (eds), *Ethical Issues in Journalism and the Media*, London: Routledge, 1992.

Belsey, Andrew and Chadwick, Ruth, 'Ethics as a vehicle for media quality', *European Journal of Communication* 10 (1995): 461–73.

Benn, Piers 'Pornography, degradation and rhetoric', *Cogito* 7 (1993): 127–34.

Bennett, T., Boyd-Bowman, S., Mercer, C. and Woollacott, J. (eds), *Popular Television and Film*, London: British Film Institute.

Berlin, Isaiah, *Four Essays on Liberty*, Oxford: Oxford University Press, 1969.

Bernays, E., *Crystallising Public Opinion*, New York: Boni and Liveright, 1923.

Bernstein, Carl and Woodward, Bob, *All the President's Men*, New York: Secker and Warburg.

Bezanson, Randall P., Cranberg, Gilbert and Soloski, John, *Libel Law and the Press*, New York: Free Press, 1987.

Birkenshaw, Patrick, *Freedom of Information: The Law, the Practice and the Ideal*, London: Weidenfeld and Nicolson, 1988.

Bok, Sissela, *Lying: Moral Choice in Public and Private Life*, London: Quartet, 1980.

Bok, Sissela, *Secrets: On the Ethics of Concealment and Revelation*, Oxford: Oxford University Press, 1982.

Bryant, Jennings and Zillman, Dolf (eds), *Perspectives on Media Effects*, Hillsdale, NJ: Erlbaum, 1986.

Calcutt, David, *Report of the Committee on Privacy and Other Matters*, Cmnd. 1102, London: HMSO, 1990.

Calcutt, David, *Review of Press Self-regulation*, Cmnd. 2135, London: HMSO, 1993.

Capa, Robert, *Slightly out of Focus*, New York: H. Holt, 1947.

Caputi, Mary, *Voluptuous Yearnings: A Feminist Theory of the Obscene*, Lanham, MD: Rowman and Littlefield, 1994.

Carroll, Noël, 'Conspiracy theories of representation', *Philosophy of the Social Sciences* 17 (1987).

Carroll, Noël, *The Philosophy of Horror*, New York: Routledge, 1990.

Carroll, Noël, *A Philosophy of Mass Art*, Oxford University Press, 1998.

Chomsky, Noam, *Necessary Illusions*, Toronto: CBC Enterprises, 1989.

Chomsky, Noam and Hermann, Edward, *Manufacturing Consent*, London: Vintage, 1994.

Christians, Clifford G., Ferré, John and Fackler, Mark, *Good News: A Social Ethics of the Press*, New York: Oxford University Press, 1993.

Christians, Clifford G., Fackler, Mark and Rotzoll, Kim B., *Media Ethics: Cases and Moral Reasoning*, 4th edn, New York: Longman, 1995.

Cohen, Elliot D. (ed.) *Philosophical Issues in Journalism*, New York: Oxford University Press, 1992.

Commission on Freedom of the Press, *A Free and Responsible Press*, Chicago: University of Chicago Press, 1947.

Cooper, Thomas W., *Communication Ethics and Global Change*, New York: Longman, 1989.

Crewe, I. and Gosschalk, B. (eds), *Political Communications: The General Election Campaign of 1992*, Cambridge: Cambridge University Press, 1995.

Curran, James (ed.), *The British Press: A Manifesto*, London: Routledge, 1978.

Curran, James and Seaton, Jean (eds), *Power without Responsibility: The Press and Broadcasting in Britain*, 4th edn, London: Routledge, 1991.

Dahlgren, Peter and Sparks, Colin (eds), *Communication and Citizenship*, London: Routledge, 1991.

Dahlgren, Peter and Sparks, Colin (eds), *Journalism and Popular Culture*, London: Sage, 1992.

Day, Louis A., *Ethics in Media Communication: Cases and Controversies*, Belmont, CA: Wadsworth, 1991.

Denton, Robert E. Jr. (ed.), *Ethical Dimensions of Political Communication*, New York: Praeger, 1991.

Deppa, Joan, *The Media and Disasters: Pan Am 103*, London: David Fulton, 1993.

Devlin, Patrick, *The Enforcement of Morals*, Oxford: Oxford University Press, 1965.

Dworkin, Andrea, *Letters from a War Zone*, London: Secker and Warburg, 1988.

Dworkin, Ronald, *A Matter of Principle*, Oxford: Clarendon Press, 1985.

Dworkin, Ronald, *Freedom's Law: The Moral Reading of the American Constitution*, Cambridge, MA: Harvard University Press, 1996.

Dyson, Kenneth and Homolka, Walter (eds), *Culture First/Promoting Standards in the New Media Age*, London: Cassell, 1996.

Eason, David L., 'On journalistic authority: the Janet Cooke scandal', *Critical Studies in Mass Communication* 3/4 (1988): 313–34.

Elliot, Deni (ed.), *Responsible Journalism*, Beverly Hills, CA: Sage, 1986.

Ellis, Anthony, 'Offense and the liberal conception of the law', *Philosophy and Public Affairs* 13 (1984): 1–23.

Ellis, John, *Visible Fictions*, London: Routledge and Kegan Paul, 1982.

Engel, Matthew, *Tickle the Public: One Hundred Years of the Popular Press*, London: Gollancz, 1996.

Ettema, James S. and Glasser, Theodore L., 'On the epistemology of investigative journalism', *Journal of Communication* 8/2 (1985): 183–206.

Evans, Harold, *Eyewitness: 25 Years Through World Press Photos*, London: Quiller Press, 1981.

Fairclough, Norman, *Media Discourse*, London and New York: Edward Arnold, 1995.

Fallows, James, *Breaking the News*, New York: Pantheon, 1996.

Feinberg, Joel, *Social Philosophy*, Englewood Cliffs, NJ: Prentice-Hall, 1973.

Feinberg, Joel, *Rights, Justice and the Bounds of Liberty: Essays in Social Philosophy*, Princeton, NJ: Princeton University Press, 1980.

Feinberg, Joel, *The Moral Limits of the Criminal Law*, vol. 2: *Offense to Others*, New York: Oxford University Press, 1985.

Feldman, D., *Civil Liberties and Human Rights*, Oxford: Clarendon Press, 1993.

Fink, Conrad, *Media Ethics*, New York: McGraw-Hill, 1988.

Fiske, John, *Television Culture*, New York: Routledge, 1987.

Fiske, John, 'Popularity and the politics of information', in P. Dahlgren and C. Sparks (eds) *Journalism and Popular Culture*, London: Sage, 1992, pp. 45–63.

Fiske, John, *Media Matters: Everyday Culture and Political Change*, Minneapolis, MN: University of Minnesota Press, 1994.

Franklin, Bob, *Newszak and News Media*, London: Arnold, 1997.

Freund, Gisèle, *Photography and Society*, London: Gordon Fraiser, 1980.

Gauntlett, David, *Moving Experiences: Understanding Television's Influences and Effects*, London: John Libbey, 1995.

Gitlin, Todd, *The Whole World is Watching*, Berkeley, CA: University of California Press, 1980.

Gluckman, Max, 'Gossip and scandal', *Current Anthropolgy* 4/3 (June 1963): 307–16.

Goldman, Alan, *The Moral Foundations of Professional Ethics*, Totowa, NJ: Rowman and Littlefield, 1980.

Goldstein, Tom, *The News at Any Cost*, New York: Simon and Schuster, 1985.

Goodman, Robert F. and Ben-Ze'ev, Aaron (eds), *Good Gossip*, Lawrence, KS: University of Kansas Press, 1994.

Goodwin, H. Eugene and Smith, Ron F., *Groping for Ethics in Journalism*, 3rd edn, Ames, IA: Iowa State University Press, 1994.

Gosschalk, B. (ed.) *Political Communications*, Cambridge: Cambridge University Press, 1995.

Graham, Gordon, *Contemporary Social Philosophy*, Oxford: Blackwell Publishers, 1988.

Gripsund, J., 'The aesthetics and the politics of melodrama', in P. Dahlgren and C. Sparks (eds) *Journalism and Popular Culture*, London: Sage, 1992, pp. 84–95.

Gross, Larry, Katz, John Stuart and Ruby, Jay (eds), *Image Ethics*, New York: Oxford University Press, 1988.

Habermas, J., *The Structural Transformation of the Public Sphere*, Cambridge: Polity, 1988.

Hargrave, Andrea Millwood, *Sex and Sexuality in Broadcasting*, London: John Libbey, 1992.

Hart, H. L. A., *Law, Liberty and Morality*, Oxford: Oxford University Press, 1963.

Hartley, John, *Understanding News*, London: Methuen, 1982.

Hausman, Carl, *Crisis of Conscience: Perspectives on Journalism Ethics*, New York: HarperCollins, 1992.

Hewitt, Patricia, *Privacy: The Information Gatherers*, London: National Council for Civil Liberties, 1977.

Hiebert, Ray Eldon (ed.), *Impact of Mass Media*, 3rd edn, New York: Longman, 1995.

Hooper, David, *Official Secrets: The Use and Abuse of the Act*, London: Secker and Warburg, 1987.

Howitt, D. and Cumberbatch, G., *Pornography: Impacts and Influences*, London: HMSO, 1990.

Hulteng, John L., *The Messanger's Motives: Ethical Problems of the Mass Media*, 2nd edn, Englewood Cliffs, NJ: Prentice-Hall, 1985.

Jones, J. Clement, *Mass Media Codes of Ethics and Councils: A Comparative International Study on Professional Standards*, Paris: Unesco, 1980.

Jones, Nicholas, *Soundbites and Spindoctors*, London: Cassell, 1995.

Kalven, Harry, Jr, *A Worthy Tradition: Freedom of Speech in America*, New York: Harper and Row, 1988.

Kant, Immanuel, *Groundwork of the Metaphysics of Morals*, in H. J. Paton (ed.) *The Moral Law*, London: Hutchinson, 1948.

Kant, Immanuel, *The Philosophy of Immanuel Kant*, Chicago: University of Chicago Press, 1949.

Karnow, Stanley, *Vietnam: A History*, New York: Viking Press, 1983.

Keane, John, *The Media and Democracy*, Oxford: Polity Press, 1991.

Keeble, Richard, *The Newspapers Handbook*, London: Routledge, 1994.

Kellner, Douglas, *Television and the Crisis of Democracy*, Boulder, CO, San Francisco and Oxford: Westview Press, 1990.

Kieran, Matthew, 'Violent films: natural born killers?', *Philosophy Now* 12 (1995): 15–18.

Kieran, Matthew, 'Art, imagination and the cultivation of morals', *Journal of Aesthetics and Art Criticism* 54 (1996): 337–51.

Kieran, Matthew, *Media Ethics: A Philosophical Approach*, Westport, CT: Praeger, 1997.

Kieran, Matthew, 'News reporting and the ideological presumption', *Journal of Communication* 47/2 (1997): 79–96.

Kieran, Matthew, Morrison, David and Svennevig, Michael, *Regulating for Changing Values: A Report for the Broadcasting Standards Commission*, London: BSC, 1997.

Klaidman, Stephen and Beauchamp, Tom L., *The Virtuous Journalist*, New York: Oxford University Press, 1987.

Knightley, Phillip, *The First Casualty: From the Crimea to Vietnam: The War*

Correspondent as Hero, Propagandist, and Myth Maker, New York: Harcourt Brace Jovanovich, 1975.

Knowlton, Steven R. and Parsons, Patrick R. (ed.), *The Journalist's Moral Compass*, Westport, CT: Praeger, 1995.

Koch, Tom, *The News as Myth*, New York: Greenwood, 1990.

Kurtz, Howard, *Media Circus*, New York: Random House, 1994.

Lambeth, Edmund B., *Committed Journalism*, 2nd edn, Bloomington, IN: Indiana University Press, 1992.

Lee, Alan, *The Origins of the Popular Press in England 1855–1914*, London: Croom Helm, 1976.

Lemert, J. B., *Criticizing the Media*, Newbury Park, CA: Sage, 1989.

Lester, Paul, *Photojournalism: An Ethical Approach*, Hillsdale, NJ: Erlbaum, 1991.

Levy, Leonard, *Blasphemy: Verbal Offense against the Sacred from Moses to Salman Rushdie*, New York: Alfred A. Knopf, 1993.

Lewis, Anthony, *Make No Law: The Sullivan Case and the First Ammendment*, New York: Vintage Books, 1991.

Lichtenberg, Judith (ed.), *Democracy and the Mass Media*, Cambridge: Cambridge University Press, 1990.

Limburg, Val E., *Electronic Media Ethics*, Boston, MA: Focal Press, 1994.

Locke, John, *Two Treatises of Government*, Cambridge: Cambridge University Press, 1963.

Locke, John, *A Letter Concerning Toleration*, New York: Prometheus, 1990.

Machiavelli, Niccolò, *The Prince*, New York: Dover, 1992.

MacKenzie, John, *Propaganda and Empire: The Manipulation of British Public Opinion 1880–1960*, Manchester: Manchester University Press, 1984.

MacKinnon, Catherine, *Only Words*, Cambridge, MA: Harvard University Press, 1993.

McLuhan, Marshall, *Understanding Media: The Extensions of Man*, London: Routledge and Kegan Paul, 1964.

McLuhan, Marshall and Fiore, Quentin, *The Medium in the Message*, Harmondsworth: Penguin Books, 1967.

McNair, Brian, *Glasnost, Perestroika and the Soviet Media*, London: Routledge, 1991.

McNair, Brian, *An Introduction to Political Communication*, London: Routledge, 1995.

McNair, Brian, *News and Journalism in the UK*, 2nd edn, London: Routledge, 1996.

McNair, Brian, 'Performance in politics and the politics of performance: public relations, the public sphere and democracy', in J. L'Etang and M. Pieczke (eds) *Critical Perspectives in Public Relations*, London: International Thomson Business Press, 1996, pp. 35–53.

McQuail, Denis, *Media Performance: Mass Communication and the Public Interest*, Newbury Park, CA: Sage, 1992.

Mander, Jerry, *Four Arguments for the Elimination of Television*, New York: Quill, 1978.

Marshall, W. L., 'Pornography and sex offenders', in D. Zillman and J. Bryant (eds) *Pornography: Research Advances and Policy Considerations*, Hillsdale, NJ: Erlbaum, 1989, pp. 185–214.

Meiklejohn, Alexander, *Free Speech and its Relation to Self-government*, New York: Harper and Row, 1948.

Merill, John C. and Barney, Ralph D. (eds) *Ethics and the Press*, New York: Hastings House, 1975.

Metz, Christian, *Psychoanalysis and Cinema: The Imaginary Signifier*, London: Methuen, 1982.

Meyer, Philip, *Ethical Journalism*, New York: Longman, 1987.

Meyerwitz, Joshua, *No Sense of Place*, Oxford: Oxford University Press, 1985.

Mill, John Stuart, *On Liberty*, Harmondsworth: Penguin Books, 1982.

Mitchell, William J., *The Reconfigured Eye: Visual Truth in the Post-photographic Era*, Cambridge, MA: MIT Press, 1992.

Moore, Roy L., *Mass Communication Law and Ethics*, Hillsdale, NJ: Erlbaum, 1994.

Morris, D., *Behind the Oval Office*, New York: Random House, 1996.

Morrison, David E. and Tumber, Howard, *Journalists at War: The Dynamics of News Reporting during the Falklands Conflict*, London: Sage, 1988.

Mulvey, Laura, *Visual and Other Pleasures*, London: Macmillan, 1989.

Newsome, Elizabeth, 'Video violence and the protection of children', Child Development Research Unit, University of Nottingham, March 1994.

Nozick, Robert, *Anarchy, State and Utopia*, Oxford: Blackwell Publishers, 1974.

Olen, Jeffrey, *Ethics in Journalism*, Englewood Cliffs, NJ: Prentice-Hall, 1988.

Paik, Haejung and Comstock, George, 'The effects of television violence on antisocial behavior: a meta-analysis', *Communication Research* 21 (1994): 516–46.

Pally, Marcia, *Sex and Sensibility: Reflections on Forbidden Mirrors and the Will to Censor*, Hopewell, NJ: Ecco Press, 1994.

Patterson, Philip and Wilkins, Lee (eds), *Media Ethics: Issues and Cases*, 2nd edn, Dubuque, IA: Wm. C. Brown, 1994.

Paul, Noel S., *Principles for the Press: A Digest of Council Decisions, 1953–1984*, London: Press Council, 1985.

Perse, Elizabeth M., 'Uses of erotica and acceptance of rape myths', *Communication Research* 21 (1994): 488–515.

Philo, Greg, *Seeing and Believing*, London: Routledge, 1990.

Plato, *Republic*, trans. D. Lee, Harmondsworth: Penguin Books, 1974.

Powes, Lucas A., Jr, *The Fourth Estate and Constitution: Freedom of the Press in America*, Berkeley and Los Angeles, CA: University of California Press, 1991.

Press Complaints Commission, *Code of Practice*, London: Press Complaints Commission, September 1994.

Press Complaints Commission, *Annual Report 1995*, London: Press Complaints Commission, 1995.

Rachlin, Allan, *News as Hegemonic Reality*, New York: Praeger, 1988.

Rawls, John, *A Theory of Justice*, Oxford: Oxford University Press, 1972.

Ricoeur, Paul, *Hermeneutics and the Human Sciences*, trans. J. B. Thompson, Cambridge: Cambridge University Press, 1981.

Ritchin, Fred, *In Our Own Image*, New York: Aperture, 1990.

Robertson, Geoffrey, *Freedom, the Individual and the Law*, Harmondsworth: Penguin, 1989.

Rodgerson, G. and Wilson, E. (eds) *Pornography and Feminism*, London: Lawrence and Wishart, 1993.

Rorty, Richard, *Contingency, Irony and Solidarity,* Cambridge: Cambridge University Press, 1989.

Rosenblum, Mort, *Who Stole the News?*, New York: John Wiley and Sons, 1993.

Rubin, Bernard, *Questioning Media Ethics*, New York: Praeger, 1978.

Schaner, Frederick, 'Uncoupling free speech', *Columbia Law Review* 92 (1992): 1321–57.

Schlesinger, Philip, *Media, State and Nation: Political Violence and Collective Identities*, London: Sage, 1991.

Schlesinger, Philip and Tumber, Howard, *Reporting Crime: The Media Politics of Criminal Justice*, Oxford: Clarendon Press, 1994.

Schoeman, Ferdinand David (ed.), *Philosophical Dimensions of Privacy: An Anthology,* Cambridge: Cambridge University Press, 1984.

Schostak, John, *Dirty Marks: The Education of Self, Media and Popular Culture*, London: Pluto, 1993.

Scruton, Roger. *The Aesthetic Understanding*, Manchester: Carcanet, 1983.

Seib, Philip, *Campaigns and Conscience: The Ethics of Political Journalism*, Vancouver, BC: University of British Columbia Press, 1994.

Seymour-Ure, Colin, *The British Press and Broadcasting Since 1945*, Oxford: Blackwell, 1991.

Shearer, Anne, *Survivors and the Media*, London: Broadcasting Standards Council and John Libbey, 1992.

Shetreet, Simon (ed.), *Free Speech and National Security,* Dordrecht: Nijhoff, 1991.

Singer, Jerome L. and Singer, Dorothy, G., *Television, Imagination and Aggression*, Hillsdale, NJ: Erlbaum, 1981.

Slater, Michael D., 'Processing social information in messages: social group familiarity, fiction versus nonfiction, and subsequent beliefs', *Communication Research* 17 (1990): 327–43.

Smith, Anthony, *The Newspaper: An International History,* London: Thames and Hudson, 1979.

Smith, Anthony (ed.), *Newspapers and Democracy: International Essays on a Changing Medium*, Cambridge, MA: MIT Press, 1980.

Smith, Anthony (ed.), *Television: An International History,* Oxford: Oxford University Press, 1995.

Smolla, Rodney, *Free Speech in an Open Society,* New York: Vintage Books, 1993.

Snoddy, Raymond, *The Good, The Bad and the Unacceptable*, London: Faber, 1992; pbk edn 1993.

Snyder, Joel and Allen, Neil Walsh, 'Photography, vision and representation', *Critical Inquiry* 2 (1975): 143–69.

Sorell, Tom, 'Art, society and morality', in O. Hanfling (ed.) *Philosophical Aesthetics*, Oxford: Blackwell Publishers, 1992, pp. 297–347.

Stephenson, Hugh, *Media Freedom and Media Regulation*, London: Association of British Editors, 1994.

Stocking, S. Holly and LaMarca, Nancy, 'How journalists describe their stories: hypotheses and assumptions in newsmaking', *Journalism Quarterly* 67 (1990): 295–301.

Strossen, Nadine, *Defending Pornography: Free Speech, Sex and the Fight for Women's Rights*, London: Abacus, 1996.

Tester, Keith, *Media, Culture and Morality,* London: Routledge, 1994.

Thompson, M. P., 'Confidence in the press', *The Conveyancer and Property Lawyer* 57 (1993): 347–58.

Thomson, J. J., 'The right to privacy', *Philosophy and Public Affairs* 4 (1975): 295–314.

Tuchman, Gaye, *Making News: A Study in the Construction of Reality*, New York: Free Press, 1978.

Tunstall, Jeremy, *The Media in Britain*, London: Constable, 1983.

Van den Haag, E., 'On Privacy', in J. R. Pennock and J. W. Chapman (eds) *Privacy: Nomos XIII*, New York: Atherton Press, 1979, p. 149.

Vaux, Kenneth L., *Ethics and the Gulf War: Religion, Rhetoric and Righteousness*, Boulder, CO: Westview, 1992.

Wacks, R., *Privacy and Press Freedom*, London: Blackstone Press, 1995.

Wakeham, J., 'The Conservative campaign: against the odds', in I. Crewe and B. Gosschalk (eds) *Political Communications: The General Election Campaign of 1992*, Cambridge: Cambridge University Press, 1995, pp. 3–8.

Waldron, Jeremy, *Liberal Rights*, New York: Cambridge University Press, 1993.

Walton, Kendall, 'Transparent pictures: on the nature of photographic realism', *Critical Inquiry* 11 (1984): 246–77.

Warburton, Nigel, 'Photographic communication', *British Journal of Aesthetics* 28 (1988): 173–81.

Warburton, Nigel, 'Seeing through "Seeing through" photographs', *Ratio* NS 1/1 (1988): 64–74.

Warburton, Nigel, 'Varieties of photographic representation', *History of Photography* 15 (1991): 203–10.

Warren, Samuel and Brandeis, Lewis, 'The right to privacy', *Harvard Law Review* 4 (1890): 205.

Weaver, Paul, *News and the Culture of Lying*, New York: Macmillan, 1994.

Williams, Bernard (ed.), *The Williams Report: Report of the Committee on Obscenity and Film Censorship*, Cmnd. 7772, London: HMSO, 1979.

Index

Printed in the United States
201934BV00011B/4-6/A

9 780415 168380

SOCIAL SELVES

THEORIES OF SELF AND SOCIETY

SECOND EDITION

IAN BURKITT

Los Angeles • London • New Delhi • Singapore

First edition published 1991 (Reprinted 1992, 1993, 1995, 2000)

SAGE Publications Ltd
1 Oliver's Yard
55 City Road
London EC1Y 1SP

SAGE Publications Inc.
2455 Teller Road
Thousand Oaks, California 91320

SAGE Publications India Pvt Ltd
B 1/I 1 Mohan Cooperative Industrial Area
Mathura Road
New Delhi 110 044

SAGE Publications Asia-Pacific Pte Ltd
33 Pekin Street #02-01
Far East Square
Singapore 048763

Library of Congress Control Number: 2007931369

British Library Cataloguing in Publication data

A catalogue record for this book is available from the British Library

ISBN 978 1 4129 1271 6
ISBN 978 1 4129 1272 3 (pbk)

Typeset by C&M Digitals (P) Ltd., Chennai, India
Printed in Great Britain by The Cromwell Press Ltd, Trowbridge, Wiltshire
Printed on paper from sustainable resources

To the memory of my father and mother,
William and Irene Mary Burkitt

CONTENTS

PREFACE TO THE SECOND EDITION AND ACKNOWLEDGEMENTS

Writing the second edition of a book is an interesting proposition. When this was first put to me by Sage my initial response was to think that I couldn't possibly go back to a task I thought I'd completed 16 years ago. But then, as I thought more about the prospect, my enthusiasm grew: so much has been written in the intervening years about self and identity that the original text was out of date in many important ways, particularly with the explosion of literature on gender and sexuality, and a revival of interest in social class. Then there is the literature on the changing nature of contemporary society in a globalized capitalist world and the effects this has had on self-identities. More than this, though, I had changed. The first edition of *Social Selves* was based on my PhD thesis, and, over the years of teaching and writing on the self, my views have subtly shifted. Because of this I chose to rewrite the whole book, rather than to graft new material onto the old. This has been more time consuming, but a much more satisfactory experience – hopefully for the reader as well as the writer.

What has also been interesting is thinking back to what was behind the writing of the original book. The seed of this was set early in my undergraduate years when one of my lecturers, Robert Ashcroft, raised the issue of what makes us into the people that we are and why we act in the ways that we do: is this something to do with us as individuals, with the society in which we find ourselves – our social position, institutional roles, or family and educational background – or in the relation between the two? This incident is itself an example of the reciprocal influence we humans have on one another: a good teacher can spark a lifetime of interest and exploration in a student. But also, as I try to point out throughout this book, everything we do is set in a social and historical context. As I began my PhD in the topic of the social self in the mid-1980s and completed the first edition of this book at the end of that decade, we were living in politically conservative times. The then British Prime Minister Margaret Thatcher had set the tone of the 1980s by declaring there was no such thing as society, only individuals and families. It seemed like a challenging time to explore the literature that suggested the opposite was true: that as individual selves we only identify our differences in a social world of interaction with others, seeing ourselves as both like and unlike some other people. But then there are the bigger questions of social similarity and difference; of power, inequality, social class, gender and sexuality. These are the themes of this book.

Appropriately in a book about social selves, whatever I have achieved hasn't been done alone. The book is a dialogue with other voices (which I hope also engages the reader) and many others have made contributions that have inspired and encouraged me. Robert Ashcroft, Brian Burkitt, Eileen Moxon and Hilary Rose all provided support in encouraging me to do the PhD which became the basis of the first edition. Richard Kilminster supervised the PhD and was a great inspiration and support, as was Keith Tester – a fellow postgraduate at Leeds University during those years – who helped share what can be the isolated task of researching and writing a thesis. Those who also commented on or helped in the preparation of the first edition of the book included David Ingleby, Ian Parker, Karen Phillips, Kathleen Temple and, lovingly remembered, Caroline Pratt.

In writing the second edition of the book I would like to thank the staff and students at Bradford University who provide the academic culture in which I work, but especially Paul Sullivan, Brid Featherstone and Friedel Weinert who took the time and trouble to read parts of the manuscript. My thanks also go to Peter Lunt who read and commented on the whole manuscript. My affection goes to Alan Scott, Charles Stones, Arvick Baghramian and Nofit Itzhak for the friendship necessary to all social beings. Social selves must, however, take individual responsibility for their actions, and whatever failings remain in the manuscript are entirely my own.

CHAPTER 1

SOCIETY AND THE SELF

Who am I? This must be one of the most frequently asked questions in the modern Western world. It seems that at key points in our lives we all address this question in one way or another. On the surface this is a deceptively easy question, because if there is one thing we ought to know it is our own self: who we are. Yet anyone who has tried to answer this question will know how difficult it is. In the modern world we are engaged in so many activities that take place in a variety of contexts with a mixture of people, we become many different things to different people. We can also be many different things to ourselves. There might not be a single answer to the question of who we are. Furthermore, if none of the varied roles we play seem to fit us, we get more confused and the question becomes more insistent: *who am I?* We then find ourselves in a search for self. But where do we look for it? 'I'm trying to find myself' is a phrase often heard from the people we encounter, and maybe many of us have said it or thought it ourselves. For those who live in Western societies, with a history of individualism, the temptation is to look inside ourselves, to examine our thoughts and feelings, as if our self-identity is a treasure locked inside, like a pearl in its shell.

Paradoxically, this search for self is rarely a lonely task. In trying to find out who we are, even if we believe the riddle is locked inside, we invariably engage others in the search for the key to ourselves; whether they are friends and family, or counsellors and therapists, we look to other people to see the image of ourselves reflected back in their words, attitudes, expressions or actions. Yet strangely we often fail to notice this, that the search for our own individual self is a social activity. In Western societies that put a high value on the individual – its freedom, autonomy, creativity, and the expression of its own individuality – we can easily overlook the role that others play in giving us the pieces with which to put together an image of our self. This is what I mean here by the notion of *social selves,* which provides the title of this book and is the conundrum I will investigate in these pages, that to become an individual self with its own unique identity, we must first participate in a world of others that is formed by history and culture. What I want to investigate is the idea of *social individuality.* This does not mean that each one of us is not an individual self, we clearly are: rather, I want to ask questions about how this self is formed in social relations with others and how it is through them, and through the relation to our own selves, that we answer the question 'who am I?'

I therefore do not intend this book to be used as a 'self help' book, in the manner of those that fill the shelves of bookstores under the heading 'popular psychology' or 'self development'. You will not find here techniques for self-analysis or exercises for addressing personal problems. Most of the book is devoted to the debates about the self that have dominated the social and human sciences; the various ways in which sociologists, philosophers and social psychologists have addressed the question of the self in the contemporary Western world. Yet each of the thinkers I discuss, along with the position I will develop here, have addressed and informed the question 'who am I?' or, more generally, 'who are we?' as human beings. Many of their ideas have permeated everyday understandings about the self, so it is impossible to think about who you are independent of the answers that these thinkers have given to the question 'who am I?'. This is also because their answers were formed in the general historical and cultural epoch that still influences our lives and selves today. However, there is no such thing as a complete answer to any question, and each thinker has left us with a series of problems still to be addressed. If it is true to say we are never quite sure of who we are as individuals, it is also true to say that collectively we are still not sure of who we are as humans.

What, then, will you learn from this book? Not exactly an answer to the question 'who am I?' but an understanding of why we even bother to ask this question, why it is so important to us, and knowledge of some of the ideas that currently shape any possible answer you could be given to this question. Before we embark on the journey through some answers to the question, first I want to make clear my own view of the issues and why I am so insistent on suggesting that we are social selves.

Social selves: a challenge to individualism

I have already begun to address the question of why I have called this book *Social Selves,* because seeing ourselves as isolated cuts off the primary connection we have to other people in the creation of self. It is not that I want to deny the fact that each one of us is a unique individual, or that individualism can be a positive value. The ideals of freedom, liberty and individual autonomy are values that can prevent us from submitting to authorities that crave too much power, seeking to subjugate free people. But like all good ideas and ideals, individualism can also have its dangers. The political thinker C. B. Macpherson characterized the type of individualism that arises in Western capitalist societies as 'possessive individualism', which means each individual is thought to be the possessor of their own skills and capacities, owing nothing to society for the development of these.[1] A free society is then seen as a market society, one in which individuals can sell their capacities on the labour market for a wage, with which they buy the goods they need to consume in order to live. But Macpherson believed that this type of individualism could be corrosive of human society, because each person is understood as bound to others only through the competitive market and nothing more.

It is also a political theory that distorts human nature, because each one of us develops our capacities in society.

For the social and human sciences, the problem of possessive individualism is the creation of a division between the individual and society. An example of this is the approach to social study known as 'methodological individualism', typified by thinkers like F. A. Hayek, Karl Popper and J. W. N. Watkins, for whom all explanations of society must be based on statements about the dispositions and actions of individuals. That is because society is not a supra-individual entity, but composed of the individuals who make it what it is. Ironically, these thinkers actually agreed with many sociologists, whom they took as the target of their critiques, believing that society was nothing more than the relations between individuals. The real source of disagreement between these two camps is the status given to social relations – whether they are seen as primary in people's lives or merely contingent upon already existing individuals. The latter position was the one adopted by methodological individualists, while sociologists and social psychologists tend to believe that social relations are primary in our experience. In the approach I develop here, I am against the methodological individualist position of seeing the individual as a primary fact, one that possesses given capacities or a determinate essence. That is because we are all born into social relations that we didn't make, and much of who and what we are is formed in that context. But I do not want to reduce individuals to the mere products of their society, for the methodological individualists are right to say that there is no society without individuals and the relations between them. I prefer Norbert Elias's solution to this problem by thinking in terms of a society of individuals.[2]

Hence, my attempt to understand humans as social selves is a way of trying to overcome this dichotomy. I want to suggest that when we ask the questions 'who am I?' or 'who are we?' we try to understand ourselves as social individuals rather than self-contained atoms. I also draw attention to the fact that I speak of social *selves,* in the plural rather than the singular, for we are all individual selves who necessarily relate to each other: there are many different selves in a society of individuals. But also, as individuals, we are multiple: I am not exactly the same person in all the different situations I act in, nor am I exactly the same person today as I was 20 years ago. This much may be uncontroversial, but why do I insist on the necessity of the concept of *social* selves? I do so for three basic reasons.

Firstly, we are born into a place and time that is not of our own making, and into a network of social relations we haven't chosen. Each one of us is born into a society composed of social relations that bear the imprint of a power structure, including a hierarchy of social classes or other groupings according to rank and status, along with a culture with its beliefs and values, such as religion, or other bodies of knowledge, like science. The position into which we are born as an individual – our family, neighbourhood, social contacts, social class, gender, ethnicity, and the beliefs and values in which we are educated – will put a sizable imprint on the self we become. Those who surround us will judge, influence and mirror an image of our self back to us in many different ways. Even those who have sought solitude in order to find themselves, wandering into the wilderness, have nevertheless come from a tradition, religious or mystical, that will guide their meditation. All cultural traditions have theories about what it is to be a person, created in a network of everyday experiences and professional or theological debates. They have their own social history and will vary between cultures, yet all will provide the basis on which the selves who populate that culture emerge, forming their self-identities by moulding them with their own particularities.

Secondly, when we try to find who we are, we often turn to some social activity to reveal that 'hidden' self. We try out different roles, jobs, education, hobbies, arts, or sporting activities, hoping to find ourselves in them. The search for self therefore involves *what we do,* the activity informing who we are through the talents and capacities it may develop. However, this raises another issue, in that the self may not be pre-given: it is not something hidden that we have to *find,* but something that has to be *made.* Self, then, is something to be created with other people in joint activities and through shared ideas, which provide the techniques of self-formation. 'Who am I?' is perhaps a mistaken question: it should be, 'who do I want to be?' or 'what shall I become?' It is not being but becoming that is the question. Note also that in both ways of making ourselves, in relations with others and in activities undertaken with others, we are not actually looking 'inward' to find ourselves, but 'outward' towards other people and joint activities. Primarily, the place where we look for ourselves is in the world we share with others, not the world we have for ourselves through reflection on thoughts and feelings.

Thirdly, the above point is underscored in the fact that who we are, or can become, is often a political issue involving rights and duties fought over within society. Becoming who we want to be, if that is possible, often involves a political struggle. This has been witnessed in recent years with the women's movement, the black power movement, and the gay, lesbian and transgender movement. The right to become a certain type of person, or to live freely as a particular person with a full complement of rights without persecution – as Asian, black, female, or gay – for many is something that has to be won, rather than something that is given. And the identities forged in such struggle are not formed prior to it, but in it. It is a very different thing today to live openly as a 'gay' man, than it was 70 years ago to live secretly as a 'homosexual'. Even when we do not think that being ourselves involves politics, this is often a misguided assumption. Those who assume that their self-identity is a given right or a natural fact – say, a straight white man in Britain – are those in a privileged position whose identities have automatic 'right of way' in most social contexts. Such people assume their privileged position, not realizing that other identities might be silenced in their presence.

These are the three main reasons why I will explore the notion of social selves and social individuality in this book, trying to understand how it is that we can only attain the state of individual self-identity in relations and activities with others. What initially looks like a contradiction in terms – social individuality – will hopefully by the end of the book look like the only sensible way to proceed in confronting the dualisms and dichotomies that theories and methodologies of individualism have left us with. However, what I will do in the rest of this chapter is say a little more about the social and philosophical heritage that has created the problem of individualism, and of the relation between society and self, along with some of the solutions it has proposed to its own problem. How has this heritage created the question 'who am I?' and what are the various answers it has devised, leaving us with a conflicting and contradictory understanding of what it is to be human?

Some Western conceptions of the individual self

Originally, there were two main sources of the self in Western culture: the concept of the person as it emerged in ancient Greco-Roman society, and Christian ideas of the soul. As the anthropologist Marcel Mauss noted in his seminal essay 'A category of the human mind: the notion of person: the notion of self '(1938),[3] the notion of 'persona' was first used in Roman culture to refer to the masks that people adopted in public ceremony. The use of masks was not restricted to ancient Rome, being common to a whole range of tribal societies as a way of marking out different roles or statuses within ritual ceremonies. What was unique to ancient Rome in its use of the term 'persona', according to Mauss, was that the notion acquired a legal status with certain rights and duties attached. The freeborn of Roman society (obviously this does not apply to slaves) became citizens of the state who had rights and responsibilities conferred upon them as persons.

In Hellenist and Roman culture the Stoic philosophers also contributed to the idea of the person as a free individual. They introduced the notion of an ethic of the self on a personal level, in which individuals made choices about who they wanted to be through their relationship with a philosophical teacher, and also by using new techniques of paying attention to, and taking care of, the self. One of these new techniques was the writing of letters to friends and teachers that recorded the details of a person's everyday life, such as their health and diet, and their general regimen for living.[4] This began a tradition of forming a 'narrative of self' that is still familiar today whenever we catch up with friends and tell them stories about what we have been doing, either in face-to-face conversation, letters, or emails. What the letters of such Stoic philosophers as Seneca, Epictetus, and Aurelius demonstrate is the beginning of narrative correspondence between people that dwells on the private world more than on the public world.[5] All these trends are evidenced in the development of biography, which starts out as a public rhetorical act – in particular, the 'encomium' or memorial speech at civic funerals – and eventually arrives at one of the first known written autobiographies, Marcus Aurelius's *To Myself*. Such a text, together with the letters of the Stoics, reveal notions of biography and narrative similar to today in that they record the events of a life (usually in chronology) as evidence of a person's character. While the events recorded are increasingly to do with the private rather than the public life of a person, what they lack is the tendency for self-analysis and revealing the 'inner' life of thoughts and feelings that we would expect today.[6] What is emerging is a private world of self-attention and care of self, but this is still based around a notion of self-mastery rather than self-analysis.[7] Self-mastery is about watching one's habits and routines for signs of immoderation – because the right of being a free citizen goes hand-in-hand with showing you can govern yourself – rather than asking the question 'who am I?'

This question looms more in Christian autobiographies, such as St Augustine's *The Confessions* (397). In this book, St Augustine recognized the struggle between good and evil in the hearts of all humans, including his own, charting his path to God through this 'inner' turmoil. While the question 'who am I?' is not explicitly asked, Mauss understands Christian records of the struggle in a soul as another step towards modern notions of the self, because with the idea that each one of us has our own soul, even if it is ridden with conflict, we come closer to a metaphysical foundation for the self. This is because the soul is conceived as something inward and indivisible, almost like a substance in itself that character-izes our own individuality, which can be divided from the body – our physical and earthly mark of difference. It could be said that Augustinian Christian ideas and practices are an important development in the turn 'inwards' in the search for self.[8]

However, it must be emphasized that when St Augustine searched to the depths of his soul, what he found there was God – the 'changeless light' of spir-itual being – and not a self. The Western notion of self begins to appear in more recognizable form with the work of the philosopher René Descartes. Like St Augustine centuries before, Descartes believed that people's higher sense of individuality is not linked to their bodies or to carnal desires and appetites: rather, for Descartes, we humans identify our existence through mental reflec-tion on our own selves, and this is what makes us unique. However, Descartes was not embarked upon some modern journey of self-discovery. The task he had set himself in his *Discourse on Method* (1637) was to lay down certain princi-ples or rules for scientific methods of thought. Thus, although his primary con-cern was for scientific methodology and not self-analysis, many contemporary philosophers still contemplate the implications for the self contained in Descartes' famous meditative discovery, 'I think therefore I am.'[9] Descartes was working in a world that no longer believed a thinker could be certain of their knowledge by identifying principles which are *external* to humanity, principles found in the order of the universe itself. Instead, knowledge was a construct of the human mind, a way of representing the world that extended beyond the mind. Yet, if this is so, how can we be sure that what we know mentally – our 'inner' representations of the world – correspond to the actuality of the external world? In the *Discourse*, Descartes began his search for certainty by pretending to doubt everything that he knew, including the evidence of his senses, and came up with the first principle of his philosophy, that:

> while I decided thus to think that everything was false, it followed necessarily
> that I who thought thus must be something; and observing that this truth: *I think*
> *therefore I am,* was so certain and so evident that all the most extravagant

suppositions of the sceptics were not capable of shaking it ... I thereby concluded that I was a substance, of which the whole essence or nature consists in thinking, and which, in order to exist, needs no place and depends on no material thing; so that this 'I', that is to say, the mind, by which I am what I am, is entirely distinct from the body, and ... that even if the body were not, it would not cease to be all that it is.[10]

A number of things flow from this proposition. Firstly, that the 'I' is a substance, the nature of which is thinking, so that self is to be found in the mind as distinct from the body, to the extent that I can imagine myself to continue even if my body ceased to exist. This conclusion is possible because Descartes saw the powers of human thought and reason to approximate God, whereas the material bodies of humans and animals were automata: machine-like entities that produced sensations and impulses. Secondly, this creates the problem known as substance dualism, for Descartes has split all of human existence in two, between the non-material mind and the material body, identifying the sense of 'I', or self-identity, purely with the mind. As mind is closer to God than to earthly things, including the human body, the self becomes a 'transcendental self': that is, something given in the infinite, rather than being created out of the finite experience of embodied individuals. Thirdly, in this move, Descartes has solved the problem of the split between the contents of the mind and the external world they represent, for no God would establish rational principles in the human mind that were incapable of independently establishing certain knowledge about the world and the universe. God was the guarantor that we can think the truth about the world, because God would not fool us.

That so much of Descartes' argument about the self and scientific reason rested in the existence of God was no accident, for it saved him coming into conflict with ecclesiastical authorities, who, along with the aristocracy, ruled society in his day. But it couldn't solve the problem of substance dualism, bequeathed to us as contemporary seekers of the self. The habit is with us to this day of seeing ourselves *either* as rational beings for whom the mind is paramount *or* as irrational beings ruled by bodily passions. After Descartes, Western philosophers became divided between Enlightenment rationalists, who emphasized the former view, and Romantics who emphasized the latter.

Yet there was an even greater fault-line in Descartes' thinking, for if you examine the above quotation carefully you will see that he has not actually managed to theorize the 'I' as a single, indivisible substance, the nature of which is thinking. In his formula, there is the 'I think' and the 'I am': two 'I's'.[11] For example, if I sit here and think about who I am, I think about the Ian Burkitt who has a distinct body, who lives in a particular place and time, who has had certain experiences throughout his life, who knows other people and is known by those same people. In short, I identify myself not purely with my thinking, but with the actual embodied individual whom I am thinking about, who at this moment is both thinking and feeling. To what extent, then, is it true to say that 'I am' entirely defined by my power for thought and could conceive of myself even without my body? If I can't do so, and it is my view that I can't, then 'I' cannot be a transcendental self. The problem with Descartes' dualism is that it cannot account for the human ability to bring seemingly diverse modes of existence together to create a unity of the material and (apparently) non-material, both in our being and in our experience of the world.[12]

For later generations of philosophers the Cartesian legacy of dualism would continue in two different strands of philosophy, which approached a resolution from its two sides, with Enlightenment rationalists emphasizing thought and reason, while Romantic thinkers privileged nature and emotion. The latter tradition can be exemplified in the work of Jean-Jacques Rousseau, who turned back to the Augustinian idea that the human self is characterized by a tumultuous struggle between good and evil. Like St Augustine, Rousseau also wrote a book of *Confessions* (1781–88), which explored his own personal contradictions throughout his life with the aim of showing that his basic motives had been good. Indeed, Rousseau is famous for his belief that humans are basically good by nature but become corrupted by society. By this he did not mean that all society was inherently evil, but that civilizations could become overly restrictive and impose artificial inequalities, diverting people from the state of nature. In this, Rousseau undoubtedly had in mind the 18th century central European society where he lived and worked, which was dominated by the aristocratic court and its elaborate code of manners. It also fostered a system in which artists and philosophers were dependent on wealthy aristocratic patrons, and no doubt this formed Rousseau's view that society could stifle the free expression of thought and feeling by the imposition of authority and artifice. Indeed, the Romantic Movement in the arts and philosophy, which gained inspiration and impetus from his writings, was based on the idea that the free expression of the creative spirit was more important than strict adherence to formal rules or traditional authorities. Charles Taylor has called this movement 'expressivist', because it understood self-identity as something to be made through an individual's creative expression.[13] The answer to the question 'who am I?' does not come from mental reflection alone, but from the expression of natural talents, feelings and impulses: from self-expression.

This radical thinking brought Rousseau into conflict with the authorities of his day, state and church: it also set him at odds with Enlightenment thinkers who believed human freedom came through reason. It wasn't that Rousseau was against reason, human society, or a civilization that incorporated rational thinking: rather, he believed that these things should serve the expression of human nature rather than dominate and stifle it. A good society cannot be bound by force of law, imposed by the upper echelons, only by people's natural sentiments for each other inclining them to act together according to a self-imposed general will. For Rousseau, the social contract should encourage relative independence and autonomy of individuals, allowing the expression of their natural self-sufficiency, thus working with nature and not against it. Conscience then becomes 'the divine voice of the soul in man' rather than a set of abstract rules that must be followed. Rousseau's Romanticism has therefore bequeathed the notion that individuals need to listen for that 'voice within' to direct us on our true and good path, both in relation to others and in seeking to express our self.

In the Enlightenment tradition, dualism was addressed from a rationalist perspective by Immanuel Kant in his *Critique of Pure Reason* (1781). Kant recognized that humans are natural beings, having sensations that provide information about the world, along with desires, needs and inclinations against which reason can appear weak.[14] Unlike Descartes, Kant does not see the rational mind as defining the whole self. He did believe, though, that it is reason, not feeling, which gives humans freedom and dignity. Without the ability to think for oneself using principles of rational thought, humans would never be critical of received wisdom, and could also be the slaves of passion. But this meant that, for Kant, the principles of reason could not be derived from human embodied experience: they cannot be learnt from current styles of thought, or else individual reason would simply mirror established forms of reasoning, with no critical distance between the two. Nor can principles of reason be extracted from the shifting data of the senses, or from the conflicting and contradictory nature of desire and emotion, which are inherently disorganized. From this, Kant concluded that reason must be *a priori,* meaning that it must be prior to the experience of any given embodied individual. If we cannot derive the principles of reason and the categories of cognitive thought from experience, then they must come from a transcendental self. Kant does not say, as does Descartes, that this transcendental self is a spark of the divine in humanity, instead he leaves open the origin of this aspect of the self. Rather, it is something that must be inferred so as to make sense of the human capacity to order and categorize the disordered sensory world, preventing us from being bombarded by a welter of sense-impressions that can never be formed into coherent thoughts. The transcendental subject therefore consists of the principles of reason and categories of thought given to all humans prior to experience and which make any ordered experience of the world possible.[15]

For Kant, then, reason is given in the human mind and is put into practice whenever humans act in the world. This applies not only to practical intelligence, but also to morality, because Kant inferred there must be an *a priori* moral law that creates a categorical imperative, guiding individuals to act in a consistently moral way. This allows society to form from the array of individual rational thinkers. However, in Kant, there are three senses in which he uses the term 'I' in answer to the question 'who am I?' Firstly, 'I' refers to the transcendental self that is capable of rational thought and can abstract itself from its embodied social, cultural and historical circumstance in order to be guided by *a priori* principles. This is Kant's notion of the 'I' as a pure ray of apperception that shines out its beam of light on the darkness and chaos of the world. Secondly, there is the embodied 'I' who puts rationality into action in practical circumstances and has an actual, empirical identity. Thirdly, there is the 'I' of moral law that has a capacity to follow moral imperatives rather than the dictates of individual desire. But Kant has difficulty in explaining how the three selves interrelate in order to achieve unity in experience.[16] He has also created a gulf between the noumenal world (the actual, practical world in which the empirical self acts) and the phenomenal world (which is the world known through the categories of thought). Ultimately, Kant has to rely on the idea that rationality is emergent in all of nature to bring the 'I' which thinks into harmony with the world it thinks about.

All the philosophers I have considered so far have in common the idea that the self is located inside the individual, either in thought or in inner nature. It follows from this that it must be an aspect of the individual self, understood as sympathy or a moral imperative, which drives the person into society with others. This has been expressed most clearly by the thinker who is often associated with a radical economic individualism: Adam Smith. In fact, in Smith's book *Theory of Moral Sentiments* (1759) he comes close to a view of the self as a social construction, laying the groundwork for philosophers, sociologists and social psychologists of the 20th century, whom I will be in dialogue with throughout this book. As part of the Scottish Enlightenment, Smith was writing in a different context to Descartes, Rousseau and Kant, in which the growing power of commercial relations in Britain during the 18th century was already beginning to challenge the traditional authority of the aristocracy and landed gentry. It was these commercial relations that Smith extolled in his more famous book *The Wealth of Nations* (1776), but it is in *Theory of Moral Sentiments* that we find him working out the psychological implications of such relations. While he did believe that each individual pursuing their own self-interest through commerce drove society to ever-greater heights of wealth and achievement, he also thought that this was not the only, or the most fundamental, human motive. Alongside self-interest, there were other aspects of human nature that incline us to be interested in the fortunes of others. These are the sentiments or sympathies we have for others that lead us to put ourselves in their shoes and imagine how they must be feeling in whatever situation they find themselves. It is not, then, the direct expression of emotion on the part of the other that calls out the same feeling in ourselves, such as grief or, especially, anger – a sentiment that Smith does not believe we instantly sympathize with – rather, it is the situation that has brought on the emotion with which we imaginatively identify, knowing how we would feel in the other's place. As Smith says, 'sympathy, therefore, does not arise so much from the view of the passion, as from that of the situation which excites it'.[17] By the same token, we expect others to sympathize with us in certain situations and feel aggrieved if they don't, seeing it as an injustice.

It is in this mutual interaction and identification with others that a view of our own self is possible, because we judge our own conduct by viewing it as through the eyes of other people. Society, then, gives us a mirror to ourselves. Furthermore, this creates for all selves what Smith calls the 'impartial spectator', which is an aspect of the self that is disengaged from our own passions, viewpoint and self-interest, as well as being disengaged from the viewpoint of any other particular person. Rather, it is the viewpoint of some general, impartial other that we take when we view our own self and behaviour. The 'I' that asks the question 'who am I?' is not for Smith an inner ray of divine light or pure apperception, but a self-reflection and awareness that can only arise in the midst of society and interaction, where we take an impartial view of ourselves based on the recognition that we are seen and judged by others. Furthermore, what we reflect upon is our actions and impulses and, through the 'I' that is an impartial spectator, these things become like the objects of our judgement. This is how the two 'I's' implicit in Cartesian philosophy come into existence, because there is the 'I' that judges and the 'I' that is being judged.[18] Yet again, this is only possible in society, where (to paraphrase that other Scot, Robert Burns) we can see ourselves as others see us.

The impartial spectator also becomes the basis of self-mastery, because through it we not only judge our own actions and impulses, we can also attempt to control them. Like the Stoics, Smith believed that self-mastery was important, but unlike the ancient Greco-Romans he did not have the elitist view that this could only be attained through a relation to a philosophical teacher: instead, everyone in society can be our teacher. This is why Smith valued commercial society so highly, because it encourages interactions with a wider range of people from all different societies and walks of life, thus broadening the view we have of the world and ourselves, increasing the scope of the impartial spectator. Interestingly, this can also be linked to the growth in popularity of the novel in the 18th and 19th centuries, as this became a tool of self-formation, expanding the identification with others through engagement with fictional characters and situations beyond the realm of one's everyday experience. Through the expanding connections to others, both real and imagined, people were exposed to greater social and individual differences, having a wider range of models to draw upon in their own self-fashioning.[19]

Although Smith did not directly influence him, the philosopher G. W. F. Hegel expanded the idea of the self as a social creation, taking it in a different direction.[20] For Hegel, the composite term 'self' is more important than the 'I', or self-consciousness, as he understood the self often to be plunged into contradiction and conflict within itself, and also periodically to be alienated from society. Contradiction, opposition, difference, and conflict, both in the self and society, is at the heart of Hegel's dialectical philosophy, for he saw these divisions as driving change in an attempt to achieve unity or resolution of contradiction at a higher level of becoming. Hegel believed that the self would not be aware of itself if it were a simple unity identical to itself: I = I cannot be the formula, for some division in the self has to occur for part of the self to be able to turn back on the other parts and become aware of them, achieving self-consciousness or self-reflection. Equally, if the self were identical with society, it would simply be absorbed into an amorphous unity, unaware of its own individual difference with others. An *historical* dialectic of contradictions between society and self must begin, within which individuals become aware of contradictions within their own selves that they are driven to resolve at a higher level of unity. Hegel's philosophy is set within a social and a historical frame, and this makes it a philosophy of becoming.

In *The Phenomenology of Spirit* (1807), Hegel traces the dialectical process of development that society and self – the universal spirit and the particular spirit – go through in becoming what they are today. He begins his history in ancient Greece where people are given the status of individuals by the laws of the state, but only as parts of the general *polis,* or political and social realm. Here, they are wholly at one with society, which determines the place and role of each individual. In Hegel's terms, the world that constitutes the self is not external to it, but is the totality of relations in which it is located. Yet in Greece, this was a limited conception of the self, because people had no notion of themselves as anything other than their place in the collective. For Hegel, as for Mauss, it was the Roman Empire that first gave to individuals the legal status of being separate persons, with duties and rights. People are no longer merely conscious of the world; they become more *self-conscious,* aware of the possibility of a degree of self-making. With the end of the Empire, as society fragments, individuals become alienated from the collective spirit of the age and begin to withdraw into a more private and personal realm. In the chaos and insecurity of the medieval period in Europe, where society collapsed into a mêlée of warring factions, the self was concerned only with the immediate necessity of survival. With no stable object outside itself to mediate its own existence, the self can find no stable reference point in its own thoughts or feelings from which to create a coherent self-identity.

In the European Middle Ages, Christianity provides a universal spiritual basis for individuals to begin to form self-consciousness as spiritual beings. However, the collective spirit as Kingdom of God is otherworldly, with individuals existing only as a partial embodiment of this spirit. As the church becomes joined in partnership with the nation-state as an agent of social authority, it sets itself above individuals as a power over them. Thus, the objective forms of universal or collective spirit set themselves against individuals, alienating them from the social world even as they participate in it. Even when reason offers itself as the guiding principle of knowledge and self-making – whether as an element of the divine in humanity, or as the transcendental self – individuals are left alone to apply this principle. Reason is to be found within and to be acted on individually, dividing people from each other and the collective spirit. Furthermore, the self is divided within itself between thought and feeling, reason and passion.

However, for Hegel, these contradictions all offer the possibility of synthesis at a higher stage, especially with the emergence of the democratic nation-state, in which humanity might be able to realize *both* a highly developed collective spirit within a social world where it feels itself to belong *and* a highly developed sense of self where people have freedom for self-development. This is because the alienated self is an unhappy consciousness, aware of its present life but also its unrealized potential. As a self always in the process of becoming, setting about resolving social and personal contradictions, it is aware of what it could be in the future as well as what it is now, driving it on to reconstruct itself right up to the point of old age and death. To Hegel, reason offers the potential for integration at a higher level, especially if it is understood as a principle of everyday organization rather than an inexplicable power beyond experience and account. This is because everyday reason allows distinct individuals to freely participate in unison within a democratic sphere. Also, if we see reason as a force of everyday life, humans must embody both reason and feeling, meaning that the two are not universally bound to exist in contradiction. In the next stage of human existence, people may be able to embody reason and feeling in the kind of harmony that people of much earlier societies could, but within a community that resolves the dialectical processes of unity, disunity, division, contradiction and alienation through a reconciliation of collective and individual self.

One of the major achievements of Hegel's work, then, has been to understand humans as social beings while retaining the notion of the self as an individual in its own right, albeit one that is the product of a dialectical historical process. In this he developed a relational understanding of the creation of the individual self, in which the totality of relations is not always bound to appear as external, but is the matrix in which we are constituted as selves. The social world only appears to oppose individuals in historical conditions of alienation, which can be addressed in new ways within the dialectical process of contradiction and resolution. However, in Hegel's historical dialectic, reason seems to appear and develop independent of human effort or design, according to its own ruse, offering possibilities for its own higher expression. Critics known as the Young Hegelians also pointed out that Hegel had posited the possibility of a resolution of contradiction through reason in theory only, and had ignored the practical and political task of setting about creating a new society that would fully overcome the separation of self and community. Numbered among this group was the young Karl Marx, whose work we will consider in the next section.

Before that, I want to consider briefly one more philosopher whose work reverberates in many current theories of the self: Friedrich Nietzsche. This is because Nietzsche did not believe that the self-conscious 'I' could be placed at the centre of human self-understanding. In *The Gay Science* (1882) he argued that consciousness is the latest development in the organic world, of which humans are part, and as such is the most unfinished and weakest part of the self. Much stronger are the human instincts, yet in civilizations humans are expected to rein in their instinctual drives in order to obey communal law and morality, or the principles of reasoned thought and behaviour. This is the origin of 'bad conscience' when humans had to suppress the instincts – the strongest part of our being – in favour of consciousness – the weakest part. It is this animal soul turned against its nature that makes the human self, because self-reflection – the turning inward to look at ourselves and the deepening of our self-analysis – is based on the drive to guard against our own desires. Nietzsche also refers to this as the 'will to power', for it creates the desire to dominate not only our own self, but other selves also. Thus, Nietzsche writes a history the direction of which is opposite to Hegel's: for Nietzsche, conflict is not resolved at a higher level in civilization through law, morality, Christianity and reason; rather, these things only weaken humans. Superficially, this looks more like Rousseau's idea that society can corrupt humans by re-directing them from nature, but there is a crucial difference. Working after the publication of Charles Darwin's *Origin of the Species* in the mid-19th century, with its ideas of the natural selection of species and the struggle for survival, Nietzsche can no longer believe that nature, including human nature, is inherently good.[21] At best, nature and human nature are amoral, with no in-built moral direction.

What this means is that human self-experience is often mistaken. When we ask the question 'who am I?' we often flatter ourselves by answering that 'I am a good person', masking some of the more unpalatable instincts that are part of our nature, which are made unconscious in this self-identification as wholly good. We also mistake the 'I' for the will to power, believing that our identity resides in our conscious power to will our behaviour, when in fact it only represents a small and fragile part of the self. However, Nietzsche does believe that there is a solution to the morass of modern civilization, represented in his ideal of the *Übermensch* (usually translated into English as 'Supermen', but perhaps more accurately as the 'Upper-man' or 'Above-man'). This is the ideal that a true self has yet to be achieved, and can only be done by those men strong enough to face up to nature, to their own passions, to the chaos and destruction in the world, and affirm it all, finding joy rather than fear in it. Such men (and Nietzsche is clear that these individuals will express masculine and virile qualities) will also free themselves from collective morality, creating themselves as a work of art according to their own laws. While this seems to be a positive affirmation of life, there is a darker side to it, for Nietzsche was not a supporter of modern democratic societies, believing that those strong enough to create a self above the common herd would become élite. It is this, along with the misuse of his philosophy by the Nazis, who took it to support their cause for a new superior race, which makes Nietzsche's philosophy controversial still.

However, his work is of contemporary importance because it challenged the emerging way of conceptualizing the self in the West. Nietzsche rejected the Christian foundations on which the self had been understood as soul (as in St Augustine) or as metaphysical substance (as in Descartes and, to a lesser degree, Kant). For Nietzsche, there is no 'thing in itself', such as a soul, at the heart of the self: rather it is made up of a number of elements that have coalesced through a series of accidents, not through any self-conscious design. Furthermore, what we take to be the self, the 'I,' is actually the will that is formed by a part of the human body turning against some of its other elements. Thus, Nietzsche also offers a materialist as opposed to a metaphysical understanding of the emergence of the illusion of self as equalling the conscious, rational 'I', another reason for his contemporary appeal.

At the end of this section, I want to make you aware of the limitations of such a brief historical overview of Western conceptions of the self as I have written above. I am painfully aware of the dangers of oversimplifying complex philosophical positions, and also that this brief history has been highly selective. I have only spoken of philosophers whose work bears relevance to ideas of the self that I will discuss throughout this book, but that does not mean that other philosophers did not have important things to say on this topic. Charles Taylor and Jerrold Seigel have both written long, more extensive and complex histories of the idea of self than I have the space or expertise to write (see the selected bibliography at the end of this chapter). I am also aware that alternative histories of the self can be written from other cultural perspectives, for example ideas of the self in Confucianism and Buddhism,[22] but again that is not my brief here: I am concerned with the self as it emerges in Western modernity. Nor should we view ideas of the self as purely a product of philosophy, because, as Hegel indicated, the changing experience of self is also due to social and historical changes, which are refracted in philosophical writings.

Indeed, this point has been made brilliantly by the sociologist Norbert Elias, who argues that the changing self-image of humans in Western Europe, beginning in the Renaissance and continuing through the Enlightenment, was only in part the product of philosophical thinking.[23] Indeed, philosophers reflected the changing times in their thinking, so that the self-image of humans they created was a response to social changes happening in their day. Some of these we have already touched upon, such as the slow erosion of church and nobility as powers that dominated society in the Middle Ages. Without the dominance of the church to authorize all of human thinking, philosophers like Descartes – who represented the rise of a new urban middle class, including academics, which was starting to establish its own freedom of thought – began to contemplate methods for the validation of knowledge independent of ecclesiastical authorities. This, however, threw individuals back onto their own resources and into contemplation of themselves, for the question arose of who are we as humans with the power to do what previously only God's representatives on earth had been allowed to do. In addition to this, Elias points out the effects of the rise in power of the nation-state and its centralized functions, and also the growth in commercial activity, resulting in what he calls the 'civilizing processes' in Western Europe: a term that refers to the shift in the balance of control of the population by means of social coercion towards greater emphasis on self-restraint of individuals acting together in daily social relations. People were now expected to show greater sensitivity towards the feelings of others, for example as expressed in the push towards more refined manners in court societies. However, this also meant that people had to constantly monitor their own feelings and expressions in the presence of others to a greater degree than before, creating a sense of deep division in humans between a rational and controlling consciousness on the one hand, and the drives, impulses and emotions on the other, which now had to be carefully watched and monitored. It is this, according to Elias, which adds to the modern human image of a self trapped inside its own casing: an 'I' that is separate from others in the 'outside' world, one which hides behind an 'external' image presented to others in order to suppress feelings or impulses that can no longer be expressed in public.

Elias's work is but one illustration of what sociologists have to contribute to understanding the emergence of the modern sense of self. I now want to turn to some other famous examples.

Sociology, social world and the self

Karl Marx, Emile Durkheim and Max Weber – three founders of the discipline of sociology – all thought that the type of self which emerged in Western modernity is inextricably bound-up with industrial capitalism. As sociologists, they did not specifically ask the question 'who am I?' but rather 'who are we?' The question is a collective one because all individuals are born into, live and die within societies. We are elements of our culture, time and place, and can never be abstracted from the social world. Even if we move from one culture to another, we simply swap one social formation for another, and it is doubtful whether we can remove every last trace of the culture of our formative years. Like the languages we learn as children, elements of it are always there ready to appear spontaneously when called on.

Karl Marx approached questions of society and self as someone who had been a young Hegelian, and who carried the influence of Hegel's philosophy throughout his life. Like Hegel, Marx believed that the social world is not something external to the self, but is the totality of relations in which the self is located and constituted. That is to say, we are all born into a social group: a social class, culture, religion, gender, ethnicity or any other social position by which we can classify ourselves. We may want to get out of that position or transcend its limitations, but we still have to work within the social framework that sets these conditions in the first place. Social relations are therefore the very essence of what it is to be a self: an individual with an identity amongst others. Again, like Hegel, Marx believed that these social conditions or relations only appear to be external to us – that is, to oppose and limit us rather than to be something living and vital to which we belong – when we are alienated from them. However, unlike Hegel, Marx did not believe that the human plight could be understood and resolved philosophically, nor that democratic society in itself provided a solution to alienation. As for philosophy, in *Theses on Feuerbach* (1845) Marx wrote that 'the philosophers have only *interpreted* the world, in various ways; the point is to *change* it'. Marx's project, then, is practical and political as well as being theoretical.

Because of this, Marx provided a view of humanity and human nature different from other philosophers, one that he characterized as 'materialist'. That meant he was concerned not just with understanding the way society and self had been conceptualized through a history of ideas, but with the way actual people have produced the conditions under which they live throughout history: their way of life, the products with which they satisfy their needs, their cultures and identities. In *The German Ideology* (1846) the Marxist view of human nature began to take shape.[24] This regarded humans as part of the natural world, and, like other animals, they must meet their needs in order to survive: they must eat, drink, and find shelter and warmth. Humans begin to distinguish themselves from other animals when they *produce* their subsistence: what they need to survive. At this point, humans no longer scavenge for food, they organize themselves into bands of hunters: they no longer rely on nature to produce edible fruit and vegetation, they cultivate crops: they no longer eat raw food, they cook it: they no longer take shelter in caves, but build shelters. Clearly, Marx regarded it as within human nature to achieve these things, but he didn't think that human nature is fixed or set, for as humans produce they change both the natural world *and* human nature. In order to hunt and cultivate crops, people organized themselves into social groups, which created a new *'mode of life'*.[25] Also, by producing, humans transformed their natural needs: they no longer needed to eat merely to satisfy hunger, but developed appetites and desires for certain types of cooked food. Through productive activity, then, nature and human nature are open to transformation.

In answering the question 'who are we?', then, Marx looked to the different ways human societies have produced their mode of life throughout history. Like Hegel, he used a dialectical method of analysing the contradictions, oppositions, differences and forms of alienation that arise in history, only Marx described this as 'historical materialism' because he wanted to study the way humans have physically produced their societies and selves in different epochs. In the early hunter-gatherer societies, people lived a tribal existence with a simple division of labour, where the land and the products of labour were communally owned. Each individual was part of the collective whole, which functioned like a family, and people shared what they produced. Contradictions and conflicts began to open up in society with property ownership, through which some individuals or groups gained power and dominance over others, who then struggled for their freedom. Property ownership is, therefore, the basis for the creation of social classes, in which certain groups of individuals gain distinction and dominance over others. In Marx's historical materialism it was this class conflict and struggle that was the motor of historical change, fuelled by changes to the way that people produce, or the 'mode of production'. Conflict between citizens and slaves, aristocrats and their subjects, feudal lords and serfs, has been the dynamic behind social change. It has also been the basis for different forms of alienation, as the totality of social relations and the products of human labour appear to stand against people as something not belonging to them. Slaves do not own their own bodies, which are bought and sold like commodities, while the feudal serf is separated from the land he or she works and the produce they grow, which is now owned by the nobility.

For Marx, class conflict and alienation reach their zenith in industrial capitalism, where the capitalist class owns the entire means of production: land, tools, technology and the labour power of the workers who work for them. The working classes do not own the means of production and can only sell their labour-power to capitalists in return for a wage. Nor do they own the products of their labour, which stand over and against them as alien objects, something they feel to have had little hand in creating. Equally, the working classes feel alienated from society as power is not lodged in any person to whom they have a direct relationship of dependence, like the feudal lord, but in the impersonal power of capital and state. As Marx claims, 'the more deeply we go back into history, the more does the individual, and hence also the producing individual, appear as dependent, as belonging to a greater whole'. With the rise of capitalist civil society in the 18th century, 'the various forms of social connectedness confront the individual as a mere means towards his private purposes, as external necessity'.[26] People then retreat from collective life, into the private world of family and friendships where they can gain sustenance.

The only solution to this alienation, for Marx, was through political transformation of capitalist society, a dialectical resolution in which the energy, vitality and productivity of capitalist industry and technology will be preserved, but in an advanced form of communal ownership where all private property and wealth will be abolished. What is more, this revolution happens through the creation of a collective self-identity. To Marx, the industrial working classes were the first exploited social class to realize their collective oppression and to organize on that basis. The Marxist historian E. P. Thompson has written a detailed history from the 18th century onward of how working people in Britain created a collective class identity through various workers' movements and trade unions, which were also a political means of achieving emancipation and greater equality. Today, in the early 21st century, where capital is more global than it was in Marx's day, its power and influence seem even more external to us, harder to identify in place and time, and more out of the reach of attempts to oppose it. Perhaps this is why events like the G8 summit – where the leaders of the capitalist countries come together to plan global economic activity – attract the most visible protests by the anti-capitalist and anti-globalization movements. And identity is still a key element at the heart of such movements. While not everyone opposed to capitalism will regard himself or herself as working class, Alberto Melucci has claimed that the new social movements are based in people's experimentations with alternative lifestyles and identities.[27] Many will be Marxists, anarchists, trade unionists, squatters, or have religious or other values through which they create an aspect of their identity.

For Marx, then, humans produce their mode of life through collective activity, and it is within this mode of life that different self-identities become possible based on the individual's place and activity within the division of labour. The individual self only begins to feel that it does not belong to the collective under conditions of alienation, where the self becomes isolated from the whole. The resolution of this dialectic of belongingness and alienation can only be found in a higher form of communal life, where self-identity would not be class-based but come from the free association of individuals who would make themselves, not as Nietzsche suggested, by laws of their own individual making, but by laws of their own collective making.

One thing that Marx has in common with Emile Durkheim is the understanding that the division of labour is fundamental to the creation of different self-identities. Marx, for example, believed that the division of labour was responsible for the rift between mind and body, reason and feeling in modern selves, for it has created the split between manual and intellectual labour, with individuals specializing in practical or intellectual skills from an early age. For both thinkers, though, the division of labour creates the range of different identities possible in any society. In *The Division of Labour in Society* (1893) Durkheim says that in simple forms of society individuals are bound together through 'mechanical solidarity', in which each individual is representative of the whole group, embodying the beliefs and values of the collective.[28] In contrast, modern Western capitalism creates and binds individuals in 'organic solidarity', in which individuals are dependent on one another because each one fulfils a different function in the division of labour. Here, individuals specialize in specific tasks and functions, creating a range of differences between people, reflected in the creation of a variety of self-identities. Indeed, it was in such a society that Mauss (Durkheim's nephew) claimed that the self becomes a basic category of thought, in the sense that it becomes one of the organizing principles of our thinking and, more broadly, of society. It forms part of what Durkheim called the 'collective consciousness': the ideas, beliefs and values formed within society, which become the basis of all individual thinking and feeling.

Because of these views Durkheim is often described as a neo-Kantian in that he saw the categories of thought existing prior to the experience of any single individual. However, rather than the categories belonging to a transcendental self, Durkheim believed they were contained within society which educates each new generation in its ideas, beliefs and values. It is not, then, some imperative of the categories that forces them upon us, rather it is society and its institutions which instil the collective consciousness in each individual. Steven Collins has pointed out, though, that Durkheim was not directly influenced by Kant but by Charles Renouvier and, through him, took on board many of Hegel's ideas.[29] This is evident in Durkheim's social and historical perspective, especially his view of individual differences emerging from an original collective whole. It also means that if the categories of thought are not transcendental, but social and historical, then they cannot be universal; they must change historically and vary between cultures. Certainly, Durkheim saw the dangers of modern individualism and relativism of thought, as it can put the collective consciousness under strain. In the modern division of labour 'each mind finds itself directed towards a different point on the horizon, reflects a different aspect of the world and, as a result, the content of men's minds differ from one subject to another'.[30]

If the modern division of labour goes too far, and people find themselves too individualized, a state of *anomie* ensues, which is a lack of moral regulation whereby individuals become isolated, without the social values to give meaning and form to their lives. These ideas led Durkheim to be ambivalent about the modern ideology of individualism, which places the highest value on the distinctiveness of each person and their freedom from the collective. Durkheim thought this had become almost like a modern religion, where the individual becomes exalted as the highest and most worthy entity. Individualism is good so far as it gives people rights and freedoms, but Durkheim argued against its utilitarian form, which states that each person pursuing their own self-interest inevitably results in the best outcome for society. To him nothing could be more destructive of social solidarity. People need to realize that it is society that guarantees individual rights in order to not always put self-interest before the interest of the group. If this can be achieved, then humanistic beliefs and the ideology of individualism can form a collective consciousness that holds modern society together.

For Durkheim, then, in answer to the question 'who are we?' he would say that modern individuals are selves characterized by their place in the division of labour: by their skills, interests, specialisms, talents, functions, knowledge, jobs, professions and social status. It is these things that create a sense of self-identity, and it is the reason why we look to change jobs or social functions when we want to change our selves and our lives. However, if we place our own individual value too highly above others, we can become isolated and disconnected from society, in a state of *anomie,* without other values or interests above ourselves to give meaning to life. In the extreme, Durkheim believed this state could lead people to commit suicide.[31] His ideas also create a view of the self that Anthony Giddens calls *homo duplex,* 'in the sense there is an opposition in every individual between egoistic impulses and those which have a "moral" connotation'.[32] That is to say, we are all double selves, one half selfishly wanting to pursue our own interests, and the other half finding joy in transcending self-centredness to reach better, higher goals that benefit others. This is why Durkheim believed that universally humans have created some form of religion through which they can transcend their own narrow self-concern and reach for higher spiritual goals within a social group. The only problem with religion, according to Durkheim, was that humans mistook the Gods they created for the real source of their self-transcendence: society.

Durkheim's theory of the social creation of modern individualism and self is inspiring and thought-provoking, but it leaves us with one central problem common to all structural or functional theories. If society forces the categories on individuals through which they think and act, and outside of which they couldn't perform these functions, how do social groups develop such categories – a collective consciousness – to begin with? As Collins points out, this *a priori* theory of classification runs into trouble, because while it claims that classification must be forced upon individuals by society, it presupposes the ability of humans to classify.[33]

While Durkheim was able to draw some positive aspect from modern forms of individualism and selfhood, this view was not echoed in Max Weber's more pessimistic ideas about modernity. Like Marx, Weber thought the modern individual self was alienated from the world as a result of the transformation of relations of personal dependence into relations of impersonality and rational calculation.[34] However, he didn't believe this to be the direct result of capitalist social relations: indeed, for Weber, the modern form of individual selfhood is derived from Christianity, especially Protestantism, and it was this that gave direct impetus to the formation of the Western style of capitalism.

In *The Protestant Ethic and the Spirit of Capitalism* (1904) Weber argued that from the 16th century onward, beginning in Geneva and Scotland, but spreading their influence outwards, the Protestant sects such as Calvinism created an ascetic ethic by which individuals ordered themselves and their behaviour; activities that were to be influential in the formation of capitalism.[35] What was important in the Protestant ethic was its denial of any magical means of salvation by the church, such as the Catholic confession in which sins could be forgiven and the soul cleansed and saved. For example, Calvinism preached a harsh doctrine of predestination, which claimed that God had already predestined the few for salvation and there was nothing that an individual could do in their life to change that. For Weber, this had two effects on individuals. First, the lack of any means of salvation meant that individuals were alienated from both God and church, as they were now abandoned in the world and left to an uncertain fate. Second, because individuals could no longer be forgiven sins, every sin counted against them and was perhaps a sign they weren't one of those chosen for salvation. Protestants now had to guard against sin and wrongdoing by ordering their lives into a progression of good works according to a rational plan. The ascetic life-plan of good deeds, hard work, frugal living and the accumulation of wealth, saved for the glory of God rather than sinfully spent and squandered, was perhaps a worldly sign that the individual was one of the chosen. As Louis Dumont has said, there is a paradox in the doctrine of predestination: although it would seem to take away the individual's control of their fate, on the contrary, it makes them more concerned with their fate, as this becomes a possible sign of election.[36]

The desire to bind all of one's life into a rational plan of work spread into all areas of life, and gradually this Protestant spirit became secularized as a general ethic. It spread into capitalist enterprises where rational methods of bookkeeping account for money spent and profits made, as well as into labour disciplines such as strict time keeping and regular working hours. More importantly, for Weber, it led to rationalization becoming the basic mode of social organization and government, with bureaucratic styles of administration that had developed earlier in countries like China, and in European institutions such as the monasteries and the military, being adopted as a general principle. To Weber, the abstractions that rule people's lives and leave them feeling alienated are not purely economic, centring on private ownership of property and accumulation of capital, but are also to do with impersonal bureaucratic systems of population management, which are rule-bound rather than person-centred. Here, individuals can come to feel like the cogs in the rational bureaucratic machine, their lives totally ordered by such systems. Weber has likened this to living in an 'iron cage', a reference made specifically about the effects of modern consumerism.

Unlike Marx, Weber saw no solution to problems of modern capitalism in a revolution of the alienated and oppressed, because he thought that socialism – in trying to distribute wealth to meet individual needs – would turn into another form of bureaucratic system. Instead, following Nietzsche, he thought that individuals, who are crushed and depleted by modern civilization, can only become true selves when they take back the power and responsibility to freely choose their own values and actions. Selfhood is therefore an ideal to be attained, rather than a fact of modern life in Western bureaucratic capitalism.

However, there are problems in Weber's understanding of the modern rationalized nature of capitalism and selfhood. Anthony Giddens has pointed to the common critique that not all countries in Europe which became capitalist in the 18th and 19th centuries were predominantly Protestant countries, and that the influence of the Protestant sects was uneven. It is hard, then, to trace any direct link between the Protestant sects and the emergence of capitalism.[37] Others have suggested that Weber overestimated the effects of asceticism on the modern self. Colin Campbell has pointed to the Pietistic tradition in Protestantism, which stressed the individual's emotional commitment to God, suggesting that the emphasis on emotion rather than rationality had an influence on the popularity of Romantic art and literature in the 19th century.[38] According to Campbell, books by Romantic writers were amongst the first items demanded and produced for mass consumption. If the Protestant ethic only encouraged the formation of ascetic selves – who denied pleasure in order to save the fruits of hard-earned labour – then modern consumerism could not be explained. Indeed, one of the characteristics of selves in contemporary capitalist societies is that they have a seemingly insatiable desire to spend money on the consumption of goods. This has led the contemporary sociologist Zygmunt Bauman to claim that modern selves are 'happy shoppers', seduced by a culture of desire rather than denial.[39] It is then a problem, in Weberian terms, to see how lone individuals can escape this system without some collective associations – such as social movements – to help build alternative ways of life and new forms of social relationships.

Indeed, it could be said about all the sociologists I have considered above, that the lines of influence they draw between contemporary forms of individualism and capitalism are uncertain. As Abercrombie, Hill and Turner have noted, individualism and capitalism both have long and separate lines of development, ones that came together in European countries to form an individualistic type of capitalism. But it need not have been that way: in Japan, for example, traditionally there has been a more collective form of capitalism.[40] Capitalism and individualism have been of mutual influence on the modern Western notion of the self, but, as Mauss showed, we can see this beginning to form in ancient Greco-Roman societies and, from that time onwards, there are multiple influences on the Western conception and experience of selfhood. There are also many possible causes of the sense of alienation – the separation from the social world and individual isolation – that some feel in Western society. I have dwelt on only a few possibilities, but from these strands we can conclude that notions of the self, in the West alone, have a complex and conflicting history of social and cultural influence.

Psychology of the self

The discipline of psychology has also been influenced by many of the ideas I have considered above. One could regard modern cognitive psychology as a direct descendant of Kant's philosophy. Cognitive psychology claims that human thought cannot be directly derived from sense experience and that there must be prior structures of thinking for humans to be able to order their thoughts and experience of the world. However, cognitive psychology does not believe in a transcendental self: rather, the structures of thought are understood to be either hard-wired into the brain at birth, or at least partly programmed in through learning. Cognitive psychology has therefore abandoned metaphysics and adopted a materialist scientific approach to the mind, based on biological science and computing. Yet there is controversy over how much mental ability is hard-wired into our brains through genetic inheritance, and how much is programmed or learned from society. Moreover, cognitive psychology cannot explain how social knowledge develops and changes, focusing instead on individual minds. Social representations theory, a branch of 'social cognition', attempts to address this problem by developing the Durkheimian notion of the collective consciousness.[41]

However, I do not propose to develop these ideas in this book. Nor do I want to dwell on 'the psychology of personality', because in this branch of psychology 'personality' has come to mean something different from the notion of self. As developed by psychologists such as Gordon Allport, Hans Eysenck, and Raymond Cattell, personality is understood as a collection of traits or types that are mainly biologically inherited, which characterize each one of us as a unique individual.[42] In this approach, different traits or types can be identified and measured to establish the nature of personality as, for example, extrovert or introvert. Again, this is not an approach I will be dealing with here, for while I do not dismiss the possibility that characteristics or temperament can be biologically inherited and socially developed, it is self-understanding I am concerned with. That is, I want to investigate how we come to identify ourselves among others as having specific characteristics, how we come to see some aspects of our personality as more important than others, and how this changes over time, both socially and individually. It could be, for example, that two different people, who know me in different contexts, develop two very different views of my personality. Which one is correct? Given that personal characteristics can vary in different situations, maybe they are both correct. But this is what the psychology of personality ignores, that we are social beings: instead, it sees the dynamic organization of each individual lying inside its biological structure, rather than being constantly recreated between people in social relationships. As Allport once said, the dynamic organization of each personality lies 'within the skin', which becomes the boundary that separates each individual.[43] Throughout this book I will provide a series of arguments against this view of personality.

For now, I want to say something about the work of Sigmund Freud, which is of greater import to other ideas I will consider in this book. Freud has also had a huge impact on self-analysis in the Western world, and beyond, through the development of psychoanalysis. As both theory and method of self-examination, this discipline has had some influence on just about every form of psychotherapy and counselling practised today. For Freud, following Nietzsche, when we ask the question 'who am I?' we reply with a partially false answer, either because we do not know who we are, or because we respond with some illusion: an ego-ideal we take to be our self, but of which it is only a small part. In Freudian theory, the vast part of the self is unknown to us, or unconscious: the conscious 'I' is like the tip of an iceberg with only the small peak visible above the water and the major part of it concealed beneath the surface.

Again, like Nietzsche, Freud believes that what we conceal are animal instincts that are largely unacceptable to our civilizations, especially in certain forms of their expression, such as sexual and aggressive instincts. These have to be either repressed in the unconscious (how many of us will admit to being an aggressive person?) or channelled into socially acceptable forms of expression. In today's civilization, to fight someone in a boxing ring, according to strict rules and under supervision, is allowed, but to attack someone in the street is not: to express one-self sexually in a loving, long-term relationship is more acceptable than to be promiscuous. For Freud civilizations develop morality and law to manage and control the human instincts, but these are so powerful that they constantly strain at the leash, building up pressure in the human self to be released. Working in the late 19th and early 20th centuries in Vienna, Freud saw many patients suffering from neuroses – obsessive, compulsive or maladapted behaviours – that he attributed to repressed sexual desires, especially among women of the time who couldn't openly express their sexuality. Freud theorized that it was the repressed aspects of the self – not only the instincts, but the ways these are culturally and historically transformed into sexual or aggressive wishes, desires, dreams and fantasies – that were causing the trouble, fighting for expression against the conscious mind and its moral conscience.

From this, Freud developed a tripartite theory of the self, divided between the ego, super-ego and id: consciousness, conscience and the unconscious. However, as Bruno Bettelheim has pointed out, it was the English translator of Freud's works who chose to use the Latin terms 'ego' and 'id' for the psychic agencies, whereas in the original German texts Freud had rendered these in everyday terms: I, above-I and it.[44] The 'I' is self-consciousness, the part of ourselves with which we identify, or the 'ideal I', whereas we regard everything we repress or deny about ourselves as not-I, or as 'it'. The 'above-I' is conscience, the moral values instilled in the self from its infant years, which watches over thoughts and feel-ings, looking to prevent the stirrings of a thought, wish or desire that is unaccept-able. Thus, for Freud, the self is like a field of conflict on which warring factions often engage: the 'it' is like a force that compels us towards the expression of its repressed content of guilty secrets or forbidden dreams and desires; the 'above-I' watching to make sure that certain desires do not emerge, and, if they do, only in acceptable form; and finally, in the middle of these two powerful forces is the 'I', the conscious self, torn between these competing demands. Like Nietzsche, Freud believed the 'I' to be the weakest and most fragile part of the self, suspended between two threatening forces: the internal 'it' powering up from the depths for satisfaction, and the external power of cultural sanctions in the form of the 'above-I', resisting 'it' with the authority of society.

However, unlike Nietzsche, Freud places himself on the side of 'I', bringing the forces of psychoanalysis to its aid. Far from wanting to see the destruction of 'I', Freud wanted self-analysis to strengthen the 'I' by enlarging its scope to encompass the 'it' and reach greater harmony with the 'above-I'. He once said that the aim of psychoanalysis was a reformation of the self, in which where 'it' was there 'I' shall be. The more we know the 'it' and its potentially destructive drives, the more we can deal with them or defuse them without becoming too repressed or fearful of parts of the self – repression and fear also being poten-tially dangerous. In *Civilization and its Discontents* (1930), written after the First World War and in the build-up to the Second, Freud expressed the view that the instincts, especially aggression, might be too powerful for any civilization to contain, leading to its eventual destruction. Again, though, Freud supported the achievements of human civilization, such as science, rationality and art, regarding them as precious but precarious in the face of human destructiveness. Freud hoped that psychoanalysis could reinforce civilization in its battle against such forces, helping the self to feel less alienated from its own drives and from society and its rules. Certainly, Freud did not believe that a communist revolution would overcome alienation and result in a better, more equal society, for revolution relies on the very destructive forces that threaten self-identity and rational thought (the 'I'), as well as all the civilized achievements Marx thought everyone should share.

Despite this, Freud's aims and hopes for psychoanalysis were frustrated. Throughout his life he worked on *The Project for a Scientific Psychology,* hoping to locate the different aspects of the human mind in neurological functions and the workings of the nervous system, but neurological science was not advanced enough at that time for Freud to ever complete the project. Instead psychoanalysis remained largely philosophical and humanistic, with Freud attempting to understand the workings of the mind and self through metaphors and allusions to ancient literature (such as his adaptation of Sophocles' play *Oedipus Rex* into the notion of the 'Oedipus complex', describing the development of the child's self and sexuality within the complexity of family relationships). And while it has had a huge impact on all forms of psychotherapy, psychoanalysis has not become the answer to all of the problems of modern civilization. If Freud set out to be the therapist to the Enlightenment, strengthening the forces of rationality against the irrational, his success has been only partial.

Furthermore, while Freud was centrally concerned with the self, often his understanding of the relationship between self and society was only a secondary consideration. Whilst he had a detailed understanding of the repression demanded in civilizations and in the family, he never fully considered the effects that others have on the formation of the self in everyday relations and interactions. Nor did Freud consider the effect of factors like social class or gender on identity (strange, given that most of his patients were middle-class women). I will consider these factors in greater detail throughout this book.

The idea of social individuality

What I will be exploring throughout the rest of this book is the idea of social individuality, which means that one cannot separate the styles of self found in different cultures from the very historical and social relationships in which they are formed. We have seen in this chapter how Western notions of the self have been formed from many diverse and contradictory cultural strands, from Roman legal theory and Greco-Roman Stoic philosophy, to the Christian theology of the metaphysical soul as a kind of self-substance, and how, in various ways, this had an effect on the type of industrial capitalism that formed in Britain and other countries of Western Europe (and later in the USA). As thinkers as diverse as Hegel,

Marx, Durkheim and Weber have pointed out, individuals also become alienated from social life when power consolidates around church and state, or certain social classes, leaving the majority divorced from the social wealth (cultural and economic) they have helped to create. But capitalism has also created the division between the public world of work and politics, on the one hand, and of private life with family and friends, on the other. The modern self feels this division to its very core, having been created within it, and is often torn by the competing demands of the two.

However, a subtle shift happened in the understanding of the self from Hegel onward, in that for him, and for other social scientists who followed, the self is no longer at the centre of the world-picture, as it was for Descartes. Understanding the self is no longer the direct concern because this has to be approached by framing the self in the wider context of social formations and their changes. This is often referred to in the contemporary literature as the de-centring of the self. Nietzsche and Freud also participated in this movement by shifting the focus of their analyses away from the self-conscious 'I' onto the unconscious 'it' from which our thoughts and feelings spring unwilled. It is this challenge I take up here in trying to understand the nature of social selves, or of social individuality, and to do it anew by way of my own theoretical synthesis.

Those who have attempted to de-centre the self have also had another aim in their sights: to challenge the founding Christian notion of the self as an inner soul or substance, one that is metaphysical because it is unseen, but nevertheless substance-like because it provides the core elements of self prior to learning or experience. Instead, for the challengers, the self is understood as created in society and is a contingent or accidental amalgamation of the different aspects of the influences that have in-formed us, literally making us who we are. I will take up this line of argument by claiming that the idea we have of ourselves as possessing an 'inner' self waiting to be revealed somewhere inside the body or mind, *feels* correct, but only as a metaphor. The metaphorical sense of having an inner self arises through a silent dialogue we constantly hold with ourselves (not necessarily going on 'in the head'), which is only possible through social relations and dialogue with others. Like Adam Smith, many believe this sense of self only arises in the communicative interactions we have with others, through which we gain knowledge of ourselves and become who we are.

However, it is my view that sometimes the movement to de-centre the self goes wrong, finding itself in a purely academic debate, because it confuses three things I have begun to draw out in this chapter.

First, the critique of individualism as a political ideology or methodology: this is the critique of individualism along the lines of Macpherson's notion of 'possessive individualism', or of the ideas of methodological individualists who believed that unique individual differences occur prior to social relations, being the building-blocks out of which society is constructed. Methodological individualism in the social sciences and in psychology is what many are against who want to understand society as existing prior to individuals, theorizing the self as a social construction. But this can also spill over into a critique of alienating forms of individualism in capitalism, such as Marx's critique, or Macpherson's more democratic adaptation of Marx's ideas.

Second, the philosophical critique of the self as substance: this is the critique of Augustinian and Cartesian ideas of the self as soul or metaphysical substance, or of contemporary theories such as the psychology of personality, which understands self to be an 'inner' organization of the organism. This is an epistemological critique of the way the individual is theorized and understood within philosophy.

Third, the investigation of the nature of self and what it is to be a self among others in the social world. It is this aspect of self I will pursue in this book, arguing that we must not confuse the critique of individualism or the epistemological critique of self as substance, with an understanding of self as it emerges in social relations and dialogues. The first and second critiques do not lead automatically to a critique of the third: that we exist as embodied beings in social relations, and, in this milieu, we become selves. I will also argue that while some ideological and metaphysical abstractions, which need to be critiqued, have acted upon individuals in everyday life, shaping self-identities, there is a reciprocal relation between political and philosophical abstraction on the one hand, and everyday life and selfhood on the other. The two inform each other, with ideas about what it is to be a self that emerge from everyday social relations seeping into concepts of the self in the social sciences, psychology and the humanities, while these concepts can then filter back into everyday understandings of who we are. I will discuss this relation of 'official' (established political or scientific) ideas of self and 'unofficial' ones (ideas and feelings that are created in everyday interactions and dialogues) throughout the book.

In anticipation of the development of my views, let me say that I understand self as a necessary part of modern Western life. Taylor has argued that to know who you are is to be oriented in moral space, to know where you stand in terms of the value commitments and identifications through which actions are determined.[45] I, however, argue that to have a sense of self and an understanding of self-identity is a means of orientation in the entire social space of Western modernity. In this space we orient our actions with one another by trying to gauge other selves: who they are and what they are thinking and feeling. Especially in the more secular and cosmopolitan places of Western modernity, where single overarching moral frameworks are starting to lose their hold, notions of the self help to orient people in their relations and activities in a society of individuals.

Notes

1. C. B. Macpherson (1962) *The Political Theory of Possessive Individualism: Hobbes to Locke.* Oxford: Clarendon Press.
2. Norbert Elias (1991) *The Society of Individuals.* Tr. Edmund Jephcott. Oxford: Basil Blackwell.
3. Marcel Mauss (1985) 'A category of the human mind: the notion of person: the notion of self', tr. W. D. Halls, in M. Carrithers, S. Collins and S. Lukes (eds), *The Category*

   of the Person: Anthropology, Philosophy, History. Cambridge: Cambridge
   University Press. pp. 1–25.
4. Michel Foucault (1988) 'Technologies of the self', in L. H. Martin, H. Gutman and
   P. H. Hutton (eds), *Technologies of the Self: A Seminar With Michel Foucault.*
   Cambridge, MA: MIT Press. pp. 16–49.
5. Mikhail Bakhtin (1981) *The Dialogic Imagination.* Tr. C. Emerson and M. Holquist.
   Austin: University of Texas Press.
6. A. Momigliano (1985) 'Marcel Mauss and the quest for the person in Greek
   biography and autobiography', in M. Carrithers, S. Collins and S. Lukes (eds), *The
   Category of the Person: Anthropology, Philosophy, History. Cambridge*: Cambridge
   University Press. pp. 83–92.
7. Michel Foucault (1988) *The Care of the Self: The History of Sexuality, Volume 3.* Tr.
   Robert Hurley. London: Penguin.
8. Charles Taylor (1989) *Sources of the Self: The Making of the Modern Identity.*
   Cambridge: Cambridge University Press.
9. Eduardo Cadava, Peter Connor and Jean-Luc Nancy (eds) (1991) *Who Comes After
   the Subject?* New York: Routledge.
10. René Descartes (1968) *Discourse on Method and the Meditations.* Tr. F. E. Sutcliffe.
    London: Penguin. pp. 53–4.
11. Jerrold Seigel (2005*) The Idea of the Self: Thought and Experience in Western
    Europe since the Seventeenth Century.* Cambridge: Cambridge University Press.
12. Anthony Kenny (1968) *Descartes: A Study of his Philosophy.* New York: Random
    House.
13. Charles Taylor, *Sources.*
14. Jerrold Seigel, *Self*, Ch. 9.
15. S. Korner (1955) *Kant.* Harmondsworth: Penguin.
16. Jerrold Seigel, *Self*, Ch. 9.
17. Adam Smith (1966) *Theory of Moral Sentiments.* New York: Augustus M. Kelley.
    p. 7.
18. Jerrold Seigel, *Self*, Ch. 5.
19. Jerrold Seigel, *Self*, pp. 159–60.
20. Jerrold Seigel, *Self*, Ch. 12.
21. R. J. Hollingdale (1965*) Nietzsche: The Man and His Philosophy.* London: Routledge &
    Kegan Paul.
22. Mark Elvin (1985) 'Between the earth and heaven: conceptions of the self in
    China', in M. Carrithers, S. Collins and S. Lukes (eds), *The Category of the Person:
    Anthropology, Philosophy, History.* Cambridge: Cambridge University Press.
    pp. 156–89.
23. Norbert Elias, *Society.*
24. Karl Marx and Frederick Engels (1970) *The German Ideology: Part One.* London:
    Lawrence & Wishart.
25. Ibid., p. 42.
26. Karl Marx (1973) *Grundrisse.* Tr. Martin Nicolaus. Harmondsworth: Penguin. p. 84.
27. Alberto Melucci (1989) *Nomads of the Present: Social Movements and Individual
    Needs in Contemporary Society.* London: Hutchinson Radius.
28. Emile Durkheim (1984) *The Division of Labour in Society.* Tr. W. D. Halls. London:
    Macmillan.
29. Steven Collins (1985) 'Categories, concepts or predicaments? Remarks on Mauss's
    use of philosophical terminology', in M. Carrithers, S. Collins and S. Lukes (eds),

The Category of the Person: Anthropology, Philosophy, History. Cambridge: Cambridge University Press. pp. 46–82.

30. Emile Durkheim (1969) 'Individualism and the Intellectuals', tr. S. and J. Lukes, *Political Studies,* XVII (1): 14-30: 26.

31. Emile Durkheim (1952) *Suicide: a Study in Sociology.* Tr. J. A. Spalding and G. Simpson. London: Routledge & Kegan Paul.

32. Anthony Giddens (1971) *Capitalism and Modern Social Theory: An Analysis of the Writings of Marx, Durkheim and Max Weber.* Cambridge: Cambridge University Press. p. 228.

33. Steven Collins, 'Categories'.

34. Derek Sayer (1991) *Capitalism and Modernity: An Excursus on Marx and Weber.* London: Routledge.

35. Max Weber (1930) *The Protestant Ethic and the Spirit of Capitalism.* Tr. Talcott Parsons. 1985 edn. London: Counterpoint.

36. Louis Dumont (1985) 'A modified view of our origins: the Christian beginnings of modern individualism', in M. Carrithers, S. Collins and S. Lukes (eds), *The Category of the Person: Anthropology, Philosophy, History.* Cambridge: Cambridge University Press. pp. 93–122.

37. Anthony Giddens (1985) 'Introduction', in Max Weber, *Protestant Ethic.* pp. vii–xxvi.

38. Colin Campbell (1987) *The Romantic Ethic and the Spirit of Modern Consumerism.* Oxford: Blackwell.

39. Zygment Bauman (2000) *Liquid Modernity.* Cambridge: Polity Press.

40. N. Abercrombie, S. Hill and B. S. Turner (1986) *Sovereign Individuals of Capitalism.* London: Allen & Unwin.

41. R. M. Farr and S. Moscovici (eds) (1984) *Social Representations.* Cambridge: Cambridge University Press.

42. G. W. Allport (1937) *Personality: A Psychological Interpretation.* London: Constable. H. J. Eysenck (1953) *The Structure of Human Personality.* London: Methuen. R. B. Cattell (1979) *Personality and Learning Theory.* New York: Springer.

43. G. W. Allport (1937) *Personality, Character and Temperament.* New York: Holt, Rinehart & Winston. p. 30.

44. Bruno Bettelheim (1985) *Freud and Man's Soul.* London: Flamingo.

45. Charles Taylor, *Sources.*

Selected bibliography

Abercrombie, N., Hill, S. and Turner, B. S. (1986) *Sovereign Individuals of Capitalism.*London: Allen & Unwin.

Bettelheim, Bruno (1985) *Freud and Man's Soul.* London: Flamingo.

Carrithers, M., Collins, S. and Lukes, S. (eds) (1985) *The Category of the Person: Anthropology, Philosophy, History.* Cambridge: Cambridge University Press.

Durkheim, Emile (1984) *The Division of Labour in Society.* Tr. W. D. Halls. London: Macmillan.

Elias, Norbert (1991) *The Society of Individuals.* Tr. Edmund Jephcott. Oxford: Basil Blackwell.

Freud, Sigmund (1930) *Civilization and its Discontents.* London: Hogarth.

Freud, Sigmund (1973) *Introductory Lectures on Psychoanalysis.* London: Penguin.

Marx, K. and Engels, F. (1970) *The German Ideology: Part One.* London: Lawrence & Wishart.

Seigel, Jerrold (2005) *The Idea of the Self: Thought and Experience in Western Europe Since the Seventeenth Century.* Cambridge: Cambridge University Press.

Taylor, Charles (1989) *Sources of the Self: The Making of the Modern Identity.* Cambridge: Cambridge University Press.

Weber, Max (1930) *The Protestant Ethic and the Spirit of Capitalism.* Tr. Talcott Parsons. London: George Allen & Unwin.

CHAPTER 2

DIALOGUE AND THE SOCIAL SELF

… no philosopher and hardly any novelist has ever managed to explain what that weird stuff, human consciousness, is really made of. Body, external objects, darty memories, warm fantasies, other minds, guilt, fear, hesitation, lies, glees, doles, breathtaking pains, a thousand things which words can only fumble at, coexist, many fused together in a single unit of consciousness. How human responsibility is possible at all could well puzzle an extra-galactic student of this weird method of proceeding through time. (Iris Murdoch, *The Black Prince*)

Much of what Iris Murdoch says above about consciousness also applies to the self and self-consciousness. It can seem like the most vague and inchoate thing to study, slipping off into indeterminacy and obscurity barely a moment after it has formed into tangibility. However, around the turn of the 20th century two remarkable schools of thought emerged that placed the social self at the heart of their thinking, attempting to explain how temporal human self-consciousness, composed of fleeting moments of sensation, perception, feeling and thought, can coalesce into some kind of temporary unity of self experience that is additive, creating the feeling of existing as a self. This unity and form of self is only achieved because we live with others in society, yet it is not reducible to the social relations and dialogue that give birth to it. Like a child that emerges from the social bonds that nurture, sustain and educate it, yet manages to become a distinct individual with its own self-identity, so all selves emerge from a social context to become unique individuals. The two schools of thought I will consider in this chapter are the pragmatists and the cultural historical school, both of which achieved a non-reductive view of the social self, but in remarkably different circumstances: the former in the USA in the late 19th and early 20th centuries, the latter in Russia in the post-1917 revolutionary period. Both schools were against the ideologies of individualism I discussed briefly in the first chapter, but did not oppose the type of everyday individuality that emerges in a world of others. Instead, they try to understand the self as embedded within its everyday relations and dialogic interactions.

Pragmatism and the self

Pragmatism was a philosophical movement that emerged in the USA in the aftermath of the American civil war, providing a way for people to cope in an increasingly modernizing capitalist society where older customs and communities were disappearing.[1] However, the pragmatists did not preach the doctrine of individual self-reliance typical of a thinker like Ralph Waldo Emerson, for whom ideally the individual was seen as free from all social bonds, able to act in ways that they alone saw fit. Instead, pragmatists thought that ideas were social, produced through dialogue within groups of interacting individuals. Ideas belong to a culture and are 'tools ... that people devise to cope with the world in which they find themselves'.[2] However, this coping involves not simply coming to terms with the world as given, but in actively transforming it to suit human purposes, to further our interests, or to better meet our needs. Ideas are tools that allow humans to be active in the world, and human consciousness is not simply a mirror image of the environment, but a creative and imaginative part of the activity that reshapes it. What we take to be truth, then, is not the knowledge that best reflects or represents a given world, but what works for us when actively pursuing our collective aims and interests. C. S. Pierce was one of the first to give this philosophy the name of pragmatism, taken from Kant's *Critique of Pure Reason* in which this type of practical knowing was referred to. However, whereas for Kant this was just one type of knowing, for the pragmatists it was the only type. This led them to oppose Kant's theory of the transcendental self, along with the notion of *a priori* categories of human thought. That is because, if knowledge is a practical tool serving human activity in the world, it must emerge from worldly experience rather than from a transcendental realm.

In this way, for pragmatists, *social activity* becomes the key to understanding knowledge, consciousness, and self, because these things emerge from it. It also means that knowledge and truth are relative, changing socially, historically and individually according to the nature of human activity, its aims and outcomes. Pragmatists therefore favoured an open democratic society in which a plurality of different views could be expressed, rather than a society of warring ideological factions. The core value here is the tolerance of different viewpoints that emerge from experience instead of an adherence to an individual viewpoint that will admit no credibility to any other, over which individuals are prepared to die or do violence to others. While pragmatism emerged in a rapidly capitalizing world, it should not be seen as a capitalist, or a peculiarly North American philosophy, for its collectivist, relativist and openly democratic spirit militates against a simple belief in free market capitalism as the only way to organize society. The pragmatists also believed in rational knowledge as a useful practical tool, not only for individuals engaged in activity, but also for governments attempting to find solutions to collective problems, and this too opposed an unfettered free market view of the world.

For my purposes here, studying the nature of the social self, there was a more important impact on the pragmatists' view of the nature of consciousness and selfhood, and that was Darwin's theory of the evolution of the species. Like Nietzsche, the pragmatists began their work in the late 19th century in the wake of Darwin's revolution, and, under his influence, they wanted to develop an understanding of self-consciousness that was materialist rather than spiritual or substantial. As Louis Menand has pointed out, what was radical about Darwin was not his evolutionism, but his materialism. This was expressed in the idea that species had evolved in a process of *natural* selection, which operates according to chance, and, as such, is blind (that is, there is no 'higher intelligence' guiding or planning the process). Also, through processes of natural and sexual selection, it is the characteristics of *individuals* that are selected in evolution, rather than those of entire species. To Menand, this means evolutionary theory is no longer interested in the conformity of an individual to an ideal type, but in the relations and interactions of individuals[3] (as in sexual selection, where individuals choose mates from a range of possible partners). Relations and interactions became important, and this had a profound impact on the pragmatists.

For William James, one of the early pragmatists, Darwin's views meant that the philosophy and psychology of consciousness had to be completely reformulated. Consciousness could no longer be seen as belonging to some inner transcendental self, but had to be understood as an evolutionary product: something that had evolved in activity as a means for humans to better adapt to the environment. James therefore redefined consciousness as an *objective function* in the active adaptation of humans to their conditions of existence, rather than as a private possession of a pre-given soul.[4] Self-consciousness is not, then, the pre-existing source of mental activity, emotions, and feelings, but rather their last and most complicated fruit.[5] This is taken further by later pragmatists such as G. H. Mead and John Dewey, who understood consciousness as a function of *social* behaviour in evolution. However, all pragmatists believe that the laws of natural selection have their limit: while they hold good biologically, the evolution of human consciousness has meant that socially we can transcend natural selection. For example, we can develop moral systems that say we should look after the sick and elderly, something that might go against the demands of natural selection.

Thus, although a late arrival in evolutionary terms, consciousness changes human nature. We are no longer simply driven by instinct and impulse, nor respond mechanically to stimuli in the environment, but can *reflect* on competing demands and possibilities presented to us and *choose* how to act. Conscious reflection on one's own activity within the group, involving choice of actions, and, with it, self-awareness, provides a loophole out of purely natural laws, even though we remain natural beings through and through.

However, for James and the other pragmatists, self-consciousness is not always the key to activity, as habit patterns much of human behaviour; habit being understood as individual variations of behaviour that are driven not by instinct or individual characteristics, but by acquisition at some stage of life. Most of our actions are done habitually, without us having to consciously think about them, and it is only where habit breaks down or is not appropriate to the task that we must become conscious of our actions and self. For James, it is the natural plasticity of the human brain which allows it to become imprinted by stimuli, by the senses, and by feelings that occur in activity, establishing neural pathways that lead to habits. But both habit and consciousness are *temporal,* changing over time. This gives further weight to the materialist thrust of James's ideas, for habit, consciousness, and self exist only in the time and space of a person's life and experience. This is expressed most clearly in James's famous characterization of the 'stream of consciousness', which indicates that human consciousness does not leap from one isolated experience into the next, but incorporates what went before into its current state, creating an additive experience. So, if thought was to pass from state a, to b, and then to c, the latter would encapsulate all three states in its awareness.[6] Like a stream, then, consciousness is always changing in time, yet accumulating experience in its flow that can be attributed to a self.

When dealing with the self, James claimed that it is a duplex composed of the 'I' which thinks – the consciousness that has emerged through evolution – and the object it thinks about, called the 'me'. Another way of conceptualizing this is seeing the 'I' as the knower and the 'me' as the known. Here James is elaborating on Descartes' dualism between the 'I think' and the 'I am', only he is explaining it in material, practical and temporal ways, rather than as a metaphysical power of reflection. However, the stream of consciousness presents us with a conundrum: it is always changing and yet whenever we say 'I' we spontaneously believe we refer to something that always remains the same. James says that 'this has led most philosophers to postulate behind the passing state of consciousness is a permanent Substance or Agent whose modification or act it is'.[7] James clearly sees this as wrong thinking, because:

> if the states of consciousness be accorded as realities, no such 'substantial' identity in the thinker need be supposed. Yesterday's and to-day's states of consciousness have no *substantial* identity, for when one is here the other is irrevocably dead and gone.[8]

However, given James's additive notion of consciousness, the passing states do amount to more than fleeting, disconnected experiences, as 'they have a *functional* identity, for they both know the same objects, and so far as the by-gone me is one of those objects, they react upon it in an identical way, greeting it and calling it *mine*'.[9] In other words, unlike Descartes' conception, there is no soul or substance behind the 'I', which is fixed and unchanging, leading logically to the conclusion 'therefore I am'. For James, thinking is empty of such substance.

Instead, the self resides in the 'I am', or in James's terms with the 'me', which is the object that consciousness reflects upon. This is the empirical self of everyday life lived with others, and although this too changes over time, it does so at a slower pace than the passing states of consciousness. According to James there are three aspects to this empirical 'me' that I reflect upon when I think about myself. First is the 'material me', especially my body by which I am identified, both by myself and by others. In everyday life, we recognize each other by our bodies, especially our faces. We would get a shock if we looked in the mirror and saw a face different from the one we usually see staring back at us. Then there are the clothes and other material possessions, such as homes and cars, by which we are identified. Because consciousness is additive, we feel the continuation of our self-identity by being in the same body, surrounded by our possessions. The American comedian Steve Wright joked that he woke up one morning in his room to find that someone had changed all his possessions for exact replicas! It would be more of a shock if we woke in our room to find ourselves surrounded by strange objects: we would begin to doubt who we were. Also included in the 'material me' is our family, who are part of us to the extent that if a member dies we feel as though we lose part of ourselves.

Secondly there is the 'social me', which is the recognition we get from others. According to James, humans are gregarious social beings who want to be noticed, and noticed *favourably,* by others. James says that 'no more fiendish punishment could be devised ... than that one should be turned loose in society and remain absolutely unnoticed by all the members thereof'.[10] Not only our continued existence, but our very existence itself, rests on being recognized by others, particularly by those we know. But James thought that we all have as many social selves as those who know us, because each of those others may see us in a different light, or see different aspects of our character depending on the social context. We may not use the same language or behaviour with our parents as we do with our friends in the street: likewise, a prison guard may be tough with prisoners but tender to his or her children. So, although the 'social me' gives some stability and continuity to identity, this is only relative, as the self changes over time and in different contexts.

Thirdly there is the 'spiritual me', which is the entire flow of the stream of consciousness about the self up to the point we are at now. Although James does not say it, this would presumably include the stories we tell about our lives, including the way our memory is ordered. He does say, though, that the 'spiritual me' includes one's psychic faculties and dispositions, and one would think that this includes our capacities, capabilities, talents and habits, through which we also know ourselves. More generally, the 'spiritual me' is a certain totality of our experience, or a slant on it, available to us at any given time as an object of conscious reflection, which also stirs certain emotions. This capacity to reflect on one's self and react to it emotionally is the core of the 'spiritual me'. As James says:

> the more *active-feeling* states of consciousness are thus the more central portions of the spiritual Me. The very core and nucleus of our self, as we know it, the very sanctuary of our life, is the sense of activity which certain inner states possess. This sense of activity is often held to be a direct revelation of the living substance of our Soul.[11]

However, what we take to be the soul or the self are not spiritual substances or essences but dynamic and loose assemblages of different aspects of our material existence, which differ from one another and are often contradictory. Here there is the clear influence of German Idealist philosophy on James (as with all the other pragmatists), especially Hegel, in that differing and contradictory elements can be formed into states of unity that unfold not only in individuals, but more generally within society. However, what is new in the pragmatists is their materialism – in which mind, reason and self are taken as matters of practical action evolving in biological organisms, rather than as Spirit or Mind emerging from the transcendental or in History – and also their lack of teleology: that is, the notion that the course of these unfolding processes will end in some Absolute state of unity. Indeed, for James, the 'I' and the 'me' interact dialectically in a process where the 'I' combines the 'mes' into a loose assemblage, but only temporarily. Because as selves we are temporal, projecting our experience from the past, through the present, and into the future, the process of change only ends when we die, never achieving Hegel's Absolute unity.

For James, as temporal selves, we are strangely perched in time. Experience is located in the present, yet a present moment is hard to grasp: it seems to slip away from us before we can fully realize what has just happened, at which point it is the past. Yet it is from this 'present' in which we live that we can look backwards and forwards through the stream of consciousness: from our past experiences and selves, reflected upon in the present, and projected into the future in the form of plans, hopes or dreams. To us humans, time becomes symbolic and is measured not only by the objective means of clocks and calendars, but by the subjective symbols of life events and changes. The sense of time comes from the flowing and changing nature of our material consciousness and self, developed and located in time and place, amongst objects and other selves, as different states or identities succeed each other. The self exists in time as a material symbolic construct.

G. H. Mead and the social self

Following James, George Herbert Mead advanced the pragmatist understanding of the self, but for him the self was much more of a social construct, even the subjective sense of 'I'. For Mead the importance of the evolutionary adaptation of consciousness was seen in a social context, where individuals not only had to adapt to the environment, but to all the other individuals in the group with whom they were engaged in joint activities. Mead's central concern, therefore, was the relationship between the activity of the social group and the formation of the individual self, and, more specifically, the role of the tools that humans have invented in evolution and social history – such as symbols, signs and language – which mediate and direct their joint activities, and form self-identities. Mead's position was shaped not only under the influence of James and Darwin, but also in a period of study in Leipzig where he became acquainted with ideas in German Idealism, specifically those of Kant and Hegel, along with the *Volkerpsychologie* (folk or social psychology) of Wilhelm Wundt, and the interpretive philosophy of Dilthey.[12] All this strengthened Mead's interest in the communicative interaction of individuals in society, the way that each member of the group adjusts their conduct by interpreting the actions of the others, and how in doing so we must reflect on the meaning of our own impulses to act and thus upon our own self. Mead was one of the first thinkers of the 20th century to explore the idea that mind and self are formed in the discourse of the social group, an idea now common in philosophy, sociology, and social psychology.

Language, however, has to have a source, a basis on which it evolves, and Mead believed that gestures are its foundation. Like other social animals, humans use gesture to signal their responses to others in the group who take the signal as a means by which to adjust their own response in the interaction. Mead's famous example of this is two boxers squaring up in the ring, watching each others' body movements as signs to where the next punch might come from and adjusting their bodies accordingly.[13] Language has grown out of body movement and gesture as a socially elaborated code of meaning, through which humans can speak or write in order to communicate with each other, and through which members of a group can adjust their actions, in conflict or cooperation. In this sense, language is a more impersonal and subtle means of communication, allowing a range of possible responses to others and to situations that are not given in nature. Now everything can become a 'significant symbol', in that it is interpreted according to socially produced systems of meaning, and the environment is composed of 'social objects': a meaningful social world that is open to a variety of interpretations. For example, as humans we still use gestures, only now these become significant symbols rather than instinctive responses, like when we give a 'thumbs-up' sign to someone to signal 'OK' or 'go ahead'. This is why Mead's ideas have become known in some quarters as 'symbolic interactionism', because symbols, signs and words that have a shared meaning for the group are now the means of mediation in social relations and activities.

In all social groups, then, whether they are small tribal units or mass industrialized nations, symbols, signs and language act as the social objects to which we respond, either as groups or as individuals in interpersonal relations. The response is governed by our interpretation or reading of the situation, as well as by knowledge of our own self: our past experience, beliefs and values (I will come to the self in a moment). It is not that humans are without instinctive responses, for Mead talked at different points in his career about the social instincts of humans,[14] and how these fall into two groups, the hostile and the friendly.[15] Key to this, though, is how these instincts become reshaped in symbolic activity, so that, for example, conflicting social groups can try to work out their anger and hostility (often caused by social factors such as prejudice, discrimination or oppression) through negotiation and peace processes rather than violence. Like Freud, Mead believed that at base humans are instinctive animals, but, unlike Freud, he thought we are constantly embedded in social processes that reconfigure instinct in response to symbols. My appetite can be stimulated by the logo of my favourite chocolate bar, or I can have a coffee with friends every 4pm, even though I may not be hungry or thirsty. These are now social activities, organized around the symbols of objects/products, time and place.

Furthermore, it is in these social activities that self-consciousness emerges, for in successfully coordinating my responses to others, I must have an awareness of my own self and the likely effect that my actions will have on others. My action becomes a sign that calls out the responses of others towards me. As Mead observed:

> In these social situations appear[s] … a consciousness of one's own attitude as an interpretation of the meaning of the social stimulus. We are conscious of our attitudes because they are responsible for the changes in conduct of other individuals. A man's reaction towards weather conditions has no influence upon the weather itself … Successful social conduct brings one into a field within which a consciousness of one's own attitudes helps towards the control of the conduct of others.[16]

However, we do not experience ourselves directly in consciousness. As James pointed out, there is no self acting behind our thoughts: the self can only be experienced as an objective, empirical fact within a world of others. For Mead, this meant that we can only experience ourselves indirectly, from the way other individuals in the group respond to our actions, or from the general standpoint of the social group taken towards ourselves. Referring to the individual, Mead stated:

> … he enters his own experience as a self or individual, not directly or immediately, not by becoming a subject to himself, but only in so far as he becomes an object to himself just as other individuals are objects to him or in his experience; and he becomes an object to himself only by taking the attitudes of other individuals towards himself within a social environment or context of experience and behavior in which both he and they are involved.[17]

Like James, Mead elaborated his theory of the self using the pronouns 'I' and 'me', the latter being the empirical social self that James referred to. However, as can be seen in the above quotation, Mead thought that we can get a sense of self only as we become social objects to other people, as we become 'mes'. The 'I' is not simply a stream of consciousness, but arises with the objective sense of 'me' as its subjective, reflective side. Before the 'I' and the 'me' start to appear in early childhood, there is only a protoplasmic consciousness, in which there is no awareness of others as distinct from self, or the objective world as distinct from the subjective one. We still experience this sense of protoplasmic consciousness as adults when we lose our self in an activity, like reading a book, watching a film in the cinema, swimming, or performing an habitual activity such as driving a car: in all such activities there are moments when we are so absorbed in the world around us or in the task at hand we lose all sense of our own self and our separation from the world. Then, we no longer sense an object or subject, an 'outside' and 'inside'. As children mature, they have an increasing sense of the presence of others in their lives who are separate beings, and who can also regard them in the same way. It is then that children can begin to take the attitude of being objects to themselves, in the way that others are objects to them, and can see themselves from an objective position, as if looking at themselves from the standpoint of an observer. In this activity, the 'I' is the attitude of the observer, the 'me' the object observed. Thus, from the very beginnings of self-awareness, the 'I' and the 'me' are locked in a dialectical interrelationship, the self-conscious person able to switch between the two stances and hold conversations between the two: the 'me' as the self 'I' look upon, the 'me' who listens when 'I' speak.

If the 'I' seems somewhat intangible, that is the way it has to be, for Mead believed, like James, that there is no substantial self that stands behind the 'I': instead, the self is the interaction of 'I' and 'me' that arises when we regard ourselves as a social object. We can think of ourselves in retrospect and use the pronoun 'I' to reflect on past actions and their motivations, as in 'why did I do that?' or 'what was I thinking of?'. In this mode, the 'I' can refer retrospectively to something we have done in a state of protoplasmic consciousness, when we were not acting with full self-awareness. But, of course, 'I' and 'me' are both pronouns: linguistic terms that arise in conversation with others when we refer to ourselves either as a subject – 'excuse me, *I* was speaking!' – or as an object – 'they just ignored me'. Mead points out that we do a similar thing when we talk to ourselves, taking the conversational positions of 'I' and 'me' in a self-dialogue that is modelled on social communication. This is the very process that we call thinking, or that we reify with the term 'mind'. Mead gives the following description of the social self and its thought:

> The self which consciously stands over against other selves thus becomes an object, an other to himself, through the very fact that he hears himself talk, and replies. The mechanism of introspection is therefore given in the social attitude which man necessarily assumes towards himself, and the mechanism of thought, insofar as thought uses symbols which are used in social intercourse, is but an inner conversation.[18]

Mead then goes on to illustrate how this 'inner' conversation – or perhaps more accurately put, conversation with oneself – is carried on in the interrelation between the 'I' position of speaker (subject) and 'me' position of hearer (object). Note also in the quotation below how Mead sees these two positions as inducing each other in the self-dialogue.

> … the stuff that goes to make up the 'me' who the 'I' addresses and whom he observes, is the experience which is induced by this action of the 'I'. If the 'I' speaks, the 'me' hears. If the 'I' strikes, the 'me' feels the blow. Here again the 'me' consciousness is of the same character as that which arises from the action of the other upon him.[19]

But this can still sound fairly mysterious, because there is always the temptation to ask 'who is the self behind the "I" when I am speaking?' as if there is a self behind the 'I'. We are lured back into the type of thinking that James saw as the pitfall of Idealist philosophy. The answer has to be that there is no self present when I am speaking, or thinking for that matter, as speaking is like a habit, a modulation of the human body, drawn out in interaction with others and with our own self. It is the bodily response to a situation or to other people that is purely natural for us – just like a gesture – but is wholly social at one and the same time. It therefore needs no self, substance, or soul to kick-start the process or to lie behind it, planning it and thinking it through. It's like talking to a friend: you don't have to plan every word you say in advance, or even think it all through before you pronounce each word: the talk comes in the interaction between you. The phenomenologist Merleau-Ponty put this well when he said that speech is one of the natural modes of expression of the human body, just like the expression of an emotion on the face, or a gesture of the body, even though these things are thoroughly imprinted and re-modulated by the social meanings embedded in our language and culture. The body acquires these cultural means as it grows and learns, and they become 'second nature' or habitual; they become our natural means of responding to each other, and to situations, as social beings. This leads Merleau-Ponty to say that 'everything is both manufactured and natural in man',[20] and I have no doubt that the pragmatists would be in full agreement.

The self, then, as 'I' and 'me', often enters the scene after the fact, after the drama has been played out, when we ask ourselves questions like 'Why did I say that?' or 'What will they think of me?' Here, we are questioning both our subjective responses to situations and the objective impressions we have left on others. We are putting together a self-image from the residue of our own responses and the likely effects they have had on others. Temporality is therefore always a factor in the relationships between the 'I' and 'me', as what is identified as 'I' in one moment – the active subject – can become the objective 'me' in the next moment. It could be said with some justification that in Mead's view *the self is temporality,* only existing in time and forever changing. However, the self is not totally absent from the experience of an interaction with others in the moment. We are often aware of our presence as selves among others in the heat of interaction, and can hold a dialogue with ourselves while we are speaking to others. We can try to stop ourselves from saying something hurtful, or adjust our tone of voice; and we can also change our bodily posture or gestures to try to change the tone of an interaction. In other words, 'I' can be aware of my actions in the moment and of the effect they are having on others, thus also being aware of their response to 'me'. Once we have self-consciousness, from early childhood onwards, the self, with its 'I' and 'me' stances, is never far from awareness.

While it is true, then, to say that the 'I' is a shifting signifier that refers to no solid, stable, or tangible entity, I do not entirely agree with Benveniste for whom the 'I' is solely a product of discourse.[21] Given what I have been saying above, following Mead, there are many different significances attached to the pronoun 'I', and it only gains significance in reference to 'me', to others (or to 'you', as Shotter puts it),[22] and with reference to our past embodied experience of protoplasmic consciousness, where self momentarily disappears. It is true to say that 'I' does not refer to an extra-discursive reality, but in saying this we must interpret the term discourse widely to include the relations and interaction between selves, and the conversations of gestures between bodies. Within this, 'I' and 'me' are stances that can be taken within communicative interaction. Furthermore, the 'me' has tangible presence as an empirical self in its body, its possessions, its life history, and the presence of these things to others.

Mead's description of the social self went deeper than this, though, for he realized that others were not only present to us in the social world, they are also present within the self. Self-consciousness is animated not only by our own embodied energy and voice, and how this relates to the objective sense of self we get from others, it is also populated by the energy and voices of others. The images of friends, family, colleagues, acquaintances or public figures known only through the media, are present in relation to our own self-image in consciousness, so that we can speak and interact with them in imagination. These others can also judge us, because they are part of the moral fabric of the social world, which operates not only according to linguistic codes, but also ethical ones. Mead believes that social values are initially communicated to the child through its parents or caretakers, so that parental figures are constantly present in the child's mind, praising or criticizing action. He says,

> ... the child can think about his conduct as good or bad only as he reacts to his own acts in the remembered words of his parents. Until this process has been developed into the abstract processes of thought, self-consciousness remains dramatic, and the self which is a fusion of the remembered actor and this accompanying chorus is somewhat loosely organized and is very clearly social. Later the inner stage changes into the forum and workshop of thought. The features and intonations of the dramatis personae fade out and the emphasis falls upon the meaning of inner speech, the imagery becomes merely the barely necessary cues. But the mechanism remains social, and at any moment may become personal.[23]

So, initially, the parents and their attitudes reflect aspects of the moral character of society and provide for the child a gateway to the wider social group. Slowly, as children begin to learn language, and more about the wider culture, they find society opening up for them more directly. For Mead, this is reflected in the way that children of different ages play together. Very young children tend to involve themselves in role play, where they can practise taking the different roles they observe in the adult world, such as homes, shops or workplaces. Or they can play out different scenarios from books, plays, TV shows, films etc., taking the part of different characters. Later, this kind of play takes on more of a story or theme in which children learn to anticipate the actions of others through interpreting the overall meaning of the story. Here, a child is showing the capacity to assume the attitudes of others, and to judge their own response to it, depending on the social meaning of the activity within the group. This ability takes another form as children learn to play games like football or hockey, which are organized by more abstract sets of rules. Children must now understand the rules of the game through participation in it, and, with that practical understanding, be able to anticipate the moves of the other players and how their own actions should fit in with them. In other words, they learn to play as a team. This reflects the growing ability of the child, developed through social activity, to take the generalized attitude of the group towards themselves and, thus, to treat themselves as an object for others. As individuals they are becoming self-aware by responding to themselves as another would through the generalized attitudes of the group.

In everyday social activity, awareness of this 'generalized other' in self-consciousness represents two things. First, it is a more generalized, impersonal stance from which to view ourselves, giving us the capacity to see ourselves and our behaviour in a less emotionally involved way. It is a power of self-consciousness through which we can detach ourselves from particular thoughts and feelings, at least *trying* to see them more objectively. Secondly, the generalized other represents the rules, laws and moral standards of society, or a section of it, which also becomes part of our self from the earliest years, as caregivers pass judgement on our behaviour. As Mead said above, gradually the voices of specific individuals telling us what to do, or what is right and wrong, fade away, and we are left with a more general understanding of social values and how others might judge us. That is not to say that thinking becomes entirely impersonal, depopulated of the images of others, only that moral understanding becomes more and more impersonal. For Mead:

> We assume the general attitude of the group, in the censor that stands at the door of our imagery and inner conversations, and in the affirmation of the laws and axioms of the universe of discourse ... Our thinking is an inner conversation in which we may be taking roles of specific acquaintances over against ourselves, but usually it is with what I have termed the 'generalized other' that we converse, and so attain the levels of abstract thinking, and that impersonality, that so-called objectivity we cherish.[24]

There is an obvious parallel here between the work of Mead and Freud because Freud also believed there was a monitor and censor in the preconscious mind, standing on the threshold between consciousness and the unconscious, censoring certain imagery from consciousness and consigning it to unconsciousness. For Freud, the monitor and censor are active even in sleep, watching over dream imagery to make sure that repressed content doesn't appear. However, the unconscious can partly bypass the night-watchman through symbolic displacement and condensation (which is why it is so hard to work out what our dreams actually mean). Mead, however, would not necessarily agree with Freud on the nature of the unconscious, and he also emphasized the social origin and working of censorship. A stronger parallel, however, can be drawn between the work of Mead and that of Adam Smith, especially with the latter's notion of the 'impartial spectator' in consciousness. Both the 'impartial spectator' and the 'generalized other' create an impersonal stance in self-consciousness by which individuals can stand back and see themselves from a greater distance, as though from the standpoint of a non-specific other, and they also reflect the morality of the group by which the self judges its own actions. Timothy Costelloe notes that while Mead never references Smith's *Theory of Moral Sentiments* in any of his publications (only *The*

Wealth of Nations), there is evidence that Mead had a broader understanding of Smith's work and could have been influenced by him. However, I think Costelloe is right to conclude that, whatever the case may be, the fact that Mead's ideas were anticipated by Smith does not undermine their originality, but places them in a broader and richer philosophical lineage.[25]

Of course, both Mead and Smith were working in the context of free market societies where commercial relations were expanding the range of contacts between different social groups, both nationally and internationally, thus expanding the range of different viewpoints available to people in society. Like Durkheim, Mead also understood that the expanding division of labour was not only multiplying the number of different roles people played in society, thus acting as the basis for a range of diverse identities, it was also expanding and increasing the different viewpoints individuals could take towards themselves through the attitudes of the many different others they encountered. But Mead was also aware of the growing inequalities appearing in society, and of the racial and ethnic tensions in the USA, which could undermine the stability of the social bond and shared meanings.[26] His personal politics, which infused his work as a pragmatist, was that of a social democrat or democratic socialist, aware of the dangers of economic inequality, prejudice of all kinds, and nationalism.[27] The pragmatist creed of a tolerant society, inclusive of a plurality of views and self-identities, is at the core of Mead's work.

This both explains and contradicts a common contemporary misconception about Mead; that because he understood society as cooperative interaction, and significant symbols to be based on shared meanings, he therefore lacked a conception of conflict, disharmony and misunderstanding. On the contrary, Mead wanted to overcome conflict and division by expanding the scope of communicative interaction, making people more tolerant of difference. But he recognized that all people will never share the same outlook or values, nor should they. Perhaps because of elements of the Hegelian influence on pragmatism, Mead saw social change and changes in social meaning as driven by contradiction and conflict. In fact, in Mead's view, social meanings and values are never stable for long, for they are constantly going through a process of destabilization and reconstruction. This occurs when a social object loses its meaning for individuals, either because it calls out contradictory responses from them, or because it becomes a source of conflict between people and their different interpretations of objects or events. Indeed, it is around these problematic cases that people become concerned about the meaning of objects or events which they would otherwise take for granted in habitual activity. It is in trying to find the solution to conflicts and problems that meaning arises, through the effort of the group (or part of it) to readjust activity towards the object and redefine its meaning. Here we see the pragmatist view of practical thought as a tool: the effort of thought in action is not aimed at gaining absolute knowledge, but is a means of adapting through change. The need to adapt and change works against the conservative function of certain aspects of social morality, in the process changing not only part of society, but also parts of the self (such as the 'me' identity and the generalized other).

Thus, in the process of reconstruction, symbols, signs and language are not only stabilizing elements, they are the means used in practical activity by instrumental thought to adapt and change. Society then becomes an ever changing and emergent organization of activities that is always somewhere in the process of reconstruction. Forms of interaction that become institutionalized and stable are only the base upon which we can act to meaningfully reconstruct society in areas of conflict. Yet the new meanings and social objects that emerge from this process only serve to throw other previously stable meanings and interactions into doubt. Society is a *process* that solidifies into stable meanings and interactions here, only to liquefy into conflict and uncertainty there. Stability in one quarter allows imaginative reconstruction in another. But reconstruction is also a social task and demands a degree of cooperation, even between old enemies. We can see the attempts to gain peace in areas of conflict throughout the world through processes of reconciliation and reconstruction – in places like South Africa, Northern Ireland, and between Palestinians and Israelis – in this light: as an attempt to create shared agreements, institutions, values, meanings and interactions in a world where previously there was only inter-group strife. In the process, new selves also become possible, as new relations and interactions are formed, and people open themselves to a greater diversity of influence. Such processes are never certain, however, and Mead would acknowledge the conservative influences that stand in their way.

Overall, then, Mead attempted to further the pragmatist project of creating an understanding of the social self and what is entailed in asking the question 'who am I?' He clarified *and* made more complex the nature of the 'I' that we seek, showing it to be a social phenomenon through and through, a pronoun with a shifting referent. Yet it is the social nature of the self as both 'I' and 'me' that grounds individuals in the social group and makes possible the attainment of self-identity. Towards the end of his life, Mead sought to further clarify the nature of self experience as embedded in temporality and social life through the use of theories of relativity, in which a common social life is 'sliced' by the different individuals within it according to their own activities, and this 'slicing' composes individual experience within the group. This is how the same social world can be experienced differently from different perspectives, yet with a common thread of experience running through so that diverse experiences can be communicable and understandable to others. Peter J. Mills believes that had Mead lived longer, this would have formed the centrepiece of his work through which he could have explored the various temporalities of society and of the selves within it.[28]

However, Mead left this project incomplete, and while he created a well-rounded theory of the social self, he was less successful in fully explaining the nature of the social process. Despite his understanding of the importance of inequalities, exclusion, prejudice and conflict in society, he had little conception of power and its effects on the self. As Brian Roberts pointed out, Mead played down the internalization of social conflict in the self through the idea of the 'generalized other'.[29] The absence of anything like a repressed unconscious in the pragmatist theory of the self, existing alongside the habitual preconscious, could also be seen as a result of not understanding the nature of self-conflict. Also missing are unpleasant emotions, such as fear and anxiety, which might haunt the conflicted or temporal self; something I will touch on in the next section by comparing Mead's understanding of the self with that of Heidegger. There is also a need to excavate the deeper layers of reflexivity in the body that, according to thinkers such as Merleau-Ponty, are the necessary foundation for the reflectivity of the self, which makes possible the experience of an 'I' and 'me'. It is to these comparisons and extensions of the pragmatist concept of the self that I now turn.

Furthering the pragmatist conception of the self

The whole pragmatist understanding of the formation of self rests on the ability of human beings to recognize the others with whom they interact, and to see themselves as if from the perspective of those others, reflecting upon themselves as they would another person. But how, from early childhood onwards, can we do this? How do human children first begin to recognize others and to understand that they can be seen and recognized by them? To be capable of doing this one would think that a child would have to have some nascent sense of its own self, in order to realize that there are other selves in the world, separate and distinct from it. Furthermore, as others begin to treat the child as a distinct, responsible agent in its own right, what is there in the child that can recognize this and respond to it? Mead already begins to provide the answer in his notion of the uniqueness of the vocal gesture, which at first may be a cry or a sound, then later the child's first words. The importance of the vocal gesture is that *it can be heard by the child* just as well as it can be heard by the others around it, and thus in spontaneously producing such gestures in the interaction with others, the child provokes a response in itself just as it provokes responses from those it interacts with. In doing this, the child becomes aware of its own presence to itself, just as it becomes aware of the responses of others to its vocal gesture. Thus, the child becomes aware of self and others through one single act, and, as its repertoire of speech and action expands, so does its awareness of self and others. These early interactions through vocal gestures prime children for later, more complex, interactions in which they will start to take the attitudes of others and see themselves from the other's perspective.

There is a striking similarity here between the ideas of the pragmatists and the French phenomenologist Maurice Merleau-Ponty.[30] For him, though, it was not just the vocal gesture that illuminated the reflexivity of the human body – that is its ability to turn back upon itself and act on itself – which provides the basis for reflectivity: the ability to consciously reflect upon oneself as an object in one's experience. For Merleau-Ponty, the whole of the human body is reflexive: I can touch one hand with the other, along with other parts of the body; I can hear myself crying or speaking; I can see myself or parts of my body and, later, recognize my reflection in mirrors. This means my body can be the touch and the touched, the noise-maker and the hearer, the seer and the visible object.[31] In these very moments, which happen in the conduct of all children, we begin to get a sense of the presence of ourselves just as we get a sense of the presence of others, as they respond to us in joint conduct. Merleau-Ponty therefore believes that the body is a 'natural self', which makes possible the social self that comes to identify itself through others.[32] Throughout our lives, though, this natural self remains the basis of who we are and everything that we do, even though it becomes socially conditioned through the acquisition of habits, which rearrange and renew the 'corporeal schema'. So, movement in space is built into the body as the child crawls, climbs, and gets a feel of the whole of its spatial arena. Later, children learn to walk upright with the help and encouragement of adults, and this becomes a habit built into the bodily self, as does the learning of language. Movement and speech are both aspects of the modulation of our bodies in the world, and both freely come in our everyday activities without us having to think or even try: they become 'natural' responses to circumstance, to others and to our own selves. Body movements and gestures, language and the way we speak, emotional responses to self and others, all become 'stable dispositional tendencies' that form our mode of expression in the world where we find ourselves. And when we express, we express not only our selves – our thoughts and feelings – but something of and about the world we are in at that moment in time, including the others with whom we interact. The expression says something about our shared situation.

The pragmatists share this view of the importance of the body in social action, especially in the fundamental place they give to habit in structuring all action. This was so for Mead, but more especially for John Dewey, for whom habit does not mean the simple repetition of acts, but a whole series of interconnected dispositions that may, under specific circumstances, lead us to act in certain ways. Until they are called out by specific social situations, habits remain latent and pure potential, although they may operate even without us being aware of it. For example, the bodily habit of walking is latent in our perception of space and distance, even when we are sat motionless. When sitting we still perceive space as one who can move around in it, and we use this habit to judge distances and the size of objects. We can 'walk around' a landscape solely in our perception of it, using the bodily habits we have acquired through life as social beings. But more than this, as stable dispositional tendencies, habits form the basis not only of perception, but also of will, desire and the self. As Dewey says:

> ... all habits are demands for certain kinds of activity; and they constitute the self. In any intelligible sense of the word will, they *are* will. They form our effective desires and they furnish us with our working capacities. They rule our thoughts, determining which shall appear and be strong and which shall pass from light into obscurity.[33]

Although habit demands a certain kind of activity, it is not a simple call for repetitive action, more a predisposition to act, so that, for example, a person predisposed to angry outbursts may commit murder only once. Nevertheless, it is those stable predispositions that form something of the basic elements of self. Such habits are not inborn but are acquired, even though they may come to feel like second nature to us. As Dewey says, 'the essence of habit is an acquired predisposition to *ways* or modes of response, not to particular acts'.[34] Furthermore, the habits are always acquired in a social context, so that they bear the stamp of the social and historical relations in which they have been learned. Dewey makes it clear that if we want to change a person's habitual dispositions, first we must change their social circumstances before we have a hope of changing their habits and self. The fact that today we take as given the idea of habits as unthinking and repetitive routines, is symptomatic of the type of society in which we live, one that demands exactly this type of activity in people's daily lives (such as unthinking work routines, for example). However, like Mead, Dewey believes that people can become aware of their habits and critically reflect on them, and this happens when a situation demands conflicting responses from individuals. Under these circumstances, people must critically reflect upon their situation in order to reconstruct it, which is how people become both socially and politically aware, demanding change to the very society that forged their habitual dispositions.

However, the pragmatists do not consider the emotional impact of human selves existing as temporal beings, constantly being subject to the forces of social and personal change. The situation of what the anthropologist Victor Turner has called 'liminality'[35] – the gap between ordered worlds, or the space between the collapse of one aspect of the social world and its reconstruction into a new form of order – can be anxiety provoking for individuals, leading them either to grasp the new and establish an alternative social world, or react against it and cling desperately to the old. This is especially so because the social order supports our dispositional tendencies, meaning that the collapse of an aspect of society also leads to the loss of an element of the self, necessitating the making of a new identity. As Heidegger points out, ultimately all temporal and reflective selves must face the inevitable reality of their own death, the knowledge of which creates anxiety throughout our lives.[36] We fear death because it means the loss of our own sense of self and presence to the world, raising the inevitability of our obliteration. However, as Joas points out, for Heidegger death anxiety is something we must all face alone, as no one else can die for us. If we are up to the task of facing death, we enter an authentic state of being, which is radically individualistic. But this means that, as Joas says, in Heidegger's conception of history and the individual life situation, he 'does not make superindividual plexuses of collective praxis really thinkable',[37] and instead sees the individual life as embedded only in fate.

Using Mead's understanding of the relativity of social and individual temporality, we can begin to think how selves deal with death anxiety through understanding that the temporality of society outstrips that of the individual. As individual selves, when our time is done, we can live on in the work we leave behind, through children, family, friends and colleagues in whose memory we still exist, living as an active participant in their self-dialogues. Individual time can be transcended in the time of the plexuses of collective praxis, and even though this may not completely eradicate death anxiety, it means that our self-demise is not the absolute end of us. Furthermore, if we take selves to be social through and through, this is a totally authentic response to our own temporal state, because, although our bodily self will die, our social self does not completely evaporate.

Finally, I want to consider the similarities and differences between pragmatism and Marxism on the question of human consciousness, language and selfhood. It is no surprise that there are similarities between pragmatist thinkers and Marx in these respects, as both sets of thinkers were influenced by a critical reaction to German Idealism. Perhaps the most profound likeness is that the pragmatists and Marx understood consciousness as practical, something that evolves from human engagement with the world. Consciousness is material rather than transcendental, a product of the practical engagement of humans in the activity of problem solving in the world. That means that consciousness is not a passive reflection of an external world (a view Marx associated with earlier, simplistic forms of materialist philosophy), nor is it totally disengaged from the world (the transcendental, idealist view), rather it is a creative and imaginative response to problems that arise in human activity. In this way consciousness is linked to human labour, which transforms the material world. Transformation is only possible because, through labour, humans can imagine and then set about making a world not given in nature. Comparing human labour to the 'labour' of other animals, Marx says:

> A spider conducts operations that resemble those of a weaver and a bee puts to shame many an architect in the construction of her cells. But what distinguishes the worst architect from the best of bees is this, that the architect raises his structure in imagination before he erects it in reality. At the end of every labour process we get a result that existed in the imagination of the labourer at its commencement.[38]

Furthermore, like Mead, Marx understands consciousness and imagination as tied to practical activity conducted socially through language. For Marx, '[l]anguage is as old as consciousness, language *is* practical consciousness … language, like consciousness, only arises from the need, the necessity, of intercourse with other men'.[39] This need for symbolic interaction emerges from the fact that humans must work together to change their material existence, so that language and the expanded consciousness it creates are inseparable from cooperative labour, and from the necessary division of labour which emerges in human groups. To organize such a division of labour, humans must have a sophisticated means of communication, and they also must become self-conscious of their own activities, along with those of others, in order to coordinate their efforts effectively. Humans then become distinguished from other animals in that 'consciousness takes the place of instinct or that his instinct is a conscious one'.[40] However, within this division of labour there also appears the division between material and mental labour, from which emerge the builders who build the structure and the architects who plan it. More importantly, for Marx, we get a division between the realm of ideas, created by priests, philosophers or moralists, and that of the reality of the mode and relations of production. Thus, ideas outstrip pure material necessity and can come into conflict or contradiction with the actually existing world, acting as a force for change. 'From now on', Marx writes, 'consciousness is in a position to emancipate itself from the world and to proceed to the formation of "pure" theory, theology, philosophy, ethics, etc.'.[41] While Marx makes clear this can only happen when social relations, including the division of labour, have come into contradiction with existing material forces of production, straining at the leash of their constraints, it nevertheless shows how Marx saw human consciousness as able to run ahead of existing material reality. It is not just a reflection on what is, even as problem solving activity, but a meditation on what could be: a world still to win, with the present open to reconstruction.

As Tom Goff points out, though, Marx was quicker than Mead or any of the other pragmatists to realize how alienating modern society can be,[42] with routine forms of work stifling the latent creativity and imagination of the majority, who are also alienated from a true voice in democratic politics. The fact that in countries like Britain and the US fewer and fewer people are voting, even though they continue to have the right to do so, shows Marx may have been more prescient in his view of the effectiveness of democracy in a capitalist society than were the pragmatists. I will pick up on many of these points in Chapter 6. For now, though, I will turn to some of the thinkers of the 'cultural historical school', who drew on ideas from Marx and from German Idealism, but moved beyond them to create a view of the self that complements and expands on that found in pragmatism.

The cultural and historical formation of self

The 'cultural historical school' was a group of thinkers that emerged in the post-1917 revolutionary period in Russia whose project was to create a non-mechanistic, non-behaviouristic Marxist psychology for the new communist society.[43] It was centred on the work of Lev Vygotsky, but included other notable academics such as A. R. Luria and A. N. Leontyev. However, the 'school' quickly ran into difficulties as Stalin rose to political power and behaviourism became the favoured psychological theory and method in Russia. Vygotsky died of tuberculosis in 1934 aged only 38, but he and the other thinkers of the 'school' gained more global recognition from the 1960s onwards with the translation of their works into English. Like Mead, the cultural historical school were focused on the formation of individuals in a meaningful world of social objects, but, following Marx, they see these objects as products of human labour as well as of symbolic and linguistic interaction. For example, A. R. Luria gathered evidence from agricultural workers in Russia to show how a more highly specialized division of labour, and use of more sophisticated technology, creates the requirement for workers to improve their literacy skills and general levels of education.[44] He concludes from this that while originally language had a very practical character, orienting groups of individuals in immediate practical tasks, it gradually became more interdependent with practice, as a 'system of codes adequate for expressing any information'. Furthermore, this illustrates that 'if humans had not possessed the capacity for labour and had not had language, they would not have developed abstract, "categorical" thinking'.[45]

For both Luria and A. N. Leontyev what this means is that labour and language are both keys to the formation of the 'higher mental functions' of individuals, as both tools and words mediate the activity through which people assimilate the powers of conceptual, reflective thinking. As Leontyev puts it, it is through team-work and communicative interaction – activities mediated by tools and signs – that these 'inter-psychological processes' can become 'intra-psychological': which is to say that when the individual masters such social activities, perform-ing them independently, they lose some of their 'external' form and become 'internal' mental processes.[46] Specifically, conceptual thought – which leads to scientific and technological ways of thinking and acting, giving people the abil-ity to lift themselves out of their present situation, and to see circumstances and themselves in a more objective light – is not a transcendental phenomenon but a product of labour and language. Concepts are social products, mastered by indi-viduals, then internalized as their own independent powers of thought. In Marx's terms, consciousness then emancipates itself from the immediacy of the world, and from the forces of natural instincts, although it can never be totally free of the social forces which enable its 'higher' forms.

This insight of Marx is a key to the thinking of Vygotsky, and to his influence on the other members of the cultural historical school. However, given that con-cepts are social products, the result of communicative interaction and joint prac-tical activity prior to individuals using them more independently, it is open to question whether the terms 'inter-psychological' and 'intra-psychological' are appropriate. I will make more of this as I go along. For now, it is worth mention-ing that Vygotsky was influenced not only by Marx, but also by the German Idealist philosopher Herder. The latter placed great emphasis on social influence in learning and education, and claimed that language was the primary medium through which children learn ideas. For Herder, adults and children are not pas-sive learners because the imitator must take up what is transmitted to them through their own active nature. For example, people bring their own shades of meaning to the language they learn. Thus, in human thought, the mind begins to work from obscure feeling, moving up through language to rationally expressed, reflective consciousness, which is required by reason to formulate abstract propo-sitions. In this way, reason becomes the centre of our being as humans, and is a higher sense than that of feeling.[47]

These influences led Vygotsky to stress the importance of the 'internalization' of speech in the psychological development of children, which enables the learn-ing of scientific concepts in school, gradually socializing the child's practical intellect.[48] Speech and conceptual thinking then move to the centre of all thought and motivation, becoming the organizing principles of individual psychology. Emotional and volitional process lie behind every thought, but speech seeks to complete these through linguistic expression. The analytical unit that Vygotsky focused on in his developmental psychology was *experience,* seeing this as the internal relation between the individual and an aspect of reality: the latter being the social world in which the child is embedded and the practices that relate it to its environment. For Vygotsky, psychological processes are located in these socio-historical forces, rather than in biology. It is socio-historical forces, especially linguistic skills acquired in the child's relationships to adults or more capable peers, which lead the child through various overlapping stages in its development. Language also transforms the 'lower mental functions', such as natural perception, into the 'higher mental functions', where words and signs determine and dominate what we perceive around us. To Vygotsky, then, signs are 'psychological tools' that remake all the natural processes of thought, just as tools used in labour remake the natural world.

As with Marx, Vygotsky understands language as transforming human consciousness, so that what we think and the way in which we think are no longer determined by instinct and biology, but by socio-historical inventions that allow humans a degree of free will. Now, humans no longer respond to stimuli in the environment, they provide their own motivation by talking themselves into, or out of, certain actions. Like Mead, then, Vygotsky understood thinking to be a form of social conversation, so that '[e]ven when we turn to mental process, their nature remains quasi-social. In their own private sphere, human beings retain the functions of social interaction.'[49] Vygotsky chose 'word meaning' as the unit of analysis to understand verbal thinking, because it could demonstrate the unity of thought and speech. That is, when we think silently to ourselves, we think in words, yet speech for oneself is different from the speech for others that we find in social interaction. Speaking silently to myself (thinking) I don't have to pronounce the words of a sentence phonetically, or certainly not all of them, as I have to do in speech for others. Instead, I can think using the meaning of a whole sentence and drop the phonetic articulation of each individual word. The vocalization of speech for oneself dies out and we can operate 'not with the word itself but with its image'.[50] So, pulling back the curtains on a morning and being hit with rays of warm sunshine, I can think 'what a sunny day' without vocalizing the words to myself: I can think purely in terms of the *meaning* of the sentence without saying it. This is how, in speech for others, we can 'know our own phrase before we pronounce it'.[51] We know the meaning of what we want to say, we have a sense of it, and then the words just come flowing from that sense. To paraphrase Vygotsky, thought is like a cloud that sheds a shower of words. But it can only do so because we think in word meaning to begin with. The syntax of speech for oneself is therefore very different from the syntax of speech for others, and Vygotsky charts these many differences, including abbreviating sentences in various ways, dropping the predicate from the sentence so only the subject of it remains, and thinking in single words alone that become saturated with the sense of all the connotations they arouse.

However, I think that Vygotsky is wrong to claim that this speech for oneself is largely monologic and that it is in some way 'inner': a 'psychological' or 'mental' phenomenon. In fact, we could see speech for oneself, what we commonly refer to as thinking, in terms of a dialogue between Mead's 'I' and 'me', the subject and object of thought. In dialogue with myself, I can take all the short-cuts in my verbal thought that Vygotsky describes, as well as in my dialogues with the images of particular others, or with the generalized other. However, as Berducci has recently claimed, that does not mean that there is always some form of mental process at work behind dialogue.[52] Nor does it mean that 'inner' speech really resides somewhere inside of the body, say 'in the head' as a 'mental' process. Rather, speech for oneself is just that and nothing more: talking to oneself silently, using different syntaxes than in speech for others. These are different linguistic practices rather than a monologue happening on an 'intra-mental' plane, which is an internalization and transformation of that happening on an 'inter-mental' plane. Just because silent speech for oneself creates the feeling that it is conducted in an internal space, largely because it is inaudible to others, doesn't mean that it is really a conversation going on somewhere inside the body or head.

Berducci goes on to say that speaking and thinking should be kept as verbs to indicate they are something that we *do,* rather than being objects we possess in our minds. We then read meanings and intentions *in* other's words, *in* their gestures or bodily movements, not by somehow inferring these things to a hidden 'mind'. It follows from this that children do not 'internalize' language: rather, in some circumstances they learn to speak and read silently to themselves, while in others they speak and read aloud. This is the meaning of what 'I' am doing in these situations; how 'I' am relating to 'me' or to others – to 'you'. Vygotsky, though, does have some interesting things to say about the transition between these different linguistic practices, or how we transform sensed meaning into speech for others. Having said this, it is no longer the case of a transition from an inner to an outer meaning, so that there always has to be an inner thought or meaning expressed in verbal speech. Rather, as Vygotsky indicates in other parts of his work, when 'I' speak, my speech flows from the situation I am in, usually from the communicative interaction with others, and this provides the context, meaning, and motive of my speech.[53]

But this must also lead us to question Vygotsky's more functionalist and hierarchical statements about the interrelationship of mental functions, in which the 'higher' mental functions come to predominate over the lower. Following Merleau-Ponty we can say that there is a *structuration* between speech, as one of the modulations of my body, and the other modulations of active perception, such as vision, touch and hearing. Vision and thought are structured like a language, not because they are completely reordered by speech, but because there is structuration and reversibility between them: the structures of movement and vision inform speech, and vice versa.[54] This is how we can express in words what we are seeing and hearing, without these perceptions first having to form themselves as mental concepts: or, indeed, we can say what we mean without first forming the meaning of it as a fully articulated concept. We say directly what we are seeing or meaning, and we can directly see or hear what others are seeing and meaning. The 'higher' psychological processes are but derivatives of embodied structurations, in which we consciously reflect on our selves, actions or the world, using and transforming socially created concepts as we do so. In that sense, they are not necessarily 'higher', nor does conceptual thinking dominate and determine all that we do.

Indeed, using the work of Mikhail Bakhtin, a Soviet linguist who began his work around the same time as Vygotsky, we can begin to clarify the continually interactive nature of speech for oneself and speech for others, and the way this is related to one's own self and that of others. For Bakhtin, in the milieu of ongoing events, dialogues, and acts, there are three basic moments: 'I-for-myself', 'I-for-others' and 'others-for-me'. These three positions are understood as central emotional-volitional moments in the flow and flux of everyday interactions.[55] More fundamentally, there are always moments of passivity and activity in life in that we find ourselves in the midst of being, part of a world not made by us as individuals, yet it is a world we also actively participate in and therefore partially remake. In life, then, there is that which is given and that which is to be achieved. As Mead would put it, the world is open to being partially reconstructed. This means that there is both passivity and activity in the constitution of the self, for just as we find ourselves in the gaze, words and gestures of others, so too are we actively engaged with our self and with others in ongoing social interactions. Key to the passive finding of oneself in others, and to the active authoring of self and others, is the dialogic relation to others ('others-for-me' and 'I-for-others') and to one's own self ('I-for-myself').

Bakhtin traces the emergence of the importance of the 'I-for-myself' – the sense we have of a core self, invisible to others – back to Ancient Greek society, through the middle ages to the contemporary world where this form of self-consciousness is illustrated by novels written in 'heteroglossic' style: that is, in a multi-vocal, dialogic style, where each character in the novel has their own voice, which addresses others and themselves in an ongoing conversation.[56] Here, the central character or hero must be 'internally complex', their own multi-voiced consciousness and self-dialogues open to the reader.

What Bakhtin is illustrating here is the historicity of the 'I-for-myself', the way that the self-dialogue and self-searching has grown in importance over the centuries in the Western world. For Bakhtin, this search for self, the asking of the question 'who am I' or 'who am I to become', is a struggle between one's own words and point of view about one's self, and the words and points of view of others. The creation of social selves is always a product of mutual authorship whereby, in action and words, we give form to others but they also give form to us. Paul Sullivan has illustrated this tension through the distinction Bakhtin makes between soul (self) and spirit: the former being the stabilization of our self-identity through the words, intonations and viewpoints of others, while the latter is our own active, perceptive, fluid sense of being in the world with others.[57] Primarily, we can only become selves in any clearly defined sense by the form that others give us. For example, the child only becomes aware of itself as an 'I-for-others' as it is addressed by its caregivers (the others-for-me). It is not just the words of the others that matter, but the vocal intonation of caregivers, which reveal their attitudes to the child: for example, of loving and affirming tones, hostile and disconfirming attitudes or cold and indifferent ones. We get a sense of who we are in these emotional intonations of others, and this situation continues through life, as the attitudes and emotions of others towards us either confirm our being, or act as a catalyst for change.

Yet alongside this there is also the sense we have of our own spirit, our active as opposed to passive and receptive way of being in the world. As we actively perceive the world around us, including the others to whom we are related, we have a sense of ourselves as open to change and receptive to new situations, fluid and unfixed. We also have the sense that we are more than our current actions, always in a process of becoming, with the potential to be something other in future. Thus, in the relation to myself (the 'I-for-myself') there is a non-coincidence in my being, or as Mead would put it a disjunction between the 'I' and the 'me'. 'I' can never say that the 'me' which exists at this moment will always remain the same, so that I never exist in full. The 'I' and 'me' never coincide, which means that the 'I-for-myself' always exists to some degree beyond the power of the words and affirmations of others. However, this constant sense of spirit, of the power and potential of active change and of being something different, remains empty until a commitment is made to specific values.

Alongside these aspects of the self, arising from social dialogue, Bakhtin also claims that there appears in discourse a *super-addressee,* a third party whose absolutely just, responsive understanding is presumed because it stands above all the dialogic participants. It is the feeling we have on entering dialogue that we can always be understood and that our words will be heard by someone. The super-addressee is like Smith's 'impartial spectator' or Mead's 'generalized other', existing in dialogue as an impersonal and just presence, acting for the self as a witness and judge of the whole person. This is the 'not-I in me', a reflection or refraction of a greater existence beyond individual selves: a sense of the impersonal words and categories through which we must pass to become an 'I-for-myself'.

Here, though, Bakhtin begins to touch on the issue of power and ethics in the struggle for self-identity, and also the struggle for integrity and unity of self among the multiple dialogues and perspectives of others; something I will focus on in more detail in the next chapter.

While Bakhtin tends to ignore the material transformations that selves effect in the world, which was the focus of the cultural historical school, he has historicized and extended the understanding of the self, an understanding which has clear links to pragmatism. He has also emphasized the importance of the self in cultural, dialogic engagement and change, and in that sense he has much to bring to an understanding of self which is compatible with the cultural historical school. Indeed, I believe that pragmatism and dialogism can add to the perspective of the cultural historical school to create what Stetsenko and Arievitch have called an ontological understanding of the self as a transformative agent in social practices.[58] In this the self is oriented to the real-life practical tasks of changing or preserving something in the world, including aspects of its own self as part of the social world. The relation to oneself, then, is not 'internal' in any sense: when we want to 'find' ourselves or change ourselves, we must engage with others in changing aspects of the world through social practice. The self is not separate from its engagement with the world, *but is constituted by the activities it performs*. We make our self as we engage in transforming the material, cultural and interpersonal world.

The self-dialogue, the talk between 'I' and 'me', the 'I-for-myself', must be revealed in its practical relevance to have a meaning within the person's major life pursuits. How we make sense of our self depends on how we contribute to the world and make a difference, no matter how small, to social life in general or to the lives of others we interact with. When we talk about finding ourselves, what we are often referring to is the search for this kind of meaningful activity, which can both make a difference to others *and* reveal the uniqueness of our self. But this also means making a moral commitment, either to some social ideal and values, or to more personal aims and goals. Yet these are all ethical activities in Bakhtin's sense that they involve the addressivity and answerability to others. Taken together, the perspectives considered in this chapter provide both a materialist and humanist ontology, in that they understand self-reflectivity as part of a practical, social engagement with real-life, material existence. In this engagement, the reflective self is not just a passive reflection of its material and social existence, but is actively engaged with others in transformation of that existence. Who we are or what we are to become is related to who we are as historical and social individuals, and how we can use the means that society and history place at our disposal to create change and make a difference. The answer to the question 'who am I?' is found in what I do.

Notes

1. Louis Menand (2002) *The Metaphysical Club*. London: Flamingo.
2. Ibid., p. xi.
3. Menand, *Metaphysical*.
4. William James (1912) 'Does consciousness exist?' in W. James, *Essays in Radical Empiricism*. London: Longmans.
5. William James (1983) *The Principles of Psychology*. Cambridge, MA: Harvard University Press.
6. Ibid.
7. William James (1961) *Psychology: The Briefer Course*. Ed. Gordon Allport. Indiana: University of Notre Dame Press, 1985. p. 63.
8. Ibid., 69
9. Ibid., pp. 69–70.
10. Ibid., p. 46.
11. Ibid., p. 48.
12. Hans Joas (1985) *G. H. Mead: A Contemporary Re-examination of his Thought* Tr. Raymond Meyer. Cambridge: Polity Press.
13. George Herbert Mead (1934) *Mind, Self and Society, from the Standpoint of a Social Behaviorist*. Chicago: University of Chicago Press.
14. G. H. Mead (1917) 'The psychology of punitive justice', in Andrew J. Reck (ed.), (1964) *Selected Writings: George Herbert Mead*. Chicago: University of Chicago Press. pp. 212–39.
15. G. H. Mead (1929) 'National-mindedness and international-mindedness', in Andrew J. Reck (ed.), (1964) *Selected Writings: George Herbert Mead*. Chicago: University of Chicago Press. pp. 355–70.

16. G. H. Mead (1910) 'Social consciousness and the consciousness of meaning', in Andrew J. Reck (ed.), (1964) *Selected Writings: George Herbert Mead.* Chicago: University of Chicago Press. pp. 123–33, p. 131.

17. G. H. Mead, *Mind, Self,* p. 138.

18. G. H. Mead (1913) 'The social self' in Andrew J. Reck (ed.), (1964) *Selected Writings: George Herbert Mead.* Chicago: University of Chicago Press. pp. 142–9, p. 146.

19. Ibid., p.143.

20. Maurice Merleau-Ponty (1962) *Phenomenology of Perception.* Tr. Colin Smith. London: Routledge. p. 189.

21. E. Benveniste (1971) *Problems in General Linguistics.* Miami, FL: University of Miami Press.

22. John Shotter (1989) 'Social accountability and the social construction of "you"', in J. Shotter and K. J. Gergen (eds), *Texts of Identity.* London: Sage. pp. 133–51.

23. G. H. Mead, 'Social self', p. 146–7.

24. G. H. Mead (1924) 'The genesis of the self and social control', in Andrew J. Reck (ed.), *Selected Writings.* pp. 267–93, p. 288.

25. Timothy M. Costelloe (1997) 'Contrast or coincidence: George Herbert Mead and Adam Smith on self and society', *History of the Human Sciences,* 10 (2): 81–109.

26. G. H. Mead, 'Punitive justice'.

27. G. H. Mead, 'National-mindedness'.

28. Peter J. Mills (1986) 'The early history of symbolic interactionism: from William James to George Herbert Mead', PhD Thesis. Leeds University.

29. Brian Roberts (1977) 'G. H. Mead: the theory and practice of his social philosophy', *Ideology and Consciousness,* 2: 81–108.

30. Trevor Butt (2004) *Understanding People.* Basingstoke: Palgrave Macmillan. Nick Crossley (1996) *Intersubjectivity: The Fabric of Social Becoming.* London: Sage.

31. Maurice Merleau-Ponty (1968) *The Visible and the Invisible.* Tr. Alphonso Lingis. Evanston: Northwestern University Press.

32. Maurice Merleau-Ponty, *Phenomenology.*

33. John Dewey (1922) *Human Nature and Conduct. The Middle Works, 1899–1924. Volume 14: 1922.* Ed. Jo Ann Boydston. Carbondale and Edwardsville: Southern Illinois University Press, 1983 edn. p. 22.

34. Ibid., p. 32.

35. Victor Turner (1974) *Dramas, Fields and Metaphors: Symbolic Action in Human Society.* Ithaca: Cornell University Press.

36. Martin Heidegger (1962) *Being and Time.* Tr. J. Macquarrie and E. Robinson. Oxford: Blackwell.

37. Hans Joas, *G. H. Mead,* p. 197.

38. Karl Marx (1867) *Capital: A Critique of Political Economy* (3 Volumes). New York: International Publishers, 1967 edn. p. 177–8.

39. Karl Marx and Frederick Engels (1970) *The German Ideology: Part One.* London: Lawrence and Wishart. p. 51.

40. Ibid., p. 51.

41. Ibid., p. 52.

42. Tom W. Goff (1980) *Marx and Mead: Contributions to a Sociology of Knowledge.* London: Routledge & Kegan Paul.

43. Bakhurst has created the notion of the 'Vygotsky school', in David Bakhurst (1991) *Consciousness and Revolution in Soviet Philosophy: From the Bolsheviks to Evald Ilyenkov.* Cambridge: Cambridge University Press.

44. A. R. Luria (1976) *Cognitive Development: Its Cultural and Social Foundations.* Cambridge, MA: Harvard University Press.
45. A. R. Luria (1981) *Language and Cognition.* New York: John Wiley. p. 27.
46. A. N. Leontyev (1972) 'The problem of activity in psychology', *Soviet Psychology,* 9: 4–33. p. 19.
47. Jerrold Seigel (2005) *The Idea of the Self: Thought and Experience in Western Europe since the Seventeenth Century.* Cambridge: Cambridge University Press. Ch. 10.
48. L. S. Vygotsky (1987) 'Thinking and speech', in *The Collected Works of L. S. Vygotsky, Volume 1: Problems of General Psychology.* Tr. N. Minick. New York and London: Plenum Press.
49. L. S. Vygotsky (1981) 'The genesis of higher mental functions', in J. V. Wertsch (ed.) *The Concept of Activity in Soviet Psychology.* Armonk: M. E. Sharpe. p. 164.
50. L. S. Vygotsky, 'Thinking', p. 262.
51. Ibid., p. 261.
52. Domenic F. Berducci (2004) 'Vygotsky through Wittgenstein: a new perspective on Vygotsky's developmental continuum', *Theory & Psychology,* 14 (3): 329–53.
53. L. S. Vygotsky, 'Thinking', p. 203.
54. Maurice Merleau-Ponty, *Visible.*
55. Mikhail M. Bakhtin (1993) *Toward a Philosophy of the Act.* Tr. V. Liapunov. Austin: University of Texas Press.
56. Mikhail M. Bakhtin (1981) *The Dialogic Imagination.* Tr. C. Emerson and M. Holquist. Austin: University of Texas Press. p. 133.
57. Paul Sullivan (2007) 'Examining the self-other dialogue through "spirit" and "soul"', *Culture & Psychology,* 13 (1): 105–28.
58. A. Stetsenko and I. M. Arievitch (2004) 'The self in cultural-historical activity theory: reclaiming the unity of social and individual dimensions of human development', *Theory & Psychology,* 14 (4): 475–503.

Selected bibliography

Bakhtin, Mikhail M. (1981) *The Dialogic Imagination.* Tr. C. Emerson and M. Holquist. Austin: University of Texas Press.

Butt, Trevor (2004) *Understanding People.* Basingstoke: Palgrave Macmillan.

Crossley, Nick (1996) *Intersubjectivity: The Fabric of Social Becoming.* London: Sage.

Joas, Hans (1985) *G. H. Mead: A Contemporary Re-examination of his Thought.* Tr. Raymond Meyer. Cambridge: Polity Press.

Reck, Andrew J. (1964) (ed.) *Selected Writings: George Herbert Mead.* Chicago: University of Chicago Press.

Stetsenko, A. and Arievitch, I. M. (2004) 'The self in cultural-historical activity theory: reclaiming the unity of social and individual dimensions of human development', *Theory & Psychology,* 14 (4): 475–503.

Sullivan, Paul (2007) 'Examining the self-other dialogue through "spirit" and "soul"', *Culture & Psychology,* 13 (1): 105–28.

Vygotsky, L. S. (1987) 'Thinking and speech', in *The Collected Works of L. S. Vygotsky, Volume 1: Problems of General Psychology.* Tr. N. Minick. New York and London: Plenum Press.

CHAPTER 3

ETHICS, SELF AND PERFORMATIVITY

So far, I hope to have established that the search for self is not a lone, individual-istic pursuit, for it involves being immersed in a society of other individuals in whose eyes we find clues to the puzzle of our self-identity. But, as touched on in the last chapter, the social interactions in which we find ourselves are infused with ethical principles about the right and wrong ways to act, and these principles also involve ideas about the kind of society we want to live in. Questions about the 'good society' intrinsically involve notions about what it is to be a good person, a proper and fully rounded human being equipped with all the capacities and abili-ties our fellow women and men expect. As suggested in the last chapter, if we are continually involved in activities that reconstruct the social world, along with the nature of our own selves, and such activities are guided by moral and political values, then the self is to a large degree formed by ethical principles. Indeed, Kant recognized that part of the self is governed by moral laws, so that asking the ques-tion 'who am I?' involves moral evaluation: am I a good or a bad person? If I feel I am bad in some way I may devise a programme of activities by which to become a better person, or I may search for ethics that allow some latitude for my bad behaviour. Either way, I am embarked on a path of ethical formation of self.

Once again, however, the moral view we have of our own self comes drenched in the words of others. From infancy, we have others' words ringing in our ears, resonating with moral evaluation and emotional intonations of approval or disap-proval: 'good boy!' or 'bad girl!'. What is more, these evaluative words and their intonations are based in certain standards of behaviour that have a social history, belonging to certain groups and forming part of their ethos, either religious or ide-ological. Such values can be in conflict with those of other groups that have dif-ferent values and beliefs about the good society or what it is to be a good person. This leads to struggle and conflict at all levels about ethical or ideological values, involving the evaluative words of others that seek to define the world and the self in different ways. For Bakhtin, this conflict exists on three levels: firstly, 'unre-solved conflict with another's word on the level of lived experience ("another's word about me")': secondly, 'on the level of ethical life (another's judgment, recognition or non-recognition by another)': and finally, 'on the level of ideology (the world views of characters understood as unresolved and unresolvable dialogue)'.[1] On the first and second levels, the conflict between children and authoritative adults over evaluative words about them – Adult, 'You are a bad boy!' Child, 'But am I really? What have I done wrong?' – occurs as children begin to separate their own voice from adults and align it with others, such as peer groups. As Mead illustrated, moral command often exists for the child in the form of the image of authority figures, usually their main caretakers, but later separates from these figures to be infused with many more increasingly generalized voices. In this light, for Bakhtin, the question 'who am I?' cannot be separated from another question: 'with whom am I?' He believed that the heroes of Dostoevsky's novels attempted to solve this problem as outlined in the quotation below, but I think this is extremely apt for children and young people attempting to create their own unique voice and self-identity in a process of separation from some authoritative people and realignment with others. The problem is, 'To find one's own voice and to orient it among other voices, to combine it with some and oppose it to others, to separate one's voice from another voice with which it has inseparably merged'.[2]

The problem for people throughout life in the making of their own self, but especially for children attempting this for the first time, is how to make and reveal ourselves, including finding our own voice – our values and beliefs – from among the words of others. It is this problem, and the dangers within it for our own sense of embodied selfhood, that I will focus on in this chapter. I want to begin, though, by looking at ideas within social constructionist psychology about the ways in which we are called by others to moral responsibility and answerability, in the process getting a sense of ourselves as autonomous agents.

The social construction of the ethical self

In the early 1970s two British social psychologists, Rom Harré and John Shotter, took up the legacy of thinkers like Mead and Bakhtin in respect of the social construction of the ethical self. For both Harré and Shotter, in their different ways, human beings only become moral selves by being interpellated, or called, by others into awareness of themselves as autonomous and responsible beings. This is done by others holding us accountable for our actions, making us answer for what we have done in terms that all other members of our culture would regard as reasonable. From the early stages of life, as soon as we have a good grasp of our language and the basic moral values of our social group, others make us explain and justify actions that are seen to be questionable in some way. 'Now why did you do that?' are words we often hear adults addressing to children, expecting from them a response that gives some reason for their action. For Harré, this is how human individuals become reasonable and responsible persons within their social groups, because the answers we give to questions about our behaviour must be couched in the knowledge of the moral rules of our culture. How our actions are judged by others will depend to some extent on how well we can explain ourselves in terms that they will find reasonable. As I noted in

Chapter 1 from the work of Marcel Mauss, in Western society since the Enlightenment the category of 'the person' has come to mean in large part an individual who is reasonable and responsible, one capable of judging and deciding upon the course of their own actions. To some extent, the modern person is therefore free to judge and choose their own actions, but by the same token they are held to be responsible for them. They have a duty to society to account for what they have done and must be capable of answering for it.

Thus in Harré's 'person centred' view of psychology, his definition of a person is that each 'is a unique embodied being, rich in attributes and powers of many kinds, having a distinct history and, importantly, being morally protected and liable to be called to account as a morally responsible actor'.[3] By moral protection Harré means something like the Kantian principle that people should be treated not as things, as means to an end, but as persons with inalienable rights and duties. These duties include the expectation we will act with moral reason, while, if we can do so, we are granted the right to be treated with dignity as a person of worth, having a degree of freedom over our own actions. However, the powers and attributes we possess as persons, capable of acting freely and responsibly, are drawn entirely from our culture, which prescribes the rules by which we must act, and provides the scripts for the different roles we play in the various contexts of everyday life. Following the sociologist Erving Goffman,[4] Harré believes that as social beings we are like actors on a stage, playing different parts in a drama, and learning the scripts by which those roles must be played. How successfully we perform our different roles will either win us the respect of our audience, for which we crave, or get us booed off stage, a disgrace that would fill us with shame. Like James and Mead, Harré thinks that each role we play contributes something to our self-identity, yet he also thinks that in learning rules, roles and scripts we acquire a social resource that is used to carry on our everyday activities, and also to account for them. The powers and attributes we have as social and moral selves are largely derived from learning these resources, something that begins in childhood as we are made to account for our actions.

Therefore, the rules and resources we learn and use to put together our actions, along with the personal characteristics, attributes and beliefs we derive from our actions and roles, plus the way others evaluate us and our behaviour, all go together to make us into the person that we are. The key to all of this, though, is language; in particular, the everyday conversation and discourse in which we are engaged. It is through such discourse that we learn to account for ourselves in acceptable ways, and also absorb the moral evaluations and judgements of others. In addition, following Vygotsky, Harré believes that language also furnishes us with the array of conceptual tools we use in order to think, which means that 'mind is no sort of entity, but a system of beliefs structured by a cluster of grammatical models'.[5] On this basis Harré has called for a 'second cognitive revolution' in psychology, because human cognition cannot be explained either transcendentally or materially – by theorizing a transcendental self or by rooting cognition in the hard-wiring of the brain – it can only be explained discursively.[6]

However, what Harré does not accommodate in his discursive psychology is the kind of conflict that Bakhtin saw as existing between the words of others about us and the way we seek to separate ourselves from some of those words and judgements, while aligning ourselves with others. In addition, he does not consider the ethical conflicts that can occur between individuals and between social groups involving relations of power and authority. What happens if groups or individuals challenge the ethical standards of reasonableness according to which we are brought to account, either on the grounds that they are biased towards certain groups, allowing them status and privilege denied to others, or because they make no personal sense, as these individuals are aligned with alternative values or beliefs? Harré seems to ignore these issues completely. And what happens to those individuals who fail to account for their actions in acceptable ways, or whose accounts are discounted on the grounds they are unreasonable: what of their moral fate? It may be more than a case of shame, discredit, and lack of self-worth, for, as we will see later in this chapter, they can be completely denied the power of embodied agency, and thus the status of persons.

Furthermore, as John Shotter points out, the discursive interactions of individuals need not be understood according to cognitive models of competence/performance in which actions are understood as structured by rules, scripts, or prior mental representations. Abandoning cognitive models to explain the self–other interaction of everyday existence, Shotter understands this as 'joint action', which is an only partially formed, always unfinished, relatively non-systematized and fluid network of dialogic relations. In dialogue, we are called to account by others, yet we respond in 'spontaneous' ways that are not determined in advance. That is, we act *into* everyday situations through a 'feel' of what is required of us, rather than from a pre-formed mental plan constructed 'in the head' prior to the events at hand. This is what Shotter refers to as 'knowing of the third kind', which is knowledge that is not clearly articulated as a mental plan or as a clearly stated emotion, but more of an intuitive feel for what to do next. However, this way of knowing and acting is also subject to the moral judgement of others who can decide whether it was ethical action or not. Like Harré, then, Shotter believes that:

> To be a person and to qualify for certain rights as a free, autonomous individual, one must be able to show in one's actions certain social competencies, that is, to fulfil certain duties and to be *accountable* to others in the sense of being able to justify one's actions to them, when challenged, in relation to the 'social reality' of the society of which one is a member. Being someone in this sense is a rhetorical achievement.[7]

And yet, to be part of a community to which we are answerable, to feel that we *belong* to it, we must be capable of doing more than reproducing it in a routine fashion. We must have the competencies and the rights to participate in it creatively as a tradition of argumentation, as a community that is continuously being contested and made anew. To belong to a community means to play a creative part in its living tradition of dialogue and argumentation. Following Bakhtin, then,

Shotter understands dialogic interrelations more as a matter of conflict and con-testation than does Harré, even though he adopts a similar understanding of the ethical social agent as discursively constructed in dialogue.

In Shotter's work, then, there is more of an acknowledgement of the issue of con-flict, of power and inequality in the formation of the ethical subject, albeit in a some-what non-specific way. For example, he talks of the unequal distribution of rights and duties in a dialogic community, but doesn't say on what basis these are unequally distributed, apart from an occasional mention of gender.[8] Shotter also speaks of the 'combat zone of the word', although this is in relation to the struggle over the rights and privileges of speakers and listeners in a dialogue, rather than the issue of whose word becomes the defining one on matters of self and world. There is also mention of a 'political economy of communicative and developmental rights', and of 'communicative ethics' that respects the person one is in dialogue with. In this, there is an acknowledgement that we should be allowed to be answer-able for our own unique position, and that we can only do so if we have been the author of it: yet there is little sense of a struggle with the words and viewpoints of others in the mutual authorship of selves, on a personal, ethical or ideological basis.

Interestingly, Shotter also talks of a 'micro-social power politics of growing up', meaning that when young children are addressed as 'you' they are not just being given information on how to act, 'they are being "in-structed" in how *to be*'.[9] That is, in mutually authoring one another, two (or more) persons in dia-logue actually 'in-form' the self of other(s), gently moulding it or aggressively pummelling it into shape with their words. In this sense, communication can be formative ontologically, creating the reality of the other's existence. For example, when a child is told, 'You shouldn't be doing *that*', they are being told not only what to do, but how they should *be* as a person. Here, Shotter recognizes that chil-dren do not only respond to such in-formation passively, for they can also utter words about themselves that challenge those of the more authoritative caregiver. His example is of a child being told, 'Stop making so much noise, *you're* shout-ing', and the child responding with, 'No *I* wasn't'. In this way, children learn the actual distribution of communicative rights and opportunities in their develop-mental situation – its social structure – and their own changing place within it.[10]

While Shotter clearly understands the struggle with the words of others in our development as selves, there are a number of things missing from his work that I want to elaborate upon here. Firstly, I want to show how socially structured posi-tions of authority in-form much of what we do in daily life, and how these can be opposed or paralleled by unofficial social formations, providing moments of structure and liminality in experience through which the self is formed. Secondly, that the ontological in-formation of selves not only involves communication, but primarily an in-habitation of the world through the body; the way body, emotion and self are in-formed through disciplines that create habitual dispositions. And finally, what is missing from Shotter's emphasis on the self–other nature of joint activity and dialogue is the more complex enfolding of conversations with the self, so that we are constantly in dialogue both with others and with our own self (the 'I' with the 'me').

First of all, let me say something about the question of social structure. Shotter is interested in what goes on in the boundary zones that exist in the margins between orderly, systemic centres of society. Everyday life is seen as existing in such a boundary zone, being a flux or hurly-burly of as yet non-systematized and non-finalized dialogues and joint actions. Yet while this is true of certain everyday interactions of a more equal and unstructured kind, such as mutual friendships, there are many examples of everyday activities in families, schools, workplaces and other institutions that are not like this. Instead, in the main, they are composed of ordered, structured and hierarchical relations, joint activities and dialogues. While I am sure that in all organizations of this nature there are places and times for more unofficial, non-systematized activities – in family leisure activities, in the school playground at playtime, in the work canteen during breaks – this doesn't mean that all everyday activities take place in this non-systematized way. In fact, everyday life can be filled with routine, and it is in what Victor Turner has called the more 'liminal' times and places that we experience more fluid and open social formations, such as rites of passage between childhood and adulthood, periods of life-crises, carnivals and festival days, or, in the modern industrialized world, in the liminoid activities of free-time, leisure-time, and holidays (see Chapter 6).

Shotter's view of dialogue as an unfinished flux of joint activity is, I think, accurate to a point, stressing the temporal, open nature of society. Yet it views temporality only in terms of the future, of the yet to be specified and formed, and not in terms of the past. It is true that Shotter pictures joint action producing unintended consequences, ones that we must deal with in any future interaction, but he does not say how these must be incorporated into the present, and, because of that, affect the future. For example, he claims that he is not interested in 'already spoken words' in the way linguists are when they study the grammatical structure of language: rather, he is concerned with 'words in their speaking', which relates to the responsive nature of dialogical or rhetorical acts. The problem is, though, that in acting responsively we still must use the system of language that is part of our culture. It doesn't mean that we can't use language in a responsive way, one that is full of feeling towards the others and events of interaction, or that there cannot be an element of spontaneity in this: it is more a case, as Merleau-Ponty said, of how we take up language as one of the modulations of our bodies, as a social system that we live through and in-habit with our body. As I claimed in the last chapter, this is as much to do with the reflexive nature of the human body as it is to do with the in-between nature of self–other joint action. But the main point I am making here is that 'already spoken words' have in-formed who we are – from very early on in life – and thus dispose us to ways of responding to others that may have apparently little relevance for a second and third party to what is currently going on in the interaction between us. 'Already spoken words' to some degree also structure what can and cannot be said in a particular social context.

This leads me to the second issue about the way that humans are embodied in the social world. For me, Shotter is right to say that mental plans do not lie behind all our actions and that in many circumstances we perform with others in the social world from a 'feel' of what is required of us. From my point of view, though, we do this through the body as a natural self, one that acquires habits and dispositions which reform the corporeal schema, creating stable dispositional tendencies. When we are called to perform actions by social situations or by the others in that situation, what is called upon are the dispositions that incline us to certain types of personal response. We do not think about how we should perform in most situations because our bodies are already disposed to certain modes of action. Obviously, this is not always the case, especially in new or strange circumstances, or in those liminal moments such as carnival, or when we are intoxicated,[11] in which cases the normal bodily habits are relaxed or released.

However, this illustrates something else about the way we in-habit the world as bodily selves: that many, though by no means all, of our habits are learned through disciplines that we have been taught by others, and in some cases have been forced upon us. The sociologist Norbert Elias has shown how what in the West is regarded as the 'civilized' or moral person, the one who is rational and reasonable in all they do, paying due regard and respect for others, is a product of a series of bodily disciplines, especially the learning of manners. Elias surveys books on manners produced in Western Europe from the 13th to the 18th century to show how standards of manners rose under the pressure of competition between different social groups, and that these manners involved an increasingly refined modulation of the human body. A well mannered person does not sit at a dinner table and fall on the dishes like a swine, but allows someone else to pick from the plate: they do not fart loudly in church, or go unwashed and give off body odour amongst others in enclosed spaces. More importantly, a well mannered person does not give full vent to their emotions in all circumstances, cowing and intimidating those around them.[12]

It is impossible for me to give the full feel of Elias's exhaustive study here, but the main point he is making is that to be regarded by others as a moral person is not just about accounting for our selves and our actions in conversations, using a rhetorical style that others recognize as reason. It is also about the way we carry and modulate our body, shown in manners and gestures, and the way we express feeling and emotion. When a caregiver says to a child, 'Stop making so much noise, you're shouting', they are in-forming the child in a deeper way than just calling it to verbal account. They are saying, implicitly, that the level of noise you're making is too much for me and for others: you must learn to modulate your body to express yourself in a more restrained, even-tempered and softer way. In a sense, we perform reason with our body, and ethics begins its work at that level, disciplining the body so that, as we mature, we become the kind of people who will take our turn in a conversation, listening to others and showing them respect, in the same way we expect others to behave towards us. In a similar vein, Aristotle pointed out that moral training begins by inculcating students in the right habits and inclinations, only later furnishing them with the discursive tools to give the right reasons for that behaviour.[13]

As I will show in the next chapter, Michel Foucault paints a darker version of bodily discipline as being integral to the strategies of power in the West. For now, we can say that the kind of discursive and ethical conflicts that Bakhtin talked about involve not only words, but also a clash of bodily habits, of different ways of in-habiting the world. Of course, these habits are not fixed forever: as Turner noted, they can be relaxed and overturned in liminal times and places, where groups of people, or even entire societies, go through significant changes of social *habitus*. Ethical standards of behaviour change throughout the life-course of individuals, as well as throughout the history of societies. They are not fixed, nor do they act as causal mechanisms, determining human behaviour in given circumstances. But they do dispose us to styles of response, meaning that such responses are not wholly dependent on the other person we are related to in the context of joint action in the moment. This is why one person can respond to the same joint activity in an entirely different way to another, despite the fact they have been raised in the same culture. And it is why, for people we know well, we have a good idea (though not a certainty) as to how they will respond to different situations.

As temporal beings, then, each moment of interaction with others contains a trace of something that is past, whether this is a body memory or habit being called into action, or a memory called to mind: that is, one we can articulate to ourselves in words or images. Yet, as it moves into the future, this moment here and now also presents the possibility of transcendence, of reconstructing joint action and the self, of each one of us becoming someone different. This is because the future is always open to some degree, allowing for the possibility of change and reconstruction. Furthermore, as I noted in the last chapter, as temporal beings we are never identical with our own selves, even the bodily self. Instead, the self is always split; as the touching or the touched, the seer or the seen, the speaker or the listener, the 'I' or the 'me'. As Bakhtin would say, the active, perceptive side of us always feels as though it can never be totally defined by current actions or performance in a social context, and that it can always become other than what we currently are. Because of this, a limit is also placed on the extent to which others can influence us, or to which we truly respond to the other, rather than to something 'going on' for our selves. In this way, any joint action, even between two people, is always a multidimensional and complex process involving not only my response to the other but also to my self. There is a dialogue going on not just between me and the other, but between the 'I' and 'me' (and the 'I' and 'me' of the other self). Because I hear myself speak and see the response my words and gestures provoke from the other, I can then modulate my body accordingly. I can lower my tone and make my manner milder, or I can up the ante by making my tone more insistent and my manner more predisposing. In doing this, I need not be consciously planning each change at the level of reflective consciousness as a fully articulated debate between 'I' and 'me', yet I can be monitoring myself at the level of bodily reflexivity (which still involves an interaction with my self).

In any joint activity, then, we can constantly switch between self-dialogues and interpersonal interchange, because we exist as an 'I-for-myself', an 'I-for-others', and there are 'others-for-me' in the world. In this, we carry forward previous modulations of the body, even though these are always open to reconstruction. As Joshua Soffer has said, '[my] sense of my own identity is relentlessly, but subtly, formed and re-formed in moving through and between myriad modalities of experience, including my moments of self-conversation, my immersion in subjects/objects of touch, sight, as well as within interpersonal interchange'.[14]

What does all this mean for the ethics of self and performance of ethical (inter)action? As I will go on to outline in the next section, using the work of Bakhtin, it means that although we learn and use languages we did not create, and are always saturated with the words and viewpoints of others, we can also talk to ourselves and be constantly working out our own position within this mêlée. We are not just held accountable by others, we can also hold our selves to account and pass judgement. At the same time, we can always question the judgements of others, either on an interpersonal basis (because we might trust our own judgement more than that of certain others), or because we question the ethical or ideological position on which their views are based, aligning ourselves instead with other groups that oppose these positions. We then perform joint activities with others by responding to their words and to the situation in which we find ourselves, yet we bring to this interactive context embodied traces of past experience as habit, disposition, memory, values and beliefs, aligned with some and against others. On this basis we are not only judged, but also the judge of others and of our selves.

The self, dialogism and ethics in Bakhtin

I have already shown how, for Bakhtin, conflict exists on the level of words said about us by others in interactions, on the level of the judgements made by others about us and the way they do or don't recognize us as fellow ethical beings, and finally on the level of ideology or world views. Within this mêlée, we have to find our own voice by combining it with some and separating it from others, especially important voices like those of parents or caregivers, in whose words and intonations our own first consciousness of self emerged. But how is it possible to find out 'who am I?' when my own consciousness of self is only possible through the words and attitudes of others? First of all, it is important to note that there are some discourses, some words and voices, which are harder to oppose than others. In this light, Bakhtin distinguishes between *authoritative discourses* and *internally persuasive discourses,* the former emanating from an ideologically authoritative source (such as religious, political or moral institutions and figures), while the latter seeks to appeal not through authority, but directly to the thoughtful life and experience of a person. Authoritative discourses *demand* that we acknowledge them, while internally persuasive discourse is affirmed through assimilation, whereby it becomes 'tightly interwoven with "one's own word"'.[15] The struggle between these two types of discourse goes on at the three levels mentioned above in this paragraph. Dialogue is therefore a continual struggle between the words of others, some authoritative, others not, that I may or may not find internally persuasive, assimilating with my own valued words, ethics or world-view. One could imagine that authoritative discourses can also become internally persuasive, but these need not necessarily be so because they demand our attention. For Bakhtin, it is an indication that thought is beginning to work in an independent, experimenting and discriminating way when it can distinguish between authoritative and persuasive discourses, and then reject those found not to be persuasive.

For a child developing its sense of self this is more difficult, as the words that have the most profound influence on the image and value it has of itself are usually those of the caregivers, whose words are authoritative. Yet parents can combine both authoritative and internally persuasive discourses: 'You'll do it because *I* [authority figure] tell you to', can be combined with or substituted by, 'It's because we love you' or 'We know what's best for you'. A child can respond to this angrily with, 'No, I won't do it and I hate you', or it can acquiesce while holding a silent, sullen resentment: in either case a child can still be internally persuaded of its caregivers' love, even though another voice is filled with anger. Because of this, Bakhtin claims that all dialogue is double-voiced, with the words and intonations of others being introduced into our own speech, taking on our own interpretation and evaluation, along with our responsive words and intonations. Furthermore, the dialogue we hold with ourselves can be divided between a first and second voice, the first being more vocal and the second more silent, a division that splits our consciousness and field of vision on the world. In the above example of the child, its first voice may say, 'I hate my caregivers for making me do this', becoming a more general view that, 'I hate them and they hate me', while the second voice is persuaded that they really do love and care for it, with the child returning that love. For this reason some young adults turn against their caregivers, aligning their voice, self-image and ethical and ideological views with others whose discourse and values they find more persuasive, re-making themselves accordingly. Others stay more closely aligned to their roots, finding their own voice and self-image within the discourse of caregivers; their words, ethics and ideology being internally persuasive.

Whatever way the child responds, it begins to find its own authentic voice and self-image by aligning itself with some discourses and opposing others. But it only does so in response to others, in the way that it reacts to the words and evaluations of others, by speaking its own words about itself (both to others and to itself) and forming its own evaluations. It is not because, as I made clear in the last chapter, there already exists a unified, completed self struggling to get out of its external casing. Rather, the child gradually comes to be in-formed by others and to in-habit the world, at the level of actions, gestures, sounds and spoken words. Through these, the self starts to form as a silent dialogue, although it is one that is never completed: as Bakhtin makes clear, there are no final words that define the world or the self absolutely: there is always something more that others can say about us, and more for us to say about our selves.

More than this, though, in Western culture people are expected to create and express an authentic or individual self-identity, one that is theirs or, at the very least, they feel comfortable with. This comes from a number of social and cultural sources we have already begun to identify. In ancient Greco-Roman culture, the writing of letters to teachers or trusted intimates and the keeping of diaries began to create a language suited for the expression of private thoughts and feelings: that is to say, a language that was not designed for public proclamations, but for the intimate whisperings of words about one's self that one might not announce in public, among strangers. Charles Taylor has also shown how Enlightenment and Romantic thinkers and artists began to create other forms of expression suited to a reasonable, rational self that could work out its own views and opinions, or to a self that could connect to its emotions and the 'voice within': its authentic sense of orientation in the world. Thus, culture not only created the tools for Westerners to shape themselves as authentic, individual voices in the world, it also called on them to be that way: in childhood and daily life people demand from one another the standards of what we call, civilized, reasonable, answerable, accountable, individualized selfhood.

However, as Taylor goes on to point out, we are called to this by others in dialogic relations, and can only affirm our authenticity by being recognized as such by others. And the very existence of the idea of authentic selfhood rests on a shared horizon of meanings – of culture and ethics – that is not an individual creation; it is one we are raised to and learn about from others.[16] Paradoxically, becoming and being an authentic individual self can only be achieved socially, through meaningful dialogic relations to others.

But there is another element to this, which can be traced back to the Middle Ages in Europe, particularly with the end of medieval social relations, when the previously unchallenged authority of the nobility and church began to be subtly critiqued by the rising middle classes. Back then such critique had to be cloaked in the form of parody or satire, as it often involved mocking and ridiculing figures of authority and, indirectly, all they stood for. This is important because the authority possessed by a person could not be taken for granted by their social role or status: these things were no longer automatically conferred on a person by their role, but instead by how well they lived up to it in the judgement of others (and no longer that of their own class alone). As Erasmus says in *The Praise of Folly* (1511) when parodying princes:

> Fashion me now a man such as princes commonly are, a man ignorant of the laws, almost an enemy of the public welfare, intent upon private gain, addicted to pleasure, a hater of learning, a hater too of liberty and truth ... measuring all things by his own desire and profit. Then put on him a golden chain, symbolizing the union of all virtues linked together; set on him a crown adorned with gems, which is to remind him that he ought to surpass others in every heroic quality ... If a prince really laid his own life alongside these symbols, I believe he would have the grace to be ashamed of his finery. He would be afraid some noisy satirist might turn the whole spectacle, suited as it is for high tragedy, into laughter and derision.[17]

While masked as parody, Erasmus's message is plain: it is not the trappings of the prince that matter – his finery, ornate symbols and what they represent – but how well he lives up to these symbols in his person and actions. How learned he is, how wise, how just, how courageous, is more important than all his wealth and status. Erasmus is expressing the values of the rising middle classes earning their place in society through commerce and intellectual achievement in newly created Universities, but he is also illustrating what is important to us here; the separation of person and social role. The self no longer coincides with itself or with its external social form: it isn't identical to a social category or type. A prince is no longer to be respected because he is a prince, but because of how well his personal qualities equip him for the role. Indeed, the finery of princes, the symbols of their power and their manners, can be mocked as inauthentic or overly conventional if, as a person, they cannot live up to the responsibilities placed on them. Self is being separated from social role or category, and people are beginning to judge others on what they see as their authentic personal qualities, which can be expressed in, yet are partly separable from, their roles.

Erasmus could only begin to speak and write this way because he was no longer completely in the employment of the court and church, but was also part of a new urban intellectual and theological group. He then found ways to circumvent the authoritative styles of expression found in his day, criticizing the nobility and ecclesiastical authorities. But he still could not express himself and the values of the group he represented directly, in an unmediated way. His writings didn't bear the stamp of the authorial voice of the church and, instead, to express his criticism, he had to use the indirect method of parody and satire, speaking in the voice of folly rather than in his own. As Bakhtin points out, it is confessional writings, especially those of the Romantics, such as Rousseau's *Confessions,* that pioneered a more directly expressive, 'personal' style of confession. Put another way, the Romantics found a way of expressing themselves in words, music and painting in which every thought, feeling and experience did not have to be expressed in the style of an authoritative discourse. Even the stoics, in the main, sent their personal letters to philosophical teachers. Bakhtin claims that where an authority rules and establishes a stabilized medium and style of expression, conventionalized discourse dominates. If there is no such medium, then multi-directional and double voiced discourse will prevail.

This means that in such cases where no single discourse establishes absolute authority, a variety of different discourses, literary styles, and modes of expression will proliferate. That is not to say that there are no authoritative discourses, only that no single one dominates the entire discursive field. Indeed, Bakhtin thought this to be the case in modern social life where there is a plethora of discourses – or as he refers to it, a heteroglossia – some of which bear the stamp of authority (scientific, religious, ethical, etc.), others less so (such as everyday conversational styles or popular culture, for example). Such heteroglossia can be evidenced in the modern novel, which doesn't draw a stylistic unity from one unified language, but from the way it *combines* the relatively autonomous languages of everyday life into the author's own developing style of work. Thus the author's own style or personality comes through in the way they combine various discourses, made up of the words of others, into their own unique voice and intonation: their own style. Just as the author brings off this feat in their writing, so do we bring off a similar feat in becoming selves, with some voices and discourses becoming so close to us they become our own, animated through our bodies and experiences, while others remain alien and at bay.

Likewise, the heroes of novels and stories can no longer be presented as fixed characters with little development viewed from the 'outside', so to speak: rather, they must be 'internally' complex, with the living core of their consciousness, their multi-voiced and double-voiced self-dialogue, open to the reader. Only then can we identify with them as a self like us, with a complex of many contradictory voices giving expression to ambivalent feelings, while stifling others. Bakhtin takes Dostoevsky as the prime example of the modern novelist, for the hero interests Dostoevsky 'as a *particular point of view on the world and on oneself,* as the position enabling a person to interpret and evaluate his own self and his surrounding reality'.[18] Here, we see the core of the ethical person as one who evaluates the world and their own self in the dialogue they keep with themselves in a world of others. According to Bakhtin, Dostoevsky never provides us with a clear answer to the question 'who is he?' about any of the heroes in his novels, because they, like we, are never finalized but always in the process of becoming. The question his heroes ask continually, though never answer completely, is 'who am I?' and 'who are you?'. The latter question is asked about the people the hero encounters. This plunges the hero into introspection, in which he dialogues with himself and with the images he believes others have of him, or with what he thinks others might say to him in an imaginary dialogue he is holding for himself. To Bakhtin, in Dostoevsky's work the hero …

> … eavesdrops on every word someone else says about him, he looks at himself, as it were, in all the mirrors of other people's consciousnesses, he knows all the possible refractions of his image in those mirrors. And he also knows his own objective definition, neutral both to the other's consciousness and to his own self consciousness, and he takes into account the point of view of a 'third person.' But he also knows that all these definitions, prejudiced as well as objective, rest in his hands and he cannot finalise them precisely because he himself perceives them; he can go beyond their limits and can thus make them inadequate.[19]

Like the heroes in these novels, we believe that others never have the final say on who we are, can never completely define us with their words or ethical judgements, because each one of us is not solely an 'I-for-others', we are also an 'I-for-myself'. As Mead showed, selves are split into an addresser and an addressee, an 'I' and a 'me', one who can speak to the self and one who answers back. But as Bakhtin illustrates above, we can do this not only in our own words, but also in the imagined words – or from the imagined viewpoints – of others. Thus, my words and the imagined words of the others blend and separate (a double-voiced consciousness) in the self-dialogue, and I can use their own words to answer them back, only blended with my own intonation depending on my response to them. So if I am having a self-dialogue with the image of someone I've actually argued with, who has called me 'stupid', I can say to myself: 'Stupid? *They're stupid.* I'll show them *I'm* not stupid'. This is what Bakhtin called the word with a 'sideways glance' at someone else's word, whereby we turn the words of others back on them through giving them our own intonation, and in so doing feel we transcend them or make them inadequate. Even the objective definition of me by authoritative groups – such as a religious evaluation or scientific classification – is not final and does not wholly define me, for there is always a word that others can say about me or that I can say about myself that can surpass these other definitions.

Yet we must not underestimate – in fact, we may know from personal experience – how difficult it is to find our own voice amidst the voices of others and their ethical evaluations. The fact that we are subject to competing voices and evaluations, and aware of how society in general – the 'generalized other' – might view us, means that our own voices are often internally divided, creating tensions in our relations to others. An example of this given by Bakhtin is of a character from one of Dostoevsky's novels, Nastasya Filippovna. No doubt aware of how society might judge her, she regards herself as a 'fallen woman' and looks for vindication in the judgement of others. When she gets vindication from particular others she argues with them, considering herself to be guilty: yet when others agree with her self-condemnation, she despises and rejects them. There are two divided voices working in her self-dialogue: the dominant one is of self-condemnation, telling her she is a 'fallen woman': the second is a more silent voice contesting this and looking for recognition and confirmation in the words and judgements of others. One could almost say the second voice is looking for strength and support in others' words, but when this is found the dominant voice takes over and starts to argue back. The problem is that Nastasya Filippovna has not found her own voice and word about herself, and cannot decide whose evaluation of her is the judgement with which she sides. Such division can only be resolved by the formation of a more unified voice that she can claim as her own.

We can see here how it is possible to identify an element of unconsciousness in the portrait of the self that Bakhtin is drawing, because the more silent voice is clearly active in what Nastasya says and does, the way she seeks recognition for it and confirmation of her self; and yet, because it cannot be fully articulated and is quickly silenced by the more dominant voice of self-condemnation, it works below full awareness. It is like someone planning suicide because they want the recognition of others, not because they really want to kill themselves. Thus, the orientation to recognition and acceptance by others is hidden by the destructive, perhaps resentful and angry, orientation. Such divided voices often involve self-concealment, where one voice is obvious, forming the *content* of speech and action, while the other is hidden or latent, forming the *structure* of speech and action.

Indeed, in confessing or revealing a hidden part of ourselves, it is often a second, previously silenced, voice that we begin to articulate more clearly in dialogue with another, looking for their response to the emergence of this voice, their confirmation or non-conformation of this aspect of ourselves. However, this is not so much a *revealing* of self as a *creating or authoring* of it in dialogue with another: we look for the words to give it form, to articulate it clearly for ourselves and for the other, and to orient it with the words and evaluations they express. In this relational way, we dialogue ourselves into existence with others. In turn, they can help us to create and articulate this aspect of our self through confirmation and dialogue, or they may not recognize it and try to deny it. Such a response could force us back into denial of that voice, or impel us to seek out others who can help us articulate it clearly with their already spoken words.

In confession with another person, we are therefore not speaking an already formed truth about ourselves, but actually creating that truth through the formation of our own voice, aligning it with some and opposing it to others. As Bakhtin claims, a single consciousness can never be self-sufficient, because 'I am conscious of myself and become myself only while revealing myself for another, through another, and with the help of another'.[20] Becoming self-enclosed by wrapping oneself up in a self-dialogue would actually be the death of the self, as that dialogue becomes impoverished and withers. To be, to exist as human, means to communicate with others at the deepest levels of mutual authoring. Echoing William James, Bakhtin believes that to be unheard, unrecognized and unseen would be absolute death for a self: thus,

> to be means to be for another, and through the other, for oneself. A person has no internal sovereign territory, he is wholly and always on the boundary; looking inside himself, he looks *into the eyes of another* or *with the eyes of another*.[21]

This is also the realm of what Martin Buber has called the 'interhuman', where individuals step outside of their current social roles, trying to see one another in the fullness of who they are, or allowing each other to become what potentially they can be.[22] As Turner has pointed out, this often happens in those liminal moments between friends and equals where we put aside roles and statuses, achieving a flash of lucid mutual recognition and understanding.[23] In such moments a high premium is placed on personal honesty, openness and lack of pretentiousness, and people aspire to a social performance aimed at mutual authoring rather than assertion of social position.

However, in Bakhtin's social ontology, the confession is an ambiguous performance, as it can be an intimate act of self-revealing to a trusted equal, or it can emerge from a social atmosphere where coercion hangs more subtly in the air. Once again turning to Dostoevsky's novels for illumination, he sees a kind of 'moral torture' inflicted on the heroes in the books, 'in order to force out of them that ultimate word of self-consciousness pushed to its extreme limits'. Dostoevsky creates around the hero 'an extremely complex and subtle atmosphere that would force him to reveal and explain himself dialogically'.[24] Ethical relations can therefore involve a coercive aspect where people try to force the truth from one another. 'I want you to tell me everything about yourself', or 'she has no secrets from me', are words we often hear spoken in everyday dialogue. Ethical coercion is also endemic within the power relations of society, in which, under various circumstances, the truth can be extracted from individuals. In courts of law we are compelled to tell the truth and can face harsh penalties for perjury if we are found to be lying. Also, a battery of experts is employed such as the police, psychiatrists, social workers or probation officers, to establish the truth of what we are saying or the moral quality of our character. Yet Bakhtin reflects on the distorted view of the self that can be formed in legal and medial/scientific discourses through a scene from Dostoevsky's novel *The Brothers Karamazov* in which Dmitry is on trial. The investigator, judge, prosecutor, defence attorney and experts (including psychologists) all attempt to fix the character of Dmitry in objectifying professional speech genres. Yet ultimately they fail, because in place of a living core to his personality filled with internal dialogues, decisions and crises, they substitute ready-made categories predetermined in words and acts by psychological laws. While in recent years branches of these professional discourses may have become more subtle, engaging with individuals seductively in order to get them to speak the truth about themselves, there is always a word and an opinion an individual can put in about him or her self, voiced silently to themselves away from professional eyes and ears. And it may well be that it is this voice and word which individuals take to be definitive of themselves at certain moments, even though this dialogue is never completely finalised.

Thus, the history and culture of the West have created a *habitus* in which it is believed that we must find our own unique self and voice, and that no one is entirely reducible to the roles, types or categories of persons that exist within the social structure. If we subtracted these things from a person, there would be something remaining that we could call the individual's self, a residue of unique humanity. Yet it is the very nature of modern Western society that creates these conditions, composed of a heteroglossia of different speech genres, roles and categorizations with no single authority to unify them, to which we are subject in being authored by others and must draw from in order to author our selves. As an ethical self I am partly authored by the words and evaluations of others, and yet, from among the varied discourses around me, I can align myself with some and seek to separate myself from others. I can also use these words to evaluate my own self, even though the words of others will have penetrated me deeply, especially those who matter most. From all of this I can begin to piece together some image of myself, either that I believe myself to be, or that I wish to be; begin to find some truth about myself, and find my own voice as I fill the words of others with my own aspirations, or respond by rejecting them and aligning myself with other voices, authoritative or persuasive.

Divided selves and divided bodies in R. D. Laing

What I have been trying to illustrate so far is the complexity of the social, interrelational process in which we become ethical selves, ones who can answer for our own actions in ways that are intelligible and reasonable to others within our culture. Furthermore, the recognition by others that we are an ethical self rests not only on the rhetorical performance of reason, but also on embodied displays of behaviour regarded as reasonable, including our manners and the way we express emotion. However, I can only become an ethical self by being in-formed as such in my relations to others, and they remain crucial in the ethical dialogues we hold throughout our lives. I am constantly aware of 'others-for-me', which is to say of other people and the fact that they are ethical beings who will judge me and the things that I do. I therefore exist first and foremost as an 'I-for-others', which is the awareness of the possible images others have of me. Derived from this, the 'I-for-myself' is the awareness I have of myself, my thoughts and feelings, and the dialogue I hold with myself, including the ethical judgements I make about myself. At any one moment of interaction there are complex, multi-directional currents in the dialogic relations between these positions. Furthermore, the self-dialogue ('I-for-myself') can become divided between different voices and ethical evaluations, some of which become dominant, while others remain more silent and below full conscious awareness.

The writer who brought out the full consequences of such divisions occurring in the dialogues between persons and with the self was R. D. Laing. In the early 1960s he wrote two influential books, *The Divided Self* and *Self and Others,* based on his work as a psychiatrist with 'psychotic patients'. It was Laing's contention that some people attract categorizations that designate them as 'mentally ill' because they display behaviour and speech that are regarded by the majority of people as unreasonable, and therefore they are discounted as persons. This behaviour is usually marked by the 'inappropriate' use of the body and bodily expressions within specific social contexts, and by speech that is disordered or unintelligible. When such people are called 'mentally ill' this further discounts their status as persons, reducing them to the object of medical study and treatment: a patient rather than an agent who is capable of answering for his or her self. Psychiatrists then further reduce their patients by seeing everything that the person does as due to a medical or biological condition, rather than being some distorted aspect of a person's being that is trying to communicate with others. Instead of a medically oriented psychiatry, Laing argued for a 'person centred' approach that tried to make sense of the person's disordered pattern of communication by putting it back into the context of their life-history and their relations to others where it has some meaning.

However, all this led Laing to certain conclusions about the nature of the embodied self and how this can become threatened and divided. His first two books are also illustrations of how the embodied self comes to feel that it is real and alive, with powers of active agency, in its dialogic relations with others. When these relations become distorted and twisted they can create unbearable tensions and divisions in the self-dialogue that renders a person disembodied, dead, and with an inability to relate to, and communicate effectively with, others.

For Laing, a necessary component of self-development is for a child or adult to have the experience of being in the loving care and attention of others. We all need to be recognized, from the earliest years onwards, as a person in our own right who is loved and valued by others who care for us. Obviously, a child has lesser degrees of autonomy when they are very young, being highly dependent on carers.

However, as they develop and mature, they need to be given more freedom from parental control and more recognition as a person in their own right. Laing does not see growing up in a rosy light, as always involving love and care, for even the closest relationships are marked with tension and conflict. Indeed, this is a necessary part of any close relationship, as those within it have to maintain their own identities as selves. All relationships, then, involve the problem of establishing closeness and distance, to maintain the healthy interdependencies of social life without a person feeling their identity becoming swamped and submerged. For children, a degree of independence is necessary for them to feel they are the author of their own actions, rather than seeing these as compelled by others or undertaken only through conformity. Put in my terms, in its everyday activities, even though these may be mainly structured by others, the child has to feel it in-habits its world and that it can express its own needs and voice in those activities.

Things can start to go wrong, according to Laing, when a vulnerable and developing sense of self becomes threatened or stifled in the relation to others, or when the child is not confirmed in its own right as a self with the power of agency. A failure to recognize the self as agent means that a child is ignored, with caregivers failing to respond in any way towards it, or that it is only praised and loved when it conforms to rules. In the latter case, being 'good' comes to mean being passive and conformist. For Laing, the sign that a child is becoming a person in its own right with some autonomous power of agency, is when it begins to break some rules and is called to account, being able to answer back in its own emerging voice. Another problem can occur if parents respond to a child's behaviour but their response is inadequate or incidental to the child's action. Here, although the action has provoked some response, it still fails to recognize or account for what the child has done, misrecognizing its agency and intention. A child may then come to feel that its actions are in some way inadequate or incidental.

In addition, if a child feels threatened by over-dominant authoritative adults, or if the adults over-encourage conformity with love, then the anxiety invoked in the emerging, vulnerable self can result in feelings of engulfment, implosion and petrification. Engulfment is where a child or adult feels invaded and swamped by others; implosion is where they feel that the power of others has destroyed their sense of self; and petrification is where they feel others have turned them into an object by responding to them as if they are a thing rather than a person. The lack of moral autonomy and positive ethical evaluation given to the child causes it to withdraw into itself, into its own self-dialogue, to live only 'within' itself. Because 'others-for-me' are threatening or engulfing, or because I am denied status as an 'I-for-others', I can only live and have value as an 'I-for-myself': this means, though, that everything that I present to others, all my performances in social situations, must be not-me: it must be a defence I hide behind. But this has disastrous consequences for the self, deadening the lived body, creating a division between self and world (including the other people within it) and an inability to create a unified voice for oneself.

First of all, in terms of the body, this has what Laing calls a 'transitional position' in the world. The body is the core and centre of my world, of all my experiences, without which I could not be alive, *and also* it is an object in the world of others. It is my body that is visible to others and by which others recognize me. Just as importantly, though, the body is what Merleau-Ponty called the 'natural self' that lives and acts in, as well as perceives, the world. If my body feels alive, real and substantial, so do I. It is the body, then, that gives my sense of being an 'I' some substance, and it is the visible object by which I can become 'me' or 'I-for-others'. If we in-habit the world with our bodies, we feel as though we belong to it to some degree, and also that we belong with others. Our actions feel vital and, at times, we can lose ourselves in them. However, for Laing's 'psychotic patients', because the body is visible to others, it becomes part of the armament or guard that keeps out external threats; it becomes everything that is not-me, no longer the centre of my world. The body then comes to feel dead, like a hollow shell: a lifeless object in the world among other lifeless objects. In 'psychosis', then, it is not only the body that feels dead and without vitality, so does the world: it too becomes a hostile and threatening place, filled with dangers that at any moment could obliterate the fragile and vulnerable self; a condition Laing calls 'ontological insecurity'.

The 'psychotic' self is therefore disembodied with a sense that the world is alien, a condition of ontological insecurity that makes the world devoid of any unquestioned certainties for the individual. The self becomes divorced from others, from the world, and from its own body. This is illustrated in the cases of two of Laing's patients: one, called James, felt that he was only a response to other people, with no self-identity of his own. To him others looked real, solid and decisive, which, when contrasted with his own fragile sense of self, made others even more threatening, leading him to withdraw from the world as a way of self-protection. Another patient, David, felt that he was always playing a part for others but could never invest anything of himself in this, or in-habit his performance with the vitality of his body. He felt he *played* at being himself and that his 'real' self was 'shut-up', living only in his dialogues with himself. The use of the word 'shut-up' is interesting because it seems to indicate that David felt that he was not only shut up in himself, never able to make real or meaningful contact with others, but that he could never really say anything, could never speak with his own voice.

While such persons feel that they live only in the dialogue with themselves, this dialogue itself becomes divided and tortuous. Laing often found that while such people had retreated from others because they felt an overwhelming sense of vulnerability, they often reported another voice expressed only to themselves, a voice of superiority over others in the 'real' world, belittling them and viewing them as unworthy of associating with. Because those considered mad often felt disembodied, they also expressed feelings of immortality and physical invulnerability, believing that whatever happened to their body would not harm the self. This only added to the feelings and voice of superiority in their self-dialogue, which drowned out the more vulnerable and fragile voice that needed recognition from others and value in their eyes. The self-dialogue becomes divided in very much the way that Bakhtin found in the works of Dostoevsky, except, unlike the heroes in those novels, none of Laing's patients could express anything of those self-dialogues to others. Their interactions and conversations with others were marked only by the presentation of a self which was everything that was not-me.

When the inner dialogue becomes divided in such an extreme way, it begins to affect the person's own relationship to themselves as an 'I' and 'me', or addresser and addressee. If the voices become radically divided, they can take on an autonomy that occasionally splits off from the sense of 'I' and 'me', becoming a semi-independent 'he' or 'she'. One of Laing's patients told him, *'She's me,* and *I'm her* all the time.' Another said, *'She's* an *I* looking for a *me'*.[25] In such cases,

> an 'I' has not ceased to exist, but it is without substance, it is disembodied, it lacks the quality of realness, and it has no identity, it has no 'me' to go with it. It may be a contradiction in terms to say that the 'I' lacks identity but this seems to be so.[26]

In the terms we have been using here we can say that if I am only an 'I-for-myself' I cannot be real, and wouldn't even exist if it were not for the dialogues around me. I have to be able to in-habit the social world with others, as an embodied self with a living sense of vitality, becoming an 'I-for-others'. Likewise, others have to be real, living selves to whom I can relate and, with some, share a sense of mutuality. Without this, others become mere objects, or fearsome entities for whom I can never be a match, forcing me to withdraw from the living world.

Thus when people express these divided self-dialogues that have no unified voice – indeed often speaking or referring to other characters that populate the self – their self-expressions are regarded as a sign of insanity. They appear to lack all reason and are unintelligible, both in the way they talk and also in the use of their body, appearing to have little control over the body and its gestures. The way the person performs with others is thought to be without sense, thereby being the manifestation of some illness. Yet Laing maintains that such 'disordered' speech and use of the body can be intelligible when put into the context of the person's life-history, including their relations to others and to themselves. Indeed, because 'psychotics' are seen as unreasonable, failing to achieve the expected standards of moral behaviour, they are discounted from intelligibility and, by the same token, discounted as persons. Being labelled as 'ill' further takes away such status, reducing them to a medical object, a 'patient' rather than an agent. Their behaviour is then interpreted as the effect of a biological condition, rather than as meaningful in the context of their own lives. This is why Laing argues for a person centred approach in psychiatry, to restore patients to the status of intelligible and meaningful moral agents.

Social relations, ethical performativity and the unconscious

For Laing, then, 'psychotics' are denied the status of ethical agents because, not only do they not display reason in their rhetorical acts, they do not display reasonableness in their embodied behaviour, failing to in-habit the world in the expected way, with acceptable styles of body control, including the production of correct speech. Furthermore, this was manifest not only in division and disjunction within self–other dialogues and relations, but also in the relation and dialogue with the person's own self. Later in his career Laing controversially suggested that such division and disjunction could be traced back to early experiences in the family, or in relations with caregivers, where he observed irregular patterns of communication and attachments between those in the family networks he studied.

Without wanting to enter into or reignite such controversy, I nevertheless think that there are important conclusions we can draw from the work of Laing. Firstly, we can say that being reasonable involves an embodied dialogical performance with and for others, and that others will judge that performance according to ethical standards inherent in the history and culture of their particular social group. Secondly, such performances are relational in that they are put on for others and must have a meaning for those with whom we act. Thirdly, we respond relationally not only to the others we currently act with, but from our experience of past relationships and from habitual disposition we have acquired in these contexts. It is from such dispositions that we come to in-habit our performances rather than just responding to others in a simple and direct way. As Kenneth Gergen has remarked, performances are constituents of relationships, and such performances are animated not only by the relationships *into* which they are directed, but by the history of relationships *from* which they, and we, are in-formed. 'Thus, when I perform I am carrying a history of relationships, manifesting them, expressing them. They *inhabit* my every motion.'[27] Fourthly, this history of relationships involves not only our relation to others, it also includes the relation we have to our own self through self-dialogues, in which some voices may operate outside of fully articulated awareness. In this sense, we are not always aware of exactly how or why we in-habit our performances in relationships in the way we do, or why they may be animated with certain emotions.

However, when we in-habit our performances with all our energy and being, they feel authentic to us. We feel as though we become whatever it is we are doing, that the part we are playing in a relationship or the action we are undertaking becomes us and we become it. Even in activities that might have some compunction to them, such as performing work for a wage, most people can put something of themselves and their energies into the role, living it if only in part. Similarly, we become ethical selves through performance in relation to others, being in-formed by them in how to behave and how to be a person. Because the words and actions of others do this in-forming, especially when we are very young children, we may not be aware of exactly how we are formed and precisely what motivates us. As the psychoanalyst Jean Laplanche has said, children are given messages by their caregivers from the earliest months of life, many of which they do not understand and which act as 'enigmatic signifiers' that children try to decode. All of us will have seen and heard children asking their caretakers the question 'Why do I have to do this?' on being given an instruction they do not fully understand the rhyme and reason for. At a deeper level, Laplanche believes that many of these enigmatic signifiers refer to prohibited sexual behaviour, but we can extrapolate this to include messages about all forms of undesirable behaviour in children, or just the evaluative intonations of caregivers signalling their approval or disapproval of certain acts. As Adam Phillips has said of Laplanche's idea:

> ... it does seem entirely plausible to imagine that parents convey far more than they intend, and that children take in, in whatever form, far more than the parents or the children suspect. In this view our lives become ... the attempted translation and retranslation of these enigmatic messages our parents left us with; and our coming to terms with the limits of our capacity for retranslation. We can never pluck out the heart of the mystery. *So what is inescapable in the genesis and development of every person is the presence inside them – the psychic force field, the aura, the atmosphere, the messages – of another person.*[28]

As Mead said, as we grow older the presence of our parents as moral figures in our consciousness dies away, and instead we are left with a generalized moral sense about ourselves and the world: as Phillips puts it above, the psychic force field, the aura, the atmosphere of their messages. And this is inescapable because, like it or not, this is part of who we are. We may not only try to translate and retranslate those messages, we may struggle against them, take up the words and evaluations of others to battle against them, try in every action to prove some lingering sense of disapproval towards us to be wrong. Still, what we respond to is something that at some time deeply in-formed the sense of who we are as a person, the sense of our own worth. Other voices in our self-dialogue might be more vocal and, thus, seemingly more dominant, forming the content of our thoughts: but the aura, the atmosphere, the trace of a distant message may structure the way we act and permeate all our relations. This was the dilemma of Nastasya Filippovna: the desire to be absolved of the generalized feeling of others' (imagined) disapproval – 'they think I'm a fallen woman' – structured her actions, yet the voice of self-condemnation always intruded as the content of her speech and thoughts, making her actions and speech contradictory and bringing her into conflict with all those with whom she entered into relationships. Likewise, Laing's patients wanted their vulnerable and divided selves to be understood, recognized and confirmed by others, but the belief that they were no one, along with the armour of an invulnerable, false and superior voice, stopped them.

As Laing comments in *Self and Others,* the unconscious is relational: it is part of a complex of relations and dialogues that is beyond the capacity of any of the performers to fully articulate and control. In any relationship or interaction, not all of me will be in communication with all of the other, only a part of me will be, and the same is true from the point of view of the other. Nor am I ever in full communication with all aspects of my self. Each one of us brings our own self into a relationship, our own core of in-formation, composed of the aura of messages, evaluations and self-dialogues: the sediment of past relationships, of antagonism between others' words about us and our own words about ourselves, including divided voices and double-sided discourse. Thus, what I attempt to project to another in a dialogic relation is an *image* of myself that may or may not correspond with the way I truly feel about myself in terms of the residues of past relationships; likewise, the other may form an image of me different from the one I am trying to project, perhaps picking up something of the aura of past relationships that has in-formed me and is carried in my embodied dispositions which are unconsciously communicated to the other. Any interaction, even between two individuals, is therefore a complex inter-relational process that cannot be characterized only by what appears to be present in the interaction of self and other. Martin Buber has attempted to list the different configurations that could be involved in the interaction of two people, Peter and Paul:

> First, there is Peter as he wishes to appear to Paul, and Paul as he wishes to appear to Peter. Then there is Peter as he really appears to Paul, that is, Paul's image of Peter, which in general does not in the least coincide with what Peter wishes Paul to see; and similarly there is the reverse situation. Further, there is Peter as he appears to himself, and Paul as he appears to himself. Lastly, there are the bodily Peter and the bodily Paul. Two living beings and six ghostly appearances, which mingle in many ways in the conversation between the two.[29]

For Buber, this illustrates the problem of being and seeming, the gulf between what we truly are and the way we appear to others, and also the difficulty of establishing truly inter-human dialogue, in which we could drop the pretence and speak to one another from the steady core of our own being. While this might seem idealistic, I would argue that Buber has illustrated something important above, which is the way that interactions are not composed of direct relations between self and other, but involve multi-directional image-work. Furthermore, as Laing points out in his comments on Buber, it also shows the way in which the unconscious – the things about our own self of which we remain consciously unaware – are the aspects of our own self with which we are not in full or honest communication (such as the voices of others or their intonations that communicate some unwanted image of ourselves). In this sense, the unconscious is not composed of biological drives that cannot be admitted into the world of civilized, decent society, ring-fenced by the defence mechanisms of morality: rather, the unconscious is made up of suppressed or silenced voices or images, the intonations and inclinations that form part of our motivation to action, while the content of our thoughts is filled with more dominant voices. Thus, as Richard Lichtman put it, 'motive and countermotive have no existence independent of each other. Both are socially constructed out of a process which construes each only in contrast with the other'.[30]

As further illustration of this, the Russian linguist Vološinov claimed that the conflict Freud noted between 'psychological forces' such as the ego, super-ego and id, involving psychic agencies in deception and non-recognition, is not possible without some form of social mediation. As a linguist, Vološinov recognized such processes as the interplay of ideological signs within a social discourse. Thus:

> The content of the human psyche – a content consisting of thoughts, feelings, desires – is given in a formulation made by consciousness and, consequently, in the formulation of human verbal discourse. Verbal discourse, not in its narrow linguistic sense, but in its broad and concrete sociological sense – *that* is the *objective milieu* in which the psyche is presented. It is here that the motives of behaviour, arguments, goals, evaluations are composed and given external expression. It is here, too, that arise the conflicts among them.[31]

In the above, Vološinov uses the term ideology in its broad sense to cover the field of social interaction and speech, so that repression of a voice or a motive can occur in the way Bakhtin described, as the clash between another's word about me and my own word about myself; or as the clash between another's ethical judgement of me, their recognition or non-recognition of me as a moral agent, and my own evaluation of my self. These conflicts must be discursive because the 'unconscious mechanism' of censorship and repression so delicately 'detects all the logical subtleties of thoughts and all the moral nuances of feelings'. It would not be possible for its 'logical, ethical, and aesthetic selection among experiences' to happen if it were a 'mechanism' of the psyche or of biology: its operation must be ideological.[32]

But Vološinov is also using the term ideology in the more classic Marxist sense to refer to the clash of world-views between social groups. To explain this he makes a distinction between 'official' and 'unofficial' ideology, the official being the established or generally accepted ideas and values within a social group, usually associated with dominant social classes, while the unofficial is the more everyday ideas and values that arise from more local interactions between people. In this context, censorship has a more political function, outlawing ideas, values, speech or images that are deemed to be socially unacceptable. The outlawed ideas, values, words or images may still be present in people's thoughts and feelings, but they are denied public expression. Vološinov also equated unofficial ideology with the early and tentative expression of new ideas and feelings that are only beginning to emerge within society, in scientific exploration or artistic endeavours, which have not yet become part of official ideology. Thus, unofficial consciousness is composed of the less systematized inner dialogues, in which playful and creative thoughts occur and occasionally sneak past the watchful eye of official consciousness.

There is, however, one final way in which unconsciousness is both relational and ideological, in that people are generally unaware of how their motives and actions appropriate the logic of the social relations and interdependencies in which they are located. Litchman refers to this as the 'structural unconscious' and gives as an example the way that individuals in capitalist society see themselves as 'self-made' men and women; their own creation, fundamentally divorced from others and in competition with them, acting out of their own self-interest. Not only does this obscure the way that we are always fundamentally interdependent with others for the very formation and sustenance of our own self, it also obscures the fact that 'self-interest and social competitiveness depend upon a general [social] structure which gives meaning to the individual acts of self-aggrandizement and which must be implicitly understood and acknowledged by the actors'.[33] Worse still, the ideology of individualism, self-made individuals and self-interest can make our need for other human beings seem like a weakness to be denied, rather than a basic condition of human existence. After all, what would be the value of the achievements of self-made individuals if no one recognized their worth and value?

This is precisely the point I have been making in this chapter; that being recognized by others as a person of worth is a social process involving the communication of judgements and values on an interpersonal, ethical and ideo-logical level. It is in such dialogue that we are first called into being as a moral agent, capable of responsible actions for which we are accountable, or denied such a status by the words and actions of others. Yet these words and actions of others in-form us not only in a cognitive sense, in the way we *think* about our-selves, they in-form our very bodily dispositions in the world, our capacities to act as a self-guided individual, and thus, still deeper, our bodily sense of being alive and in-habiting the world in a living and fully connected way. To be denied the status of ethical agent, in this sense, is to be condemned to a living death, as our sense of being a living body belonging to its world can wither and die. Yet I also hope to have shown here that multiple voices are involved in the ethical for-mation of a person, and the way in which people can develop their own sense of self, including their own unified voice about themselves, by siding with some of these voices and against others. Thus, although we are in-formed in a social world, we are never completely determined by any one of the voices or the images we receive about ourselves, especially in a society where we are exposed to many different voices. Here, there is always the possibility of becoming something different, perhaps more closely approximating an ideal we hold out for our own self.

Notes

1. Mikhail M. Bakhtin (1981) *The Dialogic Imagination*. Tr. C. Emerson and M. Holquist. Austin: University of Texas Press. p. 349.
2. Mikhail M. Bakhtin (1984) *Problems of Dostoevsky's Poetic*. Tr. Caryl Emerson. Minneapolis: University of Minnesota Press. p. 239.
3. Rom Harré (1998) *The Singular Self: An Introduction to the Psychology of Personhood*. London: Sage. p. 71.
4. Erving Goffman (1959) *The Presentation of Self in Everyday Life*. London: Allen Lane, 1969 edn.
5. Rom Harré (1983) *Personal Being: A Theory for Individual Psychology*. Oxford: Blackwell. p. 20.

6. Rom Harré and Grant Gillett (1994) *The Discursive Mind.* Thousand Oaks, CA: Sage.
7. John Shotter (1993) *Cultural Politics of Everyday Life.* Buckingham: Open University Press. p. 193.
8. Shotter, *Cultural Politics.*
9. John Shotter (1989) 'Social accountability and the social construction of "you"', in J. Shotter and K. J. Gergen (eds), *Texts of Identity.* London: Sage. pp. 133–51, p. 145.
10. Ibid., p. 145–6.
11. Tom Yardley (2005) 'Sacrificing the rational body: a phenomenological approach to voluntary intoxication', PhD Thesis. Portsmouth University.
12. Norbert Elias (1994) *The Civilizing Process.* Tr. Edmund Jephcott. Oxford: Blackwell.
13. Gerard J. Hughes (2001) *Aristotle on Ethics.* London: Routledge.
14. Joshua Soffer (2001) 'Embodied perception: redefining the social', *Theory and Psychology,* 11 (5): 655–70, p. 668.
15. Mikhail M. Bakhtin, *Dialogic,* p. 345.
16. Charles Taylor (1991) *The Ethics of Authenticity.* Cambridge, MA: Harvard University Press.
17. Desiderius Erasmus (1511) *The Praise of Folly.* Tr. Hoyt Hopewell Hudson. New Jersey: Princeton University Press, 1941 edn. p. 95.
18. Mikhail M. Bakhtin, *Problems,* p. 47.
19. Ibid., p. 53.
20. Ibid., p. 287.
21. Ibid., p. 287.
22. Martin Buber (1965) 'Elements of the interhuman', in M. Buber, *The Knowledge of Man.* Tr. Ronald Gregor Smith. London: George Allen & Unwin. pp. 72–88.
23. Victor Turner (1982) *From Ritual to Theatre: The Human Seriousness of Play.* New York: Performing Arts Journal Publications.
24. Mikhail M. Bakhtin, *Problems,* p. 54.
25. R. D. Laing (1960) *The Divided Self.* London: Penguin, 1990 edn. p. 158.
26. Ibid., p. 172.
27. Kenneth J. Gergen (1999) *An Invitation to Social Construction.* London: Sage. p. 133. My emphasis.
28. Adam Phillips (2000) *Promises, Promises.* London: Faber and Faber. p. 203. My emphasis.
29. Martin Buber, 'Elements', p. 77.
30. Richard Lichtman (1982) *The Production of Desire: The Integration of Psychoanalysis into Marxist Theory.* New York: Free Press. p. 192.
31. V. N. Vološinov (1976) *Freudianism: A Marxist Critique.* New York: Academic Press. p. 83.
32. Ibid., p. 70.
33. Richard Lichtman, *Production,* p. 232.

Selected bibliography

Bakhtin, Mikhail M. (1984) *Problems of Dostoevsky's Poetic.* Tr. Caryl Emerson. Minneapolis: University of Minnesota Press.
Buber, Martin (1965) *The Knowledge of Man.* Tr. Ronald Gregor Smith. London: George Allen & Unwin.

Elias, Norbert (1994) *The Civilizing Process.* Oxford: Blackwell.

Harré, Rom (1998) *The Singular Self: An Introduction to the Psychology of Personhood.* London: Sage.

Laing, R. D. (1960) *The Divided Self.* London: Penguin.

Laing, R. D. (1961) *Self and Others.* London: Penguin, 1971.

Lichtman, Richard (1982) *The Production of Desire: The Integration of Psychoanalysis into Marxist Theory.* New York: Free Press.

Shotter, John (1993) *Cultural Politics of Everyday Life.* Buckingham: Open University Press.

Taylor, Charles (1991) *The Ethics of Authenticity.* Cambridge, MA: Harvard University Press.

Vološinov, V. N. (1976) *Freudianism: A Marxist Critique.* New York: Academic Press.

CHAPTER 4

POWER, KNOWLEDGE AND THE SELF

As I said in the last chapter, Michel Foucault, the French philosopher and historian of systems of thought, painted a much darker version of the ethical formation of the embodied self as it occurs in the Western world than do thinkers such as Harré and Shotter. He also had an understanding of bodily discipline that ties disciplinary practice and embodiment to modern institutions of social power. More broadly, though, for Foucault, no analysis of the self can be divorced from the socially and historically situated knowledge within which human experience is constituted. When we ask the question 'who am I?' we pose it as a problem, the solution to which requires some form of knowledge that will lead us to a truer understanding of ourselves. According to Foucault, in the Western world the knowledge and social practices through which self-understanding and experience are constituted are increasingly influenced by both the natural and human sciences.

From the 18th century onwards, biologists, medical doctors, psychiatrists, psychologists, criminologists and sociologists (the list could go on) have all reshaped the knowledge and practices through which we come to solve the problem of our own self-identity and reach some kind of temporary self-understanding. In the contemporary Western world, human sexuality has become a key concept through which we search for our true selves, thinking that if we can correctly identify our sexual desires we will have found an important key to unlocking the puzzling secret of ourselves. 'Am I gay, straight or bisexual?' is the question we often pose in seeking to find the truth about ourselves. Yet Foucault points out that any answer we give to this question comes framed within a set of questions, concepts, terminology and practice that has been created by the medical and psychiatric professions ('homosexuality' and 'heterosexuality' were terms created by doctors in the 19th century). Likewise, if we are facing personal problems, difficulties, or some form of unusually severe personal distress, we may (as R. D. Laing noted) attract the diagnoses of depression, neurosis or psychosis from a medical doctor, psychiatrist or related professional worker. Even if this is not the case, and we are simply curious to learn more about ourselves, any book we pick off the shelves in a bookstore, usually under the heading of 'popular psychology', is likely to have been written by a psychologist, psychotherapist or counsellor. This leads Foucault to point out that any form of knowledge, even knowledge of the self, is linked to a form of power: to a network of scientific discourse, knowledge, professions, institutions and practices, the function of which is to classify, normalize and regulate human behaviour.

But Foucault also became concerned with the ethics through which humans, in different historical contexts, have formed a relationship to their own selves, creating styles of self-mastery or self-domination that are a micro-physics of power. He believed that in the West our modes of relating to self are characterized by self-domination, because ethical formation of the self occurs as we are subject to disciplines and to forms of expert knowledge. In this context, then, knowledge, power and the self are inextricably linked.

Foucault and the historical subjection of the subject

In the preface to one of his last books, looking back at the scope of his work over three decades, Foucault said that his project had always been to understand various modes of human experience, such as madness, criminality and sexuality, as 'the correlation of a domain of knowledge, a type of normativity and a mode of relation to the self':

> it means trying to decipher how, in Western societies, a complex experience is constituted from and around certain forms of behaviour: an experience which conjoins a field of study (with its own concepts, theories, diverse disciplines), a collection of rules (which differentiate the permissible from the forbidden, natural from monstrous, normal from pathological, what is decent from what is not, etc.), [and] a mode of relation between the individual and himself (which enables him to recognize himself ...).[1]

What this means is that Foucault's works were concerned with how human beings turn themselves into the subjects of their own thought; how, both collectively and individually, we come to examine ourselves through the knowledge we create about ourselves. However, when Foucault uses the term 'thought', he is not only referring to thought in the abstract sense, as pure theory; he uses the term in a similar way to the pragmatists, whereby thought is understood as a tool to be used in practice: it is evident in our ways of speaking, acting and relating to others. Thought is also a form of action that is manifest in the way we make judgements about what is true or false, right or wrong, and how we either accept or reject the rules we are applying in our everyday practices. For us to have an experience of self, then, we must both reflect on and *work on* ourselves and others.

In Western societies, though, our experience of being in the world and our experience of self are linked to fields of scientific study that provide concepts, categories and practices in which that experience is shaped and formed. It is also linked to rules that categorize and divide experience into good or bad, healthy or sick, normal or abnormal. For example, Foucault's first study was a history of madness, which looked at the transformation of the experience from the 16th century in Western Europe, where madness or folly was often engaged with by literary figures who used it as a voice through which to satirize or critique established authority, to the 18th century when madness was seen as the opposite of reason and thus silenced.[2] As Laing noted, doctors and psychiatrists employing scientific reason assume that the mad have nothing intelligible to say, therefore silencing them in the age of reason. For Foucault, the rise of the power of reason coincided with 'the great confinement' of the poor, elderly, infirm and criminal; the vagabonds, misfits or misplaced who were confined to the poor houses and other institutions from the 17th century onwards. Gradually, each section of this population was classified in its own right and segregated into separate institutions, with those deemed insane being confined in the madhouse. It was the medical profession who took charge of the madhouses, largely because of the initial fear that madness might be a contagious disease: however, doctors gradually began to develop the notion of mental illness that we still use today, based on a classification of symptoms and the design of forms of treatment for the various conditions.

Thus, a system of recognition of symptoms and behaviours was gradually developed which constituted itself as knowledge of 'mental illness'. But this also became a normative system for the regulation of behaviour built upon 'a whole technical, administrative, juridical, and medical apparatus whose purpose was to isolate and take custody of the insane'.[3] It was also a way of relating to oneself and others as the possible subjects of madness: in other words, the experience of madness had changed from that of being a fool, oaf, wastrel or possessed, wandering between different populations and attempting as best you could to live amongst others, to the experience of being mentally ill. That is, of being classified by doctors, magistrates or judges, and being voluntarily or involuntarily confined in an asylum where you are subject to treatment. Foucault outlines how this is actually the expression of a new form of power rather than a more humane treatment of the insane. Much is often said of how the mad were once chained to the walls of the old madhouses, their liberation symbolized by Philippe Pinel's famous act of striking off the chains of his inmates. Pinel's aim, however, was not to liberate the mad from the asylum, but – along with others like William Tuke in England – to subject them to a new form of 'moral treatment', including baths, showers and close supervision by those in charge of the institution. However, Foucault points out that the baths and cold showers were used as punishments, as was the enclosure of the mad in a world of moral judgement designed to bring home to them their guilt for the transgression of normal, rational forms of behaviour.

> Everything was organized so that the madman would recognize himself in a world of judgement that enveloped him on all sides; he must know that he is watched, judged, and condemned; from transgression to punishment, the connection must be evident, as a guilt recognized by all.[4]

The aim of such moral treatment is the internalization of guilt in the inmate's mind and the creation of a sense of remorse. It plays upon the psychological inwardness in which modern people seek to find the truth of themselves through reflection, and through which the mad person becomes aware of their guilt; an awareness from which they may return to a sense of his or her self as a free and responsible subject, able to take charge of their own behaviour in a rational way. The power of the doctor comes not from any effective cure, but from the fact that they serve as a figure displaying the authority of rational agency. The doctor appears as everything the mad person is not, but as that which the mad should and could become: rational. In this modern age, opposition to the power and authority of psychiatrists comes not from the patients themselves, but from artists and philosophers working beyond the remit of reason, or at its limits, who find a degree of freedom in which to transgress its rules and regulations. The voice of unreason can be found in the works of Nietzsche and Artaud, 'resisting by their own strength that gigantic moral imprisonment which we are in the habit of calling … the liberation of the insane'.[5]

Foucault continued analysing this style of 'punitive rationality', aimed at the recalcitrant elements of society, in his study of the prison and criminality. His aim, though, is the same: just as the study of madness tried to show how the experience of being mad and being sane (which sometimes involves a fear of madness) was linked to a new form of power and knowledge, one that involves new institutional and administrative means of dividing and regulating the population, so the experience of being criminal and law abiding involves similar mechanisms. Once again, a central theme is that the incarceration of the criminal in prisons, as opposed to the brutal physical tortures and public executions practised widely before the 17th century, is not to be regarded as a more humane form of punishment, but is the exercise of power in the form of a punitive rationality. Foucault's aim is to show how changes in the penal system and in law overlapped with the developing knowledge in the human sciences, so that the two were of reciprocal influence on each other in order to 'make the technology of power the very principle both of the humanization of the penal system and of the knowledge of man'.[6]

In punitive practices before the 17th century, the body of the condemned became the focus for what now appear to be extreme forms of physical punishment and torture, such as whippings, floggings and the public execution of the criminal, often by hanging, drawing and quartering, where the body is torn apart. For Foucault this is because the law represents the will and force of the sovereign, so that any attacks or violations of the law are thought to be attacks and violations on the person and body (the force) of the sovereign. In this context, punishment is not understood purely as redress for the victim of the crime, it is also revenge of the sovereign for the damage done to his Kingdom, over which he exercises the power of law, and to his person and body. The execution is then 'a ceremonial by which a momentarily injured sovereignty is reconstituted'.[7] Alongside this, the torture of the criminal's body is a means by which to get a confession, and so is related to extracting the truth of the crime.

Foucault notes that as we move into the 18th and 19th centuries, the truth–power relationship remains the centre of forms of punishment, but in a quite different way. Now, punitive practices try to separate the search for truth from the violence or coercion that must always be an element in any form of punishment. As sovereigns across Europe were beginning to lose their power to more impersonal forms of government and administration, power was exercised in the name of society as a whole and was legitimized as being in defence of society. Punishments were now expected to be measured against the weight of the crime, as even the criminal is a member of society, so that punishment must be seen to be just. Furthermore, the desired outcome of punishment becomes the successful reintegration of the criminal and the wayward into the law-abiding social body: it is no longer constituted by revenge against the offender's body, but aims at the reform of his or her character and the mending of their ways. This is why people now recoil at the horror of torture, not out of a new respect for the humanity of the criminal, but because there is a tendency to a more finely tuned justice that operates with greater evenness and regularity within the network of social relations that integrates and regulates the behaviour of the population. While the advantage of such a system is often thought to be its fairness and that it seeks to do justice on behalf of all, to Foucault one of its aims and effects is to spread the operation of power throughout the entire social body.

As for the prison itself, no longer is it the place for retribution against the criminal's body, it is the institutional site in which the person's character – their very *soul* – must be reformed, ready to be reintegrated into society as a useful, productive, law-abiding member. To do this, the prison became the site of a new 'microphysics' of power that no longer aimed to punish the body, but to control and discipline it: to regulate behaviour so that it could be changed and remoulded, thus changing the very character of the prisoner. This was done through detailed techniques of regulation that paid close attention to every aspect of behaviour and routine. Discipline involves a control of space in which each individual is assigned a place and a function so that they can be supervised, partitioned from others (to prevent insubordination and insurrection) and individuated. At every moment in such a regime the conduct of each individual can be supervised, watched and judged in order to calculate its qualities, merits or deficiencies. Space therefore becomes analytical, in that it is organized in order to observe, assess and record the behaviour of each prisoner so that they can be known and classified. In addition, the timetable becomes re-employed for the temporal control of activity in the prison. However, instead of being used to ensure the efficiency of actions, the timetable is now used to impose a rhythm on daily activities, and to break down each act into its elements so they can be reassembled into new ways of acting and thinking.

In all these ways, the prison aims to create new individuals, new selves, yet it does so by means of working on their bodies to discipline them.

The historical moment of the disciplines was the moment when an art of the human body was born, which was directed not only at the growth of its skills, nor at the intensification of its subjection, but at the formulation of a relation that in the mechanism itself makes it more obedient as it becomes more useful, and conversely. What was then being formed was a policy of coercions that act upon the body, a calculated manipulation of its elements, its gestures, its behaviour. The human body was entering a machinery of power that explores it, breaks it down and rearranges it. A 'political anatomy', which was also a 'mechanics of power', was being born; it defined how one may have a hold over others' bodies, not only so that they may do what one wishes, but so that they may operate as one wishes, with the techniques, speed and the efficiency that one determines. Thus discipline produces subjected and practised bodies, 'docile' bodies.[8]

Foucault makes clear that he thinks this kind of rationalized discipline is different from the kind of institutional asceticism practised in monasteries, and which spilled over into the kind of ascetic rationalization of conduct that Weber saw as operating in the Protestant ethic. Here, the aim of the discipline of ascetic practice was the mastery of each individual over his own body: in the prison it is more a matter of the control and transformation of others' bodies through the imposition of a disciplinary regime.

Nevertheless, the end product of this discipline of the body is the creation of a new individual through instilling in them techniques and habits for the control of their bodies. By separating, analysing, and differentiating each body *'discipline "makes" individuals;* it is the specific technique of a power that regards individuals both as objects and as instruments of its exercise'.[9] Thus, power does not impose itself on individuals, because 'it is already one of the prime effects of power that certain bodies, certain gestures, certain discourses, certain desires, come to be identified and constituted as individuals'.[10] Another technique for doing this is the close observation of each individual in the institution, making them visible at all times to those who are supervising them – in the case of the prison, the guards and wardens who watch over the conduct of each person, but later there will be criminologists and psychologists who will study the behaviour of prisoners, trying to 'get inside' it by understanding the mind that is supposedly 'behind' it. Therefore, surveillance becomes a key technique of discipline within the prison, and much effort is spent in the architectural design of buildings to ensure that prisoners can be watched at all times, so that no activities escape the attention of the authorities. The perfect architectural design for prisons is one in which the observers become invisible while the prisoner is constantly visible, the effect being that the prisoner never knows when he or she is being watched, and so must constantly behave as if they are under surveillance. In this way, the prisoner must constantly observe his own behaviour as an anonymous or invisible other would, regulating it according to their norms and standards.

This is very much like the 'internalization' of the 'generalized other' described by Mead, the formation of the 'impartial spectator' of Smith, or the strengthening of the 'super-ego' (the 'above-I') as detailed by Freud in his clinical work with patients. In each case, the function of the generalized sense of others, particularly the general sense of their values and possible judgements, acts to regulate actions: that is, we come to modify our own actions, to shape and design them, in ways that we feel will be approved of by the social group with which we identify. The difference in the case of Foucault is that he is detailing how in modern society, for those who seem incapable of regulating their own behaviour, a generalized sense of the moral judgements of others in the form of an impersonal authority is *imposed* on people through disciplinary power and punitive rationality.

Another of the techniques Foucault associates with this process is the examination, which places individuals in a field of surveillance and also situates them in a web of writing: that is, in documents, case notes and files that attempt to record and classify the individual, turning them into a describable, analysable object. This placed the individual under the gaze of various bodies of knowledge that could each describe them in their own particular way. For Foucault, this represents the birth of the human sciences, which emerge in the study of the details of individual case notes rather than in the grand ideas of history. It also means that in the modern world the story of an individual's life is less to be found in some heroic or epic narrative, than in the case notes of doctors, psychiatrists, psychologists or educators. (Foucault would no doubt have been fascinated by the 'record of achievement' that students are now asked to keep on themselves, compiled in association with teachers and tutors, recording all their achievements in a range of curricular and non-curricular activities from the earliest years onward). Such files and records aim at both the *objectification* and *subjection* of the individual: that is, they are turned into the object of others' gazes through the file, *and* into the object of their own gaze by coming to see themselves as a person through the knowledge and categorizations that others have made of them, getting a subjective sense of their own selves in the process. Thus, in seeking to form and regulate the behaviour of people, disciplinary power does not suppress individuality – it *creates* it in a certain form. But that form is not of a memorable person – a hero or heroine – it is in the form of a 'case'. Disciplinary technology sets out to normalize behaviour, but does so by studying and cataloguing all the varieties of individuality that exist around the norm.

All of this is the effect of the exercise of power becoming more even and regular within society so that no one totally escapes its grip. As Foucault says,

> For a long time ordinary individuality – the everyday individuality of everybody – remained below the threshold of description. To be looked at, observed, described in detail, followed from day to day by an uninterrupted writing was a privilege ... The disciplinary methods reversed this relation, lowered the threshold of describable individuality and made this description a means of control and a method of domination.[11]

However, the critique of Foucault, which I will elaborate upon later in this chapter, is that he has overextended the form of power and discipline that developed in prisons in the 18th and 19th centuries to the whole of society. The prison becomes a metaphor for disciplinary power in total, as 'the carceral archipelago transported this technique from the penal institution to the entire social body'.[12] Yet the fascination of Foucault's work is how he describes the creation of the modern self; in the case of prisons, how criminality was constituted as an object of knowledge and how 'the criminal' was created within this as a mode of experience and a type of self. In the disciplines of the prison everything was organized so that the prisoner could form a new relation to themself, one in which surveillance and regulation of their own thoughts, feelings, and behaviour plays a key role in their individuation.

In extending the notion of a disciplinary society, Foucault is also making an important statement about the formation of all selves in the contemporary Western world. Like Nietzsche, who is perhaps the greatest influence on his work, Foucault believes that there is no soul or self given to humans at birth; rather, the soul is the product of a certain historical formation of power, knowledge and discipline from the 17th century onwards. Thus,

> The history of this 'micro-physics' of the punitive power would then be a genealogy or an element in a genealogy of the modern 'soul'. Rather than seeing this soul as the reactivated remnants of an ideology, one would see it as the present correlative of a certain technology of power over the body. It would be wrong to say that the soul is an illusion, or an ideological effect. On the contrary, it exists, it has a reality, it is produced permanently around, on, within the body by the functioning of a power that is exercised on those punished – and, in a more general way, on those one supervises, trains and corrects, over madmen, children at home and at school, the colonized, over those who are stuck at a machine and supervised for the rest of their lives ... This real, non-corporal soul is not a substance; it is the element in which are articulated the effects of a certain type of power and the reference of a certain type of knowledge ...[13]

The above gives an indication as to why Foucault has a much darker view of the social formation of the responsible, accountable, rational self than social constructionists like Harré and Shotter. This is because he does not understand the individual to be solely a product of the conversation between parents and children, in which they are called to an awareness of themselves as responsible and accountable selves: instead, the micro-social power politics of growing up, and of the formation of self in general, is shot through with disciplines that act on the body, including a regime of discipline at home and school that involves a regularization of bodily activity in place and time, much like that of the prison. Thus, the micro-social power politics of becoming a self is linked by Foucault to a macro-power politics in which selves are created through discipline and knowledge in various institutional sites. In what must be the work of his most sympathetic towards Marxism, Foucault adds that these institutional disciplines prepare individual bodies for their future role as labour power, being docile, useful, manageable and productive.

However, Foucault's main allegiance was always to Nietzsche, and we can see in the above quotation how Foucault is underscoring Nietzsche's idea that there is no thing in itself, such as a soul, at the core of the self: instead, the illusion of a coherent self is formed in the 'will to power' as one instinct or impulse of the human body turns against the others. Foucault, though, is attempting to historicize this by showing that the self is not an illusion but an effect of the technologies of power and knowledge on the body, which make an individual vigilant of their own body, its actions, habits and inclinations. It is not, then, a biological instinct or impulse turning against another, but the way humans have been made the subjects of power through disciplines that inculcate the practices of self-domination.

Overall, then, Foucault attempted a historical ontology of the various ways in which humans have become subjects in the West. In using the term 'subject' to describe modern individuals, he plays on its dual meaning of being both 'subject to someone else by control and dependence, and tied to [our] own identity by a conscience or self-knowledge'.[14] This type of subjection occurs in three modes: the first emerges in relation to forms of inquiry in the humanities that have tried to gain the status of sciences, such as linguistics which studies the speaking subject, economics which studies the labouring subject – the producer of wealth – while biology studies the living subject as a product of nature and evolution.[15] The second, overlapping with the human sciences, is the institutional, administrative and legal mechanisms which attempted to divide the population and to govern it more effectively by categorizing and individualizing it. Types of madness are contrasted to sanity, forms of criminality are contrasted with responsible agency, and varieties of sickness are contrasted with health. Interestingly, Foucault points out that it is the deviant who are often investigated and individualized more than the normal: defining sanity is harder than defining madness, as we have a greater conceptual range and vocabulary to do so, and the same goes for responsibility and health (the latter being a notoriously difficult concept to pin down, usually being regarded as without illness).

A concept that Foucault uses to bring all of this together is *discourse,* something he had considerable difficulty giving a clear definition to, but which can generally be regarded as the rules that govern the language and conceptual vocabulary which (through various branches of knowledge) order the world and the relation between the things in it, and also involves the institutional sites and social practices that help to form and put in place the conceptual order of normality. Discursive practices thus delimit the field of objects, define the legitimate perspective of the agent of knowledge, and fix rules for the elaboration of concepts and theories. It thereby becomes impossible to experience or think outside of this discursive order, so that, in Foucault's more structuralist writings, the discursive order is imposed on the subject prior to all experience (in a Kantian/Hegelian fashion) through a Nietzschean 'will to knowledge' and to power. I will return to a critical consideration of this concept towards the end of this chapter.

To continue with the modes of subjection, the third identified by Foucault is the relation to self, or the way that we turn ourselves into a subject. This is best exemplified in Foucault's work on sexuality, in terms of how we have come to recognize ourselves as sexual subjects.[16] For him, the concept of sexuality became a central mode of experience of the self in the 19th century in Europe with the emergence of the various sciences of sexuality, which stemmed from medicine and psychiatry, but referred also to biology and the science of populations. However prior to this in the 17th century, there was a growing interest by various authorities in sex, particularly in the Catholic practice of confession to a pastor, in which the confessing subject was encouraged to speak in greater detail – albeit with decorum – about the details of their sex life, of their dreams and desires. It was true that people could not speak about, or be so open about, sexual behaviour as they could in the Middle Ages, yet conversely the agencies of power became more interested in sex and incited people to speak about it more, even if this was in a codified way. The pastoral concern was that people should tell of their temptations and the battles fought with their own flesh. Asking if there was a censorship of sex in this age, Foucault replies: 'there was installed rather an apparatus for producing an even greater quantity of discourse about sex, capable of functioning and taking effect in its very economy'.[17]

Furthermore, the state also becomes interested in the sex lives of the population, because in economic discourses population is identified with the production of wealth, and in biological/medical discourse sex is the means of the reproduction of population and possible control over it. Foucault calls this the emergence of 'bio-power', which is the installation of power into life itself. The health and reproduction of the populations of nation-states becomes a central concern, along with the drive to the normalization of sex, which is linked to the drive to contain and cure disease, abnormality and perversion. As with criminality, the focus of authorities was on deviant forms of sexual behaviour – the perversions – so that, 'between the state and the individual, sex became an issue, and a public issue no less; a whole web of discourses, special knowledges, analyses, and injunctions settled upon it'.[18] In the 18th century, doctors, educators and parents became concerned with the sexual activity of children, in particular masturbation in boys, which was subject to strict prohibition, and disciplines of the body were recommended to keep children's thoughts and energies from preoccupation with sex and the sensations of their own bodies.

In the 19th century, medical doctors, psychiatrists and the criminal justice system began identifying a whole range of sexual practices outside the norm of heterosexual marriage, such as homosexuality, nymphomania, sadomasochism, and so on, which they annexed as their own province of study and treatment. The body of the hysterical woman also came to be a centre of concern, with Bleuler and Freud famously diagnosing the condition (in which individuals – usually women – inexplicably lose the use of one of their limbs) as a psychological phenomenon caused by repressed sexuality. What is happening here is the production of a multiplicity of discourses on sexuality from many different quarters, which operate in a variety of institutions, all aimed at making individuals speak of their sexual practices, and of their dreams and desires. Moreover, what is being created in these discourses on sex is not simply more knowledge of a range of varied sexual practices, but an array of different *identities* based on sexual desire distributed around the norm. For example, prior to the 17th century, the act of sodomy was outlawed in canonical and civil law, but it was only the act that was prohibited: this was not yet associated with a particular identity. Sodomy could occur between a man and a woman, between two men, or with an animal. It was in the 19th century that the term homosexual was created, thus turning the homosexual into 'a personage, a past, a case history, and a childhood, in addition to being a type of life, a life form, and a morphology, with an indiscreet anatomy and possibly a mysterious physiology'.[19] In criminal law, the sodomite became a homosexual, an outlawed and excluded personage. However, while it is often said that modern society has attempted to reduce sexuality to the legitimate heterosexual couple, 'there are equal grounds for saying that it has, if not created, at least outfitted and made to proliferate, groups with multiple elements ... a distribution of points of power, hierarchized and placed opposite to one another'.[20]

Despite the growth of the sciences of sexuality, the old Christian practices of confession and self-scrutiny did not die away but were re-employed in a new setting, most famously by Freud in psychoanalytic practice. Now, instead of confessing guilty pleasures and secrets to a pastor, people analysed themselves with the aid and guidance of a therapist, to identify their desires and their own sexual nature hidden in the seemingly strange symbolism of dreams, or in the unfathomable motives behind their own consciously unwilled actions. In this context, speaking the truth of our sexuality is therefore thought of as speaking the truth of ourselves. This is why today, when we ask the question 'who am I?' we often try to answer it by finding the truth of our sexuality: yet we do this armed with the concepts and terminology of sexuality developed over three centuries in a variety of different discourses, which now forms not only knowledge of sex but also knowledge of the subject, the self, as a whole.

Unlike Freud, though, Foucault does not see sexuality as a biological life-force that has to be repressed by the power of civilization, which is often weak in the face of the primal urge it unsuccessfully seeks to contain. Instead, to Foucault, bio-power has actually infiltrated life itself and begun to analyse, classify, multiply and individuate sex. It produces sexuality rather than represses it. The aim of liberating us from modern forms of power therefore cannot proceed by attempting to liberate sexual desire, as many social movements in the 1960s aimed to do (supported by philosophers like Herbert Marcuse who took seriously Freud's idea of the repression of sex). Rather, for those who want to change society, Foucault argues that we, like him, must engage in a critical analysis of the mechanisms of power that produce our modern notions of sexuality: the forms of scientific knowledge, therapeutic and legal practices that make us who we are.

Power and knowledge, then, is not just a one-way street: it can be used by those who are its subjects in ways that authorities never envisaged, and traditions of critical rationality – in which Foucault situates himself – can be turned back on the society that has generated them. For example, while knowledge about sexuality and the creation of various sexual identities, such as homosexuality, helped to spread power and control, a reverse discourse also emerged composed of the demands of various sexual groups. In particular, homosexuals began to demand the right to have their identity recognized and legitimated by society as a whole, a movement that culminated with 'gay rights' in the 1960s, eventually leading to the de-criminalization of homosexuality and its declassification as a psychiatric illness. Relations of power and knowledge are not static, they are 'matrices of transformation' in which social groups and individuals struggle against one another. Indeed, Foucault sees relations of power as warlike, with authorities attempting to govern the conduct of the population as a whole, while other groups fight back or put up resistance, taking up certain identities and recasting them, or refusing them altogether.[21]

These struggles revolve around the question 'who are we?' and involve the refusal of certain identities – the way people have been individualized in the modern state – opposing the dividing practices that categorize and discipline individuals. Yet at the same time new alliances must be forged, with groups reclaiming and transforming their own identities within their everyday social relationships, as did gays and lesbians. I will follow up this point later in this chapter and in the next, as it is one that Foucault does not always consider in the detail it deserves.

Instead, in the second and third volumes of *The History of Sexuality*, Foucault's emphasis shifted from the technology of domination and power/knowledge, to the games of truth in which we come to recognize ourselves and constitute a relation to our self. It is through these 'games of truth' that becoming a self is historically constituted as experience and humans attempt to think their own nature. In modern Christian societies, we are led to think that the truth of ourselves resides in deciphering our own desires, having been exhorted to analyse and articulate them in order to reach this truth. In the later volumes of the study of sexuality, Foucault focuses on the societies of classical antiquity, of Greece and Rome, to understand the ethics by which citizens of those societies understood themselves. In general, they placed greater emphasis on ethical concern with the 'care of the self' rather than with 'knowledge of the self', so that ethical practices were centred on the 'arts of existence' through which people aimed to shape and transform themselves according to aesthetic values or stylistic concerns. Thus, they were focused less on morality and questions of good and bad, right and wrong, and more on the correct or pleasurable way of doing things. In this way the ancients dealt with problematizations of the self and of sex by seeking self-perfection or self-mastery, rather than searching for the truth of their inherent nature as an individual for the purpose of self-domination.

Furthermore, while many of the attitudes to be found in Christianity towards sex are prefigured in pagan culture and ethics, sex was not their overall concern. The ancient Greeks and Romans had a strict ascetic practice of moderation when it came to sex, but this was part of a wider concern with care of the self that included rules about diet, household management and the courtship of young men. There were no strict moral rules about good and bad sexual behaviour, healthy and sick acts, but ethical rules about the right way in which to conduct oneself as a free citizen (of course, this applies to the freeborn only, not to slaves). For example, love and sexual relationships between men and boys were not designated as 'homosexual', as many men who engaged in these activities were also married; nor were such relationships seen to be morally wrong. They were, however, problematized and surrounded by strict rules according to how the relationship was to be conducted. Usually, an older man would seek out a younger man as his lover, as relations between men of the same age were considered inappropriate: also, the young man had not to be 'easy' or effeminate, as the ethics of self-care involved self-mastery, power and virility. Yet Foucault believes that the art of love and courtship centred on men and boys because the relationship between men and women was set in economics and property, creating free play between those of the same sex.[22]

The main point Foucault is making, though, is that concern about sexual activity does not centre on a morality of good and bad, or anything like our contemporary notion of sexual identities, but on the correct form of sexual conduct according to ethical rules, and the correct measure of all the citizen's pleasures, whether this is to do with sex, food, or exercise. It is over-indulgence that is the problem, as this shows lack of self-mastery and virility and is a threat to health, rather than the classification of the acts one engages in. Thus Foucault concludes that the ethics of the ancient world centred on aesthetics rather than a normative rationality. As Foucault remarks about the notion of self-mastery and self-possession to be found in the Hellenistic and Imperial periods, this is not done in order to repress some element of the self or to thwart desire, but to form the self in a way that is pleasing for oneself and others.

> ... the experience of self that forms itself in this possession is not simply that of a force overcome, or a rule exercised over a power that is on the point of rebelling; it is the experience of a pleasure that one takes in oneself. The individual who has finally succeeded in gaining access to himself is, for himself, an object of pleasure.[23]

Through these studies, then, Foucault begins to draw conclusions about the ethical formation of the self that is broader than a simple concern with sex and identity. He is elucidating a different type of ethical relation to oneself that does not include a constant interrogation of self or desire to find the truth of self, but focuses on disciplines of self-mastery and self-moderation that allowed people *to create themselves* as their own object of pleasure. Furthermore, no authorities or experts intervene in this process to punish, discipline or direct the process. Foucault is not saying that we should try to emulate the ancient Greeks, as he recognizes there are aspects of their society that would be unacceptable to us today. Indeed, 'Greek ethics were linked to a purely virile society with slaves, in which the women were underdogs whose pleasure had no importance, whose sexual life had only to be oriented towards, determined by, their status as wives'.[24] What he is showing, however, is that a type of ethics is possible other than that we have today, in which pleasures do not become guilty secrets to be denied, and where the truth of the self is not sought in self-analysis and self-knowledge, but in an ethics that allows people to measure and moderate their pleasures and become the objects of their own pleasure.

In an interview with a gay magazine, Foucault spelled out the contemporary relevance of this approach, saying that gays should not relate questions of their sexuality to the problem of 'who am I?' and 'what is the secret of my desires?', but ask themselves what relationships can be invented, established and multiplied through homosexuality. In this sense, being gay is not an identity that is given; it is rather a project that has to be undertaken through building relationships of affection, tenderness, friendship, fidelity, camaraderie and compassion that current societies and institutions would find difficult to deal with in the frameworks of legalized marriage or hedonistic consumption. 'To be "gay", I think, is not to identify with the psychological traits and the visible masks of the homosexual but to try to define and develop a way of life.'[25] In other words, Foucault is suggesting the creation of a new ethics and aesthetics that makes possible new relationships and a different distribution of pleasures, which would extend beyond current gay culture. Sexuality would then be something we could create together, rather than identities generated by scientific knowledge of sex, and the positing of the discovery of the secret side of desire.

In Foucault's definition, then, ethics becomes the practice of freedom, a way of getting free of established and punitive norms, and also a way of freeing ourselves from identities given through scientific knowledge in a disciplinary society. Ethics allows us the critical distance from our own societies and selves, from which standpoint we can set about actively remaking them. In this light, Foucault returned to Immanuel Kant's essay 'What is Enlightenment?' in which he asked the questions, 'who are we today?' and 'what is to be done?' For Kant, Enlightenment is where humanity puts its own reason to use, thereby emerging from a state of immaturity in which it unquestioningly submitted itself to authority. Modernity is an attitude in which people dare to know, dare to use their own reason and judgement without looking back over their shoulders for some authority to give sanction to their thought and actions. For Foucault, Kant describes Enlightenment as the moment of autonomy when humanity puts its own reason to use: 'it is precisely at this moment that the critique is necessary, since its role is that of defining the conditions under which the use of reason is legitimate in order to determine what can be known, what must be done, and what may be hoped'.[26] The illegitimate use of reason leads to dogmatism, and it is this that Foucault aims to avoid by not creating any grand designs or schemes for the future or setting himself up as an authority whose prescriptions for a better society have to be followed to the letter. Instead, Foucault wants us to use this space of relative freedom in which a critical rationality and reflexivity can operate to analyse and critique existing power relations, as well as our own constitution as historical selves. This can lead us to reject what is no longer indispensable for the autonomous constitution of ourselves.

At the same time, though, this critical ontology has not only to be negatively concerned with the analysis of the historical limits imposed on us, it must also be a positive experiment with the possibility of going beyond those limits. To this end, Foucault turns to Baudelaire who recommended that modern individuals make themselves into works of art, like the dandy who makes his body, behaviour and style something that is his own creation. Again, through Baudelaire, Foucault is recommending an aesthetic of self-creation rather than a morality of self-searching and self-judgement: not a discovery of self, but an invention of self. Just as in the study of madness, where Foucault believed that the voice of unreason could only be heard in art and philosophy that presented the transgression of present rules and a remaking of self as a person's own creation, he is once again recommending an aesthetic of existence to combat modern forms of subjection.

Yet many questions remain about both the practicality and desirability of much of this. While Foucault has provided many insights into the creation of self in modern Western society, there are aspects of his work that also need critical attention and reconstruction.

A critical reconsideration of the Foucauldian self

As I mentioned earlier in this chapter, one of the main criticisms of Foucault's work has been that he has extended the style of disciplinary practices and punitive rationality to be found in asylums and prisons to the whole of society, where such systems do not operate so intensively. Using the work of the British cultural theorist Raymond Williams as a counterpoint to Foucault, Edward Said claimed that:

> however dominant a social system may be, the very meaning of its domination involves a limitation or selection of the activities it covers, so that by definition it cannot exhaust all social experience, which therefore always potentially contains space for alternative acts and alternative intentions which are not yet articulated as a social institution or even project.[27]

Thus, while Foucault set out to show how experience is constituted in the Western world in relation to fields of scientific knowledge and the rules of normativity, this cannot exhaust all of experience, as there is always potentially a place for the interactive creation of alternative forms of knowledge, experience and modes of relating to oneself. In the last chapter we saw how Vološinov referred to this as unofficial ideology, which is the kind of experience and knowledge of the world that can exist in the more liminal spaces of society. These spaces, which appear between or within the more formal structures of society, are ones in which we can experience what Turner called anti-structure, where society and self are more open to threats and to reconstruction. For example, Foucault himself has referred to how homosexual love is open to reformulation by gays and lesbians, and how this can be a threat to the official structures of society, especially in institutions like the military.[28]

For critics like Charles Taylor, Foucault has missed the ambivalence of disciplinary power in Western society, where disciplines are not only structures of domination imposed on others; they are also modes of self-control that provide the basis for equal participation in social action. As Taylor says of such disciplines, 'they have not only served to feed a system of control; they have also taken the form of genuine self-disciplines which have made possible new kinds of collective action characterized by more egalitarian forms of participation'.[29] Modern society finds its cohesion through common disciplines grounded on a public identity, permitting the participation of equals, rather than the total subjugation of the population to state imposed regulations. A question that remains from Foucault's work is, would an aesthetics of existence provide firmer ground for the collective participation of equals, focused as it is on the individual self as a work of art, rather than on the public identification with others?

Indeed, as I claimed in Chapter 1, Adam Smith re-interpreted the stoic ethic of self-mastery in a more democratic way for modern individuals, whereby the relation to our own selves is no longer mediated by a philosophical master because commercial society has widened the number and range of other people with whom we interact. We see ourselves, therefore, not only in the reflection of particular revered or authoritative others, but in the general reflection of broader groups of people from different backgrounds, cultures and ethnicities, who can all be our teacher and our judge. Modern commercial society thus broadens the view that we can take of our own self, rather than limiting it to the view of authorities, and also provides a broad public basis for more generalized forms of identification with others. This is why we are capable of seeing our selves in a more impartial, or perhaps more accurately in Mead's term, generalized way in contemporary society, rather than judging ourselves from the standpoint of particularized authority figures.

Michael Walzer has also picked up on the ambivalence of power in Western modernity, claiming that discourses such as that of the rule of law, with its application to all in society, can be used by the powerless just as much as by the powerful. For example, prisoners use basic notions of the rule of law when they complain about prison conditions or about punishments that go beyond what is required by their legal sentence. Thus,

> Foucault is certainly right to say that conventional truths of morality, law, medicine and psychiatry are implicated in the exercise of power ... But those same truths also regulate the exercise of power. They set limits on what can rightly be done, and they give shape and conviction to the arguments the prisoners make.[30]

What Foucault doesn't provide, then, is an account of the liberal state and the rule of law that regulates disciplinary arrangements across society. This is part of the network of power relations, but it also offers a critical perspective on all the networks of constraint, and can be used by those who are most constrained against the powers that work to limit and change them. In this way, we can see how particular selves can use discourses to articulate their own experience and sense of justice within particular contexts: they should therefore not be understood only as the *products* of power, for they clearly have some degree of autonomy – albeit socially created and regulated – in which to re-employ society's discourses and rules, be critical of the powers that work on them, and reconstruct themselves and society in the process.

This leads to a central paradox in the work of Foucault, indeed in many styles of social theory influenced by Nietzschean thinking about the self, as it wants to deconstruct the very idea of individual selfhood, which is viewed only as a creation of modern power, but then it ends up calling on some notion of the autonomous individual self, or at least a self capable of its own self-creation, as a means of overcoming the power that is said to constitute it in its entirety. The notion of an aesthetic of the self seems to evoke images of an individual with the ultimate freedom to make of his or her self what they will, without the constraints of any external authority. This requires what Jane Flax has referred to as a 'deep subjectivity' as a pre-requisite for social change, a self with the capacity for aesthetic or mystical experience.[31] Yet as Taylor has pointed out, this idea of the self also has its own historical ontology in Western thinking, being rooted in the Romantic or 'expressivist' tradition in philosophy and art that I described in Chapter 1, which forged a link between self-discovery and artistic creation. The artist was seen as a hero, as a creator of something original, and therefore one who is set against all forms of received tradition and social conformity. They are people who challenge both established artistic conventions *and* social morality more generally, pushing at the limits of what can be said and done, thereby providing new ways of seeing, thinking and living. Despite the intentions of thinkers like Foucault, this also fits into the ethics of authenticity, for the self as an original and individual creation is seen as authentic for that person, rather than as the product of social conformism. As Taylor goes on to show, self-definition and originality are then contrasted to morality and conformity, so that:

> the demands of self-truth, contact with self, harmony within ourselves could be quite different from the demands of right treatment that we were expected to accord to others. Indeed, the very idea of originality and the associated notion that the enemy of authenticity can be social conformity, forces on us the idea that authenticity will have to struggle against *some* externally imposed rules.[32]

There is, then, 'a notional difference between these two kinds of demand, that of truth to self and those of intersubjective justice'.[33] We can see these two kinds of demand at work in Foucault's later writings, when he says that gays should seek to become who they are by forging new types of relations and interactions with others. But how do we square an aesthetic of self, focused on individual stylization, with the relational demands that will inevitably be made upon us by others? Indeed, in forging new relationships, we reconstruct ourselves not only according to our own design, but within and through a dialogue with others. Also, as Taylor has commented, the ethic of authenticity requires a horizon of significance that makes it intelligible, and self-creation requires a dialogic context in which this can occur. In others words, to become our own self-creation, we need others to recognize that fact and also to highly value our originality: this is the very reason that modern people seek to be individuals in their own right, because of the positive recognition from others they can gain through it.

It is true that in his studies on ancient Greco-Roman society, Foucault does make brief references to social interaction and to people transforming themselves with the help of others. In terms of the care of self, the role of counsellor, guide, friend and teacher is seen as important. However, as Barry Smart points out, little attempt is made to elaborate on this, to explore the relationships with others at the heart of social life, the ethical significance of which cannot be confined to a relation with the self alone.[34] Care for self and care for others must somehow go together, yet Foucault's work barely explores this issue. There is also the criticism that Foucault has misread the function of ethics in classical antiquity, which was not primarily about self-fashioning, as there were normalizing forces at work here, just as there are in modern societies. Lois McNay,[35] and Cohen and Saller,[36] in their different ways, claim that whatever liberties the ancient Greco-Romans possessed in the control of their daily activities, these must be set more broadly in the network of social and political obligations demanded by others, by the state, and by law. In addition, Davidson illustrates how Stoic ethics were oriented to the norms of universal cosmic reason, which could be located in the higher regions of the self by looking inwards.[37] Perhaps in order to give an illustration of the possibility of an ascetic that did not demand conformity to some general norms, Foucault looked at ancient society in a rather selective manner.

However, what I want to focus on here in the critique of Foucault's work is the under-emphasis on relations to others, and also the over-extension of forms of scientific, medical and legal knowledge and practice to constitute the whole of experience and of the self. Certainly there is great value in Foucault's analysis of experience as constituted when the body enters the machinery of power, knowledge and discipline. It helps us to understand how many of what Merleau-Ponty called our embodied stable dispositional tendencies – movements, habits, gestures and perceptions – are actually constituted by disciplines in which we have been trained in various institutions. In schools, for example, the child's body is made to sit and pay attention to lessons, responding and participating with others in certain ways only under the instruction of a teacher or classroom assistant. All of us will have been through some experience of such discipline, in families, schools, colleges or other institutions. Yet as I have already noted, disciplinary power is not the dominant factor in all relationships, or in every place and moment of experience. For example, Mark Poster has said that Foucault has left out of his analyses the emotional dimension of our lives, particularly in our sexual and family relationships. Emotions are not just constituted by external discourses imposed on the individual; they are also constituted internally through the constellation of interactions.[38] There are, then, places and times for experiences and perceptions not wholly constituted within disciplinary power.

For example, other historical research suggests that forms of identity based on sexual orientation began to develop prior to the medicalization of sexuality in the 19th century. Randolph Trumbach has detailed how in England, France and the Dutch Republic around 1700 a group of men began to emerge who became identified as 'mollies' or 'sodomites' because their sexual desires were directed exclusively towards other adult or adolescent males. Prior to this, Trumbach argues, sexual relationships between men were conducted on similar grounds to those in ancient Greece, in that it was not uncommon for older men to court and have sex with younger men, especially adolescents. Here age was the defining feature in sexual relations, and men who had sex with other men were more often than not married, or carried on sexual relations with women. However, in 18th-century northwest Europe mollies or sodomites were singled out on the basis of their exclusive sexual attraction to, and sexual activity with, other men: in this they became almost like a third gender, separate from married men and women. Indeed, it was thought that mollies could be identified by their effeminate behaviour or by the fact that some dressed in women's clothes. In London, because of physical attacks upon them, sodomites constructed around themselves a protective subculture of meeting places and ritual behaviour. It was only towards the end of the 18th century that women who had sex with other women came to be called 'sapphists' or 'tommies' and identified by their sexual orientation and by their supposedly masculine characteristics or behaviour.[39]

Why this began to happen at the turn of the 18th century in northwest Europe no one is exactly sure, although Trumbach suggests that it was to do with the new type of relations that developed between men and women within society and the family, in which there was greater equality between the two genders. On this basis was founded the romantic courtship between prospective marriage partners, the close friendship of husbands and wives, and the loving care of children. The fear around these arrangements was that men and women were becoming less distinct, and that in the process men were becoming more feminized, a fear that was allayed by identifying a man as someone who sexually desired only women. Now, it was no longer permissible for the majority of adult males to desire both males and females, although many still did, with some acting upon it. Many married men were among the regular visitors to the 'molly-houses'. But the mollies or sodomites were themselves effeminate and so not like the majority of men. *For me, though, the important point about this is that such changing social relations, behaviour and categorization of identities, and with it the refashioning of sexual desire, was a product of the changing nature of everyday life in the 18th century and not, primarily, to do with expert discourses.* These began to emerge in the 19th century in northwest Europe, no doubt on the basis of the categorizations emerging from the socially and historically formed interactions between individuals in everyday life. Indeed, as George Chauncey has claimed, 'the invert and the normal man, the homosexual and the heterosexual, were not inventions of the elite but were popular discursive categories before they became elite discursive categories'.[40]

A number of different factors, then, appear to have shaped the changing ways in which people experienced their sexuality in northwest Europe in the 18th and 19th centuries, both in terms of identity and desire. In an article that reviews a range of historical explanations for this change, Jan Löfström suggests there are four main factors that led to the emergence of the modern homosexual: the rise of competitive capitalism, the development of expert knowledge, tensions in the gender order, and urban anonymity. Competitive capitalism ran against the grain of intimate friendships between men, who now had to be competitors in an impersonal market economy. Emotional closeness between men thus became suspect, and was replaced, as Trumbach suggested, by the new intimacy of husband and wife in the bourgeois family. This, however, created tensions in the gender order, especially with the increasing emphasis placed on the idea that male and female were two completely separate genders, as differences had to be found that demarcated men from women, one of which became a clear heterosexual orientation. The rise of urban living also created a pluralistic and relatively anonymous life-world where distinct subcultures could emerge, such as that found in London's molly-houses. Finally, at the end of the 19th century expert classification in medicine and law did have an important impact in naming and demarcating homosexual and heterosexual, as both Foucault and Jeffrey Weeks[41] have detailed, but it is not wholly accurate to say as Foucault did in Volume One of *The History of Sexuality* that this created the homosexual as a species: that is, one whose sexuality was a fundamental orientation of the self. Mollies, fairies, queens, sodomites, sapphists and tommies had existed for almost two centuries before that on the streets of London and some other major European cities (later in New York). As Löfström summarizes:

> The learned discourses of law and medicine were but one of many parameters framing the organization of homosexual experience in the life-world of urban pluralist society. In a sense, the learned theories of 'homosexual condition' were induced by the reality of people arranging their life in new ways. Of course, the learned conceptions often fed back on people's identities and experiences …[42]

It is not exactly the case, then, to claim that authorities and professions, woven into the networks of power and discourse, *constructed* homosexual identity and experience. They perhaps redistributed it around a new norm, at the centre of which was heterosexual marriage, and reclassified homosexuals as medical or psychiatric cases, making it clear they were to be seen as a deviation from the norm. In the process, they lowered the threshold of *official* description on an ordinary gay individuality that was already forming itself *unofficially* within the social relationships and interactions of everyday urban life. The official description no doubt changed homosexual experience and self-identity, but it did not wholly make it; and because of that, homosexuals and lesbians had a social basis, in their relations with others and in their changing subculture, for resistance against official classification and in the fight for rights. Lived experience and self is therefore constituted in family, friendship, acquaintances, work, the streets, and in meeting places, as well as in institutions of various sorts, thereby being composed of a heteroglossia of discourses, both unofficial and official. In these contexts, sexuality is composed by the erotic as well as by categories of identity: it is about desire for others, for bodily pleasure, mutual satisfaction, excitement, and fantasies that involve self-image and the image of others. It also encompasses emotions like love and the need for companionship. While we do not invent our sexuality for ourselves, because certain experiences of self are only possible in particular social and historical contexts – no one in the West would have been 'gay' 500 years ago – we nevertheless *in-habit* sexuality as more than just an identity: we do so as a bodily self that lives life and dreams with its flesh. Being a molly, homosexual or gay man is therefore not just to be subject to an official classification, it is also to enact a desire or fantasy in places where others of like disposition meet to share pleasures of the flesh. Merleau-Ponty was right to see sexuality as a form of bodily perception of the world.

To begin to think in this way is also to allow a more complex understanding of the self, like the one I am trying to develop here, in which the self is understood as constituted in many social contexts and by a heteroglossia of discourses within which it must struggle to find its own unified voice. As we have seen, particularly through the work of Bakhtin, becoming a self is not just about the influence of authoritative discourse, which demands to be heard and seeks to impose values and disciplines; nor is it about the self constituting itself in its own free style: rather, we become selves in a dialogic intermingling of the relation to others and the relation to ourselves. There are always 'others-for-me', and I can exist only as an 'I-for-others', in which state I can also become (under certain conditions) an 'I-for-myself'. The relation to oneself can therefore never exist without the primary relation to others. Indeed, one could argue that the relation to self is just as important for us moderns as it was for the Greeks and Romans, and that it allows us greater degrees of liberty and autonomy within the state, which seeks to impose certain normative regularities. In this context, especially in dialogic relations to others who are near equals, such as friends or colleagues, the making of self takes place in an interactive context that is not solely about self-analysis.

For example, as I claimed in the last chapter, practices like confession have dimensions to them other than those created in the relation to pastors, doctors, psychologists or counsellors. While confession can always have a coercive element to it, being surrounded by a subtle atmosphere of moral torture, with intimates it can also have the function of actually revealing or making the self. Although in one of his later lectures, Foucault revised his theory that confession was a forcible extraction of truth, being more about a speech act in which an individual 'publishes himself',[43] this idea can be developed. As Bakhtin understood, there is a language of mutual authorship in contemporary society that is not wholly determined by official scientific, medical or legal discourses, because there is a heteroglossia of linguistic styles for self-expression and the constitution of experience in which it is hard to establish any single authoritative discourse. Other discourses are always available that we may find more internally persuasive. Modern novels, popular music, films and TV shows, especially soap operas, may be equally as important in providing us with discourses that give expression to our own self, our sexuality and emotions, as scientific, medical and legal discourses. It is true, of course, that there is little separation between different discourses or speech genres, as these tend to infiltrate and influence each other. Thus, we may find the use of psychoanalytic ideas in novels and in films: yet these are not the only forms of discourse such media employ. Popular culture (and 'high' culture too) draws on the language of the everyday, developed in the streets, homes, work and leisure places, as well as on concepts taken from the sciences. In this light, it is interesting to remember Poster's remark that Foucault has generally ignored the emotional content of our sexual and social relations:

could that be because the language which gives such relationships their form and content is not to be found in scientific, philosophical, legal or any other form of official documentation studied in his genealogy, but in the everyday life and language captured in novels and other entertainments?

It is true that the lives of most modern people can be found in official documentation; in medical, educational, financial, legal, or any other form of case file owned by various agencies or by the state. But are we constituted as selves only by such documentation? Do we always recognize the description of ourselves in such files? Like Dmitry on trial in the Dostoevsky novel *The Brothers Karamazov,* described in the last chapter, we may feel that such descriptions miss the living core of dialogue, decision and doubt at the heart of ourselves, instead replacing this with categories that do not actually compose or describe our experience. There is always a word we can put in about ourselves, even if it is spoken only silently to ourselves, which says, 'You don't know me. I am not really like that'. In this instance, we have another definition of ourselves, worked out in everyday language and interaction with significant others, that provides a different viewpoint on ourselves. Indeed, as I have said, the images we have of our own self, created in dialogues with self and with others, are composed in a heteroglossia of discursive or linguistic genres and practices. The relation we have to our own self through this heteroglossic dialogue allows us some degree of distance from official forms of classification. They may surround us in a world of judgement – 'You are mad', 'You are sick', 'You are criminal', 'Return to normality' – but we also have the means, both official (such as the rule of law) and unofficial (our everyday speech genres) to challenge and contest this, judging the powers that would impose themselves upon us.

One of the responses that could be mounted to this is that Foucault has understood the seductive nature of modern power, in that it no longer comes in the form of an authoritative discourse, but as a more internally persuasive discourse. Power in modern societies is found in the forms of discourse that seek to persuade us they are good for us, that they can help us. Medicine wants to make us healthy, psychology to improve our potential, education our employability, the criminal justice system wants to make us responsible. All of this is true. Even so, I think the argument still stands that these are not the only internally persuasive discourses that play a part in the constitution of our selves. And ultimately, as Bakhtin claimed, there is never a complete description of ourselves in any form of discourse, as we are always in the process of becoming who we are, and therefore are never finalized or completed.

If we accept this view of the self, it is true to say that it is often hard to find a unified voice amidst such heteroglossia of discourses, or to be certain of any truth about ourselves. Yet perhaps we can find something like this in those moments of recognition, revealing and mutual authoring of identities I described in the last chapter, where we attempt to tell the truth about ourselves to others and to listen to their response in an open manner, recognizing who they are in the process. In this sense, the truth of ourselves is not to be found in some ultimate revelation – the absolute and final description of who we are – but in the ongoing ethical performances enacted in relations with others. This is an ongoing process occurring in interaction with others – some authoritative figures, others not – in which we find an understanding of ourselves that makes sense within our own experience. The truth of our selves, then, is not so much a revelation as an ethical practice, a way of relating to others. As Farber has said, 'I think that speaking truthfully is a more fitting ambition than speaking the truth'.[44] Although Foucault would no doubt sympathize with this more practical and modest notion of truth, the point I am making is that this does not necessarily involve an aesthetics of self: it is a way of building relationships of care and attention to others that we can practice in our everyday lives here and now, which can act as a challenge to overly authoritative forms of social and self discipline.

In this context, the confession can still be understood as a truth game, but one that, as Gardiner says, for Bakhtin,

> is indicative of the most intense and profound form of dialogue that can occur between two human beings. The confession tears away external, 'second-hand' definitions that have been foisted upon us, and reveals to the gaze of the other a naked and vulnerable self, thereby exposing the 'depths of the human soul'.[45]

Thus, in Bakhtin's social ontology, the confession is ambiguous and two-sided: it can be an intimate act of self-revealing to a trusted other, or it can emerge from a social atmosphere where coercion hangs more subtly in the air. Confession, truth-telling and the formation of self in relation to others – and to one's own self – are complex and ambivalent in the modern age.

For example, Strozier argues that had Foucault lived longer, he would have had to reassess his earlier work on the Enlightenment tradition, because thinkers like Descartes were actually describing a new form of self-relation, one in which the self is not only the subject of knowledge, and therefore subjected to it, but can take knowledge as the object of its own critical reflection. Therefore, 'the individual can now argue a unique interiority by claiming that this interiority is no longer accessible to knowledge'.[46] It is this capacity of the modern subject to know itself by a reflective relation to itself that forms the historically constituted 'essence' of modern selves and the basis of our agency. However, while the notion of the subject as subjected to knowledge and language was the deconstructive target of many French thinkers in the 1960s, including not only Foucault but also philosophers like Derrida, the notion that the Enlightenment had historically brought about the capacities for degrees of autonomous agency was often ignored (except for Foucault's late essay 'What is Enlightenment?').

Furthermore, as I indicated in Chapter 1, this deconstruction of self may be entirely misconceived, confusing political and metaphysical critiques of individualism with the existence of everyday selves. For those who critique the subject, the aim of the critique is the *metaphysical subject:* the idea that the self is transcendental, existing prior to society, history and culture. We have already seen that this philosophical notion of the subject has come in for a long and sustained critical scrutiny, not only from Nietzsche, but from the pragmatist tradition and those who follow it. Yet while Nietzsche and Foucault see the critique of the subject leading to a destruction of the very concept, the pragmatists tended to explain the self as a practical construction of the interactions of everyday life. This is not the transcendental subject of Descartes and Kant, but the practical self of everyday interaction. In this, the self is not the subject of knowledge as described by Foucault: that is, the subject who establishes a relation to himself or herself only through fields of study with their various discourses, including epistemological concepts and normative rules. In this view, the self becomes the product of Enlightenment reason and philosophy, of *episteme,* and can only be saved from that fate by the avant-garde intellectual who transgresses and deconstructs this discourse. As Flax has said, this may be nothing more than a self-serving illusion.[47]

Instead of this, pragmatism, phenomenology and Bakhtin's dialogical approach all attempt to create a socially situated understanding of the self, particularly in terms of how identities are formed, sustained and continually reconstructed with others in the everyday world. One could say this is the 'ordinary individuality' that Foucault referred to in *Discipline and Punish,* which is increasingly subject to various forms of categorization and description by the biological and human sciences, along with the disciplining of the body in various overlapping institutions. The crucial question, though, as I have already illustrated here, is the degree to which this has occurred and how we can establish and strengthen the kinds of free association between people in which reconstructed forms of selfhood can emerge.

For me, what the work of thinkers like Mead, Merleau-Ponty and Bakhtin illustrate is that there can be a critique of both individualism and the metaphysics of the self without confusing this with a complete abandonment of the concept of the self as constituted in the dialogue and interactions of social relations. In their view, the self that is formed in a reflexive and reflective relation to itself, with some degree of autonomous agency, is an everyday reality within a particular social and historical ontology. One of the great things about Foucault's work was that he showed precisely how the self comes into being only in such a social and historical ontology: yet the over-extension of his ideas on disciplinary rationality means we should use them only in a critical context to gain a more rounded understanding of the self in the contemporary Western world.

Notes

1. Michel Foucault (1986) 'Preface to *The History of Sexuality, Volume II'*, in *The Foucault Reader,* edited by Paul Rabinow. London: Penguin. pp. 333–9, pp. 333–4.
2. Michel Foucault (1967) *Madness and Civilization: A History of Insanity in the Age of Reason.* Tr. R. Howard. London: Routledge, 1987 edn.
3. Michel Foucault, 'Preface', p. 336.
4. Michel Foucault, *Madness,* p. 267.
5. Ibid., p. 278.
6. Michel Foucault (1977) *Discipline and Punish: The Birth of the Prison.* Tr. Alan Sheridan. Harmondsworth: Penguin. p. 23.
7. Ibid., p. 48

8. Ibid., pp. 137–8.
9. Ibid., p. 170. My emphasis.
10. Michel Foucault (1980) *Power/Knowledge,* edited by Colin Gordon. Brighton: Harvester Press. p. 98.
11. Michel Foucault, *Discipline*, p. 191.
12. Ibid., p. 298.
13. Ibid., p. 29.
14. Michel Foucault (1982) 'Afterword: the subject and power', in H. L. Dreyfus and P. Rabinow, *Michel Foucault: Beyond Structuralism and Hermeneutics.* Brighton: Harvester. pp. 208–26, p. 212.
15. Michel Foucault (1970) *The Order of Things: An Archaeology of the Human Sciences.* London: Routledge, 1997 edn.
16. Michel Foucault (1979) *The History of Sexuality, Volume. 1: An Introduction.* Tr. Robert Hurley. Harmondsworth: Penguin.
17. Ibid., p. 23.
18. Ibid., p. 26.
19. Ibid., p. 43.
20. Ibid., p.45.
21. Michel Foucault, 'Afterword'.
22. Michel Foucault (1986) *The Use of Pleasure: The History of Sexuality, Volume 2.* Tr. Robert Hurley. London: Penguin.
23. Michel Foucault (1988) *The Care of the Self: The History of Sexuality, Volume 3.* Tr. Robert Hurley. London: Penguin. p. 66.
24. Michel Foucault (1983) 'On the genealogy of ethics: an overview of work in progress', in Paul Rabinow (ed.), *Ethics: Subjectivity and Truth.* London: Penguin, 2000 edn. pp. 253–80, pp. 256–7.
25. Michel Foucault (1981) 'Friendship as a way of life', in Paul Rabinow (ed.), *Ethics: Subjectivity and Truth.* London: Penguin. pp. 135–40, p. 138.
26. Michel Foucault (1986) 'What is enlightenment?', in Paul Rabinow (ed.), *The Foucault Reader.* London: Penguin. pp. 32–50, p. 38.
27. Edward W. Said (1986) 'Foucault and the imagination of power', in David Couzens Hoy (ed.), *Foucault: A Critical Reader.* Oxford: Blackwell. pp. 149–55, p. 154.
28. Michel Foucault (1982/3) 'Sexual choice, sexual act', in Paul Rabinow (ed.), *Ethics: Subjectivity and Truth.* London: Penguin. 2000 edn. pp. 141–56.
29. Charles Taylor (1986) 'Foucault on freedom and truth', in David Couzens Hoy (ed.), *Foucault: A Critical Reader.* Oxford: Blackwell. pp. 69–102, p. 81–2.
30. Michael Walzer (1986) 'The politics of Michel Foucault', in David Couzens Hoy (ed.), *Foucault: A Critical Reader.* Oxford: Blackwell. pp. 51–68, p. 65.
31. Jane Flax (1990) *Thinking Fragments: Psychoanalysis, Feminism, and Postmodernism in the Contemporary West.* Berkeley: University of California Press. p. 204.
32. Charles Taylor (1991) *The Ethics of Authenticity.* Cambridge, MA: Harvard University Press. p. 63.
33. Ibid.
34. Barry Smart (1998) 'Foucault, Levinas and the subject of responsibility', in Jeremy Moss (ed.), *The Later Foucault: Politics and Philosophy.* London: Sage. pp.78–92.
35. Lois McNay (1992) *Foucault and Feminism: Power, Gender and the Self.* Cambridge: Polity Press.
36. David Cohen and Richard Saller (1994) 'Foucault on sexuality in Greco-Roman antiquity', in Jan Ellen Goldstein (ed.), *Foucault and the Writing of History.* Oxford: Blackwell. pp. 35–59.

37. Arnold I. Davidson (1994) 'Ethics as ascetics: Foucault, the history of ethics, and ancient thought', in Jan Goldstein (ed.), *Foucault and the Writing of History.* pp. 62–80.

38. Mark Poster (1986) 'Foucault and the tyranny of Greece', in David Couzens Hoy (ed.), *Foucault: A Critical Reader.* Oxford: Blackwell. pp. 205–20.

39. Randolph Trumbach (1998) *Sex and the Gender Revolution, Volume One: Heterosexuality and the Third Gender in Enlightenment London.* Chicago: University of Chicago Press.

40. George Chauncey (1994) *Gay New York: Gender, Urban Culture, and the Making of the Gay Male World, 1890–1940.* New York: Basic Books.

41. Jeffery Weeks (1977) *Coming Out: Homosexual Politics in Britain from the Nineteenth Century to the Present.* London: Quartet Books, revised edn 1990.

42. Jan Löfström (1997) 'The birth of the queen/the modern homosexual: historical explanations revisited', *The Sociological Review,* 45 (1): 24–41, p. 33–4.

43. Michel Foucault (1993) 'About the beginning of the hermeneutics of the self', in J. Carrette (ed.), *Michel Foucault: Religion and Culture.* New York: Routledge, 1999 edn. pp.158–81.

44. Cited in Adam Phillips (2000) *Promises, Promises.* London: Faber and Faber. p. 313.

45. Michael Gardiner (1996) 'Foucault, ethics and dialogue', *History of the Human Sciences,* 9 (3): 27–46, p. 39.

46. Robert M. Strozier (2002) *Foucault, Subjectivity and Identity: Historical Constructions of Subject and Self.* Detroit: Wayne State University Press. p. 19.

47. Jane Flax, *Thinking,* p. 204.

Selected bibliography

Foucault, Michel (1977) *Discipline and Punish: The Birth of the Prison.* Tr. Alan Sheridan. Harmondsworth: Penguin.

Foucault, Michel (1979) *The History of Sexuality, Volume. 1: An Introduction.* Tr. Robert Hurley. Harmondsworth: Penguin.

Foucault, Michel (1986) *The Use of Pleasure: The History of Sexuality, Volume 2.* Tr. Robert Hurley. London: Penguin.

Foucault, Michel (1988) *The Care of the Self: The History of Sexuality, Volume 3.* Tr. Robert Hurley. London: Penguin.

Foucault, Michel (2000) *Ethics: Subjectivity and Truth,* edited by Paul Rabinow. London: Penguin.

Hoy, David Couzens (ed.) (1986) *Foucault: A Critical Reader.* Oxford: Blackwell.

Löfström, Jan (1997) 'The birth of the queen/the modern homosexual: historical explanations revisited', *The Sociological Review,* 45 (1): 24–41.

Jeremy Moss (ed) (1998) *The Later Foucault: Politics and Philosophy.* London: Sage.

Robert M. Strozier (2002) *Foucault, Subjectivity and Identity: Historical Constructions of Subject and Self.* Detroit: Wayne State University Press.

Trumbach, Randolph (1998) *Sex and the Gender Revolution, Volume One: Heterosexuality and the Third Gender in Enlightenment London.* Chicago: University of Chicago Press.

CHAPTER 5

GENDER, SEXUALITY AND IDENTITY

Of all the things with which we could identify ourselves, our sex and gender would seem to be the most basic and irrefutable thing. If we were pressed to answer the question 'who am I?' we could at the very least say 'I am a man' or 'I am a woman'. That we are either one sex or the other seems to be the most basic of biological facts, which grounds our identity in physiology as either male or female. Indeed, when someone is expecting a baby, the first question we often ask them is 'do you know yet if it's a boy or a girl', probably because this question gives us the first clue as to the possible identity of the child. Yet there is so much more to both sex and gender than this, an inkling of which is given in the question asked of parents-to-be: that is, the cultural and historical weight of meaning given to sex and gender in the modern age. Indeed, as we saw in the last chapter, Michel Foucault has argued that for modern Westerners 'it is in the area of sex that we must search for the most secret and profound truths about the individual, that it is there that we can best discover what he is and what determines him'.[1] Whether a child is a boy or a girl, then, shapes our expectations of its behaviour, activities, interests, feelings, emotions, sexuality, self-identity, ways of relating to other people, and its future.

Yet because of this not everyone qualifies as being a man or a woman, or at least not a 'proper' one, because sometimes children fail to live up to these cultural expectations. When I was growing up in the 1960s I would often hear people saying of someone 'He's a *real* man', which seemed to indicate a male who was physically strong and active, athletic (usually mad on football), who was good at practical tasks rather than being overly intellectual, and didn't show too much emotion. As a boy who didn't like football, was interested in music and arts rather than sport, enjoyed doing English at school rather than sciences, and was perceived to be quiet and sensitive, I was pretty sure I didn't qualify as a 'real man'. But then where does that leave a person? If you are 'really' neither male nor female, what are you? What this illustrates is that sex and gender are more like statuses we have to attain, or identities attributed by ourselves and others, rather than natural and inescapable facts. Yet the issue is more interesting than this, because it centrally involves the human body in questions of identity, revolving around how we relate to our bodies and what we make of them and how we inhabit the world. It is because of this that we regard sex and gender as something natural to us.

Furthermore, sex and gender are also closely related to sexuality, as the division between male and female maps directly onto that between gay and straight. As I showed in the last chapter, it was precisely at that historical time and place when people were trying to make a rigid distinction between the male and female sex that some men and women were identified who were exclusively sexually attracted to others of the same sex. Such categorizations make sense only in a world unambiguously divided between men and women, where the other that you desire is clearly either male or female. The difficulty is, though, we do not live in such a world. Increasingly in the last 15–20 years social scientists have become aware of those individuals who are intersexed: that is, people born with a physiology and biology that are neither clearly male nor female. Such individuals are currently providing interesting challenges to the gender binary because they show how difficult it is for modern biological science (whether in terms of anatomy, hormones or chromosomes) to actually maintain clear divisions between the two sexes in indeterminate cases, and also because some intersexuals are now speaking out to say that they do not want to become either males or females but to live as a 'third gender', just to 'be themselves'. In so doing, they are causing us to rethink our ideas about sex and gender.

Sex and gender as identity and performance

Since the publication of Ann Oakley's book *Sex, Gender and Society* in 1972, social scientists have tended to distinguish between the terms sex and gender. Sex is taken to be a biological given, because it is thought that in all times and places people have been born as women and men, and have been able to identify themselves as such for the purposes of sexual reproduction. In contrast, gender refers to the roles, behaviours and characteristics of men and women, which we know are hugely variable across time and between different cultures. Sex, then, refers to biological fact, while gender is dependent on culture and is variable and malleable. However, this rather neat distinction has been opened to question by a number of thinkers, because gender and sex are so closely interrelated. When we meet someone we take to be a man, we not only believe that to be his gender, but also his sex. This has led the social psychologist Suzanne Kessler to argue that we should do away with the term sex and use only the term gender, because when we impute a gender to someone, sex is also included as a central element of that imputation.

Along with Wendy McKenna, Kessler argued that gender was something we attribute to others on the basis of the way they perform in social interaction – on the basis of a 'gender display' – rather than in terms of a person's physiology alone. For example, when we meet people we usually attribute a gender to them, assuming them to be either a man or a woman. Yet how do we know they are? With most people we meet we do not see their genitals (which are usually taken to be the deciding factor as to whether a person is biologically male or female), but attribute their gender in terms of other factors such as movement, behaviour, speech, dress, hairstyle, facial structure, body shape and build, and other physical features. It is a combination of all these things that decides for us whether someone is male or female. As Kessler and McKenna pointed out from their ethnomethodological research, once people have attributed a gender to someone, they are then prepared to discount other features that might call into question their attribution. So, for example, if we have decided from a range of different factors that a person is female, we are then prepared to discount the fact that she has a lower voice than most other women, thinking of her as a 'woman with a low voice'. In other words, if we have decided, on balance, that a person is either male or female, we are prepared to allow for certain features that are usually associated with the opposite sex without calling into question our primary gender attribution. We can then have women with deep voices and men with light voices, or powerful and assertive women and passive and non-assertive men. Indeed, this is usually the case, as all people have some balance of both masculine and feminine characteristics.

Along with gender attribution we also make the attribution of sex, assuming that those we have assigned as male or female have the correct body morphology, including genitalia. For example, in one of Kessler and McKenna's studies, a little boy was shown a drawing of a person with male features dressed in a business suit, then asked whether this was a man or a woman. The little boy had no problem in saying this was a man, but when asked why he thought so he replied, 'because he has a pee-pee'.[2] This was the case even though the drawing depicted the man fully dressed, with only his face and hands showing. Kessler and McKenna refer to this as the attribution of 'cultural genitals', in that what the little boy did, the rest of us also do in everyday interactions: when we have attributed a gender to someone based on cultural criteria, we then assume that behind their clothing and appearance, their physiology (and, thus, their sex) matches the gender attribution we have made.

Equally, the reproductive capacity of persons is not always important in the attribution of gender. If we were to meet a childless couple, we would make attributions of their gender in the usual ways, and we would also make the attribution of heterosexuality if their performance supported the attribution of male and female, even though we may have no evidence about their genitals or their sex life. Even if we were to find out that one of them couldn't have children for biological reasons, we would still attribute a gender to them on the basis of their overall performance rather than their biological body or capacity to reproduce. Thus, Kessler and McKenna claim that gender is a social construction, and that gender attribution depends on social interaction. In turn, attribution involves two key factors: firstly, the performance of the people whom we meet and the way they present themselves in order to convey the proper cues as to their gender: and secondly, the cultural rules that each of us has learned from childhood that provide the basis for deciding what is to be regarded as masculine and feminine. Together these things operate in a complex process of social interaction in which gender attributions are both called out and made. Yet as ethnomethodologists Kessler and McKenna believe that the rules for gender attribution are crucial in this process, as they are the cultural means (the ethno-methods) for making a gendered world.

However, there is another important aspect in the attribution of gender, which is the gender that we attribute to our own selves. This may differ radically from the attributions that others make about us. For example, two parents, along with the attendant doctors, nurses or midwife, may believe they have just witnessed the birth of a baby boy, based on the child's genitals or other biological indicators; yet that child may grow up feeling that he should really have been a girl. In this instance, he/she is making an attribution of gender in relation to his/her own self that is divergent from that being made by others. Indeed, for ethnomethodologists like Kessler and McKenna, such instances where transsexuals decide they are really of the opposite sex to the one they were born, and, at some point in their lives, seek to change sex, is a further illustration of sex as a social construction. This stems from Harold Garfinkel's classic ethnomethodological study of a male to female transsexual called 'Agnes', who was in the process of going through sexual reassignment surgery while involved in the research.[3] The conclusion that Garfinkel drew from his study of Agnes was that she was an excellent 'practical methodologist', consciously skilled and capable of producing rational and routine social situations with others in which she successfully 'passed' as a woman, even before she had her sex change operation. This often meant carefully planning events in advance and getting as much information about particular situations as possible – for example, how thorough was a medical examination required for a job she'd applied for – so that she could unquestionably pass as a 'natural woman'. In this way, a socially produced and constructed scenario is made to appear as something inherently natural.

Garfinkel went on to claim that what Agnes is doing in a consciously controlled way is nothing more than what everyone does in an unthinking, taken-for-granted way in everyday life: producing the 'naturalness' of a two-sexed world. However, far from this being a natural fact, Garfinkel believes that the production of two sexes is a 'moral fact' that we rigidly police in everyday life, sanctioning those who do not conform. Indeed, Agnes herself condemned transsexuals who did not want to assign themselves clearly to one gender or the other, along with homosexuals who did not abide by the norms of heterosexual love, regarding herself as a 'natural woman' whose male body had been a mistake, thus normalizing both her gender and her sexuality (she had a boyfriend even before her sex reassignment surgery). For Garfinkel, Agnes can teach us about how 'normal' sexuality is accomplished in everyday interaction, through displays of talk and conduct against the background of commonplace events, which we all take for granted as natural occurrences.

While Kessler and McKenna agree with Garfinkel that the production of the 'natural attitude' is important in passing as a man or a woman, they believe that attribution is more important in this process than a perfect gender performance. What they mean by this is that once people have assigned a gender to someone as a natural fact, they overlook any details in the display of gender that may contradict or be out of line with the original attribution. It is not gender that needs to be sustained through interaction, but the natural attitude, so that we take the gender displayed by those involved in the interaction as a natural, biological given. However, what Kessler and McKenna can't tell us is why biology is seen to be the deciding factor in questions of the naturalness of gender in modern social life. For this we would need to go back to Foucault and his historical research on sexuality, which outlined how biomedical discourses gained authority in the knowledge and management of the domain of sexuality and sexual reproduction in 19th century Europe. From this time onward, it was medical doctors and, more latterly, geneticists who have ultimate authority in questions of sex, sexuality and gender, deciding on matters of what makes someone male or female: indeed, medical surgeons have developed techniques that can actually *make* people into males and females, something I will return to later in this chapter.

Although they do not have a historical perspective, Kessler and McKenna nevertheless recognize the power of biological science and medicine in modern society, as well as understanding how this affects the 'natural attitude' towards gender. That is, in the West we now believe that to pass as a 'real' man or woman in social interactions is not enough: we feel we must also have the correct anatomy to go with the gender we attribute to ourselves and that we want others to attribute to us. For this reason, many male to female transsexuals take oestrogen so that they can develop breasts and more feminine features, and also have surgery to remove their penis and testes and construct a vagina, while female to male transpeople develop a masculine body and physical features by taking testosterone, and have a penis surgically constructed. Despite this, though, Kessler and McKenna argue that it is the social construction of gender in every-day interaction that provides the basis for all scientific research on gender and sex. That is because for scientists to say what biological properties belong to males and to females respectively, thus distinguishing between them – whether this is on the basis of anatomy, hormones or chromosomes – they must be able to distinguish between males and females to begin with. And on what basis do they do this? Kessler and McKenna say: on the basis of everyday cultural processes of gender attribution.

Such attribution has happened from the very beginning of biomedical research on sex and gender. For example, in Foucault's study of the 19th-century French hermaphrodite Herculine Barbin, medical records from the period show how doctors tried to ascertain her/his 'true' sex through anatomical examinations. However, when these proved inconclusive, they resorted to behaviour, tastes and sexual orientation to decide whether Herculine should really be Hercule. On physically examining Herculine (also known as Alexina), a physician called Chesnet noted her thin masculine body and flat hairy chest, but her genitals were indeterminate. He then went on to ask what should be concluded from this –

Is Alexina a woman? She has a vulva, labia majora, and a feminine urethra, independent of a sort of imperforate penis, which might be a monstrously developed clitoris. She has a vagina. True, it is very short, very narrow; but after all, what is it if not a vagina? These are completely feminine attributes. Yes, but Alexina has never menstruated; the whole upper part of her body is that of a man, and my explorations did not allow me to find a womb. Her tastes, her inclinations, draw her towards women. At night she has voluptuous sensations that are followed by a discharge of sperm; her linen is starched and stained with it. Finally, to sum up the matter, ovoid bodies and spermatic chords are found by touch in a divided scrotum. These are the real proofs of sex. We can now conclude and say: Alexina is a man, hermaphroditic, no doubt, but with an obvious predominance of masculine characteristics.[4]

Thus, while Chesnet was swayed by the fact that Herculine (Alexina) produced sperm, he was equally, if not more, convinced by her tastes and inclinations drawing her towards women: it was these factors he interpreted as 'proofs' that Herculine was 'really' and 'truly' a man. This is despite the fact that she was quite happy living as the woman she had been brought up to be, in schools and convents. Foucault comments on this by noting that prior to the dominance of medicine in matters of sex, hermaphrodites like Herculine were assumed to be of both sexes and were given that legal status, allowing for the fact they might eventually choose to favour one sex over the other. It is only when science seeks to control and determine sex that doctors assume the power and the right to assign a person's sex independent of their own wishes or choices. Indeed, Foucault notes from Herculine's memoirs how blissfully happy she seemed prior to medical intervention, living in the limbo of a 'non-identity' amongst her female companions and lovers. However, having read Herculine's memoir, I would say that she wasn't so much living in the happy limbo of a non-identity, because she had a defined personality to which other women responded positively. Rather, it seems she was a non-sex, as it is impossible to clearly define her as male or female, homosexual or heterosexual: she was not asexual, as she clearly had sexual desires for women, but one could not easily say she was lesbian, as she herself was neither male nor female. Herculine clearly does not fit contemporary categories of sex, sexuality and gender, and on being forced to make these choices by living as a man, Herculine took his/her own life, committing suicide at just 29. Prior to this it is perhaps more accurate to say that Herculine had her/his own identity that was neither clearly male or female, until the disastrous day she/he was forced to become male.

In studying more recent attempts in biological research to define people's 'true sex', Kessler and McKenna note that this too is based on prior assumptions and attributions of gender. In biochemical research, in order to distinguish different chromosomal patterns between males and females, scientists match chromosomes to people already defined as male and female. In general, most females are said to have pairs of similar looking chromosomes called XX chromosomes (because of their shape), while men have one chromosome that looks like those in females (X) paired with another shaped like a Y. So most women have XX chromosomes and most men have XY chromosomes, meaning that the Y chromosome is generally taken to be a determinant of male sex. However, as research progressed it was found that this was just the typical arrangement and that there was some variation in the pattern of chromosomes with respect to gender. In certain genetic conditions some males are found to have XX chromosomes, while females can also have a Y chromosome. But given that the Y chromosome is thought of as male, how did endocrinologists know that some people with two X chromosomes were men, while some with a Y chromosome were women? The answer would seem to be that, like the doctors who examined Herculine in the 19th century, today biochemists and geneticists make attributions of gender on the basis of a range of factors, not all of them physical or biological, including a person's appearance, behaviour, social performance, and lifestyle. As Harrison and Hood-Williams put it, commenting on genetic research:

> ... the principal feature of these studies, to which we wish to draw attention, is the apparent tautology of the work from which geneticists may never escape. A simple but glaring problem becomes clear when we ask, how did the scientists know that [some] XX subjects were males? If chromosomal theory provides the marker that determines sex these people must be women. That [they] were able to describe them as unusual men shows us that *they must already know what it is to be a man before they can confirm it genetically* ... To use Kessler and McKenna's framework, we might say that it seeks to ground in 'sex' what it has already defined through gender attribution.[5]

Indeed, chromosome testing to determine sex can produce all kinds of anomalies, with many excellent examples emerging from the testing that goes on in sports competitions. Because the possibility of athletes having surgery and taking hormones to change sex became a reality in the mid-20th century – so that a male to female transperson could take part in women's competitions and perhaps gain an unfair advantage due to having a stronger body – sporting events introduced 'sex chromosome tests' in the 1960s. Eva Klobukowska was stripped of the medals she had won at the 1964 Olympics after taking a test at the 1967 European Track and Field competitions and being declared ineligible to compete as a woman. As Kessler and McKenna report, it is likely she had some XXY cells; yet since then she has continued to live, in her own eyes and others', as a woman.[6] In this instance, through a sex chromosome test, someone was declared not to be a woman, despite the fact that they lived as a woman and thought of themself in that way, as did the others around them. So was Eva a man or a woman? Is there any basis on which an absolute, objective judgement could be made? As Kessler and McKenna say, 'biological, psychological, and social differences do not lead to our seeing two genders. Our seeing of two genders leads to the "discovery" of biological, psychological, and social differences'.[7]

This problem manifests itself most clearly in the case of intersexed babies (as a hermaphrodite like Herculine would be called today), where doctors and parents try to make judgements as to whether a child is male or female based on the child's indeterminate genitals and on some form of genetic testing. But this is because we think that genitals, chromosomes or other biological factors have some objective status that can tell us the truth about what category a child should belong to. We also assume that a child *has* to be clearly either male or female in order to have any kind of liveable life. This is why, when an intersexed baby is born, doctors advise parents on the management of the child's development:

whether to bring them up either as a boy or a girl, or to undergo surgery to make them into a male or a female. As Kessler says, 'physicians hold an incorrigible belief that female and male are the only "natural" options. This paradox highlights and calls into question the idea that female and male are biological givens compelling a culture of two genders'.[8]

In other words, when we use the term 'natural' in this context, what do we mean? Surely, babies whose sex cannot be easily determined at birth by their genitals and body morphology are as much a product of nature as those of us who were more easily assigned to a category of male or female at birth. Sometimes people might say these are 'mistakes' or 'freaks' of nature, but on what basis can humans say that? One could reply, only on the basis of a *cultural or religious belief* that there should be only two sexes. Other cultures allowed for the existence of people whose sex was not clearly male or female, such as certain indigenous American tribes who recognized not only male and female genders, but also what anthropologists called the 'berdache'. This 'third gender' was usually composed of children born as male or intersex, who were brought up to learn the traditional work of both sexes, dressed as women, and who in later life could take husbands. Some cultures like the indigenous American tribes valued the berdache and actually welcomed the birth of what we now call intersexed babies, believing them to be universal spirits that embodied both the male and the female. In later life such children often became tribal Shaman, taking up positions of power and importance in the social group, rather than finding themselves socially excluded as they are today in Western culture. Here, the birth of such children is seen as a medical problem that must be addressed: a faulty nature that must be corrected by biomedical intervention. In such a way, we actually *produce* a two-gendered world; the very 'reality' we claim exists in the first place.

However, as Kessler asks in her study of the intersexed and their medical management, what happens if we think not of 'gender ambiguity', which sounds like a problem about which something should be done, but of 'gender variability' that is a natural occurrence which includes us all. In this sense, all of us are judged, and judge ourselves, on a very narrowly defined standard of what are 'normal' genitals. Doctors often recommend surgery, or individuals seek it out, if the clitoris is thought to be too large or the penis too small. In such instances, or in the case of intersexed individuals who may have mixed genitalia, surgery is performed for cosmetic reasons, to improve *the look* of the genitals, or make them *look* like the genitals of a 'normal' man or woman, not because the genitals do not function properly. Indeed, many intersexuals have found that they are less able to get sexual satisfaction from their genitals after surgery than they did before. However, some intersexuals are now raising wider questions about their medical management from childhood onwards: these questions extend beyond the nature of medical surgery and why it is performed, to the issue of whether any surgery should happen at all until a young person is old enough to decide who and what they want to become.

As Kessler notes, while many intersexuals do want to become either men or women at some point in their lives, some are now opting to become neither, instead working for the right and recognition to live with an intersexual identity. Starting with various groups in the 1990s, such as the Intersex Society of North America, and making contact with each other through the Internet, a number of intersexuals began 'coming out' and campaigning for their right to live as intersexuals, which also included the demand that no surgery should be performed on children's sexual organs unless this was a medical necessity. Some commented on the surgery done on them as children with bitterness and rage, referring to themselves as 'improperly assigned males' or 'improperly assigned females'. Others talked of their 'sex change' to indicate the sense of loss of an intersexual status in childhood. One intersexual commented that, 'I have managed to calm down my murderous rage at [the] professionals, but probably I'll never get over what my parents did to me by trying to kill me off'. Yet others try to articulate the experience of an intersexual identity and body beyond the language and categories of the two-sexed world, someone saying that 'I wish there was a way of talking … without intrinsically distorting things, by misinterpreting them in terms of either male or female'. In this spirit, one intersexual refers to the larger-than-typical clitoris that was surgically removed in childhood as her 'phalloclit'.[9]

What is happening here amongst some intersexuals is that they are arguing for the right to exist as an identity amongst other identities in the modern world, rather than as a medical disorder. Modelling themselves on the gay movement, they are making what were once private issues – the 'problem' of their gender assignment – into public issues about gender, arguing that people should not be forced to live as either men or women, but some people should be recognized as intersexuals, transgender, or transpeople. There is, then, a struggle going on for the public recognition of such categories, and for the right of people to exercise their own judgement in terms of surgery: whether they want to be reassigned as male or female, or to live as another gender that is outside of bipolar categorization. In this light, Kessler claims that being intersexed is both a natural occurrence *and* a construction of medical and social interests. That is, because it involves the body with which one is born and the recognition of its difference from other bodies, but how that is dealt with is highly variable in social and cultural terms. On these grounds, Kessler argues that we should dispense with the notion of sex as rooted in the body, in its genitalia and underlying bio-chemistry, and instead only work with the concept of gender as something that is performed in social interaction, irrespective of the configuration of the flesh under the clothes. In this way, we would take pressure off individuals to conform to strict bodily norms, and learn the lesson of what the intersexed can teach us.

The lesson is that since the 19th century, the West has defined the 'truth' of sex too narrowly in terms of genitalia, hormones or chromosomes, and has only unconsciously recognized the value of a person's performance of their gender; the enactment of their own self-image, created amongst others. However, this does not work if we stick to the demarcation that currently exists in the social sciences between sex and gender, where sex refers to biology and the body, while gender refers to the social and cultural differences between men and women, the masculine and the feminine. As Kessler notes, gender is an interactive performance in which the body is ever-present, albeit dressed in clothes. Given this, the term gender would have to subsume everything that we currently mean when we refer to sex, being but one element in the way we are identified by others and by ourselves. Yet this might be difficult to sustain in practice, as the term sex goes right to our very core in matters of the way we in-habit or live in the world through our bodies. As I noted in the last chapter, this not only involves living as a self with an identity, it is also entangled with the way we live sex through embodied fantasy, image, desire and attraction. Sex, then, is also to do with body, sexuality and self, with gender identity only a part of this.

Another difficulty with Kessler's approach is that although it fully recognizes the power struggles between the medical profession and the intersexed, power remains completely unanalysed within her work. This is a common difficulty with all ethnomethodological or interactionist social science, that while it illuminates the minutiae of social practice, and is hugely valuable in doing so, it is often unable to link the details of everyday life within the broader frameworks of power relations and social hierarchies. It is not that this style of social science is unaware of the wider social context, just that it is often difficult to provide the linkages between local social contexts and the more global and historical vistas of power struggles.

For example, the sociologist Erving Goffman, writing just one year after the publication of Kessler and McKenna's first book, created a strikingly similar analysis of gender as produced by ritualized displays, or performances, in particular social settings. He also claimed, however, that there was a 'loose gearing' between more general social structures (such as relations of power and domination between women and men) and what goes on in the particular occasions of ritualized gender performance. Here, for Goffman, most women and many subordinate males are placed almost in the role of dependent children, with more powerful authority figures (usually men) dominating them. This domination is often expressed in the smallest of details, like a look or gesture or a manner of speaking, and these things not only symbolize the already existing social hierarchy, they actually constitute it. For Goffman, gender performances in everyday life are both the shadow and the substance of the social hierarchy, meaning that they are both cast by it *and* that they actually compose it through any number of ritualized performances within various social situations. It is not the overall power structure that characterizes gender relations in a society that gets reproduced in a specific social context, but particular features of it that the interactants deem relevant to the situation at hand. Thus, in some situations, gender might be performed in such a way as to reproduce iconic images of masculine and feminine behaviour (as men might 'do' masculinity in the army or at the rugby club), while in other situations gender displays are less distinct (in an evening on the town, the gender displays of a mixed group of friends might become more blurred). Particular social situations, and the gender performances that they entail, are not, therefore, incidental in the production and subversion of existing power relations, but central to them. The thing that Goffman finds difficult to explain is why existing power relations have the characteristics that they do: but for that, we would need a full-blown historical analysis of the changing balance of power within and between genders, and that is beyond my scope here. But others have tried to tackle this question in ways that relate to my concerns in this book.

Performance, power and context in the production of sex and gender

One of the most influential accounts of gender and sexuality to be given in recent years is that of Judith Butler. Like Kessler and McKenna (whom she never references in her early works), and also Goffman, Butler has a performative theory of gender, which is to say that gender is understood as nothing more or less than the performance of actions, behaviours and gestures that have gendered characteristics. There is no essence of male and female at the heart of our own selves which is expressed in these performances. It is the performance itself that creates the illusion that each one of us has a natural sex. In her most influential book *Gender Trouble* Butler asks the key question, 'Does being female constitute a "natural fact" or a cultural performance, or is "naturalness" constituted through discursively constrained performative acts that produce the body through and within the categories of sex?'.[10] The way Butler frames this question gives a clue as to how she sets about answering it, for she takes her reading of Foucault's concept of discourse as central to the production and reproduction of gender performance. Just as Foucault showed in *Discipline and Punish* how power works on the bodies of prisoners, not to repress instinct or desire, but to compel their bodies to signify the prohibitive law as essence, style and necessity, so Butler aims to show there is a disciplinary technology of gender that governs bodies. This comes in the form of normative regulations that compel bodies to signify in terms of the discourse on gender.

Butler's overall aim is to use the concept of discourse to tie the performance of gender to power, showing how sex – the very thing we take to be an ontological reality – is produced as discursively regulated performances. This project is revealed in the other key question she seeks to answer: 'How does language itself produce the fictive construction of "sex" that supports these various regimes of power?'.[11] In a recent book, Butler restates her project as understanding how '[g]ender is not exactly what one "is" nor is it precisely what one "has." Gender is the apparatus by which the production and normalization of masculine and feminine take place …'.[12] Gender is also a precondition for the production and maintenance of a legible humanity, for if others cannot read us as clearly male or female, our status as a human being comes into question. If we are not male or female, then what are we? Yet there is slippage in the use of the term 'gender', for as we have already seen, to talk of 'transgender' or 'transpeople' is to already move beyond the naturalized binary that the discourse on gender tries to install. This slippage also applies to the performative, as illustrated by drag, which can be seen as an ironic commentary on how gender and sex are produced by the mastery of bodily acts and gestures that signify masculinity and femininity. As an ironic commentary, drag can be subversive as it not only illustrates the performative nature of gender, it also hints at its instability by showing the possible slippage between the supposedly bounded categories of male and female, straight and gay.

More generally, Butler is arguing for a social constructionist understanding of the subject, meaning that any sense we have of being an 'I' – an active and motivated agent – does not exist prior to the structure of signification and linguistic practice within a culture, which is the precondition that enables us to speak, think and act in such a way. Furthermore, we do not come into the world as a non-gendered, non-sexed, 'I' who later acquires a gender identity: instead, from the earliest days of life we are compelled to perform as male and female according to the regulatory norms of our culture, which prescribe what doing and being male and female actually is. Like Kessler and McKenna, and also Goffman, Butler is saying that the performance creates the sense of male and female as natural facts, yet using a Foucauldian analysis she is arguing that performances are compelled by regulatory norms and the overlapping networks of knowledge and power. We can see this in the way that gender playfulness and experimentation is often tolerated in young children, who can play as the opposite sex or cross-dress – certainly in the home, where others cannot see – and yet this is only tolerated for so long: as children get older, they are expected to perform more strictly to the norms of their assigned gender and sex. For Butler, then, it is this normative regulation that actually produces gender performances, which are both iterative and improvisational; that is, they constantly repeat the gender norms in some way or improvise on them, just as a musician in performance might play a 'standard' tune in a straightforward way, or use it as the basis to improvise his or her own melody. In performing as women or men in everyday life we do exactly the same thing, by quoting the gender norms that are standard in society, or 'gender-bending' in some way by mixing together male and female signifiers.

However, Butler wants to create a more complex understanding of gender and sex than this, because she recognizes that we do not simply conform to a set of normative regulations in a self-conscious or cynical way, but are somehow deeply inscribed by these norms, which animate our bodies in their performances, creating our own sense of identification – that we *really are* a man or a woman – and shaping our sexual desires and sexuality. In my terms, Butler wants to understand how we in-habit gender and sexuality with our bodies. At the same time, though, she recognizes that bipolar categorizations of identities are unstable, because in being compelled to identify within a framework of norms that say *you must* identify *either as* male or female, gay or straight, this identification involves a repudiation of its opposite, especially if that opposite is prohibited. So men will often feel ashamed of their more feminine inclinations and feelings, thinking that they make them less masculine (less of a 'real' man), while women may feel their more masculine aspects will be frowned on because they make them less feminine: and both men and women feel they must deny any homosexual desires. In this way, gender, sex and sexuality are all interlinked, produced by the regulatory apparatus that keeps in place the heterosexual order.

However, in her book *The Psychic Life of Power* Butler is critical of Foucault for understanding the soul only as an external imprisoning frame, without exploring the sense of interiority that becoming a subject inaugurates. Yet Butler doesn't associate the psychic life with becoming a self or a person: rather she wants to explore how becoming a 'subject' in Foucault's terms – that is, being subject to others in relations of power *and* tied to our own identity by conscience or knowledge – creates the sense of an interior psyche. In Foucauldian/ Nietzschean style, Butler wants to show how power not only involves subjugation to others, but also a relation of subjection to one's own self. As Nietzsche had it, this involves a human being 'turning' against itself through a bad or guilty conscience. For Butler, this turning occurs when we are made subject to normative regulation, particularly in terms of our sexuality and gender. Using Freud's theories of psychic development, she sees this happening when children become subject to taboos and regulations regarding sexuality, such as the incest taboo that prohibits sexual relations between fathers and daughters, mothers and sons, and brothers and sisters. Prior to that, however, Freud believed there were sensual and sexual feelings between children and caregivers of both sexes, resulting from children's bodily needs and the reliance on others to meet these, that later become affectionate, de-sexualized emotional ties. Thus, for Freud, 'the child makes the person it loves into the object of all its still not properly centred sexual trends'.[13] The feminist writer Gayle Rubin pointed out that this must mean the incest taboo presupposes a prior taboo which operates against the possibility of homosexual desire.[14]

In opposition to the idea that power and normative regulation move against pre-existing desires – whether they are sexual desires or the aggressive drives which Nietzsche called the old and terrible instincts – Butler once again takes the Foucauldian position that power *produces* subjects and desires. So it is the power of the heterosexual order itself that works through taboos in order to characterize certain desires as 'heterosexual' and others 'homosexual', with the latter denigrated as 'abnormal' and the individuals identified by these desires subordinated to 'heterosexuals' and excluded from mainstream heterosexual life. Thus, the discourse that works to regulate gender and sexuality actually produces desires by naming, classifying and distributing certain desires around the norm.

For Butler, what Freud's work illustrates when channelled through a Foucauldian perspective is the discursive regulation that comes into play to institute a particular gender and sexual order, in which we become subjects or placeholders in the discursive formation, recognizing our identity and our desires in the framework of its terms and categories. Butler asks how it is that we are the kinds of beings who are vulnerable to subjugation, saying (in the third person) that the subject is '[b]ound to seek recognition of its own existence in categories, terms, and names that are not of its own making' because 'the subject seeks the sign of its own existence outside itself, in a discourse that is at once dominant and indifferent. Social categories signify subordination and existence at once'.[15]

Furthermore, subjugation occurs through the imposition of taboos and restrictions in which subjectivity is both formed and limited: that is, the subject and its psyche is formed by recognition of itself in normative discursive categories such as male and female, yet at the same time its self-knowledge is limited by what these regulations have 'foreclosed'. In particular, this is the erotic and sensuous feelings towards the caregiver of the same sex, and, thereafter, sexual feelings towards others of the same sex. Butler names this in psychoanalytic terms as a 'foreclosure' because it is not only the *object* of sexual love that has to be given up when desires get named as homosexual; it is *the love itself* that must be forever denied. This love is both unacknowledged and ungrieved, as it was never entitled to an existence. The subject is then compelled to repeat the norms of its production in gender performances, because gender is also constructed by the foreclosure of homosexual attachments. Thus, a man who feels any stirring of love or desire for another man not only has to disallow this, but he will also feel the need to accentuate his masculinity in his social performance. In this way, Butler claims that it is not enough to argue, as she had in *Gender Trouble,* that gender is only a performance, because some of the workings of gender do not show in that performance. A very feminine woman is not just performing femininity; she is also repudiating masculinity and denying homosexuality. Thus, all identity positions are produced through repudiation.

However, Butler has to admit that her understanding of the melancholic formation of gendered and sexualized subjects – melancholic because they are based on the ungrieved loss of same sex erotic attachments – is what she calls a *hyperbolic construction.* It is hyperbolic, or overstated, because it does not capture the many ways in which actual selves can experience gender and sexuality, which in phenomenological terms cannot be reduced to an equation stating that gender is stabilized through a firm heterosexuality established by disciplinary regimes requiring foreclosure and repudiation. Indeed, it is on these very grounds that Butler justifies her hyperbolic construction of gender, because its aim is the *critique* of subject positions that require repudiation to achieve stability: heterosexuality requires the foreclosure of homosexual desire and the repudiation of identifications with the opposite gender (masculinity is a repudiation of femininity, and vice versa), while in homosexuality there is a disavowal of heterosexuality. Butler wants to critique these limited subject positions and deconstruct the heterosexual order which keeps them in place, opening the possibility for more fluid attachments and identifications between humans. This is a position also taken up in the recent academic movement known as 'queer theory', which re-employs the term 'queer' to signify any form of sexuality that goes beyond the limited heterosexual order, yet at the same time doesn't attempt to fix and solidify forms of sexuality within the rigid categories of gay and straight, male and female.[16]

Once again, by taking up such a position, Butler is illustrating the slippage between linguistic categories, which also allow some leeway for subjects to improvise or subvert the heterosexual order that language supports. Furthermore, the way in which we are formed as subjects, by the 'turn' in which we establish a reflexive relation to ourselves – albeit a guilty and limited one – allows the subject some degree of power through which to establish its own agency from within a system of discursive regulation. Although as subjects we are *produced* by power, as subjects we also necessarily *assume* the power in which we have been in-formed. Furthermore, in Hegelian fashion, Butler tries to show that although subjects are only recognizable in terms that are established socially and historically, nevertheless as subjects we are not identical to ourselves. A reflexive relation always assumes a gap or a difference in which a subject can realize the power to be other than it is, or to establish a critical perspective on what it has become. Thus, we are not only bound to endlessly repeat the terms of our subjection: there are gaps and fissures in the structure of power established by discourse and language which allow for the possibility of critical and transformative agency.

For me, though, one of the major problems in Butler's approach is the way that she interprets Foucault's concept of discourse in such a narrowly linguistic way. In Foucault's work, discourse referred not only to language and the way in which the concepts and categories of knowledge were linguistically constructed, but also to the local contexts of institutions and practices that overlapped with established discourses. It is the institutional and practical contexts in which discourses are developed, deployed and resisted that is missing in Butler's work, so that terms like discourse and language often assume an abstract quality, as if they are always already established prior to human practice as the *a priori* condition for both practice and subjectivity. In addition, because she follows Foucault's position so closely in other respects, Butler incorporates into her own work many of the problems I identified in the last chapter with Foucault's position. For example, like Foucault, Butler focuses almost exclusively on 'established' or 'official' forms of discourse, along with the knowledge, concepts and categories they produce, through which we recognize ourselves and others as subjects. She therefore ignores the 'unofficial' everyday dialogues that occur between people and how, through subcultures within an urban landscape, forms of identity can be named, constructed and reconstructed. As I hope to have illustrated in the last chapter, there is a more complex mutual relation between scientific, medical and legal forms of discourse, on the one hand, and everyday dialogues, with their own names and categories for social identities, on the other.

This overly narrow interpretation of discourse as language also affects Butler's understanding of subjectivity, as the subject is conceptualized as one who is dependent on a discourse they haven't chosen, but which initiates and sustains their agency. The subject, then, is not to be confused with self or person, because it is no more than a linguistic category, a placeholder in discourse. Like Foucault, however, this means that the subject is understood only in relation to discourse, language and norms, rather than in relations with others. While Butler does say that no subject emerges without a passionate attachment to others[17] and that we come into contact with norms only through proximate and living exchanges in which we account for ourselves,[18] these are passing references in works mainly devoted to understanding subjects as inaugurated through language and norms in a more abstract, impersonal sense. Butler's concern is therefore the subject's relation to norms and language rather than to others.

For example, when Butler talks about subjects being 'interpellated' by language, she uses this concept in the sense developed by the French structuralist Louis Althusser, who meant by it that subjects are 'hailed' or called out to by ideology, and, having answered the call, are inserted into material practices as the supports of capitalist social structures.[19] For Butler, subjects are interpellated by language into the fictions of bipolar sex and gender categories. But she does not mean we are interpellated in the way Mead, Harré or Shotter did, in the sense of being called to account by others. This is important, because if we think of selves (rather than subjects) being interpellated by specific others such as caregivers, family and friends, then norms will be specific to particular contexts and highly variable depending on living exchanges with others, who will have their own personal histories and biographical trajectories, thus bringing with them variations in normative actions and expectations. These will also vary depending on the social class, generation, culture or ethnicity of the people we are interdependent with. Although I agree with Butler when she says that the norm cannot be entirely reduced to its instantiations, as it corresponds to the normalizing operation of bureaucratic and disciplinary powers,[20] I also think it is true to say that in contemporary societies we regularly encounter different institutional contexts in which norms vary widely. Also, if we contrast Butler's position with thinkers like Mead and Bakhtin, they too wanted to oppose the view of a transcendental self theorized as prior to language, understanding the self as created in living interactions and dialogues with others, finding its own voice with some and against others. Yet Mead and Bakhtin also realized that in contemporary societies there is no single authoritative discourse, so that no self is synonymous with any one social category, role or attribution, instead seeing itself through the eyes of many others with myriad perspectives. Categories, names and norms are therefore not experienced consistently with respect to any one person, and this slippage is not only linguistic – in terms of a system of signification – but also interactive and dialogic.

In terms of the categories of gender and sexuality, Butler has to admit that in a phenomenological way these are not lived and experienced in such rigid terms as her hyperbolic theory would have it, through repudiation, foreclosure and disavowal. For example, how do we explain the fact that there are many men who are comfortable with their own femininity, and nowadays many women who feel able to perform in more masculine ways? Also, how is it possible for lesbians, gay men and bisexuals to exist if same sex desire is subject to foreclosure early in childhood? Butler can always say that variation is an example of the *failure* of disciplinary regimes on every occasion to produce the subjects they require. Yet this is to cast gender and sexuality in a negative light only, as constructed from foreclosure, repudiation, disavowal or their failure. Even when gay sexuality does emerge, Butler claims it can be marked by impossibility, guilt and secrecy. While this of course is true, it is also the case that norms of gender and sexuality are changing so that, once again, this is not true in everyone's experience. The taboo on homosexuality has greatly relaxed in certain cultures so that it is now possible to express gay sexuality more freely and without guilt and shame. Perhaps this is one of the most important things that Butler's theories fail to capture; that alongside the difficulties, struggles and conflicts that can occur in expressing gender and sexuality, there are also to be found the pleasures of bodily fantasies and desires, involving joy and abandon with others.

There is also ambiguity in Butler's use of Freudian theory to explore the disciplinary taboos and prohibitions in which gender and sexuality are 'constructed,' for while this charts the drama of both sexual 'normalization' alongside its inevitable 'deviations', it still cannot account for many of the permutations and variations in sexuality and gender. For example, according to Freudian theory, in 'normal' heterosexual development the child's love for the parent of the same sex turns into admiration and they want to be like them, while their sexual desires are turned to members of the opposite sex outside the family of origin, those they want to *have*. But then how can we explain a feminine man, who at some point has presumably identified with the mother and wanted to be *like* her, wanting to *have* a woman. In other words, how do we explain in Freudian terms a feminine man who is straight? And now that the stereotype of gay men as effeminate has finally disappeared, how do we explain a masculine man loving another man – in other words, wanting both to *be* and to *have* a man? Not only does such a man (or woman in the case of a feminine lesbian) confound the Freudian framework, he (or she) also escapes the foreclosure on homosexuality, as I noted earlier. From this Butler seems to be in the paradoxical position of realizing the problems of Freudian theory, yet still reliant on it for her hyperbolic theory of gender construction through heterosexual norms.

Nevertheless, Freud's great discovery was that children are not asexual beings and that there are complex and ambivalent feelings that run within child care arrangements, between children and their caregivers, involving sensuous and erotic attachments that form in these interdependencies. As Harrison and Hood-Williams have pointed out, these erotic attachments are not designated as either heterosexual or homosexual in early childhood, as such terms really only come to be significant in puberty. In early childhood, prior to any taboo on incest, these attachments and feelings are part of what Freud called the child's still not properly centred sexual trends, so that any taboo on homosexuality at this stage would be meaningless. I would also argue that in the more varied family structures that we find today in the West, as well as across different cultures, there are multiple erotic attachments that children can form with their caregivers, alongside wide variation in the style and substance of normative regulation applied to these desires and to the performance of gender. It is, then, always possible for a variety of sexual desires and gender performances to emerge from human relationships. From this I would also say that while gender performances can change between social contexts, and, in some cases, sexuality can be more fluid, nevertheless a residue of past erotic relational attachments does persist with us as sexual desires and orientation. As Gayle Rubin has said, acquiring gender and sexuality can be like the learning of our native language and culture, in that 'most people have a home language, and home sexual and gender comfort zones that will not change much'.[21] In this sense, gender and sexuality may not be unlike other acquired, relatively stable dispositional tendencies that orient us within our world and towards other people. It may, then, be quite appropriate to speak of a 'sexual orientation' in the way we come to inhabit the world and relate ourselves to people and things.

In respect of caregivers, ambivalent emotional attachments will lead us to orient ourselves towards them in complex ways, both identifying and not identifying with them. However, as Goffman points out, an important part of gender performance and display within the parent–child complex is imagery, for children desire to imitate elements of the type of masculine or feminine images given off by parents or caregivers.[22] Furthermore, these imitative gender performances have a dialogic structure of a statement-reply kind, with a display on the part of one person calling forth an expression on the part of another. In this case interpellation is understood as a dialogic and interpersonal process (not unlike finding your own 'voice' amongst the voices of others, as I illustrated in Chapter 3) where the child and its caregivers are responding to each other's gender performance, the child responding either positively or negatively to the imagery in the gender display. The images of caregivers will not be the only gender displays the child is exposed to, especially not in today's media infused world, so that the child will have other gender displays, other imagery, through which its responses to caregivers will be mediated. Thus, in the intergenerational micro-social power politics of growing up, a child or young person can take up a position in its upbringing in which it rejects the kind of masculinity or femininity performed by its caregivers, not wanting to be that kind of man or woman. In this way, some interpellations can be refused, with the young person opting for new models of gender performance being developed by its own generation, ones in which it may feel able to find its own voice and ways of inhabiting its gender performances and sexuality, in a style that feels more authentic.

In terms of power, Goffman's viewpoint also provides an interesting counterpoint to Butler's, as in his view it is not so much the overall character of the gendered power structure, with its ideal-images of masculine and feminine, that is performed in particular social situations, but *certain context-specific features relevant to an audience*. Gender displays also provide evidence of the performer's *alignment* in a gathering, the way she or he relates to sections of the audience. As an illustration of this, one can take the range of different masculinities and femininities on display in contemporary urban gay bars in the UK. There are different bars or mixed bars frequented by fashionable young people, straight-acting men, college boys, camp boys and men, more mature men, and, more recently, 'bears' (larger, hairy men). There are also young women, sporty looking women, older women, and butch or 'fem' women. As Butler would say, these gender performances are all citations of or improvisations on normative masculinity and femininity: but they are also performances given for an audience, to call out responses from particular others involving personal and sexual attraction, and to align the performer with certain groups where they might find friendship, love and sex. There are also very different normative expectations within the gay bar that are not strictly hetero-normative, with a range of masculinity and femininity on display in both men and women that is not as evident in other walks of life, such as in the workplace. *Context and alignment, then, are hugely important in the meaning and style of performances, as well as in the selection and mixing of ideal or iconic images of masculinity and femininity used in gender displays in certain settings.* Context is also important in terms of the norms that regulate performances, as norms can vary widely both within and between different social contexts of activity.

However, sexuality is not the only factor when it comes to gay and lesbian places and the performances of gender that occur there. As Jon Binnie and Beverley Skeggs have noted from research done in the gay village in Manchester UK, social class is also an important factor as to whether gay people feel comfortable and included in 'the scene'.[23] Those interviewed in Binnie and Skeggs' study could clearly indicate which bars were frequented by particular social classes, and they saw the major threat to the gay area to be not just from parties of straight people coming to drink and enjoy themselves, but particular groups of working-class men and women – especially 'hen parties' – who were seen as drunken and vulgar. It is clear, then, that many gay people who frequent the area make distinctions between other people there, not only on the grounds of sexuality but also in terms of social class. Race is also a factor, with few places for black women in the village. Binnie and Skeggs therefore conclude that the gay community tends to reproduce not only sexual and racial divisions, but it also mirrors and reproduces the class hierarchy. For my concerns here, this means that there is much more than just the effects of sexual normativity on the performance and self-identification as gay: there is also the effect of social class, particularly on the display of the correct cosmopolitan tastes and attitudes that are so central to urban gay identity. This connects to what I will say in the next chapter about the effects of social class on self-identity. For now, though, it can be said that the signs displayed on the gay and lesbian body in its performances, refer not only to sexuality and gender, but also to class and race.

Returning to Butler's theories of gender as performative, in a recent book she advances her ideas by taking account of the effects of others on performance, placing emphasis on the *undoing* rather than the *doing* of gender, in that established gender categories come unstuck as groups make claims for recognition – such as the intersexed – that expand the definition of 'the human' beyond existing bipolar categories.[24] Here she attempts to incorporate into her work more of the Hegelian tradition that understands desire as desire for the recognition of others. Thus, Butler begins to argue that what we are doing in the performative is always a doing with or for another. Furthermore, the critical distance we can establish from norms is always a collective capacity to develop alternative norms and ideals. In doing this, groups such as lesbians, gays and intersexuals are not only asserting sexual rights, they are also struggling to be conceived as *persons* – that is, included in the category of the human as those with both a right to their existence and to a liveable life in their own terms. However, this understanding of the power of *collective* agency in gaining critical distance from established norms, sits uncomfortably with Butler's earlier stance that critical agency is located in the incommensurability of the subject – the placeholder in language – and the psyche; an incommensurability which opens up the possibility of critical reflection with the reflexive turn. This latter position is a decidedly *individual* understanding of agency, resting as it does on the nature of the psyche.

Additionally, while Butler attempts to think through the whole process of recognition, this is still couched in terms of recognition through established social and historical linguistic categories, including how these get undone. Yet, lacking an interactive or dialogical approach, the emphasis remains on the linguistic categories and how they provide the framework in which the human is recognized. In discussing the case of David Reimer, the American man whose penis was surgically removed after an accident in childhood and thereafter brought up as a girl – but whose gender always remained in question – Butler argues that Reimer's desire not to be constantly subject to categorization on the basis of his genitals, but to be recognized as a person in his own right, shows how his humanness emerges from the way he cannot be fully categorized, thus exceeding the norms of intelligibility. But this is not to exceed such norms when we consider that in Romantic discourses it is perfectly intelligible for any of us to ask to be valued in our own right, rather than as a social category. This is not a slippage that exceeds the boundaries of language, for Reimer is drawing on a discourse that is not scientific or legal in order to argue for an authentic sense of self. He is also appealing to what Martin Buber called the 'interhuman': for that historically established dialogical capacity of selves to put aside categorization and begin to author each other in a more naked and vulnerable way, as in the confession between equals.

Furthermore, the very fact that adult intersexuals have been able to speak out and rearticulate their identities and bodies, shows that as *persons* they have a sense of presence, agency and embodiment in the world that extends beyond their sexuality and gender. It is important in this context to remember how Laing argued that, from being young children, our sense of ontological presence and reality in the world depends as much upon *opposing* certain normative constraints as embodying them. Indeed, in Laing's studies, those who felt most ontologically insecure were those who had always over-conformed, who had bent to all the expectations of powerful others. Could it be possible, then, to exist as a person without having a stable gender identity or without having a certain sense of one's sex? The example of the intersexed would seem to suggest that it is, as illustrated by Herculine Barbin before she/he was forced to live as a man. As Butler puts it, in question form, 'what is it to live, breathe, attempt to love neither as fully negated nor as fully acknowledged as being'.[25]

There is, then, a question here, not so much about how fundamental gender and sex are as *aspects* of our selves, but whether it is correct to say that the person is gendered from the very beginning, while its powers of agency are being socially constituted. Freud did not seem to refer to gender or sex as being an identity, but saw masculine and feminine as 'attitudes' that could be adopted by both boys and girls. As Harrison and Hood-Williams note, for Freud the body ego of infants does not have a gender, and this, along with sexuality, only begins to centre itself at a later stage, perhaps in puberty. Furthermore, Freud's concept of identification was rather indistinct, yet he made clear that identification does not have to be with a whole person (father or mother) but could be with a trait, an act, with speech, an organ, or (as in megalomania) with the whole world.[26] I would also add, following Goffman, that it could be possible to identify with certain images of persons or aspects of their performance, or it could be bound up with someone's response to us. But more than this, as I argued in Chapter 3, when we are interpellated by parents into moral actions, we are interpellated as persons in a general sense, as well as a particular gender. While there are substantial differences in the moral demands on boys and girls, there are also large areas of similarity, such as honesty, accountability, and responsibility for one's actions. As Connell has remarked, what is often overlooked in the study of gender difference is that men and women are in many ways more similar than they are different.[27]

It is no doubt right to say, as does Butler, that to survive in this world, a person's sex has to be in some way readable and intelligible to others, otherwise they are liable to be cast into a non-existence or non-recognition by others, or, at the very worst, subject to violence and murder, as are many transpeople, gays and lesbians. By arguing for the right to exist, many of those distributed to the fringes of sexual being are arguing for their very right of survival through the recognition of others which includes them in the 'human', or in the realm of the 'interhuman'. In this way, sexual minorities not only challenge the ontological reality of two sexes, they also work to expand the definition of the 'human', in terms of who gets recognized as such by others. In doing this, however, their sense of 'I' as an autonomous agent – one who is nevertheless dependent on the recognition of others for their existence as such – is not dependent solely on the recognition of their gender, for they both claim and gain recognition on other grounds, such as their capacity as persons to articulate their position and to redefine the human. As Mead suggested, the agentive sense of being an 'I' does not refer to an identity, gendered or otherwise, but is a form of action and speech that rests on different, subtly shifting social foundations in various contexts of activity. Furthermore, as Bakhtin pointed out, this also means that the experience of being an 'I' brings with it a sense of transcendence in dialogue, that 'I' can always become something other than what I am, or what I am defined as, right now.

At the end of the day, though, the major problems in Butler's work, influential and interesting as it is, are to do with the lack of a historical and context specific understanding of sex and gender (unlike Foucault's account of sexuality). These aspects of identity are lifted out of institutionally specific social locations of practice in which identities are both formed and reconstructed. This also gives the link that Butler forms between language, power and agency an *a priori* appearance, as regulatory, normative discursive mechanisms are theorized as the power that constructs agency and identity in iterative performances, but gives little clue as to how such power could come into being and create its subjects outside of a historical and socially dynamic process in which relations and interactions are already in play. Paradoxically, while her hyperbolic theory of gender can explain and critique the establishment of heteronormativity, we get little sense of how the array of sexual persons who oppose it, or identify themselves outside of it, are possible. Linked to this, there is little acknowledgement that, in many societies, normative regulation is highly variable and not of a piece, so that the powers that work through it can also be splintered and contradictory forces that produce an array of selves. It is to this issue I now turn.

Gender order, gender regimes and dialectical pragmatics

The issue of the relationship between local contexts and overall structures of power in society is at the heart of R. W. Connell's work on gender. He has attempted to create what he calls a 'structural inventory' of the social relationships that constitute different genders, both at the level of specific locations or institutions – such as schools, workplaces, the streets – and within various branches of the state. However, at both the regional and the local level, no social formation is composed of such a tightly integrated network of relationships that they knit together to form a coherent and unified system. Rather, a structural inventory explores the complexities and contradictions in all levels and dimensions of a given situation and the social relations to be found there, all of which characterize its 'gender regime'. In contrast, the concept of the 'gender order' aims to capture the relationship between these gender regimes and how they coalesce into a hegemony of ideas about what constitutes masculine or feminine behaviour in a particular society: a hegemony that is both supported and contested.

Borrowing from the work of the Italian Marxist Antonio Gramsci, Connell takes the term 'hegemony' to mean the ascendancy of a social group or ideology that is achieved through culture, institutions and persuasion, rather than through violence or physical coercion. In these terms, for Connell, the notion of hegemonic masculinity refers to patterns of practice that inhere in a culture and its various institutions that have allowed men to dominate women (in the Western world at least) along with other subordinate men. This does not mean that all men and women conform to the hegemonic style, as there are multiple masculinities and femininities; only that, in certain historical conjunctures, for sociological reasons, certain types of masculinity become more honoured than others, or confer greater power chances on particular men. This honoured form of masculinity does, however, become normative. For example, as the power of the state in the 18th and 19th centuries changed from being based on physical coercion to a form of governance based on rational calculation and technocratic management, a hegemonic type of masculinity began to emerge that emphasized rational thinking and technical knowledge, subordinating the older 'wild' masculinity of warriors. Nevertheless, something of this older masculinity remains in specific contexts, traditionally in the armed forces and the police, although this is now being challenged with the recruitment of more women into these institutions.

Also, in the working classes, a model of masculinity as embodying physical strength and athleticism remained intact for many years, perhaps because of the manual nature of traditional working class jobs, although again this is likely to be changing in societies that are increasingly becoming de-industrialized. The book and film *Fight Club,* about a group of men who form an underground network of bare knuckle fighting clubs, can be seen as a lament for this type of 'wild' or hyper-masculinity based on physical toughness, invulnerability and an indifference to pain, that now seems to be disappearing.

What Connell is pointing out, however, is that hegemonic masculinity and 'emphasized femininity' are not natural and innate, but socially and historically created and, thus, variable between cultures, ethnicities, social classes and local contexts. Furthermore, these hegemonic forms are composed of idealized images and fantasies of masculinity and femininity held within a culture, but rarely practically embodied by any man or woman. However, in various institutions and practices, women and men, girls and boys, come to embody or rebel against aspects of hegemonic masculinity and emphasized femininity. For example, in schools the playing of sports is emphasized for boys, through which the force and skill employed in games like football or rugby are strongly cathected aspects of an adolescent boy's life – that is, the focus of both physical and mental energy – especially for those good at sport. As Connell says, for some 'it becomes a model of bodily action that has a much wider relevance than the particular game. Prowess of this kind becomes a means of judging one's degree of masculinity'.[28] Conversely, Iris Marion Young suggests that girls learn to use their bodies in a more restricted way, especially when playing sports, and this in turn leads them to underestimate their strength and physical capabilities.[29] The result is that many women use space in a less bold way than do most men, who tend to enter rooms more brashly and spread their limbs while sitting down. Of course, these trends vary widely between individual men and women, with it being possible for many women to be freer in their bodily movements and to have greater sporting prowess than some men. But the general styles of embodiment indicate the more hegemonic form of masculinity and of emphasized femininity.

One of the things that the work of thinkers like Connell and Young allows us to consider is that gender is not just a series of regulated performances, but that we are physically and emotionally cathected to our embodied performances as they constantly form and re-form our experience of sex and gender. Thus, what people find central in their experience of sex and gender is 'pleasure, pain, body-image, arousal, youth and aging, bodily contact, childbirth and suckling',[30] all those things that I have been calling our embodied ways of in-habiting the world. Because of this it is not quite accurate to say that styles and images of gender are fictions or illusions, for while they are powerful fantasies, they are nevertheless embodied and made ontologically real through various practices, such as sport, exercise, work or dieting. In this way, the 'social definition of men as holders of power is translated not only into mental body-images and fantasies, but into muscle tensions, posture, the feel and texture of the body'.[31] It is not only transpeople or the intersexed that work on their bodies to transform them, or, at the very limit of those bodies where transformation is not possible or where it does more harm than good, have to come to accept them and to articulate their embodied experience of sex and gender in new ways.

While Connell's work is useful in helping us to think through questions of the connection between power relations and the body, especially in terms of the gender order and the varied gender regimes, we must be careful about the notion of hegemonic masculinity. That is because this hegemony is constantly shifting and changing and may be composed of different models and styles of masculinity that have varied currency in different gender regimes. In this light, Demetriou has recently argued for a 'dialectical pragmatism' in approaching hegemonic masculinity, as the currently honoured forms of masculinity are not only varied, they can also draw from and mix with more peripheral types of masculinity.[32] For example, in the 1950s the honoured types of masculinity were not just represented by figures like John Wayne or Gary Cooper, they were supplemented by the likes of Marlon Brando and James Dean who were gaining popularity among young people as rebels. Furthermore, whereas the masculinity of a figure like John Wayne actively eschewed any hint of femininity or homosexuality, icons like Brando and Dean both played with, and appealed to, the fantasies and images of gay masculinity. Over the last half century this dialectical relation between hegemonic masculinities and more peripheral masculinities has intensified, especially as gay culture has had more influence in men's fashion and style. This process has intensified with the growth in popularity of 'mixed' social spaces, so that – either knowingly or unknowingly – gay and straight men are increasingly borrowing from each others' look, style and manner. While Connell and Messerschmidt are dubious that such hybridization is hegemonic at the regional or global level,[33] this seems surprising given the influence of gay culture and of gay men with the fashion and entertainment industries. This will be especially important considering the interest of many younger men in fashion and style, indicated by the growth in magazines dedicated to men's fashion, grooming and health.

Where, then, does this place us in the study of sex and gender? There is a powerful argument, backed by historical studies, that the contemporary Western belief that sex is a fundamental truth of our identities is a cultural invention of recent date (from around the 18th century onwards) and is also geographically specific. Evidence also exists that the bipolar model of sex as divided into male and female, seen as mutually exclusive biological categories, is equally recent and local, and, like the idea of sex as truth, is dependent on the growth of the biomedical sciences.[34] Furthermore, the bipolar model of sex cannot be separated from the growing cultural distinction of what today we would call gay men and lesbians, both in everyday urban life and in the late 19th century with the creation of the medical terms 'homosexuality' and 'heterosexuality'. It was only with the notion of sex as a truth about the nature of our selves that the idea was contemplated that a person's orientation towards loving people of the same sex could define their entire identity. Sex, gender and sexuality can therefore be understood historically as social and cultural creations, and, in that, they are also socially and culturally variable. For those of us in the contemporary Western world, history is currently in the making as transpeople and intersexed people challenge the truth of the bipolar model of sex and gender that we have lived with for over two centuries, arguing that there should be other genders that are recognized as fully human and allowed to survive without surgical alteration. Yet this is just one more illustration of the way in which people are not simply born to an established sex and gender, or to sexuality, but made to conform to it. The reverse side of this, however, is that there are other ways of being male and female, and of expressing one's sexuality and love, which have their own historical lineage and have survived the regulations of hegemonic powers, even as they have been affected by them.

Given this, it may be shocking to contemplate our 'own' gender as continually referencing and improvising some socially scripted performance; parts that were written long before we were born, rather than constituted by a nature we were born with. That we learn sex and gender just as we learn our native language should not be that disturbing, for, like 'our' language, the fact that we didn't invent it doesn't make it any the less our own or any the less in-habitable, in the sense that we live through it in interaction with others so that it comes to feel as much a part of us as the parts of our own body. Indeed, our bodies become refashioned in our practices and performances; they are very much part of the selves that we are becoming within the social world that gives form to our every experience. But the work of Suzanne Kessler on the intersexed illustrated something else: that as a sexed and gendered person I don't only exist as an 'I-for-others', just as they are 'others-for-me', and in the process of interaction we attribute gender to one another; as an 'I-for-myself' I also attribute a gender identity to myself, one that is selected from the range of gender options currently available in my culture, but one that may differ from the attributions that others make about me. There is, then, a degree of self-making in gender, as there is in all identity, as we are interpellated, identified and align ourselves within the range of images and voices around us, with some images and voices more in-habitable and liveable than others. These alignments are made, no doubt, on the basis of earlier interpellations and identifications that were not freely chosen, but that does not make them any the less our own.

Notes

1. Michel Foucault (1980) *Herculine Barbin, Being the Recently Discovered Memoirs of a Nineteenth-Century Hermaphrodite*. Tr. Richard McDougall. New York: Pantheon. p. x–xi.
2. Suzanne Kessler and Wendy McKenna (1978) *Gender: An Ethnomethodological Approach*. New York: John Wiley & Sons.
3. Harold Garfinkel (1967) *Studies in Ethnomethodology*. Cambridge: Polity Press, 1984 edn.
4. Michel Foucault, *Herculine*, pp. 127–8.

5. Wendy Cealey Harrison and John Hood-Williams (2002) *Beyond Sex and Gender.* London: Sage. p. 122
6. Suzanne Kessler and Wendy McKenna, *Gender,* pp. 53–54.
7. Ibid., p. 163.
8. Suzanne Kessler (1998) *Lessons from the Intersexed.* New Brunswick: Rutgers University Press. p. 13.
9. Ibid., p. 85.
10. Judith Butler (1990) *Gender Trouble: Feminism and the Subversion of Identity.* New York: Routledge. p. viii.
11. Ibid., p. ix.
12. Judith Butler (2004) *Undoing Gender.* New York: Routledge. p. 42.
13. Freud (1921) 'Group psychology and the analysis of the ego', in *The Pelican Freud Library, Volume 12: Civilization, Society and Religion.* Harmondsworth: Pelican, 1985 edn. pp. 91–178, p. 171.
14. Gayle Rubin (1975) 'The traffic in women: notes on the "political economy" of sex', in R. R. Reiter (ed.), *Towards an Anthropology of Women.* New York: Monthly Review Press.
15. Judith Butler (1997) *The Psychic Life of Power: Theories in Subjection.* California: Stanford University Press. p. 20.
16. Steven Seidman (ed.) (1996) *Queer Theory/Sociology.* Oxford: Blackwell.
17. Judith Butler, *Psychic.*
18. Judith Butler (2005) *Giving an Account of Oneself.* New York: Fordham University Press.
19. Louis Althusser (1971) *Lenin and Philosophy and Other Essays.* London: New Left Books.
20. Judith Butler, *Undoing.*
21. Gayle Rubin (1994) 'Sexual traffic (interview with Judith Butler)', *Differences: A Journal of Feminist Cultural Studies,* 6 (2–3): 62–99, p. 66.
22. Erving Goffman (1979) *Gender Advertisements.* London: Macmillan.
23. Jon Binnie and Beverley Skeggs (2004) 'Cosmopolitan knowledge and the production and consumption of sexualized space: Manchester's gay village', *Sociological Review,* 52 (1): 39–61.
24. Judith Butler, *Undoing.*
25. Judith Butler, *Undoing,* p. 58.
26. Wendy Cealey Harrison and John Hood-Williams, *Beyond,* p. 207.
27. R. W. Connell (1987) *Gender and Power: Society, the Person and Sexual Politics.* Cambridge: Polity Press.
28. Ibid., p. 85.
29. Iris Marion Young (1990) *Throwing Like a Girl and Other Essays in Feminist Philosophy and Social Theory.* Bloomington: Indiana University Press.
30. R. W. Connell, *Gender,* pp. 74–5.
31. Ibid, p. 85.
32. D. Z. Demetriou (2001) 'Connell's concept of hegemonic masculinity: a critique', *Theory and Society,* 30 (3): 337–61.
33. R. W. Connell and James W. Messerschmidt (2005) 'Hegemonic masculinity: rethinking the concept', *Gender & Society,* 19 (6): 829–59.
34. Thomas Laqueur (1990) *Making Sex: Body and Gender from the Greeks to Freud.* Cambridge, MA: Harvard University Press.

Selected bibliography

Butler, Judith (1990) *Gender Trouble: Feminism and the Subversion of Identity*.New York: Routledge.

Butler, Judith (2004) *Undoing Gender*. New York: Routledge.

Connell, R. W. and Messerschmidt, James W. (2005) 'Hegemonic masculinity: rethinking the concept', *Gender & Society*, 19 (6): 829–59.

Connell, R. W. (1987) *Gender and Power: Society, the Person and Sexual Politics*. Cambridge: Polity Press.

Goffman, Erving (1979) *Gender Advertisements*. London: Macmillan.

Harrison, Wendy Cealey and Hood-Williams, John (2002) *Beyond Sex and Gender*.London: Sage.

Kessler, Suzanne and McKenna, Wendy (1978) *Gender: An Ethnomethodological Approach*. New York: John Wiley & Sons.

Kessler, Suzanne (1998) *Lessons from the Intersexed*. New Brunswick: Rutgers University Press.

CHAPTER 6

SOCIAL RELATIONS, SOCIAL CLASS AND THE SELF

At one time, when people sought to answer the question 'who am I?' social class would likely have formed a part of their answer. A person could have said clearly that they were working class or middle class. Recently, when academics have done research on social class and gone out to interview people about their class identification, many seem reluctant or unable to give a clear definition of themselves as belonging to one particular social class. As Geoff Payne and Clare Grew say, perhaps this is because social class has become such a complex phenomenon, identified by many different dimensions of social status.[1] For psychologists researching self and identity, class was rarely a consideration, being seen as a sociological category that doesn't touch upon the 'inner' depths of a person's psychological life or their personal identity. Yet when we meet people for the first time, most of us still ask, or are asked, 'what do you do?': the question seeks information on how we spend most of our time, whether in paid or unpaid work, or unemployed. The question is so ubiquitous because finding out someone's relation to the job market tells us about the activities they engage in for the majority of their life, their skills and capacities – perhaps even their interests – how much a person might earn, their social class and status, and their lifestyle. In other words, it tells us important things about that person's identity and the ways that others view, judge and value them. Rightly or wrongly, if you were to tell someone you were a doctor, it is likely you would be given greater respect than if you were to tell them you swept the streets for a living.

In this sense, social class is about much more than what you do for a living and how much money you earn. It is about all those other elements of social interaction I have been identifying in this book, such as the way we respond to others, judging and valuing them, and how they behave in the same way towards us. It is also about fantasy and imagination: what we *desire* to be or become, and how we *imagine* others see and value us as a person. Yet social class is also about the material constraints into which we are born, affecting our life chances through things like access to education and important social contacts. In this way, social relations are *a priori* of individual experience in a *historical* sense: that is, the family into which we are born, our geographical location, neighbourhood and community relations, religion and local culture will all affect our futures in important ways, both positively – opening up opportunities for identification, assimilation, self-development or escape – and negatively – closing down access to personal and material resources, limiting life-chances and scope for self-development, shutting down opportunities for escape, and negatively affecting identifications with others. When looked at in this way, social class is absolutely central in terms of who we are and who we can become, because it affects our life chances in so many important ways and structures our biographies across time and space. And it is with this structuring of biography that I want to begin.

Social relations, biography and self

For the French Marxist Lucien Sève the biography of an individual is determined by their place within the social relations of production, and, of course, it is within that biographical trajectory that the self, or personality, is formed: the capacities, skills, needs and characteristics of the person. This standpoint leads Sève to be highly critical of the traditional psychology of the personality, which understands basic aspects of the self, such as traits, capacities and needs, to be biologically given and universal to the human species. For Sève, how individuals develop their own self is totally dependent on the social heritage they are born into, which they assimilate through work. As I noted in Chapter 1, for Marx humans produce their mode of life through the collective force of labour, and it is within the division of labour that personal differences begin to form based on the different activities, capacities and skills that people perform and develop. What people are capable of doing and how they realize their own identity will depend to a large degree on their labour activities and the role they perform in the division of labour. A person's work may give certain general clues as to their identity, such as builder, joiner, teacher, nurse, doctor, computer programmer, businessperson, and so on.

For Marx, then, humans do not make the world or their own selves through pure reflection or contemplation: we do it through practical activity and practical intelligence, in which we engage with the world, transform it, and, in the process, transform our own selves. The sense of being an 'I' is something understood not through reflection, but in what we *do* in the social world: in our actions, conversations and relations with others. By the same token, however, humans are not born into a neutral and unformed world that can be made into whatever they will it to be: rather, we are all born into a world already formed by the labour of previous generations, and this is the world with which we engage. As Marx famously put it: 'Men make their own history, but they do not make it just as they please; they do not make it under circumstances chosen by themselves, but under circumstances directly encountered, given, and transmitted from the past'.[2]

What enables us to act *and* limits the scope of our actions is the legacy handed down to us through the ensemble of social relations, including our own specific place within the division of labour and in the hierarchy of social classes. For both Marx and Sève, then, human being is always social being, for the nature and consciousness of the person can only be understood in terms of the way they appropriate and change the social heritage that is handed down to them through social relations as they unfold within history: in the process of this historically located activity, social beings also change their own nature and consciousness. In this light Marx could say that 'the human essence is no abstraction inherent in each single individual. In its reality it is the ensemble of social relations'.[3] This means that the essence of who we are is not given inside us at birth as a spirit or soul, it is always, as Sève puts it, 'excentric' to us, being contained in social relations and assimilated in different ways by different individuals depending on their place in social relations and the division of labour.

Under the influence of Marx, Sève believes that the core problem in the social sciences and in the psychology of personality is the mediation between the general movement of society through history and the lives of individuals. The development of the individual always takes place within a social logic constituted by the ensemble of social relations which form the matrices of activity in which a biographical trajectory takes shape and a self is formed. Sève is not arguing that individuals can be seen as simply the products of the social structure, because he understands that (a) we are biological creatures that are not the products of society, but are nevertheless bound by complex relations to the social structure; and (b) that we develop a practical intelligence that is never wholly subservient to social ideologies but is engaged with the practical realities of life, its contradictions and problems. Here, Sève is directly arguing against the ideas of the anti-humanist Marxist Louis Althusser (mentioned briefly in the last chapter in relation to Judith Butler), who believed that through ideologies humans are always in an *imaginary* relation to their social reality, which inserts us into social practices in such a way that we become merely the supports of the social structure. In opposition to this, Sève wants to create a scientific humanism that doesn't fall into the essentialist and idealist trap of theorizing humans as having absolute freedom within the world, but nor does it become entrapped in the structuralist fallacy of reducing humans to stage props in the drama of history. Instead, Sève understands humans to be in a 'juxtastructural' relation to society – always meshed into social relations, but never the mere unthinking products of them. To fully understand human selves, then, scientific humanism has to show how the investigation of the lives of particular individuals must always be undertaken in the context of social relations, otherwise individuals become abstracted from the very concrete historical conditions in which their lives are set. Thus, the object of any true psychology should be what Sève calls 'social individuality'. We can take the example of sex from the last chapter to illustrate what he is trying to say: our sexed body is not actually produced by the norms and fantasies of idealized masculinity or femininity, because if it was everyone would conform to the norm in both body and behaviour, with little or no sexual variation. There would be no intersexuals. However, there are intersexuals and other sexual variations, only the norms and fantasies create the conditions in which sex is experienced and through which intersexuals relate to their bodies, to themselves and to others. This is a juxtastructural relation.

If we take Sève's argument seriously, as I suggest we should, and try to understand social individuality in terms of the way that social relations and activities
translate into the logic of individual lives, what can social relations actually tell
us about individuals? First of all they can tell us something about what Sève calls
the *general forms of individuality* that develop in each historical epoch on the
basis of social relations. In capitalist social relations, for example, we have such
general forms of individuality as capitalist and worker, and in power relations
between the sexes and within the sexual division of labour we have man and
woman, straight and gay. However, such general categories are more descriptive
of the activities of social groups rather than the particular identities of the many
people who could fall within these generalized forms. Yet they can help us to
understand some of the contradictions inherent in these activities that will translate into personal dilemmas. For example, the capitalist may be torn between their
drive to accumulate capital and their desire to spend it: the worker between their
need to work to earn a living and their desire to pursue other activities they would
find more interesting or rewarding.

Secondly, for Sève, Marx's mature works also showed that alienation was not an
individual psychological condition in which a person becomes estranged from their
own inner sense of self, because the human essence was now conceived as social
relations: rather, alienation has to be understood as the separation of the vast majority of individuals who form the working classes from the social heritage they help
to create – the assimilation of which is limited for them by the constant drive to
accumulate more capital in the form of profit, rather than focus on the development
of the talents and abilities of each person. In capitalism, the need for capital accumulation constantly outweighs individuals' need for self-development. This leads
to a situation where we have, on the one hand, highly developed productive forces
in the form of technology and the application of science, and, on the other hand, the
impoverishment and alienation of a large group of workers within some of the most
advanced societies in history. For Sève, social change is brought nearer as people
fully realize that both the contradictions in their lives and the sense of alienation
that haunts them are not 'personal' problems, but the oppressions of a particular
socio-economic system that can be transformed.

Until that day, capitalist social relations will continue to structure the biographies of individual selves. They do so by structuring the *activity* and the *time* that
compose individual biographies. Because most of us have to work to earn money
and spend most of our time at work, the activities we are employed in determine
to a large degree our capacities, skills, abilities, knowledge and self-identities. It
is not simply falling under the category of some general form of individuality
such as being a worker that is important for self-identity, but it is mainly the scope
for self-development (or the lack of it) afforded by a person's work that is important. Alongside this, the time that is left over for people to engage in other activities outside of paid employment, or the alienating experience of unemployment,
is what shapes the context of people's lived experience and helps us to understand
'the whole structure and development of real human personalities'.[4] While
Foucault studied the discursive regimes that structure the organization of space

and time in the micro-social power politics of workplaces and institutions, in the process forming the individual's experience of self and world, Sève attempts to study the capitalist social relations that structure the organization of activities and time within a person's biography as it is located within various places. This gives us a broader picture of the structuring of time and activities in various places that is at the heart of a person's biography, forming their experience of self and world.

According to Sève, in capitalist social relations people have to spend most of their time at work to earn a wage, but even at work most workers' time will be spent on activities that are boring and repetitive, involving the constant re-performance of tasks that have already been learned and mastered (what Sève calls 'sector II acts'). These acts use capacities that the worker has already developed, and do not entail developing new capacities by learning new activities and skills ('sector I acts'). Furthermore, at work the time of most workers will be devoted to 'abstract activity', which is activity that is performed for the sole purpose of the accumulation of capital, rather than on 'concrete activity' that develops or uses capacities which are meaningful for the individual, enhancing their own self-development. Although Sève formed his ideas mainly in the 1960s and 70s, we can apply his approach to a modern working context such as a call centre. In this setting, workers are wired up to a telephone system which dials the numbers of people to whom the workers have to make a sales pitch for whatever product or service they are selling. Once the call centre workers have learnt about the products they are selling (often having to read from a pre-prepared script about them) and about how the telephone system works, their daily routine is spent repeating the same performance of their required activity. The purpose is not to educate or develop the capacities of the employee but to sell the products of the company so that it can make more profit.

In general, it can be said that workers in more middle-class occupations will escape some of this more soul destroying work, for their occupations, such as doctor, teacher, lecturer, lawyer, etc., will involve them in more 'sector I' activities – the learning of new knowledge, activities and capacities – and in general this will make their activities feel more concrete and less abstract: especially if they are personally meaningful, interesting and rewarding. Under these conditions middle-class people may feel more involved with their work and that it actually adds something to their lives and selves. However, no one completely escapes abstract activity and there will be aspects of everyone's activity devoted to this, whether it is salespeople having to increase the volume of their sales to make more profit, or surgeons having to perform more operations to increase efficiency for their hospital. Given the pressures of work, or the boredom and drudgery of unemployment, many people look to their leisure time for activities that are personally rewarding or pleasurable; activities that Sève calls 'intermediary' and which lead to self-development or personal satisfaction. This can be a hobby or an activity like playing sport, listening to music, spending time with friends or family, or going for a meal or a drink. As Tom Yardley shows, time spent with friends becoming intoxicated provides many individuals with those moments of what Victor Turner called anti-structure, in which people escape from the structures and disciplines of workaday routines, experiencing the possibilities and pleasures of liminal time and space.[5] However, under capitalism, time spent on personal consumption and recreation is experienced as a temporary respite, often geared more to preparing people for a return to the labour process rather than the long-term development of self.

However, as Victor Turner has pointed out, in industrial capitalism leisure time is not only *freedom from* institutional obligations, work times, routines and disciplines, experienced as a space in which to recuperate, it is also *freedom to* enter symbolic worlds of entertainment, hobbies, sport and games. This freedom to play with ideas, fantasies and materials allows people to experience some sense of transcendence over social structural limitations, and also to engage in social relations with friends that are more equal and of mutual benefit. Here, in this spontaneous equality, people can interact without a mask or a pre-set social script, although such interaction cannot be sustained for long. However, Turner admits that this is the *ideal* of leisure and that in reality it is influenced by the domain of work from which it is split. For example, entertainment and sport become a vocation for some, but only a spectator activity for many. To describe this situation, Turner distinguishes between liminal and liminoid phenomena: the former occur in all societies and involve the entire social group in ritual performance to mark the gap between ordered social worlds, as in rites of passage between different stages of life: the latter occur mainly in industrial capitalism and 'develop apart from the central economic and political processes, along the margins, in the interfaces and interstices of central and servicing institutions'.[6] The theatre is an example of a liminoid phenomenon in industrial society, as it is part of an 'entertainment industry' but is one in which the dramas of everyday life can be heightened and the underlying causes of collective experiences and tensions can be explored and critiqued. In this way, theatre can provide a liminoid space in which the rituals of everyday life can be played with, heightened, subverted, reassembled, made grotesque and critiqued. It is an experience that is both part of the time and space of industrial capitalism, yet one that finds ways to break free from it.

However, because of a lack of access to economic, cultural and social resources, many people may not have the ability to participate in such liminoid activities in their leisure time. For example, in a study of working-class mothers' support networks, Wendy Mitchell and Eileen Green found that the women's creative capacities were closely bound to wider social inequalities, so that 'their everyday experiences and discourses of motherhood, kinship and their own self-identity as a mother still remain closely interwoven with the wider socio-economic inequalities which permeate their lives'.[7] This had ramifications for their free time, for while expressing an awareness of, and a desire for, more varied leisure activities, 'their leisure was usually home based, such as watching television/reading due to childcare issues and financial considerations'.[8] Here, leisure time is perhaps experienced more as escape from daily duties than experiment with alternative ideas and ways of life.

However, we can also extend Turner's ideas of liminality to industrial capitalism by looking at the liminal periods in people's biographical time – that is, the space between structured periods in life – and the way that these are dealt with. For example, infants will go through a liminal period when leaving a full-time home environment to go to school: school leavers will experience liminality when getting their first job: the newly retired will experience liminality when first they leave work for good, needing to find activities and routines to structure their lives: and the unemployed will experience extended periods of liminality, sometimes needing to reconstruct their biographies and identities, their skills and capacities, in order to find new work, or when entering a new job or profession. Perhaps the difference between industrial societies and the non-industrial ones that Turner first studied is the lack of collective rites of passage to steer people through these liminal experiences. For example, periods of unemployment could be experienced as alienating and isolating, with an absence of people to act as guides through the experience, as well as limiting access to economic, cultural or social resources through which individuals could reconstruct their lives in meaningful ways. This is why the experience of unemployment for many is an unpleasant and meaningless lack of structure that brings on anxiety or depression. As Mead would say, in such circumstances the need is for humans to reconstruct their lives in meaningful ways, but people may lack the resources and opportunities to do this.

However, as Sève claims, time is central in all of this – whether it is routine everyday time, or the transitions, crises or breaks across the life-span – because it structures the field across which the activity of individuals unfolds within their social relations. Within a person's biography, the 'use-time' they have to devote to different activities will mark out the 'fundamental law of development' of their personality. What use-time illustrates for Sève is 'the *real* activity of the concrete individual … a reality which [people] constantly have to deal with in their life, therefore a *practical* reality, the empirical aspects of which are quite visible …'.[9] Thus, what Sève is attempting to formulate are the actual conditions of people's lives that provide *both* opportunities for self-development *and* limitations to that development due to the structure of activities and time in their biography. He wants his psychology to be not only theoretical, providing a theory of what it is to be a person, but also open to empirical application: the model of biography is something we can *use* to actually map out the biography of each individual person. In each person's use-time – the interweaving of their activities and time – we can see the disciplines to which they are subjected, the abstract and concrete nature of their activities, the extent to which they are given access to, or excluded from, the means of developing various capacities, the balance of time they have to spend on various activities, and from all of this the extent of the development of their personality.

However, Sève recognizes that in capitalism the majority of people have little control over their use-time and activities, and because of this will feel alienated to some degree in their lives. This sense of alienation is not inherent in the human condition, as most individuals will be able to escape it for some part of their lives, whether in certain aspects of concrete activity, or in the intermediary activities of interpersonal relations and interactions with others. Indeed, it is within such relations of family, friendship and community that we first experience the world as children, so that 'the concrete personality first presents itself as an ensemble of personal, indeed inter-personal, non-alienated activities, unfolding as self-expression'.[10] These are the kinds of social relations with which interactionists like Mead, and social constructionists such as Harré and Shotter, were concerned. However, even in such interactions people (including children) are subject to controls, only for Sève these are 'spontaneous controls' of the type that emerge from everyday moral encounters. There are also 'voluntary controls' that are imposed by external agencies and authorities, such as the disciplinary controls encountered in schools, workplaces and other institutions, which feel more alien to the self. Again, these controls are tied to what Foucault identified as disciplines, which make elements of the population more docile and amenable to control and management, in order to extract from them greater surplus value in the form of capital.

While all of this is greatly illuminating, helping us to put what we have already talked of in previous chapters into the context of capitalist social relations, there are nevertheless some problems with Sève's approach in many of its different aspects, especially in the divisions he creates between different types of activities and controls. If these are taken only as analytic distinctions they may be useful but problems can arise if we try to think of them in terms of practical application. For example, the distinction between spontaneous and voluntary controls is not so clear, as certain controls that apply in our interpersonal relations and interactions can have the quality of compulsion because they are imposed by authorities. An illustration would be the norms that govern our sexual and gender relations, which are not purely spontaneous in that they arise from interpersonal conduct, but as both Foucault and Butler showed they can be imposed by powers and authorities for governmental purposes rather than for the social and personal good. Indeed, in certain cases the micro-social power politics over the imposition of regulations and controls in families can lead to the severe forms of alienation and ontological insecurity that Laing noted. This means that alienation is not simply experienced as abstract activity connected with labour, because we can also become alienated from our own activities and powers of agency within interpersonal relations.

What this illustrates is Sève's major error, which is to understand the appropriation of the social heritage by individuals only in terms of their relation to the labour process: in other words, their relation to production through their place in the division of labour. This leads Sève to claim that the psychology of personality is founded on the study of social labour or it does not exist. However, as he also notes with reference to Marx's *Capital,* Marx does not believe that social labour is the human essence: rather, it is the 'particular forms of social relations' typical of each historical period (see the section on Marx in Chapter 1).[11] On this basis, Sève hopes to forestall charges of economic reductionism by claiming that in studying biographies 'one must consider the system of the division of labour in all its aspects, technical and economic, domestic, political, cultural, etc., as an ensemble of objective social facts indispensable for understanding the temporal topology of concrete personalities in a determinate society'.[12] But the problem is that this is exactly what Sève doesn't do. For example, he doesn't consider the domestic division of labour, in which caring duties done purely for the benefit of others can leave some women as depressed and unfulfilled as the most mind-numbing paid employment.[13] This omission obscures the importance of the relations of power governing sex and gender, along with the gendered division of labour, in the formation of individual biographies and selves.

As Robert Ashcroft points out, what this all means is that for many individuals the split between concrete and abstract activity is not identical with the split between concrete and abstract labour.[14] According to Sève, activities like caring for family and friends, or learning in school, would be examples of concrete activity, or certainly intermediary activity, as they are not performed for wages but for personal rewards which count towards self-development. Yet we have already noted that domestic labour can be alienated and become abstract, whether it is performed by men or women: children at school can feel alienated from their studies, and working-class students may feel academic work is too abstract and not related to their cultural background or their possible future.[15] Equally, in a more positive light, the social heritage can be appropriated outside the labour process, where vital cultural capacities of accountability, responsibility and moral judgement are learned or denied in the micro-politics of the family or interpersonal relations. Depending on the nature of these relations and the creation of a person's experience within them, these sites of micro-political relations can be experienced as entailing concrete *and* abstract activity: that is, activities or duties to which we feel a special connection and which are personally fulfilling, or alternatively activities and duties performed out of compunction and which are alienating and unfulfilling.

However, despite these criticisms, I feel that there is much of value in Sève's work, including many possibilities for its application, provided the above criticisms are used to reformulate it in a positive way. The value of the approach is that it attempts to understand the production of individual differences through biographical trajectories, involving a division of time and activities which have a concrete historical location in the social relations of capitalist society. This entails the study of actual biographies as they are divided between time for various work activities, work and leisure, domestic duties, interpersonal relations, and how the contradictions between these various activities and the capacities they create is the setting for the development or the alienation of self. Although the approach fails to highlight the capacities that are developed or destroyed in interpersonal relations – such as accountability, normative regulation and rule-breaking, and powers of agency and responsibility – nevertheless Sève does foreground exactly what others ignore: the important ways in which our lives are governed by the workings of a capitalist economy and how this structures the biography in which the self is formed (including the experience of unemployment and why it can be so negative in a world where work determines how most people spend their time and earn their money).

In addition, Sève opposes anti-humanist theories that reduce the self to a subject or illusion of ideological, linguistic or discursive systems, which are seen to construct selves in their entirety so that they act only to support and perpetuate regulative social mechanisms. For Sève, we are not just the illusions of culture, but embodied beings meshed into relations of production and reproduction, whose bodies are transformed by being empowered and disempowered in the temporal organization of the activities that make up our biography. That we can feel alienated in some areas of life, and know that this is wrong, means that we have capacities for practical intellectual engagement with the conditions of our lives, and can act to change them using capacities established in other biographical locations and activities. We are subject to norms, but different norms govern different activities within our biographies, and we can become aware of their contradictions. This does not mean that we necessarily reach a full awareness of the social conditions that structure our lives, or of the contradictions within them, nor that our lives do not involve fantasy, illusion and ideology as attempts to resolve those contradictions: however, in practical, intelligent engagement with the conditions in which we live, it is possible for humans to gain some level of insight. Indeed, without this, it would be impossible for those humans who become social scientists to analyse people's lives and the social conditions that govern them, and to write their books and articles.

Unlike Foucault, Sève realizes that the activities we perform in various institutional contexts place contradictory demands upon us in the different sectors of our biographies: the practices and disciplines of work, school or prison, may contradict the discipline of being a good mother, father, sister, brother, friend, companion or colleague. All these different activities will create different capacities and needs – technical, intellectual, communicative, interpersonal – that enable and motivate further activities. Also, the awareness of contradictions within our biographies creates the need for resolution, even if we cannot achieve this; in which case, we may lapse into alienation, destructiveness and negativity. But positive awareness and action are always a possibility.

One final aspect of Sève's work that is also worth keeping hold of is the way he attempts to correct the individualizing and pathologizing function of psychology as we know it today, which – even in its 'humanist' forms – attempts to pin alienation, depression, anger and destructiveness to *individual* trauma within a life history, usually in childhood, rather than look at the structural conditions of society that shape personal biographies and expand or limit life-chances and the scope for personal expression. Other more reductionist forms of psychology attempt to understand human behaviour and 'pathology' in terms of biology, neural-chemistry and cognitive structures, or, in the case of evolutionary psychology, by comparison to the behaviour of other animals. All these branches of psychology practice the discipline in the way that Foucault described, by selecting an *individual* case taken to be against the norm and to explore it in detail. As Sève says,

Until now psychology has sought above all to understand [the human] by way of the animal, the adult by way of the child, the normal individual by way of the sick, the total system of the personality by way of its isolated functions, and the content of this personality by way of certain forms of activity. We think the time has come to supplement this rather unfruitful effort by a real effort in the opposite direction.[16]

This effort would mean studying the social relations and activities, and the contradictions within and between them, which form all biographies and selves in capitalism, including the things that alienate and trouble us. I want to try to advance this project in the rest of this chapter by looking at the moral and emotional effects of social class relations on biographies and selves, including recent work that moves beyond the purely material structuring of class in terms of the relation of individuals to the means of production, focusing instead on cultural, social and symbolic capital as well as on material capital.

Cultural capital, social *habitus* and identity

For the French sociologist Pierre Bourdieu, the social class differences and distinctions between individuals that influence their biographical trajectories and identities are not just based in the ownership or non-ownership of material capital, or in the person's relation to the division of labour, but also depend upon the possession of cultural, social and symbolic capital. Cultural capital can come in the form of embodied states such as a person's manners or style of speech, which operate as 'second nature' without the person being conscious of it, yet give away their class background; or it can be in the form of education and qualifications, or the possession of cultural goods which tells us about a person's tastes and lifestyle that are also signs of their class position. Social capital can be the access to, or exclusion from, social networks which open up or close down opportunities in life. The value of these types of capital, however, depends on whether they can be turned into symbolic capital, which is the type of capital legitimated and recognized within particular social fields. My cultural capital as an academic may be recognized within the University system, yet would be given less value if I went to work in a factory or in business. Thus, the judgements made about us accord not only to a person's wealth or lack of it, they also depend on the various other forms of capital we possess and their relative values in different social fields. For Bourdieu, the social field is defined in terms of power, as it is the space for the relations of force between different types of capital and between agents who possess differential amounts of cultural, social and symbolic capital. Social fields therefore produce difference in terms of the distinction they confer on the holders of different types of capital, thus establishing the relations of power between them. In doing so, they also act as the principle of behaviour of the individuals and groups (the various holders of capital) within the field, forming the most real and determinate force that shapes our experience.

All of us were born into, brought up within, and live within various social fields that have formed what Bourdieu calls our '*habitus*': this is our meaningful relationship to the world which operates as a practical sense beneath awareness, shaping our perceptions and valuations of the world. At the core of the *habitus* are dispositions and tastes which incline us towards certain habitual patterns of action in relation to the world in which we live. The *habitus* begins to form in childhood through family, neighbourhood and education, which are the main social fields where we acquire cultural and social capital. Different groups and classes in society will each have a different *habitus,* which predisposes them through dispositions and habits towards specific types of practice and lifestyles. Thus:

> The structures constitutive of a particular type of environment (e.g. the material conditions of existence characteristic of a class condition) produce *habitus,* systems of durable, transposable *dispositions,* structured structures predisposed to functioning as structuring structures, that is, as principles of the generation and structuring of practices and representations.[17]

So, before individuals begin to develop the type of capacities that Sève talked of, they are influenced in the direction of their activity by the *habitus:* the dispositions and tastes that they absorb and acquire as part of their cultural conditions of life. But the *habitus* forms a limit for certain social classes, both material and cultural, on the types of activities in which they engage and the capacities they will develop. For example, Bourdieu shows how developing the type of abstract learning involved in much of higher education, and the type of appreciation required to enjoy and participate in the more abstract forms of artistic representation, depend on an absence of practical or economic necessity which favours the middle class over the working class in acquiring these capacities.[18] So the material and cultural conditions of life interrelate in forming a *habitus* in which people acquire cultural and social capital that predisposes them to certain forms of perception, appreciation and tastes, and which incline them to certain forms of activities. As illustrated by Paul Willis in his ethnographic study of adolescents in school, a large number of working-class youths feel that their learning at school is too abstract, having little concrete relevance to the realities they will face as working-class adults in their jobs and leisure pursuits. Willis finds that the main source of discontent lies in the adolescents' home-lives and their general contact with the older generation, in which little importance is placed on education in working-class culture.[19]

Thus, the cultural capital that people inherit from their family and educational background angles them in a biographical trajectory towards certain positions in the social structure, through education and work-place hierarchies, to jobs and social status, reproducing the inequalities in society. Much of this depends on the value of their cultural capital in various fields: in the style of their manners and articulation of ideas and opinions, young middle-class people can gain access more easily to higher education, whereas young working-class people may find their cultural capital of more value in practical types of occupations which require fewer academic qualifications. Indeed, dispositions within the *habitus* can be seen as the embodiment of the social relations of various fields, in terms of the relation of difference and distinction between various forms of cultural and social capital. The social heritage transmitted within social relations is therefore marked and assimilated as much through culture as through social labour, so that the cultural capital possessed by each person distinguishes them within the social hierarchy depending on how this is valued by others within various social fields. Capital does not just have a monetary value for Bourdieu, its value also depends on the evaluative judgements of others made on the basis of aesthetic, moral and normative criteria.

Indeed, partly under the influence of Bourdieu, sociologists are now beginning to write about the normative aspects of class; how much of our class position depends on the recognition or non-recognition from others – the way we are valued either positively or negatively depending on our social and cultural capital.[20] As Andrew Sayer points out, we are normative beings who judge others, and, in turn, are expected to account to others for our own behaviour. While inequalities of wealth, resources and opportunities have little to do with the moral worth of people, nevertheless they do impact on the possibility of achieving valued ways of life that bring positive recognition from others and, in the process, build self-respect. Again, access to good schools and to higher education helps to create the kind of cultural capital – in terms of qualifications, knowledge and the confident manner to articulate what you know – that is highly valued in society. Moral valuations of people, then, can be based on personal characteristics that are held to be worthy, such as honesty and integrity, which are relatively independent of a person's cultural capital: yet these are also mixed in with judgements about how someone speaks, their manners, tastes and knowledge that do relate to the cultural capital they have inherited and developed.

Bound into this network of moral evaluation are evaluations about one's own self that are, as Bakhtin showed, always dialogically related to the way we imagine that others see us. The way we value ourselves depends on the dialogical relations we have to others and the level of recognition and respect we get from them. However, as Nussbaum has pointed out, judgements are always tied to feelings and emotions, in that we will like and love the things we are attracted to, and hate, loath or feel aversion to the things we are not.[21] Both Sayer and Beverley Skeggs underline the importance of shame in class relations, as those who feel they lack the necessary social and cultural capital to gain the recognition and respect of others will also feel a sense of shame towards themselves. As Sayer claims, shame 'is a response to the imagined or actual views of others, but also a private reflexive emotion, in that it involves evaluation of the self by the self'.[22] Even if this is only an unarticulated feeling, shame may affect people in different ways, leading to a variety of responses. If someone were to feel shame because of a perceived lack of education, they may respond by resisting or rebelling against the real or imagined judgements of others, flaunting that lack or decrying the value of education generally: alternatively, they may try to conform by making up for that lack through reading or taking classes. Others may live quietly with their shame, feeling their perceived lack of education silences them in public, especially amongst others thought to be well-educated or knowledgeable.

As I have shown in previous chapters, such feelings and evaluations of the self by the self refer to what Bakhtin called the 'I-for-myself', which is the relation we develop with our own self: the images we perceive others hold of us relates to the 'I-for-others', the way that we imagine ourselves to be seen in society. However, the difference with Bakhtin's ideas is that he did not link these moral evaluations into the class structure. The same could be said of thinkers like Adam Smith and George Herbert Mead who thought that individuals internalize a sense of the moral values of their culture as an impartial spectator or generalized other. By the terms 'impartial' or 'generalized' Smith and Mead meant to indicate that the moral censor and judge that constitutes human conscience does not always take the form of any particular person, certainly not in adult life. However, as Beverley Skeggs points out, the norms that regulate our behaviour, and by which we are judged and valued, tend to be middle class norms which set the standard of respectability. In this sense they are not impartial or generalized, but are highly partial and particular: standards belonging to middle-class groups against which other classes are negatively judged. Furthermore, these moral norms apply also to gender and sexuality, which can never be separated from social class. Thus, for working-class women it is middle-class women who form the dialogical 'other' with the power to negatively judge them.[23]

In Skeggs's study of a group of working-class women attending a care course at college, she illustrates the contradictions and tensions that exist in the women's lives that form the core of their biographies and their formation as gendered/classed selves. First of all, the women in the study had limited capital to trade on the job market, except for their feminine cultural capital as unpaid labour, usually gained as carers within families. Because of their position in the division of labour, most women identified strongly with 'caring' as a positive value that was central to their self-identity. However, they strongly dis-identified as being working class, according to Skeggs, because of the negative judgements and images of working-class women, and also because their experience of being working class involved exclusion, particularly in the labour market and education. Here, their capital as working-class women is devalued and their opportunities limited, whereas as carers they possess both cultural capital and a sense of respectability.[24]

Secondly, working-class women have an ambivalent attitude to femininity, because they are often portrayed in the media as being vulgar, having excessive bodies (usually seen as overweight or inappropriately dressed), and as being sexually promiscuous. In contemporary culture a popular image of working-class women is typified by the 'hen party', through which they are represented as being drunken, noisy, badly behaved and vulgar. For Skeggs, the over-determination of her image in such a representation is an attempt to reconstruct the boundaries of regulation on working-class women through governance and self-governance.[25] Indeed, the women whom Skeggs interviewed for her book were quick to dissociate themselves from what was judged to be excessive or vulgar female behaviour. Against this image of working-class women there is the ideal representation of femininity that has existed since the 19th century in Europe, which characterizes it by ease of manner, calmness and restraint. Skeggs is quick to point out, however, that this is more of a male middle-class fantasy that is difficult for all women to attain, but perhaps more so for working-class women given the realities and constraints of their lives.

Because of their ambivalent positioning with regard to femininity, most of the working-class women in Skeggs's study identified more with ideals of glamour, largely because style is seen to be more of a working-class than a middle-class competence. However, this glamorous femininity is something that is, quite literally, 'put on': an image applied with clothes and make-up in order to stage a performance for special occasions. In this way, glamour is one of the 'styles of the flesh' in which pleasure can be gained. Yet a glamorous performance of femininity was recognized not to be necessary, or even appropriate, at all times and places, thus being limited to specific contexts such as nights out or special occasions. For everyday purposes, like going to college, femininity was not seen to be an important performance to stage, and a fellow student of the women in the study who was always glamorous and precisely turned-out – dressed up to the nines and perfectly coiffured – was taken as an object of derision. In the right context, though, glamour involved a positive valuation of self for the women, especially if they were recognized as being attractive and sexy by men. Being fancied was a positive confirmation of the women's desirability, particularly if they had no other source of confirmation of worth, such as meaningful work in which they could attain self-development and self-esteem. What this means, however, is that 'femininity' only partially encapsulated the way that women lived the category of 'woman'. Because of the contradiction in femininity, it is not a permanently habitable category for most women. Indeed, given what I said about gender performance in the last chapter, most of it depends on the social context in which people are performing and the audience they are performing for, rather than on generalized norms. It is social context that influences the way in which gender is performed within social relationships.

Thirdly, the women's relationship to heterosexuality is also contradictory and shot through with ambivalent feelings. All the women in Skeggs's study identified as heterosexual, something which should have conferred respectability on them. Yet because working-class sexuality – especially female sexuality – is seen as potentially excessive and dangerous, identification as heterosexual produces *both* normalization *and* marginalization for working-class women. Heterosexuality is a valued capital in capitalist society because of the need to reproduce the working population, which is one of the main sources for the production of wealth. Heterosexual working-class women possess this capital, yet at the same time it is devalued by old associations of the working poor with decadence and disease, and with modern media representations of excessiveness and promiscuity. For many women, sex is associated with shame and, in a society where working-class women's sexuality is associated with vulgarity and with being 'easy', the negotiation of sexual relations becomes particularly difficult. Thus, Skeggs regards sexuality as more than just a product of discursive normative regulations, because sexuality is a materiality, and the norms which regulate it are differentially institutionalized in family, work, education and leisure.

This also created a problem for the working-class women with respect to both lesbianism and feminism. To identify as lesbian, or to make any sexual choices other than those ascribed as normal female heterosexual choices, would be to risk losing their fragile sense of respectability. For middle-class women, to identify as lesbian is seen as a mark of individuality, no matter what problems it might create, whereas for working-class women it is to give up not only the possibility of becoming respectable, but also whatever power and position they may have within institutions like the family. Marriage is often a substitute for unemployment for those who lack educational capital, and many working-class girls feel that motherhood provides them with an identity in a world where it would be difficult to seek self-identity or self-development through employment. Given the position of working-class women in the division of labour and the value given to their cultural capital in various social fields, like the family and education, their heterosexuality is produced through economic and cultural incentives as a way to establish a life for themselves and a self-identity that is recognized as having some respectability. It is also for the same reasons that many working-class women do not identify with feminism, because its ideals of autonomy and independence for women could not provide them with the economic security, cultural recognition or emotional support that adopting the position of married woman or mother could. To become a feminist would also be to adopt a position identified as belonging to others; specifically, to the middle-class women who form the dialogical other with the cultural power to judge them negatively.

What Skeggs is arguing, then, is that people are not the sole authors of their identities, whether they are working class or middle class, male or female: instead, the biographical trajectories of our lives and the self-identities that are possible for us are constructed within a given social structure of power relations, capital transfers within social fields, values and representations. Who we can become as a person depends largely on our position within these social fields and the various capitals we have accumulated. Biographical life-choices and life-chances are always limited for us, although we can deploy constructive and creative strategies to generate a sense of ourselves that has some value, or to resist and have fun with the limitations placed upon us. Skeggs notes how the women in her study did this through activities like having a night on the town with the girls, which provided an occasion for them to have fun with some of the more negative images of working-class women, such as laughing loudly and joking, having a few drinks and playfully flirting with men. Thus, although the leisure activities of the working class can be limited, as the single mothers in Mitchell and Green's study recognized (referred to earlier in this chapter), there is still opportunity for people to use their creativity to create some liminal sense of freeing themselves from the normative constraints that govern most of their daily lives, or at least playing with these.

In addition, because these women, like many others, identified mainly with the activity of caring, their identities are created not so much around questions of 'who am I?' or 'what can I become?' – concerning what Foucault called 'care of the self' – but are centred on caring for others. This involves a different ethical motivation, as the ethics of care for others is orientated to relationships and dialogue, rather than to concern with the rational autonomous agent.[26] It is no coincidence that the latter has been stereotypically associated with men in Western culture, while the former has been associated with women. The association with caring can be negative as women's lives become filled with a sense of duty to others combined with a relative neglect of self. However, in a more positive light, it does create an alternative ethic of care for everyday life, and also provides the social sciences with an illustration of the intrinsically relational nature of social life, for, after all, most men are dependent in some way on the caring capacities of women, even if this goes unacknowledged in ideas of autonomous individuality.[27]

While Skeggs's work differs from Sève's in that she focuses on cultural phenomena that create divisions between social classes, leading to various exclusions and emotions like shame, she is nevertheless also concerned with the structural contradictions and ambivalences in capitalism that constrain individual biographies as they form across time and place (in various social fields), and with the construction of distinct social and personal identities within those parameters. Skeggs also underlines a key point made by Sève, that it is the nature of contradictions within everyday adult life in capitalism which defines the personality, including emotional distress and alienation, rather than the individual psychic traumas that preoccupy most psychologists who study the formation of the self.

This approach is also underlined, especially with respect to alienation, in Simon Charlesworth's phenomenological study of working class life in the town of Rotherham in northern England. Like most northern towns and cities, Rotherham established itself in the 19th and 20th centuries on the basis of industrial production, in this case the production of wrought iron and steel, and also in coal mining. During the de-industrialization of the 1980s places like Rotherham were hit hard, losing a high proportion of traditional industries that were not replaced by the boom in service sector industries, such as banking, insurance and finance, which never had a strong hold in the area. The result was large-scale unemployment, followed by a predominance of unskilled or semi-skilled work, or part-time employment, for those who could find it. But unemployment, especially youth unemployment, remains high. In the picture painted by Charlesworth, this gives the town the feeling of bleakness and despair typical of once proud working-class areas that have seen their best days disappear. As a boy who grew up in the area and as a man retains contacts there, Charlesworth immerses himself in the lived experience of those in the town, both through personal experience and in interviews with some of the residents. He then attempts a phenomenological study of the experience of being working class and living in the town, drawing on the work of Bourdieu, Merleau-Ponty and Heidegger.

Using this phenomenological approach, Charlesworth aims to show how Rotherham's social environment forms the *habitus* that grounds the working class inhabitants' embodied dispositions, perceptions of the world and capacities, including the capacity to articulate themselves. In this way, the phenomena of the social world have a personal meaning, a lived-through significance, that may not always be transparent to consciousness, but which nevertheless emerges in what people say and do – the way they discover themselves as subject to social meaning. Thus, although we may not fully understand the forces that structure our lives, our experience is nevertheless framed within the *habitus* through which we encounter these forces and which grounds our corporeal subjectivity and self-identity. Through life in a particular *place* we become imbued with a sense of the world and our position within it. This takes the form not only of self-awareness, but, more deeply, of a practical sense or pre-reflective competence, which disposes us to certain feelings, moods and perceptions of the world, and to act within it in particular ways: what Merleau-Ponty called the stable dispositional tendencies from which our actions emanate and which underlie self-consciousness. Therefore, the place where we are brought up and the place where we live is the 'world-defining context' in which social class is experienced, and it also forms the 'primordial realm in which selves take shape'.[28] Yet we must remember that place is not just made out of bricks and mortar: place is composed of *relations* – to the objects and people around us, and also to the people, real or imagined, outside of that place who judge those living within it. Place also partly determines our relation to the labour market, and is more generally a social field formed by the relation of various capitals – material, cultural and social. Thus:

> class is not a simple matter of understanding oneself through a role but a locating
> of the flesh through inhabiting a particular social realm, constituted by certain
> objects and certain relations on the basis of one's embodying incorporated forms
> that lead one to be treated factically, as an object possessed of an essence.[29]

The essence of who we are as selves is therefore, as Marx suggested, the social relations that form us: but these relations are always located and experienced within particular places – a city, a town, a village, a neighbourhood, a workplace, an institution, a family, and in places for leisure. Such places form the ontological sense of reality, so that if these places decay or are destroyed, so too are the spaces and rhythms of life, the very substance of our ontological security. According to Charlesworth, Rotherham as a place has undergone such decay, through de-industrialization, unemployment, low wages and poverty. This forms not simply an environmental backdrop to people's lives, but fundamentally changes life itself, the way that people *feel* and think about the world and themselves. The breakdown of work and daily routine shatters the rhythm of life in terms of work practices and all other areas of life linked to it, such as family life, leisure and friendships. Lingering feelings are created of a world gone wrong, in disarray, in which people literally come to feel sick. A silence envelops this world, in which people can only articulate their feelings about Rotherham in monosyllabic expressions such as the place is 'shit' or 'crap'. These are the expressions of people who have lost a sense of value in their own eyes and in the eyes of others, because their social value has fallen in terms of material capital – the value of their labour power in terms of wages – cultural capital, and social capital. Charlesworth recognizes that this is not just a problem for the working class in Rotherham, but is a problem in a globalized world where:

> Labour is unrooted, dis-embedded, being made migrant the world over, creating people so vulnerable and atomized that they carry the marks of their impoverishment in their bodies as oddity and illness. Cheap labour, scrounging a day here, a day there, a mass of bodies rendered worthless by ubiquity, fit to clean or lift, care or dig, mend or clear, yet invisible except as a threat, aliens among their own species. This condition is ontological, this is social difference, categorization, realized in the being of beings.[30]

In this way, then, social difference and categorization are lived and felt within the times and places of everyday life in which we exist as embodied beings. The damage or fulfilment we find there is carried in our bodies as movement, gesture, speech, capacities, health and illness, and as capitals, ones that in the quotation above are seen to be rendered worthless. This lack of value is marked not only by the silence of the poor, but also their invisibility to others in terms of a lack of recognition that creates an ontological non-existence. However, as Sayer points out, Bourdieu's theory of recognition is limited in terms of its concentration on capitals valued by others, such as money, status and prestige (what he calls 'external goods'), as this doesn't take account of self-satisfaction, achievement and self-development ('internal goods'), or the lack of them. One of the reasons that people may feel devalued in their own eyes is that they have little access to the type of concrete, capacity-building activity that leads to self-development and self-satisfaction. As Charlesworth says, while his is not a Marxist interpretation of working class experience:

> one of the most important reasons for this approach is to try and show that the social and cultural resources for developing one's inalienable human capacities, what Marx called one's 'species being', of coming to fruition as a person of categoric value, are inequitably distributed, with the result that the possibility of the development of capacities important to personal fulfilment are frustrated.[31]

However, while all of this is insightful and can be upheld as a general observation of working-class life, which has validity in particular places where researchers have done fieldwork, nevertheless there is a danger that working-class life is represented only in negative terms, whereas middle-class life is seen as more fulfilling and satisfying. Yet in contemporary society middle-class experience can also be filled with pressures to succeed and time-demands that lead to anxiety and depression. It can also lead, as Matthew Adams has said, to the type of leisure time commodified by consumerism that creates detachment, personal meaninglessness and dissociation, despite the possession of many different forms of cultural capital.[32] Furthermore, as Sayer points out, we can make a distinction missing in Bourdieu's work between moral and aesthetic judgements: it is the latter which are based on differential class capitals, tastes and lifestyles – such as education, taste in food, books, music and arts – while the former are more universal, to do with the relation to others irrespective of social position, in which qualities are valued such as honesty, integrity and responsibility. A person could be valued for such qualities irrespective of their social class or status. Even where certain moral standards are claimed by a specific group over and against another – let's say that the working class are harder working than the middle class – the value of hard work is still taken to be morally recognizable by all reasonable people. Therefore, moral and aesthetic standards vary in the degree to which they are class bound or universal within particular societies and cultures.

What I hope to have shown in this chapter is the way in which self-identity in all its many aspects cannot be considered separate from social class. The social relations in which we come into being as selves are class relations, which form and structure our social *habitus,* dispositions, capacities, perceptions, interests, tastes and biographical trajectory, both in the labour market and beyond it in our leisure activities and lifestyle. Class is also integrally bound up with the way we in-habit the world as gendered and as sexual beings: indeed, it is central to the way we in-habit the world as embodied beings, having formed our experience of the world from the earliest years in terms of the place we live, our cities and towns, family, neighbourhoods and friends, schools and workplaces, and the capacities and identities we create there. All these things determine the material, cultural, social and symbolic capital we develop, opening up or limiting our life-chances in various social fields and, thus, the potential for who and what we can become in future. The various capitals are also important in terms of the recognition we get from others as being a person of worth, someone to be respected; this in turn will also influence, in the dialogic fashion I have been illustrating in this book, the view we have of our own self, the way we see ourselves as a person of worth or as unworthy, and thus the way we feel about ourselves. Does our own self-image, or the image we imagine others have of us, fill us with pride or shame, or perhaps a mixture of the two? This, in turn, will influence the sense of fulfilment and satisfaction we have with our lives and selves. Thus, we can see that social class has a profound influence on the self, not just in terms of who we are but also in terms of what we can become.

Before moving on, I want to consider the way in which all the things we have been discussing in the last few chapters – gender, sexuality and social class – make up our self-identities, and how they also figure in relational performances in which we display a self-image of who we are and what we want to be. Hopefully, the following excursus will show how these things are central elements in the way we create our identities in daily life in our interrelationships with one another.

Excursus: gender, sexuality and class

The interconnection of gender, sexuality and class as aspects of self-identity that come into play in the image work of relational performances can be illustrated using a case study taken from R. D. Laing's book *Self and Others.* Here there is an account of an analytic group in which two men, Bill and Jack, collude to confirm the illusory self-identity each has constructed.[33] There were seven men in the group, most of them lower middle class except for one, but Bill and Jack are the focus of Laing's attention in his account: this centres on the issue of collusion. However my interest in this account is the way that the relationship between the men in the group raises issues of sexuality, gender and social class. According to Laing, Bill attempted to create an illusory sense of superiority about himself to hide the false premise of his essential worthlessness, while Jack had the illusion of being 'a giver', the one who quickly took the role of leader in the group, asking questions and getting others to talk. In his own eyes he was 'an independent, hard-headed, matter-of-fact, down-to-earth businessman, extremely heterosexual, although women for him were only those absent presences he talked about with "the boys"'. Conversely, 'Bill dreamt of far away places where things could be beautiful and people were refined, not vulgar and coarse like here and now'.

In reading Laing's account it is clear that when Jack leads the group discussion he usually centres this on the topic of women and the men's relationship to them. It is clear in my view that in doing this Jack is asserting the image of himself as extremely heterosexual and is warding off the undercurrents of homosexual, or, at the least, homo-social attachments that arise in a group of men who are together for the intimate purpose of revealing deeply personal things about them-selves. Bill did not participate in these discussions about women and, in the fifth session of the group, broke in on this usual discussion to say how much he dis-liked football and how he saw football fans as stupid people. Traditionally in the UK, football has been the favoured pastime of working-class men, and so it evokes strong stereotypical images of working-class masculinity. Except for Bill, all the other men in the group regularly went to football matches, including Jack, although he did admit that this was only because he wanted to be 'one of the boys'. In opposition, Bill talked about his appreciation of the arts and how he wished he knew others who could share this interest, although his aspiration was quickly shot down by Jack who commented that only very well educated people could appreciate art, a remark that struck a raw nerve with Bill who was sensitive about his lack of formal education.

In my view we can see here how the men are positioning themselves in the group interrelationships by aligning themselves to some and not others in terms of social class, their relative capitals, their aspirations, and their identifications in terms of gender and sexuality. Although Laing identifies the group as mainly middle class in terms of occupations, it is clear that most of the men in the group identify – or are trying to identify – with a working-class masculinity, and one of the group is clearly working class. On the other hand, Bill is aspiring to the middle-class intelligentsia, displaying as his cultural capital the appreciation of art. Bill also tried to show his superiority by aligning himself with Laing as the therapist, who was a member of the middle-class intelligentsia that Bill wanted to be ranked among. However, he was also frightened of Laing, whom he saw as having the education to be able to expose him as lacking in his artistic sensibili-ties or intellectual capacities. Despite this, Bill developed 'passive homosexual longings' towards Laing as the 'ideal other', which he revealed in a letter to him. What Laing points out about the group and, particularly, about Bill and Jack, is the way they confirm or disconfirm each other in their illusory sense of self. In particular, Bill's opposition to the working-class heterosexuality performed by the other men sets him apart, but it also confirms Jack as the leader and 'giver' in the group, the one who at various times draws the others together, and has the power to include or exclude Bill. In turn, Jack provides the opportunity for Bill to perform his acts of distinction, contrasting his tastes and apperceptions to those of Jack, which are deemed to be more rough and vulgar. Interestingly, the group behaved 'as if' the relationship between Bill and Jack were a sexual one, and indeed it displayed many features of a barely concealed homosexuality, with Jack asking Bill what he thought about when he masturbated. The reply was that he sometimes thought about a man, with Jack responding that he always fantasized about women. This uneasy collusion between the two often resulted in Jack being aggressive towards Bill and rejecting him, as in the remarks about education and masturbatory fantasy, yet Laing notes that there was an element of sado-masochism in their antagonism.

Thus, while Laing sees in this analytical group evidence of collusion and the maintenance of self-illusions, along with the emergence of homosexual feelings, I suggest on the basis of the position I am developing in this book that much more is behind this. In addition to the constant production and denial of homosexual feelings in the relational performances between the men (given the context of an emotionally intimate therapeutic group), there is also the performance of gender and class which are intrinsically linked to it. In performing their masculinity through talk about women and football, the men are not only warding off the homosexual feelings in the group, they are doing so by identifying themselves with a particularly working-class passion (football) and, thus, a working-class style of masculinity. Performance of class is also displayed in the men's tastes, apperceptions of the world and appreciations, especially in relation to sport and art. Bill's performance seeks to identify him as middle class in tastes and lifestyle, or at the least would-be middle class, while the others display identification with the working class. This is also evidenced in Jack's self-ideal as 'matter-of-fact' and 'down-to-earth', seeing himself as practical and manly rather than arty and pseudo-intellectual. All of this is not simply the playing of a role, but is about the way these men are immersed and embodied in the very fabric of the world; it is about how they embody a particular *habitus* and in-habit the world as sexed, gen-dered and classed, which forms the way they feel, see and think about the world and themselves: it also influences the way they relate and respond to others. Aspects of themselves that may betray the self-image they consciously wish to express – such as Bill's lack of formal education or Jack's homosexual curiosity about Bill's masturbatory fantasies – are quickly dispelled by reasserting their desired self-image in their performances.

But there are complex, unconscious feelings behind the performance of self-image that are also embedded in a person's habitus, which, in Bourdieu's terms, communicate to others far more than the performer really knows or intends. This is why human interactions and the self-identities enmeshed within them are so complex and difficult to unravel. As Laing said, the unconscious is those moments or instances when a person is not in full communication with themself, as is evident in the interaction between these men, most of whom would not admit to, or even want to articulate, their sexual feelings for other men. Instead, the projection of their own desired self-image and the way they collude with each other in the recognition and misrecognition of each other is all-important. We can also identify from this example the workings of a structural unconscious (see Chapter 3) as the men are taking up positions and alignments in the group drawing from contextually important aspects of power relations in society, involving relations of domination and subordination between sexualities, genders and social classes. I would venture to say that all of our everyday relations and interactions are like this, and that we rarely achieve those moments of what Buber called the interhuman, where we reveal ourselves to others, and also to ourselves, in all aspects of what we are as selves in the present moment. At the same time, though, it seems we are impelled by the contradictions in our lives and selves to keep moving forward in our biographies (otherwise the men used as an example here would not have been in an analytic group), to aim for greater self-development and better communication with self and others, and to become the selves we are not as yet. However, as this chapter has shown, we need more than a will to change to achieve self-fulfilment: we also need the material, cultural and social resources that allow us to do so.

Notes

1. Geoff Payne and Clare Grew (2005) 'Unpacking class ambivalence: some conceptual and methodological issues in accessing class cultures', *Sociology,* 39 (5): 893–910.
2. Karl Marx (1852) 'The eighteenth Brumaire of Louis Bonaparte', in David McLellan (ed.), *Karl Marx: Selected Writings.* Oxford: Oxford University Press, 1977. pp. 300–25, p. 300.
3. Karl Marx (1845) 'Theses on Feuerbach', in David McLellan (ed.), *Karl Marx: Selected Writings.* Oxford: Oxford University Press, 1977 edn. pp.156–58, p. 157.
4. Lucien Sève (1978) *Man in Marxist Theory and the Psychology of Personality.* Brighton: Harvester Press. p. 299.
5. Tom Yardley (2005) 'Sacrificing the rational body: a phenomenological approach to voluntary intoxication', PhD Thesis. University of Portsmouth.
6. Victor Turner (1982) *From Ritual to Theatre: The Human Seriousness of Play.* New York: Performing Arts Journal Publications. p. 54.
7. Wendy Mitchell and Eileen Green (2002) '"I don't know what I'd do without our mam": motherhood, identity and support networks', *The Sociological Review,* 50 (1): 1–22, p. 2.
8. Ibid., p. 16.
9. Sève, *Man,* p. 333.
10. Ibid, p. 341.
11. Ibid, p. 98–9.
12. Ibid., p. 274.

13. V. Beechey and E. Whitelegg (1986) *Women in Britain Today*. Milton Keyes: Open University Press.
14. Robert Ashcroft (1982) 'Conceptions of the individual and the client in social science and social work', unpublished paper. Bradford University.
15. Paul Willis (1977) *Learning to Labour: How Working Class Kids Get Working Class Jobs*. Aldershot: Gower.
16. Sève, *Man,* p. 285.
17. Pierre Bourdieu (1977) *Outline of a Theory of Practice*. Cambridge: Cambridge University Press. p. 72.
18. Pierre Bourdieu (1984) *Distinction: A Social Critique of the Judgment of Taste*. London: Routledge.
19. Paul Willis, *Learning.*
20. Special Issue on 'Class, Culture and Identity', *Sociology*, 39 (5), December 2005.
21. Martha C. Nussbaum (2001) *Upheavals of Thought: The Intelligence of Emotions*. Cambridge: Cambridge University Press.
22. Andrew Sayer (2005) 'Class, moral worth and recognition', *Sociology*, 39 (5): 947–63, p. 953.
23. Beverley Skeggs (1997) *Formations of Class and Gender: Becoming Respectable*. London: Sage.
24. Ibid.
25. Beverley Skeggs (2005) 'The making of class and gender through visualizing moral subject formation', *Sociology*, 39 (5): 965–82.
26. Carol Gilligan (1982) *In a Different Voice: Psychological Theory and Women's Development*. Cambridge, MA: Harvard University Press.
27. Valerie Walkerdine (2006) 'Minding the gap: thinking subjectivity beyond a psychic/discursive division', public lecture given in the ESRC 'Identities and Social Action' series. University of the West of England.
28. Simon J. Charlesworth (2000) *A Phenomenology of Working Class Experience*. Cambridge: Cambridge University Press. p. 65.
29. Ibid.
30. Ibid., p. 9.
31. Ibid., p. 7.
32. Matthew Adams (2007) *Self and Social Change*. London: Sage.
33. R. D. Laing (1961) *Self and Others*. Harmondsworth: Penguin, 1971 edn. pp.118–23.

Selected bibliography

Bourdieu, Pierre (1984) *Distinction: A Social Critique of the Judgment of Taste*. London: Routledge.

Charlesworth, Simon J. (2000) *A Phenomenology of Working Class Experience*. Cambridge: Cambridge University Press.

Marx, Karl (1845) 'Theses on Feuerbach', in David McLellan (ed.), *Karl Marx: Selected Writings*. Oxford: Oxford University Press, 1977 edn.

Sève, Lucien (1978) *Man in Marxist Theory and the Psychology of Personality*. Brighton: Harvester Press.

Skeggs, Beverley (1997) *Formations of Class and Gender: Becoming Respectable*. London: Sage.

Special Issue on 'Class, Culture and Identity', *Sociology*, 39 (5), December 2005.

CHAPTER 7

SELF IN CONTEMPORARY SOCIETY

One of the key themes to have emerged in social scientific writings over the last couple of decades is to do with the way that the self has changed in the midst of seismic transformations in society. It is argued that the nature of work has changed from long-term to short-term employment, and that geographical social mobility has increased because of the need to move around to find work – also because of the widening opportunities in education, employment, travel and migration – and that all of this has created a decline in generations living out their lives in the same communities, among familiar neighbours, extended family and life-long friends. The sociologist Anthony Giddens has pointed out that in a globalized world like the one we live in today, where people and organizations are linked by satellite communications, international telephone systems and the Internet, it is possible to sustain a close relationship with a family member or friend who lives half-way around the world while not knowing your next-door neighbour. It is argued that such changes in society have made it much harder to answer the question 'who am I?': indeed, we may ask this question more frequently because the contemporary world has fragmented to such an extent that the sources of our identities are no longer stable and secure. We can no longer automatically assume that jobs are secure for life, or that communities, neighbours, family and friends will always be there for us throughout our lives, come what may. All these are points of reference for our identities and, as they become less certain, so does our sense of self.

I can see these changes in my own lifetime and how they have affected me and my family. When I was growing up in Britain in the 1960s I lived with my parents in the same town that my mother was born in, which was only three miles away from the place my father was born, where his mother (my grandmother) lived. She, in turn, had lived in this town all her life and the farthest she travelled from it was 70 miles to the place where she had her honeymoon. My father had left school at 14 and worked in the same cloth mill until he retired at 65. The town I grew up in was filled with people who knew my parents, many of whom they had been to school with, and who therefore also knew me and I them. There were strangers, but not many. Few people agonized over the question 'who am I?' because they knew who they were, or at least took it for granted they did. Most of us were working class or lower middle class, male or female (even those of us not sure that we were 'real' men), and residents of the town, differentiated from each other by our interests and personal characteristics. Looking back, though, I can see now how this world was beginning to fragment even at the time when I took it for granted it would always be there. Educational opportunities were opening up which allowed some working-class people of my generation to go to university, to move away from family and hometowns, to get middle-class jobs, to travel, and, eventually, because of changes in technology and lifestyles, to become connected to others on a global rather than a local scale. We have gained so much, but also lost a lot. The town and city I live in is filled with strangers, some close friends are far away, the vocation I found as an academic is no longer a job for life and is threatened by increasing managerial control, some friends seem continually on the edge of anxiety, insecurity and depression, and the park I played in as a child, once filled with people I knew, is empty except for those walking their dogs. I think I know who I am, but I'm not certain I'll always be this way: my future may be radically different, and so may I.

What I want to do in this chapter is to explore and question some of the ideas that try to explain why the contemporary world is the way that it is, and what the implications are for the self, both in terms of the possibilities and the limitations in becoming a self, and the dilemmas faced by selves in the present-day Western world.

Social saturation and the saturated self

For Kenneth J. Gergen, one of the key factors in the transformation of the social world has been what he calls 'technologies of social saturation',[1] or the explosion of various technologies of communication. These include telecommunications systems, Internet, e-mail, possibilities for video communication or conferencing, but also the explosion in forms of media more generally, such as television and the many different television channels, cinema, DVD, computer games, newspapers and magazines. Not all these things are new, with newspapers, magazines and cinema having been around for well over a century. What is new, however, is the multiplicity and diversity of these things in the modern world: the range of media we are exposed to and its variety, communicating to us a welter of different knowledge, cultures, religions, world-views, ideas, values, lifestyles and people. The technologies of social saturation now make it possible for people to relate to a variety of different and divergent others in ways they could never do in the past. When thinkers like G. H. Mead and Mikhail Bakhtin argued that our thoughts were populated with the words and voices of others, they were thinking largely of the others we knew personally, or encountered face-to-face, or at the most characters in novels that we got to know through reading. Today, we are surrounded by a clamour of different voices, speaking different ideas and values, and representing different ways of living far beyond that of our immediate experience. In the contemporary world the media can create what appear to be intimate relationships between people who have never met, such as between celebrities and the fans that follow their every move, listen to their every word, and relate to them in highly emotional ways. For example, a few days after the death of Princess Diana, a member of the public who was laying flowers for her outside her home was interviewed by the BBC news and asked why he had turned out specially to perform this act of commemoration for a woman he had never even met? He replied that her death had meant more to him than that of his own mother. This could only happen in a world of media saturation, where some people come to feel closer to public figures, or the characters in soap operas, than they do to the actual people in their own lives. Indeed, the virtual nature of such relationships makes them more seductive, as the image of the other to whom you relate is always within your own control: they don't have to be awkward, argumentative, independent or difficult.

The point that Gergen and others are making, however, is not only that we are related to both actual and imaginary figures in the contemporary world (and even that line is blurred, as image is always blended with the actuality of another), but that the number and range of voices which animate our thoughts, or self-dialogues, has multiplied. They offer to us not only a range of different, competing, and sometimes contradictory viewpoints of the world and our own selves, but also they present us with myriad possibilities for what we could become in future. Do I want to be a Christian or a Buddhist, a socialist or a conservative, a songwriter or a singer, a blond or a brunette, or to dress like George Clooney or Brad Pitt? These are but a few of the choices that could confront us. For Gergen, then,

> as social saturation proceeds we become pastiches, imitative assemblages of each other. In memory we carry others' patterns of being with us ... selves have become increasingly populated with the character of others. We are not one, or a few, but like Walt Whitman, we 'contain multitudes.' We appear to each other as single identities, unified of whole cloth. However, with social saturation each of us comes to harbour a vast population of hidden potentials – to be a blues singer, a gypsy, an aristocrat, a criminal. All the selves lie latent, and under the right conditions may spring to life.[2]

Whereas the postmodern thinker Fredric Jameson characterized contemporary selves that are put together through pastiche as 'schizophrenic'[3] – because they are composed of multiple selves, and, as they are imitative, are depthless and emotionally void – Gergen prefers to refer to us as 'multiphrenic', because this condition is not one of clinical pathology, it is more a style of becoming a self in the postmodern world. However, like Jameson, Gergen refers to the contemporary world and to the selves that populate it as 'postmodern,' because these selves have transcended the modernist and Romantic self as described by philosophers of the 17th and 18th centuries in Europe. The modernist self is described by the philosophers of the Enlightenment as a rational creature, one who operates in the world by attempting to master the passions and to act rationally, while for the Romantics our sense of self originates from a deep inner core, an essence or voice within that tells us who we are, if only we attune to it. In opposition to this, for Gergen, the postmodern self emerges from within the processes and technologies of social saturation and is characterized by neither its rationality nor inner sense of identity, but by its *relations* to the many others to whom it is connected and of whom it is an assemblage. A number of years prior to Gergen, the postmodern philosopher Jean-François Lyotard put it in the following way:

> no self is an island; each exists in a fabric of relations that is now more complex than ever before. Young or old, man or woman, rich or poor, a person is always located at 'nodal points' of specific communication circuits, however tiny these may be. Or better, one is always located at a post through which various kinds of messages pass.[4]

For Lyotard, what characterizes the postmodern condition is that the overarching 'grand narratives' that once created some form of cohesion and unity in society and self – such as a belief in just one religion, or in the explanatory power and truthfulness of science – have fragmented into a competing number of different language games, each with their different meanings. In the complex network of postmodern social relations and communicative networks, different religions and value-systems challenge one another for our attention and allegiance, various forms of scientific explanation set out to critique one another, while we are painfully aware of the downsides of scientific and technological progress with our world threatened by global warming and the danger of the proliferation of nuclear weapons technology. In the face of all of this it is hard to believe there is one truth in which we can place our faith, or one system of values or way of living in which we can develop our sense of self-identity. According to Gergen, this means that there is a demise of the demand for rational coherence at the heart of the self, and that the sense of self-continuity and coherence disappears in the flux of social fragmentation. We therefore only *appear* to others as unified and whole identities, when just under the surface of appearance we are a fragmented and diverse assemblage of voices, demands, intentions and possibilities. While this is painful for many people who value the stability of deep and enduring social relations, nothing can hold back the tide of social change as 'continuity is replaced by contingency, unity by fragmentation, and authenticity by artfulness'[5] in people's social interactions.

Under these conditions, people can no longer take for granted that they *have* an identity, one that is given by the social circumstance of family, community or social class: rather, in fleeting, ever-changing social configurations, identity is something that is continually *made* on the spot, *in situ*. To cope with this there has to be a heightened sense of reflexivity – which, along with Hilary Lawson, Gergen takes to mean self-reflection – for we have to remake ourselves in the moment, according to what is required by the situation, and also in a chronic state of doubt. This is because we can never be certain of one truth that applies in all circumstances, or rely on a single authority whose wisdom can guide us in all matters. Each one of us must sort and assess the mass of information to which we are exposed everyday, and even if we can't make sense of most of it, we must decide what to discard and how to carry on, if only by default. Unlike some of those troubled by this state of affairs, Gergen sees the positive possibilities in it, because if the demand for personal coherence is suspended, life can be filled with greater opportunities to recreate what each one of us can become. Furthermore, freed from the illusion that each one of us is an island, we can see all our personal choices as connected to wider social relationships and to the networks of communication that bind us into them. Thus, 'an open slate emerges on which persons may inscribe, erase, and rewrite their identities as the ever-shifting, ever-expanding, and incoherent network of relationships invites or permits'.[6]

In this view, Gergen is not arguing that postmodernism is a period that comes after modernism or Romanticism, but that the three are 'perspectives' that produce different patterns of acting, ones that are in competition in the contemporary world, even if the modernist perspective – tied to scientific reason and machine metaphors – is still the dominant one. Nevertheless, the emerging postmodern consciousness calls into question the essential truths at the heart of the other two perspectives; indeed, it calls into question the whole notion of there being a single 'objective truth'. Our belief in what is true is only sustainable within a cultural perspective, so that if I am a modernist I believe in the truth value of rationality and science and the knowledge they bring, while if I am a Romantic I believe in the essential inner essence of each individual and the truth of their own emotional experiences. On the contrary, for Gergen, postmodern thought emphasizes the socially interconnected nature of personal identity and thus the social construction of the self, shifting the focus away from isolated and disconnected individuals and onto relationships. Through this lens we can reorient the focal point of Enlightenment thought away from the transcendental subject, for we 'can replace the Cartesian dictum *cogito ergo sum* with *communicamus ergo sum,* for without coordinated acts of communication, there is simply no "I" to be articulated'.[7]Because 'I' is a pronoun within a language, the purpose of which is communication *between* people, it is less clear to say 'I think therefore I am' than to say 'we communicate therefore I am'. A new discourse is therefore needed to talk about relational forms, yet this has scarcely been created. Bakhtin perhaps got close with his concept of heteroglossia, and yet Gergen points out postmodernism invites not only a heteroglossia of speaking, but also one of being. It encourages the interrelationship and free play of multiple perspectives, realities and forms of becoming a self.

While all of this is highly seductive, there are problems with Gergen's view of the emerging 'saturated self'. What is most curious is that while his account is clearly based in the writings of postmodern thinkers such as Lyotard, Jameson and Baudrillard, he makes no attempt to follow them in situating postmodern culture within a developing form of global capitalism. In particular, Jameson has argued that postmodernism is the cultural logic of multinational capitalism, and that the profit motive and the logic of capital accumulation are still fundamental laws of the Western world.[8] Capitalism has changed into a post-industrial and consumerist form, where the main product is information, media output and consumer goods, yet the logic of the system still is profit accumulation for the multinational corporations and, by implication, huge inequalities across the globe and within countries. The Marxist geographer David Harvey has written about how postmodern cities are laid out, so that poverty-stricken ghettoes are almost like distant islands in a sea of wealth creation, ones that the well-off members of society don't have to see or to visit.[9] As we noted in the last chapter, the poor and the lower classes are becoming invisible, lacking any social or moral recognition from the rest of society, which is at least partially included in the wealth-creation of contemporary capitalism. The implication of this for Gergen's thesis is that his description of the saturated self of postmodernity, one that can write, erase and rewrite its own identity from the endless array of possible modes of being, is only true for some in the contemporary world. Some others, like the residents of Rotherham in Charlesworth's study, are actually weighted down by the world in which they live, and also, being embodied and identified in that world, they are weighted down with a way of being that lacks social and cultural capital, limiting their access to other social fields and to becoming something other than the selves they currently are. Those able to write and rewrite their identities within the postmodern flux, if they exist, are the relatively affluent, educated and professional groups in society, connected up to a global rather than a limited local culture: yet as I hope to show later in this chapter, even for these selves, the contemporary world is deeply ambivalent and problematic, and they too may not be without some weight to their identity, nor without a sense of having a core self.

In addition to this, Gergen's notion of three perspectives competing in contemporary life – the Romantic, the modern and the postmodern – may be overly simplistic, as it ignores the emergence of a post-Romantic trend in the work of Nietzsche (with his influence on Heidegger, Foucault and Derrida), and also the fragmentation of the modernist tradition in the 20th century. According to Charles Taylor, only one strand of modernism expressed itself in a renewed form of Enlightenment belief in the rational core of human thought, and thus in the explanatory power of scientific reason and the 'progress' this would bring. Another form of modernism, expressed in art and philosophy, sought epiphany by shattering the notion of the self as composed of a rational core – indeed, often by removing the notion of a central organizing principle of self altogether – and instead attempted to liberate experience by opening us to the flux that is beyond the scope of control or integration.[10] Thus, impressionists, surrealists, and the cubist movement tried to create art that moved beyond the idea of a representation of reality, instead creating images that we are not aware of, or only partially aware of, in everyday perception. Others, like the symbolist poets or post-structural philosophers, shifted the centre of gravity from the unified self to the flow of language, in which meanings and identities are created and recreated in the juxtaposition of words and images that have no external or internal referent outside of the text. While it is true to say that the modernist and Romantic movements still have currency in the way we live our lives today – as in the battle between a technological world-view and an ecological one which stresses the importance of nature over the value of technological progress – it is also true that the fracturing of these world-views into modernist epiphanies and post-Romanticism have created the arena, language and imagery that have become known as postmodernism. While I don't want to get into a debate about the use of terminology here, it is important in the sense of attempting to understand the nature of the powers, institutions and social movements that create us as selves in the contemporary world. Indeed, many have argued that these social forms have to be understood as an extension of modernity, rather than a postmodernity that would be, by definition, something beyond it. The next thinker whose work I want to focus on in terms of the formation of self-identity has argued just that: all the social changes we are currently experiencing, which are changing the way we identify our selves, are due to a heightened modernity rather than to forces driving us beyond it.

Self-identities in high modernity

On the surface, the British sociologist Anthony Giddens agrees with Gergen as to the effect of contemporary social changes on self-identity, especially in terms of the growing reflexivity, or self-reflection, demanded of present-day individuals by contemporary institutions. For Giddens, however, this is because Western modernity is a post-traditional society that does not rely on customs handed down from previous generations in order to reproduce itself. Instead, systems of knowledge such as science involve the active questioning and open public debate of ideas put forward for consideration, and social life in general changes so quickly – because of scientific, technological, industrial and communications innovations – that life hardly stays the same from one generation to the next. The Enlightenment tore apart the received dogmas and inherited wisdom that had reproduced feudal society, particularly in challenging the religious doctrines that gave meaning and order to life, and the advent of industrial capitalism hastened the breaking apart of the old feudal order and power structure. Despite this, the early modern era of the 18th and 19th centuries was still centred upon some traditions inherited from the feudal period, such as the value of knowing one's place in society, the value of local community, and the sanctity of family life. In contrast to this, the period of late 20th and early 21st century society is what Giddens labels as 'late' or 'high' modernity, in which the modern project is fully becoming a post-traditional society: that is to say, even the traditions that had stabilized early modernity are now being swept away, with high levels of social class and geographic mobility breaking down class structures and local communities, and greater choice opening up in the lifestyles we can adopt.[11] This can be seen in the proliferation of different types of family structures in the present day, where still there are traditional extended or nuclear families of two heterosexual parents with two or three children, but alongside this there are single-parent families, gay and lesbian families, or families of choice that are composed of individuals who are not biologically related but choose to live like a family out of a sense of close friendship or kinship.

This signals for Giddens a change in the nature of intimate relationships, because now couples no longer stay together simply because they are married, or because they have children, and tradition forbids them to ever split up: now relationships are based on an egalitarian sense of the mutual benefits and personal satisfactions that each partner gets from the relationship. If that ceases to be the case, then a couple may decide to split. Personal relationships are now much more a matter of choice than of the demands and expectations formed by traditional ties.[12] Indeed, as Jan Löfström has pointed out, heterosexual couples are becoming more like gay and lesbian couples in this respect, as their relationships rest on personal choice and decision-making rather than on traditional institutional support and compulsion. With the growth of consumerism, the collapse of traditional family structures, and an increasingly pluralistic urban lifestyle, there is also a change of the binary categorizations that created traditional gender and sexual identities, such as the rigid distinction between men and women, gays and straights. Both Ken Plummer and Jeffrey Weeks have argued that this has led to a form of sexual or 'intimate' citizenship, in which various groups claim the right for their sexual choices and preferences to be recognized as legitimate by society.[13]

The greatest change, though, that Giddens sees in high modernity is what he calls the emergence of greater 'time-space distantiation', which describes the way in which local places are losing their central importance in structuring social relations and social actions.[14] Because of what Gergen called technologies of social saturation, it is now possible to lift social relations out of particular places and reconstitute them across global vistas of time and space. As I said in the introduction to this chapter, because of advanced communication systems such as satellite communications or the Internet, it is now possible to conduct a close relationship with family or friends who live in other countries, but not to know anything about the person living next-door. Communication systems, advanced transportation systems, and facilities like credit cards that can be used as currency or to get currency in almost any country of the world, are what Giddens calls 'disembedding mechanisms' that lift us out of local contexts and reconnect us within a globalized world. Fifty years ago, if family members or friends were to emigrate to a far-off country, this would be the occasion for tearful farewells, as loved ones said goodbye forever. Today, we may be sad or upset at such a parting, but it is not a final farewell: letters no longer take weeks or months to travel abroad, indeed we can be in touch in an instant through a long-distance phone call, an email, or through an Internet connection in which we can not only chat to the person in real-time, but also see one another with the aid of a web cam. With cheaper travel costs, we also have another foreign destination to add to our future travel plans. Even if we are not connected to others in this way, distant happenings constantly invade the locales in which we live and work, changing our consciousness of the world and our own place within it. The television in the corner of the room or on the wall constantly transmits images of famine in Africa, or a car-bomb attack in Iraq. Consciousness has become as much global as it is local.

In the wake of globalization and detraditionalization, people can no longer take for granted the ways in which they act, or what they are likely to become in future, because our lives no longer follow a preordained course. Instead, we must continually reflexively monitor and revise our biographical narratives in a chronic condition of doubt about what is the right course of action, or if we have made the correct choices. Rites of passage no longer mark the transition between different periods of life, such as the entry into adulthood, in the way they did in traditional cultures. Instead, we are catapulted through a series of social transitions over which we have little control, especially in a globalized world where we often feel that we lack power over key events in our lives. For example, if someone is made unemployed they may have little power to affect this: if they work for a company owned by a global corporation, they can no longer hold an effective protest outside the factory gates, because those who have made the decision to fold the company may meet in New York, Paris or Buenos Aires. The loss of a job not only can lead to a feeling of powerlessness, it can also bring on a life crisis or identity crisis as the person is unsure about how to reconstruct their biographical narrative in the absence of a rite of passage between the state of employment and unemployment, or what can possibly come after it. In this context, the present and the future are a risky and uncertain enterprise in which, for Giddens, risk becomes the central feature and overriding preoccupation.

Faced with situations like this, in which modern people can no longer rely on rites of passage or the wisdom of elders, people often turn to experts to guide them through times of crisis, or help them deal with the existential fears that a risk culture entails. It is no accident that in high modernity psychology has become such a popular subject at university, or that the telephone book is filled with pages of contact numbers for counsellors, psychotherapists, hypnotherapists, etc. People turn to such experts to help them deal with crises and to ward off the sense of ontological insecurity that the risks and doubts of living in high modernity can bring. When Descartes conjured up radical doubt in the form of the evil genie who tried to persuade him that he could be certain of nothing, he found ontological security and certainty in the very fact he was thinking: this persuaded him that he was an 'I' gifted with the power of rational thought and capable of dispelling the genie. But in high modernity, where science has called into question all ideas, even its own, and sees them as open to constant revision, we no longer have faith in scientific rationality as a means of dispelling doubt. Expert systems, at least, whether or not they are based on scientific knowledge, can help us deal with existential crises: we can take our sick to hospitals where they can be looked after by doctors and nurses, our dying to hospices where they will be cared for by trained staff, and our troubled children to social workers or psychologists who will try to help us deal with them.

In terms of the self, when we ask the questions 'who am I?' or 'who should I become?' or 'how should I act?' modern people often turn to therapists to help them make these decisions, mainly because the modern world is filled with many choices and possibilities about who we could become and how we can act, and there are few people around who are skilled or experienced enough to help us make these choices. Furthermore, Giddens understands the self as a reflexively created project, one that is ongoing throughout life, in which the person understands themself by creating and recreating a biographical narrative. Our identity and ontological security rest in large part on our ability to successfully keep this narrative going. Life-planning becomes all-important, which presupposes a mode of organizing time, by interpreting the past and preparing for the future. Lifestyle choices also have to be made, and here Giddens refers to the term 'lifestyle' as a more or less integrated set of practices that give material form to a particular narrative of self-identity. It is no good me trying to pass myself off as a millionaire if I don't have the lifestyle to back up my claims. Yet there are so many varied lifestyles on offer in high modernity that, once more, we have to make choices about the milieu in which we become enmeshed, or ways to deal with the variation between different lifestyle sectors.

Under post-traditionalization, then, life-span is a segment of time separated off from the lifecycle of generations, which is another difference with pre-modern societies where the individual life would always be connected to ancestors and to the younger generations. Life-span is also no longer connected to place, which does not form the parameter of experience: instead, life-span becomes separated from pre-established ties to others, such as biological kinship, and is developed as a trajectory that relates only to the individual's projects and plans. Thus, high modernity is an ambivalent social setting for an individual life and the projects of self-identity, because it has led us to a state where we have more freedom than ever before from pre-established traditions, social positions and biographical trajectories, yet we are filled with greater anxieties because we must sustain a narrative of self-identity in a world of fragmentation, doubt and risk that places our ontological security under continual strain.

However, this exposes one of the central weaknesses in Giddens's thesis, because much of it is far too generalized, and also too individualized and voluntaristic. Although Giddens makes clear that such reflexive projects of identity can only take place in high-modern society, it appears as though choices of biographical narrative and lifestyle are made independently of others, with reference only to the plans and choices of an *individual.* This ignores how Mead and Bakhtin showed identity to be always primarily based in a relational life with others, so that the way we see ourselves can never be disconnected from the way others see us – even if we respond by trying to become the opposite of what they imagine us to be. Because of this, our identities are never composed only with reference to our own projects of self, for these projects and images of what we want to be are always formulated in dialogic interaction with others.

Similarly, our biographical trajectories are not just carved out by the way that we *as individuals* choose to organize biographical time, or in the way we choose a lifestyle related to particular places. For a start, we are born *into* certain places that we do not choose, and those places with their particular *habitus* can be embodied in every muscle and fibre of our selves, in the way that Charlesworth showed in his study of the residents of Rotherham. While Giddens is no doubt right to say that places are no longer completely separate from each other as they were in pre-modern times, so that the residents of a town like Rotherham will be aware of much that goes on outside their world, that in itself does not transcend the experiential power of place. In fact one could argue that it makes the limitations of certain places even more evident to those who cannot escape them. What limits the scope for us to move between different lifestyle sectors is not any inability to make choices on the part of certain individuals, but how *transposable* our embodied dispositions and various social capitals are. With my accent, manners, bodily demeanour, dispositions, world-outlook, education, skills and capacities, will I ever get a place at *that* University, or get *that* job with *that* company, or feel comfortable living in *that* neighbourhood? If it is so unlikely, would I even think of it? While Giddens applauds Bourdieu for showing how lifestyle in the form of *habitus* is not just the *result* of class differences but one of the *structuring features* of stratification, he ignores the other side of Bourdieu's structuration: that lifestyle is *both* the result and the structuring feature of class, in that it is central to the reproduction of class differences and inequalities. Thus none of us are without limits in being able to choose our lifestyles, as so much rests on the *habitus* we were born into and that inheres in our embodied self, including our dispositions, tastes, capacities, interests and ambitions.

Similarly with the organization of time in a person's biography, Giddens proves himself too voluntaristic a theorist to fully understand its complexities. While he clearly appreciates how capitalism still remains one the key axes of globalized modernity, he fails to show how working in a capitalist world still plays a central role in the organization of biographical time, providing opportunities *and* limitations to our biographical development as selves. As I hope to have shown in the last chapter, although Lucien Sève's work is dated in many ways, it still has relevance in showing the importance of the 'use-time' we have for different types of activity in our biographies, and how work is central to the organization of that time. In contemporary capitalism, we are still far from having unlimited choice over lifestyle and biographical trajectory: indeed, many claim that in the early 21st century people are now working longer hours than ever,[15] and in the UK laws are being passed to increase the age at which people can draw their state pension to retire. Working in the contemporary capitalist world is taking more of our everyday time and consuming more of our life-span than ever before, thus shaping our biographical trajectories. Given this, the vision of greater reflexive choice of life projects could be just a chimera.

However, as Lash and Urry have pointed out, it is perhaps best to characterize contemporary society as made up of reflexivity winners and losers.[16] Like Gergen, it is not that Giddens is wrong in terms of his diagnosis of contemporary social trends, nor about their possible effects upon the self: rather, it depends upon which social groups in society we are talking about. Certainly there will be reflexivity winners who have greater choice and control over their biographical trajectories, life projects and lifestyles: inevitably these people will be those with greater cultural and social capital, in terms of education, access to knowledge and technology, social connections outside of one geographical space, usually on a global scale, and professional status, connections and wealth. On the other hand we can find reflexivity losers, who do not have access to these things, or at least not to the same extent, and whose capacity for reflexive choice and control will be limited. A more thorough and telling critique has come from Matthew Adams, for whom the reflexivity of all social actors is to be seen as limited to some degree and dependent upon the *habitus* from which they act. We need to be careful in claiming that the working classes are always *per se* limited in their capacity for reflexivity compared to the middle classes, for all of us are embedded in *habitus* that is composed to some degree of dispositions that are taken-for-granted, expressed as second-nature, and therefore pre-reflexive. To Adams, it is not so much a lack of reflexivity we find in some social groups, but different ways of being reflexive performed in relation to particular social contexts.[17] All our performances emerge from a meeting of *habitus* and social field, and any social actor will have to be reflexive to a greater or lesser extent depending on the degree of fit between their dispositions and the social situation in which they are acting. In that sense, a middle-class person would have to be more reflexive about their performance in the context of a working-class job or leisure activity among working-class people. It is perhaps the case that we tend to think of the working classes as less reflexive because it is harder for them to step outside their own social fields and gain access to those dominated by the middle classes. Because of this, greater reflexivity is not always needed. However, as Adams also points out, it is not necessarily the case that greater reflexivity is automatically a good thing: constant reflexivity could, for example, create chronic anxiety over one's performances and a preoccupation with bringing them off successfully. It could also create the state of chronic doubt or ontological insecurity which Giddens talks of, or a self-preoccupation that becomes overbearing, as displayed by many of the wealthy, self-obsessed protagonists beautifully observed in the films of Woody Allen.

In addition, Adams also spells out for us that it is one thing to be reflexive about your life projects and biographical narrative, but to actualize these projects you need access to economic or material resources. For better or worse, then, we cannot so easily separate reflexivity, and the power to put life projects into practice, from class structure and access or non-access to material resources which enable us to actualize our plans and realize or stabilize our biographical narratives. This is especially the case in a capitalist society such as the one we live in today, which tends to fragmentation of social relationships while at the same time removing many of the safety nets, such as welfare provision and benefits, put in place after the Second World War to protect individuals and communities from the destructive power of the capitalist economy.

Given the importance of contemporary global capitalism as the context in which individual biographies are set, I want to examine this more closely in terms of the effects of economic and social fragmentation on the self. While Giddens has failed to set biography and self-identity in the context of contemporary capitalism, there are others who have attempted to do so.

Self in liquid modernity and the 'new capitalism'

In the work of Zygmunt Bauman, identity in the contemporary world is linked to two main changes that have occurred in late 20th and early 21st century society: firstly, globalization has created a world in which people and capital are no longer tied to local places, but linked in a worldwide network of flows of communication, identification, travel, emigration, investment and exchange; secondly, this is interlinked with greater flexibility in people's lives, with the erosion of life-long careers and long-term work contracts, the loss of stable communities as people move around more, and the cutbacks in welfare provision as individuals are abandoned by nation-states to fend for themselves in the global market for labour. All of this adds up to what Bauman terms 'liquid modernity', labelled as such because it liquefies all solid and stable human interconnections and makes them fluid across globalized space and time. The mobile phone is a perfect emblem of liquid modernity because it allows you to be with a group of people while at the same time constantly connected to all the other people you know; wherever they may be. At any time a call may come in that disconnects you from the people you are currently with and connects you with those who are physically absent: if they report that something more interesting is going on somewhere else, you can always make your excuses and leave. In this way human relations are made fluid; always on the move, connecting and reconnecting, but never settling anywhere for long.

Indicative of this liquid modernity is the transition from what Bauman calls 'heavy capitalism' to a form of 'light capitalism'.[18] The former is characterized by the type of capitalism that first developed in the 19th and first half of the 20th centuries, when capital was very much tied to heavy industry and massive investment in plant, machinery, technology and labour. Here, the owners of factories, or any type of industrial plant, were often local people who housed labour in the immediate vicinity of their place of work. The capitalists, their plant, and the local community were stable entities located in particular places, around which labour unions formed as people were tied to a particular occupation or trade for most of their lives. In such places, labour was quite literally opposed to capital, as workers could identify a common interest, along with a common identity as a social class, and see how this was both linked to, and in contrast with, the interests of the local capitalists. On the contrary, in light capitalism capital moves on a global scale and invests in the places where it can make the most profit. It has no national identity or allegiance, and workers are often in the dark about who actually owns the company they work for. If a local workplace closes down, the workers can protest to local managers, or to local and national governments, but often this has little effect, as the decision to close can have been made in another part of the world, perhaps by an international board of directors, who remain anonymous and disconnected. Thus capital, like people, is ready to move at a moment's notice, to be liquefied in the global flows of capital, without local commitments between capitalists and workers to tie it down.

This places modern people in something of a dilemma, because in order to relate to others we must have something about our selves that is relatively substantial and unchanging, so that people can know us: yet we also must be prepared to change quickly in a fluid world that demands adaptability. There is then a contradiction 'of self-made identities which must be solid enough to be acknowledged as such and yet flexible enough not to bar freedom of future movements in the constantly changing, volatile circumstances [of liquid modernity]'.[19] Yet creating a stable identity is not easy or even desirable in this world, as the question 'who am I?' needs another to answer it, and today the others who answer are an ever-changing array of individuals. Also, to have a constant group of others always there to answer questions of identity would require commitment, something that the very nature of liquid modernity militates against. To go back to the example of the mobile phone, this has not only lessened our commitment to the others around us, as we no longer have to stick with them even through a single evening, it has also lessened their commitment to us: they can also choose to leave whenever a better offer comes in or our conversation gets boring. Thus, according to Bauman, mobile phones allow us to construct communal reference points for ourselves while on the move, but they cannot provide the kind of stable community that could give more than a temporary stability or substance to our sense of self.[20]

Indeed, for Bauman, it is those who are incapable of mobility and who have a relatively stable identity imposed upon them who are the most powerless members of liquid modernity. An excellent example would be the residents of Rotherham who were represented in Charlesworth's study that we discussed in the last chapter. They lacked the social and cultural capital to get anything but dead-end jobs or to move out of the town they found boring and deadening. They also appeared to have relatively stable identities within their communities, as lower working-class, as unskilled or semi-skilled labour, as unemployed, as benefit recipients, or as residents of Rotherham who had been there all their lives. They bore the brunt of light capitalism as they had seen traditional industries and jobs disappear, but literally they could not move with the times, only suffer their consequences. It is almost as if these people were trapped on an island that is stagnating in the moving currents of light capitalism. For Bauman, then, those who find themselves land-locked in a particular place they cannot escape are the powerless within liquid modernity, whereas it is those who can instantly move and respond to changing conditions that are the powerful. In these circumstances, power 'consists in one's own capacity to escape, to disengage, to "be elsewhere", and the right to decide the speed with which all that is done'.[21]

What this means, though, is that even for the powerful, life fragments into a series of uncoordinated episodes in which there can be no consistent or cohesive life-strategy or narrative to pull all the fragments together and make sense of them.[22] Taking this metaphor of fragmentation further, Bauman suggests that the creation of a biography that would give us some sense of self-identity is like putting together a defective jigsaw puzzle, in which some of the pieces are missing and for which there is no picture on the box to show what the end result should be like. In the contemporary world we are all a bit like this, trying to create an identity without a clear idea of what the end result will be and attempting to do this in a world that fragments our lives into disconnected episodes, or that reflects back to us diverse images of who we are in the eyes of the many disparate and disconnected people that we know. Paradoxically, it is the very conditions that make identity so difficult which also make us more preoccupied with self and identity, for, as Bauman points out, those who have an unchanging identity conferred on them at birth – one that rarely changes in an unchanging world – are those who take their identity for granted. It is only when identity has to be constantly worked and reworked for ever-changing circumstances that people become concerned or even obsessed by questions of who they are.

Bauman believes that such a change has come over society in liquid modernity, as the very process of becoming a self with its own identity has changed. We can contrast this with Foucault's position, which stated that experience is always set within authoritative discourses and knowledge that in turn construct the very embodiment of being an individual self. Yet Foucault's studies were in the main focused on the 18th and 19th centuries in Western Europe, whereas today, Bauman suggests, in a globalized world the very nature of power and authority has changed. We are no longer in the grip of a power that *coerces* every fibre of our being into the mould of a usefully embodied citizen, but rather we are amidst a power that *seduces* us through the lore of consumer goods and shopping. In the past, those wanting to confess sins would go to the priest for the therapy of confession, while those wanting to unlock the nature of their innermost desires would seek psychoanalytic therapy. Today, however, our therapy is decidedly retail, as we shop for new identities among the fashions on offer that might better suit our new job or new friends. For those who cannot afford to shop for identities, they are abandoned by social authorities to sink estates or ghettos. The change in the nature of authority is symbolized by electronic tagging, in which a criminal has an electronic device fitted to them so that their movements can be tracked. While on the surface this looks like an extension of Foucault's notion of the power of surveillance, it is in fact different: in the surveillance of the prison, there was an attempt to build a relation between guard and prisoner, and to establish a set of spatially governed routines in which the body and character of the prisoner would be reformed. In liquid modernity, no such relationship exists, as the surveillance is purely electronic, done in order to prevent the tagged from entering certain areas or breaking a curfew. In this there is no attempt to reform a self: indeed, there is no concern at all with the self of the offender. According to Bauman, this means that authorities have left identity construction to individual choices in a society dominated by the market, so that those without the spending power to choose are left behind. This characterizes the process of individualization in liquid modernity.

Despite all of this, Bauman offers some glimmer of hope for those living in liquid modernity. Firstly, globalization provides an opportunity for people to begin to identify with humanity as a whole, rather than with factional interests, as for the first time in human history all our interests begin to point in the same direction. For those opposed to various aspects of liquid modernity, the point is not to be anti-globalization but to find ways in which to control 'wild globalization'.[23] Secondly, no matter how commodified our identities might have become, commodities can never become, or take the place of, human beings. It is only other humans who can inspire our continual search for roots, kinship, friendship and love.

However, this leads us to question some of Bauman's ideas about the nature of contemporary identity, for if people are in search of roots, kinship, friendship and love there must be something about contemporary individuals that seeks to resist liquid modernity, to search out some stability, community, coherence and commitment with and amongst others, attempting to arrest the constant flows and fragmentation of life. Yet in other parts of his writings, Bauman portrays this either as a defence against globalization or as an impossibility, claiming that no consistent or cohesive life strategies can emerge in a society he characterizes variously (one could say inconsistently) as postmodernity or liquid modernity. Indeed, stability and immobility are characteristics that Bauman associates only with the poor and socially excluded. It then makes it difficult for him to explain how these might be things that all of us hanker after. Furthermore, to say that in a flexible and fluid society people simply become flexible and fluid, except for those who are excluded from society, is a simplistic form of social reductionism that seems to claim that as society changes so selves change to suit. It renders people powerless (within this theoretical position, that is) to attempt to adopt other life-strategies or choices in the face of potentially destructive social changes that fragment and destabilize, or to create any base for the kind of roots that Bauman suggests people might still want.

In addition to this I would claim that while Bauman's theories of liquid modernity are insightful, pointing up some of the important social changes that have occurred in the last 30 years, they are also over-generalized. That is not to say that a lot of the changes Bauman observes are not happening or not important; rather it is to say that the account Bauman gives of them is too one-directional and one-dimensional. For example, he assumes that those who are able to uproot at a moment's notice, to put all commitments on hold and to exist in global time, are the powerful and dominant in liquid modernity. Yet other studies show (one of which I will come to in a moment) that such people are in fact highly dissatisfied with the rootless nature of their lives and, while they are nevertheless highly paid professionals, have in fact been *forced* to move in order to keep their jobs or to find work. Others may drop out of the 'rat-race', disillusioned by overwork, over-competitiveness, or the endless flexibility demanded in the contemporary workplace. They are finding ways to create alternative life-strategies that resist the fragmentation brought about by contemporary capitalism and modernity, providing them with some coherence in their narratives of self.

Furthermore, the vision of self generated by Bauman's ideas of liquid modernity is not exactly novel. He admits that the problem of creating identities solid enough to be recognized by others yet flexible enough to be adaptable to changing circumstances is a problem that has been faced by many generations, only now the problem is more acute. It is true, of course, that all the social changes noted by Gergen, Giddens and Bauman have accentuated this problem, especially with our exposure to different and varied world-views, cultures, identities, and the accompanying multiplication of the voices with which we can dialogue and that also become the social ghosts populating our own self-dialogues. Yet perhaps we have something in common with the upheavals of the US post-civil war period in which the first wave of pragmatists were writing, whose influence inspired James and Mead to develop theories about selves that were constantly in a state of reformation and reconstruction, yet at the same time had some core of self-continuity running through them. These selves were also fragmented into many different 'mes' depending on the various situations and conversations they inhabited, but at the same time they managed to incorporate these into a sense of 'I' that created some coherence in their experiences and some sense of continuity to their selves. The 'I' is only an illusion if we take it to be the transcendental self of philosophical contemplation, or the methodological meditations of Descartes: if this transcendent essence of philosophical contemplation is taken as the object of metaphysical deconstruction by postmodernist philosophers, then it is ripe for it, because it was only ever the product of metaphysical speculation. But this is not the 'I' of which the pragmatists speak: this 'I' is the hard won sense of unity and self-identity we manage to weave from out of a diverse and contradictory realm of experience, and it comes from our practical engagement with the world, with others, and with our own selves. From my own experience, it is that part of me that can think back to when I left school over 30 years ago, with all the many things that have happened to me between then and now, which enables me to recognize the boy I was as someone very different to who I am now and yet still somehow distantly me. I could say that I was that person, even if I am not that person now, because some things endure. I will return to this question in the conclusion to this chapter. For now, I want to focus on some of the evidence to come from a recent study by Richard Sennett of the effects of what he calls the 'new capitalism' on the lives and characters of modern selves.[24]

Although Bauman refers to Sennett and some of his findings to support his thesis of liquid modernity, and indeed Sennett has some supporting evidence including the erosion of long-term employment contracts and the decline in enduring local neighbourhoods and communities, he nevertheless reaches some different conclusions to those of Bauman. These centre on the possibility of people being able to create coherent narratives about themselves and the changes that have affected them, in the process salvaging some sense of self-worth and continuity. This is despite the fact that Sennett admits that many of the factors of the 'new capitalism', such as reducing everything to the 'short-term' and tearing apart social relations through the demand for geographical mobility, have created the conditions for what he calls a 'corrosion of character' – 'character' meaning the long-term aspects of personal traits that are recognized and valued by others and by the self. Character can corrode in the new capitalism, for in a world of short-term employment contracts people are always starting over again in new jobs, work teams, and neighbourhoods, with the result that many have lost the witnesses to their days – those others in whose eyes we see ourselves and with whom we share significant events in our lives.

Indeed, for Sennett, one of the effects of the new capitalism is to create the feeling that there is 'no long-term' in life anymore, encouraging us to live in the present and accept everything as temporary. What sparked the period of observation and contemplation that led to Sennett's book *The Corrosion of Character* was a chance meeting and conversation on an aeroplane with the son of a working-class man Sennett had known from an earlier study conducted in the 1970s.[25] While the man's father had worked in the same occupation all his life and lived in roughly the same neighbourhood, his son – whom Sennett called Rico – had already had a number of jobs which entailed moving himself and his family around the USA. What this meant was relocation in various workplaces, schools and neighbourhoods, with the family never staying long enough in any one place to feel that they belonged. The constant moves involved losing friends made in particular places, relationships that were either lost or kept alive only through the Internet. The new neighbourhoods the family moved into were sociable, but people were used to the constant coming and going of neighbours, so that the social bonds formed there lacked a feeling of permanence. Indeed, Sennett's book is filled with such stories: broken narratives of people relocating in different work environments and places, constantly starting all over again. Thus, while Gergen and Giddens get excited about the positive possibilities of a myriad of mediated relationships, of global mobility and remaking life narratives, and Bauman sees the dark yet inevitable side of all this, Sennett's interviews with a number of individuals are shot through with a sense of loss.

Given this, Sennett asks crucial questions about how people can make a life and sustain a sense of self under such conditions. These include: 'How can long-term purposes be pursued in a short-term society? How can durable social relations be sustained? How can a human being develop a narrative of identity and life history in a society composed of episodes and fragments?'.[26] In particular, how do we develop 'those qualities of character which bind human beings to one another and furnish each with a sense of sustainable self [?]'.[27] This is why the new flexible capitalism can corrode character, because it eats away the very social fabric that sustains a long-term narrative of self created with others in relations of loyalty, commitment and purpose.

One strategy to salvage character, identified by Sennett, is to adopt a narrative of 'career' to create a sense of coherence, agency and responsibility in a social world that works against these very things. When he talks of career Sennett takes Lippmann's definition, which means a narrative of 'inner development, unfolding through both skill and struggle'.[28] With this there develops a sense of responsibility for one's conduct that is bound into a more long-term vision of life, one that is leading to some aim or has purpose. All aspects of the new capitalism would seem to undermine the possibility of such a narrative, and yet Sennett found people who had ostensibly been the victims of flexible capitalism developing just such a narrative. They were ex-employees of IBM, computer programmers who had been laid off when that company began to fail in the 1990s. After explaining their predicament through narratives which first of all blamed the managers of the company, then the globalization of the economy, the men eventually settled on a narrative in which they figured as having miscalculated their own careers by not seeing the trends developing in their own industry. They then began to develop narratives of career, through which they started accepting responsibility for not taking more chances in their professional lives, instead staying with IBM for the long-term company benefits (which rapidly disappeared as the company hit trouble).

Even though the theme of the narratives was failure rather than success, the programmers began to tell stories in which they figured as agents, possessed of will, choice and responsibility. In taking responsibility and agency through this narrative there is also established at its centre the sense of 'I' so common in auto-biographical stories.[29] The sense of 'I' is established in the face of conditions that demand the flexible pliant self, one who can bend and adapt to all the conditions that flexible capitalism can throw at him or her. However, as Sennett points out, these narratives are not simple acts of resistance in the face of an indifferent social, political and economic system: they speak of the deep pain that comes with failure, especially in middle age, when many find themselves considered to be past the cut and thrust of new, aggressive industries. Sennett says, 'given the destruction of hope and desire, the preservation of one's active voice is the only way to make failure bearable'.[30] This is so because, through the very structure that a narrative provides, it acts as a form of healing, a way of recovering from the wounds inflicted by a fickle world.

However, Sennett's concept of career applies only to the idea as it bears upon the world of work and the trajectory this sets us on across the life-course. Yet the notion of career can be applied to the narratives of self we develop to order our lives more generally. Indeed, Goffman used the term 'moral career' to refer 'to any social strand of any person's course through life'.[31] This course will involve a sequence of changes in a person's self and in their framework of imagery for judging self and others. Because the notion of career involves changes, an important aspect of it is the way we constantly reconstruct the view of our career when we look back over our lives. A career is never a solid or stable thing, for it is thrown into periodic states of reconstruction that select, and sometimes distort, in order to form a view of the self. According to Goffman, we often distort the facts or events of our lives to present ourselves as good or worthy. When the story cannot be presented favourably, we tend to disclaim responsibility for the way things have turned out. Instead of being the agent of the story – the 'I' who makes things happen – I become the victim of circumstance or chance. However, this was not what Sennett found; for those he interviewed the claiming of agency and responsibility was enough, in time, to help them come to terms with failure.

My own initial small-scale contribution to this literature involved an interview with a person I called 'Paul' who had faced many of the changes in his life that Giddens, Bauman and Sennett see as typical of contemporary modernity or capitalism, such as changes in career trajectory, sudden breaks in relationships, and periodic life-crises.[32] What I found through this interview was someone who felt that he could not plan far ahead, as life was unpredictable and you always had to be ready to change, yet at the same time managed to establish some continuity in his biographical narrative and in his sense of self in two main ways. First, by reconstructing his moral career through what I call a 'thick narrative', a term following what Gilbert Ryle referred to as 'thick' rather than 'thin' description.[33] That is, Paul's was a thick narrative because he did not simply recount a series of random changes that had befallen him, but instead looked for a deep sense of meaning to these changes and located the points of his own active influence over them, thereby creating a sense of 'I' in the narrative. Although there was also a counter-narrative at work in the way Paul told his story, in which there was a sense of circumstances not being within his own control, he still managed to reconstruct some meaningful sense of life-course and self out of the incoherence and happenstance of modern life.

The second way in which Paul sought to create a more stable and coherent sense of self was by locating himself very firmly within the city in which he had been brought up, and where he and significant members of his family still lived. This location in a particular place also seemed to give Paul a sense of greater weight and coherence in his sense of self. Just as he sought to create a thick narrative to make sense of his life, so Paul seemed to seek out the thickness of place in which he was densely enmeshed with friends, family and familiarity more generally. Indeed, the philosopher and social geographer Edward Casey has argued that while it is true that social relations are becoming more virtual in the contemporary world, with improvements in global telecommunications and with the advent of the Internet, people are still seeking out the 'depth' of place in which they can find physical co-presence with others and share experiences, as opposed to the 'volumetric void' of space in which the Internet is located.[34] So, although Casey would agree with the theorists we have been talking about so far, who see contemporary society – whether it is characterized as postmodernity, high-modernity, or liquid modernity – as saturated with media technologies through which social relations are disembedded from local places and globalized, he would disagree that this is diminishing the importance of place. Casey argues that the more place is levelled down by modern technology, the more individuals seek out places in which interpersonal enrichment can flourish. He gives two examples: first, the proliferation of films available on video and DVD has not meant the end of cinemas, as on the contrary more people than ever in the last 30 years are going to cinemas, finding them to be 'real places with their own sensuous density and interpersonal interest';[35] second, Internet bookselling has not brought about the demise of the bookshop, instead there are now bigger bookshops than ever, many with their own coffee bars where people can read, meet and talk. We can also add to this the interpersonal contact that most people still prefer when choosing sexual partners or looking for sexual encounters. Although a lot of meeting and dating now goes on in Internet chat rooms, many still prefer to meet others at some point for more intimate social or physical contact. As Jeffery Weeks has said, 'despite the best fantasies of prophets of the Internet and of cybersex ..., sexuality is always ultimately about interaction with others. It is through that interaction that the meanings of sexuality are shaped, and what we know as sexuality is produced'.[36]

I would argue that the creation and maintenance of places for densely enmeshed interactions, alongside virtual space and disembedded relationships, has actually created a richer environment for selves, certainly for those who can move between embodied and disembodied relations. The power of individual selves in the contemporary social world therefore seems to be constituted not so much in the ability to be totally flexible, fluid, and to have complete freedom of movement, but *to be able to choose* when to move and stay at the surface of experience or when to be rooted and search out the depth of interconnection with others in particular places. If the search for identity is a struggle to arrest the flow and solidify the fluid in order to create the thick narratives that give form to an otherwise fragmentary experience, so too is this struggle for identity expressed in the search for places that can add some weight to becoming a self. In actual places we can construct the kind of interpersonal relationships that we cannot in the thin spaces of the Internet: embodied relations in which there can develop the qualities of character that bind human beings to one another and create for each a sense of sustainable self. However, the power to do this is also tied to social class and the possession of the kind of social and cultural capital that is transposable into different places or social fields, the type of capital that does not trap you in just one particular place from which there is little chance of escape for the majority who live there.

These ideas about the density of places as a counterpoint to the thinness of space, plus the possibility of creating thick narratives of moral careers, add extra dimension to the sometimes too generalized and one-dimensional theories of postmodernity, high-modernity, or liquid modernity. They also show how it is still possible to have a relatively stable and coherent sense of self that can deal with both its own changes, contradictions and elements of disunity, *and* with the fragmentation brought on by an increasingly flexible and corrosive form of global capitalism. To think otherwise is not just to misrepresent, in a theory, the capacities of modern individuals, reducing them to being the mere reflection of existing social conditions; it is also to abandon them to an increasingly fragmented and schizoid form of capitalism, while denying them the capabilities to either combat or negotiate this increasingly hazardous social world. Instead, we can argue that the possibility for creating a sense of core self comes from two sources: first of all, from the *habitus* that is part of the core of our selves, which is the relatively stable dispositional tendencies that must be transposable and adaptable to new social fields, but endures in our bodies as a form of corporeal memory; and second, from the ability to create a unified voice that dialogues with many other voices, which carries something of their intonation and values, yet is still recognizably our own (both of these sources of core self I elaborated in Chapter 3). This means that theorists like Gergen are not necessarily wrong to suggest that modern people are saturated more than ever before with the voices of a multitude of others, but they are wrong to think this means that no core sense of self (as opposed to a unified self) is possible. We will come to this in a moment.

First, let us discuss the importance of *habitus*. As Casey notes, *habitus* is a concept that acts as the middle-term between place and self, in that certain habitual patterns of acting that are related to specific places become embodied in the self. This self is constituted by a core of habitudes 'that incorporate and continue, at both psychical and physical levels, what one has experienced in

particular places'.[37] The performances of the self in new places that it encounters are then like a reaching out to those places by transposing elements of the
habitus to them, a skilful application which allows us to embed ourselves more
completely into the life-world of ongoing experience and to in-habit it as the
particular people we are. Were it not for this capacity to transpose dispositions
from one place to another, Casey argues that the self would be 'schizoid within
and alienated without', meaning that it would have no taken-for-granted sense
of itself that could assume an ongoing experience of becoming, nor establish
the ontological security of belonging to and in-habiting, at the very least, some
places. We would also become the type of self required by each place we came
to in-habit, with nothing of our selves from past experiences to bring to them.
While Casey acknowledges that places and selves are becoming thinned out to
some degree in the contemporary world, he does nevertheless believe it possible for selves to jointly create the kind of thick places in which they can establish the densely enmeshed infrastructure of social relations. Furthermore,
children are still brought up and educated in particular places, and these inhere
in the self as habitudinal bodily memory, just as our ongoing experiences of
events in specific places leave behind their residue in our bodily sense of self.
Thus while the places in which our experiences occur might be becoming more
heterogeneous and disconnected from one another, it is still possible for our
bodies to carry their own sense of a landscape of places we have been part of,
as they remain part of us.

Secondly, this bodily sense of self that resides in our dispositions, is the precondition for the capacity to create a relatively unified voice that can sustain with
others a narrative of self: one that is not a freely chosen, socially disconnected
project of the self, but is embedded in the opportunities and limitations of the
habitus and the social and cultural capitals this has enabled us to accrue. In a way,
the fact that a narrative of self and a relatively unified inner voice are limited by
the *habitus* and filled with the voices and valuations of all the others I have
known, makes them all the more *mine,* because those places and relations to
others are what constitute *me.* As Jane Flax has pointed out, when postmodern
philosophers attack the notion of a unified self, which they claim to be a fiction,
they are actually attacking the Enlightenment modes of philosophical thinking
that associate this self with rational thought.[38] Yet we can argue that the selves of
the everyday world were never those transcendental creatures imagined in philosophy. They were the embodied selves of their own historical times and places,
partly rational but also subject to their *habitus* and the embodied dispositions and
emotions that compelled them. As Flax goes on to claim, though, those who take
deconstruction literally and call for a decentring of the self in postmodern society, seem naïve about the cohesion within their own selves that makes the increasing fragmentation of experience something other than a slide into psychosis.
Thus:

> [t]hese writers seem to confirm the very claims of those they have contempt for,
> that a sense of continuity or 'going-on-being' is so much part of the core self that

it becomes a taken-for-granted background. Persons who have a core self find the experiences of those who lack or have lacked it almost unimaginable.[39]

Even Gergen, while resisting the clinical label of schizophrenia as applying to postmodern selves, assumes that multiphrenia has meant that selves have become fragmented into a multitude of different voices with no self-identified voice to call 'I' or mine. So multiphrenics also lack a core self. But why should that be the case? Bakhtin pointed out that most of us are capable of developing a unified voice that we associate with our self, despite the fact that this emerges out of the voices, intonations and valuations of others, to such an extent that we can never totally separate our voice from the voice of others. Despite this, a voice does emerge that we can call our own, irrespective of the number of people we are in dialogue with. Just because we dialogue with many others doesn't mean that we cannot develop what we regard as our own voice – which we take as partly synonymous with the sense of 'I', expressing myself when I speak – any more than someone in conversation with many others, as opposed to just a few, is in greater danger of losing their own sense of self. We are still populated with the voices of others with which we dialogue, are questioned and challenged by those voices, thrown into periods of confusion and crisis, but out of which we can still reconstruct a meaningful sense of self-identity among others. This is what Flax refers to as a core rather than a unified self: the self does not have to be unified in order to have a core that it regards as 'I', nor does its inner voice have to be a monologue for it to develop its own unified voice among others (as opposed to a totally unified self or inner dialogue).

However, as a psychoanalyst, Flax goes on to claim that the core self ultimately resides in the deep subjectivity of the unconscious, drives and fantasy. Yet we don't have to accept the Freudian conceptualization of the self to be persuaded by the argument for a core self, for as Stevi Jackson and Sue Scott have said, instead one can focus upon that other aspect of Flax's core self – the social relations entailed in self-formation.[40] They look to Mead's ideas of the self to show how it is formed through interaction with others and through internal conversations, in which self becomes both the subject and object of its own reflection. Furthermore, the self is fragmented into many different 'mes' which, in the process of inner dialogue, can in time be resolved into a sense of 'I' that is not always present in immediate experience. Having a fragmented self with some level of disunity is not inimical to the potential for developing an ongoing and constantly reconstructed sense of core self, or 'I', to which we can refer. I would add to this the need to see this sense of core self as embodied in the relatively stable dispositional tendencies created in the social *habitus* of which we are a part or have been a part. Thus, as I hope to have shown throughout this book, the 'I' we refer to when we speak is in part a bodily sense of being in the world, of being present in a particular place to both specific and generalized others, an embodied sense of self that is fully social as classed, gendered and sexed.

Notes

1. Kenneth J. Gergen (1991) *The Saturated Self: Dilemmas of Identity in Contemporary Life*. New York: Basic Books.
2. Ibid., p. 71.
3. Fredric Jameson (1991) *Postmodernism, or, the Cultural Logic of Late Capitalism*. London: Verso.
4. Jean-François Lyotard (1984) *The Postmodern Condition: A Report on Knowledge*. Tr. Geoff Bennington and Brian Massumi. Manchester: Manchester University Press. p. 15.
5. Kenneth J. Gergen, *Saturated*, p. 181.
6. Ibid., p. 228.
7. Ibid., p. 242.
8. Jameson, *Postmodernism*.
9. David Harvey (1990) *The Condition of Postmodernity*. Oxford: Blackwell.
10. Charles Taylor (1989) *Sources of the Self: The Making of the Modern Identity*. Cambridge: Cambridge University Press.
11. Anthony Giddens (1991) *Modernity and Self-Identity: Self and Society in the Late Modern Age*. Cambridge: Polity Press.
12. Anthony Giddens (1992) *The Transformation of Intimacy*. Cambridge: Polity Press.
13. Ken Plummer (1995) *Telling Sexual Stories: Power, Change and Social Worlds*. London: Routledge. Jeffrey Weeks (1998) 'The sexual citizen', *Theory, Culture & Society*, 15 (3–4): 35–52.
14. Anthony Giddens, *Modernity*.
15. Noreena Hertz (2001) *The Silent Takeover: Global Capitalism and the Death of Democracy*. London: Heinemann.
16. Scott Lash and John Urry (1994) *Economies of Signs and Space*. London: Sage.
17. Matthew Adams (2007) *Self and Social Change*. London: Sage.
18. Zygmunt Bauman (2000) *Liquid Modernity*. Cambridge: Polity Press.
19. Ibid., pp. 49–50.
20. Zygmunt Bauman (2004) *Identity: Conversations with Benedetto Vecchi*. Cambridge: Polity Press.
21. Zygmunt Bauman, *Liquid*, p. 120.
22. Zygmunt Bauman (1995) *Life in Fragments: Essays in Postmodern Morality*. Oxford: Blackwell.
23. Zygmunt Bauman, *Identity*, p. 88.
24. Richard Sennett (1998) *The Corrosion of Character: The Personal Consequences of Work in the New Capitalism*. New York: W. W. Norton & Company.
25. Richard Sennett and J. Cobb (1977) *The Hidden Injuries of Class*. Cambridge: Cambridge University Press.
26. Richard Sennett, *Corrosion*, p. 26.
27. Ibid., p. 27.
28. Ibid., p. 120.
29. Liz Stanley (1992) *The Auto/Biographical 'I': Theory and Practice of Feminist Auto/Biography*. Manchester: Manchester University Press.
30. Sennett, *Corrosion*, p. 134.
31. Erving Goffman (1961) *Asylums: Essays on the Social Situation of Mental Patients and Other Inmates*. London: Penguin, 1991 edn. p. 119.
32. Ian Burkitt (2005) 'Situating auto/biography: biography and narrative in the times and places of everyday life', *Auto/biography*, 13: 93–110.

33. Clifford Geertz (1973) *The Interpretation of Cultures: Selected Essays*. New York: Basic Books.
34. Edward S. Casey (2001) 'Between geography and philosophy: what does it mean to be in the place-world?', *Annals of the Association of American Geographers*, 91 (4): 683–93.
35. Ibid., p. 685.
36. Jeffrey Weeks (2003) *Sexuality*, 2nd edn. London: Routledge. p. 112.
37. Edward S. Casey, 'Between', p. 686.
38. Jane Flax (1990) *Thinking Fragments: Psychoanalysis, Feminism, and Postmodernism in the Contemporary West*. Berkeley: University of California Press.
39. Ibid., p. 219.
40. Stevi Jackson and Sue Scott (2004) 'Just who do we think we are? Interactionism, modernity and the gendered reflexive self', unpublished paper.

Selected bibliography

Adams, Matthew (2007) *Self and Social Change*. London: Sage.
Bauman, Zygmunt (2000) *Liquid Modernity*. Cambridge: Polity Press.
Bauman, Zygmunt (2004) *Identity: Conversations with Benedetto Vecchi*. Cambridge: Polity Press.
Burkitt, Ian (2005) 'Situating auto/biography: biography and narrative in the times and places of everyday life', *Auto/biography,* 13: 93–110.
Casey, Edward S. (2001) 'Between geography and philosophy: what does it mean to be in the place-world?', *Annals of the Association of American Geographers*, 91 (4): 683–93.
Flax, Jane (1990) *Thinking Fragments: Psychoanalysis, Feminism, and Postmodernism in the Contemporary West*. Berkeley: University of California Press.
Gergen, Kenneth J. (1991) *The Saturated Self: Dilemmas of Identity in Contemporary Life*. New York: Basic Books.
Giddens, Anthony (1991) *Modernity and Self-Identity: Self and Society in the Late Modern Age*. Cambridge: Polity Press.
Sennett, Richard (1998) *The Corrosion of Character: The Personal Consequences of Work in the New Capitalism*. New York: W. W. Norton & Company.

CHAPTER 8

CONCLUSION

The general argument of this book has been that to truly understand ourselves and answer the question 'who am I?' we must first of all abandon the image of ourselves as self-contained monads or self-possessed individuals who can only find out about their identity by looking for and identifying some essence within them that is the secret truth of self, whether that be sexuality or some inherent personality trait. Equally, we are not individuals who are the proprietors of our own inherent capacities, owing nothing to society or to others for them. As individuals we are born into a world of social relations that have been made by previous generations, and, even though we can work to change these, nevertheless we can work only with the materials and tools we have at hand. In that sense Hegel was absolutely right to say that the world which constitutes the self is not external to it, but is the social relations it is located within. Following this, Marx, and other Marxists like Sève, showed how the human essence is not something contained inside us; it is the ensemble of social relations in which each generation is raised, learns and develops its capacities and self-identities. All the elements of identity we feel to be the core of who we are are therefore to be found, as Sève put it, 'excentric' to us within social relations. As Butler has said with respect to gender, we are 'ec-static' in that the terms in which gender identity is constructed are not authored by any one subject: they have been authored 'outside' any single subject in a sociality composed of many.

However, Sève's 'scientific humanism' set out a theory and a method for understanding not only the general forms of individuality in society, or subject positions within a discourse, but the way that individual biographies are formed within the times and places of contemporary capitalist societies. Each one of us emerges from our biographies not as a social category or cipher; we emerge as individual selves, each unique in many ways, yet similar in others: all constrained and limited by capitalist society, the overriding aim of which is the development of capital rather than the capacities of human beings. The contradictions of such a society will be reflected in the use-time of our biographies and in our selves: in the time we have for different activities, the scope we have for self-development, and the way we are related to others in our lives. This is what Sève meant by 'social individuality', a term I have taken on board and tried to develop through-out the book. However, as I argued in Chapter 6, social individuality means much more than just the way we are related to social labour within our biographies through the time spent on work or other activities in workplaces and institutions. It is also about intermediary activities and those liminal times and places in which we are related to particular others through interpersonal activities. More generally, it is also about our class position in the social hierarchy and the way that generalized – if not impartial – others value and judge us.

Social class is influential in the way our class background angles the trajectory of our biography across the life-span. Prior to the formation of capacities, the *habitus* of class background in-forms our dispositions, perceptions of the world, feelings, sensibilities, tastes and interests. Furthermore, our social class, as perceived by others, will influence how they regard us and the kind of recognition we get from them. It will colour many of the moral judgements made about us and those that we make about other people – certainly, social class influences the aesthetic judgements we make about others, their tastes and lifestyles. Thus, our dispositions, tastes, lifestyle, and the way we see and appreciate the things of the world we live in, will give away more about us than simply our personal likes and dislikes: they tell others about our likely background and education, and also about our aspirations. As I have said many times in this book, identity is not simply about who we are, but also what we want to be: the image we want to project to others and the way in which that image is supported or betrayed by our dispositions and capacities, the things we communicate to others without even realizing it. As a self always in the making, then, self-image is as much about who we want to be as about who we are, for identity is something that is both found, in terms of what we have become, and made in terms of how this can be reconstructed into what we are yet to become.

Yet this is always limited by the restraints of the material, social, cultural and symbolic capital we have access to from the earliest years. While I want to expand the notion of social individuality as developed by Sève, I want to do this within an ontology that is *both* materialist *and* humanist: that is, while I understand humans as actively and morally engaged with each other in the transformation of reality, I feel we must understand this as occurring within material constraints. We are all enabled *and* limited in terms of access to the various forms of capital through which we can realize our joint and personal projects. Thus, while I think that we still have a huge amount to learn about social selves from thinkers like Mead, who understood how we slice our individual biographies from within a plexus of supra-individual relations and practices in which we identify our own self only in interaction with others, we nevertheless must realize that this realm of everyday moral interactions is, within capitalist society, confined mainly to the times and places of what Sève referred to as intermediary activities.

Nevertheless, as both Mead and Bakhtin illustrated, everyday interaction and dialogue are vitally important, because it is in these interrelationships that we come to identify our self through the image of some of the selves around us, with some of what they represent, while setting our self against the image of others. Yet we do this only on the basis of the dispositions already forming in us as embodied selves, from the way in which we have been called into active agency by others, responding to them. Bakhtin's work, for example, is vital in illustrating how we author our identities and find for ourselves a unique voice and image, one that we can in-habit with all the vitality of the living body, with the energy of its emotional and dialogic core that is evident in every utterance. Yet no author sits down to write in the virgin snow of nowhere, from a no-place: we all have other voices circulating around us from the moment we are born, from when we ourselves could not even speak or understand. How these voices have in-formed us, with their various intonations and stances on the world, is immeasurable – we could probably never begin to fathom or decipher them. They are like the atmosphere in which we live and breathe, and one which is constantly being renewed throughout our lives by other voices, other calls made to us inviting us into different ways of being a self. The authoring of our own identity and the finding of our own voice, the one we are most sure of when we speak (a state we never completely and totally reach) is always achieved by taking from some of these voices around us and combining them in unique ways to create our own sense of self. We are therefore always immersed in the atmosphere of the social world, constantly constructing and reconstructing our selves and the society in which we are embedded.

In this way we can become an 'I-for-myself' in a world of others; but we can only do this because there are constantly 'others-for-me' all around, talking to us, acting with or against us, calling out responses or stunning us into silence. We then become an 'I-for-myself' only to the extent that we are aware of ourselves as an 'I-for-others' through the images that others communicate to us about who we are, or the images we imagine others have of us. We then use these images to author our own self-identity, one that we find to some degree in-habitable or liveable. Elements of the practices we engage in with others, including the way they influence us by their actions and words, in-form who we are before we even know it. Later, we can work on this material to try to refashion ourselves, but without it we would have no initial presence in the world, no way of being in it, living through it, and nothing about ourselves that we could reflect upon and work with. We can also draw from the voices around us, just like the author of a novel, to put together our own identity with a degree of uniqueness and originality; and in response to those other voices we can begin to find our own, one that provides a centre-point in our dialogues with our self and with others.

The darker side of this, though, as we saw from the work of Laing, is that we can be stifled and deadened as selves by the others around us: instead of being called out as social agents who act autonomously and vitally, in-habiting the world with the energy and emotion of a living body-self, we can be deadened and driven 'inwards', unable to be an 'I-for-others' in the fullest sense. In the worst cases of annihilation of self, this can lead to the kind of withdrawal from the world and sense of deadness that Laing described, as well as to the divided self-dialogues with their emotional-volitional background of rage, grandiosity, fear and impotence. But these are the kind of interpersonal forms of violence and destruction that can happen in all relationships. On a wider social scale we can also find the destruction of social worlds – the places in which the lives of social groups or classes are embedded – through wars or uncontrolled economic competition. Here, entire classes are cast into the no-places of a non-existence and, if not into actual ontological insecurity, then certainly into a world that is dead, without vitality or meaning, and into a life that is boring, monotonous and numbing. It is obviously the less powerful social groups who find themselves in such places, without a means of escape or the power to change their circumstances and selves for the better.

Authoring of self, then, is a process and a practice in which choice always occurs from a particular place, with its material and interpersonal constraints, so that the choices we make about our lives and selves are never unconstrained. But then no choice ever is unconstrained, or it would not be a choice: absolute freedom is no freedom at all, for we would be abandoned to the random working of chance. Unless I am a particular self, in-formed by my social world and the people to whom I am related, with dispositions, tastes, interests and desires, how could I ever choose? What basis would I have to make a choice with, even if I am not conscious of how that basis is formed? Without preferences, disposition, tastes or inclinations the world would be a bewildering array of objects about which I had no feelings, values or interests. On the occasions where we find it hard to make a choice, either because we have no strong feelings or because we want more than one thing, we are often reduced to sticking a pin in a list of choices. But imagine if every choice were like this: *we* would never really make any choice. The old arguments about freedom and determination, with the two as absolute opposites, were misguided as they thought that to understand selves as socially determined denied human freedom, and that in order to think about human agency – in which we regularly make personal, meaningful choices – we had to see people as somehow detached from their social circumstances, uninfluenced by others. Yet if I wasn't a determinate social self, the self of my background, learning, social class, gender and sexuality, in-formed by those I have both loved and hated, who would I be? I would be no one. And on what basis could I make any meaningful choices, even if that involves the choice to try to change what I am? I cannot think of any basis on which that could occur, other than the way I have been in-formed both actively and passively throughout my life.

In this way we can begin to develop a core rather than a unified self: that is to say, a feeling of a centre to our being, of existing as 'I' in the world, without this ever being unified into a fixed and unchanging entity that has no contradiction, indecision or univocal tensions of many different voices – both of the self and of others – clamouring to be heard. This is a core self that is never entirely sure of itself, never completed, always in the process of some degree of change, and open to the possibility – perhaps the inevitability – of reconstruction. Yet to say that this self is unstable, as many contemporary writers and thinkers do, is a misconception, because instability suggests something always on the verge of collapse. Perhaps the key term in all of this is the one used by Mead, which is *reconstruction;* as individuals we never completely construct the world or our self, because these things are constructions or compositions with so many authors: yet we are always in the process of reconstruction, of remaking who we are, along with the world in which we live. Even in contemporary society, where selves are thought of as fluid and constantly changeable, there still have to be – as Bauman claimed – some stable elements that we, and others, can recognize with some degree of consistency as a self. Without this, human social interaction – especially the most important and self-sustaining relationships like love and friendship – would be impossible. There also have to be some relatively stable dispositional tendencies on the basis of which we can act in such a diverse world.

Indeed, as Ulf Hannerz has pointed out, the modern cosmopolitan attitude is actually a disposition, most common in the middle classes, that entails an intellectual and aesthetic openness toward diverse cultural experiences, which become viewed almost as artworks to be experienced and appreciated.[1] The capacity to be adaptable and to manoeuvre skilfully between different systems of meanings is, like all capacities, one that is socially learned and situated in class background and education. It is also not only a capacity to act in a certain way, but also a status to display to others. It is wrong, then, to suggest that the kind of reflectivity demanded of modern people who are always looking, listening, intuiting and reflecting, is individualizing, as this capacity is socially founded in particular groups with a collective identity as well as individual identities. Furthermore, in this type of fluid world, the capacity for the reconstruction of identity is required more than ever. Because of this, I would suggest that the work of pragmatist thinkers like Mead is as important today for understanding the nature of social selves, as it was at the beginning of the last century.

While self, then, is very much about image, fantasy and aspiration, it is wrong to say that the self is an illusion, either in the sense of the 'I' being a fiction, or that self-identity is an illusion because it is composed of elements that do not primarily belong to the individual self. The 'I' could be said to be an illusion if it is taken to signify a fixed and unchanging kernel of self; one that radiates from an innate essence or from a transcendental self. But this is not the self that most writers – from Adam Smith to thinkers like Mead and Bakhtin – refer to when they speak about self or the sense of being 'I'. For them, self is a dialogic creation from the very beginning, involving elements of image and fantasy, yet one that is nevertheless composed in the practical realities of an everyday social world. In this sense, the self is not purely illusion, as my body-self is an important, if ever-changing, element in everyday relations and interactions. The pragmatists, including Mead, understood how the fleeting experiences of a temporal human consciousness coalesce into a temporary unity through the dialogue of the 'I' and 'me', creating an additive experience and continuing sense of self, but only in relation to others. It is the others we are related to who provide the mirror in which we create a relatively stable image of ourselves that we and others can dialogue with.

Foucault, then, was right to say that the self or soul is not the product of ideology (thus being an illusion), rather it is the product of everyday practices: only he was wrong to see the practices that create the reality of actual individuals as located only in disciplinary institutions and intersecting expert knowledges. Instead, self is as much a product of everyday practices and interactions outside such institutions, in which each one of us gets a sense of our ordinary individuality. This was illustrated with respect to gender and sexuality, especially in terms of how gay and lesbian identity has emerged as much within the subcultures of pluralistic urban societies as from the influence of medical and legal discourses. Indeed, to really understand such identities, we need to begin to understand the interrelationships between official and unofficial discourses in the formation of human selves. Furthermore, in the formation of sexual and gendered selves, the discourses and norms of official authorities are always experienced within interactive, dialogical relationships where, as Goffman noted, it is not the overall character of the power structure that is reproduced, but particular features of it deemed relevant to the social situation at hand. Thus, in some situations gender might be performed in such a way as to reproduce iconic images of masculine and feminine, while in other contexts it might be possible to subvert or play with them. Sexuality and gender identity are formed in various social contexts from infancy onwards in terms of how we are in-formed by others: those we want to *be* like and those we want to *have*. Thus, sexuality and gender are composed of a series of images, fantasies and desires that, for most people, remain not only in the imagination, but are performed with and for others. In this way, through the unique configuration of life experiences from within various social contexts, general types of social individuality become real concrete individuals who combine image, fantasy and desire in ways that signify their own distinct self.

It is wrong, however, to conclude from this idea of self composed of image and fantasy, that self is an illusion or a fiction created by language or by signifying systems which animate human practice, as if language and signification were *a priori* to historical agents. Again, self is not the product of language or signification, if the latter is thought of as some abstract system that exists outside of historical agency situated in actual places and times; rather, self is the product of dialogue as it is practised by historical agents in their everyday worlds. Here, self may be part image and fantasy, but it is also the flesh and blood of embodied dispositional tendencies, perceptions, tastes, capacities, and of desire and fantasy put into practice. This self is no illusion, but a material living being, both in and of its social world.

In terms of the notion that self is a fiction because it is composed of elements drawn from the social world, I think I have already addressed this by arguing that self can draw from the heteroglossia of social influences around it to author its own identity. This is what I have been trying to illustrate throughout this book with terms like 'social selves' or 'social individuality': that it is possible to be *both* a social being *and* an individual self. Indeed, as Charles Taylor has pointed out, the idea that self should be our own original creation – an expression of the individual's own essence and inner voice – is itself a socio-historical idea stemming from Romanticism. The selves of other times and places also had their own self-identities, created within their own social worlds, but perhaps did not give them as much thought as do we post-Romantics. They perhaps took their own identity for granted as much as they did the identities of the other people and things within their world. Today we are no longer like this; yet it could be argued that we weight our self-identity with a little bit too much significance when we could focus a little more on the world about us or on other people.

However, we must not assume that the political critique of 'possessive individualism' or the epistemological critique of transcendental self, spirit or soul, undermines the existence of selves that emerge from the social and moral interactions of everyday life. To have a self is to be able to orient oneself in the social world; to be recognized by others and to be called to account for your actions, having the capacity to reciprocate. We also 'read' others in embodied interaction, using this as a means of judging our responses to them and their possible responses to us. Selves and identities are thus the means by which we orient ourselves to one another in the social world.

Finally, then, we can say that in the face of all the efforts at an epistemological critique of the concept of self, or as Foucault put it in *The Order of Things*[2] of 'man' and his identity as a problem posed for knowledge, there is still that other strand of knowledge that attempts not metaphysical constructions of a transcendental soul, but an understanding of the various identities of human selves that are the products of relations and interactions. Foucault thought that if the knowledges that support the vision of the human self as a problem – one that can be solved only through authoritative or expert discourses – began to crumble, as under the weight of postmodern critiques, then a tide would wash over the shore and wipe the face of 'man' off the sand. This tide has already begun to lap the shores, yet there are still all the social selves walking along the beach, people with their everyday selves and identities, like each other in many ways, but in other ways a unique creation of their own biography and background set within particular social and historical times and places: creations of an interpersonal, dialogical social life. These people are you and I, products of time and place who author ourselves only in the context of the everyday social world, making ourselves in dialogic relations with others. As generations we also reconstruct ourselves and the social world in the process, so that individuals yet to be will be social selves in ways that we cannot yet dream of.

Notes

1. Ulf Hannerz (1996) *Transnational Connections: Culture, People, Places*. London: Routledge.
2. Michel Foucault (1970) *The Order of Things: An Archaeology of the Human Sciences*. London: Routledge.

INDEX

socio-historical forces 51
sociology and self 15–22
sodomites 94–5, 102–3
Soffer, Joshua 66
soul 6, 14, 35–6, 53, 89, 92–3, 123
speech
    habitual nature of 39–40
    internalization of 50–1
    see also thinking/thoughts
spirit/spirituality 6, 11–12, 53–4
'spiritual me' 35–6
St Augustine 6
stability versus social change 165, 168, 174–5,
    177, 180–1
stable dispositional tendencies 46, 64, 102,
    128, 155, 182, 184
Stetsenko, A. 54
'stream of consciousness' 34–6
Strozier, Robert M. 107
structuration 52–3
subjection of the individual 86–99, 123–4
substance dualism 7, 34
Sullivan, Paul 53
super-addressee 54
super-ego 24, 80–1, 90
surgery, sex change 114, 115, 117, 118, 119
surveillance 90–1, 92, 176
symbolic capital 148
symbolic interactionism 37, 48
sympathy 10

Taylor, Charles 8, 14, 27, 68, 99, 101, 167
temporal selves/temporality 36, 40, 44, 45,
    47–8, 65
Theory of Moral Sentiments (Smith)
    10, 42–3
Theses on Feuerbach (Marx) 16
thinking/thoughts 6–7
    as a social conversation 51
    abstract 42, 50
    and cognitive psychology 22–3
    Descarte's dualism 6–7, 34
    formed through labour and language 50
    Foucault's use of term 'thought' 86
    and reason 9
    self-dialogue 39–40, 51–2
    and verbal discourse 81
'third gender' (berdache) 118
time
    global 169, 174, 177
    leisure time 142–3
    liminal 63, 65, 143, 188

time *cont.*
    organizing biographical 170–2
    and stream of consciousness 34
    temporal selves 36, 40, 44, 45, 47–8, 65
    'time-space distantiation' 169
    use-time 172, 187
To Myself (Aurelius) 5
torture 88, 89
transcendental self 7–8, 9, 20, 32, 33, 107–8,
    126, 178
transpeople/transsexuals 114, 115, 119, 121–2,
    133–4, 135
Trumbach, Randolph 102–4
truth 32
    establishing through confession 72–3
    self-truth 97, 101, 106–7
    truth games 96, 107
    truth-power relationship 88–9, 100
    truth-telling 72–3, 107
Turner, B. S. 22
Turner, Victor 47, 63, 65, 72, 99, 143–4

unconscious 44–5, 159–60
    Freudian notion of 23–4, 42, 80–1
    relational nature of 79–81
    structural 81–2, 160
unemployment 144, 154, 155, 170
unofficial ideology 81, 99
Urry, John 172
'use-time' 144–5

verbal thinking 51–2, 81
vocal gestures 45
voice, finding own 58–9, 66–7, 71, 184, 189
voices
    divided 67, 71, 74, 80
    multiple *see* heteroglossia
    of psychotic patients 76
Volkerpsychologie (folk or social
    psychology) 36
Vološinov, V. N. 80–1
Vygotsky, Lev Semenovich 49–53

Walzer, Michael 100
wealth
    and access to opportunities 150
    accumulation of 166–7
Wealth of Nations, The (Smith) 10, 42–3
Weber, Max 20–2
Weeks, Jeffrey 104, 169, 181
Williams, Raymond 99
Willis, Paul 149